Landing of the Pilgrims at Plymouth, December 22, 1620.

THE

NEW ENGLAND GAZETTEER;

CONTAINING

DESCRIPTIONS OF ALL THE STATES, COUNTIES AND TOWNS

IN

NEW ENGLAND:

ALSO

DESCRIPTIONS OF THE PRINCIPAL MOUNTAINS, RIVERS, LAKES,
CAPES, BAYS, HARBORS, ISLANDS, AND

FASHIONABLE RESORTS

WITHIN THAT TERRITORY.

ALPHABETICALLY ARRANGED.

By JOHN HAYWARD,
Author of the Columbian Traveller, Religious Creeds, &c. &c.

FOURTH EDITION.

CLEARFIELD

Originally published
Massachusetts, 1839

Reprinted for
Clearfield Company, Inc. by
Genealogical Publishing Co., Inc.
Baltimore, Maryland
2002

International Standard Book Number: 0-8063-5163-2

Made in the United States of America

PREFACE.

THE PREPARATION of a Gazetteer ot New England, worthy the patronage of its enlightened citizens, is no easy task : those only who have attempted it can form a just conception of its difficulties. Long and wearisome journeys must be performed; hundreds of volumes and local histories must be consulted, and thousands of letters must be written.

Although a kind Providence has blessed the editor with health, and with numerous friends, in all parts of New England; yet, after a long period of devotedness, he is mortified that his work is not more complete.

It will be perceived that there are many towns, particularly in the eastern section of New England, whose names are merely mentioned; and that notices of others, in many cases, are exceedingly deficient. Had our means permitted, fair representations of the character and resources of those towns might have promoted individual and public interests; and enhanced the value of our volume. There are lakes and rivers in the northern and eastern parts of New England, whose beauty, volume of water, and hydraulic power, might vie with the Winnepisiogee and Merrimack; but whose locations and even names are but indistinctly known.

But we have the consolation to believe that a Gazetteer of New England, perfect in all its parts, is rather desired than expected. Our country is new : large portions of the territory of the New England States, are yet a wilderness, and new counties and towns are very frequently constituted.

The progress of agricultural science, and of the mechanic arts; the advancement of commerce, both at home and abroad, and the increasing success of the fisheries, united with the determination of the people of New England to connect the trade of the western oceans with, their Atlantic borders, by roads of iron, which frosts cannot impede, are so great and strong, that the most devoted geographical and statistical writers must be satisfied with following at a distance, rather than keeping pace with the rapid car of improvement in New England.

PREFACE.

In the performance of our work we have derived assistance from many valuable maps and books on New England. Among the number a respectful tribute is due, particularly, to BELKNAP's History of New Hampshire; WILLIAMSON's Maine; DWIGHT's Letters; SAVAGE's Winthrop; THATCHER's Plymouth; FOLSOM's Saco and Biddeford; BENTON and BARREY's Statistics:—HALE's Map of New England; STEVENS' Rhode Island; CARRIGAIN's New Hampshire; and GREENLEAF's Maine:—to WORCESTER's Gazetteer; THOMPSON's Vermont; PEASE and NILES' Rhode Island and Connecticut; SPOFFORD's Massachusetts, and FARMER and MOORE's Gazetteer of New Hampshire.

From the latter work, and from its authors, the lamented JOHN FARMER, Esq., a celebrated antiquarian and writer, and JACOB B. MOORE, Esq., of Concord, N. H., author of several valuable historical and miscellaneous works, we are indebted for much of that which is valuable in regard to New Hampshire.

From a beautiful volume, entitled "Connecticut Historical Collections," by JOHN WARNER BARBER, Esq., we have been permitted to enrich our pages with some of their most valuable and interesting articles.

To Heads of Departments at Washington, and to the Secretaries of the several States to which the work refers, for valuable public documents; to Postmasters; and to numerous other friends who have kindly assisted us in our labors; whose names we should feel proud to mention, were it in accordance with their wishes; we tender the acknowledgments of a grateful heart.

For the purpose of enlarging our work, as well as for its correction, our editions will be designedly small: contributions are therefore respectfully solicited.

While it is our determination to devote our time and humble talents to render our publications worthy of general approbation; we are gratified with the assurance of co-operation from eminent men in all parts of the country; and we trust with confidence to receive that patronage, which Yankees, both at home and abroad, invariably bestow on every effort whose obvious design is USEFULNESS.

BOSTON, *May*, 1839.

THE
NORTHERN REGISTER.

It was our intention to have connected this publication with the Gazetteer; but it was found that by compressing the matter, sufficiently to unite them in one volume, both would fail of the object contemplated.

A great mass of materials for the Register is already received; indeed, a considerable portion is now ready for the press; but as we have extended our plan, some months will elapse before its appearance.

The work will comprise the rise and progress of all the important literary, religious, moral and charitable institutions in New England:—an account of the Churches and Ministers in the several towns, *from their origin, and settlement to the present time*:—the rise and extent of internal improvements:—statistics of various kinds: lists of Courts, Attorneys at law, Physicians, Literary and Religious Journals, Newspapers, Banks, Postmasters, &c. &c.: to which will be added brief notices of distinguished men. In short, the Register is designed to comprise all that may be considered important and useful, in a work of this kind, in relation to New England, and which is not contained in the Gazetteer.

The number of eminent men, of every profession, who have kindly tendered the Editor their co-operation, is so great, that we feel confident that the Register will be entitled to a share of public favor.

☞ *All letters and papers for the Editor, are requested to be left at the Boston Post Office.*

NEW ENGLAND.

In presenting the public with a Gazetteer of New England, it has seemed proper to make a few introductory remarks of a general nature, on the character of its inhabitants. They may with great propriety be called *a peculiar people:* and perhaps New England and Pennsylvania are the only parts of the new world, which have been colonized by a class of men, who can be regarded in that light. The whole of Spanish and Portuguese America was organized, under the direct patronage of the mother countries, into various colonial governments, as nearly resembling those at home as the nature of the case admitted. The adventurers who sought their fortunes beyond the sea, in those golden tropical regions, carried the vices and the virtues with the laws and the manners of their native land, along with them, and underwent no farther change than was unavoidably incident to the new physical and political condition in which they were placed in America. The same remark, with nearly the same force, may be made of the Virginia colonists: they differed from Englishmen at home in no other way, than a remote and feeble colony must of necessity differ from a powerful metropolitan state. Pennsylvania was settled by a peculiar race; but its peculiarity was of that character which eventually exhausts itself; and would speedily perish but for an amalgamation, necessary though uncongenial, with the laws, the manners, and institutions of the world. If all mankind were Friends they might subsist and prosper. A colony of Friends, thrown upon a savage shore and environed by hostile influences from foreign colonial establishments, would perish, if not upheld by forces and principles different from its own. In the settlers of New England alone we find a peculiar people;—but at the same time a people whose peculiarity was founded on safe practical principles; reconcileable with the duties of life; capable of improvement in the progress of civilization, and of expanding into a powerful state, as well as of animating a poor and persecuted colony.

NEW ENGLAND.

Had not America been discovered and a tract upon our continent reserved for English colonization;—nay, further, had it not been precisely such an uninviting spot as furnished no temptation to men of prosperous fortunes, the world would have lost that noble developement of character which the fathers of New England exhibit. A tropical climate would have made it uninhabitable to Puritans; or rather would have filled it up with adventurers of a different class. A gold mine would have been a curse to the latest generation. Had the fields produced cotton and sugar, they would not have produced the men whom we venerate as the founders of the liberties of New England.

Puritanism sprang up in England, but there it could not develope itself with vigor or consist with happiness. The conflict with the hostile institutions of society was too sharp, and admitted of the cultivation of none but the militant or patient elements of character. To struggle with temporary success and to bow in permanent subjection was the necessary fate of the persecuted sect. So it was wisely ordained. Had Puritanism permanently mastered the church and the throne in England, it would have been corrupted. It would have picked up and worn the trampled diadem: it would have installed itself in the subjected church. Regarding Cromwell and the Rump Parliament as the gift of Puritanism to English liberty, it is a bequest at which we know not whether most to sigh or smile. The seed sown in England fell by the way side and the fowls came and devoured it up. The cause of political and social reform, which was conducted with self-denying wisdom and moderation in the outset, by single-hearted, honest men, degenerated as it prospered. In the moment of its triumph it sunk under the corruptions of selfishness, as a noble vessel which has braved the tempest in mid-ocean sometimes goes to pieces on the rocks as it approaches land.

But the precious seeds of liberty, civil and religious, which were sown in New England, fell upon a genial soil, and brought forth worthy and abiding fruit. Undertaking the same work which was undertaken by their brethren in England, our fathers conducted it through the days of small things, through hardships, trial, and disasters, to a triumphant issue. It is true there were greater obstacles to be encountered in England, in the resistance of established institutions. Deep rooted errors were to be torn up; the towers of feudal oppression, which had stood for centuries, were to be overthrown. But the influence of these formidable institutions was not limited to Old England. The rod of arbitrary power reached across the Atlantic. The little colonies had to struggle with the crown and the hierarchy, with the privy council and with special commissions, with writs and acts of parliament; and they had besides to struggle with the

NEW ENGLAND.

hardships of the wilderness, the dangers of the savage foe, of a sterner climate than that of their native land, the privations of a settler's life, the alternating neglect and oppression of the mother country;—but they struggled successfully with all. The reformers of abuses in England, as they claimed to be called, brought a king to the block, scattered a house of lords, and saw their great military leader clothed with all the powers of state; and in twelve years the son of that king returned to the throne, not merely by an unconditional restoration, but amidst a jubilee of national rejoicing and without one security for liberty. All the while the fathers of New England held on their even way; not betrayed into extravagance when their cause at home (as they fondly called Old England) was triumphant; nor in despair at the miserable relapse which ensued. They did not indeed live to reap the fruit of their principles and their sacrifices; and it reflects but the greater honor upon them that they persevered in their great work from a sense of duty, deep-seated, controlling, fearless, and not the less so although, while they lived, unrewarded by worldly success.

In fact the founders of New England were actuated by the only principle sufficient to produce this result. It need not be said that this was *religious* principle. How easily it is uttered of our Pilgrim fathers that they were actuated by religious principle; how little in these prosperous days do we realize all that is wrapped up in that description of their character! It is difficult to comprehend of others what we have not experienced in ourselves. That easy frame of mind which prevails among a highly favored people, in periods of halcyon prosperity, is scarcely capable of being placed in sympathy with the moral heroism, the spiritual courage, the sublime equanimity of a generation truly animated by the religious principle, exalted by persecution, and purified by hardship. Happy if in such a period we can, by diligent contemplation of the venerated men of other days, exalt our imaginations, till by conceiving we form a desire to imitate their virtues! In proportion as we do this, we shall realize the secret of their perseverance and success. They did all things through Christ strengthening them. What cannot man do when he has learned habitually and distinctly to regard this life as a preparatory scene,—a brief hour,—nay a fleeting moment, introductory to an eternal being? The fathers of New England were enabled, with their scanty means and feeble powers, to establish the foundation of institutions which will last to the end of time, for the very reason that they regarded all human interests and delights as transitory. That paradox in our moral natures which educes strength out of weakness, triumph out of self-denial, worldly power and success out of a stern preference of things not of this world, received its most illustrious confirmation in the career of the pilgrim fathers of New England.

This principle of our natures is the key to the great problem of the success which attended the forlorn hope of humanity that landed on these shores. There is indeed a fanaticism, which violates all the laws of our nature, alike the higher ulterior principles which belong to an immortal spirit, and the humbler influences which grow from the relations of ordinary life. It leads to surprising deeds; it forms characters which dazzle us with brilliant eccentricities. It is near allied to madness; often runs into it. But the religiousness of the fathers of New England was a far different principle. It was eminently *practical*. It allied itself with wise institutions of government; it sought the guidance of education; it encouraged the various pursuits of industry; it provided for the public safety and defence; and with chaste discrimination admitted the courtesies of polished life. It is difficult to say what sort of a commonwealth George Fox would have founded, had circumstances called him to assume the province of the legislator. It is most certain, that in setting up an immediate divine inspiration as the guide of every man, he maintained a principle at war with the very idea of a politcal system and all its institutions; nor is it less certain that the constitution which was actually granted to Pennsylvania, by its pure and noble-spirited proprietor, possessed little of the peculiarities of his sect but their mild, peaceful, and equitable temper. But the fathers of New England stopped short of the point where solemn conviction passes into enthusiasm. They pursued the ordinary occupations of life, planted the field, built vessels and navigated the sea, and carried on the usual mechanic arts. They made provision for protection against the Indians and the French. They organized a plan of civil government; they established by law a system of common school education, for the first time in the history of the world, and they founded a college for the avowed purpose of training up a class of educated men, well qualified to take the place of the learned and pious ministers who had emigrated with the first generation of pilgrims. These are the doings of intelligent and practical men, not of enthusiasts or fanatics; and yet they are the doings of men so resolutely bent upon the exercise of the right of worshipping God according to the dictates of their consciences, that they were willing to sacrifice to it home, fortune, and all that the mass of men hold dear.

To say that the fathers of New England were not faultless, is merely to say that they were men; to say that they established no institutions, the object of which was to bind the consciences of their successors is praise as just as it is high. If they adhered with undue tenacity to their

NEW ENGLAND.

own opinions, and failed in charity towards those who differed, they at least left their posterity free, without the attempt to secure before hand the control of minds in other ages by transmitted symbols and tests. Humanity mourns over the rigors practised towards Roger Williams, the Quakers, and the unhappy persons suspected of witchcraft; but let it not be forgotten that, as late as 1749, a witch was executed at Wurzburg, and that even in 1760 two women were thrown into the water in Leicestershire, in England, to ascertain by their sinking or swimming whether they were witches. Above all, it may deserve thoughtful enquiry, before we condemn the founders of New England, whether a class of men less stern in their principles and austere in their tempers, could have accomplished, under all the discouragements that surrounded them, against all the obstacles which stood in their way, the great work to which Providence called them,—the foundation of a family of republics, confederated under a constitution of free representative government. There is every reason to believe, great and precious as are the results of their principles, hitherto manifested to the world, that the quickening power of those principles will be more and more displayed, with every leaf that is turned in the book of Providence.

That part of the United States denominated NEW ENGLAND, comprises SIX STATES, SIXTY ONE COUNTIES, and TWELVE HUNDRED AND EIGHTY TOWNS. Their extent, divisions, and population at several periods, are as follows:

States.	Square miles	No. Counties	No. Towns.	Pop. 1790.	Pop. 1800.	Pop 1810.	Pop. 1820.	Pop. 1830.	Pop. 1837.	Pop. to sq. mile.
Me.	32,000	12	346	96,540	151,719	228,705	298,335	399,437	476,054	15
N. H.	9,280	8	224	141,885	183,858	214,460	244,161	269,328	288,746	31
Vt.	10,212	14	237	85,539	154,465	217,895	235,764	280,657	318,084	31
Mass.	7,500	14	306	378,787	422,845	472,040	523,287	610,408	701,331	94
R. I.	1,360	5	31	68,825	69,122	76,931	83,059	97,199	108,769	80
Ct.	4,674	8	136	237,946	251,002	261,942	275,202	297,675	304,755	65
	65,026	61	1,280	1,009,522	1,233,011	1,471,973	1,659,808	1,954,704	2,197,733	34

The population of Maine and Massachusetts, in 1837, is given as by a census taken in that year. The population of New Hampshire, Vermont, Rhode Island and Connecticut, for 1837, is estimated according to the ratio of increase, from 1820 to 1830.

NEW ENGLAND.

In 1830, there were in New England 1,112 persons deaf and dumb; 798 blind, and 18,668 aliens. The number of colored persons in 1820, was 20,782—1830, 21,310.

New England increased in population, from 1790, to 1800, 22.1 per cent: from 1800, to 1810, 19.3 per cent: from 1810, to 1820, 12.7 per cent: from 1820, to 1830, 17.7 per cent; and from 1830, to 1837, 12.4 cent. When it is considered, that most of the western states were originally peopled by New Englanders, and that vast numbers annually emigrate to those states, this increase of population is favorable, compared with other Atlantic states. The population of New England in 1700, is stated at 120,000; in 1755, at 345,000; and in 1775, at 714,000.

BOUNDARIES AND EXTENT. This territory is bounded north and northwest by Lower Canada, about 375 miles, and east by the Province of New Brunswick, 275 miles. Its whole eastern, southeastern and southern borders are washed by the Atlantic ocean and the waters of Long Island Sound, a distance of about 600 miles. It is bounded west by the state of New York, 280 miles. Its circumference is about 1,530 miles.

New England is situated between 41°, and 48° 12′ north latitude, and 65° 55′, and 74° 10′ west longitude from Greenwich. Its greatest length is between the sources of the Madawaska, Me., and Greenwich, Ct., about 575 miles; and its greatest breadth is between Machias, Me., and Highgate, Vt., 300 miles. Its narrowest part is between Boston and West Stockbridge, Mass., 135 miles.

NAME. During the unsuccessful attempts of Sir Walter Raleigh to plant colonies within the territory of North America, from 1584 to 1587, the whole country was called *Virginia*, in honor of Queen Elizabeth, who was then on the British throne. In 1606, James I. divided the country into two sections, *North and South Virginia;* but the French having taken possession of the Canadas, and founded Quebec, in 1608, and the Dutch having established colonies at New York and Albany, in 1613, the intermediate territory, now the New England States, was called New England, in compliment to its luxuriance and beauty, and in honor to his native land, by the celebrated John Smith, one of the first settlers of Virginia, in 1607; and who visited this coast in 1614.

The New England people are frequently called *Yankees* We are warranted in stating, from the best authority, that of the late learned HECKEWELDER, that the Lena Lenape, a tribe of Indians belonging to the Six Nations, on the arrival of our fore fathers to these shores, pronounced the word English, *Yengees*. The word was thus originally spelt, but in the course of years, in common with thousands of other Indian names and phrases, it became corrupted to *Yankee*. The first

NEW ENGLAND.

settlers of New England were *English*, or Englishmen, from Old England; and however the term *Yankee*, or *English*, may be applied to New Englanders—the descendants of the Puritans consider the term honorable to themselves, and reproachful only to those who misapply it.

SURFACE, SOIL AND PRODUCTIONS. New England is distinguished for its varied surface. Mountains in immense ranges, bold spurs, and solitary eminences; beautiful swells, extended valleys, and alluvial intervales meet the eye in every direction. Large rivers, unrivalled for their rapid courses and hydraulic power; brooks, rivulets, expansive lakes, countless ponds; and a sea coast of more than six hundred miles, decorated with delightful bays, harbors, and romantic islands, form and beautify the outline of a picture of New England.

The *soil* of New England is as varied as its surface. Loam, clay, and sand exist in all their varieties and mixtures. The soil most generally diffused through this country, is a light brown loam, mixed with gravel; fitted, in different degrees of moisture and dryness, for every production common to the climate; and capable, with proper culture, of the highest fertility.

The *agricultural productions* of this country are exceedingly numerous and valuable. The staple articles, and such as are cultivated in all their varieties, are grass, Indian corn, wheat, rye, barley, oats, beans, peas, flax, hemp, broom corn, millet, potatoes, onions, beets, carrots, turnips, squashes, melons, &c.

The *fruits* of New England, both wild and cultivated, are also numerous and abundant. Apples, pears, peaches, plums, cherries, quinces, grapes, in all their varieties; walnuts, chesnuts, Madeira nuts, butternuts; strawberries, whortleberries, blackberries, mulberries, raspberries, &c. This is but the commencement of a list of the fruits, plentiful in New England, and remarkable for their richness and flavor.

The *forests* of New England exhibit a noble variety of trees, not only delightful to the eye, but valuable for all the uses of man. The number of these is so great that a catalogue of them would cover pages.— Among the most valuable are the varieties of the pine, cedar, oak, walnut, spruce, maple, beech, birch, ash; the hemlock, hacmatack, elm, fir, &c.

The *botanical resources* of New England are not inferior to any other section of our country. Among the most beautiful native flowering shrubs are the laurel, rose, honeysuckle, and woodbine.

MINERALOGY. New England unquestionably possesses a vast and

rich variety of minerals; but until recently its people have been too busy in ploughing the ocean, or digging on its surface, to search for treasures within the bosom of its hills and valleys. A spirit of exploration however, has arisen, which promises the most favorable results. Learned and indefatigable men are in the field, and the wisdom of our legislatures will keep them there.

Granite or sienite, in all its varieties, are common in all the states: marble of various hues, varying in quality, most of which, bearing a fine polish, is abundant; coal is found in various places, and strongly suspected to exist in others. Peat is abundant on Cape Cod, where there is no wood; and it is found in meadows surrounded by forests. Copper exists in various parts of New England; and iron ore, of a pure quality, is abundant in various sections of the country. Gold and silver are said to exist, but we hope not. Fine clay, sandstone, manganese; slatestone, for roofing buildings; and various other articles for necessary use are abundant. Garnets, cobalt, rock crystals, and other minerals have been discovered in various parts of New England, and which are mentioned under their localities within the volume.

CLIMATE. The climate of New England is exceedingly various: the temperature ranges from 15° below the zero of Fahrenheit to 95° above. The mercury has been known to descend from 20° to 30° below, and to 102° above; but such cases rarely occur.

European philosophers have imagined that the coldness of this part of America was caused by our northwest winds, proceeding, as they have thought, *from the great lakes*, which are situated in the interior of North America: but since it has been discovered that the great lakes lie westward of the true N. W. point, that opinion has been exploded.

A second cause to which the coldness of these winds has been attributed, is *a chain of high mountains running from southwest to northeast*, in Canada and New Britain, at a great distance beyond the St. Lawrence. A third opinion is that of the venerated Dr. Holyoke, of Salem, who supposed that *the numerous evergreens in this country* are the source of the peculiar cold which it experiences. A fourth opinion is, that the coldness of these winds proceeds from the *forested state of the country.* Dr. Dwight entertained an opinion different from all those we have mentioned, viz: that the winds which generate the peculiar cold of this country *descend*, in most cases, *from the superior regions of the atmosphere.* The N. W. wind rarely brings snow, but when it does, the degree of cold is increased. The deepest snows fall with a N. E. wind, and storms from that quarter are most violent and of longest duration. On the mountains, the snow falls earlier and remains later than in the low

NEW ENGLAND.

grounds. On those elevated summits, the winds have greater force in driving the snow into the long and deep gullies of the mountains, where it is so consolidated, as not to be dissolved by the vernal sun. Spots of snow are seen on the south sides of mountains as late as May, and on the highest till July. A southeast storm is often as violent, but commonly shorter, than one from the northeast. If it begin with snow, it soon changes to rain. A brisk wind from the W. or S. W. with snow or rain, sometimes happens, but its duration is very short. Squalls of this kind are common in March.

One of the greatest inconveniences suffered by the inhabitants of our country, is derived from the frequent changes in the state of the atmosphere. The temperature has been known to change 44° in twenty four hours. Changes are frequent, though seldom in the same degree. Changes from wet to dry, and from dry to wet, are at times unpleasant, and probably unhealthy. There is no month in the year which is not sometimes very pleasant, and sometimes disagreeable. In a series of years, our most pleasant months are June, September and October. Often the first two, and not unfrequently the first three weeks in September are, however, very warm. From the 20th of September to the 20th of October, the weather is delightful. The temperature is mild, the air is sweet, and the sky singularly bright and beautiful. This is the period denominated the Indian Summer. Some persons think June to be a more pleasant month than either September or October. In June, there are usually a few days of intense heat. In all other respects, except the brilliancy and beauty of the heavens, this month must be confessed to have the superiority over all others. The progress of vegetation is wonderful; and it seems as if the creative hand was, in a literal sense, renewing its original plastic efforts, to adorn the world with richness and splendor. All things are alive and gay. "The little hills rejoice on every side. The pastures are clothed with flocks. The valleys are also covered with corn, and shout for joy." Health at the same time prevails in a peculiar degree. The Spring is often chilled by easterly winds and rendered uncomfortable by rains. The Winter months, when the earth is clad with its mantle of snow, is the season for relaxation and pleasure.

The number of fair days in a year compared with the cloudy, is as three to one. We have had but few meteorological journals kept. For several years past they have become more frequent, and it is hoped, that from the increasing attention to the subject, comparative results of the weather will become more numerous and exact.

NAVIGATION AND COMMERCE. The people of New England, from the first settlement of the country to the present time, have been

NEW ENGLAND.

celebrated for their fine ships, nautical prowess, and commercial spirit. Their extended Atlantic sea coast, and their noble forests of ship timber, give them as great, if not greater facilities for these enterprises, than can be found in this or any other country.

The number of vessels built in the United States in 1833, was 1,188; tonnage, 161,626 tons; of which there were built in New England 590: tonnage, 95,146. The number of seamen employed in navigation in the United States, was 67,744, of which 37,142 belonged to New England.

In consequence of the absence of both natural and artificial channels to the fertile countries on the borders of the great lakes, and west of the Alleghany mountains, the exports and imports of New England, compared with the whole of the United States, appears small; but it must be borne in mind that a large proportion of the ships and seamen employed in this commerce belong to New England, and that a vast amount of the exports from other states consist of the products of the manufacturing industry and fishery of that section of the country.

The value of the imports of New England, during the year ending 30 September, 1837, was $22,052,414. Exports, $11,878,324. The total value of the imports of the United States, in that period, was $140,989,217; of exports, $117,419,376.

During that period the American tonnage of New England, entered, compared with that of the United States, was as follows: New England, 1,944 vessels, 393,877 tons: United States, 6,024 vessels, 1,299,720 tons. During that time there were 949 vessels built in the United States; tonnage, 122,987 tons; of which 389 were built in New England, measuring 51,983 tons.

FISHERY. This important branch of industry, and one of the greatest sources of wealth to the American people, has, from time immemorial, been almost exclusively carried on by New England vessels, men, and capital.

In 1837, there were 508 vessels in the United States engaged in the whale fishery; the total tonnage was 127,239 tons; of which number 459 belonged to the New England states; measuring 115,194 tons. The same year there were 127,678 tons employed in the cod and mackerel fishery; 126,963 tons of which were owned in New England.

MANUFACTURES. From the first settlement of the country, to the general peace in Europe in 1815, New England was emphatically a commercial country. During the long wars in Europe, when the flag of the U. S. was the only passport among the belligerent nations, New England ships became the carriers of almost the whole of the eastern

NEW ENGLAND.

continent. The change from war to peace, in Europe, shook New England to its centre. It however stood firm. During a pause, in which conflicting interests in regard to the tariff on imports were settled, the resources of the country were examined, and it was found that a large portion of the capital which had been accustomed to float on every gale; and subjected to the caprice of every nation, might profitably be employed at home, in supplying our own necessities, and placing our independence on a more sure foundation. A manufacturing spirit arose in New England, whose power can only be excelled by the magnitude and grandeur of innumerable streams on which it is seen to move.

Our statistics on this highly important subject are exceedingly imperfect: those only of Massachusetts are attempted to be given. When we find that every state in New England are making rapid advances in this branch of our national wealth, particularly Rhode Island and Connecticut; and that the amount of manufactures in Massachusetts, in a single year, was $86, 282, 616, we may safely indulge the pleasing hope that the period is not distant when our exports will exceed our imports, and that our work shops will no longer remain in Europe.

ITEMS.

THERE are several items in this volume which do not strictly pertain to the general character of the work. Some of them are here noted.

Routes to the White Mountains,	See *White Mountains.*
Distances on Long Island Sound and Hudson river,	*Long I. Sound.*
Saratoga and Ballston Springs,	*White Mountains.*
Lake George, N. Y.,	"
Whitehall, N. Y.,	"
The North Eastern Boundary Question briefly stated,	*Maine.*
Confidence in God,	*Sharon, Ct.*
Troy, N. Y.,	*Long Island Sound.*
New Lebanon Springs, N. Y.,	*Hancock, Mass.*
Firmness of mind,	*Stamford, Ct.*
Catskill Mountains, N. Y.,	*Long Island Sound.*
A venerable minister,	*Hartford, Ct.*
Curious Courtship,	*Lyme, Ct.*
Bay of Fundy,	*Fundy, Bay*
St. John's, N. B.,	"
A Congregation made Prisoners,	*Darien, Ct*
Brave Women, *Dustan's Island, Gorham, Me.,* and *Dorchester, Mass*	
A good shot,	*Dalton, N. H*
Goffe and Whalley, - *Hadley, Mass.,* and *Woodbridge, Ct*	
Peddling, - - *Alexanders' Lake,* and *Berlin, Ct.*	
The " Old Black Bull,"	*Colchester, Ct.*
Prices of sundry articles in 1750,	*Gorham, Me.*
Faithful Missionaries, - *Roxbury, Mass.,* and *Haddam, Ct.*	
Burning of Fairfield,	*Fairfield, Ct.*
Mount Auburn Cemetery,	*Cambridge, Mass.*
Transplanting fish,	*Fairlee* and *Whiting, Vt.*
Obookiah,	*Cornwall, Ct.*
Large Apple Tree,	*Duxbury, Mass.*
Thermometrical observations,	*Epping, N. H.*
Fortunate Stageman,	*Belchertown, Mass.*
Tribute to female character,	*Ledyard, Ct.*
Large Pines, - *Liberty* and *Norridgewock, Me.*	
Generals Allen and Stark, *Litchfield, Ct.,* and *Manchester, N. H.*	
General Putnam and the Wolf,	*Pomfret, Ct.*
Tornadoes, *Warner* and *New London, N. H.,* and *Winchendon, Mass.*	

ITEMS.

Meteoric Stones,	See *Weston, Ct.*
Story of the Frogs,	*Windham, Ct.*
Smart Old Men,	*Whitingham Vt.*, and *Shutesbury, Mass.*
A *modest* office seeker,	*Stratford, N. H.*
Land Title settled by combat,	*Lyme, Ct.*
The "Devils Den," a good ice house,	*Sterling, Ct.*
Large Trout,	*Strong, Me.*
Floating Islands,	*Atkinson, N. H.*, and *Whitingham, Vt.*
Singular motive for marriage,	*Wethersfield, Ct.*
"Lovewell's Fight,"	*Fryeburgh, Me.*
Curious Epitaphs,	*Dorchester, Mass.*
Poised Rock,	*Farmington, N. H.*
A Turtle well marked,	*Middleborough, Mass.*
Mohegan Village,	*Montville, Ct.*
A relic of olden times,	*Ashford, Ct.*
The New Hampshire Giant,	*New Market, N. H.*
"Purgatory Cavern,"	*Sutton, Mass.*
Ice Beds,	*Wallingford, Vt*
"Satan's Kingdom,"	*New Hartford, Ct.*
Names of Towns,	*North Bridgewater, Mass.*
A "South Shore" White oak,	*Plympton, Mass.*
Tak, a slave, the captor of a British General,	*Tiverton, R. I.*
Horrible butchery of a family,	*Wethersfield, Ct.*
Penobscot Indians,	*Orono, Me.*
"The Pool,"	*Oxford, Ct*
First mail stage in the United States,	*Shrewsbury, Mass*
Indian Mound,	*Ossipee, N. H*
George III. and John Adams,	*Quincy, Mass.*
The Hermitess,	*Ridgefield, Ct.*
Tough words for stammerers,	*Roxbury*, and *Webster, Mass.*
Mineral Springs,	*Stafford, Ct.*, and *Hopkinton, Mass.*
Avalanches,	*White Mountains.*
Autumnal Foliage,	"
A worthy maiden Lady,	*Taunton, Mass.*
A Connecticut river law suit,	*Wethersfield, Ct.*
The Drum Rock,	*Warwick, R. I.*
An atrocious murder,	*Washington, Ct.*
A New England Clergyman of 1686,	*Wenham, Mass.*
Ancient Epitaphs,	*Plymouth, Mass.*, and *Windsor, Ct.*
A runaway pond,	*Glover, Vt.*
Lake scenery,	*Winnepisiogee Lake.*

NEW ENGLAND GAZETTEER.

Abbot, Me.

Piscataquis co. This town lies 76 miles N. by E. from Augusta, 130 N. by E. from Portland, and about 40 N. N. E. from Norridgewock. It is bounded N. by Monson, E. by Guilford and S. by Parkman. The Piscataquis river passes nearly through its centre. It was incorporated in 1827. Population, 1837, 649.

Abington, Mass.

Plymouth co. This town is on the high land between Massachusetts and Narraganset bays. Three rivers rise here, two of which empty into the Taunton, the other into the North. It lies 19 miles S. S. E. from Boston, 22 N. W. from Plymouth, 18 N N. E. from Taunton, and 8 S. of Weymouth landing. This town is noted for its manufactures of boots, shoes, and tacks. The total value of its manufactures, in one year, was $847,294, of which the amount of $82,000 was for tacks, and $746,794 for boots and shoes. There were 847 males and 470 females employed in the manufacture of the latter. Population, 1837, 3,057. This town was incorporated in 1712. Its Indian name was *Manamooskeagin*.

Acoakset River,

Rises on the border of the town of Fall River, and meets an arm of Buzzard's bay, at Westport, 12 miles S. W. of New Bedford, Mass.

Acton, Me.

An interior town, in the county of York, recently taken from Shapleigh. It lies near the head waters of Salmon river, by which it is divided, on the W., from New-Hampshire. It is 107 miles S. W. from Augusta, and 15 W. from Alfred. Population, 1837, 1409.

Acton, Vt.

Windham co. This town was first settled in 1781, and in 1782 it was incorporated. It has some fine brooks, but no important mill streams. It lies about 15 miles N. of Newfane, and about 90 S. of Montpelier. Population 1830, 176.

Acton, Mass.

Middlesex co. This is a pleasant farming town of good soil. The Assabet river passes through it. It is 5 miles N. W. by W. of Concord, and 21 N. W. of Boston. Incorporated 1735. Population 1837, 1071.

Acworth, N. H.

Sullivan co. This town is chiefly agricultural in its pursuits. The soil is generally good. Cold river, which rises from Cold pond in this town, affords some good mill seats. This town was formerly noted for the culture of flax, which was manufactured by some of the inhabitants into the finest linen, equal to any imported from Ireland. The town was settled in 1768, and incorporated in 1771. Population 1830, 1401.

It lies 13 miles S. of Newport, and 44 W. of Concord.

Adams, Mass.

Berkshire co. This is a flourishing agricultural and manufacturing township, comprising two villages, north and south, whose trade goes to New York. It is 40 miles E. of Troy, N. Y., 120 W. N. W. of Boston, 29 N. of Lenox, and 7 miles S. E. of Williamstown college. The Hoosack river passes through this town, and affords a great water power. There are in this town 19 cotton mills, 4 satinet factories, and 2 calico printing establishments. There are also in this town large machine shops, 4 taneries, 3 air and cupola furnaces, and manufactories of shovels, spades, hoes, forks, chairs and cabinet ware. The total value of the manufactures of this place in the year ending April 1, 1837, amounted to $1,045,417.

Between the years 1746 and 1756, this town was the scene of much Indian warfare. Traces of old *Fort Massachusetts* are still found. *Saddle Mountain*, the summit of which is called *Gray lock*, the highest of Massachusetts mountains, lies chiefly in this town, and, although it is 3,600 feet above the level of the sea, is of easy ascent. A view from *Gray lock* probably gives " an idea of vastness and even of immensity" better than any other landscape in New England, Mt. Washington, in N. H. excepted. The natural bridge on *Hudson's Brook*, in this town, is a curiosity worthy the notice of travellers. The waters of this brook have worn a fissure from 30 to 60 feet deep and 30 rods in length, through a body of white marble, or limestone, and formed a bridge of that material, 50 feet above the surface of the water. There is a cavern in this town, 30 feet long, 20 high, and 20 wide. Incorporated 1778. Population 1820 1,836—1830, 2,648—1834, 3,000—and in 1837, 4,191

Addison, Me.

Washington co. This town was incorporated in 1797. Population, 1837, 901. It lies 14 miles W. by S. from Machias, and 135 E. by N. from Augusta. Addison lies between Pleasant and Indian rivers, and near the south entrance into Mispecky reach. *Addison Point*, or Cape Split, jutting out into the sea, off which are several small islands, is the principal harbor and place of trade.

Addison County, Vt.,

Middlebury is the chief town. This county is bounded on the N. by Chittenden county; E. by Washington and Orange counties, and a part of Windsor county; S. by Rutland county, and W. by Lake Champlain. It was incorporated in 1787, and contains about 700 square miles. Large quantities of white and beautifully variegated marble, which receives a fine polish, is found in this county, and large quantities of it are quarried and transported to various markets.— This county is admirably well watered by Otter Creek, which rises near its southern boundary, and extends nearly through its centre;— by Mad and White rivers; and by Lake Champlain, which affords it many navigable privileges. The soil is good, particularly in those towns below the mountains, and bordering the lake and rivers. This county contains 22 towns. Population, 1820, 20,469—1830, 24,940. Inhabitants to a square mile, 35.

Addison, Vt.

Addison co. This is supposed to be the first place settled by the whites, in this state, west of the mountains. The town is pleasantly located on the east side of lake Champlain, and nearly opposite to Crown Point, in the state of New-York. At this place the lake is about 3 miles broad. The French,

It is said, commenced a settlement here in 1731; the same year that they erected a fort at Crown Point. The English came here about 1770. Otter Creek passes into the town, but affords no important mill site. The surface of the town is low and level. Mill and Pike rivers, are small streams, which fall into the lake opposite to Crown Point. This town lies about 12 miles W. N. W. from Middlebury, and 40 W. S. W. from Montpelier. Population 1830, 1,306.

Agamenticus Mountain,

So called, being three elevations of land in York, Me., about 4 miles from the sea, and a noted land mark for those on the coast to the northward and eastward of Portsmouth harbor. The highest summit is 673 feet above the ocean. It is said that *Saint Aspinquid* died on this mountain, in 1682, and that his funeral was celebrated by the Indians, by the sacrifice of 6711 wild animals.

Agawam, Mass.

The Indian name of a river in Wareham, and of a part of Westfield river; and the name of a village on Westfield river, 2 miles S. W. from Springfield.

Albany, Me.

Oxford co. This town was incorporated in 1803. It lies about 17 miles W. by N. from Paris, and 58 W. from Augusta. It is the source of Crooked river, which empties into Sebago Lake. Population, 1837, 598.

Albany, N. H.,

Strafford co., lies 60 miles N. by E. from Concord, and 67 N. N. W. from Dover. The principal river in Albany, is Swift river, which passes from W. to E. into the Saco, at Conway. There are several small streams in different parts of the town, furnishing convenient mill privileges. These streams were once the residence of numbers of the beaver, otter, &c.—There are several lofty hills and mountains in this town, the highest of which is called Chocorua, and is visible from a great extent of country. It received its name from *Chocorua*, an Indian, who was killed on the summit by a party of hunters in time of peace, before the settlement of the place. The predominant rock of these hills is granite—a soft, decomposing variety, in which the crystals and grains of feldspar are very large. The soil is fertile, being a sandy loam, mixed occasionally with coarse gravel. There are some fertile intervale lands on the borders of Swift river. This town has been considerably retarded by a peculiar disease which afflicts neat cattle. Young cattle cannot be reared, nor can cows or oxen be kept here for a series of years, without being attacked by a singular and fatal distemper. It commences with a loss of appetite—the animals refuse hay, grain and salt—become emaciated; an obstinate costiveness attends, but the abdomen becomes smaller than in health, and is diminished to one third its original bulk. After these symptoms have continued for an indefinite period, a brisk scouring comes on, and the animals fall away and die. Though superstition may have found a reason in the dying curse of the murdered Chocorua, philosophy has not yet ascertained a satisfactory cause for the disease. It is probably owing to the properties contained in the waters. This town was granted Nov. 6, 1766, to Clement March, Joseph Senter and others, and until the 2d July, 1833, it bore the name of Burton. Population in 1830, 325.

Albany, Vt.

Orleans co. This town was granted in the year 1781, by the name of Lutterloh; in 1815 it was changed to its present name. It is watered by a number of ponds, and by Black river and its branches. Albany lies 34 miles N. from Montpelier, and 9 S. of Irasburgh. Population, 1830, 683.

Albion, Me.

Kennebec co. This fine farming town lies on the stage road from Augusta to Bangor; 24 miles N. E. from the former, and 44 S. W. from the latter. Population, 1837, 1609. This town produced 10,728 bushels of wheat, in 1837.

Alburgh, Vt.

Grand Isle co. Settlements commenced here by emigrants from Canada, in 1782. This town lies at the N. W. corner of the state and of New England; 10 miles N. from North Hero, and 79 miles N. W. from Montpelier. It is bounded by the waters of Lake Champlain, except on the north, where it meets the Canada line, in north latitude 45°. The soil is good and finely timbered. It has a mineral spring, of some repute in scrofulous cases. Population, 1830, 1,239.

Alexander, Me.

Washington co. About 25 miles N. by W. from Machias, and S. of Baileyville, and Baring, which border on the river St. Croix. In this town are some ponds, which, with the large pond in Baring and Alexander, produce a large stream which empties into Cobscook bay. Population, 1837, 457.

Alexander's Lake.

This beautiful sheet of water, of about a mile in length and half a mile in breadth, lies in the town of Killingly, Ct., and was formerly known to the Indians by the name of *Mashapaug*. Its present name is derived from Nell Alexander, a man who settled at Killingly in 1720, and became proprietor of a large portion of the town. As this person gained his wealth in a manner which illustrates the antiquity of the propensity of the inhabitants of this state to the once honored, yet now despised employment of *peddling*, we will give the reader a short notice of his history. He came from Scotland, with a great number of other emigrants, in a ship which was to land them at Boston. Just before leaving the ship he discovered a *gold ring* upon deck, for which he could find no owner. Thus fortunately provided, after his arrival he pawned the gold ring for small articles of trade, which he peddled in Boston and Roxbury. He was very prosperous, and finally became able to redeem the author of his success, and pursue his business without embarrassment. After a few years of constant activity, he acquired sufficient property to purchase a plantation of 3,500 acres in Killingly. The gold ring was transmitted as a sort of *talisman*, to *his only son Nell*, who transferred it to *his only son Nell;* who is now living at an advanced age, and has already placed it in the hands of *his grandson Nell;* and so it will doubtless continue from *Nell* to *Nell*, agreeably to the request of the *first Nell*, until the "last knell of the race is tolled!"

A singular tradition has been handed down to us by the aborigines concerning the origin of this lake.

In ancient times, when the red men of this quarter had long enjoyed prosperity, that is, when they had found plenty of game in the woods, and fish in the ponds and rivers, they at length fixed a time for a general powwow, a sort of festival for eating, drinking, smoking, singing and dancing. The spot chosen for this purpose was a sandy hill, or mountain, covered with tall pines, occupying the situation where the lake now lies. The powwow lasted four days in succession, and was to continue longer had not the Great Spirit, enraged at the licentiousness which prevailed there, resolved to punish them. Accordingly, while the red people in immense numbers were capering about upon the summit of the mountain, it suddenly "gave way" beneath them, and sunk to a great depth, when the water from below rushed up and covered them all except *one good old squaw*, who occupied one of the peaks, which now bears the name of Loon's Island.

Mr. Barber in his admirable work entitled "*Connecticut Historical Collections*," from which this account is taken, observes, "whether the tradition is entitled to credit or not, we will do it justice by affirming that in a clear day, when there is no wind and the surface of the lake is smooth, the huge trunks and leafless branches of *gigantic pines* may be occasionally seen in the deepest part of the water, some of them reaching almost to the surface, in such huge and fantastic forms as to cause the beholder to startle!"

Alexandria, N. H.

Grafton co. A small part of Newfound lake lies in this town. Alexandria is 30 miles N. W. from Concord, and 40 S. E. from Haverhill. Population, 1830, 1,083. Incorporated, 1782. On Fowler's and Smith's rivers and several other smaller streams are about 2000 acres of intervale land, which produce flax, potatoes and grass in abundance. Other parts of the town are favorable for wheat and maize.—This town was first settled by Jonathan, John M. and William Corliss, in 1769.

Alfred, Me.

One of the shire towns of York county. It lies 24 miles N. from York, 35 S. from Portland and 86 S. W. from Augusta. Incorporated, 1808. Population, 1837, 1,360. This is a good farming town and is well watered by the higher sources of Mousum river, which meets the sea at Kennebunk. In this town is a society of those neat and industrious horticulturists and artizans, denominated "Shakers."

Alford, Mass.

Berkshire co. On the line of the state of New York, and watered by branches of Green river. Some manufactories of leather and shoes. 125 miles W. from Boston, 14 S. by W. from Lenox, and 24 E. of Hudson, N. Y. Population, 1837, 441. Incorporated, 1773.

Allenstown, N. H.

Merrimack co. On the Suncook river, 11 miles S. E. from Concord, and 38 W. from Portsmouth. The land generally is of an ordinary quality, though there are some fine farms. The town is principally covered with a growth of oak and pine timber; and great quantities of lumber are annually taken down the river. Allenstown is well watered, though no large stream passes through it. Great Bear brook furnishes the principal mill seats. Catamount hill is the highest land in town. At the E. end of this hill is a precipice of 70 feet nearly perpendicular, at the foot of which is a cavern of some extent, inclining upwards. The first settlers were Rob't Buntin and others. In 1748, while at work on the western bank of the Merrimack river, opposite the mouth of the Suncook, in company with James Carr, Mr. Buntin and his son, ten years of age, were surprised by a party of Indians. Carr attempted to escape, and was shot down. Buntin and his son, making no resistance, were not harmed; but taken through the wilderness to Canada, and sold to a French trader at Montreal; with whom they remained about eleven months, escaped, and fortunately reached home in safety. Andrew, the son, continued on his father's farm until the commencement of the revolution, when, entering the service of his country, he died in her defence at White Plains, Oct. 28, 1776. Incorporated July 2, 1831. Population, 1830, 421.

Alna, Me.

This town is situated in the county of Lincoln, 10 miles N. from Wiscasset, 54 N. E. from Portland, and 20 S. S. E. from Augusta. Incorporated 1794. Population, 1837, 1,138. This is a pleasant town and well watered by Sheepscot river.

Alstead, N. H.,

Cheshire co., is 12 miles S. E. from Charlestown, 14 N. from Keene and 50 W. by S. from Concord. This town is well watered by small streams. Cold river passes through the N. W. part; and some of the branches of Ashuelot river have their sources in this town. There are a number of ponds, the principal of which is Warren's pond;—length, 250 rods, breadth, 150. Perch and pickerel are here caught in great abundance. The soil is strong and productive, and the farms generally well cultivated. Manufactures flourish in this town, and great attention is paid to education. Alstead was originally called Newton, and was granted by charter, August 6, 1763, to Samuel Chase and 69 others. General Amos Shepard, who was for many years a member of the General Court of this state, and President of the Senate from 1797 to 1804, resided in this town, and was one of its principal inhabitants from 1777 to the time of his death, Jan. 1, 1812. By his persevering industry, his economy and correctness in business, and at the same time, by a rigid adherence to uprightness and integrity in his dealings with his fellow men, he acquired a handsome fortune, and was in many things, a pattern worthy of imitation. Population in 1830, 1,552. This town has 6000 sheep.

Alton, N. H.

Strafford co. This town lies 22 miles N. E. from Concord, and 25 N. W. from Dover, and is bounded N. by Winnepisiogee lake and bay. The town is rough and uneven; the soil hard and rocky, but productive when well cultivated. The growth of wood is chiefly oak, beech, maple and pine. The principal elevations are Mount-Major and Prospect Hill Merrymeeting bay extends S. about 1800 rods into this town, where it receives the waters of Merrymeeting river. Half-moon pond, between Alton and Barnstead, is 300 rods long and 150 wide. This town was originally called *New Durham Gore*, and was settled in 1770, by Jacob Chamberlain and others. It was incorporated Jan. 15, 1796. Population in 1830, 1,993. This town has 2000 sheep.

Amesbury, Mass.

This town is situated on the N side of Merrimack river, in the county of Essex, 40 miles N. E. from Boston, 6 N. W. from Newburyport, and 7 N. E. from Haverhill. Population, 1837, 2,567. It was taken from Salisbury in 1668, and is separated from it by Powow river, a navigable stream for vessels of 300 tons. A pond, covering about 1000 acres, back of the town, 90 feet above the sea, serves as a reservoir for a constant and extensive water power. The manufacture of flannel and satinet is very extensively pursued. The amount of those articles manufactured in the year ending April 1, 1837, was $425,000. Many vessels are built here of superior timber, and the manufacture of boots, shoes, leather, chairs, phaetons, gigs, and carryalls is very considerable. The total amount of the various manufactures of this place is about $500,000 annually. About half the population of the town is engaged in mechanical labor. Josiah Bartlett, M. D. one of the signers of the declaration of independence was born here, in 1729. He died May 19, 1795.

Amherst, Me.

Hancock co. This town is bounded on the S. by Mariaville. The head waters of Union river pass through it. It lies about 25 miles E. of Bangor. Population, 1837, 198.

Amherst, N. H.

An important town, and the seat of justice in Hillsborough county, is situated on Souhegan river. It is 23 miles S. from Concord, about the same distance from Hopkinton, 47 N. W. from Boston, 40 E. from Keene, 60 S. E. from Windsor, Vt. and 434 from Washington. Souhegan is a considerable and very important stream, and in its course to the Merrimack river from this town, affords some of the finest water privileges in the county. Babboosick, Little Babboosuck and Jo English ponds are the largest collections of water. In some parts, and particularly on Souhegan river, the soil is of an excellent quality, producing abundant crops. In other parts, on the hills elevated above the village, the soil is of a good quality, and several valuable farms are found under good cultivation. The village is pleasant and contains many handsome buildings. There is a spacious common between the two principal rows of houses, which is often used for public purposes. There is what is termed a mineral spring, about 1 1-2 miles E. of the meeting house. The water has been found useful in rheumatic complaints, and in scrofulous and scorbutic habits; for poisons by ivy, dog-wood, &c. This town was granted in 1733, by Massachusetts, to those persons living and the heirs of those not living, who were officers and soldiers in the Narragansett war of 1675. It was called *Narraganset No.3*, and afterwards *Souhegan-West*. The number of proprietors was 120, of whom a considerable number belonged to Salem, Mass. The town was incorporated Jan. 18, 1760, when it assumed the name of Amherst, in compliment to Lord Jeffrey Amherst. Among the worthy citizens of Amherst who deserve remembrance, may be mentioned Hon. Moses Nichols, a native of Reading, Mass., who was a colonel under Gen. Stark in the Battle of Bennington: Hon. Samuel Dana, a native of Brighton, Mass. Hon. William Gordon, eminent in the profession of the law.— Hon. Robert Means, who died Jan. 24, 1823, at the age of 80, was for a long period of time a resident in Amherst. He was a native of Ireland. In 1764, he came to this country, where by his industry and application to business, he acquired a large property, and great respect.

Amherst did its duty manfully during the revolutionary contest. During the first four years of that war about one in seventy of its people died in the service. The expenses of that war, to this town, "in addition of any bounties, travel, or wages given or promised by the State or the United States, was found to be in specie, £3,511." Population, 1830, 1,657.

Amherst, Mass.

Hampshire co. The college and village in this town are on elevated ground and command a very beautiful prospect of the surrounding country. Amherst was taken from Hadley, and incorporated in 1759. Population, 1837, 2,602. It lies 7 miles E. by N. from Northampton, 103 S. from Dartmouth college, and 82 miles W. from Boston. There are good mill sites in this town on two streams, which empty into the Connecticut at Hadley. Its manufactures are various, consisting of woollen cloth, boots, shoes, leather, hats, paper, chairs, cabinet ware, tin ware, axes, ploughs, palm-leaf hats, carriages, wagons, (large and

2*

small) joiners' planes, stoves, steel hammers, pistols, and *bowie knives.* Total annual amount of manufactures, about $200,000. See *Register.*

Amity, Me.

Washington co. Township No. 10, first range of townships from the east line of the state,—about 100 miles N. E. from Bangor. Incorporated 1836. Population, 1837, 130. This town has fine soil for wheat.

Amonoosuck Rivers, N. H.

Upper and *Lower.* The Upper Amonoosuck rises in the ungranted lands north of the White Mountains, and passing N. E. into Dummer, approaches to within a few miles of the Androscoggin; thence turning abruptly to the S. W. it pursues that direction and falls into Connecticut river near the centre of Northumberland. Its whole length is about 50 miles. The valley of the Upper Amonoosuck is 7 or 8 miles in breadth, and more than 20 in length: it is scooped out with great beauty, the surface gently rising to the summits of the mountains on the N. The Lower Amonoosuck rises on the W. side of the White Mountains, and after running a course of 50 miles, falls into the Connecticut just above Haverhill, by a mouth 100 yards wide. At the distance of two miles from its mouth, it receives the Wild Amonoosuck, a stream 40 yards wide, and, when raised by freshets, very swift and furious in its course. The waters of the Amonoosuck are pure, and its bed clean; the current lively, and in some places rapid. The valley of the Lower Amonoosuck is about half a mile in width, and was probably once the bed of a lake, its S. W. limit being the rise of ground at its foot, over which the waters descended in their course to the Connecticut. There is a fine fall in this river about 6 1-2 miles from the Notch of the White Mountains, where the descent is 50 feet, cut through a mass of stratified granite.

Amoskeag Falls & Village, N. H.

These falls are in the Merrimack river; between Goffstown on the W. and Manchester on the E. The whole fall of the river, within the distance of half a mile, is 54 feet, producing a great hydraulic power. A company, with a large capital, have commenced forming canals and erecting buildings for manufacturing purposes on a very extensive scale. Their plan provides for 37 mills, each containing 6000 spindles. Two canals, 2 factories, a number of dwelling houses, machine shops, &c. are now nearly completed. The canals are each a mile in length, and will, when completed, be equal to any works of the kind in our country. The *village* is in Goffstown, 16 miles below Concord and 18 miles above Nashua; delightfully situated on the banks of these majestic falls. Amoskeag is already a place of considerable business, and must eventually become the mart of large manufacturing operations. The vicinity of these falls was much frequented by the Indians. The Sachem Wonolanset resided here. The tribe under him was sometimes molested by the Mohawks, who carried terror to the hearts of all the eastern Indians. In time of war between these hostile tribes, the Indians living in the neighborhood of the falls, concealed their provisions in the large cavities of the rocks on the island in the middle of the upper part of the fall. They entertained an idea that their deity had cut out these cavities for that purpose.

Andover, Me.

Oxford co. This town was incorporated in 1804. Population, 1837, 551. It lies about 30 miles N. W. from Paris, 61 W. N. W. from Augusta, and 70 N. W. from Portland. It is finely watered by Ellis' river, a branch of the Androscoggin. This town is an extensive glebe of upland and intervale of excellent quality, surrounded by White Cap, Bald Pate, Blue and Cone mountains. The town was first settled by industrious and intelligent farmers from Essex county, Mass., in 1790, and most of its present population maintain the characteristics of their fathers.

Andover, N. H.

Merrimack co. It lies 20 miles N. W. from Concord, and about 18 E. by N. from Newport. Population, 1830, 1,324. The Blackwater in the S. W. part of the town, is the principal stream; but numerous rills and brooks find their way down the hills into the ponds or Blackwater. There are six ponds in Andover, the largest of which are Chance and Loon ponds, both picturesque, and their waters pure. The surface of this town is extremely uneven, and in some parts rocky and barren. The Ragged Mountains pass along the N., and the Kearsarge extends its base along the W. The soil is in many parts of good quality, and pleasant villages are formed in different parts of the town. This town was granted in 1746, and was called *New Breton*, in honor of the captors of Cape Breton in 1745; in which expedition several of the grantees were engaged. It retained this name until June 25, 1779, when it was incorporated by its present name. The first inhabitant of Andover was Joseph Fellows, who moved into the place in 1761: he died March 14, 1811, aged 84. Among the deceased citizens who are remembered with respect by the inhabitants, we may mention Dr. Silas Barnard, the first physician in town, a native of Bolton, Mass., who died June 25, 1795: Dr. Jacob B. Moore, a native of Georgetown, Me., born Sept., 5, 1772; settled in Andover in 1796; died Jan. 10, 1818. He possessed respectable poetical talents; was a writer on political subjects in the public papers, and was eminent in his profession. Jonathan Weare, Esq., a civil magistrate, highly respected for his integrity, died in 1816. Mr. Joseph Noyes was much honored for his charitable disposition. In 1782 a congregational church was formed and the Rev. Jossiah Babcock, of Milton, Mass., was ordained. Andover, though rough, is well adapted for grazing. It feeds about 4,000 sheep.

Andover, Vt.

Windsor co. Emigrants from Enfield, Ct., first made a permanent settlement in this town, in 1776. It was organized, as a town, in 1781. It is a mountainous township. Markhum and Terrible mountains lie in the western part. The land is uneven, the soil is hard, and the town possesses but few water privileges. Population, 1830, 975. It lies 20 miles S. W. from Windsor, 37 N. E. from Bennington, and 68 S. from Montpelier. The number of sheep in this town is about 4,500.

Andover, Mass.

Essex co. This town lies on the south side of the Merrimack river, and is well watered by the Shawsheen river; and by Great Pond and Haggett's Pond, covering an area of 721 acres. It is 20 miles N. by W. of Boston, 15 N. N. W. of Salem, 10 E. of Lowell, and 43 S. S. E. of Concord, N. H. This town was first settled in 1643. Incorporated, 1646. Population, 1837, 4,878. This town has a valuable water power, which is used for manufacturing purposes to a great extent. The value of its manufactures, for the year ending April 1, 1837, amounted to $624,450. They consisted of woollen goods, boots, shoes, leather, flax, soapstone, machinery, tin and cabinet wares, chairs and hats. This is a very beautiful town of fine soil and under excellent cultivation. It is on high ground and commands a variety of beautiful landscape. The access to Andover from Boston by the railroad, is easy and very pleasant. This town has long been celebrated for its literary and theological institutions. There is no place in New England better situated for seminaries of learning. See *Register.*

Androscoggin River,

Or *Ameriscoggin*. Its most northerly branch is the Margallaway river which receives the waters of Dead and Diamond rivers,and unites with those flowing from Umbagog lake, about a mile distant from its outlet. From this junction, the confluent stream pursues a southerly course till it approaches near the White Mountains, where it receives several considerable tributaries, and passes into Maine,N. of Mount Moriah. It there bends to the E. and S. E.; in which course, through a fertile country, it passes near the sea-coast, and turning N. runs over the falls at Brunswick, not far from Bowdoin College, into Merrymeeting bay, forming a junction with the Kennebec, 20 miles from the sea.

Ann, Cape, Mass.

See *Gloucester, Mass.*

Anson, Me.

Somerset co. Anson lies about 10 miles N. E. from Norridgewock, 112 W. from Portland, and 40 N. E. from Augusta. Incorporated, 1798. Population, 1837, 1,894. It lies at the junction of Seven Mile Brook with the Kennebec, on the western side of that river. Here are fine farms and good husbandmen. In 1837, 12,713 bushels of wheat was raised.

Antrim, N. H.

Hillsborough co. It is 20 miles N. W. from Amherst, 30 S. W. from Concord, and 67 from Boston. The E. part of Antrim lies on Contoocook river; and though somewhat hilly, is a tract of productive land, a considerable proportion of which is arable. On the river there are valuable tracts of alluvial land. The North Branch river, so called, a small stream originating from several ponds in Stoddard, furnishes several valuable mill seats and in some parts of its course, it is bordered by tracts of intervale. The W. part of the town is mountainous, but suitable for grass, and affords an extensive range of good pasturage. There are six natural ponds well stored with perch and pike. A curiosity has been discovered in the middle branch of Contoocook river, a rock, about 10 feet long and 8 feet wide, covered with a shallow coat of moss, affording sustenance to 21 different kinds of plants and shrubs, three of which produce edible fruit. Antrim was incorporated March 22, 1777. The first settlement was made by Dea. James Aiken about the year 1768. Dea. Aiken was a native of Londonderry, where he was born in 1731. He died July 27, 1817. He was a professor of the christian religion more than 60 years, and adorned it by a serious and exemplary life. Population, 1830, 1,309. Antrim has about 4,400 sheep.

Appleton, Me.

Waldo co. This town lies 20 miles S. W. from Belfast, 84 N. W. from Portland, and 35 E. by S. from Augusta. Incorporated, 1829.— Population, 1837, 839. It is situated between the head waters of the Muscongus and St. George's rivers. Considerable wheat is grown here.

Argyle, Me.

Penobscot co. This is a new town, but fertile, and flourishing in its agricultural pursuits. It produces the best of wheat. It lies 89 miles N. E. from Augusta.—Population, 1830, 326; in 1837, 601.

Arlington, Vt.

Bennington co. This town was first settled in 1763. The time of its organization is not known, as one Bisco, a tory, the town clerk in 1777, destroyed the records. It is finely watered by Green river, Mill and Warm brooks, and Roaring branch which fall into the Battenkill, at the north part of the town. These streams afford excellent mill sites, and on their banks are large bodies of superior meadow land. West and Red mountains extend through the west part of the town and supply a great variety of good timber. Excellent marble is found here;—considerable quantities of which are wrought and transported. Here is a medicinal spring, and a cavern of large dimensions. The spring is not of much note, but the cavern is a great curiosity. This is a flourishing town in both its agricultural and manufacturing pursuits. The number of sheep in this town in 1836, was 10,077. It lies 15 miles N. from Bennington, 106 S. W. from Montpelier, and 40 N. E. from Troy, N. Y. Population, 1830, 1,207.

Aroostook River.

This river rises in the interior part of Penobscot county, Me., and after traversing more than 100 miles, and receiving many and powerful tributaries in that state, it falls into the river St. Johns in New Brunswick. The lands on this river and its branches are very fertile, and are said to be equal to the celebrated Genesee lands for the culture of wheat.

Ascutney Mountain, Vt.

This mountain is situated in the towns of Windsor and Weathersfield. It is 3,116 feet above the Connecticut river, at Windsor; and 3,320 feet above the level of the sea. It consists of granite and is nearly destitute of vegetable covering. From Windsor, to the base, is 4 miles. Its ascent is generally steep, but travellers who delight to view rich and variegated scenery, will be amply rewarded for the toil of a pilgrimage to its summit.

Ashburnham, Mass.

Worcester co. This township was granted to Thomas Tileston and others of Dorchester, for services in an expedition against Canada, in the year 1690. For many years it was called "Dorchester Canada." It was incorporated as a town in 1765. Ashburnham lies on the height of land between the Connecticut and Merrimack rivers. It is watered by large ponds which furnish good mill seats. Its manufactures consist of cotton goods, boots, shoes, leather, chairs, cabinet ware, fur and palm-leaf hats; the annual value of which is about $100,000. This town is 30 miles N. from Worcester, 50 N. W. from Boston, and 35 W. from Lowell. Population, 1837, 1,758.

Ashby, Mass.

This is a pleasant town, in the county of Middlesex, on the line of N. H. It is 25 miles N. W. from Concord, 42 W. N. W. from Boston and 8 S. E. from New Ipswich, N. H. Population, 1837, 1,201. It has some manufactures of palm-leaf hats boots, shoes, chairs, wooden ware, and curled hair.

Ashfield, Mass.

Franklin co. This town was first settled in 1754, and, until its incorporation, in 1764, it was called Huntstown. Population, 1837,—1,656. This town is on elevated land between Deerfield and Westfield rivers, to each of which it sends a small tributary. It has small manufactures of leather, scythe snaiths, spirits and essences, and about

8000 sheep. It is 105 miles W. from Boston, 12 S. W. from Greenfield, and 15 N. W. from Northampton.

Ashford, Ct.

Windham co. This town was first settled in 1710. Incorporated, 1714. It is watered by several small streams which afford a water power for one cotton and three woollen factories. The surface of the town is rough and stony, but excellent for grazing. The number of sheep in this town is about 5,000. It lies 31 miles E. from Hartford, and 14 N. W. from Brooklyn. Population, 1830, 2,660. The following is said to have occurred in this town, and is told to illustrate the manners and customs of ancient times. "A concourse of people were assembled on the hill in front of the meeting house, to witness the punishment of a man who had been convicted of neglecting to go to meeting on the Sabbath for a period of three months. According to the existing law for such delinquency, the culprit was to be publicly whipped at the post. Just as the whip was about to be applied, a stranger on horseback appeared, rode up to the crowd of spectators, and enquired for what purpose they were assembled. Being informed of the state of the case, the strange gentleman rose upright in his stirrups, and with emphasis addressed the astonished multitude as follows: 'You men of Ashford, serve God as if the D...l was in you! Do you think you can *whip* the grace of God into men? Christ will have none but volunteers.' The people stared, while the speaker, probably not caring to be arraigned for contempt of court, put spurs to his horse, and was soon out of sight; nor was he ever more seen or heard of by the good people of Ashford." Col. Thomas Knowlton was a native of this town. He was at the battle of Bunker Hill, and fell at Hærlem Heights, in 1776. Washington termed him, in a general order after his death, "the gallant and brave Col. Knowlton, who would have been an honor to any country."

Ashuelot River, N. H.,

Or Ashwillet, a river in Cheshire county, which has its source in a pond in Washington. It runs in a southerly course through Marlow and Gilsum, to Keene, where it receives a considerable branch issuing from ponds in Stoddard. From Keene it proceeds to Swanzey, where it receives another considerable branch which originates in Jaffrey and Fitzwilliam. It pursues its course southerly and westerly through Winchester into Hinsdale, where, at the distance of about 3 miles from the S. line of the state, it empties into the Connecticut.

Assabet River, Mass.

This river rises in the neighborhood of Westborough;—it passes through Marlborough, Northborough and Stow, and joins Sudbury river at Concord.

Athens, Me.

Somerset co. This town was incorporated in 1803. Population, 1837, 1,424. It is about 18 miles N. N. E. from Norridgewock, 114 N. N. E. from Portland and 45 N. from Augusta. It is watered by a tributary of Kennebec river.

Athens Vt.

Windham co. This town lies 14 miles N. from Newfane, 98 S. from Montpelier, 10 W. from Bellows' Falls, and about 40 N. E. from Bennington. Population, 1830, 415. This town was first settled in 1780, by people from Rindge, N. H., and Winchendon, Mass. They encountered great hardships. "The snow was four feet deep when they came into town, and they had to beat their own path for 8 miles through the woods. A small yoke of oxen were the only domestic animals that they took with them." This is a good township of land, particularly for grazing. It has 2000 sheep. Here are productive orchards, pine timber, and a small mill stream.

Athol, Mass.

Worcester co. The Indian name of this town was *Paquoig.* This pleasant place lies 60 miles W. N. W. from Boston, 28 N. W. from Worcester, and about 24 W. from Fitchburg. Miller's river is a fine stream, and affords Athol a great water power. The manufactures of Athol consist of cotton goods, boots, shoes, leather, paper, iron castings, scythes, ploughs, cabinet ware, machinery, straw bonnets, palm leaf hats, shoe pegs, harnesses, shoe and hat boxes, pails, sashes, doors and blinds;—annual amount about $175,000. Incorporated, 1762. Population, 1837, 1,603.

Atkinson, Me.

Piscataquis co. This township was incorporated in 1819. It lies about 35 miles N. N. W. from Bangor, 132 N. E. from Portland, and 79 N. E. from Augusta. Population, 1837, 557. It is bounded on the N. by Piscataquis river. This town has a good soil. Wheat crop, 1837, 5,168 bushels.

Atkinson, N. H.

Rockingham co. It is situated 30 miles S. W. from Portsmouth, and 32 S. E. from Concord. The surface of Atkinson is uneven; the soil of a superior quality, and well cultivated. The cultivation of the apple has received much attention here, and the finest fruit is produced. Incorporated Sept. 3, 1767, by its present name, in honor of Theodore Atkinson. Several of the first settlers lived to a great age. The Rev. Stephen Peabody was the first settled minister in Atkinson. He was a native of Andover, Mass. He took an active part in the revolution, and served as chaplain in the regiment under Col. Poor, stationed at Winter-Hill. The academy in this town is one of the oldest and most respectable institutions in the state; it was incorporated Feb. 17, 1791. "In a large meadow in this town, there is an island, containing 7 or 8 acres, which was formerly loaded with valuable pine timber and other forest wood. When the meadow is overflowed, by means of an artificial dam, this island rises in the same degree as the water rises, which is sometimes six feet. Near the middle of this island, is a small pond, which has been gradually lessening ever since it was first known, and is now almost covered with verdure. In the water of this pond, there have been fish in plenty; which, when the meadow hath been flowed, have appeared there, and when the water hath been drawn off, have been left on the meadow; at which time the island settles to its usual place." Population, 1830, 555.

Attleborough, Mass.

This town lies at the N. W. corner of the county of Bristol; 12 miles N. from Providence, R. I., 8 N. W. from Taunton, and 28 S. from Boston. A branch of the Pawtucket rises here, and several other rivers pass through the town. It possesses a fine water power. It was first settled, 1644, and incorporated in 1694. Population, 1837, 2,396. The value of the manufactures at this place, for the year ending April 1, 1837, amounted to about $500,000. That of cotton goods alone to $229,571. The other manufactures consisted of boots, shoes, leather, metal buttons, combs, jewelry, clocks, planing machines, carpenter's tools, straw bonnets, chairs and cabinet ware. This town suffered much during the reign of the celebrated Indian King Philip. In 1675, Attleborough was a *frontier settlement.*

Auburn, Mass.

Worcester co. Until 1837, this town had been called Ward, in honor of General Ward, of the revolutionary army. It was incorporated in 1778. Population, 1837, 1,183. Auburn is a pleasant agricultural town. French river passes through it. It lies 5 miles S. by W. from Worcester, and 45 W. S. W. from Boston.

Augusta, Me.

This delightful town, the CAPITAL of the state, and chief town of the county of Kennebec, is in N. Lat. 44° 18′ 43″ and W. Lon. 69° 50′. It lies 146 miles N. E. from Concord, N. H.; 182 E. N. E. from Montpelier, Vt.; 163 N. N. E. from Boston, Mass.; 203 N. N. E. from Providence, R. I.; 260 N. E. from Hartford, Ct.; and 595 miles N. E. from Washington. Augusta is situated at the head of sloop navigation on Kennebec river, 43 miles from the sea. The town lies on both sides of the Kennebec, and contains an area of 8 by 6 miles. It was first settled in 1771, and incorporated in 1797. In 1836 it contained 6,300 inhabitants. Its Indian name was *Cushnoe.* There was, in its early settlement, a fort, and four block houses built of timber, to afford protection to the inhabitants from the Indians, who were then very troublesome. The fort was called *Fort Western,* and is still standing on the east bank of the river, and is now occupied as a dwelling house. This is already a very flourishing town, not only in its agricultural pursuits, but in its commerce and manufactures. The tonnage of the place is about 3000 tons. Its exports are lumber of all kinds, oats, peas, beans, hay, potatoes, wool, cider, apples, &c.— When the extent and resources of the noble Kennebec and its tributaries, above tide water, are considered, some idea may be formed of the vast quantity of lumber that must pass this place on its passage to market.

The Kennebec bridge, uniting the east and west parts of the town is a fine structure. It was built in 1799; is 520 feet in length, and cost $28,000. The town rises by an easy ascent on both sides of the river to a level surface; it is well laid out, neatly built, and contains many handsome dwelling houses. Many of the streets are decorated by trees, planted on each side;—a striking evidence of the good taste of the inhabitants.

The *State House* is a spacious and elegant structure, located upon a beautiful eminence about half a mile from the village, on the road towards Hallowell, and commands an extensive and very delightful prospect. It is built of hammered granite, or rather gneiss of a white color, and very much resembles marble, at a distance. The material of which it was built, was quarried from the spot on which it stands. It has a spacious hall for the Representatives; two of convenient size for the Senate and the Executive Departments, and rooms for all the offices immediately connected with the Government. In front is an extensive *common,* adorned with trees tastefully arranged, which, when grown into shades, will afford a delightful promenade.

The *United States' Arsenal buildings* are situated upon the east bank of the river, in view of the village, and are chiefly constructed of stone, and present a very fine appearance. The Government has expended large sums of money in their construction, and it is expected that soon the Government will make it an *Arsenal of Construction.* There are at present about 2000 stand of arms deposited here, besides cannon and other munitions of war. The Post is commanded by a captain of the Ordnance Department, aided by a Lieut. of the same corps.

The *State Insane Hospital*. This splendid granite edifice, an honor to the state and to humanity, occupies a plat of elevated ground, of seventy acres, on the east side of the river. Its situation is unrivaled for the beauty of its scenery. This building was commenced in 1836, and will probably be completed and prepared to receive patients, in 1839. It will cost the state, and some beneficent individuals, who have made liberal donations towards its erection, about $100,000. It is of the model of the *Lunatic Hospital* at Worcester, Mass., and is much admired for its external architecture and internal arrangement. The centre building and wings are 262 feet long; the centre building is 82 feet in length, 46 feet wide, 4 stories high, besides the basement and attic, having a chapel in the attic 80 by 40. The wings are 90 feet long in front, and 100 in the rear, 38 feet wide, and 3 stories high, divided into 126 rooms, 120 of which are designed for patients, the remaining 6 for water closets and other purposes, with halls between the rooms 12 feet wide running the entire length of each wing, and communicating with the dining rooms in the centre building.

The *Augusta High School*, is an elegant brick building, situated upon a beautiful eminence, 2 stories high, 65 feet long by 50 wide, having a pediment front supported by doric columns, and contains two large school rooms, beside a laboratory and four recitation rooms, and cost about $7,000.

The above is a brief sketch of the prominent features of this beautiful and flourishing town;—such as it has become by the common efforts of an intelligent and enterprising people, joined to the natural advantages of the place.

But a new era is opened to Augusta. The mighty waters of the Kennebec have been arrested in their course. That proud stream, which, for ages, has rolled its rapid current to the ocean, unimpeded by the devices of man, is destined for ages to come, to pay perpetual homage to Yankee perseverance and skill, and to lend its gigantic strength to aid the arts and sciences in supplying the wants of millions.

We may perhaps, be suspected of partiality towards this lovely Village of the East, for giving it so extended a notice;—but, as accounts of works of great public utility are interesting to most of our readers, both duty and inclination prompt us to give a brief description of the KENNEBEC DAM;—a magnificent structure;—bold in its design—curious in its workmanship,—and probably unrivaled by any work of similar character and for similar purposes, in this or any other country.

Although Augusta enjoys the pleasure of seeing this noble enterprise accomplished within its own borders, and by the energy of its own people; yet improvements of this character are by no means local in their effects. The benefits of this undertaking will be felt, not only in the valley of the Kennebec, but throughout the state.

These works were commenced in 1836, by the *Kennebec Locks and Canals Company*, and completed in September, 1837. The cost was about $300,000. They are about half a mile above the centre of the village, and were constructed under the superintendence of Col. WILLIAM BOARDMAN, of Nashua, N. H., as chief engineer, from whose report many of the following facts are elicited.

The length of the Dam, exclusive of the stone abutments and Lock, is 584 feet—the base, 127 feet—the height, 15 feet above ordinary high water mark. It is built with cribs of timber, bolted and trenailed strongly together, and is filled with ballast, to the very top. The upper slope is covered with five inch pine plank, jointed and perfectly tight; the lower with five and three inch hemlock plank.— The crest, terminating at the sluice, near the middle of the overfall, is level, and covered entirely with stone eight feet in length, and strongly secured with iron straps and bolts. The sluice, sixty feet in length, is covered in the same manner, and is about twenty inches lower than the wings. The walls of the Lock are 170 feet in length, its chamber 101 feet by 28 1-3 feet in the clear, with a single lift; the west wall serves as the eastern abutment of the Dam—it is 28 feet thick at the base, graduated to 25 at the top. The head and east walls are of corresponding strength.— Both are built wholly of granite. The face courses hammered, bed and joint, rabbitted, and laid in cement, and the rabbit filled with cement The floor of the Lock is constructed of timber fifteen inches deep, and covered with five inch pine plank, tongued and grooved, with an additional flooring of five inch hard wood plank, commencing at the head of the Lock and extending fourteen feet. The main gates of the Lock, and guard gates of the Canals, are of white oak from the Chesapeake, and the wicket gates of cast iron. The large stone piers above the Dam, for the protection of the Lock and abutments, are each 30 feet square on the base, graduated to 25 feet on the top, and about 34 feet high, and built of granite, clamped and strapped with iron.

The Canals on each side of the river are 50 feet wide in the clear, carrying 10 feet of water from the level of the top of the dam. The walls are 22 feet high, 7 1-2 feet thick at the base, and 5 feet at the top. They are finished as far as, and including, the guard gates. The gates are of great strength, built of heavy oak timber, and in the most substantial manner, revolving in stone coins, with which stone and sheet-piling is connected, extending across and 25 feet into each bank, and driven 10 feet below the bottom of the Canals.

The walls on the banks of the river, above and below the Dam, extending about 500 feet, are of the same height as the Canal walls, and 8 feet thick at the base. On the upper side of the Dam is a sheet of timber-piling, tongued and grooved, and either resting on the bare ledge, or driven as far as they could be made to penetrate into the solid bed which covers a portion of its surface, and is connected with the piling which passes under and across the Lock into the east bank, and also with that which is driven in the west bank of the river.— Above this, and extending to the top of the Dam, so as to cover the entire planking of the upper slope, is a mass of gravel from 20 to 30 feet deep.

2,500,000 feet of timber and about 25 tons of iron have been used in constructing the Dam, and about 75,000 tons of ballast have been deposited in it.

The Lock, Piers, River and Mill walls, with the Canal walls, extending to and including the guard gates, contain about 800,000 cubic feet of stone.

During the progress of the work, and especially while the course of the river was contracted to a space of 17 feet wide by 24 deep (a time peculiarly favorable for forming an estimate, and rarely offered in a stream of this magnitude) repeated observations were made upon the velocity of the current, and at no time was there found a less quantity than 2,500 cubic feet per second. It is proper to add that the seasons of 1836 and 1837, were both remarkable for the small quantity of water running in all the streams in this vicinity.

The pond formed by this Dam covers 1200 acres. It is 16 1-2 miles in length, and its average depth is 16 feet.

Augusta presents advantages for manufacturing establishments, equal, if not superior to any in New England. It is located in the heart of a large and powerful state, rapidly increasing in population and wealth; surrounded by a fertile country, rich in every necessary agricultural product, and stored with granite, clay, lumber, lime, iron ore—every building material; all of which are found near the spot, and at very low prices.

The facilities afforded at this place, for transportation, are of inestimable value to a large manufacturing town. Cotton and other raw materials, and manufactured goods, may be transported by water, to and from the very doors of the mills. At no distant period the great eastern railroad from Boston and Portland will pass through this town, in its course to Bangor. At this time, steamboats pass from Augusta to Boston in eleven hours.

The greatest consideration, however, in regard to Augusta, as a manufacturing town, is its *unfailing supply of water*. The main branch of the Kennebec is the outlet of an immense lake, with numerous powerful tributaries, connected with other lakes or large reservoirs of water. On its passage to Augusta, Dead river, Seven Mile Brook, the Sandy, Sebasticook, and many other less powerful streams pay their tribute to it. Indeed, all the waters of the extensive valley of the Kennebec, above the Dam, meet at this place. It may be said with safety, that this place possesses a water power amply sufficient to drive 200,000 spindles, day and night, throughout the year; and an almost inexhaustable *surplus* power from November to July.

Preparations are making for the erection of buildings for extensive manufacturing operations.

Aurora, Me.

Hancock co. This town lies 106 miles from Augusta. With a population of only 140, this town produced, in 1837, among its agricultural products, 855 bushels of wheat.

Averill, Vt.

Essex co. This town lies on the Canada line, about 30 miles N. of Guildhall. It has several large ponds and a branch of Nulhegan river. Some of these waters pass to the Connecticut, and some to the river St. Francis. The soil of Averill is cold and broken, with few cultivators.

Avon, Me.

Franklin co. Avon lies 35 miles W. by N. from Norridgewock, and 50 N. N. W. from Augusta. It was incorporated in 1802. Population, 1837, 767. It is watered by some of the head branches of Sandy river. In 1837, this town produced 3,220 bushels of wheat.

Avon, Ct.

Hartford co. This town was taken from Farmington, in 1830. Population, 1,025. It lies between two mountainous ridges and has considerable rich level land on the borders of Farmington river. This is a handsome agricultural town and possesses some very beautiful scenery. The view from *Monte Video*, on Talcott mountain, nearly 1000 feet above the waters of the Connecticut, is quite enchanting.— "Wardsworth's Tower," or Monte Video, is much resorted to by parties of pleasure in summer months. Avon is 6 miles N. from Farmington, and 9 W. N. W. from Hartford.

Bachelder, Me.

Oxford co. This township lies between two mountains on the line of New Hampshire, 20 miles W. by N. from Paris, and 60 W. from Augusta.

Baileyville, Me.

Washington co. This town is on the line of New Brunswick, about 45 miles N. by W. from Machias, and 80 E. N. E. from Bangor. Incorporated, 1828. Population, 1837, 331. Baileyville is watered on the E. by the St. Croix, and on the N. by the outlet of Schoodic lakes.

Baker's River, N. H.

Baker's river, a considerable stream in Grafton county, is formed of two branches. The N. branch has its source near Moosehillock mountain in Coventry. It runs southerly through Warren into Wentworth, where it unites with the S. branch which originates in Orange. After the union of these branches, the river pursues a S. E. and an easterly course through the S. part of Rumney and the N. part of Plymouth, where it forms a junction with Pemigewaset river just above Plymouth village. It was on this river, in the township of Rumney, that General Stark was captured by the Indians, on the 28th of April, 1752.

Bakersfield, Vt.,

Franklin co., lies 30 miles N. E. from Burlington, 38 N. N. W. from Montpelier, and 15 miles E. from St. Albans. Branches of Missisque river pass through it. This town is well timbered with hard wood, the land is warm, but somewhat broken. 4,000 sheep. First settled about 1789. Population, 1830, 1,087.

Baldwin, Me.

Cumberland co. This town is bounded E. by Sebago pond and W. by Saco river. It contains a number of ponds, affording fish of various kinds. Baldwin was incorporated in 1802. Population, 1837, 1,133. It is 26 miles W. S. W. from Portland.

Baltimore, Vt.

Windsor co. This town was taken from Cavendish in 1793. Hawk mountain is the division line. The soil is warm but stony. 1,200 sheep. An abundance of gneiss and granite is found here. It is 10 miles N. W. from Windsor and about 65 S. from Montpelier. Population, 1830, 179.

Bangor, Me.

This is the chief town of Penobscot county. It lies in N. lat. 44° 47' 50''., W. long. 68° 47'. It lies 66 miles E. N. E. from Augusta, 120 N. E. by E. from Portland, 230 N. E. from Boston, Mass., 115 S. from Eastport, and 675 N. E. from Washington. The first settlement in this place, by the whites, was made in the winter of 1769—1770. In 1772, the Plantation, Kenduskeag, as it was then called, consisted of twelve families. In 1790, the population of Bangor was 169; in 1800, 277; in 1810, 850; in 1820, 1,221; in 1830, 2,868, and in 1837, 9,201. This place is situated at the head of navigation on the west side of Penobscot river, 30 miles N. by E. from Belfast bay, 60 to Matawamkeag Point, 120 to Houlton, and about 60 miles from the open sea. The compact part of the population reside on both sides of Kenduskeag stream, about 190 yards in width at its mouth, over which are three bridges, and on which, at the foot of the falls, about a mile from the city, are numerous mills. The bridge across the Penobscot, 100 rods above the mouth of the Kenduskeag, is about 440 yards in length. It cost $50,000. The basin at and below the mouth of the Kenduskeag, where the shipping lie to receive their cargoes, is 90 rods in width, and affords good anchorage. The tide generally rises about 17 feet. Ship building is extensively pursued at this place; but commerce in lumber, of all the various kinds in use, is the principal occupation of the inhabitants. An immense amount of that article is annually rafted down the rivers, and transported to almost all parts of the world. Bangor is the greatest depot for lumber on the continent of America.

On the Penobscot river and its tributary streams, above Bangor, are more than 250 saw-mills, capable of cutting at least two hundred million feet of boards a year; all of which, except what is used in building, must be shipped at the harbor of Bangor. The value of the boards, timber, clapboards, shingles, oars, scantling, wood, &c., shipped at this port, varies from a million to a million and a half of dollars, annually. About 1200 vessels of about 110 tons burthen are annually employed during the season of navigation, in freighting lumber, timber, &c., to various places. There are belonging to this place, about 100 sail of coasting vessels, 50 engaged in foreign commerce, and 15 or 20 other vessels engaged in the fisheries.

Bangor was incorporated as a town in 1791. In 1834 it became a city. Its government is under a Mayor and seven Aldermen, who constitute the upper Board; and twenty-one Common Council men, who, when they have elected a President, constitute the lower Board. A city court sets every Monday.

The site of the city is pleasant, commanding fine views of the rivers and the adjoining country. The buildings, both public and private, are constructed with neatness and taste, and some in a style of superior elegance. Conveyances for travellers from the city are frequent and comfortable; both by land and water. A railroad is in operation to Oldtown, 12 miles, and steamboats ply to and from Portland and Boston, during the season of navigation, which generally continues eight months in the year. The great eastern railroad from Boston will doubtless reach this eastern city before the lapse of many years.

On the banks of the Penobscot, within the city, three miles above the mouth of the Kenduskeag, is what is called "Fort Hill," the site of a fortification, supposed to be the ancient "Negas," destroyed by Captain Heath, with a party of men, in 1725, who, it is said, "fell on a village of about 50 Indian houses, and committed them to the flames. The Indians becoming alarmed, deserted them."

Bangor is on one of the noblest rivers in the Northern States;—the product of an almost innumerable number of tributary streams. Nature has seated Bangor at the natural outlet of these mighty waters, as the mart of one of the most extensive, and one of the richest alluvial basins east of the Ohio valley. It is true that this section of country is in a high degree of latitude, and that the icy chains of winter are felt with greater force and for a longer period than in more southern climes. But this seeming disadvantage is more than compensated by the unrivalled purity of the air and water,—two of the indispensable requisitions of health and longevity. There is probably no portion of country in the world where the great staples of wheat, beef and wool can be produced with greater facility; where surplus produce can find a market at less expense, or where the industrious agriculturalist can reap a more sure reward. When the present population of this immense territory, extending from tide water to Madawaska, is compared with that of older settlements of a less fertile soil, of less navigable facilities, and in nearly as high a degree of latitude, the mind is favorably struck with the flattering prospects of the valley of the Penobscot, and with pleasing anticipations of the prosperity of its city. See *Register.*

Baring, Me.

Washington co. This town is bounded N. by the St. Croix river, E. by Calais and Robinston, and W. by a large and beautiful pond which empties into the St. Croix. Incorporated, 1825. Population, 1837, 286. The railroad from Calais, 4 miles, will soon be completed to this place. 209 miles N. E. by E. from Augusta.

Barkhampstead, Ct.

Litchfield co. This town is watered by branches of Farmington river. The soil is more particularly adapted to grazing: considerable beef and the products of the dairy are sent to market. It is 26 miles N. W. from Hartford, and 20 N. N. E. from Litchfield. Population, 1830, 1,715. First settled, 1746. Incorporated, 1779. Granite, iron ore and limestone are found here. The hilly part of the town presents some fine scenery. *Hitchcockville,* north of the centre of the town, is a flourishing manufacturing village, with great water privileges.

Barnard, Me.

All the knowledge we can obtain in regard to this town is, that it lies in the county of Piscataquis, 108 miles from Augusta;—that in 1837, there were 132 people in the town, and that they raised 444 bushels of wheat, the same year;—that this town received $264 of the surplus revenue;—that in 1837, Augustus W. Walker and others, obtained an act of the legislature for quarrying slate, and that Stephen Palmer is, or was, Postmaster.

Now, the good people of Barnard are hereby respectfully requested to give the editor their *latitude and longitude,* and other necessary information for future editions. Citizens of other towns, similarly situated, and of *all towns,* who may wish more full descriptions of their resources, &c. than we are able, at present, to give, are also requested to forward their communications.

Barnard, Vt.

Windsor co. First settled, 1774. Incorporated, 1778. Population, 1830, 1,881. It is watered by Broad Brook which empties into White river in Sharon; and by Locust Creek, which also empties into White river in Bethel. On this Creek, during the revolutionary war, there was erected a Fort, where the militia of this and other towns were stationed as a defence against Indian depredations—they having surprised and carried to Canada a number of its first settlers, in 1780. In the centre of this town is the village, and a beautiful pond, from which issues a stream on which there are mills. On this Creek is an establishment for the manufacture of starch from potatoes. This stream joins its waters with the Creek one mile from the pond. The surface of this town is hilly. The soil is well adapted to grazing; and there are but few towns that turn off yearly more cattle, butter and cheese, sheep and wool. The number of sheep is about 6,000. It lies 10 miles north of Woodstock, and 40 miles south of Montpelier.

It is stated as a singular fact, that the firing on Bunker Hill, on the 17th of June, 1775, was distinctly heard in this town, 130 miles N. W. from Charlestown.

Barnet, Vt.

Caledonia co. This town lies on Connecticut river, at the 15 mile falls, and opposite to Lyman, N. H. It has a good soil, and is an excellent farming town, with slate and iron ore. It lies 35 miles E. from Montpelier, 10 S. by E. from Danville, and 65 N. by E. from Windsor. Population, in 1830, 1,764.—

First settled, about 1763. Many of the inhabitants are of Scotch descent. This town has a great water power on Passumpsic and Stevens' rivers. On the latter, are falls of 100 feet, in the distance of 10 rods. This water power is improved by three flannel and other manufactories. There are a number of pleasant and fertile islands in the river between this place and Lyman, and some beautiful ponds in Barnet, which afford fish of various kinds. This is quite a romantic place, and lies at the head of navigation on the Connecticut river. In 1835, the product of the farms, carried to market, amounted to $26,381. One farmer sold 3,000 lbs. of butter, and 3,000 lbs. of pork. There are about 4,000 sheep in the town.

Barnstable County Mass.

Barnstable is the chief town.—This county was incorporated, 1685. Population, 1820, 24,046—1830, 28,525—and in 1837, 31,109; area, about 330 square miles. This county includes the whole of Cape Cod, extending E. and N. into the Atlantic ocean, and which Gosnold discovered in 1602. It is bounded N. W. by Plymouth county, and W. by Buzzard's bay. Cape Cod lies in the form of an arm,half open; the elbow is at Chatham, 20 miles E. of Barnstable; the hand, the wrist inclining inward, is at Race Point, 33 miles N. by W. of Chatham. The whole length of the Cape is 65 miles, and the average breadth about 5. This county is principally diluvium. Below the town of Barnstable the county is quite sandy, so much so that the people are generally dependant on Boston and other towns for a large proportion of their meats and breadstuffs. This deficit is amply compensated by the unrivalled privileges enjoyed, and well improved by them, in the cod, mackerel and other fisheries. This county has but little wood, but it is well stored with peat. About two millions of dollars are invested in the manufacture of salt. There were manufactured in this county in the year ending April 1, 1837, 669,064 bushels of salt, valued at $219,870. The manufactures of cotton and woollen goods, boots, shoes, iron castings, glass, cabinet and tin wares, cordage, &c., amounted to $496,602. There are in this county 370 vessels employed in the whale, cod and mackerel fishery. The tonnage, 24,378 tons. The value of the fishery, in one year previous to April, 1837, was $557,737. Tonnage of the District, 1836, 30,278 tons. The annual amount of tonnage of vessels built is about 1,000 tons; value, $63,318. Total annual value of the fisheries and manufactures, $1,-337,527. The number of sheep in the county in 1837, was 7,332.

Barnstable county is noted for its fine sailors and men of superior nautical talents. The ladies are celebrated for their fair complexions and good housewifery; but are peculiarly subject to the vicissitudes pertaining to a maritime situation. By a statement recently made, it appears that there were in this county nearly a thousand widows living, who had lost their husbands by the dangers of the sea. In two towns, (Harwich and Wellfleet,) there were 223 widows who had thus lost their companions. This county has 13 towns; and 91 inhabitants to a square mile.

Barnstable, Mass.

This is the chief town of Barnstable county, and a port of entry. It is 65 miles from Boston. *Sandy Neck*, on the N. side, forms a good harbor for vessels of 8 feet of water. *Hyannis*, on the S. side, 6 miles S. E. of Barnstable C. H., is now a good harbor; but by an expensive *Breakwater*, constructing at that place by the U. S. government, it will soon become perfectly safe from all winds, for all classes of vessels navigating the Sound, and passing round the Cape. The "Pilgrim Fathers" landed here, Nov. 11, 1620, and borrowed some corn of the *Mattacheeset* Indians. The celebrated patriot, James Otis, was born here, Feb. 5, 1725. He died at Andover, May 23, 1783. The manufacture of salt was commenced here as early as 1779. It then sold for $6 a bushel. There was made 27,125 bushels of salt in this town in 1837. Between 50 and 60 sail of fishing and coasting vessels belong to this place. This town has numerous ponds, a considerable water power, some fine upland, and extensive salt marshes. The manufacture of vessels, salt, boots, shoes, hats, leather, cabinet ware, chairs, and wooden ware, amounted in one year to $56,562. Pop. 1837, 4,017.

Barnstead, N. H.

Strafford co. This town lies 26 miles W. by N. from Dover, 36 N. W. from Portsmouth, and 20 N. E. from Concord. Incorporated, 1767. Population, 1830, 2,047. Barnstead is not mountainous, but has large swells of land, good for grazing. About 2,500 sheep are kept here. The soil is easy and productive. There are several ponds in this town—the largest are the two Suncook ponds, which lie near each other, Brindle pond, and Half-moon pond, on Alton line. These waters are stocked with fish, and are discharged into the Suncook. Barnstead was granted May 20, 1727, to the Rev. Joseph Adams and others. Settlements commenced in 1767.

Barre, Vt.

A pleasant and flourishing town in Washington county, six miles S. of Montpelier, and 48 N. by W. of Windsor. This is considered one of the best farming towns in the state. Large quantities of pot and pearl ashes, beef, pork, butter and cheese, are annually taken from this place to Boston market. About 7,000 sheep are kept here. It is well watered by Stevens' and Jail, branches of Onion river, which afford good mill privileges. Inexhaustible quantities of granite are found here, of the excellent quality with which the capitol at Montpelier is built. This is a great thoroughfare for travellers, particularly for large teams from the north to Boston, by the Gulf road. A large number of these noted six and eight horse teams are owned here. Barre was first settled in 1788. Present population, about 2,500.

Barre, Mass.

Worcester co. This excellent agricultural township is on high land, and is well watered, particularly by Ware river, on which are many mills. The manufactures of Barre for the year ending April 1, 1837, amounted to about $365,000. The articles manufactured were woollen and cotton goods, ($161,600) copper pumps, boots, shoes, carriages, leather, palm-leaf hats, ($167,200) straw bonnets, axes, scythes, and gunpowder. Large quantities of beef, butter, cheese, &c., are annually sent from this town to Boston market. It was incorporated in 1774. Population, 1837, 2,713. It lies 65 miles W. by S. from Boston, 24 N. by W. from Worcester, and 15 N. E. from Ware. Barre took its name in honor of Col. Barre, an eloquent friend of America in the British Parliament.

Barrington, N. H.

Strafford co. It lies 20 miles N. W. from Portsmouth, 10 W. from Dover, and 30 E. from Concord. The surface of Barrington is somewhat broken and rocky, the soil being principally a gravelly loam.— The town is abundantly supplied with ponds, of which there are no less than thirteen of considerable magnitude, from whence issue streams affording excellent mill seats. At one of these mill seats, on the Isinglass river, is a perpendicular fall of 30 feet. There is, about two miles from the centre of the town, a remarkable cavern, or fissure in a rock, commonly called the *Devil's den*. The entrance is on the side of a hill, and is sufficiently large to admit a person in a stooping posture. Having entered 5 feet in a horizontal direction, there is a descent of 4 or 5 feet, on an angle of 45°, large enough only to admit the body of a middling sized man. After squeezing through this passage, you enter a chamber 60 feet in length, from 10 to 15 in height, and from 3 to 8 in width.— Communicating with this, are several other fissures of equal height, and from 10 to 15 in length. Barrington was incorporated May 10, 1722, and the settlement commenced in 1732. Population, 1830, 1,895.

Barrington, R. I.

Bristol co. This small town, of about 8 square miles, originally belonged to Massachusetts. It was attached to Rhode Island in 1746, and incorporated in 1771. It is bounded southerly by Narraganset bay, and is well watered by Palmer's river, and by an inlet of Warren river, over which is a bridge. The soil of the town is of a fertile, sandy loam, and quite productive. Large quantities of sea-weed are collected on its shores. A large tract in Barrington, called "the cove," now covered with water to a considerable depth, is supposed to have once been a forest, as timber and fuel are obtained from its bottom. Some salt is made in this town, and shell and other fish are abundant. Barrington lies 8 miles E. S. E. from Providence, and about 7 miles N. by W. from Bristol. Population, 1830, 612.

Bartlett, N. H.,

Coos co., is 45 miles S. E. from Lancaster, 82 N. N. E. from Concord, and 85 N. N. W. from Portsmouth. It lies at the foot of the White Mountains, on the eastern side. Its soil is various, and, on the Saco, in some parts, good. This river meanders through the centre of the town. Bartlett was incorporated June 16, 1790. Population, 1830, 644.

Barton, Vt.

Orleans co. This town derived its name from Gen. William Barton, of R. I., and was first settled in 1796. The town is well watered by *Barton river*, which rises in Glover, and empties into Memphremagog lake. Here are several ponds containing good fish. Barton is a thriving town, with a good hydraulic power, and about 3,000 sheep. It lies 9 miles S. E. from Irasburgh, and 40 N. E. from Montpelier. Population, 1830, 729.

Basin Harbor, Vt.

See *Ferrisburgh*.

Baskahegan River, Me.

This river rises in a large lake of the same name, in the county of Washington, near the line of New Brunswick; it passes westerly 15 or 20 miles, and falls into the Matawamkeag, a tributary of the Penobscot.

Bath, Me.,

In the county of Lincoln, is situated on the west bank of Kennebec river, 12 miles from the sea, 32 N. E. of Portland, and 31 S. from Augusta. It is bounded E. by Kennebec river, S. by Phipsburg, W. by New Meadows river and Brunswick, and N. by Merrymeeting bay. Population, in 1830, 3,773; in 1835, 4,200, and in 1837, 4,523. Incorporated, 1780. An attempt was made by a missionary to settle this place, and preach to the fishermen, as early as 1670. But the Indians would not permit it. A permanent settlement was made in

1756. The principal business of Bath is commerce, trade and shipbuilding, for which it is admirably well located. There belonged to this port in 1835, 26 ships, 32 brigs, 54 schooners, and smaller vessels. Tonnage of the district of Bath, including the waters of Kennebec river, in 1837, 41,728 tons. Total number of vessels belonging to the district of Bath, in 1835, 37 ships, 94 brigs, 195 schooners, 10 sloops, and 1 steam-boat. Total, 337. The harbor of Bath is seldom obstructed by ice. Regular lines of steamboats ply between this place and Portland and Boston, about three-fourths of the year.

Bath, N. H.,

Grafton co., on Connecticut river, is 32 miles N. of Dartmouth College, 82 N. W. of Concord, and 9 N. of Haverhill. Bath is pleasantly situated in the vale of the Connecticut, between the Green mountains on the W., and the White Mountains on the E., by which it is effectually shielded from high winds and long storms. The Amonoosuck river waters the S. E. part, affording many fine mill seats and water privileges. The Amonoosuck has a very convenient fall at the village, calculated to accommodate machinery to any extent. Two mills for the manufacture of cassimere, and other machinery, are already erected. At the principal village, (which is very pleasant,) there is a considerable bridge over the Amonoosuck, of 350 feet in length, built in 1807. The soil on the hills is generally a reddish loam, on a bed of marl, or hard pan. In the valleys, it is alluvial. About one-sixth part of the whole town is intervale land. Much improvement has been made in the agriculture of this place: 550 sheep are kept here. The town was granted, 1761, and the first settlement was made in 1765, by John Herriman from Haverhill, Mass. Population, 1830, 1,627.

Battenkill River,

This river is about 45 miles in length. It rises in Dorset, and passing Manchester, Sunderland and Arlington, it receives Roaring Brook and other tributaries in Vermont; it then passes into the state of New York, and falls into the Hudson, three miles below Fort Miller, and about 35 miles N. from Albany, N. Y.

Bays and Harbors.

The bays and harbors in New England are generally mentioned under the places pertaining to them.

Bear Camp River, N. H.,

Is formed of several branches rising on the south side of Sandwich and Albany mountains. The two principal branches unite in Ossipee, and fall into Ossipee lake on its western border.

Bear River, Me.,

Rises in the highlands, near Umbagog lake, passes Newry, and empties into the Androscoggin, opposite to Bethel.

Becket, Mass.,

An elevated farming township on the Green mountain range, in Berkshire county. Westfield, Farmington and Housatonick rivers receive the waters of several ponds in this town. It has some small manufactures, and about 7,000 sheep. The town was incorporated in 1765, and lies 110 miles W. from Boston, 15 E. S. E. from Lenox, and 23 W. from Northampton. Population, 1837, 957.

Beddington, Me.

Washington co. There are several ponds in this town, which are among the head waters of Pleasant and Narraguagus rivers. Incorporated, 1833. Population, 1837, 169.

It lies 35 miles N. W. from Machias, and about 40 E. from Bangor.

Bedford, N. H.

This is a pleasant town in Hillsborough county. It is 8 miles N. E. from Amherst, 20 S. by E. from Concord. Merrimack and Piscataquoag are the only rivers in this town. The latter passes through its N. E. corner, where there is the pleasant and flourishing village of *Piscataquoag*. This town has considerable very productive intervale land. It has been noted for the cultivation of hops and for its fine domestic manufactures. On the W. line of Bedford, are a remarkable gulf and precipice, which are objects of curiosity. A considerable brook passes over the precipice, and falls about 200 feet within the distance of 100 yards. Here are found several excavations in solid stone, which are sufficiently large to contain many persons. In mineralogy, this town affords a great variety of specimens. Iron ore is found in different places, and in several varieties. Sulphuret of iron, imbedded in common granite, and red oxide of iron, combined with alumine, are common. Black lead, pyritous copper, schorl, hornblende, epidote, talc, mica, black, yellow and green gneiss, crystallized quartz, &c. are found here. The first child born in town was Silas Barron, son of Capt. Moses Barron, in 1741. The town was incorporated, May 19, 1750. Bedford was the residence of many Indians in former times. Near Goffe's falls is a spot of ground, about ten rods long and four wide, which is supposed to have been an Indian burial place. Population, 1830, 1,554.

Bedford, Mass.

This is a pleasant town in Middlesex county, and the source of Shawsheen river. This town was formerly parts of Concord and Billerica, and was incorporated in 1729. Population, 1837, 858. It lies 15 miles N. W. from Boston, and 5 N E. from Concord. Bedford is bound ed N. by Concord river. It has some manufactures; principally of boots and shoes.

Belchertown, Mass.,

A beautiful town in Hampshire county, originally called "Cold Spring," 75 miles W. from Boston, 11 E. from Northampton, and 27 E. from Pittsfield. Population, 1837, 2,598. First settled, 1732. Incorporated, 1761. The soil of the town is of an excellent quality, and well improved. Large quantities of wool is grown in this town. It is separated from Ware by Swift river, on the N. The principal manufacture is that of pleasure wagons, of which about 600 are annually made. Mr. A. Shumway, of this place, has driven the stage between Belchertown and Northampton 25 successive years. In that period he made 15,000 trips, travelled 218,400 miles, and carried at least 124,000 passengers; yet, although his hours of travelling were early in the morning and late in the evening, he never broke a limb, overturned his coach, or met with any serious accident whatever, during his whole career.

Belfast, Me.,

Is the chief town of Waldo county, and a port of entry, and is beautifully situated on Belfast bay, on the W. side of Penobscot river. It lies 40 miles E. from Augusta, 30 S. from Bangor, 30 N. from Thomaston, and, across Belfast bay, 12 W. from Castine. The town was incorporated in 1773, but not permanently settled until about the year 1785. There is considerable good land in Belfast. In 1837 it produced 3,492 bushels of as good wheat as ever grew on the prairies of the "boundless West." The Paasaggassawakeag river passes near the centre of the town, and adds much to the appearance of the place. The harbor is very good—it is guarded by Long and Sears' islands, and has anchorage for a great number of vessels of the largest class. The proximity of Belfast to the sea, its site in relation to Penobscot river, and its excellent harbor, which was never known to have been obstructed by ice, but twice, (1780—1815,) gives it peculiar advantages for foreign commerce, the coasting trade, and the fisheries. Considerable ship building is carried on at this place. The tonnage of the district of Belfast in 1837, was 29,342 tons. The principal exports are lumber and fish. Population, 1810, 1,259; 1820, 2,026; 1830, 3,077, and in 1837, about 4,000. Belfast, although irregularly built, is a pleasant town, and is an important *winter* mart of the trade of Penobscot river.

Belgrade, Me.

Kennebec co. In this town are parts of three large and beautiful ponds or lakes, well stored with fish. They are connected with each other, and find an outlet at Waterville. The scenery on the borders of these waters is truly delightful. It produced in 1837, 6,340 bushels of wheat. Belgrade was incorporated in 1796. Population, 1837, 1,483. It lies 10 miles N. E. from Augusta, and 69 N. by E. from Portland. The village at *Belgrade Mills*, 6 miles from the centre of the town, and 16 miles from Augusta, is a very flourishing place.

Bellamy Bank, N. H.

A river, one branch of which issues from Chesley's pond, in Barrington, and the other from low and marshy lands in the vicinity; these unite in Madbury, and after meandering through the town, the waters fall into the Piscataqua, on the W. side of Dover Neck, where the stream is called *Back* river.

Bellingham, Mass.

Norfolk co. The soil of this town is light and sandy, and not very good for agricultural purposes. It is finely watered by Charles river, and has a good hydraulic power. Its manufactures, consisting of cotton and woollen goods, straw bonnets, boots and shoes, amounted, in one year, to $127,837. It lies 18 miles S. W. from Dedham, 17 N. by W. from Providence, R. I., and 28 S. W. from Boston. Population, 1837, 1,159. Incorporated, 1719. Iron ore is found here.

Bellows' Falls.

See *Walpole, N. H.*

Belmont, Me.

This town is well watered by the Paasaggassawakeag, which rises there in a pond of that name, and empties at Belfast, about 6 miles N. It lies 34 miles E. by N. from Augusta. In 1837, Belmont produced 3,435 bushels of wheat, and considerable wool. Waldo county.

Belvidere, Vt.

Lamoille co. A mountainous township on the west side of the Green Mountains, 32 miles N. E. from Burlington, 32 N. from Montpelier, 27 E. by S. from St. Albans, and watered by branches of Lamoille river. Incorporated, 1791. Population, 1830, 185.

Bennington County, Vt.

Bennington and *Manchester* are the chief towns. This is the oldest county in Vt., on the west side of the Green Mountains. It is bounded on the north by Rutland county, on the east by Windham county, on the south by Berkshire county, Mass., and on the west by the state of New York. It is 39 miles long and 20 wide. Area, 610 square miles. Population, in 1820, 16,125; 1830, 17,468. Inhabitants to square mile, 28. The low lands are excellent, and produce good crops, but the largest portion of the county is mountainous, and fit only for grazing. Many streams rise in the mountains and descend to the ocean, some by the Hudson and some by the Connecticut, affording a great hydraulic power. Lead and iron ores of good quality are found in this county, and large quarries of beautiful white marble. The number of sheep in this county in 1837 was 69,828.

Bennington, Vt.

One of the chief towns of Bennington county. It lies 120 miles S. W. by S. from Montpelier, 25 S. from Manchester, and 20 east from Troy, N. Y. Population, 1830, 3,419. Present population, about 4,200. First settled,1761. The town is situated high above the great rivers and the ocean, yet we find it of good alluvial soil, delightfully encircled by ever-green mountains. It abounds in iron ore, manganese, ochre and marble. The streams are numerous and afford excellent mill sites. The products of the soil consist of all the varieties common to New England. Great attention is paid to the rearing of sheep: about 7000 of those useful animals feed on the hills and valleys. There are in Bennington, 6 cotton and 3 woollen factories, a very extensive iron foundry, 2 furnaces, a paper mill, flouring mills, &c. The public schools justly sustain an elevated rank. Bennington is finely located for the muses. On the border of this town, about 6 miles W. of the court house, the gallant Stark, with a small band of "Green Mountain Boys," celebrated for their bravery, gained an important victory over the British, August 16, 1777. The fame of that battle is as imperishable as the mountains which overshadow the ground. Shame to the country:—there is not a stone to mark the spot!

Benson, Vt.

Rutland co. This town, on Lake Champlain, was first settled in 1783. Population, 1830, 1,493. It lies 84 miles E. from Montpelier, 20 W. N. W. from Rutland, and opposite to Putnam, N. Y. The lake at this place is about a mile in width. The town has some streams affording mill sites, but none of great importance. The waters are generally brackish and unpleasant. A stream issues from a swamp in this town, and after running a short distance, passes through the base of a high hill, a distance of more than half a mile. Benson has good pine, maple, walnut, oak and beech timber, and a bog of marl resembling fuller's earth. There are about 14,000 sheep in this town.

Berkley, Mass.

Bristol co. Berkley lies 37 miles S. from Boston, 18 E. from Providence, and 5 S. from Taunton. Population, in 1837, 878. Taken from Dighton in 1735, from which it is separated by Taunton river. Some coasting vessels belong to this place, and some ship building is carried on. *Assonet village*, on Taunton river, is the principal place of business. The soil is light and sandy.

Berkshire County, Mass.

Lenox is the chief town. This county was incorporated in 1770. Population, 1820, 35,666; 1830, 37,825, and in 1837, 39,101; area, 860 square miles. Bounded N. by Bennington county, Vt., W. by Rensselaer and Columbia counties, N. Y., S. by Litchfield county, Ct., and E. by Franklin, Hampshire and Hampden counties. This county is rough and hilly in many parts, but it affords considerable very fine land, and produces much wool, all sorts of grain, and exports great quantities of beef, pork, butter, &c. The number of sheep in this county in 1837, was 136,962. Berkshire

NEW ENGLAND GAZETTEER.

is the most elevated county in the state. The Green and Taughkannic Mountains cross it from N. to S.; the average height of which is about 1,200 feet above the level of the sea. The Housatonick and Hoosick are its chief rivers. The former empties into Long Island Sound; the latter into the Hudson: 29 towns; 45 inhabitants to a square mile. "This county possesses, in rich and inexhaustible abundance, three of the most important articles of the commerce of the world, *Iron*, *Marble* and *Lime*, and its wood and water power are fully sufficient to enable it to fit them for the purposes of life." The tonnage of this county to its marts of trade, principally on the Hudson, amounted, in 1834, to no less than 34,075 tons. At the present time it probably exceeds 40,000 tons. The enterprize of a railroad from Boston to Albany will soon be accomplished, and cannot fail of being exceedingly beneficial, not only to this county, but to the commonwealth at large.

Berkshire, Vt.

Franklin co. Elihu M. Royce, son of Stephen Royce, was the first child born in this town. That event occurred in 1793. On Missisque and Trout rivers, which water this town, is some fine intervale land. Pike river, from Canada, affords Berkshire a great water power. This town lies 50 miles N. W. from Montpelier, 22 N. E. by E. from St. Albans, and 31 N. E. by N. from Burlington. Population, 1830, 1,308. About 3,000 sheep.

Berlin, Me.

Oxford co. This town is bounded E. by Phillips, S. by Weld and W. by Byron. It lies 100 miles N. from Portland, 45 N. W. from Augusta, and about 40 N. from Paris. Population, 1837, 470. Wheat crop, same year, 2,175 bushels.

Berlin, N. H.

Coos co. This town, from 1771 to 1829, was called Maynesborough. The Androscoggin and Amonoosuck rivers pass through it. It is about 20 miles E. from Lancaster, and 125 N. from Concord. Population, 1830, 73.

Berlin, Vt.

This is a pleasant town in Washington county, watered by Onion and Dog rivers, Stevens' branch, and a number of ponds, furnishing good mill sites, and excellent fishing. The land is somewhat broken, but of strong soil and good for tillage. Considerable manufactures are produced in this town, and about 6,000 sheep. There is a mineral spring here of little note. First settled in 1786. Population, 1830, 1,664.— Berlin is bounded N. by Montpelier and E. by Barre.

Berlin, Mass.

Worcester co. Taken from Bolton, in 1734. Population, 1837, 724. It lies 15 miles N. E. from Worcester, 31 W. by N. from Boston, and 7 S. E. from Lancaster. A branch of the Assabet affords this town good water privileges. Large quantities of hops are produced here; some wool, and some baskets.

Berlin, Ct.

Hartford co. Taken from Farmington, in 1785. Population, 1830, 3,047. This town lies 11 miles S. from Hartford, and 23 N. from New Haven. The surface of Berlin is hilly, but productive of grass, grain and fruits. There are in the town about 2,000 sheep. The villages of *Worthington* and *New Britain* are very pleasant, and the manufactures of brass, tin and other wares, there pursued, are very extensive and flourishing. The first manufacture of tin ware in this country was commenced at this place, in about the year 1770, by Edward Patterson, a native of Ireland. Mr. Patterson peddled his

Bernardston, Mass.

Franklin co. This is a township of superior land for agricultural purposes, considerably elevated, between Fall and Connecticut rivers. It was formerly called *Fall Town*. There was a fort here in 1746, when this part of the county was peopled mostly by Indians. It was incorporated, by its present name, in 1764. It lies 96 miles W. by N. from Boston, and 7 N. from Greenfield. Population, 1837, 878. Bald and West mountains afford delightful scenery:—the former is 630 feet above the waters of the Connecticut. Here are springs containing magnesia, sulphur and iron. Bernardston produced, in one year, 16,000 bushels of corn and rye, and 5,000 barrels of cider. There are 3,022 sheep in this town, and some manufactures of shoes, leather, palm-leaf hats, and scythe snaiths.

Berwick, Me.

York co. This town lies on the E. side of Salmon river, about 14 miles S. S. W. from Alfred, 45 S. W. from Portland, and 98 S. W. from Augusta. Berwick has considerable trade in lumber. Incorporated, 1713. Population, 1837, 1,799.

Bethany, Ct.

New Haven co. Taken from Woodbridge, in 1832. It lies 10 miles N. by W. from New Haven. Some portions of this town is good land and well cultivated, but a large part of it is mountainous, and fit only for the growth of wood. Beacon mountain, between Bethany and Naugatuck river, presents some wild and picturesque features.

Bethel, Me.

Oxford co. Incorporated in 1796. Population, 1837, 1,864. Bethel lies 18 miles N. W. from Paris, 61 N. W. from Portland, and 63 W. from Augusta. This town is bounded N. and W. by Androscoggin river, and S. by Greenwood. This is a fine farming town, and produced 5,214 bushels of wheat in 1837.

Bethel, Vt.

Windsor co. This town was first settled in 1780, and was the first town chartered by the government of Vermont. It lies 31 miles S. by W. from Montpelier, and 30 N. W. from Windsor. Population, 1830, 1,240. Bethel is watered by branches of White river, and possesses good mill sites. Soap stone is found here in great quantities and of good quality: much of it is sawed and transported. Garnet in small, but perfect crystals, is also common. The surface of Bethel is broken and mountainous, but the soil is warm and good for grazing. It has about 8,000 sheep. Considerable business is done at both villages, *East* and *West;* the latter is the largest.

Bethel, Ct.

Fairfield co. This is a pleasant and flourishing village, in the town of Danbury, and about 3 miles N. W. from the centre of that town. There are about fifty dwelling houses in the village, and about thirty work shops or factories. The manufacture of hats and combs is the principal business of the place, and large quantities of both are annually transported to Boston, New York and other places.

Bethlehem, N. H.,

Grafton co., is bounded N. by Whitefield and Dalton, E. by Carroll and ungranted land, S. by Franconia and Lisbon, and N. W. by Littleton. It is watered by Great Amonoosuck river. The soil produces good crops of grass and grain. There is plenty of pine timber and sugar maple. Iron ore, both of the mountain and bog kind, has been occasionally found. Two mineral springs have been discovered.— Bethlehem was settled in 1790. It was incorporated Dec. 27, 1799. Population, 1830, 665.

Bethlehem, Ct.

Litchfield co. This town is 38 miles W. S. W. from Hartford, 32 N. W. by W. from New Haven, and 8 S. from Litchfield. It was taken from Woodbury in 1787. It is hilly, with a gravelly loam, and fit for grazing and the growth of rye. It has 2,000 sheep. Population, 1830, 906. The town is watered by Pomperaug river, a branch of the Housatonick.

Beverly, Mass.

Essex co. This town lies N. of Salem, and is united to it by a bridge across the North river, built in 1788, 1,500 feet in length. The people of this town are noted for their enterprise in commerce and the fisheries. There are some merchant vessels belonging to this place, about 50 sail of fishermen, and 20 coasters. The annual value of the fisheries at Beverly is about $100,000. The manufactures, consisting of Brittania ware, tin and cabinet wares, chairs, hats, boots, hair, mustard and bricks, amounted in one year to about $120,000. The prosperity of this town has not suffered by the growth of luxury or excess of trade; its fisheries and manufacturing concerns are steady and progressive. First settled, 1626. Incorporated, 1688. Population, 1830, 4,079—1837, 4,609. Among many distinguished men who have lived and died at Beverly, was Captain Thomas Lothrop, who commanded the "Flower of Essex," a company of young men from this county, and who were, with their leader, almost wholly cut off by the Indians, at Bloody Brook, in 1675.

Biddeford, Me.

York co. On the S. side of Saco river, and connected with the town of Saco by a bridge. The town extends down the river to the sea, and includes a point of land called "Fletcher's Neck," off which are several small islands; on one of which, Wood Island, is a revolving light. This is a good township for agricultural pursuits, the coasting trade, ship building, and the fishery. It lies 38 miles N. E. from York, 15 S. W. from Portland, and 69 S. W. from Augusta. First permanently settled, 1630. Incorporated, 1718. Population, 1837, 2,278. See *Saco*.

Billerica, Mass.

Middlesex co. This town is watered by the Concord and Shawsheen rivers, and has a pleasant village, on high ground, near the centre. Its soil is good and well improved. The Middlesex canal and the Boston and Lowell rail road pass through the easterly part of the town. First settled, 1653. Incorporated, 1655. Population, 1837, 1,498. Here are some manufactures of woolen cloth, boots, leather, wooden ware, straw bonnets, shaving and splitting knives, bed binding, soft soap, and spirits. Billerica lies 18 miles N. W. from Boston, 7 S. S. E. from Lowell, and 7 N. E. by N. from Concord.

Bingham, Me.

Somerset co. On the eastern bank of Kennebec river, opposite to Concord, 26 miles N. from Norridgewock, 118 N. N. E. from Portland, and 55 N. from Augusta. Incorporated, 1812. Population, 1837, 701. In 1837, 2,548 bushels of wheat was raised in this town.

Black Rivers.

Black river, in *Windsor county, Vt.* is 35 miles in length. It rises in Plymouth, passes Ludlow, Cavendish and Weathersfield, and falls into the Connecticut at Springfield. This river passes through many natural ponds, and affords a great number of mill seats.

Black river, in *Orleans county, Vt.* is about 30 miles in length. It rises in some ponds in Craftsbury, and passing through Albany, Irasburg, and Coventry, it falls into Memphremagog lake at Salem.

Black river, in *Somerset county, Me.* is one of the head branches of the Walloostook.

Blackstone River, Mass.

The most inland branch of this river rises between Paxton and Holden. It passes Worcester, and the ponds in Shrewsbury pay it the tribute of their waters. After passing Auburn, Grafton, Millbury, Sutton, Northbridge, Uxbridge and Mendon, it passes into the state of Rhode Island, where it changes its name to Pawtucket, and meets the tide waters in Providence river.

Blackwater River, N. H.

Blackwater river, N. H. so called from its dark appearance, is formed by two small streams, one of which rises in Danbury, and the other issues from Pleasant pond, in New London. These branches unite soon after crossing the W. line of Andover, and form the Blackwater, which passes through the S. W. part of that town; from thence through the W. part of the towns of Salisbury and Boscawen into Hopkinton, where it empties into Contoocook river.

Blanchard, Me.

Somerset co. This town lies 116 miles from Augusta. In 1837, 795 bushels of wheat was raised here. Population, same year, 261. See *Barnard, Me.*

Blandford, Mass.

Hampden co. Branches of Westfield river rise in this town and give it a good water power. Blandford was incorporated in 1741. It was originally settled by a company from the north of Ireland. It lies 114 miles W. by S. from Boston, and 15 W. by N. from Springfield. Population, 1837, 1,443. The manufactures of the place consist of woolen cloth, paper and leather. Annual amount, $50,500. The agricultural products sent to market in 1836, amounted to $22,340. There were in the town 1,535 cows and 1,822 merino sheep.

Block Island, R. I.

See *New Shoreham.*

Bloody Brook, Mass.

See *Deerfield.*

Bloomfield, Me.

Somerset co. This town was incorporated in 1814, and lies on Kennebec river, 33 miles N. from Augusta and 7 below Norridgewock, opposite to Skowhegan. Population, 1837, 1,053. Bloomfield is a fine township of land, and produced in 1837 5,080 bushels of wheat.

Bloomfield, Vt.

Essex co. Bloomfield lies on the W. side of Connecticut river, and is also watered by branches of the Nulhegan. Population, 1830, 150. It is about 20 miles N. from Guildhall, and 60 N. E. from Montpelier.

Bloomfield, Ct.

Hartford co. This was formerly a parish in Windsor, called Wintonbury. It derived its name from the circumstance of the parish being formed from Windsor, Farmington and Simsbury; the name Win-ton-bury being a part of the name of each of those towns. It was incorporated into a town in 1835. The inhabitants enjoy a fine soil, and cultivate it with great industry, producing large crops of grass and grain, with an abundance of choice fruit. It lies about six miles N. from Hartford. Population, about 1,400.

Blue Hill and Bay, Me.

Hancock co. The town lies at the head of a large bay, of the same name, 12 miles E. from Castine, and 78 E. from Augusta. There are several large ponds in Blue Hill, and a hill of 960 feet in height, from which delightful marine scenery is presented. Incorporated 1789. Population, 1837, 1,808. The bay has Long and other islands inside; and outside, Burntcoat, and a group of smaller islands. Blue Hill bay is connected with Penobscot bay and river by a passage between the islands and main land, of about 12 miles. It lies about 16 miles W. from Frenchman's bay.

Blue Hills.

The first range of mountains on the eastern coast of New Hampshire and Maine; and the elevated lands in Milton, Mass. are thus denominated, in consequence of their blue or cloud-like appearance, at a distance, on the ocean.

Boar's Head, N. H.

See *Hampton.*

Bolton, Vt.

Chittenden co. Population, 1830, 452. 17 miles S. E. from Burlington, and 17 N. W. from Montpelier. Incorporated, 1763. Bolton lies on the western side of the Green Mountains. Onion river passes through the town, on the banks of which most of the inhabitants reside.

Bolton, Mass.

A good farming town in the county of Worcester, 31 miles W. by N. from Boston, and 15 N. N. E. from Worcester. Incorporated, 1738. Population, 1837, 1,185. It lies between Concord and Nashua rivers. Here are good limestone, and small manufactures of boots, shoes, leather and combs.

Bolton, Ct.

Tolland co. This town lies 14 miles E. from Hartford, and 10 miles S. by W. from Tolland. Population, 1830, 744. The soil is a coarse, hard, gravelly loam, fit only for grazing. It is within the granite region of the eastern section of the state. The Bolton Stone Quarry is quite noted. "The stone is a species of slate, of a brilliant light gray color, composed of mica and quartz, and is excellent for flagging and other purposes. It is extensively used in the principal cities of the United States. For strength it exceeds any other known in this country, and the demand for it is rapidly increasing." The supply is inexhaustible.

Boon Island, Me.,

A ledge of rocks, with a lighthouse thereon; about 9 miles E. from Kittery. Near this island the steamboat New England, on her passage from Boston to Gardiner, met a fatal disaster, by coming in contact with a loaded coaster, on the night of the 31st of May, 1838, by which many valuable lives were jeopardized.

Boothbay, Me.

Lincoln co. This town is bounded W. by the mouth of Sheepscot river, N. by Edgecomb, E. by Damariscotta river, and S. by the ocean. It is nearly surrounded by water, and is noted for its excellent harbor. Its maritime situation renders it a place of considerable business in the coasting trade and fisheries. This town lies 39 miles S. S. E. from Augusta, 12 E. N. E. from Wiscasset, 60 E. N. E. from Portland, and about 40 miles S. W. by W. from Owl's Head, by water. Boothbay is a fine watering place, and many visit it, in summer months, for health or pleasure. Here may be found all the enjoyments of sea air and bathing; fishing and fowling; ocean and island scenery; for which *Nahant*, in Massachusetts bay, is justly celebrated. Incorporated, 1764. Population, 1837, 2,562.

Boscawen, N. H.

Merrimack co. Boscawen is situated between Concord and Salisbury, on the W. side of Merrimack river. Boscawen is 8 miles N. W. from Concord. Besides the Merrimack, the west part of this town is watered by Blackwater river, running nearly parallel with the former, through the whole extent of the town, and about five miles distant from it. It is not a large stream, but very important, both on account of the fertile fields of champaign on its borders, and the numerous water privileges it affords. There are two ponds of some note. Great pond, near the centre of the town, Long pond, in the west part, and mill seats at the outlet of each. Boscawen is of a deep, productive soil, affording many excellent farms delightfully situated. The surface, when viewed from its highest parts, appears uncommonly level. From the numerous streams of living water, and from the peculiar direction of the swells of the hills, this town probably derives that pure air and uniform temperature which are so conducive to health. The principal village is in the east section of the town. It is situated on a spacious street nearly two miles in length, very straight and level. Here the eye of the traveller is attracted and delighted by the fertile intervales and windings of the river Merrimack. There is another village on a pleasant eminence near the west meeting house. Boscawen was granted by Massachusetts in 1733. The proprietors gave to it the name of *Contoocook*, after the Indian name of the river. It received its present name when it was incorporated, April 22, 1760, from Edward Boscawen, a celebrated English admiral then on the American station. The first settlement commenced early in the season of 1734. Abigail Danforth was the first child born in the town. The Indians made frequent predatory incursions on the inhabitants. See *Duston's Island.*

Among the deceased citizens of this place entitled to respectful notice, are, *George Jackman*, Esq., the first town clerk, who continued in office 36 years. He was appointed a justice of the peace under Geo. II. and continued in that office during all successive changes down to 1818.

Rev. *Samuel Wood*, D. D., for more than half a century the minister of Boscawen, was distinguished for his learning and piety.

Hon. *Ezekiel Webster*, a native of Salisbury, resided here many years. He was an eminent barrister at law, of extraordinary talents, and great private worth. He died in the court house, at Concord, April 10, 1829, aged 49, beloved and lamented by all who knew his character. Population, 1830, 2,093.

BOSTON.

County of Suffolk. The ancient city of BOSTON, the capital of Massachusetts, and of New England, and the birth place of American Freedom, is naturally divided into three sections—*Old Boston, South Boston*, and *East Boston*, situated at the western extremity of Massachusetts Bay. The peninsula on which Old Boston is built, extends from Roxbury, on the south, to Winnesimet Ferry, on the north, and is nearly surrounded by the waters of Boston harbor on the east, and Charles river on the north and west. Its length is nearly three miles, and its average breadth about one mile. It originally contained about 700 acres, but its territory has been greatly extended, by filling up around its borders. Its surface is quite uneven. It has numerous eminences, rising from 50 to 110 feet above the sea, affording admirable sites for building, and giving to it a peculiarly romantic appearance. It is in north Lat. 42° 21' 23" and west Lon. 71° 4' 9". It lies 163 miles S. S. W. from Augusta, Me.; 63 S. S. E. from Concord, N. H.; 160 S. E. by S. from Montpelier, Vt.; 158 E. (19' S.) from Albany, N. Y.; 40 N. N. E. from Providence, R. I.; 97 E. N. E. from Hartford, Ct.; 207 N. E. by E. from New York, and 432 miles N. E. by E. from Washington. Its Indian name was *Shawmut*. It was called by the first settlers *Tramount, Tremont*, or *Trimountain*, from three hills nearly in its centre. It took its present name on the 7th of Sept., 1630, in honor of the Rev. John Cotton, second minister of the first church, who came from Boston, in England. The original proprietor of this territory was *John Blackstone*, who, soon after its settlement by Winthrop and others, removed to Rhode Island. Boston was incorporated as a city, February 23, 1822.

South Boston.

This part of Boston was set off from Dorchester, by legislative enactment, March the 6th, 1804. It is bounded south by Dorchester Bay, and spreads about two miles on the south side of the harbor, above the forts. It contains about 600 acres, and is laid out into regular streets and squares. The surface of this part of Boston is exceedingly picturesque. In about the centre of this tract, and about two miles from the City Hall, the memorable "Dorchester Heights" rear their heads 130 feet above the sea, from which is presented a splendid view of Boston, its harbor, and the surrounding country. It is connected with Old Boston by two bridges. This part of Boston is rapidly increasing in population and wealth. The *Washington House*, near the "Heights," is a noble building, and a delightful residence

East Boston.

This section of the city, until recently, had been called *Noddle's Island*. It lies about 660 yards N. E. from Old Boston, and about the same distance from Charlestown. It is divided from Chelsea by *Chelsea Creek*, 600 feet wide, over which is a bridge, and from which is an excellent road to the Salem turnpike. The Eastern rail-road, to Salem, Newburyport, &c., commences at East Boston. The island contains about 660 acres of land, and a large body of flats. It was purchased by a company of enterprizing gentlemen in 1832. They were incorporated in March, 1833, and the first house was commenced in October of the same year. A steam-boat ferry is established between this place and Old Boston, starting from each side every five minutes. The time occupied in crossing is about three minutes. A ferry is about being established between this island and Charlestown. The surface of the island is pleasingly variegated, and affords delightful sites for dwelling houses and gardens at moderate prices. This place is well located for manufactories of various kinds; particularly for ship building, and all those branches of mechanics connected with navigation.

The *Maverick Hotel* is a large and splendid building, occupying a commodious site. This house is named in honor of Samuel Maverick, who owned the island and resided there in 1630, and who is said to have made " some figure in the history of after times—a man of very loving and courteous behavior, and very ready to entertain strangers."

Boston Harbor,

Extends across Light House Channel and Broad Sound, from Point Alderton on Nantasket, to Point Shirley in Chelsea, a distance, between the islands, of about 4 miles. It is safe, and of ample capacity for the largest navy. The most important part of this harbor is entered by a narrow pass, between two and three miles below the city and Navy Yard; and is well protected by two powerful forts—Independence and Warren. The outer harbor, below these forts, will shortly be protected by a very powerful fortress now erecting on George's Island, at a great expense, by the government of the United States. Boston harbor contains many islands of great beauty, and is the reservoir of the *Mystic, Charles, Neponset, Manatiquot* and other rivers. Its borders are environed by the towns of Hull, Hingham, Weymouth, Braintree, Quincy, Dorchester, Roxbury, Brookline, Cambridge, Charlestown, and Chelsea; and the numerous small bays, coves and inlets, indenting their shores, give great variety, and add much to the scenery of this delightful harbor.

Owing to the almost insular situation of Boston, and its limited extent, its population appears small. But it must be considered that the neighboring towns of Quincy, Dorchester, Milton, Roxbury, Brookline, Brighton, Watertown, Cambridge, Charlestown, Medford, Malden, and Chelsea, although not included in the city charter, are component parts of the city, and are as much associated with it in all its commercial, manufacturing, literary, and social relations and feelings, as Greenwich, Manhattanville, and Harlem are with the city of New York; or Southwark and the Northern Liberties with Philadelphia.

The population of Boston in 1700, was 7,000—1722, 10,567—1765, 15,520—1790, 18,038—1800, 24,937—1810, 33,250—1820, 43,298—1830, 61,391, and in 1837, 80,325.

Avenues.

The peninsular situation of Boston requires many artificial avenues to and from the surrounding country. Until 1786, the "Neck," between Boston and Roxbury, one mile and 117 feet in length, was the only passage to it by land. On the 17th June, of that year, the *Charles River Bridge*, leading from Boston to Charlestown, was opened for travel. It was incorporated, March 9, 1785. This bridge is 1,503 feet in length, 42 in breadth, and cost $50,000. Net revenue in 1834, $9,383. This bridge by its charter becomes state property in 1856.

West Boston Bridge, leading to Cambridge, was opened on the 23d of November, 1793. It was incorporated March 9, 1792. Length of the bridge, 2,758 feet—abutment and causeway, 3,432—total length, 6,190 feet. Cost, $76,667. Net revenue in 1834, $12,928. This bridge will become state property in 1879.

South Boston Bridge, leading from Boston Neck to South Boston, was incorporated March 6, 1804, and opened for travel in July, 1805. Length, 1,550 feet—width, 40. It cost the proprietors about $50,000. It is now city property—free.

Canal Bridge, from Boston to Lechmere Point, in East Cambridge, was incorporated February 27, 1807, and opened for travel in August, 1809. Length, 2,796 feet—width, 40. A lateral bridge extends from this to *Prison Point*, Charlestown. Length, 1,820—width, 35 feet. Net receipts in 1834, $3,173. This bridge will become state property in 1879.

The Western Avenue, leading from Beacon street to *Sewell's Point*, in Brookline, was incorporated June 14, 1814, and commenced in 1818. It was opened for travel, July 2, 1821. This avenue is a substantial dam across Charles river bay, about a mile and a half in length, and from 60 to 100 feet in width. This dam encloses about 600 acres of flats, over which the tide formerly flowed from 7 to 10 feet. A partition dam divides this enclosure, and forms, by the aid of flood and ebb gates, a full and receiving basin; thereby producing, at all times, a great hydraulic power. The cross dam also forms an excellent avenue from the main dam to Roxbury. Cost, about $700,000. Net receipts in 1834, $6,133. The proprietors of this avenue claim a perpetual franchise.

Boston Free Bridge, from Sea street to South Boston. Incorporated, March 4, 1826—completed, 1828. Length, 500—width, 38 feet. Built by proprietors of lands in the vicinity. City property.

Warren Bridge, leading to Charlestown. Length, 1,390 feet—width, 44. Incorporated March 12, 1828, and opened on the December following. It is now state property. The net receipts of this bridge in 1834, were $16,427.

All the above avenues are lighted with lamps, when necessary, and make a beautiful appearance.

Public Buildings.

Some of those of the most prominent character only can be mentioned.

The City Hall, or "the Old State House," on State and Washington streets, now occupied by the city government, Post-Office, Reading-Room, &c., is 110 feet in length, 38 in breadth, and 3 stories high. Two buildings on this spot have been destroyed by fire. The first was built in 1659, the second in 1714, and the present in 1748. Until the erection of the present State House, this building had ever been used for governmental purposes, both colonial and state.

Faneuil Hall, or the "Cradle of Liberty," in Dock Square, is three stories high, 100 feet by 80, and was the gift of Peter Faneuil, Esq. to the town, in 1742. The building was enlarged in 1805, and until the new Market was built the lower part of it was used for meat stalls. It is now improved for stores. The *Hall* is 76 feet square, 28 feet high, and has deep galleries on three sides. It is adorned with superb paintings of patriots, warriors and statesmen. The third story is improved for armories.

State House. This building is on an open square, on Beacon-street, fronting the malls and common. Its foundation is 110 feet above the level of the sea. It was commenced in 1795, and completed and occupied in 1798. Cost, $133,333. Length, 173 feet—breadth, 61. On the area of the lower hall stands the beautiful *Statue of Washington*, by Chantry. From the top of the dome on this building, 52 feet in diameter, and 230 feet above the level of the harbor, the whole city appears beneath, with all its *crooked streets*, its extended avenues, its splendid buildings, and the malls and common, crossed with romantic walks, and shaded by centurian elms. On the north and west the county of Middlesex presents its numerous villas, and a rich array of agricultural taste and beauty. Here are viewed the hallowed halls of Harvard, and the sacred field of Bunker. On the south the county of Norfolk appears, with its granite hills and luxuriant vales, chequered with a thousand farm houses, cottages, and splendid mansions. On the east, the city, with its lofty spires, the harbor and the ocean, all conspire to render this the most enchanting scene west of the Bay of Naples.

The *Massachusetts Hospital* is on an open plot of ground of 4 acres, at the western part of the city, on the banks of Charles river. It is 168 feet in length, and 54 in breadth. Commenced in 1818, completed in 1821. This building is of granite, and is a beautiful monument of taste and beneficence.

Faneuil Hall Market. The corner stone of this superb granite building was laid on the 27th of April 1825, and completed in 1827. Cost, $150,000, exclusive of land. It extends east of Faneuil Hall, on Dock square, 536 feet, and is 50 feet in width. The centre part of the building, 74 by 55, projects two or three feet on the north and south, and rises 77 feet from the ground, to a beautiful dome. The wings are 31 feet, and two stories high. The lower floor is exclusively appropriated as a meat, fish and vegetable market. The upper story is one vast hall, arranged to be divided into compartments for ware-rooms and large sales. On the sides of this building are *North Market street*, 65, and *South Market street*, 102 feet in width; on each of which is a range of spacious ware-houses, with granite fronts. On the east, across Commercial street, is a commodious wharf, belonging to the city. The hall, in the centre of the building is called *Quincy Hall*, in honor of Josiah Quincy, L.L. D., the late indefatigable mayor of the city, and now president of Harvard University.

Tremont House. This superb hotel, on Tremont and Beacon streets, was commenced on the 4th of July, 1828, and completed 16th of October, 1829. Its granite front on Tremont street is 160 feet, and 3 stories high. The wings are four stories high; that on Beacon street is 84 by 34 feet; and that on the south, fronting an open square, is 110 by 40 feet. This building contains 180 rooms. The dining hall is 70 by 31, and 14 feet high. Cost, $68,000, without the land.

New Court House. The corner stone of this building, in Court square, between Court and School streets, for the accommodation of all the courts of law for the county, city, and the United States, offices of record, &c., was laid Sept. 28, 1833. It is of cut, or hewn granite, from the Quincy quarry. Its length is 175 feet 10 inches;—width, 53 feet 10 inches, and height 57 feet 3 inches. A portico of nearly the same model of the Doric portico at Athens, adorns its north and south fronts. There are four columns of fluted granite at each of these porticos, measuring 25 feet 4 inches in length, and 4 feet 5 inches in diameter. **They weigh 25 tons each.** The interior contains four court rooms, 50 feet by 40, and large and commodious offices for all the respective departments.

Houses of Industry, Correction, and Reformation. These houses are delightfully situated on a plot of ground of about 61 acres, situated at South Boston, on the margin of the harbor, and near the brow of Dorchester Heights.

Trinity Church, in Summer street, *St. Paul's Church* and the *Masonic Temple*, in Tremont street, the *Washington Bank*, in Washington street, the granite building lately erected by the Suffolk Bank, the *United States Bank*, in State street, and the *Steeple* of Park street Church, are some of the best specimens of architecture in Boston.

Schools and Institutions.

The first settlers of New England were exceedingly tenacious of their civil and religious rights, and they well knew that *knowledge* was an all-powerful engine to preserve those rights, and transmit them to their posterity. They therefore very early laid the foundation of those *free schools*, of which all the sons and daughters of New England are justly proud. Exclusive of Infant and Sabbath school scholars, about a quarter part of the population of Boston is kept at school throughout the year, at an annual expense of about $200,000. Boston is not only celebrated for its schools, but for its munificent donations in support of its institutions for moral, religious, and literary purposes. Since the year 1800, not less than two millions of dollars have thus been appropriated by the citizens of Boston.

New England Institution for the Education of the Blind.

This Institution was incorporated in 1829; but, little was accomplished until 1832, when Dr. Howe returned from Europe accompanied by a blind teacher; manifesting that zeal in the cause of the blind which had distinguished his philanthropic labors, in another sphere, in a distant land. He opened a school with six blind young scholars. The progress of those children was so great, and the value of an Institution of the kind so apparent, that legislatures and citizens, generally, became much interested. By public and private donations, particularly by the influence of ladies in several parts of New England, and by the munificent gift of a splendid building in Pearl street, by the Hon. Thomas H. Perkins, the Institution has increased, both in reputation and funds, with unparalleled success. The scholars are instructed in all those branches common in other schools, and some of them in the higher branches of literature. Music is the study of all. Mechanical labors are taught and enjoyed by the pupils. Musical instruments of all kinds, and other implements are provided for their convenience and use. A printing press is established, and several books have been printed in embossed letters, which are superior to any in Europe. It is exceedingly delightful to see these interesting youth, whose lives once seemed a dreary waste, and to witness their improvement in acquiring useful knowledge, partaking of all those recreations, natural and proper for their age, sex, and condition, and fitting themselves for useful stations in society. The Institution is managed by a board of trustees, and is patronized by the governments of all the New England States.

Eye and Ear Infirmary.

This Institution was commenced in Boston, by Drs. Jeffries and Reynolds, in 1824, from a conviction of its utility and importance, derived from what they had seen and known of similar establishments in Europe. Those gentlemen conducted the establishment at their own expense for some time, during which large numbers received the most important benefits. In 1827, by the philanthropic exertions of those, and other gentlemen, an act of incorporation was obtained, and some funds were raised. As early as 1828, 2,610 cases were treated at the Infirmary, of which about five-sixths were cured. Of these cases about one-sixth were for diseases of the ear. Since that time the number of applicants has increased annually; and this Institution, whose merits are not surpassed by any other in the city, has now a beautiful and commodious building in Bowdoin square for the reception of patients.

Theatres.

The *Boston Theatre*, on Federal and Franklin streets, was first opened February 3, 1794. It was burnt, February 2, 1798; it was re-built, and re-opened on the 29th of October, the same year. It is of brick, 152 feet long, 61 wide, and 40 high. This building is now denominated "The Odeon," and is consecrated to the worship of God. A huge wooden building was erected on Tremont street, and opened as the "Hay-Market Theatre," December 26, 1796. The citizens in its neighborhood being fearful of its conflagration, caused its demolition, by subscription, and the block of elegant brick dwelling-houses, near, and north of Boylston street, now occupy the spot.

The *Tremont Theatre*, on Tremont street, is a very neat building, with a granite front 135 feet by 79. It was commenced in July, and opened September 24, 1827. Cost, about $120,000.

The *National Theatre*, at the junction of Portland and Traverse streets, near the Warren bridge, was constructed in 1831. This building was first used for equestrian performances.

Boston Common.

This is considered one of the most delightful promenades in the world. It comprises about 75 acres of land, of variegated surface, beautifully shaded by trees of various kinds, particularly in the malls, or walks which surround it. Some of those trees were planted more than a hundred years ago. The malls are wide, beveled, graveled, and smooth; the waters of Charles river, and the romantic scenery beyond it, are in prospect. The whole is enclosed by an iron fence, on the outside of which are wide streets and beautiful buildings. The distance around the malls and common is about a mile. This plot of ground is so held by the city, that it can never be appropriated to any other than its present healthful and pleasing purposes.

The foundation of a large and splendid BOTANIC GARDEN was laid in 1837, by the subscription of funds for that purpose. It is located on the city lands, on the west side of the Common. This will be a great ornament to the city, and an honor to the taste and judgment of its projectors.

Finances.

The public debt of the city of Boston on the 1st of May, 1837, was $1,497,200. The receipts, during the financial year, from the 30th of April, 1836, to 30th April, 1837, was $926,350—the expenditures, $904,065. Besides the public property in public buildings, city and other wharves, &c. &c., both improved for city purposes, and rented, the city has about 7,000,000 square feet of land on the Neck, exclusive of streets, public squares, and malls, and a very large property in other lands in various parts of the city, which are rapidly increasing in value. The amount of this property cannot be stated, but it is known greatly to exceed the city debt, exclusive of that part which is wanted for the uses of the city.

Commerce.

The citizens of Boston have ever sustained a high rank for their commercial enterprise. After whitening every sea with their canvass, and extending their commerce with all nations of the globe, they are now looking *westward* and *northward*, and constructing new and artificial channels, to enable them not only to compete with other Atlantic cities for the already immense commerce of the western world, but to intercept it on its passage down the St. Lawrence.

The number of vessels entered at this port the year ending September 30, 1837, was 1,544—tonnage, 242,277 tons—crews, 11,503:—cleared, 1,367, tonnage, 184,373 tons—crews, 9,177. The registered, enrolled and licensed tonnage of this port, the same year, was 201,005 tons. A large amount of tonnage, owned at Boston, is registered at southern ports.

Commercial Accommodations.

There is probably no place in the world better accommodated for commercial operations than Boston. The whole length of the harbor on the east and north is lined with about 200 docks and wharves. A few of them only can be noticed.

India Wharf, at the foot of *Fort Hill*, was constructed in 1805. It extends into the harbor 980 feet, and is 246 to 280 feet in width. In the centre is a range of 39 stores, 22 by 80, and 4 stories in height.

Central Wharf, between India and Long wharves, was built in 1816. In the centre are 54 ware-houses, 23 by 50, 4 stories high. It is 1,379 feet in length, and 150 in width. Over a spacious hall in the centre of this range of stores, is one of the best observatories in the United States.

North of this is *Long Wharf*, at the foot of State street, commenced in 1710. This wharf extends into the harbor 1,800 feet, is 200 feet in width, and has 76 spacious ware-houses. About the centre of this wharf is a well of fresh water, 90 feet in depth.

Passing the City wharf on the north, we come to *Commercial Wharf*, 1,100 feet in length, and 160 in width. On the centre of this wharf is a range of 34 granite ware-houses, 25 by 60 feet, and are unequalled by any thing of the kind in the United States for convenience or grandeur. Cost, $500,000.

On the west, and in front of this tier of wharves, which run into the harbor nearly parallel to each other, are *India* and *Commercial streets*, having the east end of Faneuil Hall Market nearly in the centre. These streets are wide; they serve as wharves, and their west sides are covered with large and convenient stores. It is contemplated to extend India street, on the south, to the Free Bridge on Sea street; and Commercial street, on the north, to Winnesimet Ferry. (See Hale's Map of Boston.)

The *Marine Railways*, established in 1826, at the north part of the city, afford great accommodations to those engaged in navigation. A new and splendid Custom House is now erecting on India street, between Long and Central wharves. An Exchange, for the accommodation of merchants, and a new City Hall, are contemplated.

Manufactures.

Although Boston has never been considered a manufacturing city, yet, since the general peace in Europe, in 1815, and the passage of the present tariff laws, in 1833, its manufacturing interests have considerably increased.

The following are the manufactures of Boston for the year ending April 1, 1837, with the value of each, the number of hands employed, and the amount of capital invested, so far as can be ascertained.

It may be proper to observe, that the following account is doubtless

NEW ENGLAND GAZETTEER.

accurate, as far it extends, but it is known that in some towns in Massachusetts the whole amount of their manufactures has not been stated by the assessors.

ARTICLES.	Value.	Hands employ'd Males.	Females.	Capital Invested.
Boots and Shoes,	$102,641	304	55	
Leather,	228,000	50		$60,000
Hats,	194,673	95	68	
Iron Castings,	272,000	289		665,000
Axes,	7,500	8		2,000
Glass,	48,000	77		47,000
Chairs and Cabinet Ware,	148,100	164		
Combs,	41,000	25	16	121,000
Tin Ware,	112,032	116		
Spirits,	926,856	19		
Straw Bonnets,	182,450		438	
Vessels, (average for 5 years,)	124,400	17		
Axletrees,	10,000	6		6,000
Beer,	12,000	8		30,000
Soap and Candles,	93,000	29		125,000
Whale Oil,	135,000	16		100,000
Copper and Brass,	756,754	200		316,300
Organs and Piano-fortes,	302,700	220		163,500
Brushes,	93,000	79	59	38,000
Gold and Silver Leaf,	43,000	22	14	11,200
Carriages and Harnesses,	318,805	298		82,200
Refined Sugar,	976,454	92		303,653
Silver Ware and Jewelry,	228,100	88		111,050
Chain Cables,	60,000	20		75,000
Umbrellas,	65,000	37	26	36,500
Saddles, Trunks and Whips,	177,000	120	17	83,000
Granite, Marble, &c.	336,000	400		165,500
Machinery,	326,000	287		183,775
Blank Books and Stationary,	78,000	43	7	49,000
Gas,	100,000	40		375,000
Looking Glasses and Frames,	147,500	42		55,600
Lasts,	40,000	29		18,000
Neck Stocks, &c.	122,000	21	435	58,200
Types and Stereotypes,	157,000	185	30	140,000
Printed Books,	925,000	500	400	850,000
Clothing,	1,887,666	542	2402	769,094
Hard Ware,	40,000	29		18,000
Baskets, &c.	93,000	138		38,000
Totals,	$10,010,631	4,655	3,967	

Fisheries.

The city of Boston is so limited, in regard to territory, as to be excluded, in a great measure, from participating in the fisheries. Much capital of the Bostonians is, however, invested, at the out ports, in this important branch of the resources of the wealth of New England. During

NEW ENGLAND GAZETTEER.

the year ending April 1, 1837, there were belonging to this city four vessels engaged in the whale fishery, and 152 in the cod and mackerel fisheries, employing 1,919 hands. Total tonnage, 11,253 tons. Total proceeds, $824,898. Capital employed, $748,200.

Health.

To judge of the health of a city we must compare its bills of mortality, for a series of years, with those of some other city. We have ever believed that the climate of Boston, and of New England generally, was as conductive to health as any portion of our country; but having heard it often asserted that the climate of Boston was more favorable to some diseases, particularly those of a pulmonary character, or what is commonly called *consumption*, than that of our sister city New York, we have examined with great care the authenticated bills of mortality of each city for five successive years, (1830—1834, inclusive.) The population of Boston, in 1830, was 61,391—of New York, 202,589—a fraction less than 3 1-3 in New York to 1 in Boston. From 1820 to 1830, the average increase of the population of Boston was a fraction less than 4 per cent. per annum—that of New York a fraction less than 6 1-3 per cent. per annum. The aggregate number of deaths in Boston during those five years, was 7,340—New York, 35,087 :—a fraction more than 4 2-3 in New York to 1 in Boston. In that period, the aggregate number of deaths in Boston, by *consumption*, was 1,128—in New York 6,124 :—more than 5 1-3 in New York to 1 in Boston.

Fires.

Boston, in common with all large towns which are chiefly built of wood, has suffered very much by fire. Fifty years ago the buildings in the town were principally of that material; but by efficient measures adopted by the citizens, particularly the law of 1803, prohibiting the construction of wooden buildings of a greater height than 10 feet, a large portion of the old buildings have been taken down, and their places, with thousands of others on new sites, now present to that destructive element solid walls of brick and stone. A few of the most memorable fires are here given. In October 1711, a fire broke out in Williams' Court and destroyed most of the buildings on both sides of Cornhill, now Washington street, from School street to Market square. On the 20th of March 1760, 174 dwelling-houses, 175 ware-houses, shops, &c. were burnt. This fire was in the centre of the town, (Cornhill, State and Congress streets to Fort Hill,) and the amount of property consumed, was estimated at £100,000 sterling. April 24, 1787, a fire commenced in Beach street, and extending south, destroyed about 60 dwelling-houses, 40 other buildings, and the church in Hollis street. July 30, 1794. Seven rope-walks, between Pearl and Atkinson streets, and about 90 other buildings in that neighborhood were destroyed. Loss estimated at more than $200,000.

On the 3d of November, 1818, the *Boston Exchange Coffee-House,* in Congress-square, was destroyed by fire. This building covered 12,753 feet of land. It was 7 stories high, and from the floor to the top of the dome was 83 feet. It contained 210 apartments, and cost about half a million of dollars. The conflagration occurred in the evening, and the sight was awfully sublime.

On the 7th of July, 1824, at noon, (the wind blowing almost a gale,) 15 costly dwelling-houses were burnt, on Beacon, Charles and Chesnut streets.

A very destructive fire commenced on Doane street, April 7th, 1824, when 53 large ware-houses, in that part of the city, with a great amount of merchandize, were destroyed.

A number of buildings, containing about 35 lawyers' offices, and 20 stores and shops, on Court street, were burnt, Nov. 10, 1825.

During five years, 1830—1834, inclusive, there were 226 fires—the amount of property destroyed was $274,278 :—of which $140,943 was insured. The most destructive fires were in 1833. In that year 71 fires occurred, $89,970 value of property was destroyed, of which $57,040 was insured.

The present Fire Department was organized in 1826. It is always in the most perfect state of preparation for service. Attached to this department are 24 engines, and 16,000 feet of hose. By the most powerful of these engines, with 250 feet of hose, water can be thrown over the *grasshopper,* on the cupola of Faneuil Hall, 84 feet above the pavement.

Water.

The subject of pure water for all the various uses of life has ever been one of the first and most important considerations with settlers in all countries. It frequently happens that those places most suitable for commerce are the least favorable to the ready acquirement of that indispensable element; consequently the ingenuity and skill of man have devised and executed those stupendous aqueducts, and tanks or reservoirs, both in ancient and modern times, which have made some of the most desolate parts of the globe the greatest marts of trade and most splendid cities. Governor Winthrop and his associates located themselves at Charlestown, and would have continued there had not the waters of *Shawmut* been more agreable to their tastes. Their change of situation, on that account, is no compliment to their chemical knowledge, for the waters of Charlestown are decidedly the best. Possibly " the magic of a name" might have influenced them; for *Shawmut,* in the Indian language, is said to mean " springs of living waters."

The city council, in 1834, took the long neglected subject of introducing soft and pure water into the city, into consideration. By analyses of the waters of Boston, one of the best wells in the city was found to contain 3.6 grains of the salts of sulphate of lime, muriate of soda and muriate of lime, to the pound of water. The well is 30 feet deep, and is situate high on the side of a hill. Some wells were found to contain 7.5 grains of the above salts, and many others a much greater quantity of noxious matter. An able engineer stated that in October 1834, there were 2,767 wells in the city; of which number 2,085 were drinkable, and 682 bad; and that only 7 of the whole number were occasionally used for washing. The engineer also stated that "all the dug or Artesian wells of Boston, are in strata of different materials in very irregular position, so that whatever may be the success in making one well, no certain result can be predicated upon another trial at a short distance from the first. The wells in town are polluted by the dirty water at the surface being absorbed, settling and mingling with the veins below; or are adulterated by mixture with little streams of sea-water."

The Boston Aqueduct Corporation commenced operations for conveying water into the city from Jamaica pond, in Roxbury, in 1795. The distance from Boston to the pond is four miles, and the number of feet of logs laid in the city is 72,000, or about 18 miles. The greatest quantity of water that can be supplied from this source is 50,000 gallons daily, and the greatest height it can be raised in the city is 49 feet above tide-water. According to the estimates of the quantity of water used in London and Philadelphia, about 28 gallons daily would be required for every person in the city. This includes all that is commonly used for stables, washing streets, the extinguishment of fires, for manufacturing, and all other purposes. The quantity of water necessary for the present population is therefore about 2,500,000 gallons, daily. Spot pond in Stoneham, 8 miles from the city; Mystic pond in Charlestown and Medford, 7 miles; Long pond, in Natick, 16 miles; or the waters of Charles river, taken at Watertown, 7 miles from the city, would almost inundate the misnamed *Shawmut* with soft and pure water, at an expense of about a million of dollars. Philadelphia, by her incomparable water works, has added a lustre to her bright name; New York is following her noble example, by bringing the Croton river, 45 miles, to the centre of the city, at an expense of five millions of dollars; and Boston cannot much longer remain insensible of the value of pure water, to the health and comfort of its people.

Antiquities.

Boston was described by Johnson in his "Wonder Working Providence," about the year 1663, in the following words:—

"Invironed it is with brinish floods, saving one small Istmos, which gives free access to the neighboring towns by land, on the south side, on the northwest and northeast. Two constant fairs are kept for daily trafique thereunto. The form of this town is like a *heart*, naturally situated for fortifications, having two hills on the frontier part thereof next the sea, the one well fortified on the superficies thereof, with store of great artillery well mounted. The other hath a very strong battery built of whole timber, and filled with earth; at the descent of the hill, in the extreme poynt thereof betwixt these two strong arms lies a cove or bay, on which the chief part of this town is built, overtopped with a third hill; all these like overtopping towers, keep a constant watch to see the approach of foreign dangers, being furnished with a beacon and loud babbling guns to give notice by their redoubled echo to all the sister towns. The chief edifice of this city-like town is *crowded* on the sea-banks, and wharfed out with great labour and cost; the buildings beautiful and large, some fairly set forth with brick tile, stone and slate, and orderly placed with semely streets, whose continual enlargement presageth some sumptuous city. But now behold the admirable acts of Christ, at this his people's landing; the hideous thickets in this place were such that wolves and bears nurst up their young from the eyes of all beholders, in those very places where the streets are full of girls and boys, sporting up and down with continued concourse of people. Good store of shipping is here yearly built, and some very fair ones. This town is the very mart of the land; Dutch, French, and Portugalls come here to trafique."

Present condition of Boston.

Perhaps at no period since the settlement of Boston has its prosperity been so flattering as for the last seven years. It is true that Boston increased in population and wealth with great rapidity during the wars in Europe, from 1794 to 1807. But that growth was unnatural and contingent; it depended solely on the caprice of the belligerent powers, who viewed us rather as servants to their necessities, than with respect.

The present state of things is altogether different. The world is at peace. We look for no besieged city to supply with bread, neither do we seek to run the gauntlet of a blockading squadron to furnish a starving country with the growth and produce of its own colonies. We now rely on our own resources—agriculture, manufactures, the fisheries, and commerce with all nations with whom we can exchange our commodities at fair prices. So long as we are blessed with union, good schools, good laws, and with all those moral, religious and charitable institutions, which tend to make mankind wiser and better, our city, under Providence, will continue on in the forward path to prosperity and happiness.

The location of Boston always gave it the command of a greater coasting trade than any other port in the United States; but the great arteries to an immense, wide-spread and rapidly increasing interior commerce were never opened until the rail-roads to the north, the west, the south, and the east were constructed and in operation. By these devices of human wisdom, and by the continuance of the two former—crossing the waters of our own Connecticut to the noble Hudson, and piercing the centre of a large and fertile country, to the outlet of the great western oceans on the banks of the St. Lawrence, Boston, with its enterprize and wealth, located 160 miles nearer the British capital than New York, cannot fail of sustaining a fair and successful competition for this trade with any city on the American continent.

Motto of the City.

Sicut patribus sit Deus nobis.

AS GOD WAS WITH OUR FATHERS, SO MAY HE BE WITH US.

Bow, N. H.,

Merrimack co., was originally laid out nine miles square, comprehending a great portion of the territory now constituting Pembroke and Concord. It is bounded N. E. by Merrimack river, which divides it from Pembroke, S. E. by Hooksett, S. W. by Dunbarton, N. W. by Concord and a part of Hopkinton. The soil is very uneven and hard, but productive when well managed. There is but one pond of any size, called Turee pond. Turkey river empties into the Merrimack at Turkey falls, near the N. E. part of Bow. About a mile below are Garven's falls, now passable by locks on Bow side. Bow canal is situated on the Merrimack, 3 miles below Concord; the perpendicular measurement around which it is carried is 25 feet—its length 1-3 of a mile. It passes through a ledge of granite, and is for the most part imperishable. Its cost was $13,860; and about $2,000 of its first income were appropriated towards clearing channels through Turkey falls, &c. Pop. 1830, 1,065.

Samuel Welch, the oldest native citizen of New Hampshire, died in Bow on the 5th of April, 1823, at the age of 113 years. He was born at Kingston, Sept. 1st, 1710, where he spent the early part of his life; he lived subsequently a while at Pembroke; but for 50 years preceding his death he resided at Bow, in an obscure corner, and steadily cultivated his little farm, till the frosts of a century had whitened his locks, and the chills of a hundred winters had benumbed his frame. His life was marked by no extraordinary vicissitude—he was never in battle, or in any public service; he was a man of industry and temperance.

Bowback Mountain.

See *Stratford, N. H.*

Bowdoin, Me.

Lincoln co. This agricultural township is bounded on the S. E. by Bowdoinham, and S. by Topsham. It was incorporated in 1788, and lies 17 miles W. from Wiscasset, 37 N. N. E. from Portland, and

20 S. S. W. from Augusta. Population, 1837, 2,173.

Bowdoinham, Me.

Lincoln co. A pleasant town on the west side of Kennebec river, and north of Topsham. Here is considerable business in the lumber trade and ship building. Twenty miles S. by W. from Augusta, and 12 N. from Bath. Population, 1837, 2,218. Incorporated, 1762.

Boxborough, Mass.

Middlesex co. Incorporated,1783. Population, 1837, 433. Some shoes, palm-leaf hats and straw bonnets are manufactured in this town, and large quantities of hops are grown. It lies 25 miles N. W. by W. from Boston, and 9 W. by N. from Concord. Good lime-stone is found here.

Boxford, Mass.

Essex co. This town lies 26 miles N. from Boston, 13 S. W. from Newburyport, and 10 W. by N. from Ipswich. The annual amount of manufactures of cotton wicking, boots, shoes and ploughs is about $100,000. Population, 1837, 964. Incorporated, 1685.

Boylston, Mass.

Worcester co. Incorporated,1786. Population, 1837, 821. It lies 40 miles W. from Boston, and 8 N. by E. from Worcester. Boylston is watered by Nashua river, and has iron ore and a ledge of crystalized quartz. Here are some manufactures of combs, palm-leaf hats, boots and shoes;—several ponds and fine fish.

Bozrah, Ct.

New London co. This town was taken from Norwich in 1786. It was formerly called New Concord. It lies 33 miles E. S. E. from Hartford, and 5 W. from Norwich. The soil is a gravelly loam, rich and fertile. It is watered by Yantic river, on which are two pleasant and flourishing villages, *Bozrahville* and *Fitchville*, at both of which are manufactories for cotton. This town experienced a terrible hail storm on the 15th of July, 1799, by which much property was lost and many cattle injured. The hail fell in immense quantities, some particles of which measured six inches in circumference. Population, 1830, 1,073.

Bradford, Me.

Penobscot co. This town lies 87 miles from Augusta. 4,944 bushels of wheat was raised here in 1837, with a population of 770.— See *Barnard, Me.*

Bradford, N. H.

Merrimack co. Situated about midway between the Merrimack and Connecticut rivers, bounded N. by Newbury and Sutton,E. by Warner, S. by Henniker and Hillsborough, W. by Washington; is 31 miles from Amherst, 25 from Concord, and 80 from Boston. This town is watered by small streams, which principally issue from ponds,—of which the largest is Todd's pond, lying in Bradford and Newbury. This pond is supplied with water from the hills and mountains in Newbury. In it are a number of floating islands, which are deemed objects of curiosity. Its outlet forms the northern branch of Warner river. Pleasant, or Bradford pond, is on the E. side of the town. It is about 550 rods long and 150 wide. It communicates with Warner river by an outlet at the N. end of it. In this pond are several islands, which, with the rugged declivities on the E. bank, the waters below, and the cottages and cultivated fields on the west bank, present to view, in the summer season, a wild and variegated landscape. Many parts of Bradford are hilly. A large proportion of the town, however, lies in a valley, about three miles in width. Near the Sunapee mountains, on the N. W., is an extensive plain, more than a mile long and about half a mile wide. The soil differs in quality. It is light, loamy or rough. In the easterly part are valuable stone quarries. Bradford was granted to John Peirce and George Jaffrey, in 1765. Its first settlement was made in 1771, by Dea. William Presbury and his family. They were soon followed by several inhabitants from Bradford in Mass., from which circumstance it derived its name. It was incorporated Sept. 27, 1787, and is mentioned in the act as including New Bradford, Washington Gore, and part of Washington. Population in 1830, 1,285.

Bradford, Vt.

Orange co. This town lies on the W. side of Connecticut river, 25 miles S. E. from Montpelier, 7 S. from Newbury, and 15 E. N. E. from Chelsea. Population, 1830, 1,507. Bradford is a pleasant farming town, of good soil, and is well watered by Wait's river. About 4,500 sheep.

Bradford, Mass.

Essex co. This is a very pleasant town on the south side of Merrimack river, and united to Haverhill by a bridge of 650 feet in length. The surface of the town is uneven and the soil various; but much of the land is of a superior quality. Several of the hills exhibit beautiful scenery. Bradford is celebrated for its excellent schools and seminaries of learning. Here are several ponds, good fishing, and a pleasant stream of water. Some bricks are made here, and considerable leather tanned; but the principal manufacture of the place is of boots and shoes, of which, during the year ending April 1, 1837, the value of $381,748 was made. Total amount of manufactures that year, $394,448. Hands employed, 1,096. Incorporated, 1675. Population, 1837, 2275. This town lies 28 miles N. from Boston, 10 W. S. W. from Newburyport, 18 N. by W. from Salem, and about 18 miles N. E. from Lowell. A branch of the Boston and Lowell rail-road passes through Bradford to Haverhill.

Bradley, Me.

Penobscot co. First settled, 1796. Incorporated, 1835. Population, 1837, 338. See *Barnard, Me.*

Bradleyvale, Vt.,

An unincorporated township in Caledonia county, chartered in 1791, containing about 4000 acres. Moose river passes through it. It is bounded on the west by Kirby. Most of the land is on a mountain. It never had more than 21 inhabitants.

Braintree, Vt.

Orange co. This is a good farming town, and produces considerable butter, cheese, beef and pork. It lies 21 miles S. from Montpelier, and 14 W. by S. from Chelsea. Population, 1830, 1209. Branches of White river pass through the town.

Braintree, Mass.

Norfolk co. This town formerly included Quincy and Randolph, and was first called *Mount Wollaston.* It is celebrated for the antiquity of its settlement, (1625) and for the eminent men it has produced, both in church and state. The surface of the town is variegated by hill and dale, presenting many delightful views of Boston, its harbor and the adjacent country. The soil is a strong gravelly loam, and very productive. Excellent granite abounds here, of which large quantities are annually quarried and transported; and some of the best merchant ships are built of native white oak and cedar. The holley tree (Ilex aquifolium) is indigenous. Indications of coal have been so strong as to warrant an attempt at mining. The Manatiquot river, which rises in Randolph, after meandering through this town and receiving the waters of Great and Little ponds, meets the tide waters of Boston harbor, at Braintree landing, on Weymouth Fore river, 11 miles from Boston. At this place there is considerable trade in lumber and bread stuffs, and some navigation is employed in the coasting trade and fisheries. The manufactures of Braintree consist of boots, shoes, cotton and woolen goods, paper, leather, nails, axes, cotton ginns, chocolate, carriages, granite, straw bonnets, tin ware, and vessels. The value of these articles of manufacture, for the year ending April 1, 1837, amounted to $371,937. The value of boots and shoes amounted to $202,363, and gave employment to 850 persons. The Manatiquot affords this town excellent mill sites; some of which lie near ship navigation, and are very valuable. Braintree was incorporated in 1640. It lies 10 miles S. by E. from Boston, and 12 S. E. from Dedham. Population, 1830, 1,752; 1837, 2,237.

Brandon, Vt.

This is a flourishing town in Rutland county, 40 miles S. W. from Montpelier, 16 N. by W. from Rutland, and 16 S. from Middlebury. It was first settled in 1775, and organized in 1784. Population, 1830, 1,940. Brandon is finely watered by Otter creek, Mill river, and Spring pond; on which streams are good mill seats. Some of the land is level, with rather a light soil, but that on Otter creek is the best alluvial. Bog iron ore, of an excellent quality, is found here; copperas and marble are also found. There are two curious caverns in this town. The largest contains two apartments, each from 16 to 20 feet square. It is entered by descending from the surface about 20 feet. They are formed of limestone.

Branford, Ct.

New Haven co. An uneven township, of strong soil, on Long Island Sound, about 7 miles E. from New Haven. Thimble islands and Indian islands lie within the limits of the town. Here are fish of various kinds, a small stream of water, a harbor, and some vessels engaged in the fishery. The town was settled in 1644. Population, 1830, 2,332. A beautiful pond, called Saltonstall's lake, lies between Branford and East Haven.

Brattleborough, Vt.

Windham co. This town is situated in the southeasterly quarter of the state and county; is bounded E. by Connecticut river, S. by Vernon and Guilford, W. by Marlboro', and N. by Dummerston. At the N. E. section of the town is the site of the once famous military post, *Fort Dummer*, nothing of which is now retained but the name, *Dummer Meadows*. At the mouth of Whetstone brook is a commodious landing place for river craft. Brattleborough is connected with Hinsdale and Chesterfield by a handsome covered bridge, spanning the Connecticut, and terminating at its western abutment in the east village, where the north, the south, the east, and the west lines of mail stages concentrate. The town and vicinity are noticed for their salubrious air, pure water, and fine mountain scenery. It is watered on the east by the Connecticut, and is intersected by West river, Whetstone brook, and numerous smaller streams. There are many sites for water power on the larger streams, unoccupied, and inviting to enterprize. The east village is the *general business mart* for the surrounding towns. Of its own internal business and industry, one instance is given of many of less amount. "The Brattleboro'

Typographic Co." was incorporated Oct. 26, 1336. Capital, $150,000. The Company is extensively engaged in the manufacture of paper and books. Their paper mill is furnished with the best machinery, and is capable of turning out from 40 to 50 reams of the largest printing paper, or from 150 to 200 reams of letter paper per day. Their printing office contains eight power presses. There are employed in the establishment from 60 to 70 male and female operatives. So great are their facilities, that they have taken rags and manufactured them into paper, and printed it, on the same day. Probably there is no establishment in the country which combines so many facilities for carrying on the book business as this. The Company publish a variety of bibles and other valuable works. The value of business done at this establishment, in 1836, is stated to have amounted to $500,000.

It is presumed that this village, according to its size, is second to none in the state for business or wealth. The surface of the town is diversified by hills, vales, and plains; is of good soil, and generally well improved. It is 12 miles S. E. from Newfane, 96 S. from Montpelier, 90 W. of Boston, and 76 E. N. E. from Albany. Population, 1820, 2,017—1830, 2,141.

Bremen, Me.

Lincoln co. This town was formerly a part of Bristol. It is bounded N. by Nobleborough, west by Bristol, south by Pemmaquid point in Bristol, and east by Muscongus island in Muscongus bay. It lies about 40 miles S. E. from Augusta, and 15 E. S. E. from Wiscasset, and possesses great navigable privileges. Population, 1837, 773.

Brentwood, N. H.

Rockingham co. Brentwood is bounded E. by Exeter, N. by Epping, W. by Poplin, and S. by Kingston. The soil is better adapted to grass than grain, although some improvements have been made in its qualities. Exeter river passes nearly through the centre of the town, and there are other streams of less magnitude connecting with it. Pick-pocket falls, on Exeter river, are in this town, and near them are situated an extensive cotton factory, and a number of mills. A card factory has been established here, which promises to be of great utility; and also an iron furnace for casting machinery. Quantities of iron ore have been found, and it was formerly worked with success. Vitriol, combined in masses with sulphur, has also been found here. Brentwood was incorporated June 26, 1742. Population, in 1830, 891.

Brewer, Me.

Penobscot co. Brewer lies on the Penobscot river, opposite to the city of Bangor. It was taken from Orington in 1812. Population, in 1837, 1,622. It is watered by the Segeunkedunk, on which are mills of various kinds. Considerable quantities of lumber, hay, potatoes, tanners' bark and wood, are annually exported from this town. The town was named in compliment to Col. John Brewer, one of the first settlers, from Worcester, Mass. The navigable privileges at this place are equal to those at Bangor.

Brewster, Mass.

Barnstable co. This town was the Indian *Sawkatucket*. It was taken from Harwich, in 1830, and took its name from Elder Brewster, one of the first settlers of Plymouth; a man of great learning and piety, who died, 1644. In common with all the towns on Cape Cod, a large number of ship-masters, sailing to foreign ports, belong here. From three ponds in this town, covering about 1,000 acres, a never-failing stream of water is produced, on which are a cotton mill, carding mill, machine shop and other small mills. The value of the manufactures of cotton goods, boots, shoes, leather, axes, chairs, cabinet and tin wares, lampblack, Epsom and common salts, amounted, in one year, to $52,072. Product of the cod and mackerel fishery, $9,050. Brewster lies on the north side of the Cape, 16 miles E. by N. from Barnstable, and 6 N. N. W. from Chatham. Population, 1837, 1,534. Here are about 1,000 sheep.

Bridgeport, Ct.

Fairfield co. The town of Bridgeport was formerly a part of Stratford, and was incorporated by its present name in 1821. It contains about 10 square miles, of a strong and fertile soil, under excellent cultivation. That part of Bridgeport where the city now stands was called the village of Newfield, until 1800, when it was incorporated as a borough by its present name. In 1836 it became a city. This is one of those beautiful and flourishing places in New England, the pride of Yankees and the admiration of strangers. It is located on an elevated plain, on the west side of an arm of Long Island Sound, and commands extended views of Long Island and the surrounding country. The city is built in a style of great neatness and some elegance. The harbor is safe, but the navigation for large vessels is impeded by a bar at its mouth, of about 13 feet draught of water at high tides. A large business is done here in the coasting trade; some in foreign commerce, and some in the whale and other fisheries. The city is watered by the Pequanock, affording some water power. There is a commodious bridge across the harbor, 412 yards in length, with a draw for the passage of vessels. This is an important manufacturing city, particularly of saddlery and carriages, of which a very large amount is annually made and transported. A rail-road from this place is in contemplation, to pass up the Housatonick river, and meet the Boston and Albany rail-road at West Stockbridge, in Mass. The population of the borough of Bridgeport, in 1830, was 1,800. The present population of the city exceeds 4,000. Bridgeport lies 62 miles N. E. from New York, 17 S. W. from New Haven, and 4 E. by N. from Fairfield. The distance from this place to Setauket, on Long Island, across the Sound, is about 18 miles.

Bridgeton, Me.,

Cumberland co., is pleasantly situated on the border of Long pond, and near the head of navigation to Portland, by the Cumberland and Oxford canal. The distance from this place to Portland, by navigable waters, is about 50 miles. The soil of Bridgeton is good, and produced in 1837 4,000 bushels of wheat. Its location affords it great facilities for inland trade. Long pond is about 10 miles in length and 1 in breadth. It empties into Crooked river, which passes into Sebago pond. This town lies 74 miles S. W. by W. from Augusta, and 40 N. W. from Portland, by the road. Population, 1837, 1,863.

Bridgewater, N. H.

Grafton co. Originally part of New Chester; now Hill, was incorporated, 1788. It is bounded N. by Plymouth and Hebron, on the E. by Pemigewasset river, dividing it from part of Holderness and New Hampton, on the S. by Bristol, and on the W. by Newfound pond, which separates it from Alexandria. The soil is well adapted to grazing, and few townships in this vicinity exceed it in this respect. The Mayhew turnpike passes through the W. part, near Newfound pond, and the main road from Concord to Plymouth through the

E. part near Pemigewasset river. The first settlement was made in 1766, by Thomas Crawford, Esq., when the tract comprised the whole of New Chester, Bridgewater, and Bristol. Population, in 1830, 783.

Bridgewater, Vt.

Windsor co. This town is bounded E. by Woodstock, and lies 45 miles S. from Montpelier, 17 N. W. from Windsor, and 60 N. E. from Bennington. Population, 1820, 1,125; 1830, 2,320. The settlement of the town commenced in 1780. In 1785 the town was organized. There are many good mill seats in this town, on Waterqueechy river, and considerable fine intervale lies on the borders of that stream. The high lands are good, and produce valuable crops. It feeds about 6,000 sheep. Here are found iron ore, garnets, rock crystal, mica slate, gneiss, limestone, quartz, and excellent soapstone. In 1822, a *living frog* was taken from 26 feet below the surface of the ground, about 30 rods from the river.

Bridgewater, Mass.

Plymouth co. This township was formerly very large. It is now divided into four distinct towns. Not content with attaching the cardinal points of the compass to the names of three divisions of this ancient and respectable town, this remnant of the old territory is often improperly called *South* Bridgewater. The Indian name of this township was *Nunketest*. Bridgewater contains some very good land, and is well watered by branches of Taunton river. It lies 27 miles S. by E. from Boston, 20 S. S. W. from Plymouth, and 17 S. from Weymouth landing. Population, 1830, 1,855; 1837, 2,092. This town was first settled in 1651, and incorporated in 1656. The settlements were nearly all destroyed by the Indians, in 1676. Manufacturing operations commenced here at an early period. Hugh Orr, an eminent Scotchman, carried on the manufacture of cannon and small arms during the revolutionary war. The present manufactures consist of boots, shoes, hats, paper, anchors, bar iron (from native ore,) iron castings, nails, tacks, axes, cotton ginns, straw bonnets, &c. The value of these manufactures, in one year, amounted to about $250,-000, and gave employment to 400 hands.

Bridport, Vt.

Addison co. Bridport was first settled in 1768, and organized as a town in 1785. It is bounded on the W. by lake Champlain, and is opposite to Crown Point, in the state of New York. It is 12 miles W. by S. from Middlebury, 37 S. from Burlington, and 45 S. W. from Montpelier. Population,1830,1,774. The surface is nearly level, with a loamy soil and sandstone. The water is bad to the taste, and contains Epsom salts. It has a harbor on the lake, and the business of the town is considerable. Across the lake to Crown Point is about 2 miles. A visit to the ruins of this ancient fortress, so renowned in the annals of the revolutionary war, and elevated 47 feet above the level of the lake, is a great treat to the contemplative traveller, or the lover of splendid scenery. From these warlike ruins to those of Ticonderoga, is 15 miles, S.

Brighton, Me.

This town is situated in the county of Somerset and bounded by Athens on the S. It was incorporated in 1816, and is 120 miles N. N. W. from Portland, 50 N. from Augusta, and about 30 W. from Dover. Population, 1837, 798. The same year it produced 5,203 bushels of wheat.

Brighton, Vt.

A town in Essex county. Population, 1830, 105. See *Barnard. Me.*

Brighton, Mass.

Middlesex co. This was formerly a part of Cambridge, and called "Little Cambridge" until its incorporation in 1807. It lies 5 miles S. W. from Boston, 13 S. E. from Concord, 25 E. from Worcester, 8 N. by E. from Dedham, and 15 N. W. by N. from Weymouth landing. Population, 1830, 972; 1837, 1,337. The western and northern boundaries of this town are washed by Charles river. The soil is excellent and highly cultivated, and, in common with all the towns in the vicinity of Boston, Brighton has become the residence of many people of wealth and taste, who possess beautiful country seats and splendid gardens. Winship's garden is noted throughout the country for its nursery of fruit-trees and shrubbery, and for its grand display of plants and flowers of every variety. Brighton is the largest cattle market in New England. Monday is the market day, when sellers and buyers meet in throngs to traffic in live stock, both for slaughter and domestic use. The sales in 1830 and 1837 are here given.

1830.	*No.*	*Value.*
Beef cattle,	37,767,	$977,990.
Store do.	13,635,	154,564.
Sheep,	132,697,	215,618.
Swine,	19,639,	70,971.
	203,783,	$1,419,143.

1837.	*No.*	*Value.*
Beef cattle,	32,664,	$1,567,872.
Store do.	16,210,	486,480.
Sheep,	110,206,	275,515.
Swine,	17,052,	119,364.
	176,132,	$2,449,231.

Brimfield, Mass.

Hampden co. This town lies 19 miles E. by N. from Springfield, 50 W. N. W. from Providence, R. I., and 70 W. by S. from Boston. Population, 1837, 1,590. First settled, 1714. Incorporated, 1731. This is a fine farming town, with a good soil, and is well watered by Chickopee and Quinebaugh rivers. The articles manufactured in this town, in one year, amounted to $105,262. The manufactures consisted of cotton goods, boots, shoes, leather, palm-leaf hats, chairs and cabinet ware. The value of wool grown, in one year, was $4,067.

Bristol County, Mass.

Taunton and *New Bedford* are the county towns.

The surface of this county is somewhat broken, but generally level. Its soil in many parts is of an inferior quality. There are 12,468 sheep. Area, 600 square miles. It has a maritime coast of considerable extent, and its people are extensively engaged in navigation. The tonnage of the two districts in this county (New Bedford and Dighton) is 94,163 tons. This county gives rise to many important streams that fall into Massachusetts and Narraganset bays, and its water power is abundant in almost every town. It abounds in excellent iron ore, and in no section of our country, of its extent, are more extensive manufactures of that material, for almost all the uses of man. This county is bounded N. by Norfolk co., E. by Plymouth co., S. E. by Buzzard's bay, and W. by the counties of Providence, Bristol, and Newport, R. I. In king Philip's time this part of the country was called *Pawcunnawcutt*. It was incorporated in 1685. Population, in 1820, 40,903; 1830, 49,474; and in 1837, 58,152: 97 inhabitants to a square mile. Value of the manufactures, for the year ending April 1, 1837, $7,929,479. Product of the fishery, $2,183,656. The Taunton and Pawtucket are its chief rivers.

Bristol County, R. I.

Bristol is the chief town. The territory of this smallest county in New England, except the county of Suffolk, in Massachusetts, belonged to the colony of Massachusetts until 1746. It is bounded on the N. by Bristol county, Mass., E. by Mount Hope bay, and S. and W. by the upper waters of Narraganset bay. Area, 25 square miles. The location of this county, on the beautiful waters of Mount Hope and Narraganset bays, affords it unrivalled facilities for navigation. The soil is generally a deep gravelly loam and very fertile, producing various kinds of grain and fruits; and has about 4,000 sheep. The rocks are mostly granite. Bristol county affords some of the best scenery in New England, and is otherwise interesting as being, for many years, the residence of the brave and cruel Philip. Population, 1830, 5,466: 218 inhabitants to a square mile.

Bristol, Me.

Lincoln co. This town is bounded N. by Nobleborough and Bremen, W. by Damariscotta river, S. by the sea, and E. by Muscongus bay. "Bristol Mills," so called, is the centre of the town, or the chief place of business. The town is finely watered by the Damariscotta and Pemmaquid, and possesses great hydraulic power and navigable facilities. There are a number of islands in the waters around Bristol, which make a beautiful appearance; some of them are quite large, and inhabited. The surface of Bristol is not mountainous, but elevated, with a good soil. A number of square rigged vessels belong to this town; about 20 sail are engaged in the coasting trade, and a great number of smaller vessels are employed in the bank and shore fisheries. Bristol lies 15 miles S. E. from Wiscasset, 60 N. E. from Portland, and 32 S. E. from Augusta. Population, 1837, 2,788. This town was incorporated in 1765. There was a temporary settlement here as early as 1625. In an old fort, on the banks of the Pemmaquid, once called William Henry, and afterwards Frederick George, built of stone, in 1692, and taken by the French in 1696, "are found grave stones of a very early date, and streets regularly laid out and paved, in the vicinity of the fort. On the side of the river, opposite to the fort, tan pits have been discovered, the plank remaining in a state of preservation. In other places coffins have been dug up, which bear indubitable evidence of a remote antiquity." "A considerable portion of the inhabitants of Bristol are of Irish extraction, a small part of Scotch, a few of German and English. The predominant characteristics of the inhabitants are frankness and hospitality, a generous liberality of sentiment, and an ardent love of liberty and independence. There are few of that class of men who are esteemed opulent. The most wealthy are those who labor daily with their hands, and raise by their own individual exertions the bread they consume. On the other hand, the population of the miserably poor is very small, and the town is burthened with but few paupers." Bristol was the residence of Commodore Samuel Tucker, distinguished for his bravery in the revolutionary war.

Bristol, N. H.

Bristol, in the S. E. part of Grafton county, is bounded N. by Bridgewater, E. by Pemigewasset river, and W. by Hill. It is 16 miles S. from Plymouth, and 30 N. from Concord. The land is hilly, but has, in general, a good soil. Newfound pond, about 6 miles in length and from 2 to 3 miles in width, lies in this town and in Hebron. Its waters are discharged through Newfound river, a stream about 2 miles long and 100 feet wide, into Pemigewasset river. At the confluence of these rivers is a pleasant village, a cotton factory, and a number of valuable mill seats. Bristol was taken from Bridgewater and New Chester, and incorporated June 24, 1819. The first settlement was made in 1770. Population, in 1830, 799.

Bristol, Vt.

Addison co. It is 25 miles S. W. from Montpelier, 11 N. from Middlebury, and 25 S. E. from Burlington. The town is mountainous; some parts of it, about the "Hog's Back" and "South Mountain," are unfit for cultivation. On the west side of the mountains is some fine land. About 2,200 sheep are kept here. Bristol is watered by New Haven river, Baldwin and Lewis' creek, and some beautiful natural ponds. Here is a good water power, and some manufactures. Population, in 1830, 1,247.

Bristol, R. I.

This is the chief town of Bristol county; the *Pocanocket* of the Indians. It is delightfully situated on the waters of Narraganset and Mount Hope bays, in lat. 41° 39' 53" N., lon. 71° 19' W. It lies 15 miles S. from Providence, 15 N. from Newport, and 56 S. S. W. from Boston. Its navigable advantages are unrivalled. The commerce of this place is not so extensive as formerly; still there is considerable maritime trade. It has 18 vessels engaged in the whale fishery, 15 or 20 sail in the merchant service, and a large number in the coasting trade. The amount of tonnage in this district in 1837, was 16,627 tons. Much of the capital of this town is employed in manufacturing concerns at other places. The town comprises an area of about 12 square miles, including Mount Hope, once the residence of the celebrated king Philip. The soil is a deep, gravelly loam, very fertile and productive. Great quantities of onions are produced here; the cultivation of which gives a lucrative employment to a great number of the inhabitants. Population, in 1830, 3,054.

Mount Hope lies about 2 miles N. E. of the court house. It is of a conical form, and though not more than 300 feet above tide water, presents a view of great interest and beauty.

Mount Hope bay is an arm of Narraganset bay: it extends N. E. from Bristol to Fall river and Somerset, and receives the waters of Taunton river.

Bristol, Ct.

Hartford co. This town was taken from Farmington in 1785. It is watered by some streams which flow into Farmington river, and there are found within its limits iron and copper ores, and granite. The copper mine is very rich and productive, and will probably become a source of great wealth. "The surface of the town is uneven and hilly, and the soil is a gravelly loam, and considerably fertile, producing all kinds of grain, grass and fruit, common to this region. This is a manufacturing town, and the inhabitants are distinguished for their enterprize and industry. There are at present sixteen clock factories, in which nearly 100,000 brass and wooden clocks have been manufactured in a single year. The manufacture of buttons is also carried on in this place." Bristol is 16 miles W. by S. from Hartford, and 28 N. from New Haven. Population, 1830, 1,707; 1837, about 2,500.

Brookfield, N. H.

Strafford co. It is 45 miles from Concord, and 90 from Boston; was originally a part of Middleton, from which it was separated and incorporated Dec. 30, 1794. The soil is good. Cook's pond is the source of the W. branch of Salmon-Fall river. There is also another small pond, covering about 15 acres, directly on the top of Moose mountain, which has always about the same quantity of water, and a variety of fish in it. Population, in 1830, 679.

Brookfield, Vt.

Orange co. On the high lands between Onion and White rivers; 40 miles N. by W. from Windsor, 16 S. from Montpelier, and bounded by Chelsea on the S. E. It is watered by a number of ponds and springs, but has no important mill privileges. This is a fine grazing town, and feeds about 10,000 sheep. The products of the dairy are considerable. Here are some manufactures, and an inexhaustible bed of marl, from which lime is made. The town was first settled in 1779, and organized in 1781. Population, 1830, 1,677.

Brookfield, Mass.

Worcester co. The Indian *Quaboag*, a large, fertile and beautiful township, in two parishes, well watered by several large ponds, which give rise to a principal branch of Chickopee river. For about forty years after its first settlement, in 1660, this town suffered exceedingly by the Indians. The ponds afford fine fish of various kinds, and in this town is a mineral spring of some celebrity. It lies 58 miles W. from Boston, 18 W. from Worcester, and 7 E. from Ware. Incorporated, 1673. Population, 1830, 2,342; 1837, 2,514. The agricultural products of this town are butter, cheese, wool, and fine beef cattle. The manufactures consist of boots, shoes, leather, iron castings, ploughs, chairs, cabinet ware, palmleaf hats, silver plate, shoe makers rolling and shingle machines, sleighs, carpenters' hammers, coach wrenches, sewing silk, and wooden legs. These manufactures, for the year ending April 1, 1837, amounted to $248,502, exclusive of the silk.

Brookfield, Ct.

Fairfield co. This town lies 33 miles S. W. from New Haven, 24 N. by W. from Fairfield, and 6 N. by E. from Danbury. It was taken from New Milford, Danbury, and Newtown, in 1788, and named after the first minister, Rev. Thomas Brooks, who was ordained when the church was organized, in 1758. The surface of the town is somewhat broken, but the soil is strong, and well adapted to the culture of grain. The rocks in many parts of the town are limestone, and afford marble. The N. E. boundary is washed by the Housatonick river, over which is a bridge to Milford; and Still river passes nearly through its centre. Fish, particularly shad, are taken in its waters. Population, 1830, 1,261.

Brookline, N. H.

Hillsborough co. On the S. line of the state. It is 7 miles from Amherst, 35 from Concord, and 43 from Boston. Nisitissit is the only river in Brookline. It rises in the N. E. part of Mason; passes through the S. part of Milford into Brookline, pursuing a S. E. course to Potanipo pond. From the pond it runs S. E. to Hollis, passing through the S. W. corner of that town into Pepperell, where it empties into Nashua river. Potanipo, or Tanapus pond, is situated near the meeting house. It is about a mile long and one third of a mile wide. Brookline formerly belonged to Massachusetts. It was incorporated March 30, 1769, by the name of *Raby*. In Nov. 1798, the name was altered by an act of the legislature to Brookline. Population, in 1830, 627.

Brookline, Vt.

Windham co. Set off from Putney and Athens in 1794. The easterly part of the town is elevated and unproductive. A deep valley runs through the town, in which is some good land. Its principal stream is Grassy brook, a branch of West river. An extensive bed of porcelain clay is found here. Population, 1830, 376. 35 miles S. from Windsor, 10 N. E. from Newfane, and 18 N. from Brattleborough.

Brookline, Mass.

Norfolk co. This delightful town is connected with Boston by the mill-dam across Charles river bay; one of the most beautiful and expensive avenues leading to the city. It is distant from Boston about 5 miles S. W., and from Dedham 5 miles N. N. E. Incorporated, 1705. Population, 1837, 1,083. This town is remarkable for its varied surface, high state of cultivation, elegant country seats and gardens, excellent roads, and for its rich and picturesque scenery. Many gentlemen of taste and fortune make this their residence.

Brooklyn, Ct.

Shire town of Windham co. This town is finely watered by Quinnebaug river, and Blackwell's stream. It was taken from Pomfret and Canterbury in 1786. The land is uneven, and somewhat stony; but the soil is strong, producing in abundance all the varieties common to a fertile grazing country. This town lies 30 miles E. from Hartford, 44 W. from Providence, R. I., and about 20 N. by E. from Norwich. Population, 1830, 1,451.— Good landscapes are obtained from the Gray Mare and Tetnuck hills. Here is a cave called the *Lion's Den*, and a mineral spring of some notoriety. The celebrated hero, General Israel Putnam, lived many years and died in this town. He was born at Salem, Mass., Jan. 7, 1718. He died May 29, 1790.

Speaking of this brave man, Dr. Dwight observes, " During the gayest and most thoughtless period of his life, he regarded religion with profound reverence, and read the scriptures with the greatest attention."

Brooks, Me.

Waldo co. This town is 11 miles N. N. W. from Belfast, and 45 N. E. from Augusta. It produced in 1837, 3,475 bushels of wheat. From *Paqsaggassawakeag* pond issues a stream of the same name, which passes into Belfast bay. First settled, 1798. Incorporated, 1816. Population, 1837, 800.

Brooksville, Me.

Hancock co. On the E. side of Penobscot bay, opposite to Islesborough and Castine. It is bounded on the N. by an arm of that bay, and includes cape Rosico. This town is well located for navigation and the fisheries. It lies 80 miles E. from Augusta, and about 25 S. E. from Ellsworth. Population, 1837, 1,192. Incorporated, 1817.

Brownfield, Me.

Oxford co. Bounded E. by Sacc river, and contains several ponds and streams; 81 miles S. E. from Augusta, and 30 S. W. from Paris. Incorporated, 1802. Population, 1837, 1,178.

Brownington, Vt.

Orleans co. Willoughby river, a branch of Barton river, furnishes this town with a good mill stream. It lies 45 miles N. N. E. from Montpelier, and 57 N. E. from Burlington. Chartered, 1790. Population, 1830, 412. It is divided from Irasburg, on the W., by Barton river. In this town are about 1,500 sheep.

Brownville, Me.

Piscataquis co. Bounded on the N. and E. by Pleasant river, S. by Williamsburgh, and W. by Vaughan. Incorporated, 1824. Population, 1837, 532. It lies about 20 miles N. from Dover, 97 N. N. E. from Augusta, and 171 N. N. E. from Portland. This is a good township of land, and produced, in 1837, 3,252 bushels of wheat.

Brunswick, Me.

Cumberland co. This town is on the S. side of Androscoggin river, and connected with Topsham by a substantial bridge. It is 27 miles N. E. from Portland, 30 S. of Augusta, and 8 W. from Bath. Population, in 1830, 3,747; and in 1837, 4,136. It lies at the head of the tide waters, where vessels of 400 tons are built. Vast quantities of timber and logs descend the Androscoggin to this place, and lumber of all kinds is sent to Bath in gondolas, or transported by land to the sea board. A rail-road, of about 4 miles in length, is contemplated, for the transportation of lumber. There are 30 board saw mills at this place, exclusive of those in Topsham. Two cotton and woolen factories were erected here; but they were both burnt in 1824. Another factory was built in 1834, calculated for 4,000 spindles. It is of stone, five stories high, and 174 by 45 feet. Other factories are contemplated. This place, possessing such an exhaustless water power, and situated on navigable waters, and on a large and beautiful river, extending 140 miles into the heart of a fertile and healthy country, cannot fail of very soon becoming one of our largest manufacturing towns.

Brunswick was first settled in 1627, and incorporated in 1739. It has been the scene of much savage aggression. See *Register*.

Brunswick, Vt.

Essex co. This town was first settled in 1780. Population, 1830, 160. It lies on the W. side of Connecticut river, and has some excellent mill sites on the waters of Nulhegan river, and Wheeler and Paul's streams. There are some beautiful ponds in town, and a mineral spring said to contain medicinal virtues. It is 55 miles N. E. from Montpelier, 14 N. from Guildhall, and opposite to Stratford, N. H.

Buckfield, Me.

Oxford co. This town is finely watered by a branch of Androscoggin river. It is bounded on the W. by Paris, and is 34 miles W. by S. from Augusta, and 50 N. by W. from Portland. Population, 1837, 1,618. The soil of this town is very good. Among its agricultural products, in 1837, it yielded 5,613 bushels of wheat.

Buckland, Mass.

Franklin co. This is a pleasant town and is separated from Charlemont by Deerfield river. It lies 102 miles W. by N. from Boston, 10 W. from Greenfield, and 20 E. S. E. from Adams. Incorporated, 1779. Population, 1837, 1,051.—This is a good farming town, and produces a considerable quantity of wool.

Bucksport, Me.

Hancock co. This town lies on the E. side of Penobscot river, 15 miles below Bangor, 61 N. E. by E. from Augusta, and about 18 W. by N. from Ellsworth. It has a fine harbor for vessels of the largest class, and which is seldom obstructed by ice. The soil is good, and the town is watered by a number of ponds and streams. Considerable shipping belong to this place, and the trade is quite extensive, particularly in the lumber business. It has some manufactures. From 1792 to 1816, Bucksport was called *Buckstown*. This is a very beautiful town, elevated, healthy, and flourishing. It is situated just above the head of Orphan's island,

Burke, Vt.

Caledonia co. A mountain, 3,500 feet in height, divides this town from Victory, on the E. Branches of Passumpsic river pass through it, and afford a good water power. This is a place of some manufactures, particularly of oil stones. This stone *(novaculite)* is found on an island in Memphremagog lake.— The stones are brought in their rough state, and their quality is said to equal those from Turkey. The soil of the town is good, and abounds with hard-wood and evergreens. A large number of sheep are kept here. Burke was first settled in 1780. Population, 1830, 866. It lies 40 miles N. E. from Montpelier, and 19 N. E. from Danville.

Burlington, Me.

Penobscot co. The number of inhabitants in this town in 1837, was 277. They produced the same year 2,106 bushels of wheat. See *Barnard, Me.*

Burlington, Vt.

This is the chief town in the county of Chittenden. It is delightfully situated upon the tongue of land formed by the confluence of the Winooski, or Onion river, with lake Champlain. This is the most important town in Vermont. It lies in lat. 44° 27' N. and in lon. 73° 15' W. It is 38 miles W. N. W. from Montpelier, 62 S. by E. from St. Johns, L. C., 80 S. S. E. from Montreal, 70 N. from Whitehall, 22 S. E. from Plattsburgh, 10 miles across the lake to Port Kent, N. Y. and 440 from Washington.

Although some beginnings were made before that event, no permanent settlement was effected in this township till about the close of the revolution in 1783. The town was organized by the election of town officers about the year 1786. The surface of the township is agreeably diversified, and is so much elevated above the lake that the air is pure and wholesome.

This town is not surpassed in beauty of location by any one in New England. It lies on the east shore of Burlington bay, and occupies a gentle declivity, descending towards the west and terminated by the waters of the lake. The principal streets, running east and west are one mile in length, and these are intersected at right angles by streets running north and south, and cutting the whole village into regular squares. A large share of the business on lake Champlain centres at this place, and the town is rapidly increasing in wealth and consequence. There are regular daily lines of steam-boats between this place and Whitehall, between this and St. Johns and between this and Plattsburgh, besides numerous arrivals of irregular boats, sloops, &c. Three extensive wharves, with store-houses, have been constructed and most of the merchandize designed for the north-eastern section of Vermont is landed here. The trade is principally with the city of New York, although Montreal and Troy have a share. For the safety of the navigation, a light-house has been erected on Juniper island, at the entrance of Burlington bay, and for the security of the harbor, a breakwater has been commenced here at the expense of the general government. There are four lines of mail stages which arrive and depart daily, besides three or four others which come in and go out twice or thrice a week.

The public buildings are six churches, the University of Vermont, the Episcopal Institute, the court house, two banks, the Academy and two female seminaries. The University consists of four spacious edifices, located upon the summit at the eastern extremity of the village, more than 250 feet above the level of the lake, and commands one of the finest prospects in the United States. The village, the lake, with its bays and islands —its steam-boats and sloops,—the Winooski river, dashing through frightful chasms and then winding among the beautiful meadows, and the distant and lofty mountains which form the great outline, render the view from the dome of the University one of the most variegated and interesting to be met with in our country.

As a part of Burlington may be mentioned the village called "Winooski City." It is situated on both sides of the Winooski river, partly in Burlington and partly in Colchester, and is one mile from the village of Burlington. The water power here is sufficient for propelling almost any amount of machinery, and is beginning to be employed to some purpose. Besides two saw mills, a large grist mill, a machine shop and numerous smaller works, there is a large satinet factory and an extensive block factory now in successful operation, and a woolen factory of the first class is to commence running the present season. A substantial covered bridge connects the two sides of the river; a handsome church, and several stores have been erected, and 'Winooski City' bids fair to become a place of business and importance. See *Register*.

Burlington, Mass.

Middlesex co. This town is watered by Vine brook, a branch of the Shawsheen river. It lies 11 miles S. E. from Lowell, 10 N. E. from Concord, and 13 N. W. by N. from Boston. Population, 1837, 522. Some shoes are made here. The soil is light, and suitable for the growth of rye and hops.

Burlington, Ct.

Hartford co. An agricultural township, with a soil of gravelly loam, pleasantly diversified by hills and vales, 17 miles W. from Hartford, and 36 N. from New Haven. Population, 1830, 1,301. It is watered by Farmington river, and was taken from Bristol in 1806. This town has some manufactures, and has been noted for the equality of its inhabitants, in regard to property.

Burnham, Me.

Waldo co. It lies 37 miles N. E. from Augusta, and about 30 N. W. from Belfast. It is bounded S. W. by Sebasticook river, and E. by Troy. Incorporated, 1824. Population, 1837, 602. It produced 2,297 bushels of wheat in 1837.

Burnham's River, N. H.

See *Lyman, N. H.*

Burnt Coat Island, Me.

Hancock co. A large island, surrounded by others of a smaller size, lying off Blue Hill bay, E. by S. from Deer island about 13 miles, and about 6 miles S. by W. from the town of Mount Desert. It has a light-house and good harbors, and is a fine location for the shore fishery.

Burrilville, R. I.

Providence co. This town was taken from Gloucester in 1806. It is finely watered by Branch river, with many branches; one branch of which rises in Allum pond, partly in this town and partly in Douglas, Mass. This river is an important tributary to the Blackstone. Manufacturing villages are scattered over this large town in almost every direction, and a vast amount of manufactures of various kinds is annually produced. The face of the town is rough, but the soil is adapted to grazing, and produces large quantities of beef, pork, butter, cheese, &c. Herring and Eddy's ponds are pleasant sheets of water. Burrilville lies 24 miles

N. W. from Providence, and 27 S. by E. from Worcester. Population, 1830, 2,196.

Buxton, Me.

York co. This town is bounded on the S. W. by Saco river. At this place the Saco falls about 80 feet, and produces a great hydraulic power, which is partly improved for manufacturing establishments. It lies 8 miles N. W. from Saco, 16 N. E. from Alfred, 18 W. from Portland, and 71 S. W. from Augusta. Incorporated, 1772. Population, 1837, 2,883.

Buzzard's Bay, Mass.

This bay lies N. W. from Dukes county, W. from Barnstable county, and S. by E. from the counties of Plymouth and Bristol. The length of the bay is about 30 miles from N. E. to S. W., and its average breadth about 7 miles. From the head of this bay, across Cape Cod to Massachusetts bay, (the place proposed for a canal,) is 5 miles.

Byfield, Mass.

See *Newbury*.

Byram River.

See *Greenwich*, Ct.

Byron, Me.

Oxford co. See *Barnard, Me.*

Cabot, Vt.

Caledonia co. On the height of land between Onion and Connecticut rivers. "The Plain" is delightfully situated, having the Green and White mountains in prospect. Several branches of the Onion river water this town, and afford it some water power. Here is Jo and Molly's pond, and a sulphur spring. The surface is broken and hard, but good for sheep, of which about 6,000 are reared. The town was first settled in 1785. The first females who came here came on snow-shoes. This is the birth place of *Zerah Colburn*, the celebrated mathematician. Cabot lies 12 miles N. E. from Montpelier, and bounded E. by Danville. Population, 1830, 1,304.

Calais, Me.

Washington co. At the head of navigation on the Schoodic, or St. Croix river, nearly opposite to St. Andrews, N. B. The *Upper* village, or *Mill Town*, is about two miles from tide water. At the *Lower* village, below the falls, is a bridge to the British side. Calais lies 28 miles above Eastport, about 35 N. by E. from Machias, and 204 E. N. E. from Augusta. This is a great mart for lumber of all kinds. About 40 saw mills and other machinery are in operation by the great fall of the river. The tide rises here about 20 feet, and large vessels ascend to the lower village. A rail-road is in operation between the two villages; it is to extend to Baring. Incorporated, 1809. Population, 1830, 1,686; 1837, 3,027.

Calais, Vt.

Washington co. Abijah Wheelock and others first settled this town in 1787. It lies 36 miles E. by S. from Burlington, and 12 N. E. from Montpelier. Population, 1830, 1,539. Calais has a number of streams, branches of Onion river, and several fine ponds. Two thousand pounds of trout have been taken in a season. There is some manufacturing carried on in the town, and it feeds about 6,000 sheep.

Caledonia County, Vt.

Danville is the chief town.— Bounded E. by Connecticut river and Essex county; S. by Orange county; W. by Washington county, and N. by the county of Orleans. It contains about 700 square miles. Population, 1820, 16,669; 1830, 19,943. Inhabitants to a square mile, 28. Incorporated, 1792. The eastern range of the Green mountains extends through the western part of the county. It is watered by many fine streams, but the Connecticut and Passumpsic are its chief rivers. A large part of the county is high and good land; that along the rivers is excellent. It produces wheat and other grain, beef cattle, horses, and about 60,000 sheep. There are some sulphur springs in this county; limestone and granite are abundant.

Cambridge, Me.

Somerset co. In the year 1837 the town had a population of 421, and raised, the same year, 2,890 bushels of wheat. See *Barnard, Me.*

Cambridge, N. H.

Coos co., is an uninhabited township, of 23,160 acres, granted May 19, 1773, to Nathaniel Rogers and others. It is bounded N. by the township of Errol and Umbagog lake, E. by the state of Maine, S. by Success and Milan, and W. by Dummer. This tract has an uneven surface, but might be advantageously cultivated. Several streams rise here, and fall into the Ameriscoggin, which passes through the N. W. part of the town.

Cambridge, Vt.

Lamoille co. It lies 30 miles N. W. from Montpelier, and about 16 W. from Hydepark. Population, 1830, 1,613. First settled, 1783. The Lamoille and other streams afford this town a good water power. There is some good intervale in the town, but the land is rough, and chiefly valuable for grazing: it feeds about 7,000 sheep.

Cambridge, Mass.

Middlesex co. This town may be divided into three parts: *Old Cambridge*, the seat of the most ancient and best endowed college, in the United States, is 3 miles from West Boston bridge, which divides Cambridge from Boston. *Cambridge-Port* is a compact, flourishing village, about midway between the University and the bridge. *East Cambridge* is of newer growth, and is a very flourishing place. It is the seat of the county courts, and is immediately connected with Boston by Canal bridge and the viaduct of the Boston and Lowell rail-road, over Charles river. This town was incorporated by the name of Newton in 1630. It took the name of Cambridge in 1638. The first printing press in America was established here, by Stephen Day, in 1639. The first work printed was the "Freeman's Oath." In this town are various and extensive manufactories. They consist of glass, hats, leather, boots and shoes, shoe blacking, tin ware, chairs and cabinet ware, rail-road cars, chaises, coaches, and other carriages; iron axletrees, harnesses, organs, carpenters' tools, clothing, pumps and blocks, cigars, brass and britannia ware, bricks, ropes and twine, soap, brushes, varnish, confectionary, stamped and stained paper, stoves, sheet iron, glue, pocket books, and medicine. The value of these manufactures the year ending April 1, 1837, amounted to $930,066. The amount of glass, which is considered of admirable quality, exceeded $450,000. Cambridge is very pleasant, although not so elevated as some of the neighboring towns. Besides the buildings of the University, it contains the United States' arsenal, other handsome public buildings, and many very elegant private residences. Pop. 1830, 1,072; 1837, 7,631. See *Register.*

Mount Auburn Cemetery, lies about a mile W. of the University, in the towns of Cambridge and Watertown. It contains about 100 acres of land, and is laid out with gravelled walks, and planted and embellished with all the varieties of trees, shrubbery, and flowers. Lots of ground, of 300 square feet, at suitable distances along the winding passages, are appropriated as family burial places, with the perpetual right to purchasers of enclosing, decorating, and using them for that purpose. Numerous monuments of exquisite workmanship are already erected, which add, if possible, to the melancholy grandeur of the scene. It is an enchanting spot;—a magnificent resting place of the dead. This cemetery was dedicated Sept. 24, 1831. We cannot deny ourselves the gratification of quoting a few lines from the *descriptive* part of Judge *Story's* admirable address on that occasion.

"A rural cemetery seems to combine in itself all the advantages which can be proposed to gratify human feelings, or tranquilize human fears; to secure the best religious influences, and to cherish all those associations which cast a cheerful light over the darkness of the grave.

"And what spot can be more appropriate than this, for such a purpose? Nature seems to point it out with significant energy, as the favorite retirement for the dead.— There are around us all the varied features of her beauty and grandeur—the forest-crowned height; the abrupt acclivity; the sheltered valley; the deep glen; the grassy glade, and the silent grove. Here are the lofty oak, the beech, that ' wreaths its old fantastic roots so high,' the rustling pine, and the drooping willow,—the tree, that sheds its pale leaves with every autumn, a fit emblem of our own transitory bloom; and the evergreen, with its perennial shoots, instructing us, that ' the wintry blast of death kills not the buds of virtue.' Here is the thick shrubbery, to protect and conceal the new-made grave; and there is the wild-flower creeping along the narrow path, and planting its seeds in the upturned earth. All around us there breaths a solemn calm, as if we were in the bosom of a wilderness, broken only by the breeze as it murmurs through the tops of the forest, or by the notes of the warbler, pouring forth his matin or his evening song.

"Ascend but a few steps, and what a change of scenery to surprise and delight us. We seem, as it were, in an instant, to pass from the confines of death to the bright and balmy regions of life. Below us flows the winding Charles, with its rippling current, like the stream of time hastening to the ocean of eternity. In the distance, the city,— at once the object of our admiration and our love,—rears its proud eminences, its glittering spires, its lofty towers, its graceful mansions, its curling smoke, its crowded haunts of business and pleasure, which speak to the eye, and yet leave a noiseless loneliness on the ear.— Again we turn, and the walls of our venerable University rise before us, with many a recollection of happy days passed there in the interchange of study and friendship, and many a grateful thought of the affluence of its learning, which has adorned and nourished the literature of our country.— Again we turn, and the cultivated farm, the neat cottage, the village church, the sparkling lake, the rich valley, and the distant hills, are before us through opening vistas; and we breathe amidst the fresh and varied labors of man.

"There is, therefore, within our reach, every variety of natural and artificial scenery, which is fitted to awaken emotions of the highest and most affecting character. We stand, as it were, upon the borders of two worlds; and as the mood of our minds may be, we may gather lessons of profound wisdom by contrasting the one with the other, or indulge in the dreams of hope and ambition, or solace our hearts by melancholy meditations."

Camden, Me.

Waldo co. This sea-port is finely located for navigation, with two beautiful harbors, on the W. side of Penobscot bay, 10 miles N. from Thomaston, 17 S. from Belfast, and 40 E. S. E. from Augusta. Population, 1837, 2,991. This place has some navigation engaged in the coasting trade and fisheries, and considerable ship building is carried on; but the principal business is the manufacture of lime from inexhaustible quarries of marble, or lime stone. About 200,000 casks of lime is annually shipped from this place to all parts of the United States. This lime is noted for making a cement of a superior quality. The Megunticook river waters a part of the town, and gives it a great water power, which might be well applied to manufacturing purposes. From a mountain in the rear of the town a beautiful prospect is presented of Penobscot bay and its numerous islands. Camden is a pleasant retreat in summer months.

Camel's Back Mountain, Vt.

This most elevated summit of the Green mountains lies in Huntington, 17 miles W. from Montpelier, 25 N. E. from Middlebury, and 20 S. E. from Burlington. It is 4,188 feet above the sea.

Campton, N. H.,

Grafton co., Is bounded N. by Thornton, E. by Sandwich, S. by Holderness and Plymouth, W. by Rumney; is 50 miles from Concord, and 75 from Portsmouth. Its surface is broken and uneven, abounding with rocky ledges, and having several mountainous tracts. Besides Pemigewasset river, running N. and S. through nearly the centre of the town, it is watered by Mad and Beebe's rivers, which fall into the Pemigewasset on the E., and by West Branch river and Bog brook on the W. The land in the valleys is generally good, and there is some good intervale. The high land is good for grazing. The forest trees are mostly deciduous. No white oak or pitch pine is found N. of the centre of the town. Iron ore of an inferior quality is found in some places. The towns of Campton and Rumney were both granted in Oct. 1761, to Capt. Jabez Spencer, of East Haddam, Conn., but he dying before a settlement was effected, his heirs, in conjunction with others, obtained a new charter, Jan. 5, 1767. The first settlement was made in 1765, by two families of the names of Fox and Taylor. The proprietors held their first meeting Nov. 2, 1769, and the inhabitants theirs, Dec. 16, 1771. From the circumstance of the first proprietors building a *camp* when they went to survey Campton and Rumney, this town derives its name. In the revolutionary war, this town, though in its infancy, furnished nine or ten soldiers, five of whom died in the service, and three were living in 1822. Population, in 1830, 1,318.

Canaan, Me.

Somerset co. This town was first settled in 1774, and incorporated in 1788. It formerly embraced the territory of Skowhegan and Bloomfield. It is a good farming town, and produced, in 1837, 5,444 bushels of wheat. It lies on the east side of Kennebec river, 13 miles E. from Norridgewock, and 34 N. from Augusta. Population, 1837, 1,347.

Canaan, N. H.

Grafton co. Bounded N. by Dame's gore, which separates it from Dorchester, E. by Orange, S. by Enfield, and W. by Hanover, and is situated on the height of land between the rivers Connecticut and Merrimack. It is 16 miles E. from Dartmouth college, 30 S. E. from Haverhill, 25 S. W. from Plymouth, and 40 N. W. from Concord. The only stream of consequence is the Mascomy, which rises in the N.W. part of Dorchester, and after a meandering course of 8 or 10 miles, falls into Mascomy pond in Enfield. Indian stream river rises in the S. E. corner of Dorchester, and running about 8 miles, mingles with the waters of Mascomy, near the centre of the town. Heart pond, so called from its figure, is situated in the centre of the town, and upon a swell of land so elevated that at a distance it presents the appearance of a sheet of water on a hill. It is about 500 rods in length and 200 in width, and the only natural curiosity of any note, is the mound, or bank of earth, which nearly surrounds this pond. It is from 4 to 5 feet high; and from its uniform height and regular construction would seem to be the work of art; but from frequent annual observation, it is found to have been produced by the drifting of the ice when breaking up in the spring. Besides this, there are Goose, Clark's, Mud and Bear ponds. The land is not so broken as in some of the adjoining towns. There is but little not capable of cultivation. The soil is tolerably fertile, and produces wheat, rye, corn, flax, &c. Canaan was granted by charter, July 9, 1761, to 62 persons, all of whom except ten belonged to Connecticut. It derived its name from Canaan in that state. The first permanent settlement was made in the winter, in 1766 or 7, by John Scofield, who conveyed what effects he possessed the distance of 14 miles over a crust of snow upon a handsled. Among others of the first settlers, were George Harris, Thomas Miner, Joshua Harris, and Samuel Jones. The first proprietors' meeting was held July 19, 1768. Population, in 1830, 1,429.

Canaan, Vt.

Essex co. Bounded N. by Canada, and E. by Stewartstown, N. H.; 31 miles N. from Guildhall, and 112 N. E. from Montpelier. First settled, 1785. Population, 1830, 373. The land in this town is broken and cold. Leed's pond produces an abundance of fish. Canaan produces more fish than grain.

Canaan, Ct.

Litchfield co. First settled in 1733. Incorporated, 1739. Canaan lies 41 miles N. W. from Hartford, and 18 N. N. W. from Litchfield. Population, 1830, 2,301. The town lies on the E. side of Housatonick river, opposite to Salisbury. A ledge of limestone rocks crosses the river at this place, about 30 rods in length, causing a perpendicular fall of 60 feet. The river is rapid, both above and below this beautiful cataract. The whole descent of the river, in Canaan, is about 130 feet, "nobly arranged and distributed, and comprehending a remarkable variety of beauty and grandeur." The township is mountainous, with some arable land along the streams. About 4,000 sheep are kept here. This section of country is noted for its excellent mutton. Limestone and iron ore are abundant; the latter is of a very fine quality. Iron works, on an extensive scale, are established here; a satinet factory and other machinery.

Canals in New England.

See *Register*.

Candia, N. H.,

Rockingham co., Was detached from the N. part of Chester and incorporated, 1763. The soil is naturally hard of cultivation; but the industry of the inhabitants has made it fruitful. It was originally covered with a thick growth of oak, ash, maple, birch, &c. The site of this town is elevated, and commands an extensive view of the rich scenery of the adjacent country—the

White Hills, the Wachusett, and other mountains, the lights on Plum island, and the ocean being visible. In the W. part of the town is a ridge of land extending from N. to S., which is the highest elevation between Merrimack river and the ocean. On the E. side of this ridge, two branches of Lamprey river take their rise. Candia lies 15 miles from Concord. This town among others contributed largely to the attainment of independence; and the names of 69 soldiers of the revolution are found on its records. The inhabitants are mostly industrious farmers, many of whom are wealthy. Population, 1830, 1,362.

Canterbury, N. H.

Merrimack co. Canterbury, though an uneven township, is not mountainous. The soil is generally good; the more uneven parts affording excellent pasturage. There are no large streams in this town; but several ponds give rise to smaller streams, furnishing good mill sites, and near which are cut great quantities of hay. Two bridges over the Merrimack connect this town with Boscawen. The town was settled about 1727, and for a long time the inhabitants were exposed to the inroads of the savages. The husbandman cleared and tilled his land under the protection of a guard, uncertain whether the seed he committed to the ground might not be watered by his blood, or that of an enemy. Canterbury lies 8 miles N. from Concord. Population, 1836, 1663.

The Hon. ABIEL FOSTER deserves a particular notice. He possessed in a great degree the esteem and confidence of the people; and soon after he left the pastoral care of the church, he was called to arduous duties as a magistrate and legislator. In 1783, he was elected to Congress; and for three years was a member of that body under the old confederation. He was successively returned a member for nearly all the time until 1804; when he retired to private life and domestic traquillity. He was an ardent lover of his country, and faithfully served his constituents—by whom his memory will long be cherished. He died in Feb., 1806. Canterbury, from its elevated situation, has ever been a healthy town.

In the S. E. part of this town, on an elevated and beautiful site, is the village of the "SHAKERS." At present it consists of more than two hundred members. They have a meeting-house open at all times of public worship, where any discreet and decent spectator is allowed to attend. They have a "Trustees' Office," where all their public business is transacted, and where strangers are at first received on their visits to the society. They have also neat dwelling-houses, of two and three stories, and several workshops both for men and women. Their mills and various kinds of machinery are moved by water on an artificial stream. They manufacture many articles for sale, which are remarkable for neatness and durability. Their gardens are perhaps the most productive of any in the country; and indeed all their improved lands exhibit the pleasing effects of industry and rural economy. They cultivate garden seeds and take much pains to propagate those of the best kind.—They occupy more than 1,500 acres of land, lying principally in a body, which they have 'consecrated to the Lord,' and which they enjoy in common. They cheerfully pay their proportion of public taxes, and share all the burthens of government, except the bearing of arms, which they deem to be contrary to the gospel; and in return they claim from government only that protection and support guarantied to other citizens. The income of their manufactures, together with their agricultural products, yields their temporal support; and what they become possessed of more than is necessary to their wants, they devote to charitable purposes, agreeably to their church covenant. It should be mentioned as a practice highly creditable to this sect, that the members of their societies never make use of ardent spirits, except in cases of sickness, being aware of the evils intemperance brings upon society. Another practice not unworthy of imitation is, they refuse to be trusted even in the smallest sum. They transact their secular concerns with great uprightness; and though they may have suffered reproach from their singularity of life and manners, they have become a proverb for industry, justice and benevolence.

For a particular account of the religious tenets of this singular people, see *Religious Creeds and Statistics.*

Canterbury, Ct.

Windham co. The first settlers of this town were principally from Dorchester, Mass. and its neighborhood. They came here about the year 1690. The soil of the town is a gravelly loam, generally fertile and productive. It lies 40 miles E. by S. from Hartford, and 6 S. from Brooklyn. Population, 1830, 1,881. The Quinnebaug is here a large and beautiful stream. It annually overflows its banks, and fertilizes a large tract upon its borders. There is fine fishing in Bates' pond. Considerable excitement manifested itself in this town, in 1832, in consequence of a Miss Crandall proposing to open a school for the instruction of " Young ladies and little misses of color."— Although no one seemed to question the purity of Miss Crandall's motives, yet the people doubted the expediency of the measure.

Canton, Me.

Oxford co. Incorporated, 1821. Population, 1837, 827. It lies on both sides of the Androscoggin river, 32 miles W. N. W. from Augusta, and 24 N. E. from Paris. Canton produced, in 1837, 3,114 bushels of wheat.

Canton, Mass.

Norfolk co. Neponset river and several large ponds give this town a great water power. It lies 15 miles S. W. from Boston, and 5 S. by E. from Dedham. Incorporated, 1797. Population, 1830, 1,517; 1837, 2,185. The manufactures of Canton the year ending 1st of April, 1837, amounted to $695,180. They consisted of cotton and woolen goods, shoes, palm-leaf hats, copper, wicking, thread, candlesticks, hoes, iron castings, trying squares, and " shapes." The bells manufactured at this place are of superior metal and sound. This place is easily approached from the capital by the Boston and Providence rail-road. The viaduct, or bridge, on that road at this place, cost the company about $80,000. It is of massive hewn granite, 600 feet in length ; 63 feet above the foundation, on 6 arches, with a succession of arches at top. It is an admirable piece of workmanship.

Canton, Ct.

Hartford co. First settled, 1740. Incorporated, 1806. Population, 1830, 1,437. *Collinsville* is the principal village in the town, at which a large amount of axes, of a superior quality, are annually made. It lies 16 miles N. W. by W. from Hartford, and 16 N. E. from Litchfield. This village presents a beautiful appearance, and is a noble specimen of individual enterprize. The soil of Canton is coarse and stony, and the surface hilly. Farmington river passes through its S. W. corner.

Carlisle, Mass.

Middlesex co. This town lies

20 miles N. W. from Boston, and 5 N. from Concord. Incorporated, 1805. Population, 1837, 596. It is bounded S. E. by Concord river. This is a poor town, and its manufactures are very trifling.

Carmel, Me.

Penobscot co. Population, 1837, 510. Growth of wheat, same year, 1,890 bushels. 71 miles from Augusta. See *Sowadabscook Stream.*

Carroll, N. H.

A township in Coos county, lying at the base of the White Mountains, on the N. W., having Jefferson and Whitefield N., Whitefield and Bethlehem W., and the ungranted lands, and Nash and Sawyer's Location on the S. It was granted Feb. 8, 1772, to Sir Thomas Wentworth, Bart., Rev. Samuel Langdon, and 81 others. Its surface is uneven, and its appearance dreary.—Population, in 1830, 108.

Carthage, Me.

Franklin co. Incorporated, 1826. Population, 1837, 455. 46 miles from Augusta, and 73 from Portland. See *Barnard, Me.*

Carver, Mass.

Plymouth co. Set off from Plymouth in 1790. Population, 1837, 990. 38 miles S. E. from Boston, and 8 S. W. by S. from Plymouth. There are a number of pleasant ponds in this town. The soil is not very productive. The manufactures of Carver consist of iron castings, boots, shoes, boxes, and willow baskets; annual amount about $50,000.

Casco Bay, Me.

This is one of the finest bays on the American coast. Its western boundary is Cape Elizabeth; its eastern, Cape Small Point. The distance between those capes is about 20 miles. Its indentation does not exceed 15 miles. Within it are some of the best harbors in the world. It is said that Casco bay contains as many islands as there are days in the year; however that may be, we know that they are very numerous, some very large, fertile, and well cultivated; and that a survey of them from the high grounds in Portland, Falmouth, Cumberland, or Yarmouth, affords a treat of island and ocean scenery of transcendent beauty.

Castine, Me.

Hancock co. Castine derived its name from a French baron of that name, who resided here upwards of twenty years after 1667. This peninsula, jutting out into Belfast bay, at the mouth of Penobscot river, was formerly called "Major Biguyduce," pronounced, *Bagaduce.* The peninsula embraces 2,500 acres of land, and was first settled by the English, in 1760. The British occupied this place in both of the wars with the U. S. It was the shire, or chief town, of the county from 1789 to 1838, when the courts were removed to Ellsworth. Castine possesses an excellent maritime position, but its trade from the country is limited, being cut off by the more inland towns. Its trade, however, is considerable. The lumber and coasting trade, with the fisheries, give active employment to its people. 78 miles E. from Augusta, and about 25 S. W. from Ellsworth. Population, 1830, 1,155; 1837, 1,168.

Castleton, Vt.

Rutland, co. This is a flourishing town, watered by a river of the same name; 11 miles W. from Rutland, 72 S. W. from Montpelier, and 14 E. from Whitehall. Population, 1830, 1,783. First settled, 1770. The surface of the town is rough and hilly, but there is some rich land. It feeds about 9,000 sheep. Mill streams abound in Castleton, on which are a woolen and other manufacturing establishments. Lake Bombazine, 7 miles in length and 2 in breadth, is chiefly in this town. It is stored with fish, and has an island near its centre of exquisite beauty. The village of Castleton is elevated, neatly built, and presents a great variety of rich and beautiful scenery.

Cavendish, Vt.

Windsor co. There are two flourishing villages in Cavendish, *Dutton's village* and *Proctorsville*. It is watered by Black river and Twenty Mile Stream, which afford a good hydraulic power. Here are in operation 4 large woolen factories, iron works, manufactures of tin, and many other branches of mechanics. Along the streams the soil is excellent; the high land is good, but best adapted to grazing. Here are about 6,000 sheep. The channel of Black river, at the falls, has been worn down 100 feet. The effects of the water, at this place, are very curious. Hawk's mountain separates this town from Baltimore. Cavendish, in common with most of the towns in Vermont, presents a great variety of mountain scenery. It lies 10 miles S. W. from Windsor, and 60 S. from Montpelier. First settled, 1769. Population, 1830, 1,498.

Centre-Harbor, N. H.,

Strafford co., is pleasantly situated between Winnepisiogee and Squam lakes; distant from Concord, 39 miles, Portsmouth 60, Boston 104. Measley pond is partly in this town. Squam lake furnishes fine trout, and has several islands valuable for grazing. The soil is very good, mostly a rich loam. Centre Harbor is a delightful resting place, during the warm season, of tourists, to the White Mountains, and the great resort of those, visiting the Winnepisiogee lake and the great natural curiosities in the adjoining town of Moultonborough. The first settlements were made by Ebenezer Chamberlain, in 1765, and Col. Joseph Senter, in 1767. Population, in 1830, 577.

Champlain Lake.

This delightful expanse of water is the boundary line between New York and Vermont. Vermont embraces about two thirds of its surface. New York is on the W. side, and the counties of Franklin, Chittenden, Addison, and a part of Rutland, in the state of Vermont, lie on the E. At the N. it extends a few miles into Lower Canada, and receives the waters of Pike river. It discharges into the St. Lawrence by the Richelieu, Sorel, or Chambly river. Among its tributaries from Vermont are the Missisque, Lamoille, Onion, Otter, and Pawlet rivers. From New York it receives the waters of the Chazy, Saranac, Sable, Bouquet, and Wood rivers, and of Lake George. Its length is about 130 miles: its breadth varies from 1 to 12 miles: average breadth about 3 miles. It abounds with salmon, trout, pickerel and other fish. It is navigable for vessels of 90 tons burthen, and splendid steamboats are continually plying, in the season of navigation, from Whitehall, along its beautiful shores, to St. John's in Canada.—This lake contains about 60 islands, is remarkable for its splendid scenery, and renowned in ancient and modern stories for its scenes of warlike achievements. Lake Champlain is a great resort, both for business and pleasure.

In the *Register*, under *Burlington*, may be found some notes for travellers.

Chaplin, Ct.

Windham co. Taken from Mansfield, Hampton and Windham, in 1832. It is watered by Natchaug river, which passes nearly through its centre. The town is small, but the soil is good, and populated by industrious farmers, who, by their practice of keeping a large number of sheep, seem to be convinced of the fact that wool is one of the most important staples of New England. It lies 10 miles W. by N. from Brooklyn, and 30 E. by N. from Hartford.

Charlemont, Mass.

Franklin co. Deerfield river meanders through this town, and gives it a good water power. Garrisons were erected here in 1754, against the savage French and Indians. Their remains are now visible. Incorporated, 1765. Population, 1837, 994. It lies 110 miles W. N. W. from Boston, and 14 W. by N. from Greenfield. Although this is a mountainous township, it contains much valuable land. It maintains about 5,000 merino and other sheep. Its manufactures consist of boots, shoes, leather, iron castings, axes, hoes, palm-leaf hats, saddlery, scythe snaiths, and lather boxes.

Charles Rivers.

Charles river, in Massachusetts, is the *Quinobequin* of the Indians. This river rises on the borders of Hopkinton and Milford, and after meandering through Bellingham, Franklin, Medway, Medfield, Sherburne, Dover, Dedham, Needham, Natick, Newton, Waltham and Watertown, it meets the tide waters, and forms a part of Boston harbor. It is navigable to Watertown, 7 miles W. from Boston.

Charles river, in R. I., has its source in Warden's pond, in South Kingston, and empties into the Pawcatuck, at Westerly.

Charleston, Me.

Penobscot co. At the source of Pushaw lake. Bounded W. by Garland. It lies 25 miles S. W. from Belfast, and 73 N. W. from Augusta. This township is fine wheat land; it yielded, in 1837, 7,606 bushels. Incorporated, 1811. Population, 1837, 1,140.

Charleston, Vt.

Orleans co. Echo pond, the outlet of lake Seymour, waters this town. Lake Seymour is a large sheet of water, and passes N. into lake Memphremagog. Charleston lies about 35 miles N.E. from Hyde-park, 55 N. N. E. from Montpelier, and 15 S. of Canada line. Population, 1830, 564.

Charlestown, N. H.,

Sullivan co., is situated on Connecticut river, 51 miles from Concord, 100 from Boston, 100 from Albany, 110 from Hartford, Conn., and 18 miles from Windsor, Vt. The only rivers in Charlestown are the Connecticut and Little Sugar rivers. In the former, there are three islands within the limits of this town, the largest of which contains about ten acres, and is called Sartwell's island. The others contain about six acres each, and have a rich loamy soil. Sartwell's island is under a high cultivation. There are no falls in this river within the limits of Charlestown which interrupt the boat navigation, although some little inconvenience is experienced in low water from what are called "Sugar river bars." Little Sugar river waters the north part of Charlestown, and empties into Connecticut river about two miles south of the S. line of Claremont. This town has but few factory or mill privileges. The soil is extremely various. West of the great road leading from Walpole to Claremont, are not less than 1,500 acres of fine intervale land, generally of a deep, rich and loamy soil, and favorable for the culture and growth of most of the various kinds of grass and grain. In the E. and N. E. parts of the town, the soil of the upland is good—the natural growth of wood, consisting principally of beech, birch, oak, maple and hemlock. There is a ridge of hard, broken, and in some parts stony, land, east of the river road, extending almost the whole length of the town, and which is considered unfit for settlements. The south part of the town appears to have a different soil, and is favorable for yielding the lighter grains. Charlestown contains two parishes, which are divided by a line running from Cheshire bridge S. 87° E., to the corner of Acworth and Unity. In the south parish, there is a handsome village, delightfully situated, at the distance of about half a mile from Connecticut river, and parallel with it. In the north parish is a meeting-house and a small village. Cheshire bridge, about 2 miles N. of the S. meeting-house, connects this town with Springfield, Vt. From this bridge Cheshire turnpike leads southerly through the principal village, to Keene. Charlestown was granted by Massachusetts, Dec. 31, 1735, by the name of *Number* 4, which is sometimes applied to it at the present day.

On the 2d July, 1753, No. 4 was incorporated by the name of Charlestown. The charter was granted by Gov. Benning Wentworth to Joseph Wells, Phinehas Stevens and others, who were purchasers under the old grantees. In 1754, the French war commenced—and the inhabitants were obliged to take up their residence in the fort. The first settlers of Charlestown, like the first inhabitants of almost every frontier town in New England, were, prior to 1760, the victims of savage cruelty. For twenty years after the first settlement, their neighbors on the N. were the French in Canada, on the W. the Dutch, near the Hudson, on the E. the settlements on Merrimack river, and on the S. few were found until arrived at Northfield, in Massachusetts, a distance of more than 40 miles. The Indians were at peace but a small portion of that time. From their infancy, the settlers had been familiar with danger, and had acquired a hardihood unknown to posterity. When they attended public worship, or cultivated their lands, they sallied from the fort prepared for battle, and worshipped or labored under the protection of a sentinel. In their warfare, the Indians preferred prisoners to scalps, and few were killed but those who attempted to escape, or appeared too formidable to be encountered with success. The first child born in Charlestown was Elizabeth, the daughter of Isaac Parker. She was born 1744, and died in 1806.— Charlestown has been favored with a number of eminent men, only one of which we have room to mention. Capt. PHINEHAS STEVENS was one of the first settlers. The town when in its infancy was protected by his intrepidity. He was a native of Sudbury, Mass., from whence his father removed to Rutland. At the age of 16, while his father was making hay, he, with three little brothers, followed him to the meadows. They were ambushed by the Indians, who killed two of his brothers, took him prisoner, and were preparing to kill his youngest brother, a child four years old. He, by signs to the Indians, made them understand if they would spare him, he would carry him on his back—and he carried him to Canada. They were redeemed and both returned. He received several commissions from Gov. Shirley, and rendered important services in protecting the frontiers. In 1747, when Charlestown was abandoned by the inhabitants, he was ordered to occupy the fort with 30 men. On the 4th of April, he was attacked by 400 French and Indians, under Mons. Debeline. The assault lasted three days. Indian stratagem and French skill, with fire applied to every combustible about the fort, had not the desired effect. The heroic band were not appalled. They refused to capitulate. At length an interview between the commanders took place. The Frenchman shewed his forces, and described the horrid massacre that must ensue unless the fort was surrendered. "My men are not afraid to die," was the answer made by Capt. Stevens. The attack continued with increased fury until the end of the third day, when the enemy returned to Canada, and left Capt. Stevens in possession of the fort. Capt. Stevens, for his gallantry on this occasion, was presented by Sir Charles Knowles with an elegant sword; and from this circumstance the township, when it was incorporated, in 1753, took the name of Charlestown. Population, in 1830, 1,778.

Charlestown, Mass.

Middlesex co. The Indian name of this town was *Mishawun*. First settled, 1628. Incorporated, 1629. Population, 1820, 6,591; 1830, 8,787; 1837, 10,101. Charlestown is a peninsula, formed by Charles and Mystic rivers, and is united to Boston by Charles and Warren bridges. It is also united to Boston as a port of entry, and in its various commercial and manufacturing pursuits. This town is noted for its sacrifices in the cause of liberty; and its soil will ever be dear to the patriot's bosom. The town is not so regularly laid out as Philadelphia, yet it is neatly built, and contains many elegant public and private edifices. The streets are wide and airy, and many of them have recently been planted with trees for shade. Considerable shipping is owned here, engaged in foreign and domestic commerce. The annual value of the cod and mackerel fisheries is about $40,000. The value of the manufactures, in Charlestown, the year ending April 1, 1837, exclusive of a large amount of leather, was $390,000. The articles manufactured were as follows: soap, candles, boots, shoes, hats, morocco, chairs, cabinet ware, vessels, combs, tin ware, and spirits.

The United States' Navy Yard was first established in this town about the year 1798. The yard is situated on the N. side of Charles river, on a plot of ground of about 60 acres. It is enclosed by a high wall of durable masonry, and contains several ware-houses, dwelling-houses for the officers, and a large amount of naval stores, live oak and other timber. It also contains three large ship-houses, in which are the Vermont and Carolina of 74, and the Cumberland frigate of 44 guns. These ships can be launched and ready for sea in a very short time.

The dry dock at this place is of hewn granite, and of unrivalled masonry. It is 341 feet in length, 80 in width, and 30 in depth. It cost $670,089. This dock was completed and received the *Constitution* on the 24th of June, 1833.— Connected with this establishment are a naval hospital and magazine, at Chelsea, and a large ropewalk in the yard; other additions are contemplated. This is considered one of the best naval depots in the United States.

McLean Asylum. This establishment is located on a beautiful rise of ground, in Charlestown, near East Cambridge, and about a mile and a half from the City Hall, in Boston. The buildings are large, and exceedingly well adapted to their philanthropic design. They cost about $186,000. This House was opened for patients on the 6th of October, 1818.

Belonging to, and surrounding this Asylum, are about 15 acres of land, appropriated to courts and gardens. These are laid out with gravelled walks. The former are furnished with summer houses, and the latter are ornamented with groves of fruit and ornamental trees, shrubbery and flowers. Surrounding the lower garden and within the enclosure, is a carriage path, where patients are taken to ride. In the centre is a small fresh water pond, containing several hundred gold and silver fish, and immediately contiguous is a summer house, where the patients at times resort for games and amusements.

The system of moral treatment adopted and pursued, is founded upon principles of elevated benevolence and philanthropy, and an acquaintance with human nature and the capabilities and wants of the insane. The previous tastes, habits and pursuits, and the present inclinations and feelings of each individual, are habitually consulted. A library for the use of the patients has been purchased, and those of them who are disposed to read, are permitted at stated periods to send in their names and the number of the book desired; the list is examined and approved by the physician, and the books are distributed by the librarian. In the same way, writing materials are distributed, and patients are engaged in keeping journals—writing sketches of their lives—poetry—addressing letters to their friends, drawing, &c. Some engage in games, as bowling—throwing the ring--battledore—graces—jumping the rope—chess—draughts—back gammon, &c., or are occupied in walking and riding into the country, or in making fishing excursions in the company of their attendants; while others are working on the farm and in the garden. The female patients, besides being employed in various kinds of needle and ornamental work, are engaged in various domestic labors. The quiet and convalescent patients regularly attend the religious exercises of the family, and a portion of them join in the vocal and instrumental music of the occasion; a part of this number also attend church on the Sabbath, in company with the nurses and attendants, and dine with the family. A regulated intercourse with the family and society is regarded as an important auxiliary in the means of cure, and on suitable occasions they are invited into the house, where parties are made for their special amusement and benefit.

JOHN McLLEAN, Esq., late of Boston, an eminent merchant, bequeathed a large amount of property to this institution; hence its name.

Bunker Hill Monument. On the 17th of June, 1825, the corner stone of an *Obelisk* was laid on the heights in this town, by the illustrious La Fayette, to commemorate the battle between the Americans and British on the 17th of June, 1775. In that battle, 449 Americans and 1,055 Britons were slain. Charlestown was burnt by the British the same day. The site of the Monument is 62 feet above the level of the sea. It is of hewn granite, and, when completed, will be 30 feet square at the base, 15 feet square at the top, and 220 feet in height. It is now raised about 60 feet, and will probably be completed in one or two years. The cost of it will be about $100,000.

The State Prison. This institution was founded in 1800, and soon after located on a point of land in this town, near East Cambridge, and which is connected with Canal bridge by a lateral bridge of 1,820 feet in length. After having struggled with many and great difficulties attendant on the establishment of an institution so entirely new; the state, by the agency of suitable men, have so placed it as to effect all the objects proposed, without any expense to the commonwealth,

Charlestown, R. I.

Washington co. Charlestown lies on the sea, opposite to Block Island. It has five large ponds, which cover an area of 7 square miles.—Charlestown and Conaquetogue ponds are salt water, and Posquisett, Watchaug and Cochumpaug are fresh water. These waters afford a great variety of fish. Near the sea, the land is arable, but the interior of the town is more fit for the growth of wood. This town contains the graves of the remnant of the tribe of the once powerful and dreaded Naraganset Indians. They possessed a considerable tract of land in this town, but owing to a dislike to agricultural pursuits, and by intermarriages with the whites and negroes, their race as a distinct people has long since become extinct. Charles river passes through the town, and gives it mill privileges. Charlestown lies about 8 miles W. S. W. from South Kingston, and 40 S. W. from Providence. Population, 1830, 1,284.

Charlotte, Me.

Washington co. Incorporated, 1825. Population, 1837, 612. About 25 miles N. W. from Machias, and 184 E. by N. from Augusta. Charlotte contains a pond, the waters of which pass through Dennysville and empty in Cobscook bay.

Charlotte, Vt.

This is a pleasant town, in Chittenden county, on lake Champlain, and opposite to Essex, N. Y. In Essex, about 3 miles across the lake, is *Split Rock*, a great natural curiosity. Charlotte lies 49 miles W. of Montpelier, 11 S. of Burlington and 21 N. W. of Middlebury. A part of this town gradually slopes toward the lake, and is very productive. Its trade is chiefly with Canada. From the principal village, "The Four Corners," the lake, and the mountains that skirt its borders, present a very romantic appearance. Population, in 1830, 1,702.

Charlton, Mass.

Worcester co. Charlton was set off from Oxford, 1754. It lies 53 miles S. W. from Boston, and 12 W. N. W. from Worcester. Population, 1837, 2,469. There is a cotton mill in this town, and some manufactures of leather and shoes.

Chatham, N. H.,

Strafford co., is situated on the E. side of the White Mountains, and adjoining the line which divides this state from Maine. It has Conway on the S., Bartlett and Jackson on the W., Mount Royse on the N. Chatham was granted to Peter Livius and others, Feb. 7, 1767. There are several ponds in Chatham, and some considerable streams. The surface is mountainous and rocky, and can never sustain a great population. Between Chatham and Jackson, Carter's mountain rises so high as to prevent the opening a road between the two towns; so that in holding an intercourse with the rest of the county, the inhabitants are obliged to pass through part of the state of Maine. Population, in 1830, 419.

Chatham, Mass.,

Barnstable co., lies on the elbow of Cape Cod, south side. Pleasant bay, inside of Chatham beach, forms a good harbor. Chatham is 20 miles E. from Barnstable, and 32 S. S. E. from Provincetown. Incorporated, 1712. Population, 1837, 2,271. The value of the cod and mackerel fisheries, for the year ending April 1, 1837, was $56,100;—value of salt made, $8,220;—value of boots and shoes made, $1,500. There are, belonging to this place, about 20 sail of fishermen and 30 coasters.

Chatham, Ct.

Middlesex co. The township of Chatham embraces Chatham parish, (formerly East Middletown,) the greater part of Middle Haddam parish, the parish of East Hampton and a part of the parish of West Chester. It lies 16 miles S. from Hartford, and opposite to Middletown, from which it was taken in 1767. Population, 1830, 3,646. Chatham is watered by Salmon and Pine brooks and several ponds.—*Job's* pond, about 2 miles in circumference, has no outlet. It rises and falls about 15 feet. It rises for six or twelve months, and then falls about the same period. It is highest in the driest season of the year, and lowest when there is most rain. It is from 40 to 60 feet deep. Chatham is noted for its valuable quarries of freestone. "For forty years past it has been extensively improved, and the stone, to the depth of thirty feet from the surface, are now removed over an area of an acre and a half, back from the river. The stone in this quarry is covered in some places with four or five feet of earth, and in others with four or five feet more of shelly rock. It is not perfectly solid, but lies in blocks, eight or ten feet thick, and fifty and sixty feet long. The seams and joints facilitate the process of removing these from their beds; and when removed, they are reduced by the wedge and chisel to any size or form which is wished. In this quarry thirty hands have been employed for several years, eight months in the year, and from four to six teams. The quantity of stone prepared for market, and sold to the inhabitants of this and the neighboring towns, and exported to distant parts of the country, has been very great; and has yielded a handsome profit. Fifty rods south of this quarry an opening was made about 1783, now spreading over half an acre. Here the stone is covered with about ten feet of earth. In this opening as many as twelve hands have been sometimes employed. Vessels come to this and the above quarry, and load from the bank. The bed of stone in which these and the smaller openings in the neighborhood have been made is immense, and lies at different depths from the surface in different places. It has been discovered in sinking wells, for half a mile in northern and southern directions, and has been opened at a greater distance eastward. Wherever found, the stone possesses the same general properties, but varies, like the freestone in Middletown, in the fineness of its texture."

Chelmsford, Mass.

Middlesex co. On the south side of Merrimack river, and connected with Dracut by a bridge.— First settled, 1753. Incorporated, 1655. Population, 1837, 1,613. It lies 25 miles N. W. from Boston, and 4 S. W. from Lowell. Chelmsford abounds in limestone and granite; considerable of the latter is transported to Boston by the Middlesex canal, which passes through the town. The manufactures of this town, during the year ending April 1, 1837, amounted to about $100,000;—principally of glass and iron.

Chelsea, Vt.

County town of Orange county. First settled, 1785. Chelsea is a township of good land, with a pleasant village in the centre. It is watered by the head branches of White river and has a good hydraulic power. Its manufactures consist of cassimere, satinet, leather, iron, &c. Chelsea produces all the various commodities common to the climate, and feeds about 6,000 sheep. It lies 20 miles S. by E. from Montpelier. Population, 1830, 1,958.

Chelsea, Mass.

Suffolk co. This town was formerly a ward of Boston. Incorporated, 1738. Population, 1837, 1,659. The centre of the town lies from Boston about 3 miles N. E., across Charles river, and 3 miles E. of Charlestown. The manufactures of Chelsea consist of upholstery, stone ware, snuff, segars, wood and copper engravings, carriages, bricks, vessels, salt, boots, shoes, &c.;—annual value, about $90,000.

The *United States Marine Hospital* in this town, is on a large plot of ground, in a delightful and airy situation, and affords a comfortable retreat for sick and disabled seamen. Point Shirley, extending southeasterly, forms the northern part of Boston harbor. Winnesimet Ferry, leading from the foot of Hanover street, in Boston, to this town, is probably the oldest establishment of the kind in America. The first grant was given to Thomas Williams, in 1631. The distance across Charles river is about a mile and a half. Neat and commodious steam-boats are continually running across this delightful stream, making the *Winnesimet* of the Indians the *Hoboken* of Boston.

Cherryfield, Me.

Washington co. At the head of tide water, on both sides of Narraguagus river, with a handsome village, and considerable trade. Incorporated, 1815. Population, 1837, 1,000. 116 miles E. by N. from Augusta, and about 35 W. from Machias.

Cheshire County, N. H.

Cheshire is one of the western counties in this state. Its length is 31 miles: its greatest breadth 26 miles: and its least breadth 15. It is bounded N. by the county of Sullivan, E. by Hillsborough county, S. by the state of Massachusetts, and W. by Vermont. This county contains 727 square miles. Throughout the whole extent on the west, it is watered by the Connecticut, the western bank of which forms the boundary line between New Hampshire and Vermont. Ashuelot river is a considerable stream, and is tributary to Connecticut river. It has its source from a pond in Washington, and after receiving two branches in Keene and Swanzey, and several smaller streams in Winchester, empties into Connecticut river at Hinsdale. Spafford's Lake, a beautiful collection of water, of about 8 miles in circumference, is situated in Chesterfield. There is a pleasant island in the lake, containing about eight acres. The Grand Monadnock, in Dublin and Jaffrey, is the highest mountain, its attitude having been repeatedly found to be more than 3,000 feet above the level of the sea. Bellows' 'Falls' in Connecticut river, at Walpole, have been regarded as one of the greatest natural curiosities in this county.

The earliest settlement in this county was made about the year 1732, at Hinsdale, then a part of Northfield, and under the government of Massachusetts. The county was formed March 19, 1771, and it probably received its name from Cheshire, one of the western counties in England. The population of Cheshire county in 1790, was 19,665, in 1800, 24,288, in 1810, 24,673, in 1820, 26,843, in 1830, 27,016. It has 22 towns:—39 inhabitants to a square mile. *Keene*, the chief town, is nearly in the centre of the county, and lies in N. lat. 42° 57'.

Cheshire, Mass.

Berkshire co. Cheshire has rendered itself worthy of its name by its production of cheese of fine flavor and quality. In 1801, the good people of this place sent a cheese to Mr. Jefferson, weighing about

1200 pounds. The value of wool, the growth of 1836, sold for $5,522. The Hoosack river passes through the town. Although a mountainous township, the soil has been rendered productive by the industry of the people. It has some manufactures of leather and shoes. 125 miles W. N. W. from Boston, and 16 N. by E. from Lenox. Population, 1837, 924. Incorporated, 1793.

Cheshire, Ct.

New Haven co. Taken from Wallingford in 1780. It lies 14 miles N. from New Haven, and 25 S. E. from Hartford. Population, 1830, 1,780. The Quinnipiac river and Farmington canal pass through the town. Cheshire has an uneven, but good soil, with a very pleasant village, and an Episcopal academy, 54 by 34 feet;—a brick building of considerable taste. Agriculture is the chief occupation of the inhabitants.

Chester, Me.

Penobscot co. Incorporated, 1834. Population, 1837, 323. See *Barnard, Me.*

Chester, N. H.,

Rockingham co., is 17 miles W. S. W. from Exeter, 30 W. S. W. from Portsmouth, 17 N. W. from Haverhill, and 23 S. E. from Concord. A branch of Exeter river, called "The Branch," flows through the N. E. part of Chester, beside which there is no stream deserving mention. Massabesick pond is the largest body of fresh water in the county, and contains about 1,500 acres. The line between this town and Manchester passes more than 2 miles through the westerly part of this pond. The Indians had a settlement of 10 or 12 wigwams on an island in this pond, vestiges of which, it is said, may still be seen. A considerable portion of the town possesses a good soil, and many of the large swells yield in fertility to none in the state. There are several large and valuable meadows. In this town are two caves, sometimes visited by strangers. That which was earliest noticed, is situated in Mine hill, near the east side of Massabesick pond. The entrance is about 5 feet high and 2 1-2 wide. The cavern extends into the hill, in a northern direction, about 80 feet, of sufficient dimensions to admit a person to pass. Its form is very irregular, and its height and breadth various, from 2 to 12 feet. The other is in the westerly side of Rattlesnake hill, in the S. W. part of the town, in a ledge of coarse granite, nearly 40 feet high. It has two entrances. The north entrance is about 11 feet high and 4 broad. Native sulphur is found in this town in small quantities, imbedded in tremolite. Granite and gneiss are the prevailing rocks, and handsome specimens of graphic granite are sometimes found. The village in this town is pleasant, and stands chiefly on a long street. It is the principal place of business in this part of the county, and is situated on an elevated rise, commanding one of the most extensive prospects in New England. From this hill, the ocean, though more than 20 miles distant, may, in a clear day, be distinctly seen. Population, 1830, 2,039. Incorporated, 1722.

Chester, Vt.

Windsor co. First settled, 1764. Population, 1830, 2,320. Three considerable streams form William's river and give Chester a good water power. The land is uneven, but fertile and productive. This is a very pleasant town, with two handsome villages, manufactures of various kinds, and about 10,000 sheep. This is a great thoroughfare for travellers from the eastern part of New England to the Hudson river, near Troy, N. Y. The passage over the Green Mountains, from Chester to Manchester, is considered the best.

In this part of the state. Chester lies 16 miles S. S. W. from Windsor, 79 S. from Montpelier, and about 30 E. N. E. from Manchester.

Chester, Mass.

Hampden co. This is a mountainous township, but good for grazing. In 1837, it had 3,720 sheep; their wool weighed 10,325 pounds, and sold for $5,818. There are 2 cotton mills in Chester, 3 tanneries, and a window blind factory. Total amount of manufactures, in one year, $47,975. Branches of Westfield river pass through the town. Incorporated, 1765. Population, 1837, 1,290. 115 miles W. by S. from Boston, and 20 N. W. from Springfield.

Chesterfield, N. H.,

Cheshire co., is 11 miles S. W. from Keene, and 65 S. W. from Concord. Few towns on Connecticut river have so little intervale land. For the whole six miles that it lies upon the river, the hills approach near the river's side. There is much good upland, well adapted for grazing and the production of Indian corn. The chief articles carried to market are beef, pork, butter and cheese. Cat's Bane brook is a stream of great importance, as it furnishes many mill seats. Spafford's lake is a beautiful collection of water, situated about one mile N. from the meeting-house. It contains a surface of about 526 acres. It is fed by springs in its bosom. Its waters are remarkably clear and pure, its bed being a white sand. In this lake there is an island of about six acres, which forms a delightful retreat. On its E. side issues a stream called Partridge's brook, sufficiently large to carry the machinery of a cotton factory, saw-mills, &c. West river mountain lies in this town and Hinsdale. It is supposed to have been once subject to a volcanic eruption, and there is at present a considerable quantity of lava near its crater. It is said by those who live near the mountain, that it frequently trembles, and a rumbling noise is heard in its bowels. Chesterfield has 3 villages. The principal one, leading from Hartford to Hanover, is situated near the centre of the town, and 3 miles E. from Connecticut river. Here are several dwelling-houses, the meeting-house and a flourishing academy, which was opened Aug. 14, 1794. The first settlement was made Nov. 25, 1761, on the banks of the Connecticut, by Moses Smith and William Thomas, with their families. At that period, the river afforded abundance of shad and salmon, and the forests were well stocked with deer, bears and other game, so that the inhabitants did not experience those privations so common in new settlements. Population, 1830, 2,040.

Chesterfield, Mass.

Hampshire co. A township of rough, elevated land, 97 miles W. from Boston, and 11 W. N. W. from Northampton; watered by a branch of Westfield river. It has a good water power, 1 woolen mill, 2 tanneries, some curious minerals, and a water course, worn very deep through solid rock. Population, 1837, 1,158. There were sheared in Chesterfield, in 1837, 7,100 sheep, producing 20,800 pounds of wool, valued at $12,480. A noble example.

Chesterville, Me.

Franklin co. Wilson's stream passes through this town, and empties below the falls of Sandy river. First settled, 1782. Incorporated, 1802. Population, 1837, 1,040.—This is an excellent township of land. It yielded, in 1837, 4,046 bushels of wheat. It lies about 24 miles N. E. from Augusta, and 12 N. E. from Farmington.

Chesuncook Lake, Me.,

In the county of Piscataquis, is a large sheet of water through which the Penobscot river passes. It also receives the Kahkoguamook and Umbazookskus rivers. This lake is about 25 miles long and 3 miles wide. The country around this fine lake is very fertile, and as well adapted to the growing of wool and wheat as any portion of the globe. Its central point is about 130 miles W. N. W. from Augusta.

Chichester, N. H.,

Merrimack co., is situated 8 miles E. from Concord. It was granted May 20, 1727, to Nathaniel Gookin and others; but the settlement was not commenced until 1758, when Paul Morrill settled in the woods. The soil is good, and richly repays the cultivator. There is little waste land, nor are there any considerable elevations. The east part of the town is watered by the Suncook river, which affords its mill seats and some productive intervale.—Population, 1830, 1,084. In various parts of the town are still to be seen traces of Indian settlements; and implements of stone, chisels, axes, &c., have frequently been found. The vicinity was once the residence of a powerful tribe, the Penacooks, and their plantations of corn, &c., were made on the banks of the Suncook.

Chickopee River, Mass.

This river rises in Spencer, Leicester and Paxton, and receives the waters of Quaboag pond, in Brookfield. It passes through Warren. At Palmer it receives the waters of Ware and Swift rivers, and enters the Connecticut at the N. part of Springfield, 7 miles S. from South Hadley.

Chilmark, Mass.

Dukes co. This town lies on the S. and W. part of Martha's Vineyard. *Gay Head*, in this town, is the south point of the island; it is 150 feet above the sea, and is crowned with one of the five lighthouses in this county. *Gay Head* is about 60 miles E N. E. of Montauk, on Long Island, and bears marks of having been subject to volcanic eruptions. The place abounds in specimens of minerals worthy the notice of geologists. This part of the island is inhabited by some descendants of the native Indians, who own part of the lands. There is some salt manufactured at this place, and about 7,000 sheep are kept. Chilmark was incorporated in 1714. Population, 1837, 700. It lies 92 miles S. E. from Boston, 33 W. from Nantucket, 23 S. E. by S. from New Bedford, and 12 S. W. by S. from Edgarton.

China, Me.

Kennebec co. This is a township of excellent land, which produced, in 1837, 12,953 bushels of wheat. China is watered by a lake, or "Twelve Mile Pond," a fine miniature of the beautiful Skaneateles, in the state of New York. At the outlet of this pond, into the Kennebec, are excellent mill privileges. On the bank of the pond is a very flourishing village, a steam saw-mill, and an academy. A visit to this place, Albion, Clinton, Dixmont, and the neighboring towns, where wheat is worth a dollar and a half a bushel in the barn, is a good specific against the *western fever*. A trip from Boston to China and back again may be performed in the same number of hours that it takes to go up either of the canals 100 miles, *towards* an unseen country. China lies 20 miles N. E. from Augusta, 48 S. W. from Bangor, and 138 from Boston. Population, 1837, 2,641.

Chittenden County, Vt.

Burlington is the chief town. This county is bounded N. by

Franklin county, E. by Washington county, S. by Addison county, and W. by Champlain lake. Area, 500 square miles. Population, 1820, 16,055; 1830, 21,765. Population to a square mile, about 44. A few settlements commenced in this county before the revolution, but they were all abandoned during the war. Incorporated, 1782. Its soil varies from rich alluvial meadows to light and sandy plains. The beautiful Champlain washing its western boundary gives it great facilities for trade to New York and Canada. Its agricultural and manufacturing products are considerable. In 1837 there were in this county about 80,000 sheep. Lamoille river passes through its N.W. corner, and Onion river pierces its centre. These streams, with several others of smaller size, afford the county a good water power.

Chittenden, Vt.

Rutland co. Most of the lands in this town lie on the Green mountains. Some of the branches of White river pass through it. Near the head of the Philadelphia branch, so called, is a mineral spring, said to contain some good qualities.— *Manganese* of an excellent quality is found here. In 1837 there were in Chittenden about 700 people, and 3,000 sheep. About 12 miles N. by E. from Rutland, and 40 N. by E. from Montpelier.

Claremont, N. H.,

Sullivan co., is 12 miles N. from Charlestown, 8 W. from Newport, 47 N. N. W. from Concord, and 97 W. N. W. from Portsmouth. This town is watered by Connecticut and Sugar rivers, besides numerous brooks and rivulets. Claremont is a fine undulating tract of territory, covered with a rich gravelly loam, converted into the best meadows and pastures. The hills are sloping acclivities, crowned with elegant summits. The intervals on the rivers are rich and luxuriant. The agricultural products are large and valuable. The houses and buildings present a very favorable appearance, and indicate the wealth and prosperity of the town. In this town are a number of manufactories of cloth, paper, leather, &c. Claremont was granted in 1764.— In this town are fine beds of iron ore and limestone. It received its name from the country seat of Lord Clive, an English general. The first settlement was made in 1762, by Moses Spafford and David Lynde. Many eminent men have resided in this town. The Hon. *Caleb Ellis* came to reside in Claremont about 1800. In 1804, he was chosen a member of congress from this state; in 1809 and 1810, a member of the executive council: in 1812, an elector of president and vice-president of the U. S. In 1813, he was appointed judge of the superior court, in which office he remained till his death, May 9, 1816, aged 49. Population, 1830, 2,526.

Clarenden, Vt.

Rutland co. Otter creek, Mill and Cold rivers and several brooks give this town good mill privileges. Here are good marble, a mineral spring, and a curious cave. The soil is a gravelly loam, with considerable alluvial meadow along its streams. There are some manufacturing establishments in Clarenden, and about 13,000 sheep. Population, 1830, 1,585. It lies 55 miles S. from Montpelier, and 7 S. from Rutland.

Clarksburgh, Mass.

Berkshire co. A branch of Hoosick river passes through this mountainous township. It lies 125 miles W. by N. from Boston, and 27 N. by E. from Lenox. Incorporated, 1798. Population, 1837, 386. Clarksburgh has a small cotton mill, 5 saw mills, and 255 sheep.

Clarksville, N. H.

This town was incorporated in 1832. It had before that time borne the name of the *First College Grant.* It was granted to the trustees of Dartmouth College, Feb. 5, 1789. It contains 40,960 acres, and is situated on Connecticut river, in Coos county, N. of Stewartstown. Its population, in 1830, was 88.

Clinton, Me.

Kennebec co. This fine township is bounded on the E. by Kennebec river. The Sebasticook passes through the town, and, at the falls on that river, affords it a great hydraulic power. It has a neat and pleasant village on the bank of the Sebasticook, some manufactures, and large agricultural products. In 1837 this town produced a considerable quantity of wool, and 10,807 bushels of wheat. Incorporated, 1795. Population, 1837, 2,642. Clinton lies 24 miles N. by E. from Augusta, and about 12 S. by E. from Skowhegan.

Cobbessecontee Waters, Me.

The pond is a fine sheet of water, lying W. of Hallowell, and connected with smaller ponds in Monmouth, Winthrop, Readfield, and Mount Vernon. The outlet of the pond is a river of the same name, which passes into a beautiful pond we see on the stage road in Richmond, and empties into the Kennebec at Gardiner. These waters afford a great hydraulic power, an abundance of fish, and much delightful scenery.

Cobscook Bay, Me.

A large bay, the recipient of a number of large ponds, on the S. W. side of Eastport, in Passamaquoddy bay. See *Eastport.*

Cod, Cape and Bay.

Having briefly described this cape, under *Barnstable county,* we have only to add that Cape Cod light is in N. lat. 42° 2' 22''; W. lon. 70° 4' 22''.

Cape Cod bay is in Massachusetts bay, and is formed by the half extended arm of the cape. See *Barnstable county.*

Cohasset, Mass.

Norfolk co. A town on Massachusetts bay, noted for its rocky coast and numerous shipwrecks. 6 miles E. from Hingham, 20 E. by S. from Dedham, and about 16 S. E. from Boston, by water. Incorporated, 1770. Population, 1837, 1,331. This place has about 40 sail of merchant, coasting and fishing vessels, and a large tide-water power. Cohasset has become a great resort for citizens and strangers, in summer months, to enjoy the marine scenery, exhilarating air, and all those pleasures for which *Nahant* is celebrated. The value of the fisheries, for the year ending April 1, 1837, was $75,536. The value of salt, vessels, boots, shoes, and wooden ware manufactured, was $35,920.

Colchester, Vt.,

Chittenden co., is pleasantly situated at the head of a bay on the E. side of lake Champlain, 36 miles N. W. from Montpelier, and 6 N. from Burlington. This town is well watered by Onion river, and some smaller streams. Colchester has some good and some poor land, some trade on the lake, and about 4,000 sheep. First settled by Gen. Ira Allen, in 1774. Population, 1830, 1,489.

Colchester, Ct.

New London co. This is a pleasant town; the site of Bacon academy. It lies 20 miles N. W. from New London, and 23 S. E. from Hartford. First settled, 1701. Population, 1830, 2,068. The surface of the town is uneven, with a strong gravelly soil. Excellent iron ore is found here.

Rev. *John Bulkley*, a grandson of president Chauncy, was the first settled minister in this place. Mr. Bulkley was a very distinguished scholar. He died in 1731. He published a curious treatise, in which he contended that the Indians had no just claims to any lands but such as they had subdued and improved by their own labor. The following story is told in an old book. "The Rev. Mr. Bulkley of Colchester, Conn., was famous in his day as a casuist and sage counsellor. A church in his neighborhood had fallen into unhappy divisions and contentions, which they were unable to adjust among themselves. They deputed one of their number to the venerable Bulkley, for his services, with a request that he would send it to them in writing. The matters were taken into serious consideration, and the advice, with much deliberation, committed to writing. It so happened, that Mr. Bulkley had a farm in an extreme part of the town, upon which he entrusted a tenant. In superscribing the two letters, the one for the church was directed to the tenant, and the one for the tenant to the church. The church was convened to hear the advice which was to settle all their disputes. The moderator read as follows: *You will see to the repair of the fences, that they be built high and strong, and you will take special care of the old black bull.* This mystical advice puzzled the church at first, but an interpreter among the more discerning ones was soon found, who said, Brethren, this is the very advice we most need; the directions to repair the fences is to admonish us to take good heed in the admission and government of our members: we must guard the church by our Master's laws, and keep out strange cattle from the fold. And we must in a particular manner set a watchful guard over the *Devil*, the old black bull, who has done so much hurt of late. All perceived the wisdom and fitness of Mr. Bulkley's advice, and resolved to be governed by it. The consequence was, all the animosities subsided, and harmony was restored to the long afflicted church."

Colebrook, N. H.,

Coos co., on Connecticut river, about 35 miles N. of Lancaster. It is watered by the Mohawk river and Beaver brook. The soil here is rich, and capable of culture. Intervales of good quality stretch along the Connecticut. Colebrook was originally granted to Sir George Colebrook and others, and was incorporated Dec. 1, 1790. There is an academy in this town, incorporated in 1833. Population, 1830, 542.

Colebrook, Ct.

Litchfield co. An elevated township of a hard gravelly soil and uneven surface, on the line of Massachusetts; 31 miles N. W. from Hartford, and 18 N. E. from Litchfield. The eastern part of the town is watered by Farmington river. Here are a number of good mill seats, and a manufactory of broadcloth. The village is very pleasant, having Mount Pisgah in the rear. First settled, 1765. Population, 1830, 1,332.

Coleraine, Mass.

Franklin co. This town was first settled by a colony from the north of Ireland, about the year 1736. It lies 105 miles N. W. from Boston, and 9 N. W. from Greenfield. It is watered by a branch of Deerfield river, which produces a water power for 3 cotton mills and several other manufactories. The manufactures consist of cotton goods, iron castings, leather, hats, chairs, cabinet ware, ploughs, spades, shovels, forks, and hoes; total value, in one year, $91,000. This is a fine grazing township, and produced, in 1837, 16,123 pounds of wool, valued at $9,132, the fleeces of 5,754 sheep. Population, 1837, 1,998.

Colleges in New England.

See *Register*.

Columbia, Me.

Washington co. At the head of tide water, on the W. side of Pleasant river. It is a very large township, well provided with mill seats, and was settled soon after the revolutionary war. It lies 15 miles W. from Machias, and 120 E. by N. from Augusta. Columbia has considerable trade, particularly in lumber. Population, 1837, 793.

Columbia, N. H.,

In the county of Coos, lies on the E. bank of Connecticut river, 30 miles N. of Lancaster, and 147 N. of Concord. The surface of the town is quite uneven, the mountains of Stratford lying along the S. From these a number of streams descend north-westerly into the Connecticut, furnishing many fine mill seats. There are also several small ponds in town. On the borders of one, called Lime pond, vast quantities of shells are found, from which a species of lime is made that answers for some uses. It was incorporated 1797. Population, 1830, 442.

Columbia, Ct.

Tolland co. Taken from Lebanon, in 1800. It is 22 miles E. from Hartford, and about 14 S. by E. from Tolland. Population, 1830, 962. Columbia is watered by a branch of the Willimantic, and has a satinet factory, and other operations by water. The surface is uneven; the soil hard and gravelly, but excellent for grazing. In this place, about the year 1741, the Rev. Dr. Eleazar Wheelock, the first president of Dartmouth College, opened a school for the instruction of Indian youth. He removed his family and pupils to Hanover, N. H., in the autumn of 1770. The snow was very deep, and Hanover was a wilderness. "Sometimes standing in the open air, at the head of his numerous family, Dr. Wheelock presented to God their morning and evening prayers: the surrounding forests, for the first time, reverberated the solemn sounds of supplication and praise." This good man died in 1779, aged 69.

Concord, Me.

Somerset co. Incorporated in 1821. Population, 1837, 524. Concord lies on the W. side of Kennebec river, 55 miles N. from Augusta, and about 20 N. from Norridgewock. This is a good township, and produced, in 1837, 3,121 bushels of wheat.

Concord, N. H.

The capitol of the state, and shire town of the county of Merrimack. It lies on both sides of the Merrimack river, in N. lat. 43° 12′ 29″, and W. lon. 71° 29′; and is 146 miles S. W. from Augusta, Me.; 97 S. E. from Montpelier, Vt.; 153 N. E. from Albany, N. Y.; 65 N. N. W. from Boston, Mass.; 103 N. from Providence, R. I.; 129 N. N. E. from Hartford, Conn., and 474 N. E. by E. from Washington. There are five ponds in Concord, the largest of which are Turkey, in the S. W., and Long pond in the N. W. parts of the town, on the streams passing from which are some valuable mills and privileges. The Contoocook river enters the W. corner of the town, and uniting with the Merrimack on the N. W. line, forms at its junction the celebrated *Duston's Island*. On the borders of the Merrimack, which is the principal river of this region, are rich intervale lands, highly valued by the inhabitants, and well cultivated. Soon after entering

Concord, the river passes over Sewall's falls, or rapids, below which is Sewall's island. From thence the river has no natural obstruction until it reaches the falls at the S. E. extremity of the town, where is a water power, now owned by the Amoskeag Manufacturing Company, almost sufficient to move the machinery of another Lowell.— Locks are here constructed, and navigation by boats has been open since 1815 during the boating season, adding much to the business and importance of the place. The river is about 100 yards wide opposite the town; but during the great freshets which sometimes occur here, the river rises 20 feet above the ordinary level, presenting to the eye a body of water a mile in width. There are two handsome bridges thrown across the river.

The principal village, and seat of most of the business of the town, is on the western side of the river, extending nearly two miles between the two bridges; and is one of the most healthy and pleasantly situated villages in New England. The state house, state prison and court house, and five very commodious and handsome structures for public worship, are in this village. The state house occupies a beautiful site in the centre of the village, and is constructed of hewn granite. It is 126 feet in length, 49 in width, 50 feet of the centre of the building having a projection of 4 feet on each front. It rises two stories above the basement. The height from the ground to the eagle on the top of the cupola is 120 feet. The cost of the building and appendages, $80,000. The state prison is also a solid structure of massive granite. On the east side of the river, is the second principal village, where the Sewall's Falls Locks and Canal Company, recently chartered, have commenced their works, which, by taking the waters of the river in a canal from Sewall's falls, will create a vast and valuable water power at this village, that must ultimately prove of immense importance to the town. Another handsome village has grown up in the west part of the town. The intercourse with Lowell and Boston, by way of the canal on the Merrimack, has been open since 1815, and a very large amount of business in freights has been done on the river. The Concord rail-road, to connect with the Lowell rail-road, has also been surveyed, and will doubtless soon be put in progress. This is a link in the great chain of northern railways, which must ultimately extend from Boston to connect with the western waters at the outlet of lake Ontario. The importance of extending the rail-road to the heart of New Hampshire has by no means been fully estimated by the public. Concord is the great thoroughfare for travellers from the north, and the freight by horses and baggage wagons is immense.

The soil of this town is generally good, and the intervales very productive. Large masses of granite suitable for the purposes of building exist here, the most important of which is *The New Hampshire Ledge,* a name by which in an act of incorporation an immense mass of granite in the N.W. part of the town has been designated. This ledge is situated about 1 1-2 miles N. W. of the state house, and about 200 rods distant from Merrimack river, which is navigable to this place with boats. The course of the ledge is from N. E. to S. W. and its rise about 45° from a plane of the horizon, and its height about 350 feet. It presents a surface of massive primitive granite, of more than 4,500 square rods. The rift of this stone is very perfect, smooth and regular; spots are easily made to the depth of 12 to 20 feet, and of almost any required length. And unlike much of the building stone now in the

THE NEW HAMPSHIRE GRANITE LEDGE.

Concord, N.H.

market, it has been ascertained by a recent examination (made by Mr. A. H. Hayes, of Roxbury, Mass., and other eminent chemists and geologists,) that the stone from this quarry is perfectly free from those oxides, or other mineral substances, which on exposure to the atmosphere, mar the beauty of much of the New England granite. This stone quarries easily; the great elevation and dip of the ledge, and its proximity to the river, giving it facilities of working and transportation, it is believed unequalled. From the base of the ledge to the bank of the Merrimack, a rail-way is contemplated, the proprietors of the ledge having already obtained a charter for that purpose. As the great facility of transportation by way of the river to the markets, becomes known, together with the fact, that the upward freight would, during a great portion of the year, go far towards remunerating the cost of transportation of this stone to the seaboard—the situation, extent, and value of this quarry will be seen and appreciated. On several large perpendicular faces of the ledge, protected by shelving rocks from vegetable stains, but exposed for ages perhaps to the atmosphere, the stone is found to be entirely free from any coloring or stain, preserving its natural color. The amount of the whole mass, when wrought, can scarcely be estimated. This representation is derived from gentlemen of Concord not at all interested in the quarry, and is here given, with the sole qualification, that if the quality of the stone is as pure as is stated, there is no danger of over-estimating the value of the quarry. A specimen of this granite is with the editor for examination. Concord, originally called *Penacook*, was granted by Massachusetts to a company of settlers, 17th Jan., 1725, and the settlement began the year following. In 1733, the plantation was incorporated by the name of *Rumford*, which name it retained until 7th June, 1765, when the town was incorporated by its present name. This town suffered much from incursions of the savages. Several of the inhabitants were killed, and others taken into captivity, between the years 1740 and 1750. The manufactures of Concord are numerous and valuable. They consist of books, furniture of all kinds, boots, shoes, granite, lumber, and a variety of other articles. The manufacture of books is very extensive, and annually increasing.

Population in 1775, 1,052; in 1790, 1,747; in 1800, 2,052; in 1810, 2,393; in 1820, 2,838; and in 1830, 3,727. The present population is between 4 and 5 thousand.

Among the early inhabitants and distinguished citizens of this town, may be mentioned the following:

Hon. TIMOTHY WALKER, son of the first minister of Concord, an active patriot during the revolution, member of the convention of 1784, a legislator, and judge of the common pleas. He died May 5, 1822, aged 85.

Dr. PHILIP CARRIGAIN, an eminent physician, who died in 1806.

Hon. THOMAS W. THOMPSON, a distinguished lawyer and politician, who died 1 Oct., 1821, aged 57.

Sir BENJAMIN THOMPSON (known to the world as COUNT RUMFORD) settled and married here in early life.

JOHN FARMER, ESQ., an eminent antiquary and genealogist, resided here for the last seventeen years of his life, and died 13 Aug., 1838, aged 49. Mr. Farmer's health was always exceedingly delicate: he therefore, partly of necessity and partly of choice, adopted a very sedentary mode of life. He collected around him books of ancient date—gathered together early records of towns—notices of the first settlers of the country—inquired into the names, ages, characters, and deaths of distinguished men of every profession—entered into extensive correspondence with men who might be able to furnish him with facts relative to the subjects of his inquiry. In short, Mr. Farmer soon became known as an ANTIQUARIAN, distinguished far beyond all his fellow citizens, for exact knowledge of facts and events relative to the history of New England. His mind was a wonderful repository of names and dates and particular incidents, not stored up indeed for private gratification, but always open for the benefit of others. So general and well established was his reputation for *accuracy*, that his authority was relied on, as decisive in historical and genealogical facts.

Feelings of personal attachment and obligations for numerous invaluable tokens of friendship, received by the editor, would seem to require a full length portrait of the character of this distinguished man and estimable christian—even in a work of this kind; and it should be given, had not an abler pen performed that act of justice. See *American Quarterly Register.*

Concord, Vt.

Essex co. First settled, 1788. Population, 1830, 1,031. On the W. side of Connecticut river: 38 miles E. by N. from Montpelier, and 18 S. W. from Guildhall. Moose river, a branch of the Passumpsic, waters the north part of the town. Hall's and Mile ponds are beautiful sheets of water, and afford a variety of fish. The soil of the town is pretty good, and keeps about 3,000 sheep.

Concord, Mass.

One of the chief towns of Middlesex county. This town is situated on the river of the same name, 17 miles W. N. W. from Boston, 14 S. S. W. from Lowell, and 30 E. N. E. from Worcester. Incorporated, 1635. Population, 1820, 1,788; 1837, 2,023. This town was the first inland settlement in the colony of Massachusetts Bay. The township was originally six miles square, and derives its name from the harmony in which it was purchased of the natives. Its Indian title was *Musketaquid.* It took an active part in the prosecution of the war against king Philip, in 1675-6, and in April of the latter year, 10 or 12 of its citizens were killed, in the attack made by the Indians on the neighboring town of Sudbury. The general court has frequently held its sessions in this town, and in the year 1774 the provincial congress selected it as their place of meeting. On the 19th of April, 1775, a detachment of British troops, sent out by Gen. Gage for the purpose of seizing a quantity of military stores which were deposited here by the province, were met at the North bridge by the citizens of Concord and the neighboring towns, and forcibly repulsed. It was at this spot that the first regular and effectual resistance was made, and the first British life was taken, in the war of the revolution. The graves of two of the British soldiers, who were killed at this place, are still marked, and a suitable monument is erected near the site of the bridge, to commemorate the event. The monument is of granite, in the form of an obelisk; its height about 25 feet; the base, which is square, is a large block 5 1-2 feet broad, and about 3 in height. On the west side of the next block, is inlaid a slab of white Italian marble, on which is engraved the following inscription:—

Here,
On the 19th of April, 1775,
Was made
The first forcible resistance
To British aggression.
On the opposite Bank,
Stood the American Militia.
Here stood the invading Army,
And on this spot
The first of the enemy fell
In the War of that Revolution
Which gave
Independence
To these United States.

In gratitude to God,
And
In the love of freedom,
This Monument
Was erected
A. D. 1836.

The manufactures of Concord consist of cotton goods, satinet and flannel, boots, shoes, hats, ploughs, lead pipe, chairs and cabinet ware. The whole value, in one year, exclusive of cotton goods, amounted to $156,012.

Concord River.

This river is formed by the union of Assabet and Sudbury rivers at Concord: after passing through the towns of Bedford, Billerica, and Chelmsford, it falls into the Merrimack between Lowell and Tewksbury. This river furnishes the Middlesex canal with most of its waters.

Connanicut Island.

See *Jamestown, R. I.*

CONNECTICUT.

This state is bounded N. by Massachusetts, E. by Rhode Island, S. by Long Island Sound, and W. by New York. Situated between 40° 58′ and 42° 1′ N. lat., and 72° 37′ and 71° 43′ W. lon.

The territory of Connecticut was formerly two colonies—*Connecticut* and *New Haven.* The colony of Connecticut was planted by citizens of Massachusetts, at Windsor, in 1633, and at Hartford and Wethersfield, in 1635 and 1636. The colony of New Haven was settled by Englishmen, in 1638. In 1665, the two colonies were united by a charter granted by Charles the Second. This charter was the basis of the government till 1818, when the present constitution was formed.

The executive power of this State is vested in a Governor, and a Lieutenant-Governor, who is also President of the Senate.

The legislative power is vested in a Senate and a House of Representatives, which together are called *The General Assembly.* The Senate consists of not less than 18 and not more than 24 members. Most of the towns may choose two Representatives; the others one each. All the above are elected annually by the people on the first Monday of April. The General Assembly has one stated session in each year, commencing on the first Wednesday in May. These sessions are held alternately, in the years of even numbers at New Haven, and in the years of odd numbers at Hartford.

The electors are all the white male citizens, of twenty-one years of age, who have resided in the town in which they vote six months next preceding, and have a freehold estate of the value of seven dollars; or who have performed regular military duty in said town for one year next previous to the voting; or who shall have paid a tax within a year of his voting. Those entitled to be electors, before voting must be qualified by taking the oath prescribed by law.

No person is obliged to join any religious society; but having joined one he is liable by law to pay his proportion of the charges for its support. He may separate himself from such society by leaving with the clerk thereof notice of his determination to close his connexion with them.

The judicial department of the government embraces the Supreme Court of Errors, the Superior Court, a County Court in each county, a City Court in each city, a Court of Probate in each probate district, and as in other states in New England, an indefinite number of Justices of the Peace in each county.

The Supreme Court of Errors consists of five Judges, who are appointed by the General Assembly, and hold their offices during good behavior, but not after seventy years of age. They are subject to removal by impeachment, and by the Governor, on the address of two thirds of the members of each House of the General Assembly. This court has final and exclusive jurisdiction of writs of error, brought to revise the judgment on decrees of the Superior Court, in law or equity, wherein

NEW ENGLAND GAZETTEER.

the errors complained of appear from the files and records. It holds one term in each county annually. Though this body, *as a court*, has cognizance only of writs of error, yet, as all the members are Judges of the Superior Court, a convenient opportunity is afforded, while they are thus assembled, for hearing arguments on motions for new trials and cases stated. These, of course, occupy a considerable portion of the term. The opinions of the Judges upon them are given by way of *advice to* the Superior Court, in which the cases are respectively pending. This advice is always followed, it being understood as settling the law.

A Judge of the Superior Court of Errors, designated by that court for the purpose, constitutes the Superior Court; two terms of which are held in each county annually. This court has cognizance of civil actions at law brought by appeal from the County, City, and Probate Courts, and of suits for relief in chancery, wherein the value of the matter in demand exceeds $335. In criminal causes it has exclusive jurisdiction of offences punishable with death or imprisonment for life; and, concurrent with the County Courts, of all other offences not committed to the jurisdiction of the Justices of the Peace. It has also cognizance of writs of error brought to revise the decisions of inferior tribunals; of petitions for divorce, and of writs of *scire facias, audita querela,* and petitions for new trials relative to matters in or issuing from the court. In capital cases, the Judge holding the court is to call to his assistance one or more of the other Judges.

The County Courts consist of one Chief Judge and two Associate Judges, who are appointed annually by the General Assembly. This court has original jurisdiction of all civil actions at law, wherein the value of the matter in demand exceeds $35, and appellate jurisdiction of all such actions wherein the value in demand exceeds $7. It has also original and final jurisdiction of suits for relief in equity, wherein the value in demand does not exceed $335, except suits for relief against a judgment rendered on a cause depending at law in the Superior Court.

In criminal jurisdiction, it has cognizance of all offences above the jurisdiction of a Justice of the Peace, and not exclusively within that of the Superior Court. It is also vested with powers relative to the laying out of roads, granting licences, the appointment of surveyors, &c.

Justices of the Peace have cognizance of all actions at law of a civil nature, wherein the value in demand does not exceed $35, and of all offences and crimes punishable by fine not exceeding $7, or by imprisonment not exceeding thirty days, or both.

In each of the six cities—Hartford, New Haven, New London, Norwich, Middletown, and Bridgeport—there is a City Court, consisting of the Mayor and two senior Aldermen, having cognizance of all civil actions wherein the title of land is not concerned.

Succession of Governors since the Union of the Colonies under the Charter in 1665.

John Winthrop, 1665—1676. William Leet, 1676—1683. Robert Treat, 1683—1698. Fitz-John Winthrop, 1698—1707. Gurdon Saltonstall, 1708—1724. Joseph Talcott, 1725—1741. Jonathan Law, 1742—1751. Roger Wolcott, 1751—1754. Thomas Fitch, 1754—1766. William Pitkin, 1766—1769. Jonathan Trumbull, 1769—1784. Matthew Griswold, 1784—1786. Samuel Huntington, 1786—1795. Oliver Wolcott, 1796, 1797. Jonathan Trumbull, 1798—1809. John Treadwell, 1809—1811. Roger Griswold, 1811, 1812. John Cotton Smith, 1813—1817. Oliver Wolcott, 1817—1827. Gideon Tomlinson, 1827—1831. John S. Peters, 1831—1833. Henry W. Edwards, 1833, 1834. Samuel A. Foot, 1834—1836. Henry W. Edwards, 1836—

Succession of Chief Justices.

Richard Law, 1785—1789. Eliphalet Dyer, 1789—1793. Andrew Adams, 1793—1797. Jesse Root, 1798—1807. Stephen M. Mitchell, 1807—1814. Tapping Reeve, 1814, 1815. Zephaniah Swift, 1815—1819. Stephen T. Hosmer, 1819—1833. David Daggett, 1833—1835. Thomas S. Williams, 1835—

Connecticut is divided into the eight following counties—Hartford, New Haven, New London, Fairfield, Windham, Litchfield, Middlesex, and Tolland. The face of the state is greatly diversified by hills and valleys. In general it is so exceeding undulating or uneven, as to present an everchanging variety of objects. The ranges of mountains from the north, which terminate near New Haven, are not remarkable for their elevation in this state. Connecticut is finely watered by the noble river from which it derives its name, by the Thames, Housatonick, Naugatuck, and other smaller streams. The soil varies from a gravelly loam on the hills, to a rich and exceedingly fertile alluvial in the valleys. The former is more particularly adapted to grazing, the latter to tillage. These lands, in possession of an industrious class of freemen, yield, in great abundance, all the varieties of products common to a northern climate. The mineral resources of the state are not yet fully developed; but iron and copper ores of excellent qualities are found; also, lead, cobalt, marble and freestone. The mineral waters at Stafford are the most celebrated. Manufacturing establishments are scattered over the state, on its numerous delightful streams; and foreign commerce, the coasting trade, and fisheries, enjoy an enviable position on the waters of Long Island Sound.

Blessed with a salubrious climate and fertile country, the people of Connecticut probably enjoy as much happiness as is allotted to any part of the human family. Her population is always full, and although her domain is not extensive, no Atlantic state has sent so many of her children, or so large a share of intellectual wealth, to the western country, as Connecticut.

If the love of liberty, literature and the arts, of social feeling and moral worth has an asylum on earth, Connecticut may boast that it is to be found within her bosom. See *Register*.

Connecticut River.

This beautiful river, the *Quonektacut* of the Indians, and the pride of the Yankees, has it sources in New Hampshire and the mountainous tracts in Lower Canada. Its name in the Indian language is said to signify *Long River*, or, as some render it, *River of Pines*. Its general course is north and south. After forming the boundary line between New Hampshire and Vermont, it crosses the western part of Massachusetts, passes the state of Connecticut, nearly in its centre; and, after a fall of 1,600 feet, from its head, north of latitude 45°, it falls into Long Island Sound, in latitude 41° 16′. The breadth of this river, at its entrance into Vermont, is about 150 feet, and in its course of 60 miles it increases to about 390 feet. In Massachusetts and Connecticut, its breadth may be estimated from 450 to 1,050 feet. It is navigable to Hartford, 45 miles, for vessels of considerable burthen, and to Middletown, 30 miles from the sea, for vessels drawing 12 feet of water. By means of canals and other improvements, it has been made navigable for boats to Fifteen Mile Falls, nearly 250 miles above Hartford. The most considerable rapids in this river, are Bellows' Falls, the falls of Queechy, just below the mouth of Waterqueechy river; the White river falls, below Hanover, and the Fifteen Mile Falls, in N. H. and Vt.;—the falls at Montague and South Hadley, in Mass., and the falls at Enfield, in Ct., where it meets the tide water. The perpendicular height of the falls which have been overcome by dams and locks between Springfield, in Mass., and Hanover, in N. H., a distance of 130 miles, is 240 feet. Bars of sand and gravel extend across this river in various places, over which boats with difficulty pass in low water. The most important tributaries to the Connecticut, in New Hampshire, are Upper and Lower Amonoosuck, Israel's, John's, Mascomy, Sugar, and Ashuelot rivers: in Vermont, Nulhegan, Passumpsic, Wells, Wait's, Ompomponoosuck, White, Waterqueechy, Black, Williams, Sexton's, and West rivers: in Massachusetts, Miller's, Deerfield, Agawam, Chickopee, and Westfield rivers; and the Farmington, in Connecticut.

The intervales are generally spread upon one or both sides of the river, nearly on a level with its banks, and extending from half a mile to five miles in breadth; but its borders are in some places high, rocky and precipitous. In the spring it overflows its banks, and, through its winding course of nearly 400 miles, forms and fertilizes a vast tract of rich meadow. In point of length, utility, and beauty, this river forms a distinguished feature of New England.

Large quantities of shad are taken in this river, but the salmon, which formerly were very plenty, have entirely disappeared. Connecticut river passes through a basin or valley of about 12,000 square miles; it is decorated, on each side, with towns and villages of superior beauty, and presents to the eye a wonderful variety of enchanting scenery.

Connecticut Lake,

The source of one of the principal branches of Connecticut river, is situated in latitude 45° 2'; and is 5 1-2 miles in length, and 2 1-2 in width. It is supplied by several small streams, rising in the highlands north of the lake.

Contoocook River, N. H.,

A stream of considerable length and importance, waters most of the towns in the W. part of the county of Hillsborough. It has its origin from several ponds in Jaffrey and Rindge, and in its course north receives numerous streams from Dublin, Peterborough, Sharon, Nelson, Stoddard, Washington, Antrim, Deering, and Hillsborough. In Hillsborough it takes a N. E. and easterly direction, and proceeds through Henniker to Hopkinton, where it receives Warner and Blackwater rivers. From Hopkinton, it pursues a meandering course through Concord, and discharges itself into the Merrimack between Concord and Boscawen. Near the mouth of this river is *Duston's Island,* celebrated as the spot where Mrs. Duston destroyed several Indians, in 1698.

Conway, N. H.,

Strafford co., on Saco river, is 72 miles N. N. E. from Concord, 60 N. by W. from Dover, and 57 N. W. from Portland, Me. Swift river, a considerable and very rapid stream, Pequawkett river, and a stream taking its rise in Walker's pond, the two last affording mill privileges, discharge themselves into Saco river in this town. Saco river here is from 10 to 12 rods wide, and about 2 feet deep; its current rapid and broken by falls. This river has been known to rise 27 and even 30 feet in the course of 24 hours. The largest collections of water in Conway are a part of Walker's pond, and Little Pequawkett pond, which lie in the south part of the town. There is a detached block of granite on the southern side of Pine hill, the largest perhaps in the state. A spring near the centre of the town, on the bank of Cold brook, strongly impregnated with sulphur, has been visited frequently by the infirm, and in many instances found beneficial. There are also in this town large quantities of magnesia and fuller's earth. The intervale along the river is from 50 to 220 rods wide. The plain, when properly cultivated, produces large crops of corn and rye. Conway is quite a resort for travellers from the east and south to the White Mountains. From Conway village to Crawford's house, at the Notch, is 34 miles N. W. Daniel Foster, in 1765, obtained a grant of this township, containing 21,040 acres, on condition that each grantee should pay a rent of one ear of Indian corn annually for the space of ten years, if demanded. Pop. 1830, 1,601.

Conway, Mass.

Franklin co. This town is divided from Shelburne, on the north, by Deerfield river. It lies 100 miles W. by N. from Boston, and 7 S. W. from Greenfield. Incorporated,

1767. Population, 1837, 1,445. A tributary of Deerfield river passes its northern border. The manufactures of Conway consist of cotton and woolen goods, leather, boots, shoes, hats, chairs and cabinet ware. Total amount, year ending April 1, 1837, $22,475. The value of wool grown, the same year, was $5,072, comprising 4,830 fleeces, weighing 14,490 pounds.

Cooper, Me.

Washington co. Denny's river, emptying into Meddybemps lake, and both discharging into the river St. Croix at Baring, water the north part of this town. It lies 164 miles E. N. E. from Augusta, and about 36 miles N. from Machias. Population, 1837, 571.

Coos County, N. H.

Coos is the largest county in New Hampshire, and within its limits are situated the contested Indian Stream territory and the greater part of the ungranted lands. Large portions of this county are exceedingly mountainous, cannot be cultivated, and will probably never be settled. This county extends from lat. 43° 58' to the extreme north part of the state—being 76 miles in length, and having a mean width of about 20 miles. The area of this county is estimated to contain 1600 square miles, or, in round numbers, 1,000,000 of acres. It is bounded N. by Lower Canada, E. by Maine, S. by the county of Strafford, W. by Grafton county and the state of Vermont. Besides the stupendous pile of the White Mountains, which distinguishes this county, there are several other mountains of no inconsiderable height. Those in Shelburne, Jackson and Chatham, on the east side of the White Mountains, are bold and abrupt. The Peak and Bowback mountains in Stratford; the elevations in Dixville, Columbia and Kilkenny; Pilot and Mill mountains in Stark; Cape Horn in Northumberland, and Pondicherry, S. W. of Jefferson, are all of considerable magnitude, and partake of the grandeur of the White Hills. In the neighborhood of high mountains are generally found the sources of our greater rivers. Three of the principal rivers of New England, the Connecticut, Androscoggin and Saco, take their rise in this county. There are numerous other streams which become tributary to these rivers, the principal of which are the Mohawk, Amonoosuck, Israel's and John's rivers. The Margallaway, after receiving the waters of Dead and Diamond rivers, unites with the Androscoggin, near Umbagog lake. This lake lies principally in Maine. Lake Connecticut is situated north of the 45th degree of latitude, and is one of the sources of Connecticut river. The largest pond in this county lies N. of lake Connecticut, and is connected with it by an outlet.

The first settlement in the county was made at Lancaster in 1763. The county was incorporated Dec. 24, 1803, and the name is of Indian origin, although the same name occurs in the New Testament. The population in 1820 was 5,549; and in 1830, 8,390. Coos contains 23 towns, and five inhabitants to a square mile. Lancaster, Shiretown.

Corinna, Me.

Somerset co. Situated 53 miles W. N. W. from Augusta, and about 35 N. W. from Norridgewock. Incorporated, 1816. Population, 1837, 1,513. In 1837, 8,864 bushels of wheat were raised in this valuable township.

Corinth, Me.

Penobscot co. This delightful township lies 81 miles N. W. by W. from Augusta, and about 25 S. W. from Bangor. It is watered by

Kenduskeag stream, and produced, in 1837, 9,017 bushels of wheat. Population, same year, 1,232.

Corinth, Vt.

Orange co. Two branches of Wait's river water this town. It is 20 miles S. E. from Montpelier, and 10 N. E. from Chelsea. First settled, 1777. Population, 1830, 1,953. Corinth is pleasant, with a rough, strong soil, and very healthy; it has some water power and keeps about 7,000 sheep.

Cornish, Me.

York co. Bounded N. by the Saco and Great Ossipee rivers. 83 miles S. W. from Augusta, 32 W. by N. from Portland, and 25 N. from Alfred. Incorporated, 1794. Population, 1837, 1,180. Cornish produces good crops of wheat and some wool.

Cornish, N. H.,

Sullivan co., is 17 miles N. from Charlestown, 50 N. W. by W. from Concord, and 12 N. W. from Newport. Connecticut river waters the west part of this town, and by means of a bridge connects Cornish with Windsor, Vt. The soil is generally fertile. The town is hilly, with the exception of that part which lies on the river. Blow-me-down and Bryant's brooks are the only streams of any magnitude—these afford good mill privileges, which are improved for a woolen factory, a large number of saw, and other mills. The agricultural products of this town are very considerable. Cornish was granted June 21, 1763, to Rev. Samuel McClintock, of Greenland, and 69 others. The town was settled in 1765.—Population, 1830, 1,687.

Cornville, Me.

Somerset co. This town is well watered by the Wessaransett river, a branch of the Kennebec. There is much choice land in Cornville. A few of the inhabitants, in 1837, by way of experiment, raised 7000 bushels of wheat. Incorporated, 1798. Population, 1837, 2,112. Bounded S. by Skowhegan: 38 miles N. from Augusta, and about 13 N. E. from Norridgewock.

Cornwall, Vt.

Addison co. This is a level township of excellent land, watered by Otter creek and Lemonfair river, without any good mill sites. Notwithstanding there is a very large swamp in this town, the people are healthy, and many live to a very great age. Very beautiful calcareous spar, in rhomboidal crystals, is found here. The population of Cornwall, in 1830, was 1,264. The number of sheep, in 1837, was about 16,000. It lies 60 miles S. W. from Montpelier, and bounded N. E. by Middlebury. First settled, 1774.

Cornwall, Ct.

Litchfield co. This mountainous township lies on the east side of Housatonick river, 38 miles W. from Hartford, 48 N. from New Haven, and 13 N. by W. from Litchfield. First settled, 1740. Population, 1830, 1,714. The scenery about the south village is very beautiful. "The cheerful appearance of the church and the little cluster of white buildings surrounding it, at the bottom of a deep valley, is uncommonly pleasing. The mountains and lofty hills which rise immediately on almost every side, shutting out, in a sense, the most of the world from this apparently retired spot, present a bold and most striking feature in the landscape." This village is the place where a Foreign Mission School was established in 1818. "This school had its rise from the attempt to qualify Obookiah, a pious Owyheean youth, and others, for missionaries to their native lands. Obookiah was brought to this country in 1808, and came to New Haven. While here, Samuel J. Mills, a student in Yale College, and other pious persons, commiserating his condition, instructed him in the Christian religion.— Obookiah soon became hopefully pious, and strongly advocated a mission to his countrymen. Other natives of his island were found, and a school was established for their benefit at Cornwall. In 1820, the number of pupils in this school was 29, of whom 19 were American Indians, and 6 from the islands of the Pacific ocean. Obookiah sickened and died in Cornwall in 1818. The following is the inscription on his monument in the village grave yard.

"In memory of *Henry Obookiah*, a native of Owyhee. His arrival in this country gave rise to the Foreign Mission School, of which he was a worthy member. He was once an Idolater, and was designed for a Pagan Priest; but by the grace of God, and by the prayers and instructions of pious friends, he became a Christian. He was eminent for piety and missionary zeal. When almost prepared to return to his native isle to preach the gospel, God took him to himself. In his last sickness he wept and prayed for *Owyhee*, but was submissive. He died without fear, with a heavenly smile on his countenance and glory in his soul, Feb. 17th, 1818, aged 26."

Coventry, N. H.,

Grafton co., is 70 miles N. N. W. from Concord, and 12 E. S. E. from Haverhill. This town is watered by branches of Oliverian brook and Wild Amonoosuck rivers. In the S. E. part of Coventry is Moosehillock mountain. Owl-head mountain lies in the W. part of this town. Coventry presents a rough and mountainous aspect, and the soil in several parts is not capable of cultivation. This town was granted Jan. 31, 1764, to Theophilus Fitch and others, and was settled after the commencement of the revolutionary war. Population, 1830, 441.

Coventry, Vt.

Orleans co. This is a good township of land, and is watered by Barton's and Black rivers, two good mill streams, running north into Memphremagog lake. First settled, 1800. Population, 1830, 728. The south part of the lake lies in Coventry, and gives it some trade to Canada. Here are about 2,500 sheep. Coventry lies 47 miles N. by E. from Montpelier, and has Irasburgh on the south.

Coventry, R. I.

Kent co. This is a very large township, extending to the north line of Connecticut, and admirably watered by numerous ponds and by Flat river, an important branch of the Pawtucket. Coventry has long been noted for the number and variety of its manufactures, particularly of cotton and wool. The soil of the town is well adapted to agricultural pursuits: it is well improved, and a large amount of the products of the dairy, &c., is annually produced. There are a number of pleasant villages in Coventry, all of which are flourishing, both in manufacturing and trade. This town was distinguished for its patriotism during the revolutionary contest. Coventry was incorporated in 1742. It lies 10 miles S. W. from Providence, and 8 N. W. from East Greenwich. Population, 1830, 3,851.

Coventry, Ct.

Tolland co. The Wangombog, a beautiful pond, and the Skungamug, Hop and Willimantic rivers, give Coventry a good water power. In the south part of the town are two cotton and two woolen manufactories, a machine shop and other important mechanical operations by water. This town was the gift of

Mohegan Sachem, and was first settled in 1700. The surface is uneven, and the soil a gravelly loam. Coventry lies 18 miles E. from Hartford, and bounded N. by Tolland. Population, 1830, 2,119. This town is celebrated as the birth place of Capt. NATHAN HALE, who volunteered his services to Washington to discover the position of the enemy on Long Island. He fell a martyr to American liberty, Sept. 22, 1776, aged 22.

LORENZO DOW, an itinerant preacher, celebrated for his eccentricity was born in Coventry, October, 16, 1777. It is said that during the 38 years of his ministry he travelled in this and foreign countries two hundred thousand miles. He died at Georgetown, D. C., Feb. 2, 1834.

Craftsbury, Vt.

Orleans co. Col. Ebenezer Crafts was the father of this little republic. He died, much honored, in 1810, aged 70. Craftsbury was settled in 1789. It lies 25 miles S. of the Canada line, 25 miles N. from Montpelier, and about 15 S. S. W. from Irasburgh. Population, 1830, 982. This town is finely watered by Black river, Wild Branch, and 5 large natural ponds well stored with trout. The village in the centre of the town is elevated, commanding a delightful prospect.

Cranberry Islands.

Hancock co. These islands were attached to the town of Mount Desert until 1830, when they were incorporated. They lie a few miles E. by S. from Mount Desert, and embrace Great and Little Cranberry, Sutton's and Baker's islands. These islands afford good harbors, and are well located for the shore fishery. Population, 1837, 183.

Cranston, R. I.

Providence co. The soil of this town is more favorable for the production of fruits and vegetables than for grain. Some parts of the town are very fertile, but considerable of the land is rough and uneven. Providence market is supplied with a considerable amount of the products of the town. The manufacture of cotton is very extensively pursued. The water power of the Pawtuxet and Powchasset are constant and abundant. Cranston is a very pleasant town, and its proximity to Providence, (only five miles south west) gives it peculiar privileges. Population, 1830, 2,653.

Crawford, Me.

Washington co. Incorporated, 1828. This is a good township of land, and was formerly called Adams. A large pond in Crawford and a part of another are the sources of a branch of East Machias river. Population, 1837, 311. Located about 30 miles N. from Machias and 140 E. N. E. from Augusta.

Crooked River, Me.,

Rises in ponds in Oxford county; passes through Harrison, Otisfield, and Raymond, and joins the outlet of Long pond into Sebago lake.

Cross Island, Me.

A large island, off Machias bay, attached to the town of Cutler.

Croydon, N. H.,

Sullivan co., is 44 miles N. N. W. from Concord, and 8 N. from Newport. The N. branch of Sugar river waters this town. On this stream is a woolen factory and other mills. Croydon mountain is of considerable elevation, on which are two small ponds. The soil of Croydon is moist and rocky, and produces valuable crops. Croydon was granted by charter to Samuel Chase, and others, May 31, 1763. It was settled in 1766. Population, 1830, 1,057.

Cumberland County, Me.

Portland, chief town. Bounded N. by Oxford county, E. by Lincoln county, S. by the Atlantic ocean, and W. by York county and a part of Oxford. Area about 990 square miles. Population, 1820, 49,445; 1830, 60,113; 1837, 67,619. This is an excellent county of land, and under good cultivation. The commerce and manufactures of Portland and neighboring towns is very extensive. Casco bay is within the county, and affords it unrivalled privileges for navigation and the fisheries. It is watered by several large mill streams; and the Cumberland and Oxford canal to Sebago lake, within the county, gives to its chief town considerable inland trade. In 1837 there were 37,803 bushels of wheat raised in the county, and it contained 71,000 sheep.

Cumberland, Me.

Cumberland co. Set off from the westerly part of North Yarmouth in 1821. Population, 1837, 1,525. 54 miles S. W. from Augusta, and 10 N. from Portland. Cumberland is pleasantly situated on Casco bay, and enjoys many navigable facilities.

Cumberland, R. I.

Providence co. The manufacture of cotton and boat building is extensively pursued in this town. Pawtucket, Mill and Peter's rivers, and Abbot's run, afford the town a good hydraulic power. There is some good land in Cumberland, producing a variety of articles for Providence market; from which it is distant 8 miles N. Population, 1830, 3,675. See *Smithfield.*

Cummington, Mass.

Hampshire co. Located 110 miles W. from Boston, and 20 W. N. W. from Northampton. Incorporated, 1779. Population, 1837, 1,204. In this town are good mill seats on Westfield river. It is a mountainous township but excellent for grazing. It produced, in 1837, 12,486 pounds of merino wool, the weight of 4,162 fleeces, valued at $7,492. The manufactures of Cummington consist of cotton and woolen goods, leather, palm-leaf hats, and scythe snaiths. Total value, in one year, $98,000. Iron ore and soapstone.

Cushing, Me.

Lincoln co. Situated on Saint George's river, opposite to the town of St. George; 45 miles N. E. from Augusta, and about 12 miles S. from Warren. This place was settled by emigrants from Ireland, as early as 1733. Here was the celebrated stone fort, erected by Maj. Burton. Incorporated, 1789. Population, 1837, 732.

Cutler, Me.

Washington co. Bounded S. by the Atlantic Ocean, and about 20 miles S. W. from W. Quoddy Head. It contains Little Machias bay and Little river, and is bounded W. by Machias bay. Cutler has a good harbor, and a population of 667 164 miles E. by N. from Augusta, and 10 S. E. from Machias.

Dalton, N. H.,

Coos co., lies between Lancaster and Littleton, on Connecticut river, and is 110 miles N. by W. from Concord. The Great, or Fifteen Mile Falls, on Connecticut river, commence in Dalton, and rush tumultuously along its northwest boundary. The town is also watered by John's river and several large brooks. The western and southern parts of this town are hilly. Along the borders of John's river the majestic white pine abounds. The soil on the highlands is deep, and well adapted to grazing—is generally good, and in some parts easy of cultivation. Blake's pond, the only one in town, lies at the S. E. corner. Moses Blake and Walter Bloss were the first settlers of Dalton, and, with their families, for a long time the only inhabitants. Dalton was incorporated Nov. 4, 1784. Population, 1830, 532.

Blake was a famous hunter, and the moose which frequented the pond called by his name often fell by the accuracy of his shots. Blake and Capt. Bucknam, (one of the first settlers of Lancaster,) on a hunting excursion, fired at a mark, on a small bet. Bucknam fired first, and cut, at the distance of twenty rods, near the centre of a mark not larger than a dollar. Blake then fired, and on going to the tree on which the mark was made, no trace of the ball could be discovered. Bucknam exulted: "Cut out your ball," said Blake, "and you'll find mine o'top on't." The operation being performed, the two balls were found, the one safely lodged upon the other.

Dalton, Mass.

Berkshire co. Dalton lies 120 miles W. from Boston, and 13 N. by E. from Lenox. Incorporated, 1784. Population, 1837, 830. It is watered by the E. branch of Housatonick river. Its manufactures consist of woolen cloth, iron castings, paper, ($37,500,) leather, boots and shoes. Total amount in one year, $47,815. In 1837, the product of 4,238 sheep was 11,852 pounds of wool, valued at $5,725.

Damariscotta River, Me.

This river has its source in ponds in Jefferson and Nobleborough; its general course is southerly between Newcastle, Edgecomb and Boothbay, on the west, and Bristol on the east. It is navigable for vessels of any burthen 16 miles, to the bridge which crosses it between Newcastle and Nobleborough. Large quantities of lumber descend, and many merchant ships are built on this broad and navigable arm of the sea.

Dana, Mass.

Worcester co. Dana lies 65 miles W. from Boston, and 27 W. N. W. from Worcester. A branch of Swift river passes through the town.— Some leather is tanned in Dana; and 70,000 palm-leaf hats were made in 1836, valued at $10,500. Incorporated, 1781. Population, 1837, 660.

Danbury, N. H.,

Is in the S. part of Grafton county, and lies in the form of a diamond. It is 16 miles S. by W. from Plymouth, and 30 N. W. from Concord. This town is generally hilly, although there are some intervales. In the N. E. part is a large hill. The eastern section is watered by Smith's river. The first settlement was made in Nov. 1771, and incorporated June 18, 1795. Population, 1830, 786.

Danbury, Ct.

One of the shire towns of Fairfield county. Danbury, the *Pahquioque* of the Indians, was first settled in 1684. The soil of the town is good, and agreeably diversified by hills and valleys. The borough or village is very pleasantly situated in a valley, and is memorable for its sacrifices in the revolutionary war. It was nearly destroyed by the British, with a large amount of continental stores, April, 1777. It lies 22 miles N. from Norwalk, 36 S. S. W. from Litchfield, and 55 S. W. by W. from Hartford.

ROBERT SANDEMAN, the founder of a religious sect, died at Danbury in 1771, aged 53. See *Bethel, Ct.*

Danby, Vt.

Rutland co. Situated near the head waters of Otter creek, 17 miles S. from Rutland, and 68 S. S. W. from Montpelier. First settled, 1768. Population, 1830, 1,362.— The surface of the town is rough

NEW ENGLAND GAZETTEER.

and mountainous, but productive of extraordinary feed for cattle. Some of the best dairies in the country are in Danby. Large quantities of butter and cheese, of superior quality, are annually sent to market. There are some curious caverns in this town,—one of great depth.

Danvers, Mass.

Essex co. This flourishing town lies 2 miles N. W. from Salem, to which it was attached until 1757, and called "Salem Village." It is very pleasant, and has some mill and navigable privileges. The manufactures, for the year ending April 1, 1837, amounted to $854,300. The articles manufactured were boots and shoes ($435,900,) leather, ($264,400,) nails, bricks, pottery ware, glue, lasts, morocco, chocolate, shoe pegs, shoe and soap boxes, soap and candles. Population, 1830, 4,228; 1837, 4,804.

Danville, Me.

Cumberland co. This town, formerly called *Pejepsco*, was set off from the westerly part of North Yarmouth, in 1802. Population, 1837, 1,282. It lies 32 miles S. W. from Augusta, and 29 N. from Portland. Farming is the principal business of the inhabitants;—they raised, in 1837, 1,218 bushels of wheat.

Danville, N. H.

Rockingham co. It was incorporated February 22, 1760; formerly a part of Kingston, and until recently known by the name of Hawke. The soil is uneven, but in some parts good. Acchusnut river passes over the north west corner. Long pond lies in the east part, and Cub pond on the west side. The first settlements were made by Jonathan Sanborn, Jacob Hook, and others, between 1735 and 1739. Danville lies 33 miles S. E. of Concord, and 10 S. W. of Exeter. Population, 1830, 528.

Danville, Vt.

Chief town of Caledonia county. Danville village is very pleasantly situated near the centre of the town, and is surrounded by a beautiful farming country: first settled, 1784. Charles Hacket brought the first woman into town, in 1785. Population, 1830, 2,631. It lies 28 miles N. E. from Montpelier. Here is a medicinal spring; and Jo's pond, covering 1,000 acres, lies mostly in the town. Several tributaries of the Passumpsic give the town a good water power. This is a place of considerable manufactures and domestic trade.

Darien, Ct.

Fairfield co. Until 1820, Darien was a parish in the town of Stamford. The soil is excellent, and well adapted to tillage and grazing. It lies 5 miles W. from Norwalk, and 42 S. W. from New Haven. Population, 1830, 1,201.

During divine service, on Sunday, 22d of July, 1781, a party of British troops surrounded the meeting house at this place, and made the whole congregation prisoners. The males were tied, two and two, and the Rev. Moses Mather, D. D., a man distinguished for his learning and piety, placed at their head. They were marched to the shore, taken to Long Island, and afterwards to New York, where they suffered a cruel imprisonment.— Some of them never returned.

Dartmouth, Mass.

Bristol co. The *Aponiganset* of the Indians. A sea-port on Buzzard's bay, on the W. side of Accushnet river, 56 miles S. from Boston, and 3 W. from New Bedford. Incorporated, 1664. Population, 1837, 3,958. There are 5 vessels belonging to this place engaged in the whaling business, and a number in coasting, and other fisheries. The product of the whale, cod and mackerel fisheries the year ending April 1, 1837, amounted to $93,108. The value of wool grown was $2,110. The value of salt manufactured, of vessels built, of leather tanned, and of boots and shoes made, was $27,910.

Dead Rivers.

Dead river, in Maine, is an important tributary to the Kennebec. It rises on the border of Lower Canada, in the county of Franklin. It passes in a S. E. direction 40 or 50 miles; then N. about 10; it then changes to the E., and after passing about 15 miles it falls into the Kennebec, about 20 miles below Moose Head lake. The lands on Dead river and its numerous tributaries are very fertile and heavily wooded.

Dead Stream, in Maine, is a considerable tributary to the Penobscot, from the west. It empties at Orono, opposite to the Indian village.

Dead river, in New Hampshire, rises in the N. W. corner of the state, in Coos county, and after receiving several tributaries it falls into the Margallaway.

Deanfield, Me.

Located at the N. W. corner of Hancock county, between Passadumkeag river and Olammon stream. See *Barnard, Me.*

Dearborn, Me.

Kennebec co. The soil of this town is excellent, particularly around Great pond, which covers a large portion of the surface, and has a number of islands of great beauty. This pond is connected with other large sheets of water in Belgrade, Mount Vernon, and Rome, which render this part of the county highly picturesque. Dearborn was incorporated in 1812. Population, 1837, 799. 15 miles N. from Augusta.

Dedham, Me.

Hancock co. Incorporated, 1837. It is bounded on the W. by Ellsworth. Union river passes through its N. W. corner. In 1837 it had a population of 427, and produced 1,550 bushels of wheat.

Dedham, Mass.

Norfolk co. County town. This town is on Charles river, with a good water power. It is 10 miles S. W. from Boston, 35 E. from Worcester, 35 N. W. from Plymouth, 26 N. by W. from Taunton, and 30 N. E. from Providence. It has a beautiful court house of hewn granite. Its Indian name was *Tiot*. A railroad from the centre of the town meets the Boston and Providence rail-road, about two miles at the eastward. The manufactures of Dedham the year ending April 1, 1837, amounted to $510,755. They consisted of cotton and woolen goods, leather, boots, shoes, paper, marbled paper, iron castings, chairs, cabinet wares, straw bonnets, palm-leaf hats, and silk goods. The value of silk goods manufactured was $10,000. Dedham village is very pleasant, and possesses every inducement to render it a desirable residence for the mechanic or man of leisure. Population, 1837, 3,532

Deerfield, N. H.,

Rockingham co., is 18 miles E. S. E. from Concord, and 30 W. by N. from Portsmouth. This town has a number of very pleasant ponds which afford fish of various kinds. Moulton's pond is situated at the W. part of the town. This pond, although small, is noted on account of its having no visible inlet, and therefore is supposed to be supplied by a subterraneous passage, as the water is always of nearly an equal depth. The outlets of the pond run in opposite directions. This pond is also remarkable on account of having been often sounded without discovering any bottom. A branch of Lamprey river passes S. and S. E. through Deerfield. The surface of this town is uneven, the soil durable and fertile, although hard to cultivate. The Tuckaway, between Deerfield and Nottingham, the Saddleback, between Deerfield and Northwood, and Fort mountain on the W., are the principal elevations. In the W. part of this town, on the southerly side of a ridge of rocks which extend 3-4 of a mile, is a natural formation in the rock, for sixty years designated as the "Indian Camp." Its sides are irregular, and the top is covered by a canopy of granite projecting about 14 feet, affording a shelter from the sun and rain. On the E. side of this camp is a natural flight of steps, or stones resembling steps, by which persons may easily ascend to the top of the rock. Deerfield was once a place of favorite resort for deer, great numbers of which were taken. While the petition for the town was pending, a Mr. Batchelder killed a deer, and presenting it to Gov. Wentworth, obtained the act under the name of *Deer-field.* The town was settled in 1756 and 1758, by John Robertson, Benjamin Batchelder and others. During the Indian wars the inhabitants lived in garrisons, but no serious mischiefs were experienced. Population, 1830, 2,086.

Deerfield, Mass.

Franklin co. At the junction of Connecticut and Deerfield rivers, on the west side of the former, and on both sides of the latter. The *Pocumtuck* of the Indians. It is 95 miles W. by N. from Boston, 4 S. from Greenfield, and 17 N. from Northampton. First settled, 1668. Incorporated, 1682. Population, in 1837, 1,952. A very pleasant town, and a place of considerable commerce. The manufactures of this place, for one year, amounted to $147,190. They consisted of leather, boots, shoes, cutlery,($100,000) chairs, cabinet ware, palm-leaf hats, lead pipe, hair cloth and beds, wagons and carriages, pocket books, wallets, and corn-brooms. The value of wool grown, the same year, (1836) was $2,708. From the mountains in this vicinity, delightful views are obtained. *Deerfield Mountain* is 700 feet above the plain. *Sugar Loaf Mountain* rears its conical peak of red sandstone 500 feet above the river, and overlooks the ground of many sanguinary battles between the whites and Indians. This is a place of great interest. While the traveller lingers here, enjoying the beautiful scenery, and hospitality of the people of this quiet town, he cannot fail of contrasting the present scenes with those of former years: particularly with that at *Bloody Brook,* in 1675, when a company of 90 young men from the county of Essex were slain by ruthless savages. A monument, commemorating this event, was erected in 1838.

Deerfield River.

This beautiful and important Indian stream joins the Connecticut between Greenfield and Deerfield. It rises in the high grounds of Windham county, near Stratton, Dover and Somerset, Vermont; and proceeding in a S. E. course, it passes through Monroe, Florida, Rowe, Charlemont, Hawley, Buckland, Shelburne and Conway. The most important tributaries to this stream are *Cold* river; a river from Heath and Coleraine; one from Leyden, via Greenfield; and a river from Conway. Its whole length is about 50 miles. In some places Deerfield river is rapid, and its banks very precipitous. Its passage through the mountains is very curious and romantic.

Deering, N. H.,

Hillsborough co., 23 miles S. W. from Concord, and 22 N. W. from Amherst. It is diversified with hills and valleys; is well watered, and its soil is favorable to the several purposes of agriculture. There are three ponds, Dudley, Pecker's, and Fulton's. The two former are sources of the N. branch of Piscataquog river. There are some manufactures in this town, and bricks are made in a considerable quantity. Deering was incorporated Jan. 17, 1774. The name was given by Gov. John Wentworth, in honor of his wife, whose maiden name was Dering. The first permanent settlement was made in 1765, by Alexander Robinson. Population, 1830, 1,227.

Deer Isle, Me.

Hancock co. This town is constituted of three principal Islands—Deer Island, Little Deer Island, and the Isle of Haut. They comprise about 17,000 acres, and were inhabited before the revolutionary war. Incorporated, 1789. Population, 1837, 2,473. The principal island lies about 2 miles S. W. from Sedgewick harbor, and 95 miles E. by S. from Augusta. These islands have good harbors, and are well located for the shore fishery. Although they are situated near the sea they produce good crops and wheat.

Deer Islands, N. H.

In Connecticut river, between Lyman and Barnet, Vt., are five in number. The largest contains 88 acres.

Denmark, Me.

Oxford co. Incorporated, 1807. Population, 1837, 1,082. It lies 85 miles S. W. by W. from Augusta, about 28 S. W. from Paris, and 47 N. W. from Portland. Denmark is finely watered by Saco river and several beautiful ponds. The principal business of the inhabitants is agricultural, for which they have a fertile soil, and which produced, in 1837, 2,560 bushels of wheat.

Dennis, Mass.

Barnstable co. This town crosses the cape, and was taken from Yarmouth in 1793. Population, 1837, 2,750. It lies 8 miles E. by N. from Barnstable, and 7 W. from Harwich. The first salt produced by solar evaporation in this country was made in this town, by John Sears and others, in 1776. About 7,000 tons of shipping belong to this town, principally engaged in fishing and coasting, and all manned by natives of the town. *Bass river,* rising from a pond, affords a small water power. 150 ship-masters belong to this town, sailing from various ports in the Union. The products of the cod and mackerel fishing, in one year, amounted to $50,899. The manufacture of common salt, Epsom salts, vessels, and lampblack, amounted to $25,975.

Dennysville, Me.

Washington co. This town is bounded on the S. by Cobscook bay, and watered by a river of the same name. It lies 172 miles E. N. E. from Augusta, and 22 N. E. from Machias. Population, 1837, 349.

Derby, Vt.

Orleans co. First settled, 1795. It is bounded on the N. by Lower Canada, and on the W. by Memphremagog lake. Clyde river, the outlet of Salem pond, affords it a good water power. This town is very pleasant, level and fertile;— it has some manufactures;—the farmers are industrious and rear a large number of sheep. Derby is 50 miles N. N. E. from Montpelier, and 15 N. N.E. from Irasburgh. Population, 1830, 1,469.

Derby, Ct.

New Haven co. The Indian name of this town was *Paugasset.* It was purchased of the Indians, and incorporated in 1675. The surface of the town is uneven, with some fertile meadow on the banks of the rivers. Derby is watered by the Housatonick and Naugatuck rivers. Derby Landing, Smithville and Humphreysville, are the principal places of business.

The *Landing* is on the east side of the Housatonick, just below the junction of that river with the Naugatuck, and is 8 miles N. W. from New Haven, and 14 from the mouth of the river at Stratford, on Long Island Sound. Vessels of 10 feet draught of water can pass to the Landing, from which wood and other commodities are transported by water.

Smithville is located in view of the Landing, and commands a beautiful prospect. It has extensive manufactures of copper, in sheets and wire, augurs, carriage springs and axletrees, nails and tacks, flannels, satinets, and other operations by the waters of the Naugatuck, passing through a canal of about a mile in length. This village was commenced in 1834, and is very flourishing.

Humphreysville is located in a small valley, on the Naugatuck river, about 4 miles from the Landing. The Humphreysville Manufacturing Company was incorporated in 1810. The building is 4 stories high and 100 feet long. In this village and around it is some of the most beautiful and romantic scenery in New England. This village derived its name from the Hon. DAVID HUMPHREYS, a native of Derby, a poet, an aid to Washington, and a minister to Spain. He died at New Haven, February 21, 1818, aged 66.

Derry, N. H.

Rockingham co. A fine grazing township, taken from Londonderry in 1828. The principal manufactures are linen thread and cloth, palm-leaf hats and shoes. The village is very handsome, and a great thoroughfare for travellers. The soil is very productive, and the inhabitants are remarkable for their industry, general wealth and longevity. Derry lies 18 miles W. S. W. from Exeter, and 25 S. E. from Concord. Population, 1830, 2,176.

Dexter, Me.

Penobscot co. This town was first settled in 1801. Incorporated, 1815. It lies 67 miles N. E. from Augusta, and 35 N. W. from Bangor. Population, 1837, 1,401. Dexter is a valuable township of land. The farmers reap a rich reward for their labors. In 1837, 7000 bushels of wheat was raised. In this town is a pond covering 500 acres, at the outlet of which are mills and a beautiful village.

Diamond River, N. H.

Diamond river has its principal source in Diamond pond, in Stewartstown. From thence it passes through Dixville, and after receiving several tributaries, falls into the Dead river near its junction with the Margallaway.

Dighton, Mass.

Bristol co. A port of entry, on the west side of Taunton river, opposite to Berkley. Population, 1837, 1,453. 40 miles S. from Boston, 8 S. from Taunton, and 20 N. W. by W. from New Bedford. There are in this place three cotton factories, a woolen mill, a furnace, and other iron works. Tonnage of the district, 9,032 tons. The noted "Dighton Rock," so called, on which are inscriptions difficult to decypher, in fact lies on the Berkley side of the river. The value of cotton and woolen goods, boots and shoes, pig iron and wooden ware manufactured, and vessels built in Dighton, in one year, was $30,000.

Dixfield, Me.

Oxford co. This is a good farming town on the north bank of the Androscoggin river, 42 miles N. W. by W. from Augusta, and 25 N. by E. from Paris. Incorporated, 1803. Population, 1837, 1,148. In 1837, 5,522 bushels of wheat was raised in Dixfield.

Dixmont, Me.

Penobscot co. This town derived its name from Dr. Elijah Dix, late of Boston, one of the original proprietors, and from a hill or mountain in the town, beautifully wooded to its summit. It is on the height of land between the Kennebec and Penobscot. The surface of the town is undulating; the soil excellent and of easy cultivation. It annually produces large quantities of hay, some corn, rye and wool.— In 1837, a bounty of $649 40 was obtained for raising 932 1-2 bushels of wheat. There is a pond in the town and some mill privileges. Dixmont lies 44 miles N. E. from Augusta, and 24 S. W. from Bangor. Incorporated, 1807. Population, 1830, 1,323.

Dixville, N. H.,

Coos co., was granted in 1805, to the late Col. Timothy Dix, jr., of Boscawen. It comprises 31,023 acres of uneven land. Numerous streams meander through this town from the surrounding heights. Dixville lies about 40 miles N. N. E. from Lancaster. In 1810 it had a population of 12; and in 1830, of only 2.

Dorchester, N. H.,

Grafton co., is situated on the highlands between Connecticut and Merrimack rivers, 12 miles from the former, and 8 from the latter. It is 23 miles S. by E. from Haverhill, 50 N. W. from Concord, and 90 N. W. by W. from Portsmouth. The principal streams are the S. branch of Baker's river, a branch of Mascomy, and Rocky branch. There are two considerable ponds, both in the W. part of the town. The soil in some parts is very fertile; particularly the intervales on the branch of Baker's river. The highlands are very uneven, and the greater part rocky. First settled about the year 1772. Population, 1830, 702.

Dorchester, Mass.

Norfolk co. This ancient and respectable town lies on Dorchester bay, in Boston harbor, 5 miles S. from Boston, and 7 N. E. from Dedham. Population, 1837, 4,564. It was first settled by a party of Puritans from England. These pilgrims landed from the ship Mary and John, at Nantasket, on the 11th of June, 1630, and on the 17th day of that month they located themselves at the Indian *Mattapan,* and called it Dorchester, in honor of their pious and learned friend, the Rev. John White, of Dorchester, 120 miles W. from London. The town was incorporated on the 7th of September following, and included most of the territory of the towns of Milton, Canton, Stoughton, Sharon, and that part of Boston on which stand "Dorchester Heights," memorable for their sudden conversion into a fortress, for the protection of Boston harbor, by order of Washington, on the night of March 4, 1776. These lands were obtained from the Indians by purchase, not by combat. The present limits of the town are about 6 by 3 1-2 miles. Dorchester furnished pioneers for the settlement of many parts of the country. A party from this town crossed the trackless wilderness in 14 days, and settled Hartford, on Connecticut river, in 1635. In 1695, another party emigrated from this place, and settled Dorchester, in South Carolina, and afterwards Medway, in Georgia. The soil of Dorchester is rocky, but very fertile and under a high state of cultivation. It is exceedingly productive, particularly of vegetables, fruits and flowers. Its surface is greatly variegated, presenting a continual succession of picturesque and delightful views of the country, city, and sea. Its hill-tops and valleys are decked with farm houses and tasteful villas, and no where can be found the union of town and country enjoyments more complete. The beautiful Neponset washes the whole of the southern border of the town, and besides its navigable privileges, affords it a large and valuable water power. The first water mill in America was erected in this town, in 1633; and here, about the same time, the cod fishery, the boast of New England, was first commenced. There are now 4 vessels employed in the whale, and 16 in the cod and other fisheries. Total tonnage, 2,210 tons. Capital invested, $190,000. Product, in one year, $138,349. The manufactures of Dorchester consist of cotton goods, boots, shoes, hats, paper, cabinet ware, block tin, tin ware, leather, wearing apparel, soap, candles, chocolate, and playing cards; the aggregate amount of which, in one year, was $457,400.

The first settlers of Dorchester came a regularly organized church, with its pastor and officers. They soon erected a house of public worship; but it is a singular fact that "none can tell the precise spot where the first meeting-house was located, nor does a single stone remain to designate the site of the original burying ground." There are, however, some mementos of olden times. The earliest date in the present ancient cemetery that can be distinctly traced, is 1644. We copy the following from among many singular effusions, found on the grave-stones in that cemetery, in commemoration of the dead.

"Here lies our Captain and Major of Suffolk was withal,
A Godly Magistrate was he and Major General,
Two troops of horse with him here came, such worth his love did crave,
Ten companies of foot also, mourning marched to his grave.
Let all that read be sure to keep the faith as he has done;
With Christ he lives now crowned, his name was Humphrey Atherton."

On the grave of three brothers, by the name of Clarke.

"Here lies three Clarks, their accounts are even,
Entered on earth, carried up to heaven."

Johnson, in his "Wonder Working Providence," thus speaks of Dorchester in 1654.

"The forme of this Towne is almost like a Serpent turning her head to the Northward; over against Tompson's Island, and the Castle, her body and wings being chiefly built on, are filled somewhat thick of Houses, onely that one of her Wings is clift, her Tayle being of such large extent that Shee can hardly draw it after her. Her houses for dwelling are about one hundred and forty; Orchards and Gardens, full of Fruit-trees, plenty of Corne Land, although much of it hath been long in tillage, yet hath it ordinarily good crops; the number of trees are near upon 1500. Cowes and other Cattell of that kinde about 450. Thus hath the Lord been pleased to increase his poore dispersed people, whose number in this Flock are near about 150. Their first Pastor called to feede them was the Reverend and godly Mr. Maveruck."

Among the first settlers of Dorchester was George Minot, a ruling elder of the church for thirty years. He erected a dwelling-house in that part of Dorchester where the pleasant village of Neponset now stands. That house is now standing, and is doubtless one of the oldest houses in the country. It is in good repair, and has ever remained in possession of Mr. Minot's lineal descendants. Mr. Minot died December 24, 1671, aged 78. This house is more celebrated for the female heroism displayed within its walls, than for its antiquity. A party of Narraganset Indians, hunting on the borders of Neponset river, stopped at elder Minot's house and demanded food and drink. On being refused they threatened vengeance, and the sachem, or chief of the party, left an Indian in ambush to watch an opportunity to effect it. Soon after, in the absence of all the family, except a young woman and two small children, the Indian attacked the house and fired at the young woman, but missed his mark. The girl placed the children under two brass kettles and bade them be silent. She then loaded Mr. Minot's gun and shot the Indian in the shoulder. He again attacked the house, and in attempting to enter the window, the girl threw a shovel full of live coals into his face and lodged them in his blanket. On this the Indian fled. The next day he was found dead in the woods. The Indian's name was Chickataubut, but not the Narraganset sachem of that name. The government of Massachusetts bay presented this brave young woman with a silver wristband, on which her name was engraved, with this motto,— "*She slew the Narrhaganset hunter.*"

Dorset, Vt.

Bennington co. This town was first settled in 1768, and organized the following year. Paulet and Battenkill rivers rise in this town, and, with the waters of Otter creek, which pass the northern part, afford some mill privileges, which are used for manufacturing purposes. There are two mountains partly in this town, the Dorset and Equinox.

There is a cavern in the south part of the town of some note. It is entered by an aperture nearly 10 feet square, " which opens into a spacious room nine rods in length and four wide. At the further end of this apartment are two openings which are about 30 feet apart. The one on the right is three feet from the floor, and is about 20 inches by six feet in length. It leads to an apartment 20 feet long, 12 wide and 12 high. From this room there is an opening sufficient to admit a man to pass through sideways about 20 feet, when it opens into a large hall 80 feet long and 30 wide. The other aperture from the first room is about as large as a common door, and leads to an apartment 12 feet square, out of which is a passage to another considerable room, in which is a spring of water. This cavern is said to have been explored 40 or 50 rods without arriving at the end." Dorset lies 26 miles N. from Burlington and 91 S. S. W. from Montpelier. Population, 1830, 1,507.

Douglas, Mass.

Worcester co. This town lies 47 miles W. S. W. from Boston, 17 S. E. from Worcester, and 21 N. W. from Providence. Population, 1830, 1,742. Here is good meadow land, iron ore, and valuable water privileges on Mumford river. In this town was manufactured, in 1836, $55,000 value of cotton goods; boots and shoes, $5,250; leather, $1,500; and $116,400 of axes and hatchets; besides large quantities of hatchet handles and shoe lasts. Incorporated, 1731.

Dover, Me.

Piscataquis co. Bounded N. by Piscataquis river, S. by Garland, W. by Sangerville and E. by Atkinson. It lies 77 miles N. by E. from Augusta, and about 35 miles N. W. from Bangor. Incorporated, 1822. Population, 1837, 1,042. Dover is the shire town of this new county, and remarkable for its beauty. It produced, in 1837, 10,290 bushels of wheat.

Dover, N. H.

This is one of the most interesting and important towns in New Hampshire. It is one of the county towns of Strafford county, and lies 40 miles E. from Concord, 12 N. W. by N. from Portsmouth, and 45 S. W. from Portland. Population, 1830, 5,549. The principal streams of Dover, are the Cocheco, and Bellamy Bank, or *Back* river. They take a S. E. course through the town, and unite with other waters to form the Piscataqua.

Cocheco, or *Quochecho* river, has its rise from several small streams in New Durham, which unite in Farmington, whence the river meanders through Rochester, there receiving the Isinglass, a tributary, and thence passes through Dover into the Newichwannock, or Salmon Fall river, the principal branch of the Piscataqua. The Cocheco is a beautiful river, and very important to the inhabitants of Rochester and Dover. Passing over this town in any direction, the traveller finds no rugged mountains, nor extensive barren plains, but occasionally ascends gentle swells of land, from the height of which the eye meets some delightful object; a winding stream, a well cultivated farm, or a distant village. In the S. part of the town is a neck of land about 2 miles long and half a mile broad, having Piscataqua on one side, and Back river on the other. From the road on either hand, the land gradually descends to the rivers. It commands a very delightful, variegated, and extensive prospect of bays, adjacent shores, and distant mountains. On this neck the first settlement of the town was made, in 1623, by a company in England, whose design it was to plant a colony, and establish a fishery around the Piscataqua; for which purpose they sent over, with several others, Edward and William Hilton, fishmongers, of London. These men commenced their operations on the Neck at a place by the Indians called *Winichahanat*, which they called *Northam*, and afterwards *Dover*. For several years, this spot embraced the principal part of the population of the town; here was erected the first meeting-house, afterwards surrounded with an entrenchment, and flankarts, the remains of which are still visible; here the people assembled to worship, and to transact their public business. In process of time, the business and population of the town began to centre around Cocheco falls, about 4 miles N. W. from the neck. These falls are in the river whose name they bear, and give to the water that passes over them a sudden descent of 32 1-2 feet. Situate at the head of navigation, about 12 miles from the ocean, having a fertile country on the north, west, and south, they are considered among the most valuable in New England. Around these falls the beautiful village of Dover is situated, containing many handsome buildings.

The Dover "Cotton Factory Company," at Cocheco falls, was incorporated in 1820. They have one brick mill of 420 feet by 45, 7 stories high, and two other mills of the same material, 154 by 43 feet, one 5 and the other 6 stories high.— These mills contain 25,040 spindles and 768 looms, and manufacture annually 5,000,000 yards of cotton cloth; the principal part of which is bleached, and printed into calico by the company. This company employ a capital of more than a million of dollars, and about 1,000 persons. There are other manufacturing establishments at Dover, but this is the principal.

A society of Friends was established here at an early period, and formerly comprised about one third of the population.

A congregational church was organized in 1638. A Mr. Leverich, a worthy puritan, was their first minister, and probably the first ordained minister that preached the gospel in New Hampshire. Mr. Leverich soon removed, and until the settlement of the pious Daniel Maud, in 1642, the church was much oppressed by the bad character of their ministers.

The Rev. JEREMY BELKNAP, D. D. the celebrated historian of New Hampshire, was ordained in this town in 1767. He removed to Boston, and was settled there April 4, 1787. He died in Boston, June 20, 1798, aged 54.

This town in its early years was greatly frequented by the Indians; and experienced many sufferings in their repeated attacks upon the inhabitants. In 1675, Maj. Waldron by a stratagem secured about 200 Indians at Dover, who had at times exhibited signs of hostility. Seven or eight of them, who had been guilty of some atrocities, were immediately hanged, and the rest sold into slavery. The Indians abroad regarded this act of Waldron as a breach of faith, and swore against him implacable revenge. In 1689, after a lapse of 13 years, they determined to execute their project. Previous to the fatal night (27th of June) some hints had been thrown out by the squaws, but they were either misunderstood or disregarded; and the people suffered them to sleep in their garrisons as usual. In the stillness of night the doors of the garrisons were opened, and the Indians, at a concerted signal, rose from their lurking places, and rushed upon the defenceless inhabitants. Waldron, though 80 years of age, made a gallant defence, but was overwhelmed by the superior numbers of his adversaries, who literally cut him to pieces. In this affair, 23 persons were killed, and 29 made prisoners. The Indians were soon overtaken and nearly the whole party destroyed.

Dover, Vt.

Windham co. This town was a part of Wardsborough, until 1810. It lies 12 miles N. W. from Brattleborough, 17 N. E. from Bennington, and 120 S. by W. from Montpelier. The land in Dover is high and uneven;—more fit for pasturage than tillage. It is the source of several branches of West, and a branch of Deerfield river. Serpentine and chlorite slate are found here. Population, 1830, 831.

Dover, Mass.

Norfolk co. Dover lies 5 miles W. from Dedham, and 14 S. S. W. from Boston. It was taken from Dedham in 1784. This town is bounded northerly by Charles river, and in it are manufactures of nails, iron hoops and rods, ploughs, brushes, boots and shoes. Total amount of manufactures in 1836, $99,558. The surface of Dover is uneven, and a large part of it covered with wood. Population, 1837, 518.

Down East, Me.

We crave the favor of a letter from our friends "Down East." See Barnard, Me.

Dracut, Mass.

Middlesex co. Dracut is united to Lowell by a bridge over Merrimack river. The town is pleasantly situated on the N. side, on the line of N. H., with a tolerable soil and some water power, by Beaver river. It lies 27 miles N. from Boston, and 16 N. by E. from Concord. Incorporated, 1701. Population, 1837, 1,898. The manufactures of Dracut consist of woolen goods, leather, cutlery, boots and shoes. Annual amount, exclusive of woolen goods, about $25,000.

Dresden, Me.

Lincoln co. On the E. bank of Kennebec river, near the head of Swan Island, 9 miles N. W. from Wiscasset, 14 S. from Augusta, and 59 N. E. from Portland. This is a large agricultural township, with some trade on the river. Previous to the division of the county, in 1789, Dresden was the shire town or place where all the courts in Maine were holden, E. of Kennebec river. Dresden was incorporated as a town in 1794. Population, 1837, 1,570.

Drewsville, N. H.

See *Walpole.*

Dublin, N. H.

Cheshire co. It is 10 miles E. by S. from Keene, and 50 S. W. from Concord. Dublin is situated on the height of land between Connecticut and Merrimack rivers. Its streams are small; those on the W. side run into the Ashuelot, those on the E. into Contoocook river. The rain which falls on the roof of the church is shared by the rivers.— There is a pond near the middle of the town called Centre pond, one mile in length and about the same in breadth. A large portion of the Grand Monadnock lies in the N. W. part of Dublin, and near the centre of the town is Breed's mountain. Monadnock was formerly covered with a growth of small timber and shrubbery, but fires having run over it at different times, it presents little more than ragged rocks. Between the rocks, however, there are low whortleberry bushes, which produce great quantities of fruit of a very rich flavor. The season for ripening is the latter part of August, and to those who ascend the summit at this season they are peculiarly grateful. This mountain is not difficult of access. The view from its summit is sublime. Its height is 3,718 feet above the level of the sea. The land in general is much better for grazing than tillage. The late Rev. Edward Sprague bequeathed nearly 8,000 dollars for the support of public schools, the annual interest of which is to be applied to this object. He also left the town $5,000, the interest of which, paid quarterly, is to be applied to the support of an ordained congregational minister, who shall statedly preach in Dublin. The first settlements were in 1762, by John Alexander, and others. Population, 1830, 1,218.

Dudley, Mass.

Worcester co. This good farming town was called by the Indians *Chabanakongkomum.* It is finely watered by the Quinnebaug and other streams, and possesses excellent mill privileges. During the year ending April 1, 1837, the value of the manufactures of Dudley amounted to $346,826. The articles manufactured were woolen goods, leather, shoes, scythe snaiths, chairs, and cabinet ware. The value of wool grown was $1,585.

Dudley lies 55 miles S. W. from Boston, 18 S. from Worcester, and 34 N. W. from Providence. Incorporated, 1731. Population, 1837, 1,415.

Duke's County, Mass.

Edgarton is the county town. This county is formed of the islands of Martha's Vineyard, Chappequiddic, Elizabeth Islands, and No Man's Land—the latter of which is the southern extremity of Massachusetts. These islands lie off and S. of Barnstable county and Buzzard's bay, and contain about 120 square miles. The principal island, Martha's Vineyard, the Indian *Nope,* or *Capawock,* was first settled by the whites, at Edgarton, in 1641, and is 21 miles in length and 6 in breadth. Although a large portion of this county is woodland, and many of the people engaged in the fisheries and coasting trade, yet considerable exports are annually made of wool, woolen cloth, salt and grain. This county suffered much during the revolutionary war. In 1778, the people were compelled to surrender their fire arms and 2,300 head of cattle to the British. Incorporated, 1695. Population, 1820, 3,292; 1830, 3,518; 1837, 3,785: 32 inhabitants to a square mile. There were on these islands, in 1837, 11,281 sheep.

Dummer, N. H.,

Coos co., is bounded N by Millsfield and Errol, and comprises 23,040 acres. It was granted March 8, 1773, and is watered by the Ammonoosuck and Androscoggin.—Population, 1830, 65.

Dummerston, Vt.

Windham co. West river passes through this town and gives it a good water power. The surface is rough and hilly, but adapted to grazing. Black mountain, near the centre, is a vast body of granite. Good slate for buildings, and primitive limestone are found. There are in Dummerston some manufacturing concerns, and a considerable number of sheep. Population, 1830, 1,592: 90 miles S. from Montpelier, and 8 S. E. from Newfane.

Dunbarton, N. H.

Merrimack co. This town lies 9 miles S. W. from Concord, and 7 S. E. from Hopkinton. Population, 1830, 1,067. The situation of the town is somewhat elevated, though there are but few hills, nor any mountains. The air is clear, the water is good, and the health of its inhabitants is seldom interrupted by sickness. The soil is good, peculiarly suited for corn, wheat and orcharding. Almost every lot in town is capable of making a good farm. The farmers here have good buildings and are excellent husbandmen. The advantages in point of water privileges are not great. The inhabitants are principally descendants of Scotch Irish, so called, from the North of Ireland. Their posterity still retain many traits of character peculiar to that people. Dunbarton was granted in 1751, to Archibald Stark and others. Its present name is derived from *Dumbarton*, in Scotland, from whence Stark emigrated. The first settlement was made about 1749. William Stinson, born in Ireland, came to Londonderry with his father. He was much respected and was a useful man. James Rogers was from Ireland, and father to Major Robert Rogers. He was shot in the woods, being mistaken for a bear.

Dunmore Lake, Vt.

See *Salisbury*.

Dunstable, Mass.

Middlesex co. Nashua river waters the N. W. part of the town, and passes into Nashua, N. H. The surface of the town is level;—some part of it is good land, but generally it is light and sandy. It has no manufactures, and only 315 sheep. Population, 1837, 570. Incorporated, 1683. Dunstable lies 27 miles N. W. from Boston, 18 N. by W. from Concord, and 6 S. from Nashua.

Durham, Me.

Cumberland co. Located on the S. side of Androscoggin river, and united with Lisbon by a bridge. This is a township of good land, and farming is the principal occupation of the inhabitants. Durham lies 25 miles N. from Portland and 31 S. W. from Augusta. Population, 1837, 1,832. Incorporated, 1789.

Durham, N. H.,

Strafford co., is 32 miles E. by S. from Concord, 11 W. N. W. from Portsmouth, and 7 S. from Dover. Population, 1830, 1,606. The situation of this town, upon the Piscataqua and its branches, is very favorable both as to water power and transportation. Oyster river, one of the branches of the Piscataqua, issues from Wheelwright's pond, in Lee, and after running nearly its whole course in Durham, furnishing in its progress several convenient mill seats, falls into the main river near Piscataqua bridge. This bridge is 2,600 feet in length and 40 in width. It cost $65,400. The tide flows in this branch of the river up to the falls near the meeting-house in the village, where business to a large amount is annually transacted. This village is a very central depot for the lumber and produce of the adjacent country. Lamprey river, another branch of the Piscataqua, runs through the westerly part of this town, over several falls remarkably well adapted for mill seats, into the town of New Market, where it falls into the Great Bay. Upon both sides of Oyster river, a deep argillaceous loam prevails, which is peculiarly favorable to the production of the grasses, of which very heavy crops are cut, and hay is an article of considerable export. Extensive ledges of excellent granite, with which this town abounds, have been the source of much profitable employment to the inhabitants. A large block of detached granite in the southeast part of this town was formerly placed in a very singular situation. Its weight was 60 or 70 tons, and it was poised so exactly upon two other stones as to be visibly moved by the wind. It was some years since dislodged from this extraordinary position by the barbarous curiosity of some visitors. Durham was originally a part of Dover; but soon after its settlement was formed into a distinct parish by the name of *Oyster river*, from the stream which passes through it. From the abundance of excellent oysters found in its waters, this river probably derived its name, and it was a famous rendezvous of the Indians. For many years this place suffered exceedingly by Indian depredations and murders. In 1694, when a large part of the inhabitants had marched to the westward, the Indians, who were dispersed in the woods about Oyster river, having diligently observed the number of men in one of the garrisons, rushed upon eighteen of them, as they were going to their morning devotions, and having cut off their retreat to the house, put them all to death except one, who fortunately escaped. They then attacked the house, in which there were only two boys, beside the women and children. The boys kept them off for some time and wounded several of them. At length the Indians set fire to the house and even then the boys would not surrender till the Indians had promised to spare their lives. The latter, however, perfidiously murdered three or four children, one of whom they fixed upon a sharp stake in the view of its mother. The next spring the Indians narrowly watched the frontiers, to determine the safest and most vulnerable points of attack. The settlement at Oyster river was selected for destruction. Here were twelve garrisoned houses, amply sufficient for the reception of the inhabitants; but not apprehending any danger, many of the families remained in their unfortified houses, and those who were in the garrisons were indifferently prepared for a siege, as they were destitute of powder. The enemy approached the place undiscovered and halted near the falls. One John Dean, whose house stood near the falls, happening to rise very early for a journey before the dawn of day, was shot as he came out of his door. The attack now commenced on all points where the enemy was ready. The enemy entered the house of a Mr. Adams without resistance, where they murdered fourteen persons, whose graves can still be traced. The house of John Buss, the minister, was destroyed together with his valuable library. He was absent at the time, and his wife and family fled to the woods. Many other cruelties were perpetrated, when the Indians, fearing that the inhabitants from the neighboring settlements would collect against them, retreated, having killed or captured between 90 and 100 persons, and destroyed 20 houses, 5 of which were garrisoned. Minute accounts of these disasters are given in Belknap's valuable History of New Hampshire, to which the reader is referred. The first preacher who statedly officiated in Durham was John Buss; but he never was ordained. He died 1736, at the age of 108. Rev. Hugh Adams settled March 26, 1718.

Maj. Gen. JOHN SULLIVAN, of the revolutionary army, was a resident of this town, and died here Jan. 23, 1795. He was a native of Berwick, Me.; was a distinguished commander during the war; was president of the state three years, and afterwards district judge of New Hampshire. On all occasions he proved himself the firm supporter of the rights of the country.

Durham, Ct.

Middlesex co. This town was first settled in 1698. Its Indian name was *Coginchaug*. It lies 7 miles S. by W. from Middletown, and 20 S. from Hartford. Population, 1830, 1,116. Agriculture is the principal employment of the people of Durham, for which they have rather an uneven but fertile soil. "This town has been distinguished many years for a very fine breed of cattle. Two oxen, presented by some of the inhabitants to General Washington, furnished a dinner for all the officers of the American army at Valley Forge, and all their servants. These oxen were driven almost five hundred miles, through a country nearly exhausted of its forage; yet one of them, a steer, five years old, weighed two thousand two hundred and seventy pounds."

Capt. Israel Camp, a noted psalmodist died in Durham, in 1778.

Duston's Island, N. H.

This small island in the Merrimack at the mouth of Contoocook river, between Concord and Boscawen, has become celebrated on account of an exploit of a lady whose name it bears. On the 15th March, 1698, the Indians made a descent on Haverhill, Mass. where they took Mrs. Hannah Duston, who was confined to her bed with an infant only six days old, and attended by her nurse, Mary Niff. The Indians took Mrs. Duston from her bed and carried her away with the nurse and infant. They soon despatched the latter by dashing its head against a tree. When they had proceeded as far as this island, which has been justly called Duston's island, on their way to an Indian town situate a considerable distance above, the Indians informed the women that they must be stripped and run the gauntlet through the village on their arrival. Mrs. Duston and her nurse had been assigned to a family consisting of two stout men, three women, and seven children, or young Indians, besides an English boy who had been taken from Worcester. Mrs. Duston, aware of the cruelties that awaited her, formed the design of exterminating the whole family, and prevailed upon the nurse and the boy to assist her in their destruction. A little before day, finding the whole company in a sound sleep, she awoke her confederates, and with the Indian hatchets despatched ten of the twelve. One of the women whom they thought they had killed made her escape, and a favorite boy they designedly left. Mrs. Duston and her companions arrived safe home with the scalps, though their danger from the enemy and from famine in travelling so far, must have been great. The general court of Massachusetts made her a grant of £50, and she received many other valuable presents.

Duxbury, Vt.

Washington co. This town lies on the S. side of Onion river, and is watered by several of its branches. The land along Onion river is good, but the greater part of the township is mountainous and unfit for cultivation. Duxbury lies 12 miles W. from Montpelier. First settled, 1786. Population, 1830, 651.

Duxbury, Mass.

Plymouth co. This town lies on Massachusetts bay in Plymouth harbor. It is 29 miles S. E. from Boston and 6 N. from Plymouth. Duxbury affords some good land, a good water power and a great variety of scenery. Its Indian name was *Matakeeset*. Ship building, the coasting trade and fisheries is the chief business of the place. In 1837, it had 46 vessels employed in the cod and mackerel fishery, the product of which amounted to $69,548. Value of vessels built, $169,048. The value of woolen cloth, leather, boots, shoes, salt, iron, brass castings and tin ware manufactured, amounted to $105,787. Some attention is paid here to rearing sheep, and the manufacture of cordage.

There is in Duxbury an apple tree noted for its age, size and fruitfulness. It is upwards of a hundred years old. It is forty feet in height, and its circumference, eight inches from the ground, is 16 feet. Its fruit, in one year, has made 10 barrels of cider, besides 30 bushels for the cellar. Population, 1837, 2,789.

Dyer's Bay, Me.

See *Steuben*.

Eagle Lake, Me.

This large lake is in the county of Penobscot, between the Aroostook and St. John's rivers. It is connected with some lakes of smaller size. The general outlet is north by Chipquedopskook river, about 14 miles in length, into the river St. John. Great quantities of logs are taken to this outlet, sawed and sent to New Brunswick.

East Bridgewater, Mass.

Plymouth co. This town lies on a branch of Taunton river, and was, until 1823, a part of the ancient Bridgewater. It is 24 miles S. by E. from Boston and 17 S. W. from Plymouth. Population, 1830, 1,653—1837, 1,927. East Bridgewater has a good water power, and manufactured the year ending April 1, 1837, $414,044 value of goods. The articles consisted of cotton goods, boots, shoes, leather, bar iron, nails, tacks, lead pipe, chaises, window blinds, sashes and shoe boxes.

Eastbrook, Me.

Hancock co. Incorporated, 1837. See "*Down East.*"

East Greenwich, R. I.

Shire town of Kent co. This town was incorporated in 1677, and is pleasantly located on Narraganset bay, 13 miles S. from Providence, and comprises an excellent harbor for ships of 500 tons burthen. A number of vessels are owned here, and the coasting trade and fisheries give employment to many of the inhabitants. The town is watered by Maskachug and Hunt's rivers, on which are cotton mills and other manufactories. The soil of the town is rather rough and stony, but it yields good crops of corn, barley and potatoes. East Greenwich is noted for excellent fruit and cider.

The "Kentish Guards" was established here in 1774, and proved a nursery of distinguished officers, of which the celebrated General Nathaniel Greene was one. Across the bay, to Bristol, is about 8 miles. Population, 1830, 1,591.

East Haddam, Ct.

Middlesex co. A town of considerable trade and manufacturing enterprise, on the east side of the Connecticut, and at the outlet of Salmon river. It lies 18 miles above the mouth of Connecticut river, 14 below Middletown, and 30 S. S. E. from Hartford. The soil is hilly and rocky, and more fit for grazing than tillage. Considerable business is done here in the shad fishery. It is supposed that more leather is made in this than in any other town in the state. This place has fine water privileges, both for navigation and manufactures. A short distance from the centre of the town is a pond covering 1,000 acres. On the river formed by the outlet of this pond, the water is precipitated over rocks nearly 70 feet perpendicular. The scenery around these falls is beautiful, and worthy of particular notice.

There are 6 cotton mills in East Haddam, two of which manufacture twine.

Leesville, on Salmon river, and *Mechanicsville*, on Moodus river, a branch of Salmon river, are very flourishing settlements.

This place, the Indian *Mackimoodus*, is remarkable for frequent slight shocks of earthquakes, producing singular noises, which the Indians attributed to the anger of their gods towards the white men. It is said that some valuable geological discoveries have recently been made in this quarter. The town was first settled in 1685, but not incorporated until 1724. Population, in 1835, about 3,000. This is the birth place of many distinguished men. The venerable Nathaniel Emmons, D. D., of Franklin, Mass. was born here.

Eastham, Mass.,

Barnstable co., on a narrow part of the cape, 23 miles E. by N. from Barnstable. Population in 1837, 1,059. First settled, 1644. Incorporated, 1646. The product of the cod and mackerel fishery in 1836, was $30,900. The value of salt, boots, shoes and palm-leaf hats manufactured, was $10,561.

Easthampton, Mass.

Hampshire co. This is a pleasant town on the W. side of Connecticut river. The Hampshire and Hampden canal passes through it. In the year ending April 1, 1837, $40,000 worth of lasting buttons were manufactured; also cotton goods, leather, boots and shoes, to the amount of $15,300 : 5 miles S. from Northampton. Pop. 1837, 793.

East Hartford, Ct.

Hartford co. This town is situated opposite to Hartford, and connected with it by a bridge across Connecticut river. The soil of the town is generally fertile, but the alluvial meadows on the border of the river, of which there is a large tract, is of a superior quality. The agricultural products of this town are very considerable. Hackanum river furnishes the town with a good water power, on which are valuable manufacturing establishments particularly of paper. East Hartford is noted for its manufactures in former years. The first powder mill in this country, it is said, was erected here in 1775. Anchors, mill screws, nail rods, gunpowder, paper, snuff and glass were manufactured here in 1784. The early settlers found the ferocious and warlike tribe of Podunk Indians in this neighborhood. One sachem commanded two hundred bowmen. This is a very pleasant town. The main street, which is very long and wide, is delightfully shaded by stately elms. East Hartford was taken from Hartford in 1784. Population, 1830, 3,537.

East Haven, Vt.

Essex co. Moose river rises in

...terly part of this town and the Passumpsic passes through the westerly part. The land is mountainous and most of it unfit for cultivation. It lies 45 miles N. from Montpelier First settled, 1790. Population, 1830, 33.

East Haven, Ct.

New Haven co. This town was taken from New Haven, in 1785, and is connected with New Haven by a bridge. Population, 1830, 1,229. It has good navigable privileges, and is watered by Quinnipiac river. It has some trade, but the principal employment of the inhabitants is agriculture and fishing.

This was a great resort for the Indians in former years. On *Grave Hill* was an Indian fort and cemetery. Bones of Indians of a large size, and domestic and warlike implements for savage use, have been found here. The *Indian Well*, in a granite rock, on an island in Stony river, is a curiosity. It is about 30 inches in diameter, very smooth at the bottom. It is now about 5 feet in depth, but formerly it was deeper. It was evidently formed by the attrition of sand and pebbles which passed over this rock, it being at some former period, the bed of the river. East Haven is pleasantly located, and commands a fine prospect of Long Island Sound.

East Kingston, N. H.

Rockingham co. Its soil is of an excellent quality, and well adapted to the cultivation of grain and grass. Powow river crosses the S. W. part of this town, having its sources in the ponds of Kingston. The town was incorporated Nov. 17, 1738. Rev. Peter Coffin was settled here in 1739. Population, 1830, 442. It lies 40 miles S. E. by E. from Concord, and 20 S. S. W. from Portsmouth.

East Machias, Me.

Washington co. This is a flourishing town on navigable waters. It was incorporated in 1826, and is the eastern part of Old Machias. It lies on both sides of East Machias river, 149 miles E. by N. from Augusta. Population, 1837, 1,282. East Machias has a great water power, a large number of mills, and a very pleasant village. It is extensively engaged in the lumber trade.

Easton, Mass.

Bristol co. Two branches of Taunton river water this town, on which are a woolen and 4 cotton mills, and various iron works. The manufactures consist of cotton and woolen goods, pig iron, iron castings, wire, boots, shoes, shovels, spades, forks, hoes, cutlery, palm-leaf hats, straw bonnets, surveyors' instruments and shoe pegs:—the value of which in one year (exclusive of woolen cloth, boots and shoes,) amounted to 207,100. The manufacture of shovels, spades, forks and hoes, amounted to $108,000. Easton lies 22 miles S. from Boston and 10 N. by W. from Taunton. Incorporated, 1725. Population, 1837, 1,976.

Eastport, Me.

Washington co. The township of Eastport embraces and is constituted of Moose, Dudley's, Frederick and Patmos islands, the chief of which, whereon the village of Eastport stands, is Moose island, in sight of, and but a short distance from, Indian and Campo Bello islands, belonging to the British. Eastport is a beautiful harbor in Passamaquoddy bay, on the eastern boundary of the United States, and noted for smuggling adventures by strangers visiting the place during the embargo and war. It is about 7 miles N. by W. from West Quoddy Head, 176 E. by N. from Augusta, and about 30 E. N. E. from Machias. The tide is very rapid, and rises 25 feet. There are two long bridges connecting Moose island with Dennysville and Perry; each cost $10,000. Eastport and Lubec are the chief towns in Passamaquoddy bay, and are extensively engaged in the fisheries, and the trade of the extensive waters of the river St. Croix and Bay of Fundy. Tonnage of Passamaquoddy bay, 10,712. *Cobscook Bay* and its tributary waters, on the west, give to Eastport a large trade in lumber. Moose Island contains 2,150 acres of rough land. It was first settled in 1780. In 1790 it contained only 244 inhabitants. There are now on the Island a handsome village, containing 60 wharves, 80 stores, 5 meeting-houses, a United States garrison, and 5,000 inhabitants.

East Windsor, Ct.

Hartford co. First settled 1680. Taken from Windsor, 1768. This is an excellent township of land. Its extensive meadows on the east side of Connecticut river are of uncommon fertility and beauty. Among the various agricultural products with which this town abounds, tobacco has been cultivated with success, and manufactured. It is said that 70,000 bushels of rye has been raised in a season. Scantic river, a considerable mill stream, passes through the north part of the town, and gives it the name of *Scantic*. The village of *Wapping* is in the S. E. section of the town. The principal street, about a mile back of the river, is the village, running the whole length of the town, wide, neatly built and beautifully shaded. East Windsor lies 8 miles N. from Hartford. Population, 1830, 2,129.

Eaton, N. H.,

Strafford co., lies 60 miles N. E. from Concord and 55 N. N. E. from Dover, and is bounded E. by Maine. Population, 1830, 1,432. The soil of the uplands, which are quite uneven, is moderately good, and the plains furnish excellent pine timber. There are several small ponds in this town. Eaton was granted Nov. 7, 1776, to Clement March and 65 others.

Eddington, Me.

Penobscot co. This town lies on the east side of Penobscot river, 6 miles above, and N. N. E. from Bangor, and 70 N. E. by E. from Augusta. The village is pleasantly situated at the "Bend" of the river. The soil of the town is good and well wooded. It produced, in 1837, 2,414 bushels of wheat. Population, 1837, 558.

Eden, Me.,

Hancock co., situated on the north part of the island of Mount Desert, and taken from the town of Mount Desert (which formerly comprised the whole island) 1795. First settled, 1763. Eden lies 92 miles E. from Augusta, and about 18 S. by E. from Ellsworth. Population, 1837, 1,024. The town has a good soil, good harbors, and possesses great advantages for the shore fishery. It is said that 500 bushels of cranberries have been picked in Eden in a season. Cranberry isles lie on the coast, about 3 miles south.

Eden, Vt.

Lamoille co. This township was granted to " Col. Seth Warner and his associates, our worthy friends, the officers and soldiers of his regiment in the line of the continental army," August 28, 1781. " Our friends," for their patriotic services, certainly deserved a better township than this, for it is mountainous, rocky and cold; it is however good for grazing, and produces some fine beef cattle and sheep. It is watered by Green river and Wild Branch. Several ponds in the town afford good fishing. Eden lies 30 miles N. from Montpelier, and is bounded S. by Hydepark. Population, 1830, 461.

NEW ENGLAND GAZETTEER.

Edgartown, Mass.

Dukes co. County town and port of entry on the island of Martha's Vineyard—91 miles S. E. from Boston, 20 N. W. by W. from Nantucket, 28 S. E. by E. from New Bedford, 20 S. from Falmouth, and 495 from Washington. First settled, 1641. Incorporated, 1671. Population, 1837, 1,625. Edgartown (Old Town) harbor is on the east side of the town, in lat. 41° 25′ N.; lon. 70° 25′ W. This township includes the fertile island of Chappequiddick, on the southeast, on which are some Indians. This island is 5 miles in length and 2 1-2 in breadth. It is very pleasant and forms Old Town harbor. Eight whale ships belong to this place, and a number of coasting vessels. This is said to be the only place in the state where *grouse* are native. The value of sperm oil imported, in the year ending April 1, 1837, was $65,598. The value of salt, oil casks, boats and hats manufactured the same year, was $7,260. The value of wool, the product of 2,150 sheep, was $1,590.

Edgecomb, Me.

Lincoln co. This town is bounded by Damariscotta river on the E. and Sheepscot river on the W., and lies nearly opposite to Wiscasset across the latter river. 26 miles S. S. E. from Augusta. Population, 1837, 1,282. This town enjoys great facilities for navigation, the fisheries, ship building and the lumber business. It is a place of considerable trade. First settled, 1744.

Edinburgh, Me.

Penobscot co. Incorporated, 1835. Population, 1837, 89. See "Down East."

Edmonds, Me.,

Washington co., situated between Cobscook bay and East Machias. Population, 1837, 205. See "Down East."

Effingham, N. H.

Strafford co. There are several mountains of considerable elevation in this town. The Ossipee river passes through the town, over which is a toll-bridge. Province pond lies between Effingham and Wakefield. Effingham was settled a few years prior to the revolution. It was then known by the name of *Leavitt's Town*. Incorporated, Aug. 18, 1778. Effingham borders W. on Ossipee lake and E. on Maine. It lies 58 miles N. E. from Concord and 25 N. E. by E. from Gilford. Population, 1830, 1,911.

Egremont, Mass.

Berkshire co. A mountainous township, watered by branches of Housatonick river. Incorporated, 1760. 140 miles W. from Boston and 15 S. S. W. from Lenox. Population, 1837, 968. The manufactures of Egremont consist of wheat flour, leather, boots, shoes, harnesses, stone, (sawed,) chairs and cabinet ware. Total amount in one year, $29,100. Value of 1,790 fleeces of wool, $2,770.

Elizabeth, Cape, Me.

This celebrated cape lies in the town of Cape Elizabeth, and forms the western limits of Casco bay. Near the point of the cape is a light-house, 50 feet in height, in N. lat. 43° 33′, W. lon. 70° 11′. For the *town* of CAPE ELIZABETH, see *Register*.

Elizabeth Islands, Mass.

These islands are attached to Dukes county, and lie between Buzzard's bay and Vineyard sound. They are 16 in number. The largest, Nashawn and Nashawenna, are inhabited. Gosnold, the discoverer of Cape Cod, spent the winter of 1602-3, on one of these islands.

Ellington, Ct.

Tolland co. Ellington was taken from East Windsor in 1786, and was that part of East Windsor called the *Great Marsh*. The soil is light and dry, but considerably fertile. It is generally level, but the eastern part is hilly and mountainous. Formerly the lands in this town were held in low estimation, but by the industry of the people in their cultivation they have risen in character and value. "The scenery in this town embraces considerable variety and is uncommonly interesting and beautiful." The " Ellington School" for boys, situated in a very neat village, is in high repute. Population, 1830, 1,455. Ellington lies 12 miles N. E. from Hartford, and is bounded S. E. by Tolland.

Elliot, Me.

York co. This town lies on the N. W. of Kittery of which it constituted a part until 1810. It adjoins Salmon Fall river on the S. W. by which it is separated from New Hampshire—and is bounded N. by South Berwick, and E. by York. It is a good farming town and probably contains as great a proportion of valuable tillage land as any in the county according to its size. Population, 1837, 1,859. Elliot is 108 miles S. W. from Augusta.

Elliotsville, Me.

Somerset co. This place is 81 miles from Augusta. See " Down East."

Ellis' Rivers.

Ellis' river, in *Maine*, is a tributary to the Androscoggin. It rises N. of Rumford, in the county of Oxford, and passes through that town. Ellis' river, in *New Hampshire*, rises on the E. side of the White mountains, in several small streams, near the sources of Peabody river, and separating into two streams which again unite, it falls into the Saco at Bartlett.

Elligo Pond, Vt.

This beautiful sheet of water, two miles in length and half a mile in breadth, lies partly in Craftsbury and partly in Greensborough, Orleans county: Its northern outlet passes to Black river; its southern to the Lamoille. There are two small islands in the lake. This was a favorite resort for the Indians, and now attracts numerous lovers of fine trout and delightful scenery to its borders.

Ellsworth, Me.

Chief town of Hancock co. This is a pleasant and flourishing town on both sides of Union river, at the head of navigation. The village is principally on the E. side, where there is a good bridge across the river, 3 miles above the entrance of the river into the waters connected with Blue Hill bay. The tide rises at the bridge 10 or 12 feet, and Ellsworth possesses an enviable position for maritime and inland trade. The location of the courts for this county was changed from Castine to this place in 1838. The court house is eligibly situated on the W. side of the river. Ellsworth is quite an agricultural township. It has a good soil, and considerable attention is given to the growth of wheat and wool. It lies 81 miles E. by N. from Augusta, and 30 N. E. by E. from Bangor. Population, 1830, 1,385—1837, 2,195.

Ellsworth, N. H.,

Grafton co., is 52 miles N. N. W. from Concord and 20 S. E. from Haverhill. Population, 1830, 234. It is a mountainous tract of territory. The most prominent elevation is Carr's mountain. A small stream issues from West Branch pond and runs into the Pemigewasset at Campton. The soil, though in some parts sterile, produces wheat, rye and corn. Maple sugar is made here, and clover seed is raised in considerable quantities. This town, formerly called *Trecothick*, was granted May 1, 1769, to Barlow Trecothick.

Elmore, Vt.

Lamoille co. First settled, 1790. Elmore lies 16 miles N. from Montpelier and 10 S. from Hydepark. Population, 1830, 442. There are five ponds in this town, the waters of which, the town being very high, descend partly to Lamoille and partly to Onion rivers. Some cattle and some wool are sent to market.

Embden, Me.

Somerset co. A fine township of land with two pleasant villages, on the W. side of Kennebec river. Seven Mile brook passes through the S. W. corner of the town.— Embden produced, in 1837, 6,400 bushels of wheat and considerable wool. Incorporated, 1804. Population, 1837, 1,048. It is 46 miles N. N. W. from Augusta and about 18 miles N. by W. from Norridgewock.

Enfield, Me.

Penobscot co. Incorporated, 1835. See "Down East."

Enfield, N. H.

Grafton co. Enfield comprises 24,060 acres, of which about 2,500 acres are water. It is 10 miles S. E. from Dartmouth College and 40 N. W. from Concord. Its surface is diversified with hills and valleys, and watered by a variety of ponds and streams, stored with fish of every species common to the country. Mascomy pond, which has acquired from travellers the appellation of Pleasant pond, is a beautiful collection of water, 4 miles in length and of various breadth, interspersed with islands and checkered with inlets. Its eastern banks are covered with trees; the hills gradually rise one above another for some distance. Along the western bank, between the pond and Mont Calm, within a few rods of the water, extends the turnpike road, the whole distance through a beautiful village, shaded to the N. on either side by a growth of trees. Mascomy river empties into this pond in the N. W. part. This pond is supposed to have once been much higher than it now is, and the plain and villages to the south are supposed to have been the bed of it. This fact is sufficiently evident from the ancient shore still remaining round the pond, about 30 feet above high water, and from logs having been frequently found 12 feet below the surface of the plain once flowed. On the W. bank, near the southern extremity, is the Shakers' settlement, situated on a fertile plain.— The structure of the buildings, tho' not lofty, are neat and convenient. They occupy about 1,000 acres of land, and their number consists of about 240. They are agriculturalists and mechanics. Garden seeds are grown, and wooden ware, whips, corn brooms, leather, and various other articles, are manufactured by them with peculiar neatness. See *Canterbury*.

Mountain pond, on the summit of Mont Calm, is 200 rods long, and 100 wide. At the outlets of the ponds are mills of various kinds. The town was formerly called *Relhan*, and was incorporated by charter, granted to Jedediah Dana and others, July 4th, 1761. Population, 1830, 1,492.

Enfield, Mass.

Hampshire co. Swift river passes through this town, and adds much to its beauty and importance.— The manufactures of this place, the year ending April 1, 1837, amounted to $182,669. The articles consisted of cotton and woolen goods, leather, boots, shoes, hats, hoes, shingle machines, palm-leaf hats, wool cards, cotton batting and wicking. The value of wool grown was $1,090. Enfield lies 71 miles W. from Boston, and 15 E. from Northampton. Population, 1837, 1,058.

Enfield, Ct.

Hartford co. This town was first settled, 1681, by emigrants from Salem, Mass.: it formerly belonged to Mass. and was a part of Springfield. The first bridge across Connecticut river was built in 1808, connecting Enfield with Suffield. The surface is generally level and the soil moist and fertile. The street, where most of the inhabitants reside, is very pleasant, wide and well shaded. The village near the river was commenced about 1831, at which the manufacture of carpeting is extensively pursued. About 120 looms are employed, making about 800 yards daily. The manufacture of ploughs is also an important pursuit in Enfield. It is watered by Scantick river. Population, 1830, 2,129. It is 18 miles N. from Hartford, and 8 S. from Springfield, Mass.

Englishman's Bay, Me.

This bay is a few miles W. of Machias bay, in Washington county. It receives the waters of Chandler's river, a considerable stream: it contains a number of islands, and furnishes many fine harbors Head harbor, an island off Jonesborough, is its western limits.

Enosburgh, Vt.

Franklin co. Missisque, Trout and other streams give this town excellent water privileges, and manufacturing establishments flourish. The surface of the town is pleasantly diversified by hills and valleys, and well adapted for grazing. The products of the town are cattle, butter, cheese and wool.— First settled, 1797. Population, 1830, 1,560. Enosburgh lies 43 miles N. by E. from Montpelier, and 20 N. E. from St. Albans.

Epping, N. H.,

Rockingham co., lies 29 miles S. E. from Concord, 20 W. from Portsmouth, and 8 N. W. from Exeter. It was formerly a part of Exeter, and was incorporated Feb. 12, 1741. The town contains 12,760 acres, being nearly 20 square miles. The soil, in general, is very good, and well suited to raise the various productions that grow in the state. Lamprey river, at the west, receives the Patuckaway, and runs through the whole length of the town. Another river runs through the N. part of the town, and from that circumstance is called North river. By observations taken at 6 in the forenoon, at 1 and 9 o'clock in the afternoon, from Fahrenheit's thermometer placed in the open air, 13 feet from the ground, and where the sun does not shine on the thermometer, the annual average of heat for 10 years in succession, was 44 1-12°. During that period the annual average of rain that fell, was 2 feet 10 inches, and of snow, 6 feet 7 inches.

WILLIAM PLUMER, one of its most distinguished and estimable citizens, resides in this town. A considerable portion of his life has been employed in the service of the people, in the several stations of representative and senator in the legislature, president of the senate, speaker of the house of representatives, representative and senator in congress, and for four years as chief-magistrate of the state. Population, 1830, 1,268.

Epsom, N. H.

Merrimack co. This town lies 12 miles E. from Concord. Population, 1830, 1,418. The surface of the town is generally uneven. The principal eminences are called M'Coy's, Fort, Nat's, and Nottingham mountains. The soil is in general good, and well adapted for grazing or grain. Great and Little Suncook are the only streams deserving the name of rivers. Here are three ponds, Chesnut, Round, and Odiorne's. Brown oxide, and sulphuret of iron are found, the latter most frequently in its decomposed state. Varieties of quartz, feldspar and schorl are also found. An alluvial deposite has been discovered, which has been ascertained to be terra de senna; it constitutes a very handsome and durable paint for cabinet work. Epsom was granted May 18, 1727, to Theodore Atkinson and others. Like all other frontier towns, Epsom was exposed, in its early settlement, to the Indians.

Maj. ANDREW M'CLARY, a native of this town, fell at the battle of Breed's Hill, June 17, 1775. Like the illustrious Roman, he left his plough on the news of the massacre at Lexington, and in the action when he lost his life displayed great coolness and bravery.

Errol, N. H.

Coos co. This town is situated on the W. of Umbagog lake. It contains about 35,000 acres, of which 2,500 are water. Several considerable streams here unite with the Androscoggin. Errol was granted Feb. 28, 1774, to Timothy Ruggles and others. Population, 1830, 32. It lies about 30 miles N. N. E. from Lancaster.

Erving, Mass.

Franklin co. This township remained unincorporated until April 17, 1838. Previously it had been known by the name of "Erving's Grant." It is bounded S. by Miller's and W. by Connecticut rivers. Erving contains some excellent land, and a great water power. The year previous to its incorporation, the manufactures of the town, consisting of satinet, boots, shoes, palm-leaf hats, &c., amounted to $35,185. Population, 1837, 292. Erving lies 95 miles N. N. W. from Boston, and 10 E. from Greenfield.

Essex County, Vt.

Guildhall is the county town. This county is bounded N. by Lower Canada, W. by the counties of Orleans and Caledonia, and S. and E. by Connecticut river. Area 680 square miles. This is considered the poorest county in the state; but although much of the land is hilly and mountainous, there is considerable good soil, and a large portion of it is well adapted for grazing. There were, in 1836, about 8,000 sheep in the county, and a considerable number of beef cattle and horses were sent to market. The principal streams are the Nulhegan, which is exclusively in Essex county;—the Passumpsic, Moose and Clyde. Incorporated, 1792. Population, 1820, 3,334; 1830, 3,981. About 6 inhabitants to a square mile.

Essex County, Mass.

Salem, Ipswich, and Newburyport are the shire towns. This county is bounded N. W. by Rockingham county, New Hampshire, S. W. by Middlesex county, E. and N. E. by the Atlantic ocean, and S. E. by Massachusetts bay. There is much good land in this county, but its surface is rocky and uneven. It has an extensive sea coast, indented with numerous bays, inlets, and capacious harbors. It is more densely populated than any county of its size in the United States. It has great wealth, and its commerce and fisheries are unrivalled by any section of country, of its extent, on the globe. Population, 1820, 73,930; 1830, 82,887, and in 1837, 93,689. This county comprises an area of 360 square miles;—the number of inhabitants to a square mile is 260. Essex county, although of stubborn soil, has many very delightful farms, and furnishes great quantities of hay and vegetables for market. It has many beautiful ponds and commanding elevations, and its seaboard is the delight of every beholder. However fruitful the citizens may have rendered the soil by their industry, this county is essentially a commercial and manufacturing section of New England. The tonnage of the five districts, in 1837, was 85,933 tons. The amount of manufactures, for the year ending April 1, 1837, was $10,216,300; and the amount of the whale, cod and mackerel fisheries, amounted to $1,378,144. The principal rivers in Essex county are the Merrimack and Shawsheen. Essex county was incorporated in 1643, and has given birth to some of the most distinguished merchants in the United States. Among many others may be mentioned WILLIAM GRAY, ISRAEL THORNDIKE, and WILLIAM PARSONS.

Essex, Vt.

Chittenden co. This town is finely watered by Onion river on the S. and Brown's river, a branch of the Lamoille, on the N. It is also watered by other smaller streams. At Hubbell's falls, on Onion river, are admirable mill sites, at which are manufactures of some extent. The surface of the town is level; a considerable portion of the soil is dry and somewhat sandy, but produces good crops of corn and rye. Along Onion river are some tracts of beautiful intervale. Essex was first settled in 1783. It lies 31 miles N. W. from Montpelier, and 8 N. N. E. from Burlington. Population, 1830, 1,664.

Essex, Mass.

Essex co. This town lies at the head of Chebacco river, running into Squam bay, 13 miles N. E. from Boston, and 5 miles S. E. from Ipswich, from which it was taken in 1819. Many vessels of 50 to 120 tons are built in this town, and many small vessels are employed in the coasting trade and the fisheries.—The manufactures of vessels, leather, boots, shoes, bar iron, barrels, cordage, pumps and blocks, in the year ending April 1, 1837, amounted to $102,271. The tonnage employed in the cod and mackerel fishery was 878 tons. Population, 1837, 1,402. Essex is a pleasant and flourishing town.

Etna, Me.

Penobscot co. This is an excellent farming town with no important streams. It lies 63 miles N. E. from Augusta, 17 W. from Bangor, and bounded by Dixmont on the S. Incorporated, 1820. Population, 1830, 362—1837, 626. Etna is fine wheat land: it produced, in 1837, 2,421 bushels.

Exeter, Me.

Penobscot co. Exeter is 65 miles N. N. E. from Augusta, and 25 S. W. from Bangor. It was incorporated in 1811. Population, 1830, 1,438— 1837, 1,920. At the "Four Corners," in the northerly part of the town, is a pleasant village with considerable trade and some mills. The people of Exeter in 1837, with a soil not above mediocrity, proved without effort, by raising 12,058 bushels of wheat, that the state of Maine is abundantly able, by means within itself, to supply the whole family of Yankees with bread stuffs, and have some to spare to their western brethren.

Exeter, N. H.

Rockingham co. This beautiful town lies 40 miles S. E. by E. from Concord and 14 S. W. from Portsmouth. The compact part of the town lies about the falls, which separate the fresh from the tide water of a branch of the Piscataqua, called by the natives Swamscot, and now known by the name of Exeter river. Above the falls this stream assumes the name of Great river, to distinguish it from one of it' smaller branches, called Little river. Great river has its source in Chester, whence it runs through several towns before it meets the tide water in the centre of Exeter. On this river are many valuable mill privileges.

The Exeter Cotton Manufacturing Company commenced operations April 1, 1830. Their principal building is of brick, 175 feet by 45. They have 5,000 spindles, employ 212 girls and 40 men and boys. They manufacture annually about 1,400,000 yards of sheeting. They consume about 1,200 bales of cotton, 300 cords of wood and 22,500 pounds of potatoe starch annually. They have a steam engine, 40 horse power, to operate when the water power fails. This probably consumes annually about 150 chaldrons of Sidney coal. The capital invested in lands, buildings, machinery, &c. is about $210,000.

A powder mill has been in operation about two years, and will manufacture from 130 to 150 tons of powder annually.

The manufacture of potatoe starch was commenced in 1824. The establishment has been twice burnt, but is rebuilt with brick, and starch is now manufactured from wheat as well as from potatoes. The amount of sales of starch and gum is about $10,000 annually.

In the westerly part of the town is a paper mill, which manufactures paper to the value of $20,000 annually. The manufacture of books, blank books, &c. in Exeter, is very extensive. About $100,000 value of shoes and boots are made annually, and a large amount of leather. There are also establishments for the manufacture of morocco leather, carriages, of various kinds, brushes, tin and pottery wares. The soil of Exeter is in general good, though comprehending every variety, from that of the best quality to the least productive. Like most towns in the state, it is essentially agricultural, and the improvement in the style of husbandry has been very great. The number of industrious and enterprising mechanics, to whom Exeter is indebted for her prosperity, is very rapidly increasing. See *Register.*

Phillips' academy, in Exeter, was founded by the liberal donations of John Phillips, LL. D., in 1781, who at his death, in 1795, bequeathed to the institution a large portion of his estate.

BENJAMIN ABBOTT, LL. D. has discharged the duties of principal with distinguished ability for more than fifty years. The building stands on a plain, near the centre of the town, and is well provided with accommodations for the different branches of instruction, and a large hall for declamation and the annual exhibitions.

The settlement of Exeter commenced in 1638, by John Wheelwright and others, who formed themselves into a body politic, chose their magistrates, and bound the people to obedience. Their laws were made in popular assemblies; and the combination thus entered into subsisted about three years. From 1675 to 1712, Exeter, like most of the early settlements, suffered from the attacks of the Indians.

Hon. SAMUEL TENNEY, M. D. was an original member of the N. H. Medical Society, its vice president several years, and a member of congress in 1800 and 1804.

Gen. NATHANIEL PEABODY was an original member of the N. H. medical society; was a member of the old congress; a senator of the N. H. legislature in 1792; and speaker of the house in 1793.

Hon. NICHOLAS GILMAN was a member of the old congress, and a senator in congress from 1805 to his death in 1814.

Gen. NATHANIEL FOLSOM was a member of the old congress, and a valuable revolutionary officer.

Hon. JEREMIAH SMITH, a native of Peterborough, was one of the first representatives to congress under the Federal government, was appointed Judge of S. C. of N. H. in 1802, was chief justice, and continued such till 1809, when he was elected governor. He was appointed chief justice of S. J. C. in 1813.

Hon. JOHN TAYLOR GILMAN, a descendant of one of the principal settlers at Exeter, was an active supporter of the revolution; a member of the old congress; filled at times the offices of representative and state treasurer; and for fourteen years, between 1794 and 1816, was governor of the state.

Exeter has at all periods of its history possessed eminent and useful men; and some of the first lawyers and jurists, antiquarians and scholars, have received their early education at its literary institution. Population, 1830, 2,759.

Exeter, R. I.

Washington co. This is an agricultural and manufacturing town, situated 24 miles S. W. from Providence, and from its centre about 10 miles N. W. from South Kingston. The town is very large, being 12 by 5 miles. The surface is much diversified by hills and valleys; the soil is a gravelly loam, and very productive of all the varieties common to the climate. The products of the dairy are considerable.—Branches of Wood river give this town a good water power, which is well improved by cotton mills and other manufactories. Exeter was incorporated in 1743. Population, 1830, 2,383.

Fairfax, Vt.

Franklin co. Bounded S. by Lamoille river: 37 miles N. W. from Montpelier, and 12 S. E. from St. Albans. First settled, 1763. Population, 1830, 1,729. By Parmelee's and Stone's brooks, Brown's river, and the Lamoille, this town enjoys a good water power. The falls on Lamoille river, at this place, are singular and worthy of the traveller's notice. The land is generally level and of a good quality. A considerable amount of agricultural products is sent to market, and about 6,000 sheep are reared. There are some manufactures at the falls. Fairfax is a place of considerable business.

Fairfield, Me.

Somerset co. This beautiful township is located on the W. side of Kennebec river, and S. of Bloomfield. Fairfield is the most southern township in the county. It is watered by a small stream running into the Kennebec, and by a branch of Waterville river. This town is favored with a fine soil, and navigable privileges to Augusta. It has a pleasant village, considerable trade, and, in 1837, produced 11,531 bushels of wheat, and a large quantity of wool. Population, 1837, 2,203. Distant from Augusta, 26 miles N., and from Norridgewock, 19 S. E. Incorporated, 1788.

Fairfield, Vt.

Franklin co. This town was first settled in 1739. It is well watered by Smithfield pond, Fairfield river, Black creek, and branches of Missisque river, and abounds in mill sites. Fairfield has a good strong soil and generally suitable for cultivation. It is a pleasant place, with some trade and considerable manufactures. It produces good beef cattle and horses, and pastures about 7,000 sheep. Population, 1830, 2,270. Fairfield lies 45 miles N. W. from Montpelier, 27 N. N. E. from Burlington, and is bounded W. by St. Albans.

Fairfield County, Ct.

Fairfield and *Danbury* are the shire towns. This county is bounded N. by Litchfield county, N. E. and E. by Housatonick river, S. E. and S. by Long Island Sound, and

W. by the state of New York. This is a fine farming section of country, agreeably diversified in regard to surface, with a strong fertile soil, and possesses great natural agricultural resources. Fairfield county extends nearly 40 miles on Long Island Sound, and enjoys great facilities for navigation and the fisheries. The beautiful Housatonick washes its northeastern boundary, and the Saugatuck, Norwalk, Mill, Pequonuck and other rivers afford it an ample water power. The manufacturing interests of the county are valuable and increasing. It contains many villages of superior beauty, and abounds in scenery of an interesting character. First settled, 1639. Area, 630 square miles. Population, 1820, 42,739; 1830, 46,950; 75 inhabitants to a square mile. In 1837 there were in this county about 22,000 sheep.

Fairfield, Ct.

Shire town, Fairfield co. This ancient and patriotic town comprises three parishes, *Fairfield*, the seat of justice, *Green's Farms* and *Greenfield*. Fairfield lies 21 miles S. W. from New Haven, and 58 N. E. from New York. Population, 1830, 4,246. Its Indian name was *Unquowa*. The surface of the town is undulating and very pleasant. The soil is fertile, well cultivated and productive of wheat and rye, and a great variety of fruits and vegetables for New York market. Black Rock harbor is safe and easy of entrance for vessels drawing 19 feet of water at common tides. The tide usually rises in Long Island Sound about 5 feet. There is but little water power in Fairfield, except that produced by the tide. The tonnage of Fairfield district, in 1837, was 11,988 tons. The principal business in navigation is the coasting trade.

In the year 1637, the tract of country which now forms the town of Fairfield was discovered by captain Mason and the troops of Massachusetts and Connecticut under his command, when they pursued the Pequots to the swamp in this town, bearing the name of " Pequot Swamp." This is the spot made memorable by the great fight that took place there, between those troops and the Pequots, terminating in the almost entire destruction of that once powerful and warlike nation of savages. There are no Indian marks left by which this swamp can be traced as the place of their extermination, except a mound of earth in the centre of it, considered as a place of safety, evidently the effect of art, with a raised foot path leading from it to the surrounding high grounds. In that expedition this region attracted the notice of adventurers. In the year 1639 a few families removed hither from Windsor, commenced a settlement, and, in a short period afterwards, were joined by several persons from Watertown and Concord, Mass. After Connecticut obtained her charter, the general assembly granted these people a patent, then including the towns now Reading and Weston.

Fairfield is distinguished for its ardent attachment to American liberty, and for its sacrifices during the contest for independence. In 1779, when Tryon, a British governor, demanded a surrender of the town, under a threat of its destruction, the answer of the inhabitants was, " We will never voluntarily lay down our arms till we have obtained the object for which they have been taken up. The village is in your power; plunder and burn it if you will, and take along with your plunder the infamy of which it cannot be divested."

" On the 7th July, 1779, governor Tryon, with a large and vengeful army, sailed from New Haven to Fairfield; and the next morning disembarked upon the beach. A few militia assembled to oppose them; and, in a desultory, scattered manner, fought with great intrepidity through most of the day. They killed some; took several prisoners; and wounded more. But the expedition was so sudden and unexpected, that the efforts, made in this manner, were necessarily fruitless. The town was plundered; a great part of the houses, together with the two churches, the court house, jail, and school houses, were burnt. The barns had been just filled with wheat, and other produce. The inhabitants, therefore, were turned out into the world, almost literally destitute.

"While the town was in flames, a thunder storm overspread the heavens, just as night came on. The conflagration of near two hundred houses illumined the earth, the skirts of the clouds, and the waves of the Sound, with an union of gloom and grandeur, at once inexpressibly awful and magnificent. The sky speedily was hung with the deepest darkness, wherever the clouds were not tinged by the melancholy lustre of the flames. At intervals the lightnings blazed with a livid and terrible splendor. The thunder rolled above. Beneath, the roaring of the fires filled up the intervals with a deep and hollow sound, which seemed to be the protracted murmur of the thunder, reverberated from one end of heaven to the other. Add to this convulsion of the elements, and these dreadful effects of vindictive and wanton devastation, the trembling of the earth; the sharp sound of muskets, occasionally discharged; the groans, here and there, of the wounded and dying; and the shouts of triumph: then place before your eyes crowds of the miserable sufferers, mingled with bodies of the militia, and from the neighboring hills taking a farewell prospect of their property and their dwellings, their happiness and their hopes; and you will form a just but imperfect picture of the burning of Fairfield. It needed no great effort of imagination to believe that the final day had arrived; and that amid this funeral darkness, the morning would speedily dawn, to which no night would ever succeed; the graves yield up their inhabitants; and the trial commence, at which was to be finally settled the destiny of man.

"The next morning the troops re-embarked; and, proceeding to Green's Farms, set fire to the church, and consumed it; together with fifteen dwelling houses, eleven barns, and several stores."

Fairhaven, Vt.

Rutland co. First settled, 1779. Population, 1830, 675. The soil is generally productive, particularly along the banks of the streams. It is watered by Castleton and Poultney rivers, the former of which receives the waters of lake Bombazine, a large pond between Fairhaven and Castleton. On these streams are considerable falls, and mill sites. Fairhaven lies 16 miles W. from Rutland, and 9 N. E. from Whitehall, N. Y.

Fairhaven, Mass.

Bristol co. This pleasant town was taken from New Bedford, in 1812. It lies across Acushnett river, about a mile east of New Bedford. It is united to New Bedford by a bridge 3,960 feet in length, and is associated with it in many of its enterprises. First settled, 1764. Population, 1830, 3,034; 1837, 3,649. There are 37 vessels belonging to this place engaged in the whale fishery, the tonnage of which is 11,564 tons. The value of whale oil and bone imported into this place the year ending April 1, 1837, was $322,272. The number of hands employed in the fishery was 945. Capital invested, $957,000. The Acushnett produces some water power, on which are two cotton mills, a paper mill, and other operations by water. The value of cotton goods, leather, boots, shoes, tin ware, vessels, salt, wooden ware, chairs and cabinet ware manufactured, amounted to $40,363.

Fairlee, Vt.

Orange co. A rough and mountainous township, with very little productive land, on the west side of Connecticut river, and connected with Orford, N. H. by a bridge across that river. First settled, 1768. Population, 1830, 656. This town lies about 17 miles E. S. E. from Chelsea, and 31 S. E. from Montpelier.

Fairlee pond is two miles in length and about three fourths of a mile wide. It formerly had no fish. Some years ago a gentleman placed some pickerel in it, and the legislature passed a law protecting the fish from molestation for two years. Since that time the pond has had an abundance of pickerel of good size and quality.

Fall River, Mass.

Bristol co. This town took the name of *Troy*, in 1803. It was formerly a part of Freetown. In 1834, the name was changed to that of the river within its borders, at the union of which and Taunton river the town is very pleasantly situated. This town is without a parallel on the continent of America, in regard to the union of hydraulic powers and navigable facilities. Fall river rises in Wattuppa ponds; one of which is 11 miles in length and 1 in breadth. These ponds are produced by perpetual springs, and lie about two miles east of the town. The descent of this river is 136 feet. The volume of water is constant, not liable to excess, and of sufficient power for the largest manufactories.

The harbor on Taunton river is safe and easy of access, and of sufficient depth of water for the largest ships. Six ships from this port are engaged in the whale fishery. It has also some merchant and coasting vessels. A marine rail-way was constructed here in 1834.

This town has an abundance of fine granite, equal to the Quincy. A rail-road is in progress to meet the Boston and Providence, at Seekonk, 13 miles.

The *Pocasset Hotel*, belonging to a company of gentlemen, is a splendid building, constructed in 1833. No house in the country affords better accommodations. A regular steamboat line is established between this place and Providence:—distance, by water, 28 miles.

The value of the manufactures of Fall River for the, year ending April 1, 1837, amounted to $2,863,378, exclusive of large manufactures of machinery, iron hoops and rods, stoves, brass, copper, and tin wares. The ten cotton mills produced 7,767,614 yards of cloth, valued at $668,028. The woolen mill produced 150,000 yards of cloth, valued at $180,000. The other articles manufactured consisted of leather, boots, shoes, iron castings, hats, nails, chairs, cabinet ware and vessels. The two print works printed twelve million yards of calico. The number of hands employed in all the factories was 1,819. The product of the whale fishery, the same year, was $68,700. Hands employed in the fishery, 120.

Fall River lies 49 miles S. from Boston, 17 S. from Taunton, 14 W. from New Bedford, 18 S. E. from Providence, R. I. and 190 E. from New York. Population, in 1820, 1,594; 1830, 4,159; 1837, 6,352.—The surface of Fall River is elevated, rough and uneven, and considered a healthy location for a manufacturing town.

Falmouth, Me.

Cumberland co. This is a pleasant town at the head of Casco bay,

6 miles N. from Portland, and 47 S. W. from Augusta. It is watered by Presumscut river, and has a number of vessels employed in coasting and fishing. The soil on the whole coast of Maine is not so fertile as in the interior parts of the state, yet Falmouth comprises a considerable quantity of good land. The town was incorporated as early as 1718, and included the territory of the city of Portland until 1786. Population, 1837, 2,068.

Falmouth, Mass.

Barnstable co. A pleasant town on Vineyard Sound. There are belonging to this town 9 whale-ships, and about 40 sail in the coasting trade and fishery. Two streams afford a water power, on which are two woolen mills and other manufactories. There are about 40 ponds in this town, some salt and some fresh:—these, with the views of the islands in the Sound, form a variety of agreeable scenery. "Wood's Hole" harbor, at the S. W. extremity of the town, is a good harbor and much frequented by vessels, and by invalids in search of health. The value of oil imported into Falmouth, the year ending April 1, 1837, amounted to $146,600. The value of vessels, salt, woolen goods, boots, shoes and leather, manufactured the same year, was $58,657. Falmouth lies 71 miles S. E. by E. from Boston, and 22 S. W. from Barnstable. "Woods' Hole" is 4 miles W. from the centre of the town; and "Holmes' Hole" harbor, on Martha's Vineyard, is 6 miles S. Population, 1837, 2,580. Incorporated, 1686.

Farmington, Me.

County town of Franklin co. This very beautiful town lies 29 miles N. W. from Augusta, and is watered by Sandy and Little Norridgewock rivers. At the union of these rivers are excellent mill privileges, and a delightful village, the seat of justice. Farther up the Sandy, about 5 miles, is another beautiful village, the seat of a flourishing academy. The soil of Farmington being of a superior quality, the inhabitants are induced to devote much attention to agricultural pursuits; yet it is a place of some manufactures, and considerable trade in lumber and other merchandize. The agricultural products of Farmington are various and valuable. In 1837 it produced 12,406 bushels of as good wheat as ever grew on the banks of the Ohio. Incorporated, 1794. Population, 1837, 2,507.

Farmington, N. H.,

Strafford co., was formerly a part of Rochester, but was incorporated as a distinct town, Dec. 1, 1798. It lies 36 miles E. N. E. from Concord, and 17 N. W. by N. from Dover. The Cocheco meanders through the N. E. part of the town. The Blue hills or Frost mountains extend nearly through the town under different names. From the summit of the ridge in the S. E. part, ships may be seen by the naked eye off Portsmouth harbor; while to the N. and W. the White Hills and the Monadnock, with hundreds of smaller mountains, meet the eye of the beholder. There is, not far from the village in Farmington, a rock supposed to weigh from 60 to 80 tons, so exactly poised on other rocks, that it may be caused to vibrate several inches by the hand. At the bank of the Cocheco, a little more than a mile S. E. from the principal village, is a place called the *Dock*, so named from the circumstance that the first settlers usually deposited their lumber here to be floated down the river. This name is some times ignorantly applied to the village.

Hon. AARON WINGATE, for many years a member of the legislature, a counsellor from 1797 to 1803, and for sometime chief-justice of the common pleas in Strafford, died here in 1822, aged 78 years. Population, 1830, 1,465.

Farmington, Ct.

Hartford co. The first settlers of this town were from Hartford, being emigrants from the neighborhood of Boston, Mass. They located themselves, in 1640, on the luxuriant meadows of the Tunxis, or Farmington river, 10 miles W. from Hartford. The township was purchased of the Tunxis Indians, a numerous and warlike tribe. At its incorporation, in 1645, the township comprised fifteen miles square; since which the pleasant towns of Southington, Berlin, Bristol, Burlington and Avon have been taken from the original territory of Farmington.

Farmington river rises in the high lands in the N. part of Litchfield county, and after meandering delightfully through the towns of New Hartford and Burlington, in a S. E. direction, it changes its course at Farmington to the N., and passing Avon and Simsbury to the border of Granby, it again turns abruptly to the E. and meets the Connecticut at Windsor. This is a beautiful and fertilizing stream, and gives to the towns through which it passes, but particularly to Farmington, large tracts of rich alluvial meadows.

Farmington village is a delightful place, on an elevated plain, surrounded by high hills. The street is about two miles in length, beautifully shaded, and contains, besides two churches and an academy, about 100 neat dwelling houses, some of which are tasteful and elegant. The Farmington canal passes through the village.

Round Hill, in the meadows, near the village, is a natural curiosity. It rises abruptly, to the height of 60 feet, is nearly circular in its form and covers 12 acres. It is thought that this hill was formerly an island in the centre of a lake, which covered the whole of the present meadows. The population of Farmington has varied but little from 2,000 within the last 30 years.

Fayette, Me.

Kennebec co. This town contains some beautiful ponds and is the source of a branch of Sandy river. It lies 17 miles W. N. W. from Augusta, and is bounded E. by Readfield. Incorporated, 1795.— Population, 1837, 1,006. This is a good township of land; it produced, in 1837, 4,438 bushels of wheat and some wool.

Fayston, Vt.

Washington co. Fayston is generally too mountainous to be much cultivated. Along the borders of some of the branches of Mad river, which rise here, is some arable land. It lies 16 miles W. S. W. from Montpelier, and 25 S. E. from Burlington. First settled, 1798. Population, 1830, 458.

Ferdinand, Vt.

Essex co. This town was chartered in 1761, and contains 23 square miles; it is bounded S. E. by Maidstone. Paul's stream affords it a good water power, but the land is so mountainous, rocky, cold and swampy that people do not choose to cultivate it.

Ferrisburgh, Vt.

Addison co. This township possesses a good soil, an excellent water power by Otter, Little Otter, and Lewis creeks; and navigable privileges on the waters of the outlets of those creeks and lake Champlain. Basin Harbor in this town is deep and well protected from winds, and is a place of considerable navigation and commercial importance. Across the lake to Essex, N. Y. is about two miles. Large crops of grain are produced here, and Ferrisburgh is noted for its fine butter, cheese, pork, and fat cattle.

There are some woolen and other manufactures on its streams, and about 10,000 sheep graze in its pastures. Large quantities of fish are annually taken in the season of spring. First settled, 1784. Population, 1830, 1,822. Ferrisburgh lies 19 miles S. from Burlington, 16 N. W. from Middlebury, and 34 W. from Montpelier.

Fitchburgh, Mass.

Worcester co. This township was first granted by "the Great and General Court of His Majesty's Province of Massachusetts Bay, Nov. 4, 1719." The township thus granted included the territory of some of the neighboring towns. The town was incorporated in 1764. A large branch of the Nashua and two smaller streams pass through the town, and afford it an extensive and constant water power. Over the Nashua, in the distance of two miles, are eleven dams for the accommodation of manufactories. This is a very flourishing town, and exhibits in a striking manner the effect of water power on the increase, wealth and respectability of many of our interior towns. There are many valuable mill sites at this place still unimproved. In the immediate vicinity of the principal village is an immense quarry of excellent granite. This town lies 47 miles W. N. W. from Boston, 24 N. from Worcester, 30 W. by S. from Lowell, and 60 N. E. from Springfield. There are in Fitchburgh 4 cotton, 3 woolen, and 2 paper mills. The manufactures for the year ending April 1, 1837, amounted to $429,640. The manufactures consisted of cotton and woolen goods, paper, leather, boots, shoes, hats, scythes, bellows, palm-leaf hats, straw bonnets, chairs, tin and cabinet wares. The surface of the town is hilly, but the soil is strong and productive. Population, 1830, 2,169; 1837, 2,662.

Fitzwilliam, N. H.

Cheshire co. Fitzwilliam lies 13 miles S. E. from Keene, 60 S. W. from Concord, and 65 N. W. from Boston. Camp and Priest brooks, running in a S. direction, are the principal streams. South pond, 230 rods long and of various width, Sip's pond, 200 rods long and 100 wide; Rockwood's pond and Collin's pond, are the only natural collections of water. The surface of this town is hilly: the soil is rocky. There is a considerable quantity of very productive and highly valuable meadow land. The soil is suitable for grazing and tillage. Beef, pork, butter and cheese are the staples. The farmers have of late turned their attention to the raising of sheep. Near the centre of the town is a large hill, remarkable for the beautifully romantic prospect it affords. Gap mountain, which at a distance, appears to be a part of the Monadnock, and on which are found various kinds of stones suitable for whetstones, lies partly in Troy and partly in the N. E. part of Fitzwilliam. Population, 1830, 1,229.

Fletcher, Vt.

Franklin co. There are some small streams in this town and some manufacturing operations. The soil is broken, hard, and not very productive. It lies 22 miles N. N. E from Montpelier, and about 18 S. E from St. Albans. Population, 1830, 793.

Florida, Mass.

Berkshire co. A mountainous township, 125 miles W. by N. from Boston, 27 N. N. E. from Lenox, and 7 E. from Adams. Florida is watered by Deerfield river, and exhibits some fine Alpine scenery. Population, 1837, 457. Inc. 1805.

Foster, R. I.

Providence co. This is a large agricultural and manufacturing town, finely watered by Hemlock brook, Ponongansett and Moosup rivers. The surface of the town, in many parts, is rough and uneven, but the soil is well calculated for the productions of the dairy. In the western part are extensive forests of valuable timber. There are a number of pleasant villages on the borders of the numerous streams, most of which are largely engaged in manufacturing operations, particularly of cotton. Foster was first settled in 1717; incorporated in 1781, and named in compliment to the Hon. THEODORE FOSTER, formerly a senator of the United States. It lies 15 miles W. by S. from Providence, and 50 E. from Hartford, Ct. Population, 1830, 2,672.

Foxborough, Mass.

Norfolk co. This town was taken from Dorchester in 1778. It is watered by Rumford and Cocasset rivers, branches of the Taunton, on which are mills of various kinds. The manufactures of Foxborough the year ending April 1, 1837, amounted to $231,136:—they consisted of cotton and woolen goods, boots, shoes, leather, iron castings, straw bonnets, shovels, spades, hoes and forks. Foxborough lies 24 miles S. S.W. from Boston,15 S. from Dedham, and 18 E. N. E. from Providence, R. I. Population, 1830, 1,099; 1837, 1,416.

Foxcroft, Me.

Piscataquis co. This town is situated on the north side of Piscataquis river, opposite to Dover. The soil of the town is capable of producing all the varieties common to the climate. A part of Sebec pond lies in the north part of the town. In 1837, 5,574 bushels of wheat was raised. This is a fine section of country for the growth of beef and wool. Foxcroft was first settled in 1805, and was named in compliment to the Hon. Joseph E. Foxcroft. The village, with an academy, is very pleasantly located on the bank of the river, and has the appearance of prosperity. Foxcroft lies 77 miles N. N. E. from Augusta.—Population, 1830, 677; 1837, 907. Incorporated, 1812.

Fox Islands, Me.

See *Vinalhaven*.

Framingham, Mass.

Middlesex co. A large and flourishing manufacturing town, with a fine soil, and pleasant ponds:—20 miles W. S. W. from Boston, and 13 S. S. W. from Concord. The ponds and Sudbury river give this town a good water power. The value of the manufactures, the year ending April 1, 1837, amounted to $421,111. The articles manufactured were 268,640 yards of woolen cloth, valued at $311,800; boots, shoes, leather, hats, paper,($46,000) straw bonnets, chairs, tin and cabinet wares. Framingham is a delightful town, and approached by the rail-road with great ease. It has become an agreeable resort for fishing, fowling and other rural sports. Incorporated, 1700. Population, in 1830, 2,313 ; 1837, 2,881.

Francestown, N. H.

Hillsborough co. It is 12 miles N. W. from Amherst, and 27 S. W. from Concord. The two S. branches of the Piscataquog rise in this town; the largest branch from Pleasant pond, the other from Haunted pond. The former branch passes near the village in Francestown. Pleasant and Haunted ponds are considerable collections of water. The land is uneven, and in many parts stony, but the qualities of the soil are warm and moist. There are some small intervales, which are very productive. About 7,000 sheep are kept here. The streams of water are not large, and almost every mill is situated on rivers that take their rise from hills and ponds within the limits of the town. The highest land is Crotched mountain, the summit of which is more than 600 feet above the level of the common in the centre of the town. One of the summits of this mountain is covered with wood; the other is almost a solid ledge of rocks, affording a very extensive prospect to the S. W. There is in the easterly part of this town a very extensive and valuable quarry of freestone. It is of a dark greyish color, and when polished strongly resembles the variegated marble of Vermont. In the N. part of this town black lead has been found of a good quality—and in the S. part some beautiful specimens of rock crystal. The common garnet is met with in various places. On the N. side of Haunted pond, there is a bar of 20 rods in length, 6 feet high, and 3 or 4 feet through; but for what purpose or by what means this barrier was raised, is a matter of conjecture only. The local situation of this town is very eligible for business, being near the centre of the county, and on the great thoroughfare from Windsor to Boston, and on a leading road from the S. W. part of the state to Concord. The village is very pleasant, neatly built and flourishing. Francestown derived its name from *Frances*, the wife of the last Gov. Wentworth. The first settlement was made about 1760, by John Carson, a Scotchman.

Mr. JAMES WOODBURY, who died March 3, 1823, at the age of 85, closed his life in this town. He was an active soldier in the old French war, and engaged by the side of Gen. Wolfe, when he was killed at the memorable siege of Quebec. He was one of the truly invincible *rangers* under the immortal Stark, and discharged every duty in a prompt and courageous manner. Population, 1830, 1541.

Franconia, N. H.

Grafton co. It is 28 miles N. E. from Haverhill, and 74 N. from Concord. A large proportion of this town is mountainous. Its streams are branches of the Lower Amonoosuck river, and rise on the mountainous tracts to the east. Here are several ponds: one of which, called Ferrin's pond, is the source of the middle branch of Pemigewasset river. The mountains adjoining the Notch, through which the road passes, are most conspicuous. These are called Mounts La Fayette and Jackson. On the latter is the celebrated "Profile," or "Old Man of the Mountain." It is situated on a peak of solid rock, 1,000 feet in height and almost perpendicular. On this peak, nature, in her wildest mood, exhibits the profile of the human face, of which every feature is delineated with wonderful exactness. The Franconia mountain pass presents to the traveller some of the wildest scenery in our country, and must ever remain a great thoroughfare between the upper waters of the Connecticut river and the ocean.

There are two iron establishments in this town. The lower works are situated on the S. branch of Amonoosuck river, and are owned by the New Hampshire Iron Factory Company; incorporated, Dec. 18, 1805, which was composed principally of gentlemen in Salem and Boston. Their establishment is very extensive, consisting of a blast furnace, erected in 1808, an air furnace, a forge and trip-hammer shop. There are also near, or connected with the establishment, grain and saw-mills, a large store, several shops, and other buildings, which make a small village. The ore is obtained from a mountain in the east part of Lisbon, N. H., three miles from the furnace, and is considered the richest in the United States, yielding from 56 to 63 per cent; and the mine is said to be inexhaustible. First settled, 1774. Population, 1830, 447.

NEW ENGLAND GAZETTEER.

Frankfort, Me.

Waldo co. This excellent township of land is situated on the W. side of Penobscot river, 57 miles N. E. by E. from Augusta, 12 S. from Bangor, and 18 N. from Belfast. It is well watered by Marsh river, on which are two beautiful villages. The largest village is near the Penobscot, on Marsh bay. The other village is at the head of the tide, on Marsh river, about 4 miles S. W. from the Penobscot, and is accommodated with excellent mill privileges. The location of Frankfort is exceeding favorable to the navigation and trade of Penobscot river, particularly so in the winter season, as it is the highest point on the river to which vessels can ascend during the icy season of the year. The prospects of Frankfort in its commercial and agricultural pursuits are very promising: indeed it bids fair to become an important depot on one of our largest rivers. Among the agricultural products of this town, in 1837, was 9,330 bushels of wheat. Population, 1830, 2,487; 1837, 3,223. Incorporated, 1789.

Franklin County, Me.

Farmington is the county town. This county was incorporated March 20, 1838.

The following is the legislative description of its territory:

"The towns of New Sharon, Chesterville, Wilton, Temple and Farmington in the county of Kennebec; and Jay, Carthage, Weld, Berlin, Madrid, townships numbered six, letter E. and D. in the county of Oxford, thence extending northerly from the north-west corner of letter D. on the line betwixt townships numbered three and four, through the several ranges of townships to Canada line, so as to include three tiers of townships west of the west line of the Bingham Purchase in said county of Oxford; and Industry, New Vineyard, Strong, Avon, Phillips, Freeman, Salem, Kingfield, townships numbered four in the first range west of Kingfield, three and four in the second range, and the south half of township numbered four in the third range of the Bingham Purchase, in the county of Somerset, be and hereby are, &c."

This county is therefore bounded N. by Lower Canada, E. by the county of Somerset, S. by Kennebec and Oxford counties, and W. by Oxford county. This county has no navigable waters, but is interspersed with numerous ponds and mill streams. Its surface is generally undulating, with some mountainous tracts. Its soil, for the most part, is excellent, and cannot fail in remunerating the industrious farmer by its products of wheat, beef, and wool.

Franklin County, Vt.

St. Albans, county town. This county is bounded N. by Lower Canada, E. by Orleans county, S. E. and S. by Lamoille county, S. by Chittenden county, and W. by lake Champlain. Incorporated, 1792. Population, 1830, 22,034. The Missisque river passes through the northern part of the county, and the Lamoille its most southern section. The principal part of the trade of this county goes to Canada, by lake Champlain, which affords it many facilities in transportation. Although the surface is somewhat broken and in some parts mountainous, yet the soil is productive of wheat and grass. Many cattle are annually taken from this county to market, and in 1837 it had 63,000 sheep. In this county, marble and iron ore of excellent qualities are found.

Franklin County, Mass.

Greenfield, county town. Bounded N. by Windham county, Vt., and a part of Cheshire county, N. H.

E. by Worcester county, S. by Hampshire county, and W. by Berkshire county. Area, 650 square miles. The Connecticut river passes nearly through the centre of this county. It produces, in great abundance, all sorts of grain, fruits and vegetables common to its climate; and exports considerable quantities of beef, pork, and products of the dairy. Manufactures are increasing in value and importance; and this county yields to no other in the state in the extent of its hydraulic powers, or in the richness and variety of its scenery. There are 44 inhabitants to a square mile. Chief rivers, Connecticut, Deerfield, and Miller's. Taken from Hampshire county in 1811. Population, 1820, 29,268; 1830, 29,344; 1837, 28,655. The value of the manufactures of this county, for the year ending April 1, 1837, was $787,900. The value of wool grown, the product of 55,713 fleeces, was $70,513.

Franklin, Me.

Hancock co. Franklin lies at the head of Taunton bay, the most northerly waters of Frenchman's bay. It is bounded S. by Sullivan, and contains several large ponds and good mill sites. Franklin is about 15 miles E. from Ellsworth. Population, 1837, 474. Incorporated, 1825.

Franklin, N. H.

Merrimack co. This town was incorporated in 1828, from parts of the towns of Salisbury, Andover, Sanbornton, and Northfield: is 18 miles from Concord, 63 from Portsmouth, and 78 from Boston. Franklin is a place of considerable and increasing business: has a cotton factory, two paper mills, an iron foundry, and other manufacturing establishments. The junction of the Winnepisiogee and Pemigewasset rivers, in this town, form the noble Merrimack, creating on both streams an extensive and valuable water power. It is probable that within a few years the river will be rendered navigable, by means of locks and canals, as far up as Franklin, in which event it would become one of the most flourishing interior towns in New Hampshire. Population, in 1830, 1,370.

Franklin, Vt.

Franklin co. This town was formerly called Huntsburgh, and was first settled in 1789. It lies 50 miles N. W. from Montpelier, 17 N. N. E. from St. Albans, and bounded N. by Canada. The surface of the town is rough, but the soil is tolerably well adapted for sheep, of which about 3,500 are kept. Population, 1830, 1,129.

Franklin, Mass.

Norfolk co. Charles river and its branches afford Franklin a good water power. It was taken from Wrentham in 1778. There are five cotton mills in the town, and manufactures of straw bonnets, shoes, boots, boxes and boats; total amount of manufactures in one year, $210,472, of which $160,186 were for straw bonnets, for which this town is celebrated. Franklin lies 27 miles S. W. by S. from Boston, and 17 S. S. W. from Dedham. Population, 1837, 1,696.

Franklin, Ct.

New London co. Shetucket river separates this town from Lisbon. The surface of Franklin is uneven; the soil a gravelly loam, more fit for grazing than tillage. There is a woolen factory on Beaver brook, a branch of the Shetucket, but the chief business of the people is rearing sheep, and other agricultural pursuits. Population, 1830, 1,194. It lies 34 miles E. S. E. from Hartford, and 7 N. by W. from Norwich. Franklin was taken from Norwich in 1786.

Freedom, Me.

Waldo co. Previous to its incorporation, in 1813, the territory of Freedom was called "Beaver Hill." It was first settled in 1794. It is a good township of land, and bounded W. by Albion, and E. by Knox. It is about 20 miles E. S. E. from Belfast, and 25 N. E. from Augusta. Freedom, in 1837, with a population of 1,058, produced 6,084 bushels of wheat.

Freedom, N. H.

Strafford co. This town, formerly *North Effingham*, was incorporated by its present name, Dec. 6, 1832. It is an uneven township, but has some good farms. It is bounded in part by the Ossipee lake, and river, which discharge eastwardly into the Saco. Distant 60 miles N. N. E. from Concord. Population, in 1833, about 900.

Freeman, Me.

Franklin co. This small town of only 17,000 acres, most of which is woodland, with a population of 805, produced 6,485 bushels of wheat in 1837. Freeman is the source of a small branch of Sandy river. It lies 62 miles N. W. from Augusta, and 15 N. from Farmington.

Freeport, Me.

Cumberland co. This is a respectable town with a pleasant village, and small harbor at the head of Casco bay, on the road from Portland to Brunswick, 18 miles N. by E. from the former, 9 S. W. from the latter, and 36 S. S. W. from Augusta. Freeport was taken from North Yarmouth in 1789, and was formerly called the *Harraseeket Settlement*, from the name of the river that passes through it. This is a place of some navigation, ship building, and agricultural enterprize. Population, 1837, 2,659.

Freetown, Mass.

Bristol co. This town lies on the E. side of Taunton river, 8 miles S. from Taunton, 12 N. by W. from New Bedford, and 40 S. from Boston. First settled, 1659. Incorporated, 1683. Population, 1837, 1,779. It is watered by a branch of Taunton river, and has some navigation. The manufactures of Freetown consist of iron castings, cutlery, axes, shovels, spades, hoes, forks, nails, leather, boots, shoes, vessels, chairs, and cabinet ware. Total amount, in one year, $43,820. The soil is light, and keeps, among other cattle, about 1,000 sheep.

French River.

This river rises in Leicester, Mass. It passes through Auburn, Oxford, and Dudley; it then enters the state of Connecticut and joins the Quinebaugh at Thompson. Some French protestants settled on this river in 1685.

Frenchman's Bay, Me.

This important bay, in the county of Hancock, containing a number of excellent harbors and beautiful islands, is bounded W. by Baker's island, one of the Cranberry islands, and E. by a peninsula in Goldsborough, on the W. side of which is Musquito harbor. The distance across this bay, from Baker's island to Goldsborough point, is 10 miles. This bay juts in from the Atlantic ocean about 20 miles, and is environed by the towns of Eden, Trenton, Hancock, Franklin, Sullivan, and Goldsborough, and is the recipient of many valuable streams. It is easy of access, never obstructed by ice, and is one of the best retreats in a storm on the American coast.

Friendship, Me.

Lincoln co. This is an Atlantic town, containing several islands, at the head of Muscongus bay. It was formerly called the *Meduncook*

Settlement, as lying between a river of that name and the Muscongus. Friendship is a place of considerable navigation and trade. It lies 48 miles S. E. from Augusta, and 10 miles S. W. from Warren. Population, 1837, 662.

Fryeburgh, Me.

Oxford co. This interesting and pleasant town lies on both sides of Saco river, on the line of New Hampshire. The uplands are not remarkable for their fertility, but the intervales on the Saco are of the choicest kind. Fryeburgh is only 6 miles square, yet the Saco here is so fantastic in its course that it winds itself between 30 and 40 miles within its limits. This town, the Indian *Pequawket*, lies 75 miles W. N. W. from Augusta, 47 N. W. from Portland, and 28 S. W. from Paris.—Population, 1837, 1,444. Incorporated, 1777. The principal village is situated on a plain, surrounded by lofty hills, and watered by the Saco: it bears evident marks of antiquity, and has an academy "with a cabinet of rare curiosities, collected with much diligence."—Lovewell's pond lies a short distance from the village. This beautiful sheet of water, now the resort for innocent amusements, was once the scene of bloody combat, and of the overthrow of a powerful Indian tribe.

The story of *Lovewell's Fight* has been told thousands of times, but as it is identified with the town of which we treat, we quote a brief notice of the event from the North American Review.

"It was on the 18th of April, 1725, that Capt. John Lovewell, of Dunstable, Massachusetts, with 34 men, fought a famous Indian chief, named Paugus, at the head of about 80 savages, near the shores of a pond in Pequawket. Lovewell's men were determined to conquer or die, although out-numbered by the Indians more than one half. They fought till Lovewell and Paugus were killed, and all Lovewell's men but nine were either killed or wounded dangerously. The savages having lost, as was supposed, 60 of their number out of 80, and being convinced of the fierce and determined resolution of their foes, at length retreated and left them masters of the ground. The scene of this desperate and bloody action, which took place in the town which is now called Fryeburgh, is often visited with interest to this day, and the names of those who fell, and those who survived, are yet repeated with emotions of grateful exultation."

Fundy, Bay of.

This bay washes a part of the eastern shore of Maine; and as it is an important channel of commerce between the United States and the British provinces of New Brunswick and Nova Scotia, it may be useful to notice it. This large and important bay sets up N. E. round cape Sable, the most southern point of Nova Scotia, in N. lat. 43° 24', W. lon. 65° 39', and crosses to the shore of Maine a little W. of Frenchman's bay. From the mouth of Frenchman's bay to Cape Sable is about 150 miles; from Eastport to St. John's, N. B. is 60 miles; from St. John's to Annapolis, in a bay of that name, on the Nova Scotia side, is 40 miles; from thence to Halifax, by land, is 80 miles. From Eastport direct to Annapolis, across the bay, is about 70 miles. The Bay of Fundy is divided near its head by cape Chignecto. The N. W. part is called Chignecto bay; the S. E. part the Basin of Mines. From Eastport to Cumberland, at the head of Chignecto bay, is about 170 miles; to Windsor, at the head of the Basin of Mines, is about 150. From Windsor to Halifax in N. lat. 44° 39' 20'', W. lon. 63° 36' 40'', is 45 miles.

The commerce on this bay with our friends and neighbors, the English, is very considerable. While they receive bread stuffs and other productions of our soil, we are indebted to them for vast quantities of grindstones and gypsum to sharpen our tools and renovate the soil. The gypsum is principally from the Basin of Mines;—it lies embedded in elevated masses along the shores of the bay;—it is easily quarried and taken on board of vessels by the sides of the cliffs. This gypsum is of a fine quality, and it is doubtful whether any has been discovered in our own country as good.

The grindstones from Cumberland, or Chignecto bay, are every where celebrated. The source is inexhaustible, and the manufacture immense.

The tides in the bay of Fundy are supposed to rise to a greater height than in any other part of the world. Their elevation increases as you ascend the bay. At Eastport they rise 25 feet; at St. John's 30; at Cape Split, 55; at Windsor, 60, and at Cumberland, at the head of Chignecto bay, they rise to the enormous height of 71 feet. These tides announce themselves some time before their approach, by a sound resembling that of a rushing wind in a forest: they dash against the shore with a reddish hue, the color of the clay bottom over which they pass, with frightful violence; at first, to the height of from 8 to 10 feet, overwhelming all within their reach.

There are but few islands within this bay. Grand Menan, and a cluster of small islands round it, off West Quoddy Head, and Campo Bello, near Eastport, are the principal. They belong to the British. A small island about 5 miles off the S. W. part of cape Chignecto, called *Isle de Haut*, contains beautiful specimens of asbestos.

The rapidity of the tides within this bay, the fogs which frequently prevail, and the absence of good harbors between Eastport and St. John's, and from St. John's to cape Chignecto, render the navigation difficult and often dangerous.

The harbor of St. John's is easy of access, safe, and of sufficient expanse for a large fleet of any draught of water. The city of St. John's contains about 15,000 inhabitants. It is located at the outlet of the great river whose name it bears, in N. lat. 45° 20', W. lon. 66°. This city is a very flourishing place. It is the largest resource for timber and lumber that Queen Victoria has in her possessions.

St. John's river rises in Canada and the northern part of Maine. It receives the Madawaska, St. Francis, Aroostook, and many other valuable tributaries, from Maine; it waters a large portion of its northern territory, and bears many valuable productions of that state to its mouth. "This river is 350 miles long; the tide flows up about 80 miles; it is navigable for boats 200 miles, and for sloops of 50 tons 80 miles. This river and its branches water a large tract of excellent country. About 30 miles from its mouth commences a fine level country of rich meadow lands, well clothed with timber. The river furnishes a great quantity of salmon, bass and sturgeon. About a mile above the city of St. John's is the only entrance into this river. It is about 80 or 100 yards wide, 400 yards long, called the falls of the river. It being narrow, and a ridge of rocks running across the bottom of the channel, on which there are not above 17 feet of water, it is not sufficiently spacious to discharge the fresh waters of the river above. The common tides here rising above 20 feet, the waters of the river at low water are about 20 feet higher than the waters of the sea; at high water the waters of the sea are about 5 feet higher than those of the river: so that at every tide there are two falls, one outwards and one inwards. The only time of passing with safety is when the waters of the river and of the sea are level, which is twice in a tide, and continues only about 20 minutes each time."

Frederickton, the capital of New Brunswick, lies on this river, 80 miles from its mouth, in N. lat. 46° 3', W. lon. 66° 45'.

Gardiner, Me.

Kennebec co. Gardiner was formerly a part of Pittston, and lies on the W. side of Kennebec river, 6 miles S. from Augusta, and 4 below Hallowell. It is located at the head of large navigation, and in regard to its commerce, manufacturing and agricultural interests, it is considered one of the most flourishing towns in Maine. It was incorporated in 1803, and was named in honor of Dr. SYLVESTER GARDINER, one of the proprietors of the old Plymouth patent.

The *Cobbessecontee waters* meet the Kennebec river at this place, and produce a water power of great usefulness and extent. Here are mills for sawing lumber of all dimensions, and here are vessels of from 80 to 120 tons burthen, lading it for transportation to its various markets. Here are also manufactures of various other kinds. This town, Hallowell and Augusta, lie in a most favored section of our country. What we have said in regard to the location of Hallowell and Augusta, may be applied to Gardiner. These towns are on the same side of a noble river, united by the same interests and feelings, and will soon be connected by a rail-road passing between them. The village of Gardiner is very pleasant. The business part lying on the river, is full of activity and enterprise. The buildings, on a gentle rise from the river, are beautifully located. They command a delightful prospect, and some of them are of superior architecture. Population, 1837, 3,709. The present population is about 5,000.

Gardner, Mass.

Worcester co. Otter river, a considerable stream, a branch of Miller's river, rises partly in this town, and affords good mill seats. On this river is some good intervale land; the high lands are rough, but good for grazing. The value of palm-leaf hats, straw bonnets, chairs, cabinet and wooden wares, leather, boots and shoes, manufactured in one year, amounted to $132,272. The cabinet ware and chairs amounted to $109,000. Gardner was incorporated in 1785, and lies 54 miles N. W. by W. from Boston, and 23 N. W. by N. from Worcester. Population, 1837, 1,276.

A church was formed here in 1786, and the Rev. Jonathan Osgood was ordained. He died in 1825, after sustaining the vocations of *pastor, physician* and *school master*, 30 years.

Garland, Me.

Penobscot co. Garland is watered by some of the head branches of Kenduskeag stream. It lies 74 miles N. E. by N. from Augusta, and 27 N. W. from Bangor. Incorporated, 1811. Population, 1830, 621; 1837, 932. This is an excellent township of land; it produced, in 1837, 6,521 bushels of wheat.

Gay Head, Mass.

See *Chilmark*.

Georgetown, Me.

Lincoln co. Georgetown is constituted of two considerable islands lying at the mouth of Kennebec river. These islands have Kennebec river on the W., Sheepscot river on the E., and separated from Woolwich on the N. by a navigable passage between those two rivers. It is a little below Bath, on the opposite shore. This is one of the most ancient settlements in Maine. The town was incorporated in 1716. Population, 1837, 1,355. It lies 46 miles S. from Augusta, and 12 S. W. from Wiscasset. This town has excellent harbors, and possesses peculiar privileges for all occupations connected with navigation and the fisheries.

Georgetown, Mass.

Essex co. Georgetown was the W. part of Rowley. It was called *New Rowley* for some years, until its incorporation as a separate town, in 1838. Georgetown is watered by a branch of Parker's river, and is almost entirely engaged in manufactures and the mechanic arts. It is a pleasant town and highly flourishing. Population, about 1,500. It lies 30 miles N. from Boston, and 10 S. W. from Newburyport. The people of Georgetown are probably more extensively engaged in the manufacture of boots and shoes than at any other place, of its population, in America. The value of boots and shoes manufactured, and leather tanned, is said to exceed $500,000 annually.

Georgia, Vt.

Franklin co. Population, 1830, 1,897. Georgia lies 40 miles N. W. from Montpelier, and 8 S. from St. Albans. First settled, 1784. The soil of Georgia is various but generally fertile. It feeds about 11,000 sheep. The Lamoille passes through the S. E. corner of the town, which, with other streams, give it an ample water power. This is a place of considerable trade and some manufactures. Over *Stone Bridge brook* is a stone bridge,—a curious piece of nature's mechanism. Georgia is washed on the W. by Lake Champlain: the village is pleasantly located, and commands some very pretty lake and mountain scenery.

Gilead, Me.

Oxford co. Between two mountains on both sides of Androscoggin river. There is some good land on the river, but the chief part of the township is fit only for grazing. The expense of transportation of fuel down the mountains, in a slippery time, is very trifling. Gilead lies 71 miles W. from Augusta, and 25 S. S. W. from Paris. Incorporated, 1804. Population, 1837, 374.

Gilford, N. H.,

One of the four shire towns for Strafford county, is situated on the S. side of Winnepisiogee lake. This town lies 26 miles N. N. E. from Concord, and 48 N. W. from Portsmouth. The soil is generally productive. There are two ponds in this town, Little and Chattleborough. Gunstock and Mile's rivers, rising in Suncook mountains and flowing N. into the lake, are the principal streams. The N. source of the Suncook river is on the S. of these mountains, which extend in a lofty pile over the E. part of the town, from Gilmanton line nearly to the lake. There are seven islands in the lake, belonging to Gilford, one of which has been connected to the main land by a bridge 30 rods in length. This town, which was formerly a part of Gilmanton, was incorporated June 16, 1812. It was settled in 1778.—Here are manufactories of cotton goods, besides other useful mills and machinery. Four bridges across the Winnepisiogee connect the town with Meredith. The village at this place is thriving and pleasant. Population, 1830, 1,872.

Gill, Mass.

Franklin co. A mountainous township on the W. side of Connecticut river; 86 miles W. by N. from Boston, and 5 E. N. E. from Greenfield. Gill contains a fine tract of rich intervale on a bend of the Connecticut. The people are generally engaged in farming. The town is divided from Greenfield by Fall river. It has some manufactures of combs, wooden ware, leather and palm-leaf hats. The fleeces of 1,809 sheep weighed 5,627 pounds, and were valued, in 1837, at $2,214. Population, 1837, 809. Taken from Deerfield in 1793.

Gilmanton, N. H.

One of the shire towns in Strafford county, 17 miles N. N. E. from Concord, and 45 W. N. W. from Portsmouth. It is bounded N. and N. E. by Gilford and Alton. Population, 1830, 3,816. Beside the Winnepisiogee, this town is watered by the Suncook and Soucook rivers, which have their sources in Gilmanton. The Suncook rises in a pond near the top of one of the Suncook mountains, elevated 900 feet above its base. The water of this pond falls into another at the foot of the mountain, of 1 mile in length and 1-2 mile wide. Passing from this, it falls into another, covering about 500 acres, from which it meanders through the town, receiving several streams in its course. The Soucook rises from Loon, Rocky and Shellcamp ponds, in the S. part of the town. This town is very hilly and rocky. The soil is hard, but fruitful, when properly cultivated. The geology of this town presents many varieties.—There are several springs in Gilmanton, termed mineral; one of which has proved efficacious in cutaneous and bilious affections. This town was granted May 20, 1727, to 24 persons of the name of Gilman, and 152 others. In Dec. 1761, Benjamin and John Mudgett, with their families, settled here. Dorothy Weed, the first child, was born here Oct. 13, 1762. An academy was founded here in 1764. Its productive funds are about $11,000. The theological seminary at this place is connected with the academy, and is a flourishing institution.

Gilsum, N. H.

A small township in Cheshire county, situated about 10 miles E. from the Connecticut. The soil is, in many parts, fertile, and produces good crops of grass and grain. Ashuelot river runs through this town and affords a good supply of water for mills, which is improved for cotton and other manufactures. Gilsum was granted July 13, 1763, to Messrs. Gilbert, Sumner and others. From the combination of the first syllables of the names of these men, it derives the name of Gil-sum. The first settlement was made in 1764. Gilsum lies 55 miles S. W. by W. from Concord, and about 9 N. from Keene. Population, 1830, 642.

Glenburn, Me.

Penobscot co. This territory was called *Dutton*, from 1822 to 1837. It lies 76 miles N. E. from Augusta, and 10 N. N. W. from Bangor. Population, 1837, 717. Glenburn is situated on both sides of the great bend of Kenduskeag stream. It has a water power, but the inhabitants are mostly farmers. The soil is good, and considerable wheat is raised.

Glastenbury, Vt.

Bennington co. This is a township of 40 square miles of mountainous land, more fit for the residence of wild beasts than human beings. It is 9 miles N. E. from Bennington. Population, 1830, 59.

Glastenbury, Ct.

Hartford co. This town, previous to its incorporation in 1690, had been attached to Wethersfield. It lies on the east side of Connecticut river opposite to Wethersfield, 8 miles S. from Hartford. It has some fine land on Connecticut river. The face of the uplands is rough but generally productive. About a mile and a half from Connecticut river, and 8 miles from Chatham freestone quarry, in a romantic spot between the hills, is a beautiful village connected with the Hartford Manufacturing Company. Roaring brook, at this place, passes through a very narrow defile, affording a great and constant water power. Cotton is manufactured here to a considerable extent, and the village is very flourishing. From the hills around this village a great variety of delightful scenery is observable. Population, 1830, 2,980.

"In the eastern part of the town there is a pond of about a mile in circumference, called 'Diamond pond,' from the circumstance of there being small pebbles or stones around its margin, having a peculiar brilliancy. Near the centre of the town there is a mineral spring, which, though it has acquired no celebrity abroad, has been thought by men of science who have examined it, to possess valuable medicinal qualities; and for more than one hundred years has been known by the name of the 'Pool of Neipseic.'"

Gloucester, Mass.

Essex co. This is a maritime township, comprising the whole of Cape Ann, and celebrated for the enterprise of its people in the fisheries and commercial pursuits. It is one of the oldest fishing establishments in the state. This cape extends about 8 miles into the sea, and forms the northern boundary of Massachusetts bay. Its harbor is capacious, easy of access at any season, and of sufficient water for ships of great burthen. Gloucester harbor and the chief settlements are on the south side. Sandy and Squam bays lie on the north side, about 4 miles from the south harbor, and afford harbors for small vessels. The lights on Thatcher's island bear about northeast 6 miles from East Point, the eastern boundary of Gloucester harbor. As early as 1794 the exports from this place, in one year, amounted to $230,000. Here are immense quarries of light and grayish granite, which is split with great ease, and in large regularly formed blocks. This stone is of a fine grain, is easily dressed, and can be put on board of vessels with little expense. The demand for this stone is rapidly increasing, and the quarrying, hammering, and transporting it gives employment to many men and vessels. The canal across the neck of the cape has failed of that success which was anticipated. The manufacture of palm-leaf hats, boots, shoes, hats, vessels, chairs, tin and cabinet wares, in the year ending April 1, 1837, amounted to $46,726. In that year there were 221 vessels employed in the cod and mackerel fishery, the tonnage of which was 9,824 tons. They took 55,181 quintals of cod fish, and 43,934 barrels of mackerel: 113,-760 bushels of salt was used, and 1,580 hands employed. The value of the cod and mackerel taken was $522,082. There are belonging to this place a great number of vessels engaged in foreign and domestic trade. The total tonnage of the district in 1837 was 18,802 tons. This town lies in N. lat. 42° 36′, W. lon. 70° 40′, and was incorporated in 1639. Population, 1820, 6,384; 1830, 7,513; 1837, 8,822. It lies 29 miles N. E. from Boston, and 16 N. E. by E. from Salem. Gloucester is a very pleasant town, and a delightful retreat in summer months.

Gloucester, R. I.

Providence co. This large and respectable manufacturing town lies 16 miles W. S. W. from Providence, and 50 E. by N. from Hartford. First settled, 1700. Incorporated, 1730. The surface of the town is somewhat broken by hills, but the soil is well adapted to agricultural purposes, particularly to grazing. Gloucester furnishes large supplies of various products for market. There are fine forests in several parts of the town, and large quantities of ship and other timber are conveyed to Providence and other places. The Chepachet and some smaller streams give Gloucester a good water power. Manufacturing establishments are very numerous, and Gloucester yields to but few towns in New England in the value of this branch of industry, particularly in the manufacture of cotton. Population, 1830, 2,522.

Glover, Vt.

Orleans co. Glover was first settled in 1797. It lies 33 miles N. N. E. from Montpelier, and 12 S. by E. from Irasburgh. The town is hilly, and the soil is more fit for grazing than tillage. There are about 3,200 sheep in the town. There are in the town branches of Barton's, Passumpsic, Lamoille, and Black rivers, and several ponds. On these streams are some manufactures, but none of any great importance. Population, 1830, 902.

We copy an account of the *running off* of Long Pond, from Thompson's valuable Gazetteer of Vermont.

"Long pond was situated partly in this township and partly in Greensborough. This pond was one and a half miles long, and about half a mile wide, and discharged its waters to the south, forming one of the head branches of the river Lamoille. On the 6th of June, 1810, about 60 persons went to this pond for the purpose of opening an outlet to the north into Barton river, that the mills, on that stream, might receive an occasional supply of water. A small channel was excavated, and the water commenced running in a northerly direction. It happened that the northern barrier of the pond consisted entirely of quicksand, except an encrusting of clay next the water. The sand was immediately removed by the current, and a large channel formed. The basin formed by the encrusting of clay was incapable of sustaining the incumbent mass of waters, and it brake. The whole pond immediately took a northerly course, and, in fifteen minutes from this time, its bed was left entirely bare. It was discharged so suddenly that the country below was instantly inundated. The deluge advanced like a wall of waters, 60 or 70 feet in height, and 20 rods in width, leveling the forests and the hills, and filling up the valleys, and sweeping off mills, houses, barns, fences, cattle, horses and sheep as it passed, for the distance of more than ten miles, and barely giving the inhabitants sufficient notice of its approach to escape with their lives into the mountains. A rock, supposed to weigh more than 100 tons, was removed half a mile from its bed. The waters removed so rapidly as to reach Memphremagog lake, distance 27 miles, in about six hours from the time they left the pond. Nothing now remains of the pond but its bed, a part of which is cultivated and a part overgrown with bushes and wild grass, with a small brook running through it, which is now the head branch of Barton river. The channel through which the waters escaped is 127 feet in depth and several rods in width. A pond, some distance below, was, at first, entirely filled with sand, which has since settled down, and it is now about one half its former dimensions. Marks of the ravages are still to be seen through nearly the whole course of Barton river."

Goffstown, N. H.,

Hillsborough co., is 12 miles N.

by E. from Amherst, and 16 S. from Concord. Piscataquog river, the tributary branches of which unite near the W. line of the town, runs through its centre in an E. direction, and falls into Merrimack river at Piscataquog village in Bedford. Large quantities of lumber are annually floated down this river to the Merrimack, and most of the mill privileges are derived from this valuable stream. There are two considerable elevations in the S. W. part of the town, which obtained from the Indians the name of *Un-can-nu-nuc*. On the rivers are considerable tracts of valuable intervale. Back from the rivers commence extensive plains, easy of cultivation, and producing abundant crops of Indian corn and rye. From these plains the land rises on each side of Piscataquog river into large swells. In this town there is an extensive cotton factory. The Goffstown Manufacturing Company are erecting a large woolen factory at a flourishing village, in the W. part of the town, on Piscataquog river. Population, 1830, 2,213.

Dr. JONATHAN GOVE, a man distinguished for his urbanity, his talents and professional skill, resided in this town. He was one of the oldest practitioners of medicine in the county. He was many years an active member of the legislature.

Goldsborough, Me.

Hancock co. This is a large township, on the Atlantic ocean, containing a number of excellent harbors, and nearly surrounded by water. It is admirably located for all the various pursuits in navigation. Goldsborough harbor, on the E. side of the town, is capacious and easy of approach by almost any wind. Frenchman's bay extends on the W. side of the town and affords it many commercial advantages. It lies 99 miles E. from Augusta, 27 S. E. from Ellsworth, and is bounded by Sullivan on the N. Incorporated, 1789. Population, 1830, 880; 1837, 1,047.

Gorham, Me.

Cumberland co. This town is watered on the N. E. side by Presumpscut river, and the Cumberland and Oxford canal. It is 9 miles W. N. W. from Portland, and 63 S. W. from Augusta. Gorham was first settled in 1736, by John Phinney and others from Barnstable county, Mass. Maine was at that time almost a wilderness. Portland, Saco and Scarborough were very feeble in consequence of the depredations of the Indians. These people endured great privations, and for many years were in constant apprehension of attack by the savages. "The wives and daughters of the first settlers of Gorham shared in all the toils and wants of their husbands and fathers; they used to labor in the field, carry burdens, go to mill, and aid in defence of their property. One time when most of the men were away, the Indians attacked the fort, and the wife of Hugh McLellan rallied the women in the garrison, shut the gates, mounted the walls, fired upon the Indians, and by her courage and activity baffled the enemy till succor arrived."

Rev. Solomon Lombard, a native of Truro, Mass., was the first settled minister. His annual salary was £53, 6s. 8d. He was ordained Dec. 26, 1750. One hundred and twenty dollars were raised to defray the expenses of the ordination. We copy the following from the list of supplies for that occasion, to show the prices of some articles at that period.

1 barrel of flour,	£14	7s.	6d.
3 bushels of apples,	2	8	0
2 barrels of cider,	9	0	0
2 gallons of brandy,	5	0	0
1 bottle of vinegar,	0	5	0
2 cheeses, 6d. per lb.			

54½ lbs. of pork, 7d. per lb.
6 candles, £0 1s. 0d.
1 oz. of nutmegs, 0 1 0
8 fowls, 1 16 0
29 lbs. sugar, 8 14 0
1 tea pot, 1 10 0
4 gallons of rum, 5 4 0
2 bushels cranberries, 2 0 0
1 lb. of tea, 0 10 0
1 lb. of ginger, 0 2 0
6 gals. molasses, 2s. 8d. per gal.
4 oz. of pepper, 0 0 6

Gorham is very pleasantly located: its soil is of a superior quality: it has a flourishing academy, on a solid foundation: it is a place of considerable trade, and of extensive manufactures of cotton, wool, leather, starch, and gunpowder. Gorham has produced many men of talents, among which were eminent jurists and statesmen. It is noted for its attachment to the principles of the revolution.

From 1807 to 1834, twenty persons died in Gorham, whose average age was 94 years. Population, 1837, 3,022.

Gorham, N. H.,

Coos co., is a rough and unproductive township lying on the northerly base of the White mountains, and bounded E. by Shelburne, N. by Berlin, and W. by Randolph, and is 96 miles N. from Concord. Several streams descend from the mountains through this town into the Androscoggin. It was formerly called *Shelburne Addition*, but was incorporated by its present name June 18, 1836. Population in 1830, 111.

Goshen, N. H.,

Sullivan co., is bounded N. by Newport and Wendell, E. by Newbury, S. by Washington, and W. by Lempster and Unity. It is 42 miles W. by N. from Concord. Croydon turnpike passes through Goshen. From Sunapee mountain, lying in the E. part of this town, spring many small streams, which unite in forming Sugar river. Rand's pond is in the N. E. part of the town. The soil is particularly calculated for the production of grass. It was incorporated Dec. 27, 1791. The first settlement was made about the year 1769, by Capt. Benjamin Rand, William Lang, and Daniel Grindle, whose sufferings and hardships were very great. The crops of the first settlers were greatly injured, and sometimes entirely destroyed by early frosts. In such cases they procured grain from Walpole and other places. At a certain time of scarcity, Capt. Rand went to that place after grain, and being detained by a violent snow storm, his family was obliged to live without provision for six days, during which time Mrs. Rand sustained one of his children, 5 years old, by the milk from her breast, having a short time before buried her infant child. Population in 1830, 772.

Goshen, Vt.

Addison co. First settled, 1800. Population, 1830, 555. Goshen lies 30 miles S. W. from Montpelier, and 15 S. E. from Middlebury. Leicester and Philadelphia rivers supply the town with mill privileges. The lands along the rivers are very good, but in general they are too mountainous for profitable cultivation. Some minerals are found in this town.

Goshen, Mass.

Hampshire co. A mountainous town, 103 miles W. by N. from Boston, and 12 N. W. from Northampton. Some valuable minerals are found here, such as emeralds, lead, and tin. The manufactures of Goshen are small, chiefly of boots and shoes. The value of 3,048 fleeces of wool, produced in 1837, was sold for $4,500. Population, 1837, 560.

Goshen, Ct.

Litchfield co. First settled, 1738.

Incorporated, 1749. Population, 1830, 1,734. Goshen lies 6 miles N. from Litchfield, 42 N. N. W. from New Haven, and 32 W. from Hartford. Great attention is paid in this town to the education of youth. Ivy mountain, in Goshen, is considered the most elevated point of land in the state; its summit presents an extensive and delightful prospect. "Goshen is the most elevated township in the state, but not generally mountainous; the surface being undulating, affording an interesting diversity of hills and vales. The soil is a gravelly loam, deep, strong and fertile, admirably adapted for grazing. This is one of the best towns for the dairy business in the state. Large quantities of cheese are annually made, the fame of which is widely and justly celebrated, and the inhabitants are generally in prosperous circumstances. In neatness, in and about their dwellings, and in the appearance of general comfort and prosperity, they are not exceeded, if equalled, by any town in the state."

Gosport, N. H.

See *Isles of Shoals*.

Grafton County, N. H.

Haverhill and *Plymouth* are the county towns.

This county extends from lat. 43° 27' to 44° 22' N. It is 58 miles in length, and its greatest breadth is 30 miles. It contains 828,623 acres, besides a large tract of ungranted land. It is bounded N. by the county of Coos, E. by Strafford, S. by Merrimack, and W. by the state of Vermont. Grafton county is watered by Connecticut river, on which are several pleasant and flourishing towns; by Pemigewasset, and Lower Amonoosuck rivers, and by many smaller streams.— Squam and Newfound lakes are the largest collections of water. The former, of which a considerable part lies in Strafford county, has been much celebrated for its picturesque beauties. Its numerous angular projections, the variety of its islands covered with wood, and the vicinity of lofty mountains, render it an object peculiarly interesting. There are numerous elevations which come under the name of mountains. Those of the most importance are Gardner's in Lyman, Peaked in Bethlehem, Moosehillock in Coventry, Cushman's and the Blue mount in Peeling, Carr's in Warren and Ellsworth, Moose in Hanover, and Cardigan in Orange.

A large portion of Grafton county is mountainous and hilly, but this circumstance does not prevent its productiveness. It presents fine tracts for pasturage, a large proportion of arable land, and on the rivers, extensive and fertile intervales.

This county is emphatically a wool growing county, and there were, in 1837, more than 120,000 sheep within its borders.

The first settlement in this county was made at Lebanon, and this was the first settlement on Connecticut river north of Charlestown. It was constituted a county, March 19, 1771, and received its name in honor of Augustus Henry Fitzroy, Duke of Grafton. Population in 1775, 3,597; in 1790, 12,449; in 1800, 20,171; in 1810, 28,462; in 1820, 32,989; and in 1830, 38,691.

Grafton, N. H.,

Grafton co., is bounded N. E. by Orange, S. E. by Danbury, S. W. by Springfield, and N. W. by Enfield. It is 36 miles N. W. from Concord, and 13 S. E. from Dartmouth college. It is watered by branches of Smith's and Mascomy rivers. Heard's river, a small tributary to Smith's river, waters the S. E. part. There are 5 ponds. The largest, containing from 200 to 300 acres, is called Grafton pond. Two are named Mud ponds. The surface of Grafton is very hilly, in some parts very mountainous; and the soil is so rocky as, in many places, to be unfit for cultivation. There are, however, some good tracts of land. The Grafton turnpike, leading from Andover to Orford bridge, passes through the E. part, and the 4th N. H. turnpike, from Concord to Hanover, through the W. part. In this town there is a remarkable ledge, called the Pinnacle, on the S. side of which the ground rises by a gradual ascent to the summit; but on the N. side, it falls nearly 150 feet, within the distance of 6 or 8 feet. Isinglass, as it is commonly called, is found in a state of great purity in Glass Hill mountain. It adheres in the form of lamina to rocks of white and yellow quartz. The usual size of these lamina is about 6 inches square, but some have been found much larger. It requires much labor to obtain this glass, which, when prepared, is transported to Boston, and from thence exported to England. It is found on the E. side of the mountain, which is 200 feet high. Grafton was granted Aug. 14, 1761, to Ephraim Sherman and others.—The first permanent settlement was made in May, 1772, by Capt. Joseph Hoyt, from Poplin. Capt. Alexander Pixley and wife were the second family who settled here. Incorporated in 1778. Population in 1830, 1,207.

Grafton, Vt.

Windham co. Grafton is finely watered by Sexton's river, which is formed in the town by the union of several streams; and by a branch of Williams' river. On these streams are manufactures of woolen and other goods. Soap-stone of an excellent quality is very abundant in this place. It is manufactured by water power for various uses to a great extent: it is bored for aqueducts and sold at a very low price. This town contains two pleasant and flourishing villages, and a great variety of mineral treasure. Its surface is uneven with a strong and productive soil. Grafton was first settled, 1780. Population, 1830, 1,439. It lies 90 miles S. from Montpelier, and 18 N. from Newfane.

Grafton, Mass.

Worcester co. This important manufacturing town, the *Hassanamisco* of the Indians, was incorporated in 1735. It lies 36 miles S. W. by W. from Boston, and 9 S. E. from Worcester. Population, 1830, 1,889; 1837, 2,910. Blackstone river and several large ponds give this town a constant and valuable water power. There are 5 cotton and 1 woolen mills. The total amount of the manufactures of Grafton, the year ending April 1, 1837, was $1,052,448. The manufactures consisted of cotton and woolen goods, boots, shoes, leather, scythes, chairs, tin, cabinet and wooden wares, shoe tools and bricks. The manufacture of boots and shoes amounted to $614,141, employing 1,392 males and females. Grafton has a fine soil, is beautifully located, and exceedingly flourishing.

Granby, Vt.

Essex co. This town is nearly allied to *Ferdinand*, both in location and the character of the soil. Granby lies the next town S. of it, and 97 people, it is said, reside within the limits of Granby.

Granby, Mass.

Hampshire co. This town lies 90 miles W. by S. from Boston, and 9 S. E. from Northampton. Incorporated, 1768. It has good fish ponds and two small streams. There are two woolen mills in the town and 2,067 sheep. The wool, in 1837, sold for $3,670. Population, 1837, 922. It is said that copper ore of a good quality is found in Granby.

Granby, Ct.

Hartford co. This town was incorporated in 1786, and was that part of Simsbury which contains the famous Simsbury mines; the old state prison of Connecticut. The cavern, once occupied as a prison, is now worked, as formerly, as a copper mine. This odious place, unfit for the residence of the worst of criminals, is 16 miles N. N. W. from Hartford. The pit or cavern is more than 50 feet in depth, dark, damp and dismal. The worst stigma that can be cast on the good people of Connecticut is, that this infernal region was suffered to remain nearly 40 years the abode of their fellow beings. There are some hills in Granby of considerable elevation. *Barn door hills* rise between four and five hundred feet, and have the appearance of having been separated by some convulsion of nature. *Turkey hills* and *Salmon brook* are pleasant villages, and have the appearance of prosperity. Farmington river waters the former, and a branch of that river, the latter. Population, 1830, 2,722.

Grand Isle County, Vt.

North Hero is the county town. This county comprises a group of islands in Lake Champlain, and a point of land jutting into the N. part of that lake on the S. side of the Canada line, on which Alburgh is situated. This county contains about 80 square miles: most of the land is level and excellent for grazing and tillage. This county has no considerable streams, but its navigable facilities are very great. It was first settled about the close of the revolutionary war. Incorporated, 1802. It contained, in 1837, about 16,000 sheep. Population, 1820, 3,527; 1830, 3,696. Population to a square mile, 46.

Grand Isle, Vt.

Grand Isle co. This town is bounded on all sides by Lake Champlain except on the S., where it is bounded by South Hero, from which it was taken in 1809. It lies 50 miles N. W. from Montpelier, and 18 N. by W. from Burlington.— First settled, 1783. Population, 1830, 643. The soil of the town is very fertile; it produces fine crops of grain and an abundance of fruit and cider. Marble, lime-stone, rock crystals, &c., are found here, and Grand Isle contains the only water mill in the county. This is a fine place for fishing and fowling.

Grand Lake.

This is a large collection of water, lying partly in the county of Washington, Me., and partly in New Brunswick. It contains a large number of islands: it receives the waters of many small lakes and rivers, and is the chief source of the river St. Croix. It lies about 90 miles N. E. from Bangor.

Grantham, N. H.,

Sullivan co., is bounded N. by Enfield, E. by Springfield, S. by Croydon, and W. by Plainfield, which separates it from Connecticut river. It is 12 miles S. E. from Dartmouth college, and 45 N. W. from Concord. There are 7 or 8 ponds, the largest of which lies in the S. E. part of the town and is called Eastman's pond, containing nearly 300 acres. Another, lying near the centre of the town, contains nearly 200 acres. Croydon mountain extends through the westerly part of Grantham in a direction from S. W. to N. E. The soil is productive, especially on the W. of the mountain. It seems to be more favorable for wheat than any other species of grain. The mountain affords good pasturage, and the lower land yields grass in abundance. On the E. side of the mountain is a spring supposed to possess medicinal qualities, visited by hundreds of valetudinarians in the summer season. On the summit of Croydon mountain is a natural pond, containing about 50 acres. This town was first granted July 11, 1761, but the proprietors not fulfilling the conditions of the charter, it was forfeited. In 1767, it was re-granted to Col. William Symmes and 63 others, by the name of *Grantham*. Incorporated in 1761. Population, in 1830, 1,079.

Granville, Vt.

Addison co. See *Barnard, Me.*

Granville, Mass.

Hampden co. This is a mountainous township, 110 miles W. S. W. from Boston, and 14 W. from Springfield. It contains good soapstone and 1,500 sheep. The wool sold in 1837 for $2,572. There are some manufactures in Granville of pocket books, boots, shoes, leather, and silver ware. Although the land is high, the soil in many parts is very good and productive. The village is very pleasant. Incorporated, 1754. Population, 1837, 1,439.

Gray, Me.

Cumberland co. This is a fine farming town, watered by branches of North Yarmouth and Presumpscot rivers, and containing a large part of Little Sebago pond. It lies 17 miles N. by W. from Portland and 44 S. W. from Augusta. Incorporated, 1778. Population, 1837, 1,671. Gray is a pleasant town and a place of considerable trade and some manufactures.

Great Barrington, Mass.

Berkshire co. A very pleasant town in the valley of Housatonick river, 125 miles W. by S. from Boston, and 14 S. from Lenox. Incorporated, 1761. Population, 1837, 2,440. Monument mountain, in this town, is quite lofty: it presents some wild and picturesque scenery. Here are good iron ore, beautifully variegated marble, and a good mill stream. The soil on the banks of the Housatonick is fertile and the uplands are well adapted for grazing. The manufactures consist of cotton and woolen goods, boots, shoes, leather, hats, pig iron, lasts, tin ware, bevils and guages. Total amount of manufactures in one year, $122,369. This town the same year (1837) produced 2,657 fleeces of merino wool, valued at $3,321.

Great-Bays, N. H.

The largest is that lying E. from New Market, formed by the united waters of Swamscot, Winnicut, and Lamprey rivers. It is 4 miles wide, and at some seasons is picturesque as connected with the surrounding scenery. This bay has Newington on the E., Greenland and Stratham on the S., and New Market and Durham W.: its waters pass N. E. through Little bay, where Oyster river unites with the current which passes into the Piscataqua.

Great-Bay, between Sanbornton and Meredith, is a body of water, connected with Winnepisiogee lake, and discharging its waters into Winnepisiogee river. Round and Long bays are situated between the lake and Great Bay, and there are two small bays on the river below

Great Island, N. H.

See *New Castle.*

Great Works Stream, Me.

This stream has a number of tributaries, and is an important branch of the Penobscot. It has many sites for mills, and falls into the Penobscot, on the E. side, opposite to the Indian settlement at Oldtown. At its confluence with the Penobscot there is a considerable village.

There is another stream of this name, which rises in York county, and passes to Salmon Fall river, at South Berwick.

Greene, Me.

Kennebec co. Greene has several ponds, but no good mill privileges. It lies on the E. side of Androscoggin river, 6 miles above Lewiston, and 22 S. W. from Augusta. It is an excellent farming town, and produced, in 1837, 3,278 bushels of wheat. Incorporated, 1788. Population, 1837, 1,366.

Greenbush, Me.

Penobscot co. This territory was called the *Olammon Plantation*, until its incorporation in 1834.— Olammon stream, one of the most beautiful tributaries of the Penobscot, joins that river, on the E. side, in Greenbush, affording an extensive hydraulic power. Greenbush is a flourishing place, and lies about 25 miles N. by E. from Bangor. Population, 1830, 333; 1837, 666.

Greenfield, Me.

Hancock co. This town was incorporated in 1834. It was No. 38 on the *Bingham Purchase*. See "Down East."

Greenfield, N. H.,

Hillsborough co., is bounded N. by Francestown and Society-Land, E. by Francestown and Lyndeborough, S. by Lyndeborough and Temple, and W. by Peterborough and Hancock. It is 14 miles W. N. W. from Amherst, and 38 S. W. from Concord. Contoocook river forms part of the W. boundary, and separates this town from Hancock. The soil is generally fertile. The hills afford excellent pasturage; the valleys and plains are favorable for grain. Hops are raised in great abundance. A part of Crotched mountain rises from the N. part, and part of Lyndeborough mountain from the S. and E. sections of this town. There are some valuable meadows; in one of them have been found many Indian relics, from which it is conjectured that it was a favorite spot of the sons of the forest. There are five ponds; the largest about one mile in length, and one third of its length in width. The first settlement commenced in 1771, by Capt. Alexander Parker, Major A. Whittemore, Simeon Fletcher, and others. It was incorporated June 15, 1791. Population, in 1830, 946.

Greenfield, Mass.

County town, Franklin co. This town lies on the W. side of Connecticut river, and is washed by Green river, an excellent mill stream, a branch of the Deerfield. The village is situated about 2 miles from Connecticut river, and is very beautiful and flourishing. There is a woolen mill in Greenfield with four sets of machinery; and manufactures of boots, shoes, leather, hats, iron castings, chairs, cabinet and tin wares, saddles, harnesses, trunks, stove and lead aqueduct pipe, iron work, guns, pistols, rifles, coaches, wagons, books, &c. The total amount of manufactures, for the year ending April 1, 1837, was $164,844. The value of wool, the product of 2,153 fleeces, sheared in 1837, was $3,404. There is an academy for young ladies in this town, a farming school for young men, and some iron and copper ores. Greenfield lies 95 miles W. by N. from Boston, and 22 N. from Northampton. Incorporated, 1753. Population, 1830, 1,540; 1837, 1,840

Greenland, N. H.,

Rockingham co., is situated five miles W.S.W. from Portsmouth, and 45 E.S.E. from Concord: it is bounded N. by the Great-Bay and Newington, E. by Portsmouth and Rye, S. by North-Hampton, and W. by Stratham. The soil is remarkably good. The orchards and gardens of this town are valuable, and yield annual profits to the farmers.— Greenland, originally a part of Portsmouth, was incorporated as a distinct town in 1703. Settlements commenced early, and in 1705 there were 320 inhabitants.

Rev. SAMUEL M'CLINTOCK, D. D., who died in the 48th year of his ministry, was born at Medford, Mass., May 1, 1732; graduated at the New Jersey college in 1751; ordained in 1756; and died April 27, 1804, aged 72. His father was a native of Ireland. Dr. M'Clintock was a sound divine, eminent as a preacher, and distinguished for his attachment to the cause of his country. He served as a chaplain in the army of the revolution. Population in 1830, 681.

Green Mountains.

This range of mountains rises in Lower Canada. They pass nearly through the centre of Vermont, from N. to S., and the westerly parts of the states of Massachusetts and Connecticut, and terminate near New Haven, on Long Island Sound. From their green appearance they give the name to Vermont, and decrease in height as they approach the south. The north peak, in Mansfield, Vt., is the greatest elevation, being 4,279 feet above the surface of lake Champlain.

Green Rivers.

Green, or Quodotchquoik river, in the N. E. part of Penobscot county, *Maine*, is an important branch of the St. John's, and joins that river about 24 miles W. from the line of New Brunswick.

Green river, in *Massachusetts*, rises in the high lands at the N. W. corner of Berkshire county; it passes N. W. through Williamstown, and the S. W. corner of Vermont, and joins the Hoosick in N. Y.

There are several smaller streams in New England of the same name.

Greensborough, Vt.

Orleans co. William Scott Shepard, born March 25, 1789, was the first white child brought forth in this town. For his good fortune in this respect, the proprietors of the township gave him 100 acres of land. "Beautiful lake" and several other lakes and ponds in this town, form a part of the head waters of the river Lamoille. This town is well timbered: the surface is not very elevated; the soil in general is good, particularly for grazing. It produces some fine cattle, and keeps about 4,000 sheep. Population, 1830, 734.

Greenville, Me.

Piscataquis co. The "Haskell Plantation," incorporated in 1836. 109 miles from Augusta. Population, 1837, 132. See "Down East."

Greenwich, Mass.

Hampshire co. There are a number of ponds in this town, by which, and Swift river passing through it, a good water power is acquired. There is a woolen mill in the town, and manufactures of shoes, boots, palm-leaf hats, and scythes. Incorporated, 1754. Population, 1837, 842. Greenwich lies 75 miles W. from Boston, and 17 N. E. from Northampton.

Greenwich, Ct.

Fairfield co. The settlement of this town commenced in 1640, and was incorporated by Stuyvesant, the Dutch governor at New York, in 1665. Greenwich comprises three parishes or villages,—West Greenwich, Greenwich on the E. and Stanwich on the N. West Greenwich, on *Horse Neck*, so called from a peninsula on the Sound formerly used as a horse pasture, is the largest and most important part of the town. Greenwich is watered by Byran river, the boundary line between the town and state of New York, and the most southern part of New England. At the outlet of Byran river, on the New York side, is a place called *Sawpits*, a noted landing place on the Sound, 28 miles

N. E from New York. Miannus creek and other smaller streams water the town.

A great battle took place between the Dutch and Indians at Horse Neck, in 1646. The action was long and severe, both parties fighting with much obstinacy. The Dutch with much difficulty kept the field, and the Indians withdrew. Great numbers were slain on both sides, and the graves of the dead, for a century or more, appeared like a number of small hills.

"Putnam's Hill is situated in West Greenwich, about five miles W. from Stamford, on the main road to New York. This place is celebrated for the daring exploit of General Putnam, who descended this precipice when pursued by the British dragoons."

Greenwich is a rough and uneven township, with a productive soil. It presents some wild scenery along the road, and many beautiful views of Long Island Sound. It lies 48 miles W. S. W. from New Haven, and 20 W. S. W. from Fairfield. Population, 1830, 3,805.

Greenwood, Me.

Oxford co. Incorporated, 1815. Population, 1837, 754. It lies 58 miles W. by S. from Augusta, and 7 N. W. from Paris. This is a township of excellent land. The inhabitants are generally engaged in agricultural pursuits.

Griswold, Ct.

New London co. This town was taken from Preston in 1815, and is separated from Lisbon by Quennebaugh river. The Pochaug, a sluggish stream, passes through the town. The principal village, which is very neat and pretty, containing about 900 inhabitants, is called *Jewett City*. The *city* lies on the east side of the Quennebaug, at this place a very powerful stream, and contains three extensive cotton factories, a church, bank, and a number of handsome buildings.— This little city is said to be very prosperous in its manufacturing and commercial concerns. It lies 8 miles N. E. from Norwich, and 46 E. S. E. from Hartford. There are other manufactories of cotton in this town, and some of wool. The surface of Griswold is hilly; its soil a gravelly loam: some produce is sent to market, and about 3,000 sheep are kept. Population, 1830, 2,212.

Groton, N. H.,

Grafton co., is bound N. by Rumney, E. by Hebron, S. by Orange, and W. by Dorchester. It is 10 miles S. W. from Plymouth, 45 N. W. from Concord, and 15 S. E. from Hanover. The north part is watered by a branch of Baker's river, and the southerly part has several small streams, which fall into Newfound lake. There is but one pond of any consequence lying wholly in this town, and that is situated about a mile N. E. of the meetinghouse. Groton was granted July 8, 1761, to George Abbot and others by the name of *Cockermouth*. It was re-granted, about five years afterwards, to Col. John Hale and others, and the first settlement was commenced in 1770. Incorporated by the name of Groton, Dec. 1796. Population, in 1830, 689.

Groton, Vt.

Caledonia co. First settled, 1787. Wells river and its branches afford this town a good water power.— There are a number of ponds in Groton, well stored with excellent fish, some of which are large and handsome. The soil of the town is generally hard, but there is some choice land along the streams, and good timber.

The wife of a Mr. Page, of this town, in the year 1819, produced *four* lusty "green mountain boys" at a birth. When domestic manufactures of this description and amount, are adduced as evidence of the prosperity of a town, it is useless to talk about water power, cotton factories, or wool growing. Groton lies 16 miles E. by S. from Montpelier, and 15 S. by W. from Danville. Population, 1830, 836.

Groton, Mass.

Middlesex co. This is a delightful town, with an extraordinary good soil; 32 miles N. W. from Boston, and 13 W. by S. from Lowell. Groton was settled soon after Concord. It was for some years a frontier settlement, and much exposed to the Indians. In 1676, the town was attacked by 400 Indians, and all the buildings plundered and burnt, except four garrison houses. The town is finely watered by the Nashua and Squancook rivers and a number of beautiful ponds. The buildings are in a style of great neatness and taste, and some of elegance. This town has a female seminary of high reputation, and a number of moral and religious institutions. The local beauties of Groton and its facilities for education are so great as to induce many wealthy families to made it their residence. The manufactures of Groton consist of paper, axletrees, soap-stone pumps, mathematical instruments, clothing, palm-leaf hats, chairs, cabinet ware, leather, boots and shoes. Incorporated, 1655. Population, 1830, 2,057.

Groton, Ct.

New London co. Groton lies at the mouth of the river Thames, in the harbor of New London, and opposite to that city, on the E. The lands are generally hilly and rocky, with some fertile tracts on the margin of the Thames. There are several villages, *Groton Bank*, opposite New London, *Portersville*, on Mystic river, and *Pequonnuck*. The Pequonnuck and Mystic rivers pass through the town, and empty into Long Island Sound. A number of whale ships and coasting vessels are owned in this town. This is a place of some trade, and considerable quantities of the produce of the county is shipped to New York market. Ship building is carried on to a considerable extent, on the Mystic, which is navigable for large vessels about two miles from the Sound. About 300 men and boys are employed in navigation.

Previous to its incorporation, in 1705, Groton was a part of New-London. Population, 1830, 4,705.

" Groton will ever be memorable as the theatre of the most important and interesting military transactions which have taken place in the state. In the early settlement of the country, the fate of Connecticut was decided by the sword on Pequot hill, within the limits of this town, and the Pequots, the most haughty and warlike tribe of savages in New England, effectually crushed by a single blow, and their existence as a nation annihilated. In the war of the revolution, another of the 'high places of Groton became an Aceldama', and the flower of her sons were sacrificed to the vengeance of an infuriated enemy.

" On the 6th of September, 1781, a body of British troops, about 800 in number, under the command of Lieut. Col. Eyre, landed on the Groton side, opposite the lighthouse, and having found a lame boy collecting cattle, compelled him to show them the cart path to the fort. They landed about 9 o'clock in the morning of a most delightful day, clear and still. Fort Griswold was under the command of Lieut. Col. William Ledyard, brother of the celebrated traveller of the same name. He resided on Groton bank, opposite New London, and was much beloved and respected by his neighbors. On the advance of the enemy, Col. Ledyard, having but about 150 men with him in the fort, sent out an officer to get assistance, as there were a number of hundreds of people collected in the vicinity: this officer, by drinking too much, became intoxicated, and no reinforcement was obtained. On the rejection of a summons to surrender, the British extended their lines, so that they were scattered over the fields, and rushed on to the attack with trailed arms, under the fire of the Americans, to the assault of the fort on three sides. Having effected a lodgment in the ditch, they cut away the pickets, and having scaling ladders, they entered the fort and knocked away the gate on the inside. While the British were in the ditch, they had cold shot thrown on them, and as they were entering the embrazures, the garrison changed their weapons and fought desperately with spears or pikes, 15 or 16 feet in length, which did considerable execution. Unfortunately they had lent the greater part of the pikes belonging to the fort to a privateer a few days before. Major Montgomery was hoisted up on the walls of the fort by his soldiers. As he was flourishing his sword on his entrance, he was mortally wounded by Jordan Freeman, a colored man, who pierced him through with a spear. Another officer was killed by a musket ball, while in the fort. As he fell, he exclaimed: '*Put every one to death, don't spare one.*' Col. Ledyard, finding further resistance useless, presented his sword to an officer, who asked him who commanded the fort. 'I did,' said Col. Ledyard, 'but you do now.' The officer (Capt. Bloomfield) took his sword and plunged it into his bosom. Col. Ledyard fell on his face and instantly expired. An indiscriminate massacre now took place, till a British officer exclaimed: '*My soul cannot bear such destruction,*' and ordered a parley to be beat. Such had been the butchery in the fort, that it was *over shoes in blood* in some parts of the parade ground. Soon after the surrender, a wagon was loaded with wounded Americans, and set off down the hill; it struck an apple tree with great force, and knocked several of these bleeding men out, and caused their instant death. One of these distressed men having been thrown out of the wagon, and while crawling towards the fence on his hands and knees, was brutally knocked on the head by the butt end of a musket, by one of the refugees who were attached to the British army. The British embarked at the foot of the hill, near the ferry, and took off a number of prisoners with them. As they left the fort, they set fire to a train, intending to blow up the magazine, in which were about 100 barrels of powder. Fortunately it was extinguished by our people, who entered the fort soon after the enemy left it. It is stated that the enemy lost in the attack on the fort 54 killed and 143 wounded, several of whom afterwards died of their wounds. The killed of the enemy were buried by their comrades at the gate of the fort, and were so slightly covered that many of their legs and arms remained above ground. Our people who were killed at the fort, were stripped, and so disfigured, covered with blood and dust, that with the exception of two or three, they could not be recognized by their friends, except by some particular marks on their persons."

The monument on Groton Heights, in commemoration of the destruction of Groton and New London by the traitor Arnold, "has its foundation stone at an elevation of about 130 feet above tide water: the monument itself is one hundred and twenty seven feet in height. The pedestal rises about eighteen or twenty feet, and is twenty three feet square: on the pedestal rises an obelisk square, ninety two feet in height, twenty two feet square at its base, and eleven feet at the top. It is ascended by one hundred and sixty five stone steps, inserted into the outer wall, rising in a circular form, their inner ends supported by an iron rail and bannister. The monument is constructed of granite, of which there is an abundance in the vicinity. The expense of its erection was eleven thousand dollars; this amount was raised by a lottery, granted by the state for this purpose.

The following is the inscription, on marble, placed over the entrance of the monument.

" This Monument
was erected under the patronage
of the
State of Connecticut,
A. D. 1830,
and in the 55th year of the Independence of the U. S. A.
In memory of the brave Patriots
who fell
in the massacre at Fort Griswold,
near this spot,
on the 6th of September, A. D. 1781,
when the
British, under the command
of the traitor, Benedict Arnold,
burnt the towns of
New London and Groton,
and spread desolation and woe
throughout this region."

Guildhall, Vt.

County town of Essex co. Guildhall is situated on the W. side of Connecticut river, and is united to Lancaster, N. H., by two bridges across the river. The town is watered by several small streams.— The soil of the town is quite uneven and stony, except a tract of intervale on the river. Cow and Burnside mountains are considerable elevations, and afford excellent views of the meanderings of the Connecticut. Guildhall lies 50 miles N. E. from Montpelier, and 90 N. by E. from Windsor. First settled, 1789. Population, 1830, 481.

Guilford, Me.

Piscataquis co. This town is finely watered by the Piscataquis and some of its upper branches. It is of fine soil, and produced in 1837, 4,965 bushels of wheat. It has a pleasant village, a number of mills, and considerable trade. Guilford is 71 miles N. by E. from Augusta, 45 N. W. from Bangor, and 12 N. W. from Dover. Incorporated, 1816. Population, 1837, 799.

Guilford, Vt.

Windham co. This town was first permanently settled in 1760. It lies 125 miles S. from Montpelier, 15 S. by E. from Newfane, and 30 E. from Bennington. Population, 1830, 1,760. The people of this town took an active part in defending the rights of Vermont against the claims of jurisdiction set up by the state of New York, about the years 1783-4. Guilford produced a number of patriots in this as also in the revolutionary cause. The soil of the town is warm and fertile, exceedingly productive of grain, fruits, maple sugar, butter, cheese, pork, sheep, horses, and beef cattle. It has good mill seats on Green river and branches of Broad brook, a number of manufactories, a medicinal spring, and various kinds of minerals.

Guilford, Ct.

New Haven co. This town, the *Menunkatuc* of the Indians, was first settled in 1639. The town was settled by a party of Non-Conformists from England, at the head of which was the Rev. Henry Whitfield. Mr. Whitfield's house, built of stone, in 1640, is now standing, occupied, and in good repair. The cement used in building it, is said to be harder than the stone itself. This building was used by the first settlers as a fort and place of refuge against the attacks of the natives.

The first marriage in the town was solemnized in this building. The *treat* on the occasion was *pork* and *peas*. Guilford *borough* was incorporated in 1815. It is handsomely located two miles from Long Island Sound, on a tract of alluvial plain, and near a small stream called the Menunkatuc. The buildings in the borough are neat, but somewhat antiquated in their appearance.—Guilford is a place of resort for sea air and bathing. The accommodations are very good. The scenery in the vicinity of Sachem's Head is wild and picturesque. The soil of Guilford is well adapted to agricultural pursuits, to which, and some coasting trade, the principal part of the inhabitants are devoted. It lies 16 miles E. from New Haven, and 36 S. from Hartford. Population, 1830, 2,344.

Haddam, Ct.

One of the county towns of Middlesex co. Incorporated, 1668. This town lies on both sides of Connecticut river. Haddam Society, on the W. side, is the largest part of the town, and the seat of justice. That part of Haddam on the E. side is called Haddam Neck. There is but little alluvial land in Haddam. The principal part of the township is hilly and stony, with considerable forests. There are valuable quarries of granite on both sides of the river. About 150 men are annually employed in quarrying it, and about $70,000 worth of stone is annually exported. There are many vessels built at Haddam. The timber in this quarter of the county is well adapted for that purpose. The village of Haddam is pleasant, and has a good prospect of the river. It lies 23 miles S. from Hartford, and 8 S. E. from Middletown. Population, 1830, 2,830.

DAVID BRAINERD, the devoted missionary among the Indians, first drew his breath in Haddam.

"If the greatness of a character is to be estimated by the object it pursues, the danger it braves, the difficulties it encounters, and the purity and energy of its motives, David Brainerd is one of the greatest characters that ever appeared in the world. Compared with this standard of greatness, what little things are the Alexanders, the Cæsars, the conquerors of the whole earth. A nobler object no human or angelic mind could ever propose to itself than to promote the glory of the great Governor of the Universe, in studying and laboring to diffuse purity and happiness among his unholy and miserable creatures.

"'His life and diary among the Indians,' says a celebrated English divine, 'exhibits a perfect pattern of the qualities which should distinguish the instructor of rude and barbarous tribes; the most invincible patience and self denial, the profoundest humility, exquisite prudence, indefatigable industry, and such a devotedness to God, or rather such an absorption of the whole soul in zeal for the divine glory and the salvation of men, as is scarcely paralleled since the age of the apostles.'"

This faithful servant of Christ died at the house of the Rev. Jonathan Edwards, at Northampton, Mass., October 10, 1747, aged 30.

Hadley, Mass.

Hampshire co. This is a pleasant town on the E. bank of Connecticut river, and unites with Northampton by a beautiful bridge, 1,080 feet in length. It was first settled in 1647. Incorporated, 1661. Population, 1837, 1,305. It lies 88 miles W. from Boston. Two small streams afford the town some water power. Hadley contains a large and fertile tract of alluvial meadow. The village, situated on the river, is pleasant, and contains many neat and valuable buildings.

Hadley was a retreat of the celebrated Goffe and Whalley, two of the judges who condemned Charles I. for execution. They remained secluded here more than fifteen years, when Whalley died. Goffe died and was buried at New Haven, Ct., some years after.

The manufactures of Hadley consist of leather, boots, shoes, hats, glue, palm-leaf hats, wire, chairs, cabinet ware, brooms, and brushes. Total value the year ending April 1, 1837, $117,850. This town is celebrated for raising broom corn. The value of brooms manufactured was $39,248. A considerable quantity of the unmanufactured material was sent to other places.

Halifax, Vt.

Windham co. This township is rather elevated, but of good soil, finely adapted for grazing. It is a place of considerable trade, and of manufactures on its numerous streams. Its principal streams are Green river and a branch of the Deerfield. There are some handsome falls of water in Halifax, and a curious cave called *Dun's Den*. The productions of the town are butter, cheese, pork, sheep and other cattle. The cause of education flourishes here, and the people are generally independent cultivators of the soil. Halifax lies 125 miles S. from Montpelier, and 15 S. from Newfane. First settled, 1761.—Population, 1830, 1,562.

Halifax, Mass.

Plymouth co. The Indian name of this place was *Monponset*. It lies 28 miles S. S. E. from Boston, and 12 W. by S. from Plymouth. The surface of the town is generally level, with considerable good soil. Monponset and other ponds are large collections of water, and the sources of valuable mill privileges. There are a cotton and woolen mill in the town, and manufactures of shoes and straw braid;—total annual amount of manufactures about $150,000. Halifax was incorporated in 1734. Population, 1837, 781.

Hallowell, Me.

Kennebec co. Hallowell is delightfully situated on both sides of Kennebec river, between Augusta and Gardiner, two miles below the former and four miles above the latter. The principal village is on the W. side of the river. The streets run parallel with the river, and the ground ascends 200 feet from the lower street, or business part of the village. On this street are 60 commodious stores, constructed principally of brick. Most of the dwelling houses are on the back or elevated streets: they are built, as are the churches, with great taste, and being surrounded by beautiful groves, make a fine appearance. The varied views of the river, the neighboring towns, and of a fertile country of hills and vales, presented from the high grounds on each side of the village, form an exhibition of scenery of uncommon excellence. Hallowell is about 3 miles in width, and extends back on each side of the river 5 miles. It was incorporated in 1771, and included all the territory of Augusta and a part of Gardiner. From this place the brave but traitorous Arnold marched on an expedition against Canada, in 1776.

There is one water mill in the town; two saw mills, an iron foundry and machine shop, worked by steam. Steam boats ply from this place to Portland and Boston, during the season of navigation. There is considerable tonnage at this place: a number of vessels are engaged in the freighting business, and others run as packets to various places.

The principal exports are lumber, granite, and all the common productions of a fertile northern climate. The granite quarries at Hallowell have been worked for fifteen years with great success.

The granite is of a light color and easily wrought: in some years $100,000 worth of it has been transported. Vessels drawing 9 feet of water can come to the wharves in the centre of the village. As Hallowell and Augusta are so closely united in all their various interests and pursuits, a repetition of what we have said of the favorable position of Augusta, and of its future prospects, is unnecessary. With common success in our national affairs, and with a continuation of that spirit of enterprize, every day manifested on the banks of the Kennebec, it requires no *Mormon spectacles* to foresee that within a very few years there will be a continuous village from the Kennebec dam to the mouth of the Cobbesseeontee. Population, 1820, 2,919; 1830, 3,964. The present population is about 5,000.

Hallowell was, for many years, the residence of BENJAMIN VAUGHAN, LL. D. a gentleman highly distinguished for his learning, public benefactions and private virtues.

Hall's Stream, N. H.,

Rises in the highlands which separate that state from the British dominions, and forms the N. W. boundary between New Hampshire and Lower Canada, from its source to its junction with the Connecticut at Stewartstown.

Hamden, Ct.

New Haven co. This town was taken from New Haven in 1786, from which it lies about 6 miles N. It is situated between the East and West Rock ranges of mountains, the southern terminus of the Green mountain range. The soil in many parts is easy of cultivation, but in general it is more adapted to grazing than tillage. Minerals are found here, among which are specimens of very pure copper. Mill river affords numerous sites for water works.

Whitneysville, about two miles from New Haven, is admirably located for manufacturing opperations. The manufactures at the *Carmel works*, consist of paper, carriages, coach and eliptic springs, steps, axletrees, brass work, &c. Mount Carmel, a noted elevation, 8 miles N. from New Haven, exhibits an extensive prospect. Population, 1830, 1,669.

Hamilton, Mass.

Essex co. This is a beautiful farming town, and most of the inhabitants are employed in cultivating it. There are some vessels built here, and some manufactures of leather, boots, and shoes. The town is quite small. Population, 1837, 827. Taken from Ipswich in 1793. It lies 8 miles N. by E. from Salem.

Hampden, Me.

Penobscot co. Hampden lies on the west side of Penobscot, below and adjoining Bangor. It is also watered by the Sowadabscook river, a large and valuable mill stream. This is an important township in its commerce on the Penobscot, its manufacture of lumber, and its agricultural productions. It is one of the most flourishing towns on the river. The quantity of wheat produced by the farmers, in 1837, was 5,664 bushels. Population, 1830, 2,020; 1837, 2,520. Hampden is 6 miles S. from Bangor, and 62 E. N. E. from Augusta.

Hampden County, Mass.

Springfield is the chief town. This county is very fertile and well cultivated, and in common with all the counties on Connecticut river, it presents a rich array of delightful scenery. Its rivers afford an abundant water power; and this county has become noted for its various and extensive manufactures. Much inland trade is brought to the banks of the Connecticut, and large exports are made from this county, the product both of the soil and mechanical labor. This county was taken from Hampshire county in 1812. Population, 1820, 28,021; 1830, 31,640; 1837, 33,627. Area, 585 square miles. Bounded S. by Tolland and Hartford counties, Connecticut; W. by Berkshire county; N. by Hampshire county, and E. by Worcester county: 57 inhabitants to a square mile. The Connecticut, Westfield, Chickopee, and Quinebaugh are its chief rivers.

The value of the manufactures of this county, the year ending April 1, 1837, was $3,056,302. The value of wool, the product of 29,950 sheep, was $44,786.

Hampshire County, Mass.

Northampton is the chief town. This ancient county, although its limits have been greatly reduced by the production of Franklin and Hampden counties, is still increasing in agricultural, commercial and manufacturing strength. Located in the centre of the alluvial basin of the noble Connecticut; blessed with a rich and variegated soil, and great water power, this must ever remain one of the most independent counties in New England.— Area, 532 square miles. Population, 1820, 26,447; 1830, 30,210; 1837, 30,413. Incorporated, 1662. This county is bounded S. by Hampden, W. by Berkshire, N. by Franklin, and E. by Worcester counties: 57 inhabitants to a square mile. The Connecticut, Westfield, and Swift, are its chief rivers. The manufactures of this county, the year ending April 1, 1837, amounted to $2,335,652. The value of wool, the fleeces of 64,274 sheep, amounted to $103,751.

Hampstead, N. H.,

Rockingham co., lies partly on the height of land between Merrimack and Piscataqua rivers. Most of the waters descend S W. into the Merrimack through Spiggot river, which flows from Wash pond, near the centre of the town. Angly pond is in the N. E. part of the town, the waters of which pass into Powow river. Island pond, in the S. W. part of the town, contains a valuable farm of 300 acres. The town was granted by Gov. Benning Wentworth, January 19, 1749, and named by him after a pleasant village five miles N. of London, England. He reserved the island before mentioned for his own farm. Population in 1830, 913.

Hampton, Me.

See "Down East."

Hampton, N. H.,

Rockingham co., lies on the seacoast, bounded N. E. by North-Hampton, S. E. by the Atlantic, S. W. by Hampton Falls, N. W. by Hampton Falls and part of Exeter Distant 13 miles S. W. from Portsmouth, 7 S. E. from Exeter, and 50 S. E. from Concord. The soil is well adapted to tillage and mowing, and about one fifth of the territory is a salt marsh. Hampton is pleasantly situated; many eminences in the town affording romantic views of the ocean, Isles of Shoals, and sea-coast from Cape Ann to Portsmouth. Its beaches have long been the resort of invalids and parties of pleasure, and are little inferior to the famous Nahant beach near Boston.

Boar's Head is an abrupt eminence extending into the sea, and dividing the beaches about half way between the river's mouth and the N. E. corner of the town. On the N. beach are numerous fish-houses, from which the winter and summer fisheries have been carried on with much success. Great quantities of the winter fish are carried frozen into the interior, and to Vermont and Canada.

The Indian name of this town was *Winnicumet;* it was first settled in 1638, by emigrants from the county of Norfolk, England. The first house was erected in 1635, by Nicholas Easton, and was called the Bound-house. The town was incorporated in 1636, and then included within its limits what now constitutes the towns of North Hampton, Hampton Falls, Kensington and Seabrook. This town was formerly the scene of Indian depredations. On the 17th Aug. 1703, a party of Indians killed 5 persons in Hampton, among whom was a widow Mussey, celebrated as a preacher among the Friends. The Hon. CHRISTOPHER TOPPAN died here in Feb., 1819, aged 84: he was a very useful and distinguished citizen. Population in 1830, 1,103.

Hampton, Ct.

Windham co. This town was taken from Windham and Pomfret in 1786. The people are generally agriculturalists, with a good strong soil of an uneven surface. The village is pleasantly situated on high ground, 35 miles E. from Hartford and 6 from Brooklyn. Hampton has good mill seats on a branch of Shetucket river. Population, 1830, 1,101.

Hampton Falls, N. H.,

Rockingham co., is situated 45 miles S. E. from Concord, and 16 S. W. from Portsmouth. The soil is generally good. Hampton Falls was originally a part of Hampton, from which it was separated and incorporated, in 1712. Population, 1830, 582.

Hancock County, Me.

Ellsworth is the chief town. This county is bounded N. by Penobscot county, E. by Washington county, S. by the Atlantic ocean, and W. by Penobscot bay and river, and a part by Penobscot county. Its extent on the ocean is between 50 and 60 miles: it comprises numerous islands of great beauty, some of which are large, fertile and well cultivated; it comprises also numerous bays, and a vast number of coves, inlets and spacious harbors.

Perhaps there is no district of its extent on the American coast, that offers greater facilities for navigation, in all its various branches, than the county of Hancock. The tonnage of Frenchman's bay, in this county, in 1837, was 13,184 tons. The soil of the county is generally of an excellent quality, particularly in the interior. There are a great number of ponds in the county: every section of it is watered by mill streams, and Union river, nearly in its centre, affords the interior part great facilities for transportation. This county contains an area of about 1,850 square miles. Population, 1830, 24,347; 1837, 28,120. Population to a square mile, 15. This county produced, in 1837, 21,446 bushels of wheat, and contained 38,870 sheep.

Hancock, Me.

Hancock co. This town was taken from Sullivan and Trenton in 1828. It is situated between those towns, and is nearly surrounded by the head waters of Frenchman's bay. It is a place of some navigation; 85 miles E. from Augusta, and bounded easterly by Ellsworth. Population, 1837, 653.

Hancock, N. H.

Hillsborough co. It is 35 miles from Concord, 22 from Amherst, and 19 from Keene. The W. part of the town is mountainous, but affords excellent pasturing and many good farms. The other parts of the town are agreeably diversified with plains, hills and valleys. On the Contoocook, and some of its tributary streams, there are several tracts of excellent intervale. There are two considerable ponds, one of which is in the centre, a few rods N. of the meeting-house. There is a cotton factory, a paper mill, and several other manufacturing establishments here; also a flourishing academy. Hancock was incorporated Nov. 5, 1779. It was named after Gov. Hancock, of Boston, who was one of the original proprietors. The first settlement was begun in 1764. Population, 1830, 1,316.

Hancock, Vt.

Addison co. Several branches of Otter creek rise in this town. Hancock is wholly on the mountains, and most of the land fit only for grazing. First settled, 1778. Population, 1830, 472. It lies 30 miles S. W. from Montpelier, and 15 S. E. from Middlebury.

Hancock, Mass.

Berkshire co. This is a mountainous township, on the line of the state of New York, the source of the Housatonick, and the residence of a family of "Shakers." It lies 129 miles W. from Boston, 15 N. by W. from Lenox, and 5 E. from New Lebanon, New York. Incorporated, 1776. Population, 1837, 975.

There are one cotton and three woolen mills in the town, and some manufactures of leather, boots, shoes, iron castings, and wooden ware. The value of 5,445 fleeces of wool, sheared in 1837, amounted to $11,544.

As we are so near the lovely valley of New Lebanon, its tepid springs, and a large family of our friends, the SHAKERS, we must be permitted to cross the line a moment, "just to take a look."

New Lebanon, New York, is in the county of Columbia, and situated in a delightful valley, surrounded by cultivated hills, which present scenery greatly variegated and peculiarly pleasing.

A community of Shakers, of between 500 and 600, own about 3,000 acres of excellent land in this township, which is highly improved by this industrious, hospitable, and curious people. Their village is about two miles southeast of the springs.

The Springs are on the side of a hill, and are so abundant as to supply a small water power. The waters are tasteless, pure as crystal, and appear to differ in no respect from other pure mountain waters, except in temperature, which is always at 72° of Fahrenheit.

This is a great resort for visitors from all directions:—some to enjoy the romantic scenery with which this region abounds, and others the benign influence of the waters. The public resorts are well located, and afford excellent accommodations. New Lebanon is 134 miles W. from Boston, 24 E. from Albany, 25 N. E. from Hudson, 7 W. from Pittsfield, 23 S. by W. from Williamstown, 156 N. by E. from New York, and 68 N. W. by W. from Hartford. Ct.

Hanover, N. H.

Grafton co. The Connecticut river separates it from Norwich, Vermont. It is 53 miles N. W. from Concord, and 102 from Portsmouth. In this town there is no river nor any considerable stream besides the Connecticut. Mink brook, running in a S. W. direction, Slate brook in a W. course, and Goose-Pond brook in the N. E. part of the town, are among the principal streams. Neither of them is large enough for permanent mill privileges. There are several small islands in Connecticut river within the limits of Hanover, the largest of which is Parker's island, containing about 20 acres. There are no natural ponds. The surface of Hanover is agreeably diversified with hills and valleys, and the greatest part is suitable for farms. There is but a small proportion of waste land; less, perhaps, than in any other town in Grafton county. It is estimated that nearly one half is under improvement. Moose mountain is a considerable elevation, extending across the town from N. to S., at the distance of about five miles from Connecticut river. A handsome bridge connects the S. W. part of the town with Norwich. The principal village is in the S. W. corner of the town, on a beautiful and extensive plain, half a mile from Connecticut river, and 180 feet above the level of its waters. Vegetable substances are found in different parts of this plain at a depth of from 50 to 80 feet. The principal houses are erected round a square, level area, of 12 acres. The remainder stand on different streets, leading from the green in all directions.

In this pleasant village is located Dartmouth College. See *Register.*

Among the worthy men who have finished their earthly career in this place, may be mentioned the following:

Rev. ELEAZAR WHEELOCK, D. D., who died April 24, 1779, aged 69.

Hon. JOHN WHEELOCK, LL. D., president of the college 35 years, who died April 4, 1817, aged 63.

Hon. BEZALEEL WOODWARD, who died Aug. 1804.

Rev. JOHN SMITH, D. D., who died April, 1809.

Hon. JOHN HUBBARD, who died in Sept. 1810.

Rev. FRANCIS BROWN, D. D., who died July 27, 1820, aged 36. These gentlemen were all connected with the college. Population, 1830, 2,361.

Hanover, Mass.

Plymouth co. Hanover is bounded S. by North river, which furnishes good mill sites. It was incorporated in 1727. It lies 23 miles S. E. from Boston, and 12 N. W. from Plymouth. The manufactures of Hanover consist of bar iron, iron castings, anchors, ploughs, vessels, tacks, leather, boots, shoes, and woolen cloth: total annual amount, about $75,000. Pop. 1837, 1,435.

Hanson, Mass.

Plymouth co. This town is watered by a branch of North river and several ponds. It was taken from Pembroke in 1820, and lies in the vicinity of large beds of excellent iron ore. The manufactures of Hanson consist of ship anchors and knees, nails, carriage springs, iron castings, leather, shoes, sawed boxes and shingles: total annual amount, about $70,000. Population, 1837, 1,058. It lies 24 miles S. S. E. from Boston, and 15 N. N. W. from Plymouth.

Hardwick, Vt.

Caledonia co. Hardwick is finely watered by Lamoille river, which gives the town valuable mill sites, and which are well improved for manufacturing purposes. The soil of the town is generally very good, and produces a variety of exports. Between six and seven thousand sheep, and many other cattle, are kept in the town, a large amount of which are annually fattened and sent to market.

Among the first settlers of the town, in 1790, was Mr. Gideon Sabin, whose wife became the mother of 26 children. Population, 1830, 1,216. Hardwick lies 20 miles N. N. E. from Montpelier, and 13 N. W. from Danville.

Hardwick, Mass.

Worcester co. Ware river and a smaller stream pass through the S. part of this town, and furnish good mill privileges. It lies 62 miles W. from Boston and 22 W. by N. from Worcester. Incorporated, 1738. Population, 1837, 1,818.— There are 2 paper mills in the town, and manufactures of straw bonnets, palm-leaf hats, boots, shoes, ploughs, leather, chairs and cabinet ware: annual amount about $50,000.—

Hardwick is a pleasant town, of good soil, with a fine fish pond.

Harmony, Me.

Somerset co. This town has an excellent soil, and is well watered by a large and beautiful pond, and by other sources of Sebasticook river. In 1837 it had a population of 1,048, and produced 6,836 bushels of wheat. It was incorporated in 1803, and lies 53 miles N. by E. from Augusta, and 23 N. E. from Norridgewock.

Harpswell, Me.

Cumberland co. This township comprises a promontory in Casco bay, formerly *Merryconeag*, and several islands surrounding it, the largest of which is called *Sebascodegan*. The waters which enclose this territory are so situated, at the northern and eastern extremity of Casco bay, that a canal of about a mile in length would unite them with Kennebec river, near Bath. The soil of Harpswell is very fertile, and the location delightful in summer. It is a resort for invalids and parties of pleasure. The people are principally engaged in farming and fishing. It lies 22 miles N. E. from Portland by water, and 4 miles S. E. from Brunswick. Incorporated, 1758. Population, 1837, 1,344.

Harrington, Me.

Washington co. This town is bounded on the S. and E. by the waters of Narraguagus bay, and W. by the river of that name. It has good mill privileges, excellent harbors, considerable navigation and trade. Incorporated, 1797. Population, 1830, 1,118; 1837, 1,354.— Harrington lies 118 miles E. from Augusta, and 25 W. S. W. from Machias.

Harrison, Me.

Cumberland co. Crooked river passes the E. side of this town, and the waters of Long pond are its western boundary. This is a good township of land, and produced, in 1837, 3,180 bushels of wheat. Incorporated, 1805. Population, 1837, 1,161. Harrison has Otisfield on the E., and is 75 miles W. S. W. from Augusta, and 45 N. W. from Portland.

Hartford, Me.

Oxford co. This excellent township is watered by ponds and small streams, and produced, in 1837, 9,318 bushels of wheat. It lies 31 miles W. from Augusta, and 15 N. E. from Paris. Population, 1830, 1,453. Incorporated, 1798.

Hartford, Vt.

Windsor co. This town is on the west side of the Connecticut, and is otherwise finely watered by White and Waterqueechy rivers. It lies 42 miles S. S. E. from Montpelier, and 14 N. from Windsor. First settled, 1764. Population, 1830, 2,044. The surface of the town is uneven, but the soil is rich, warm, and very productive. The two principal villages are pleasantly located on the banks of the rivers that meet the Connecticut at this place, both of which are flourishing in manufactures and trade. Many cattle, beside pork, butter, cheese, &c., are sent to market from Hartford. In 1837 it had 13,207 sheep.

Hartford County, Ct.

Hartford is the chief town. This county is bounded N. by Hampden county, Mass., E. by Tolland county, S. by the counties of Middlesex and New Haven, and W. by the county of Litchfield. This is considered the most important and valuable county in the state, in regard to the variety and richness of its soil, and the high state of culture it has attained. It was constituted in 1666, since which, Tolland county and parts of Middlesex, Windham, Litchfield, and New

London have been detached. Its present limits comprise an area of about 727 square miles. Besides the Connecticut, which traverses its whole length, the Farmington, Hackanum, Podunk, Scantic, and other streams, water the county in almost every direction. On these streams important manufacturing establishments have sprung up, and unite with the agricultural interest and river trade in rendering this county the centre of a large and flourishing business. In 1837 there were in the county 29,576 sheep. Population, 1820, 47,261; 1830, 51,141: 70 inhabitants to a square mile.

Hartford, Ct.

The first English settlement in Hartford was commenced in 1635, by Mr. John Steel and his associates from Newtown, (now Cambridge) in Massachusetts. The main body of the first settlers, with Mr. Hooker at their head, did not arrive till the following year.

"About the beginning of June, (says Dr. Trumbull,) Mr. Hooker, Mr. Stone, and about one hundred men, women and children, took their departure from Cambridge, and traveled more than a hundred miles, through a hideous and trackless wilderness, to Hartford. They had no guide but their compass, and made their way over mountains, through swamps, thickets and rivers, which were not passable but with great difficulty. They had no cover but the heavens, nor any lodgings but those that simple nature afforded them. They drove with them a hundred and sixty head of cattle, and by the way subsisted on the milk of their cows. Mrs. Hooker was borne through the wilderness upon a litter. The people carried their packs, arms, and some utensils. They were nearly a fortnight on their journey. This adventure was the more remarkable, as many of the company were persons of figure, who had lived in England, in honor, affluence and delicacy, and were entire strangers to fatigue and danger."

The Indian name of Hartford was *Suckiag.* A deed appears to have been given by *Sunckquasson,* the sachem of the place, about 1636, to Samuel Stone and William Goodwin, who appear to have acted in behalf of the first settlers.

The town of Hartford is bounded N. by Windsor and Bloomfield, E. by Connecticut river, S. by Wethersfield, and W. by Farmington and Avon. It is about six miles in length from north to south, and averages about five in breadth. The western part of the town has a soil of red gravelly earth, very rich and productive. That part near the river is covered with a strong clay, or a rich black mould. The latter is principally in the valuable tract of meadow adjacent to Connecticut river.

HARTFORD CITY, incorporated in 1784, is over a mile in length upon the river, and about three fourths of a mile in breadth. The alluvial flat upon the river is narrow, being from 40 to 100 rods, and is connected with the upland by a very gradual elevation. It is situated on the west side of Connecticut river, 45 miles from its mouth. It is in N. lat. 41° 45′ 59″, W. lon. 72° 40′. It is 260 miles S. W. from Augusta, Maine; 139 S. S. W. from Concord, New Hampshire; 205 S. from Montpelier, Vermont; 97 W. S. W. from Boston, Massachusetts; 64 W. from Providence, Rhode Island; 110 N. E. from the city of New York, and 335 E. from Washington.

The legislature of the state assembles alternately at Hartford and New Haven, the odd years at Hartford. The city is rather irregularly laid out, and is divided at the S. part by Mill, or Little river. Across this stream a fine bridge of freestone has been thrown, which connects the two parts of the city. This structure is 100 feet wide, supported by a single arch, 7 feet in thickness at the base, and 3 feet 3 inches at the centre, the chord or span of which is 104 feet; elevation from the bed of the river to the top of the arch, 30 feet 9 inches. Another bridge, across Connecticut river, 1,000 feet long, and which cost over $100,000, unites the city with East Hartford. Hartford is very advantageously situated for business, is surrounded by an extensive and wealthy district, and communicates with the towns and villages on the Connecticut above by small steam-boats, two of which, for passengers, ply daily between Hartford and Springfield. The remainder are employed in towing flat bottomed boats, of 15 to 30 tons burthen, as far as Wells' river, 220 miles above the city. The coasting trade is very considerable, and there is some foreign trade carried on. A daily line of steam-boats pass between Hartford and New York. The manufactures of this city exceed $900,000 per annum; among these are various manufactures of tin, copper, and sheet iron; block tin and pewter ware; printing presses and ink; a manufactory of iron machinery; iron foundries, saddlery, carriages, joiners' tools, paper-hangings, looking-glasses, umbrellas, stone ware, a brewery, a web manufactory, cabinet furniture, boots and shoes, hats, clothing for exportation, soap and candles, manufactories of machine and other wire cards, operated by dogs, &c. More than twice as many books, it is stated, are published here, annually, as are manufactured in any other place of equal population in the United States.

The city is well built, and contains many elegant public and private edifices. The state-house, in which are the public offices of the state, is surmounted by a cupola, and is a very handsome and spacious building. The city hall, built for city purposes, is also spacious and elegant; it has two fronts, with porticos,—supported each by six massive columns. The American Asylum for the deaf and dumb, the Retreat for the insane, and Washington College, are all beautifully located, in the immediate vicinity of the city. The population within the city limits, in September, 1835, was nine thousand and eight hundred.

"*The American Asylum* for the education and instruction of deaf and dumb persons, was founded by an association of gentlemen in Hartford, Conn., in 1815. Their attention was called to this important charity by a case of deafness in the family of one of their number. An interesting child of the late Dr. Cogswell, who had lost her hearing at the age of two years, and her speech soon after, was, under Providence, the cause of its establishment. Her father, ever ready to sympathize with the afflicted, and prompt to relieve human suffering, embraced in his plans for the education of his own daughter, all who might be similarly unfortunate.— The co-operation of the benevolent was easily secured, and measures were taken to obtain from Europe a knowledge of the difficult art, unknown in this country, of teaching written language through the medium of signs, to the deaf and dumb. For this purpose, the Rev. Thomas H. Gallaudet visited England and Scotland, and applied at the institutions in those countries for instruction in their system; but meeting with unexpected difficulties, he repaired to France, and obtained, at the Royal Institution at Paris, those qualifications for an instructor of the deaf and dumb, which a selfish and mistaken policy had refused him in Great Britain. Accompanied by Mr. Laurent

Clerc, himself deaf and dumb, and for several years a successful teacher under the Abbe Sicard, Mr. Gallaudet returned to this country in August, 1816. The Asylum had, in May preceding, been incorporated by the state legislature. Some months were spent by Messrs. Gallaudet and Clerc in obtaining funds for the benefit of the institution, and in the spring of 1817 the Asylum was opened for the reception of those for whom it was designed, and the course of instruction commenced with seven pupils.

"As the knowledge of the institution extended, and the facilities for obtaining its advantages were multiplied, the number of pupils increased from seven to one hundred and forty, which for several years past has not been much above the average number; and since its commencement, in 1817, to 1837, instruction has been imparted to four hundred and seventy-seven deaf and dumb persons.

"In 1819, Congress granted the institution a township of land in Alabama, the proceeds of which have been invested as a permanent fund. The principal building was erected in 1820, and the pupils removed to it in the spring of the following year. It is one hundred and thirty feet long, fifty feet wide, and, including the basement, four stories high. Other buildings have been subsequently erected, as the increasing number of pupils made it necessary; the principal of which is a dining hall and workshops for the male pupils. Attached to the institution are eight or ten acres of land, which afford ample room for exercise, and the cultivation of vegetables and fruits for the pupils.

"The system of instruction adopted at this institution is substantially the same as that of the French school at Paris. It has, however, been materially improved and modified by Mr. Gallaudet and his associates. This system, and indeed every other rational system of teaching the deaf and dumb, is based upon the natural language of signs. By this we mean those gestures which a deaf and dumb person will naturally use to express his ideas, and to make known his wants previous to instruction. These gestures and signs are rather *pictorial*, that is, an exact outline of the object, delineated by the hands in the air; or *descriptive*, giving an idea of an object by presenting some of its prominent and striking features; or *conventional*, such as may have been agreed upon by a deaf and dumb person and his associates. As there are very few objects which can be expressed with sufficient clearness by the delineation of its outline alone, a descriptive sign is usually connected with it. Thus, in making a sign for a *book*, the outline is first delineated by the fore finger of both hands. To this is added the descriptive signs of opening a book, placing it before the eyes, and moving the lips as in reading. It may therefore simplify the classification of natural signs if the first two divisions be united; and it will be sufficiently accurate to say that all the signs used by the deaf and dumb are either *descriptive* or *conventional*. By far the greater part of these signs belong to the former class; as it includes the signs for most common objects, actions and emotions. A deaf and dumb child constructs his language upon the same principle as the child who can hear; that of imitation.

"In the school-room, the instructor makes use of *natural signs* to communicate ideas to his pupils, of *systematic signs* to enable them to translate their own into written language; of the *manual alphabet*, or signs of the hand, corresponding to the letters of the alphabet; and of *written symbols* to express the grammatical relations of words.

"The pupils usually remain at

the Asylum four or five years, in which time an intelligent child will acquire a knowledge of the common operations of arithmetic, of geography, grammar, history, biography, and of written language, so as to enable him to understand the Scriptures, and books written in a familiar style. He will of course be able to converse with others by writing, and to manage his own affairs as a farmer or mechanic. There are workshops connected with the institution, in which the boys have the opportunity of learning a trade, and many of them, by devoting four hours each day to this object, become skillful workmen, and when they leave the Asylum find no difficulty in supporting themselves. The annual charge to each pupil is one hundred dollars.

"The department of instruction is under the control of the principal of the institution, who has also a general oversight of the other departments. The pupils are distributed into eight or nine classes, the immediate care of which is committed to the same number of assistant instructors. When out of school, the pupils are under the care of a steward and matron."

Retreat for the Insane. "This nstitution is situated on a commandng eminence, at the distance of a mile and a quarter, in a southwesterly direction, from the State House in Hartford. It was opened April 1, 1824. The elevation overlooks an ample range of fertile country, presenting on every side a most interesting landscape, adorned with every beauty of rural scenery, that can be found in rich and cultivated fields, and meadows of unrivalled verdure; in extensive groves and picturesque groups of forest, fruit and ornamental trees; and above all, in the charming diversity of level, sloping and undulating surfaces, terminating by distant hills, and more distant mountains.

"This site was selected as one pre-eminently calculated to attract and engage the attention, and soothe and appease the morbid fancies and feelings of the patient whose faculties are not sunk below or raised above the sphere of relations that originally existed. And if he is not beyond the reach of genial sensations, connected with external objects, he will undoubtedly feel the conscious evidence that this situation most happily unites the tranquilizing influence of seclusion and retirement, with the cheering effect of an animated picture of active life, continually passing in review before his eyes, while himself is remote, and secure from the annoyance of its bustle and noise.

"The edifice for the accommodation of the patients, and those who have the care of them, is constructed of unhewn free-stone, covered with a smooth, white, water-proof cement. Its style of architecture is perfectly plain and simple, and interests only by its symmetrical beauty, and perhaps by the idea it impresses of durability and strength, derived from the massy solidity of its materials. Yet notwithstanding these, its general aspect is remarkably airy and cheerful, from the amplitude of its lights, and the brilliant whiteness of its exterior. The whole building is divided into commodious and spacious apartments, adapted to various descriptions of cases, according to their sex, nature and disease, habits of life, and the wishes of their friends. The male and female apartments are entirely separated, and either sex is completely secluded from the view of the other. Rooms are provided in both male and female apartments for the accommodation of the sick, where they are removed from any annoyance, and can continually receive the kind attentions of their immediate relations and friends. Attached to the building are about seventeen acres of excellent land, the principal part of which is laid out in walks, ornamental grounds and extensive gardens. With each wing and block of the building is connected a court-yard, encompassed by high fences, and handsomely laid out, designed to afford the benefit of exercise, pastime and fresh air, to those who cannot safely be allowed to range abroad." The mode of treatment at this institution is similar to that adopted at the *McLean* Asylum, Charlestown, Mass.

"*Washington College.* This institution was founded in 1826 It has two edifices of free stone; one 148 feet long by 43 wide, and 4 stories high, containing 48 rooms; the other 87 feet by 55, and 3 stories high, containing the chapel, library, mineralogical cabinet, philosophical chamber, laboratory and recitation rooms. See *Register.*

The Charter Oak. This tree stands on the beautiful elevation which rises above the south meadows, a few rods north of the ancient seat of the Wyllys family. The tree is still in a vigorous state, and may flourish for another century.

"That venerable tree, which concealed the charter of our rights," says a daughter of Secretary Wyllys, "stands at the foot of Wyllys hill. The first inhabitant of that name found it standing in the height of its glory. Age seems to have curtailed its branches, yet it is not exceeded in the height of its coloring, or richness of its foliage. The trunk measures twenty one feet in circumference, and near seven in diameter. The cavity, which was the asylum of our charter, was near the roots, and large enough to admit a child. Within the space of eight years, that cavity has closed, as if it had fulfilled the divine purpose for which it had been reared."

The story of the "Charter Oak" is thus told by Mr. Barber.

" Sir Edmund Andros being appointed the first governor-general over New England, arrived in Boston in Dec. 1686. From this place he wrote to the colony of Connecticut to resign their charter, but without success. " 'The assembly met as usual, in October, and the government continued according to charter, until the last of the month. About this time, Sir Edmund, with his suite and more than sixty regular troops, came to Hartford when the assembly were sitting, and demanded the charter, and declared the government under it to be dissolved. The assembly were extremely reluctant and slow with respect to any resolve to surrender the charter, or with respect to any motion to bring it forth. The tradition is, that governor Treat strongly represented the great expense and hardships of the colonists in planting the country; the blood and treasure which they had expended in defending it, both against the savages and foreigners; to what hardships he himself had been exposed for that purpose; and that it was like giving up his life, now to surrender the patent and privileges so dearly bought and so long enjoyed. The important affair was debated and kept in suspense until the evening, when the charter was brought and laid upon the table where the assembly were sitting. By this time great numbers of people were assembled, and men sufficiently bold to enterprise whatever might be necessary or expedient. The lights were instantly extinguished, and one Capt. Wadsworth, of Hartford, in the most silent and secret manner, carried off the charter, and secreted it in a large hollow tree, fronting the house of Hon. Samuel Wyllys, then one of the magistrates of the colony. The people all appeared peaceable and orderly. The candles were officiously re-lighted, but the patent was gone, and no discovery could be made of it, or the persons who carried it away.'"

West Hartford, or, as it was formerly called, *West Division*, is a fine tract of land. The inhabitants are mostly substantial farmers, and the general appearance of the place denotes an unusual share of equalized wealth and prosperity. The venerable NATHAN PERKINS, D. D., still continues his labors in the ministry in this place. In 1833, his sixtieth anniversary sermon was published. In that sermon he says, "I am now the oldest officiating minister of the gospel in this state, and, as far as I can learn, in the United States. And I cannot learn, from the history of churches in Connecticut, that there has ever been an instance of one of its ministers preaching for sixty years uninterruptedly to the same congregation."

Dr. Perkins stated, as we are informed, that from the commencement of his ministry, that in his church there had been one thousand deaths and one thousand baptisms—that he had delivered four thousand written sermons, and three thousand extemporaneous ones, on other occasions of worship—that he had attended sixty ordinations and installations, and had preached 20 ordination sermons, twelve of which had been published by request; that he had attended one hundred ecclesiastical councils, to heal difficulties in the churches, and that he had fitted for college one hundred and fifty students, and more than thirty for the gospel ministry.

Hartland, Me.

Somerset co. This excellent township is watered on its eastern boundary by one of the principal branches of Sebasticook river. The inhabitants are principally engaged in agricultural pursuits, and the soil richly rewards them for their industry. Hartland produced 4,836 bushels of wheat in 1837, some wool and other valuable commodities. It was incorporated in 1820. Population, 1837, 890. It lies 42 miles N. by E. from Augusta, and 18 N. E. from Norridgewock.

Hartland, Vt.

Windsor co. Timothy Lull was the father of this flourishing republic. He took his family from Dummerston, up Connecticut river about 50 miles, in a log canoe, in 1763. He landed at the mouth of a beautiful stream, called *Lull's Brook*. His nearest neighbors were more than 20 miles distant. He commenced a settlement on Lull's Brook, and, after acquiring a handsome property, died there at the age of 81. Timothy Lull, jr., was the first child born in the town.—On the occasion of his birth, a midwife was drawn 23 miles on a hand sled.

This is a rich farming town, pleasantly diversified by hills and valleys. Hartland produces many cattle: ten thousand sheep graze in its pastures. It lies on the west bank of Connecticut river. Waterqueechy river, at the N. part of the town, and Lull's Brook, at the S., give it a water power of great value. On these streams are neat villages and flourishing manufacturing establishments. Hartland lies 50 miles S. S. E. from Montpelier and 9 N. from Windsor. Population, 1830, 2,503.

Hartland, Ct.

Hartford co. This town is 22 miles N. W. from Hartford. It lies in a mountainous part of the state: most of the land is cold and fit only for grazing. A branch of Farmington river passes through the town, and forms what is called *Hartland hollow*, a deep ravine, presenting some bold and picturesque scenery. Hartland was incorporated in 1761. First settled, 1753. Population, 1830, 1,221.

Harvard, Mass.

Worcester co. This town was taken from Stow, Groton and Lancaster, in 1732. It is washed on the W. side by Nashua river. It lies 30 miles N. W. from Boston, 20 N. E. from Worcester, and 13 W. from Concord. Here are two large ponds with fine fish, and quarries of slate used for monuments.

About 200 of that industrious sect, called shakers, reside here, and own a considerable tract of excellent land. They live about 3 miles N. E. from the centre of the town, and supply the market with a great variety of wares, fruits, seeds, herbs, &c. &c., the product of their mechanical ingenuity and horticultural skill.

There are three paper mills in Harvard, and manufactures of palm-leaf hats, boots, shoes, leather and grave stones: annual value about $40,000. Large quantities of hops have been raised in this place.— Population, 1837, 1,566.

Harwich, Mass.,

Barnstable co., on the S. side of Cape Cod, 14 miles E. from Barnstable. Incorporated, 1694. Population, 1830, 2,464; 1837, 2,771. On Herring river, the outlet of Long pond, are cotton and other mills. Some vessels are built here and some salt manufactured. The product of the cod and mackerel fishery the year ending April 1, 1837, was $33,000. Harwich is a pleasant town: the village makes a good appearance from the sea.

Harwinton, Ct.

Litchfield co. Har-win-ton derived its name from three syllables taken from the names of Hartford, Windsor and Farmington. It was first settled in 1731; incorporated, 1737. Population, 1830, 1,516. It lies 23 miles W. from Hartford, 40 N. by W. from New Haven, and 8 E. from Litchfield. Harwinton is situated on high ground, abounding with granite rocks and more fit for grazing than tillage.

Hatfield, Mass.

Hampshire co. This is a wealthy agricultural township, noted for its good soil and fine beef cattle. It lies on the W. side of Connecticut river, 5 miles N. from Northampton, and 95 W. from Boston.— Incorporated, 1670. Population, 1837, 937. The manufactures of the town consist of corn brooms, boots, shoes, palm-leaf hats, and carriages; annual value about $50,000.

There is an elm tree in Hatfield which is said to measure, two feet from the ground, thirty four feet in circumference.

Haverhill, N. H.,

Grafton co., is one of the shire towns. It lies 31 miles N. W. from Plymouth, and 70 N. N. W. from Concord. It is watered by Oliverian and Hazen brooks. Haverhill is a pleasant town. The soil is suited to every species of cultivation. There is a quarry of granite suitable for mill stones and buildings, and a bed of iron ore, on the W. side of Coventry, bordering this town.

The principal village is at the S. W. angle of the town, and known by the name of *Haverhill Corner.* There is a beautiful common in this village, laid out in an oblong square, around which the buildings regularly stand. The site is a handsome elevation, overlooking the adjacent country many miles N. and S., and not less than 6 or 7 miles E. and W. From the street, the ground slopes with unusual elegance to the W., and is succeeded by broad intervales. The prospect here is delightful. There is another village at the N. W. angle of the town, on a street nearly a mile in length, straight and very level.

Haverhill was granted, 1764. Its first settlement was made in 1764, by Capt. John Hazen, who settled on the Little Ox Bow, near where there had formerly been an Indian fort and burying ground, and where many Indian skulls and relics have been found. Several of the early settlers were from Newbury and Haverhill, Mass., and from the last place, this town derived its name. Its former name was *Lower Coos*.

Hon. MOSES Dow was one of the most distinguished citizens of this place.

Hon. CHARLES JOHNSTON, who died March 5, 1813, aged 76, resided here. He was a valuable officer in the revolution, and was many years judge of probate in Grafton county.

Hon. James Woodward and Hon. Ezekiel Ladd were among the early settlers, and were judges of the old county court. Population, in 1830, 2,153.

Haverhill, Mass.

Essex co. This ancient, respectable and flourishing manufacturing town, lies on the N. side of the Merrimack river, at the head of navigation, and united to Bradford by two beautiful bridges. It is 30 miles N. from Boston, 31 N. N. W. from Salem, 12 W. by S. from Newburyport, 18 N. E. from Lowell, 30 S. W. from Portsmouth, N. H. and 40 S. E. from Concord, N. H. Little river passing through the town affords a good hydraulic power, on which are manufacturing establishments of various kinds. The manufactures consist of woolen goods, leather, boots, shoes, hats, shovels, spades, forks, hoes, chairs, cabinet ware, combs, ploughs, tin ware, vessels, palm-leaf hats, shoe lasts, spirits, morocco leather, chaises and harnesses: total amount the year ending April 1, 1837, $1,357,526.

Haverhill is delightfully located, handsomely built, and has been the birth place and residence of many of the most valuable and distinguished citizens of New England. Haverhill is so situated as to command an extensive inland trade: it is easily approached from Boston by the Andover and Wilmington rail-road, which is extending to Exeter, N. H., and from thence to Maine.

Haverhill, the Indian *Pentuckett*, was first settled in 1641: it was a frontier settlement for nearly half a century and suffered great calamities by savage depredations.

It was incorporated in 1645.—Population, 1820, 3,070; 1830, 3,896; 1837, 4,726.

Hawley, Mass.

Franklin co. Hawley is on elevated ground, and watered by branches of Deerfield river. The soil is good for grazing, and feeds about 3,000 sheep. A considerable quantity of leather is tanned in this town. Incorporated, 1792. Population, 1837, 995. Hawley has good iron ore and some iron works. It lies 107 miles W. by N. from Boston, and 14 W. by S. from Greenfield.

Haynesville, Me.

Washington county. See "Down East."

Heath, Mass.

Franklin co. A mountainous township good for grazing sheep, of which 2,312 were kept in 1837. There are in Heath some manufactures of leather, boots, shoes and palm-leaf hats. Incorporated, 1785. Population, 1837, 953. It lies 125 miles W. N. W. from Boston, and 13 W. N. W. from Greenfield.

Hebron, Me.

Oxford co. This is a good farming town, lying S. E. from Paris about 7 miles, and 42 W. S. W. from Augusta. Incorporated, 1792. Population, 1837, 972.

Hebron, N. H.,

Grafton co., lies 9 miles S. W.

from Plymouth, and 40 N. W. from Concord. A considerable part of Newfound lake lies in the S. E. part of this town. It has no river, nor any important streams. Nearly one half of this town was included in the grant of Cockermouth, now Groton. The remaining part was taken from Plymouth. It was incorporated, 1792. Population in 1830, 538.

Hebron, Ct.

Tolland co. Hop river, a branch of the Willimantic, waters this town. The village of Hebron, with its Gothic church, 20 miles S. E. from Hartford, and 14 S. from Tolland, is pleasant and commands a good prospect. There are in the town 2 cotton, 1 woolen, and 1 paper, mills; a large iron furnace and other manufactories. The surface of the town is hilly, but fertile. North pond in the S. part of the town is a handsome sheet of water. Hebron was first settled, 1704. Incorporated, 1707. Population, 1830, 1,939.

Henniker, N. H.

Merrimack co. It is 23 miles N. W. from Amherst, and 15 W. from Concord. Contoocook river passes easterly through its centre, and divides the town into nearly equal portions of territory and population. Its course is rather circuitous, and in many places presents scenes of considerable interest and beauty. Few places afford better prospects for the successful operation of water machinery than this. There are several ponds of considerable size. Long pond is the largest, being between 1 and 2 miles in length, and from 40 to 80 rods wide—situated 1 mile N. of the centre village. Craney hill is the principal elevation, and embraces a large portion of territory on the S. of the town. It is mostly in a state of cultivation. The soil of the hills is favorable for wheat—the valleys produce good crops of corn.

Henniker was granted in 1752, under the name of *Number 6*. Its settlement commenced in 1761. It was incorporated in 1768, when it received its present name from Gov. Wentworth, in honor of his friend Henniker, probably John Henniker, Esq., a merchant in London and a member of the British parliament at that time. Population, in 1830, 1,725.

Hermon, Me.

Penobscot co. A good township of land, 7 miles W. from Bangor. A large pond and the Sowadabscook river water its S. W. corner. In 1837, 1,870 bushel of wheat was raised. Incorporated, 1814. Population, 1837, 535.

Highgate, Vt.

Franklin co. This town lies on the E. side of Lake Champlain, at the N. W. corner of New England, and of the United States. It is 60 miles N. W. from Montpelier, and 12 N. from St. Albans. First settled, about 1784. The soil is generally sandy, in some parts swampy. Bog iron ore, of a good quality, is found here. There are many mill privileges in Highgate, particularly at a fall of the river Missisque, where are iron works, and other manufactories. The scenery at this place is quite wild and picturesque. Population, 1830, 2,038. Highgate is a place of considerable trade with Canada, and down the lake.

Hill, N. H.

Grafton co. This town is 24 miles N. N. W. from Concord, and 44 S. S. E. from Haverhill. It is watered by Pemigewasset and Smith's rivers, and several small streams. Eagle pond is the only one of note. Ragged mountain is a considerable elevation, and but little inferior to Kearsarge. Viewed from the summit of the neighboring hills, this town appears very uneven, yet there are many fine tracts converted into productive farms. The soil in some parts is rich and fertile—it is generally good. There is at the S. E. section of the town, a flourishing village, situated on a spacious street 1 mile in length.

This town was granted Sept. 14, 1753, to 87 proprietors, who held their first meeting at Chester, and as the greater part of the inhabitants belonged to that place, it was called New Chester; which name it retained until Jan. 1837, when it was changed to the name of HILL, in compliment to the then governor Hill. The first settlement was in 1768.

In Dec. 1820, six children of Mr. William Follansbee were consumed in the flames of his house, while he and his wife were absent. Incorporated, 1778. Population, 1830, 1,090.

Hillsborough County, N. H.

Amherst is the shire town. Hillsborough has Merrimack county on the N., Rockingham on the E., the state of Massachusetts on the S., and Cheshire county on the W. The surface of this county is generally uneven, though there are but few lofty mountains. Lyndeborough mountain, in the township of Lyndeborough, the Unconoonock, in Goffstown, Crotched, in Francestown and Society Land, are of considerable altitude.

This section of New Hampshire is well watered. The noble and majestic Merrimack passes its southeastern border. At Nashua, the Nashua, a beautiful stream from Massachusetts, discharges its waters into the Merrimack. North of the Nashua, the Souhegan and Piscataquog, streams of much value and consequence to the manufacturing interests, discharge themselves into the Merrimack; the former in the township of Merrimack, the latter in Bedford. Part of a large collection of water, denominated a lake, the Massabesick, on the E. boundary of Manchester. Besides these there are numerous ponds, interspersed through the whole extent of territory. Some of the largest of these are Gregg's pond, in Antrim, Pleasant pond, in Francestown, Babboosuck pond, in Amherst, and Potanipo, in Brookline. There are several mineral springs which have been found serviceable in cutaneous affections, but no one has yet acquired general celebrity. Minerals have been found in various places, but not in great abundance.

This county possesses many advantages for manufactu.ing establishments, and it is gratifying to find that many of its citizens are turning their attention to this branch of national and individual wealth.

The settlement of this county was made at Nashua, lately Dunstable, some years before the war with king Philip, in 1675. It was constituted a county by an act of the General Assembly, 19 March, 1771. It received its name from the Earl of Hillsborough, one of the privy council of George III. The population, in 1775, was 13,132; in 1790, 24,536; in 1800, 31,260; in 1810, 34,410; in 1820, 35,761; and in 1830, 37,762. In 1837, there were 45,511 sheep in this county.

Hillsborough, N. H.

Hillsborough co. It is 23 miles N. W. from Amherst, 24 W. S. W. from Concord. This town is well watered. Contoocook river passes through the S. E. corner, and affords several excellent water privileges. Hillsborough river has its source from ponds in Washington; runs in a S. E. course through the whole extent of Hillsborough, receiving the outlets of several ponds on the E., and forms a junction with the Contoocook, on the S. line of this town. The land here is uneven, but it affords many good farms. There is a pleasant village on the 2d New Hampshire turnpike, which passes N. W. through this town, containing a number of dwelling houses, stores, mills, and a cotton and woolen factory.

Hillsborough was formerly known by the name of *Number* 7 of frontier towns. The first settlement was made in 1741. The first children born in Hillsborough were John M'Calley and Mary Gibson, who intermarried, and received as a gift a tract of land, from the principal proprietor. It was incorporated in 1772. Population, 1830, 1,792.

Hinesburgh, Vt.

Chittenden co. Platt river and Lewis creek water this town. A part of the town is mountainous, but the soil is generally very good, particularly for grazing. About 9,000 sheep are kept here, and some products of the farms are exported. Hinesburgh contains a pleasant village, and numerous manufacturing operations are found on its streams. First settled about 1785. Population, 1830, 1,669. It lies 13 miles S. S. E. from Burlington, and 26 W. from Montpelier.

Hingham, Mass.

Plymouth co. A pleasant town on Boston harbor, and an agreeable resort for citizens and strangers. It lies 11 miles S. E. from Boston, by water, and 14 by land. Hingham cove is 5 miles S. W. from Nantasket beach, about 6 W. from Cohasset harbor, and 24 N. N. W. from Plymouth. First settled, 1633. Incorporated, 1635. Population, in 1830, 3,357; 1837, 3,445.

Major-general BENJAMIN LINCOLN, was born in this town, Jan. 23, 1733; he died May 9, 1810.

This town is remarkable for its healthiness and longevity. During 50 years, 8 persons died in one house, whose average age was 84 years.

About 80 sail of vessels belong to this place, which are engaged in the cod and mackerel fishery, and coasting trade;—aggregate tonnage about 5,000 tons.

In this town is an iron foundry, considerable ship building, a steam bucket factory; and large quantities of other wooden wares are manufactured, and some salt.

The amount of manufactures of Hingham, for the year ending April 1, 1837, was $237,078. They consisted of leather, boots, shoes, iron castings, hats, ploughs, cabinet, tin and wooden wares, silk, salt, vessels, umbrellas, spars and blocks, cordage, carriages, hammers, and hatchets. The product of the cod and mackerel fishery, the same year, was $113,700. Total amount of the fishery and manufactures $350,778.

Derby Academy, a free school, and the *Willard* Private Academy, are highly respectable seminaries, and promise great privileges to parents.

A commodious steam-boat plies between this and Boston, in summer months, two or three times a day. The hotels are large, and furnish excellent accommodations. Baker's Hill presents extensive and delightful views of Boston harbor. An excursion to Hingham is very pleasant.

Hinsdale, N. H.

Cheshire co. It is 75 miles S. W. by W. from Concord. It is well watered with springs and rivulets of the purest water. The Connecticut washes its western border; and the Ashuelot runs through the centre, forming a junction with the Connecticut, a little below the great bend, called Cooper's point. Kilburn brook rises in Pisgah mountain, runs S. and falls into Ashuelot river. Ash-swamp brook rises in West river mountain, runs a S. W. course, and falls into the Connecticut, near the side of Hinsdale's fort.

There are several islands in the Connecticut in this town. On the N. line of Hinsdale, is West river mountain, which extends from the banks of the Connecticut, E. across the whole width of the town. Its greatest elevation is at the W. end. President Dwight states the height above low water mark to be from 800 to 900 feet. In this mountain is found iron ore, and some other minerals and fossils. South of Ashuelot, is Stebbins' hill, a tract of excellent land, and principally in a high state of cultivation. The intervales here are extensive, and of an excellent quality. On the point of a hill, not far from Connecticut river, there is to be seen the remains of an Indian fortification, constructed prior to the settlement of the town. There is a deep trench drawn across the hill, to separate it from the plain back, and is continued to the river.

Hinsdale was incorporated in 1753. It was originally a part of Northfield, and was settled as early as 1683. The former name of this place was *Fort Dummer* and *Bridgman's Fort*. This town encountered all the difficulties of the Indian wars, and struggled with other hardships incident to frontier settlements, begun in the wilderness and remote from cultivated lands. Population, 1830, 937.

Hinsdale, Mass.

Berkshire co. Hinsdale is the source of a branch of Housatonick river. It is an elevated township, and well adapted for grazing.— There are two woolen mills in Hinsdale, and manufactures of boots, shoes, leather, hats, chairs, and cabinet ware: total amount in one year $86,550. The value of 11,020 fleeces of wool, sheared in Hinsdale in 1837, weighing 32,116 pounds, was $19,266. This town was incorporated in 1804. Population, 1837, 832. It lies 125 miles W. from Boston, and 15 N. N. W. from Lenox.

Hiram, Me.

Oxford co. This town lies on both sides of a branch of Saco river, 86 miles W. S. W. from Augusta, and 40 S. W. from Paris. The township is fertile and productive of wool and wheat. Incorporated, 1807. Population, 1830, 1,148.

Hodgdon, Me.

Washington co. Incorporated, 1832: 179 miles from Augusta. In 1837, with a population of 552, it produced 3,184 bushels of wheat. See "Down East."

Holden, Mass.

Worcester co. This town is finely watered by branches of Blackstone and Nashua rivers. It has a valuable water power on Quinipoxet river. It has some good meadow land on the borders of the streams. There are 5 cotton and 2 woolen mills in the town, and manufactures of leather, boots, shoes, straw bonnets, and palm-leaf hats; total amount of the manufactures for the year ending April 1, 1837, $201,960. Holden is 48 miles W. from Boston, and 6 N. W. from Worcester. Incorporated, 1740.— Population, 1837, 1,789.

Holderness, N. H.

Grafton co. It is 65 miles N. W. from Portsmouth, and 40 N. from Concord. The soil is hard and not easily cultivated, but when subdued is tolerably productive. From the sap of the sugar maple, a considerable quantity of sugar is made. The Pemigewasset imparts a portion of its benefits to this place, and there are various other streams which serve to fertilize the soil, and to furnish mill seats. Squam river, the outlet of Squam ponds, runs in a S. W. direction and empties into the Pemigewasset near the S. W.

angle of the town. This stream affords excellent mill privileges, having on it 2 paper mills and other machinery. There are 3 ponds or lakes.

The road from Plymouth through this place to Winnepisiogee lake, and along the borders of that lake to Wolfeborough is highly interesting; displaying scenery which is scarcely equalled in this part of our country. Holderness was first granted in 1751. The first settlement was made about the year 1763. Population, 1830, 1,429.

Holland, Vt.

Orleans co. This is an excellent township of land, producing in great abundance all the varieties common to the climate. Previous to the year 1800, it was a wilderness. It is bounded N. by Canada: 56 miles N. N. E. from Montpelier and 20 N. E. from Irasburgh. Population, 1830, 432.

Holland, Mass.

Hampden co. Holland was taken from Brimfield in 1785. It lies 70 miles S. W. by W. from Boston, and 20 E. by S. from Springfield. Population, 1837, 495. Holland has several ponds, and is otherwise watered by Quinnebaugh river. There is a cotton mill in the town, and 658 sheep.

Hollis, Me.

York co. This town lies on the W. bank of Saco river, and contains numerous mill sites. Incorporated, 1812. Population, 1837, 2,374. It lies 72 miles S. W. from Augusta, and 30 N. from York.

Hollis, N. H.

Hillsborough co. It is 8 miles S. from Amherst, and 36 S. from Concord. Nashua river waters the S. E. part, and Nisitissit crosses the S. W. extremity. There are 4 ponds, known by the name of Flint's, Penichook, Long and Rocky ponds. There is a pleasant village near the centre of the town, on a site somewhat elevated. The original name of Hollis was *Nisitissit*, its Indian name. The first settlement was made in 1731. It was incorporated in April, 1746.— The name is either derived from Thomas Hollis, a distinguished benefactor of Harvard college, or from the Duke of New Castle. Population, 1830, 1,501.

Holliston, Mass.

Middlesex co. First settled, 1710. Incorporated, 1724. Population in 1837, 1,775. It lies 24 miles S. W. by W. from Boston, and 21 S. from Concord. There is a woolen mill in the town, and some manufactures of boots, shoes, leather, chairs and cabinet ware, combs, ploughs, straw bonnets, books, clothing, wagons and harnesses: total value in one year $335,948. The value of boots and shoes amounted to $241,626, employing 461 hands. Holliston is watered by a small branch of Charles river.

Holmes' Hole, Mass.

See *Tisbury*.

Hooksett, N. H.

Merrimack co. It lies nine miles S. S. E. from Concord. The river Merrimack, whose course here is nearly N. and S., passes through this town a little W. of the centre. Here are those beautiful falls, known by the name of Hooksett Falls.— The descent of water is about 16 feet perpendicular in 80 rods. A high rock divides the stream, and a smaller rock lies between that and the western shore. There is a pleasant village on the W. side of the river. There is a strong and well built bridge over Merrimack river. Hooksett canal is in this town. It is 1-4 of a mile long—the fall is 16 feet perpendicular. Hooksett was detached from Chester, Goffstown and Dunbarton, and incorporated as a separate town in June, 1822. On the E. side of the river is an extensive cotton factory, owned by the Amoskeag Company. Population, 1830, 880.

Hoosack River and Mountain.

Two branches of the *Hoosack*, *Hosick*, or *Hoosick* river, rise in New England: one in the high lands in the county of Berkshire, Mass.; the other in the mountainous tracts of Bennington county, Vt. These branches unite near Hoosack Falls, in the state of New York, about 3 miles W. of the celebrated Bennington battle ground. Hoosack river meets the Hudson at Schagthicoke, 15 miles N. of Troy, N. Y. This stream, in many places, is exceedingly rapid in its course, and affords a great number of mill sites.

Hoosack mountain lies principally in Clarksburgh and Berkshire, Mass., and is the source of a branch of Hoosack river. Its elevation is from 1,500 to 2,000 feet from its base.

Hope, Me.

Waldo co. Hope is a township of choice land, having Camden and Megunticook lake on its south-eastern border. It lies 44 miles E. S. E. from Augusta, and 16 S. by W. from Belfast. Hope produced in 1837, 3,142 bushels of wheat. Population, same year, 1,733. Incorporated, 1804.

Hopkinton, N. H.

Merrimack co. It is 28 miles N. from Amherst, 7 W. from Concord, 46 N. E. from Keene, 30 S. E. from Newport, 50 W. from Portsmouth, and 65 N. N. W. from Boston. Contoocook river flows from Henniker into the south-westerly part of this town, and meanders in a N. E. direction. In its course it receives Warner and Blackwater rivers, and several large brooks, and empties into Merrimack river at Concord. On these streams are some valuable tracts of intervale and meadow lands. The principal village in Hopkinton is 7 miles from the state-house in Concord. In this town the county jail is located. In the W. part of the town is a thriving village on the Contoocook river, known as *Hill's Bridge*, or *Contoocookville*, where is a valuable water power, and several mills. Hopkinton was granted Jan. 16, 1735, to John Jones and others, and was called *Number 5*, and afterwards *New-Hopkinton*. The first settlement was made about 1740, by emigrants from Hopkinton, Mass. This town suffered from Indian depredations. Population in 1830, 2,474.

Hopkinton, Mass.

Middlesex county. Branches of Charles and Mill rivers rise in this town, on which are manufacturing establishments. There are 3 cotton mills in Hopkinton, and manufactures of boots and shoes, ($152,300,) leather, ploughs, and straw bonnets: total value, the year ending April 1, 1837, $217,550. The town was incorporated in 1715. Population, 1830, 1,809; 1837, 2,166.

The mineral spring in this town has become celebrated. It contains carbonic acid, and carbonate of lime and iron. It is situated near White Hall pond, which abounds in fine fish of various kinds. The Boston and Worcester rail road passes within 3 1-2 miles of it, at Westborough, and it is 7 miles from the Blackstone canal, at Northbridge. It is 30 miles W. S. W. from Boston, 14 E. by S. from Worcester, and 30 N. by W. from Providence, R. I. There is a large and convenient hotel at this place, at which visitors for health or pleasure are kindly entertained. A trip to Hopkinton springs is both pleasant and fashionable.

Hopkinton, R. I.

Washington co. Wood river, a valuable mill stream, passes through this town, on which are cotton and woolen mills, iron works, and various other manufactories. The soil of the town is generally well adapted for grazing, and the cultivation of grain. It produces large quantities of fruit and excellent cider. Shad and alewives are taken in Pawcatuck river. There are several ponds within the town. Considerable wood and timber are sent to market from this place.

Hopkinton City, at the south part of the town, on the Tommaquaug branch of Charles river, is very pleasant and flourishing. It lies 35 miles S. W. from Providence, and 15 W. from South Kingston. Hopkinton was first settled in 1660. Incorporated, 1757. Population, 1830, 1,777.

Houlton, Me.

Washington co. This town is situated on the east line of the state and of the United States, on the border of the Province of New Brunswick. It lies 120 miles N. N. E. from Bangor, and about 75 W. N. W. from Frederickton, the capital of New Brunswick. The town was first settled in 1808, and for twenty years it was entirely cut off from all communication with the western part of the state by a dense wilderness of nearly 100 miles in extent.

In 1829, a military post, the "Hancock Barracks," was established here by the U. S. government, and in 1834 the military and state roads between Bangor and Houlton were completed and opened for travel. The great thoroughfare between the United States and the British Province of New Brunswick is through this town. The roads between Bangor and Houlton are excellent: stages pass and repass from Bangor through Houlton to Frederickton, three times a week. Frederickton is 80 miles N. N. W. from St. Johns. A good road between Houlton and Calais, on the river St. Croix, about 90 miles distant, is now open for travel. This town is well watered by branches of Meduxnekeag river, which empties into the St. John's. The garrison is located about a mile north of the village, and has generally contained four companies of infantry. In this town the courts of probate are held, and the office of registry of deeds kept for the northern district of Washington county.

The soil of Houlton and its vicinity is of a superior quality. Twenty-five bushels of wheat to the acre is an average crop: 40 bushels to the acre is frequently obtained.—Houlton, with a population of 667, raised 5,869 bushels of wheat in the year 1837.

We have heard it is said, that persons might go so far " down east" as to "jump off." If Houlton is the *jumping off place*, we advise some of our western brethren to go and view the precipice.

Housatonick River.

The sources of this river are in the towns of Lanesborough and Windsor, Berkshire county, Mass. The two branches meet at Pittsfield, where the river forms; it then passes south, through Berkshire county, and enters the state of Connecticut. After meandering through the county of Litchfield, in that state, it separates the counties of New Haven and Fairfield, and meets the tide water at Derby, 14 miles above its entrance into Long Island Sound. The source of this mountain stream is more than 1,000 feet above the ocean; and in its course, of nearly 150 miles, it affords numerous mill sites, and presents many pleasant and well cultivated towns. The volume of water of this river is not very large except in seasons of freshet, when the rains from the mountains that environ its borders, inundate the valleys and greatly fertilize the soil. The scenery on the Housatonick is exceedingly beautiful; in some places it is enchanting. The romantic cataract at Canaan, Conn., of 66 feet perpendicular, is well worthy the notice of travellers. The Indian name of this river, signifies *over the mountains*. A vocabulary of Indian names, so beautiful and expressive, would be not only curious but valuable.

Howland, Me.

Penobscot co. This is a large township of good land, in which the Piscataquis and Seboois rivers form a junction: at the mouth of the former, about 50 rods from the Penobscot, are several saw mills. The banks of the river are low and very beautiful. Howland was incorporated in 1826. It lies 117 miles N. E. from Augusta, and 34 N. from Bangor. Population, 1830, 329; 1837, 507.

Hubbardston, Vt.

Rutland co. Elizabeth Hickok, the daughter of Elizabeth and Uriah Hickok, was the first white child born in this town. This event occurred in 1774. The face of the town is uneven, and in some parts mountainous. It is watered by several ponds, the largest of which, lying partly in Sudbury, is *Gregory's pond*, the outlet of which is called *Hubbardston river*. This river empties into Lake Champlain at West Haven and is an excellent mill stream. The village at the northwesterly part of the town is pleasant and flourishing: it contains mills for the manufacture of various articles.

Hubbardston lies 50 miles S. W. from Montpelier, and 10 N. W. from Rutland. Population, 1830, 865.

Hubbardston, Mass.

Worcester co. Hubbardston is on elevated ground, and the source of several branches of Ware river. There is much unimproved water power in the town. There are considerable tracts of valuable meadow land, and the uplands are good for grazing. It was incorporated in 1767. Population, 1837, 1,780. The manufactures of the town consist of copperas, leather, boots,shoes, palm-leaf hats, chairs, cabinet and wooden wares. Hubbardston lies 54 miles W. from Boston, and 22 S. from Worcester.

Hudson, N. H.

Hillsborough co. This town lies 17 miles S. E. from Amherst, and 38 S. from Concord. The land here is of easy cultivation. On the river are fine intervales, of a deep rich soil. Distant from the river, the land is hilly and somewhat broken. There are two ponds, known by the name of Little Massabesick, and Otternick ponds. This town was included in the grant of Dunstable, and was settled as early as 1710. The first settlements were made on the banks of the river, where the Indians had cleared fields for cultivating corn. The first inhabitants lived in garrisons. While the men were abroad in the fields and forests, the women and children were lodged in these places of security. Near the Indian cornfields have been found cinders of a blacksmith's forge, which have led to the conjecture that they employed a smith to manufacture their implements of war and agriculture. Incorporated, 1746, by the name of Nottingham-West, which it retained until July 1, 1830, when it was changed to Hudson. Population in 1830, 1,282.

Hull, Mass.

Plymouth co. Hull was first settled about the year 1625. Incorporated, 1644. Population, 1837, 180. This town comprises the peninsula of Nantasket, which forms the S. E. side of Boston harbor. It extends N. by W. from Cohasset, 5 miles, and is celebrated for its beautiful beach, 4 miles in length, and for its shell fish and sea fowl. The town lies between two hills of fine land, near point Alderton, opposite Boston light-house. It lies 9 miles E. S. E. from Boston, by water, and 22 by land, via Hingham. On one of the hills in this place, is a well 90 feet in depth, which is frequently almost full of water. Capital invested in the manufacture of salt, $12,500.

Hull is remarkable for the unanimity which always prevails among its inhabitants in their deliberative assemblies, and for a spirit of compromise manifest on all occasions in their selection of public servants.

Huntington, Vt.

Chittenden co. First settled, 1786. Population, in 1830, 929.—Huntington lies 20 miles W. from Montpelier, and 15 S. E. from Burlington. *Huntington river* passes through this town; it is a branch of Onion river, is rapid in its course, affording several towns an abundant water power. The soil of Huntington is poor: its surface is generally too hilly for cultivation.—Camel's Back mountain lies in the eastern part of the town.

Huntington, Ct.

Fairfield co. This is a township of uneven surface, but well adapted to agricultural purposes, to which the inhabitants are principally devoted. Huntington was incorporated in 1789. It lies 4 miles W. from Derby Landing, 12 N. E. from Fairfield, and 12 W. from New Haven. Population, 1830, 1,371.

Hyannis Harbor, Mass.

See *Barnstable*.

Hyde Park, Vt.

Lamoille co. County town. The Lamoille, Green, and other rivers give this town a great water power, some of which is advantageously improved. The soil is generally of a good quality and easily cultivated. It lies 24 miles N. from Montpelier, and 32 N. E. from Burlington. Population, 1830, 823. First settled, 1787.

Indian Rivers.

Indian river, Me., Washington county, is a small stream in the town of Addison.

Indian stream, N. H., Coos county, is the principal and most northerly source of Connecticut river, rising in the highlands near the N. limit of the state, and pursuing almost a direct S. W. course to its junction with the E. branch flowing from lake Connecticut.

Indian river, Vt., rises in Rupert, and falls into the Pawlet. Another stream of this name, in Vt., rises in Essex, and falls into Colchester bay.

Indian Stream Territory.

Is a tract in New Hampshire N of lat. 45°, extending to the British possessions in L. Canada. It was surveyed in 1805, and contains 160,363 acres. Lake Connecticut and several considerable ponds are situated within this tract.

Industry, Me.

Franklin co. This town borders N. W. on Sandy river, and is a valuable tract of land. It lies 32 miles N. W. from Augusta, and is bounded S. W. by Farmington. Industry was incorporated in 1803: it has a pleasant village and raised, in 1837, 6,078 bushels of wheat, with a population of 1,014.

Ipswich, Mass.

Essex co. This is one of the shire towns of the county, and a port of entry, on a river of the same name, sometimes called *Agawam*, the Indian name of the place. Ipswich village is very pleasant, and the country around it is well cultivated, and beautifully variegated. There is a cotton mill in the town, and a number of vessels are engaged in the coasting trade and fishery. The manufactures consist of cotton goods, hosiery, vessels, leather, boots, shoes, chairs, and cabinet ware:—total annual amount, about $120,000. Ipswich is 12 miles N. by E. from Salem, 10 S. from Newburyport, and 26 N. E. by N. from Boston. First settled, 1633. Incorporated, 1634. Population, 1820, 2,553 : 1837, 2,855.

Ira, Vt.

Rutland co. This township is elevated: it contains good land for rearing cattle: it has about 5,000 sheep. Castleton river and Ira brook wash a part of the town, but afford no valuable mill privileges. Ira lies 60 miles S. S. W. from Montpelier, and 8 S. W. from Rutland. Population, 1830, 442.

Irasburgh, Vt.

Shire town of Orleans county. This township was granted to Ira Allen and others, in 1781. It was first settled in 1799. Population, 1830, 860. It lies 40 miles N. by E. from Montpelier, and 30 N. by W. from Danville. The surface of the town is undulating, with an easy soil to cultivate, and generally fertile. Black and Barton rivers water the town, but move too sluggishly to produce any valuable power.

Isinglass River, N. H.,

Takes its rise from Long pond in Barrington, and Bow pond in Strafford, and, after receiving the waters of several other ponds, unites with the Cocheco near the S. part of Rochester.

Isles of Shoals.

These islands, 8 miles from the mouth of Portsmouth harbor, N. H. are seven in number, viz: Hog, Smutty Nose, Star, Duck, White, Malaga, and Londonner islands. Hog contains 350 acres of rock, and its greatest elevation is 57 feet above high water mark. Smutty Nose contains about 250 acres of rock and soil—greatest elevation 45 feet. Star island contains about 180 acres of rock and soil, and its height is 55 feet. These islands, as a town, are called *Gosport.* Star and Smutty Nose are inhabited by fishermen, who carry on considerable business in their way; supplying Portsmouth and the neighboring towns with fresh fish, and sending large quantities of cured fish to Boston and other places. The celebrated dun fish are found here, which have heretofore been considered a distinct species of the cod. They differ however from the common cod only in the circumstance of their being caught and cured in winter. Star island and Smutty Nose are connected by a *sea wall,* built at the expense of government, for the purpose of breaking a strong south east current passing between them, and forming a safe anchorage on the north west side of it. These objects have been attained, and the miniature fleet of the Shoalers, riding at anchor in this artificial harbor, is no unpleasant sight. Smutty Nose and Malaga are connected by a sea wall, built at the expense of Mr. Haley, "the King of the Shoals." This wall, 14 rods in length, 13 feet in height, and from 20 to 30 feet in width, effectually secures Haley's inlet and wharf from the easterly storms, although the waves not unfrequently break over it in a severe storm. These islands are composed of ledges of gneiss, bearing evidence of their igneous origin, as they are often traversed by veins of quartz, trap, and iron stone.

There are a few spots of dry soil upon them under cultivation. The Shoals are a pleasant resort for water parties, and their delightful bracing air, cannot be otherwise than advantageous to those who are in want of pure sea breezes. The present population is about 100.

These islands were discovered by the celebrated John Smith, in 1614, and were named by him *Smith's Isles.* The line between Maine and New Hampshire passes through these islands, leaving the largest on the side of Maine. Upon all of them are chasms in the rocks, having the appearance of being caused by earthquakes. The most remarkable is on Star island, (Gosport) in which one Betty Moody secreted herself when the Indians visited the island and took away many female captives; and thence called to this day "*Betty Moody's hole.*" For more than a century previous to the revolution, these islands were populous, containing from 300 to 600 souls. They had a court-house on Haley's island; a meeting-house, first on Hog island, and afterwards on Star island. From 3 to 4 thousand quintals fish were annually caught and cured here, and 7 or 8 schooners, besides numerous boats, were employed in the business. The business has since very greatly decreased.

William Pepperell and a Mr. Gibbons, from Topsham, England, were among the first settlers at the Shoals; the former an ancestor of the celebrated Sir William Pepperell.

A woman. of the name of Pulsey, died in Gosport, in 1795, aged 90. In her life time she kept two cows. The hay on which they fed in winter, she used to cut in summer, among the rocks, with a *knife*, with her own hands. Her cows, it was said, were always in good order. They were taken from her, but paid for, by the British, in 1775, and killed, to the no small grief of the good old woman.

Islesborough, Me.

Waldo co. This town comprises a large and fertile island, in Penob- scot bay, and several islands in its vicinity. This island has excellent harbors, and is much frequented by fishermen and coasters. The inhabitants are independent farmers and fishermen, who are accustomed to render their insular situation a place of comfort to the wayfarer, or the invalid in pursuit of ocean breezes. Islesborough lies 10 miles S. E. from Belfast, and 56 E. from Augusta. Incorporated, 1789.— Population, 1837, 674.

Israel's River, N. H.,

Coos co., is formed by the waters which descend in cataracts from the summits of Mounts Adams and Jefferson, and running N. W. it passes through Randolph and Jefferson, discharging itself into the Connecticut near the centre of Lancaster. It is a beautiful stream, and received its name from Israel Glines, a hunter, who with his brother frequented these regions, long before the settlement of the county.

Jackson, Me.

Waldo co. An interior township of good land that produced, in 1837, 4,893 bushels of as fine wheat as can be raised in Tennessee. Population, same year, 523. Jackson is 49 miles N. E. from Augusta, and 15 N. N. W. from Belfast. Incorporated, 1818.

Jackson, N. H.,

Coos co., situated on the E. side of the White mountains. The surface of the town is uneven, but the soil is rich and productive. It is watered principally by the two branches of Ellis' river, passing from the N. and uniting on the S. border near Spruce mountain.— The principal elevations are called Black, Baldface, and Thorn mountains. Benjamin Copp was the first settler; he moved into Jackson in 1779, and with his family buffeted the terrors of the wilderness fourteen years, before any other person settled there. The town was incorporated December 4, 1800, by the name of *Adams*, which name it retained until 1829, when it was changed to Jackson. Population, in 1830, 515.

Jaffrey, N. H.

Cheshire co. This town lies 62 miles N. W. from Boston, and 40 S. W. by S. from Concord. The Grand Monadnock is situated in the N. W. part of this town and in Dublin. Innumerable streams of water issue from the mountain. Those which issue from the western side discharge themselves into the Connecticut river; those from the eastern form the head waters of Contoocook river. The largest stream rises about 100 rods from the summit, and descends in a S. E. direction. With this brook, the thirsty and fatigued visitors of the mountain associate the most pleasing recollections. The uneven soil of Jaffrey, affording numerous meadows, and early and rich pastures, is peculiarly adapted to raising cattle. There are several ponds in this town. Out of 3, issue streams sufficient to carry mills erected near their outlets. In the largest, which is 400 rods long, and 140 wide, is an island comprising about 10 acres. About 1 1-2 miles S. E. from the mountain is the " Monadnock mineral spring." The spring is slightly impregnated with carbonate of iron and sulphate of soda. It preserves so uniform a temperature as never to have been known to freeze. Where the spring issues from the earth, yellow ochre is thrown out. In this town are a cotton and woolen factory, and various mills. The first permanent settlement was made in 1758. Jaffrey was incorporated in 1773, receiving its name from George Jaffrey, Esq., of Portsmouth, one of the original proprietors. Population in 1830, 1,354.

Jamaica, Vt.

Windham co. West river waters this town, and gives good mill seats. At a pleasant village near the centre of the town are valuable manufacturing establishments. The surface of the town is very uneven; in some parts mountainous, but the soil is generally good and productive. Lime-stone of a good quality is found here. Jamaica was first settled in 1780. Population, 1830, 1,523. It lies 90 miles S. from Montpelier, and 14 N. W. from Newfane.

Jamestown, R. I.

Newport co. This town comprises *Connanicut*, a beautiful island in Narraganset bay, about 8 miles in length: its average breadth is about a mile. The soil is a rich loam, and peculiarly adapted for grazing and the production of Indian corn and barley.

The inhabitants of this island are remarkable for their industry and agricultural skill, which, united with the fertility of the soil and the location of the island, renders it a delightful place. The distance from the town or island to Newport and South Kingston, is about a mile each way; to each of those places a ferry is established. The island was purchased of the Indians in 1657. Jamestown was incorporated in 1678. Population, 1830, 415.

Jay, Me.

Franklin co. Jay lies at a bend of Androscoggin river, 29 miles W. by N. from Augusta, and 12 S. S. W. from Farmington. There is much valuable land in Jay. The inhabitants are principally farmers, and cultivate the soil with much industry. The town produced, in 1837, 8,129 bushels of wheat, and considerable wool. Population, 1830, 1,276; 1837, 1,685. Incorporated, 1795.

Jay, Vt.

Orleans co. A part of this town is very mountainous—Jay's peak lying in the S. W. part; the other part is good arable land, and would produce good crops if well cultivated. A number of streams issue from the mountain and produce an ample water power. Jay was chartered in 1792, but it was not permanently settled until about 1816. It lies 50 miles N. from Montpelier, and 15 N. W. from Irasburgh. Population, 1830, 196.

Jefferson, Me.

Lincoln co. This town lies at the head of Damariscotta river, and embraces a large body of water. It is otherwise watered by several ponds producing streams for mill seats, which give to Jefferson great facilities for sawing and transporting lumber. This is a flourishing town in its trade and agricultural pursuits; it produced 3,361 bushels of wheat in 1837. Incorporated, 1807. Population, 1837, 2,246. It lies 28 miles E. S. E. from Augusta, and 15 N. E. from Wiscasset.

Jefferson, N. H.

Coos co. Pondicherry pond, in this town, is about 200 rods in diameter, and is the principal source of John's river. Pondicherry bay is about 200 rods wide and 100 long. Mount Pliny lies in the easterly part of this town, and around its base there is excellent grazing and tillage land. On the S. W. side of this mountain are several fine farms, which command a most delightful view of the White mountains. Israel's river passes through Jefferson from S. E. to N. W., and here receives a considerable branch. The town was first settled about the year 1773. Jefferson is 77 miles N. from Concord, and 9 S. E. from Lancaster. Population, 1830, 495.

Jerico, Vt.

Chittenden co. First settled, 1774. Population, 1830, 1,654. Jerico lies 25 miles N. W. from Montpelier, and 12 E. from Burlington. This town lies on the N. side of Onion river, and is otherwise finely supplied with mill seats by Brown's river and other streams. The soil varies in quality, from good intervale, on the streams, to common grazing pastures, on the hills. There is a pleasant village at the falls, on Brown's river, and some manufactories.

Johnson, Vt.

Lamoille co. Johnson was first settled in 1784, by a revolutionary hero, of the name of Samuel Eaton. Mr. Eaton frequently passed through this township, while scouting between Connecticut river and lake Champlain; and several times encamped on the same flat which he afterwards occupied as a farm, it being a beautiful tract of intervale. Like many other settlers of this state, he had many difficulties to encounter. In indigent circumstances, and with a numerous family, he loaded his little all upon an old horse, and set out in search of that favorite spot which he had selected in his more youthful days. He had to travel nearly 70 miles through the wilderness, guided by the trees which had been marked by the scouts, and opening a path as he passed along. He depended, for some time after he arrived at Johnson, entirely upon hunting and fishing for the support of himself and family.

The river Lamoille enters this township near the southeast corner, and running westerly about two miles, through a rich tract of intervale, falls over a ledge of rocks about 15 feet in height into a basin below. This is called *M'Connel's falls.* Thence it runs northwesterly over a bed of rocks, about 100 rods, narrowing its channel and increasing its velocity, when it forms a whirlpool and sinks under a barrier of rocks, which extends across the river. The arch is of solid rock, is about eight feet wide, and at low water is passed over by footmen with safety. The water rises below through numerous apertures, exhibiting the appearance of the boiling of a pot.

The surface of this township is uneven, being thrown into ridges, which are covered with hemlock, spruce and hard wood. The soil is a dark, or yellow loam, mixed with a light sand, is easily tilled, and very productive. The alluvial flats are considerably extensive, but back from the river the lands are, in some parts rather stony. In the northeastern part has been discovered a quantity of soapstone.

The village, in Johnson, is very pleasant, and contains a number of mills, for the manufacture of various articles. Johnson lies 28 miles N. by W. from Montpelier, and 6 N. W. from Hyde Park. Population, 1830, 1,079.

Johnston, R. I.

Providence co. This town lies 5 miles W. from Providence, from which it was taken in 1759. It is pleasantly variegated by hills and vales, with a soil adapted to the culture of corn and barley, and particularly to all sorts of vegetables and fruits, of which large quantities are annually sent to Providence market. The quarries of freestone in Johnston are valuable; they supply the wants, not only of the city and immediate vicinity, but distant places, with that useful material. The Wonasquatucket and Pochasset rivers with their tributary streams give this town a good hydraulic power. Beautiful manufacturing villages are scattered along the banks of these waters, presenting to the eye of the traveller the pleasant union of our agricultural and manufacturing interests. Population, 1830, 2,113.

Jonesborough, Me.

Washington co. This town has Chandler's river and the head of Englishman's bay on the E., Jonesport on the S., and the town of Addison on the W. Incorporated, 1809. Population, 1837, 435. It lies 134 miles E. by N. from Augusta, and 12 S. W. from Machias.

Jonesport, Me.

Washington co. Taken from Jonesborough in 1836, and is bounded N. by Jonesborough, E. by Englishman's bay, S. by Mispeeky reach, and W. by Addison bay and harbor. This place has an excellent harbor, and is finely located for ship building, the fisheries and coasting trade. It lies 138 miles E. by N. from Augusta, and 16 S. W. from Machias. Population, 1837, 581 Beal and Head islands lie off S. from Jonesport.

Judith Point, R. I.

A noted headland in South Kingston, 11 miles S. S.W. from Newport, in N. lat. 41° 24', W. lon. 71° 35'. A light-house was erected here in 1810, the tower of which is 35 feet in height. This point opens to the ocean about midway between Vineyard and Long Island Sounds.— When off this place, travellers unaccustomed to the sea frequently experience some little inconvenience for a few miles. From this light, Montauk, on Long Island, bears about S. W. 30 miles, and Gay Head, on Martha's Vineyard, about E. by S., 35 miles.

Katahdin Mountain, Me.

This celebrated mountain, the greatest elevation in the state, lies between the eastern and western branches of Penobscot river, in the county of Piscataquis, about eighty miles N. N. W. from Bangor, and 120 N. N. E. from Augusta. Dr. Jackson has ascertained its height to be 5,300 feet above the level of the sea. The Indians had a notion that this mountain was the abode of supernatural beings. It is steep and rugged, and stands in almost solitary grandeur. It may be seen in a clear day from Bangor. Those who have visited its summit pronounce the scenery unrivalled in sublimity.

Kearsarge Mountain, N. H.,

In the county of Merrimack, situated between the towns of Sutton and Salisbury, extending into both towns. The line between Wilmot and Warner passes over the summit. Kearsarge is elevated 2,461 feet above the level of the sea, and is the highest mountain in Merrimack county. Its summit is now a bare mass of granite, presenting an irregular and broken surface; the sides are covered with a thick growth of wood. The prospect from this mountain, in a clear sky, is very wide and beautiful.

Keene, N. H.,

Chief town of Cheshire co., is one of the most flourishing towns in N. H. It is 80 miles W. N. W. from Boston, 60 S. from Dartmouth college, 43 S. S. E. from Windsor, Vt., 40 W. from Amherst, and 55 W. S. W. from Concord. The soil is of various kinds and generally good.

Ashuelot river has its source in a pond in Washington, and discharges itself into the Connecticut, at Hinsdale, 20 miles distant from Keene. Keene has been called one of the "prettiest villages" in New England; and president Dwight. in his travels, pronounces it one of the pleasantest inland towns he had seen. The principal village is situated on a flat, E. of the Ashuelot, nearly equidistant from that and the upland. It is particularly entitled to notice for the extent, width, and uniform level of its streets. The main street, extending one mile in a straight line, is almost a perfect level, and is well ornamented with trees. The buildings are good and well arranged; some of them are elegant. Keene is a place of considerable business. It has 2 glass houses, a woolen factory, iron foundry, and many other valuable manufacturing establishments. Its first settlement commenced about the year 1734, by Jeremiah Hall and others. Its original name was *Upper Ashuelot*. It was incorporated with its present name, April 11, 1753, which is derived from Sir Benjamin Keene, British minister at Spain, and contemporary with Gov. B. Wentworth.

In 1736 the settlement had so increased, that a meeting-house was erected and in two years after, a minister was settled. But the usual scourge, which attended the frontier settlements, visited this town. In 1745 the Indians killed Josiah Fisher, a deacon of the church: in 1746, they attacked the fort, the only protection of the inhabitants. They were, however, discovered by Capt. Ephraim Dorman in season to prevent their taking it.— He was attacked by two Indians, but defended himself successfully against them, and reached the fort. An action ensued, in which John Bullard was killed; Mrs. M'Kenney, who being out of the fort, was stabbed and died; and Nathan Blake taken prisoner, carried to Canada, where he remained two years. Mr. Blake afterwards returned to Keene, where he lived till his death, in 1811, at the age of 99 years and 5 months. When he was 94 he married a widow of 60. The Indians burnt all the buildings in the settlement, including the meeting-house. The inhabitants continued in the fort until April, 1747, when the town was abandoned. In 1753 they returned, and re-commenced their settlements. In 1755 the Indians again attacked the fort. Their number was great, and the onset violent, but the vigilance and courage of

Capt. Syms successfully defended it. After burning several buildings, killing cattle, &c., they withdrew. They again invaded the town, but with little success.

Col. ISAAC WYMAN, an active and influential man, marched the first detachment of men from this town, in the war of the revolution, and was present at the battle of Breed's Hill. Population, in 1830, 2,374.

Kenduskeag Stream, Me.

This stream rises in Dexter and Garland, and after meandering very circuitously through Corinth, Levant and Dutton, it falls into the Penobscot river, at the centre of the city of Bangor. This is a valuable mill stream; it has numerous tributaries; its banks are fertile, romantic and beautiful.

Kennebec River, Me.

The first source of this important river is *Moose Head lake*, of which it is the outlet. From thence it passes in a S. W. course nearly 20 miles, where it receives the waters of *Dead river;* it then proceeds S. to Starks, about 40 miles, where it receives the waters of the *Sandy:* here it changes its course easterly, about 12 miles, passing Norridgewock and Skowhegan: it then again changes its course to the S. till it receives the waters of the *Sebasticook*, about 15 miles: it continues to descend in nearly a S. course to Hallowell, about 20 miles; here it inclines to the E. a few miles, and then resuming a S. course, and passing through Merrymeeting bay, where it receives the Androscoggin river, it passes Bath and meets the ocean. The whole length of this river, from Moose Head lake to the sea, is about 150 miles. The tributaries already named are the most considerable ; but there are many others that would be considered important rivers in other sections of country. The whole fall of this river is more than 1,000 feet, and its hydraulic power, with that of its tributaries, is incalculable.

We are enabled to state that the average, or *mean* time, of the closing of this river by i e, at Hallowell, for 45 successive years, was December 12th, and of its opening, April 3d. The most remarkable years were, 1792, when the river closed November 4th, and opened April 1st, the following year; and 1831, when it closed January 10th, and opened April 13th, 1832. Since the year 1786 the Kennebec has not been obstructed by ice in any spring after the 20th of April.

Kennebec County, Me.

AUGUSTA is the shire town. This county is bounded N. by Franklin, Somerset, and Penobscot counties, E. by Waldo and a part of Lincoln counties, S. by Lincoln county, and W. by Oxford county. This county is watered by numerous ponds and rivers, but principally by the noble Kennebec, which passes nearly through its centre, from which the name of the county is derived. The face of the county is undulating, not hilly; its soil is of a superior quality, producing, in great abundance, all the variety of grasses, grains, vegetables and fruits common to its climate. The union of hydraulic power with navigable waters, which this county enjoys; its fertility, locality, and other natural advantages, render it a highly favored section of our country.—Area, about 1,050 square miles. In 1837 this county contained 101,238 sheep, and produced 186,876 bushels of wheat. Population, 1837, 62,-375 : 59 inhabitants to a square mile.

Kennebunk, Me.

York co. This town is situated on the S. W. side of the Kennebunk river, and is regarded as one of the pleasantest towns in New England. Population, 1837, 2,343. In former years the business of the town was mostly of a commercial character, there being a large number of vessels owned here, which were engaged in the West India trade. But this trade is now nearly abandoned, and the navigation is engaged in the freighting, coasting, and fishing business. Ship building has been carried on here to a great extent, for about seventy years, and some of the finest ships in the country have been built in this place within the last few years. There is one large cotton factory in operation, and other privileges for large manufacturing establishments on the Kennebunk, and the Mousum, a pleasant stream which meets the ocean in this town. Kennebunk is a port of entry: tonnage of the district, in 1837, 6,964 tons. Incorporated, 1820. It lies 80 miles S. W. from Augusta, 25 S. W. from Portland, and 15 N. N. E. from York.

Kennebunk Port, Me.,

York co., is situated on the N. E. side of the Kennebunk river. This town was formerly extensively engaged in the West India trade, but its navigation is now employed in the freighting, coasting, and fishing business. The extensive granite quarries here are likely to become a source of considerable business. The stone, bearing a strong resemblance to the Quincy, finds a ready market where granite is made use of in building. Thirty years ago, this town, and Kennebunk, on the opposite side of the river, were the most active and busy ports in Maine; but the tide of emigration has carried off most of the young men, leaving a surplus of girls; so that whatever activity there now is in the place, is of a domestic character, not creating that noise and bustle incident to the operations of the other sex. Kennebunk Port lies about 4 miles N. E. from Kennebunk. This town and Kennebunk are much united in maritime pursuits, and both enjoy a good harbor for shipping. Population, 1837, 2,730.

Kensington, N. H.,

Rockingham co., is 45 miles N. from Boston, 15 S. W. from Portsmouth, and 40 S. E. from Concord. This town has no streams of any note; its surface is pretty even. Kensington was settled at an early period, and was originally a part of Hampton, from which it was detached in 1737. Population, 1830, 717.

Kent County, R. I.

East Greenwich is the county town. Kent county is bounded N. by Providence county, E. by Providence bay, S. by Washington county, and W. by the state of Connecticut. The surface of the county is generally rough and uneven: in the eastern part are tracts of level land. The soil is either a gravelly or sandy loam, and very productive of Indian grain, rye, fruits, and vegetables. The grazing business is extensively pursued in this county. The Pawtuxet and Flat rivers are the principal, but a number of large ponds produce smaller streams in abundance. The manufacturing interests of this county, particularly of cotton and wool, are very extensive, and probably pursued with as much spirit and success as in any portion of the state. Some navigation is employed on the bay in the coasting trade and fishery. Kent county comprises an area of 186 square miles. Population, 1820, 10,228; 1830, 12,789. Population to a square mile, 69.

Kent, Ct.

Litchfield co. First settled, 1738. Incorporated, 1739. Population, 1830, 2,001. Kent is 50 miles W. from Hartford, 50 N. W. from New Haven, and 15 W. from Litchfield. This is a mountainous township, with some fine land on the banks of the Housatonick, which passes through its western border. Good iron ore is found here. There are three furnaces in town, but the manufacture of iron is not so extensive as formerly. The Housatonick, calm and still, winding gracefully at the foot of a high and rugged mountain, renders the scenery from the neat and quiet village, highly picturesque and beautiful.

"There is in this town," says Dr. Trumbull, "convincing evidence that it was a grand seat of the native inhabitants of this country, before Indians, who more lately inhabited it, had any residence in it. There are arrow heads, stone pots, and a sort of knives, and various kinds of utensils, frequently found by the English, of such curious workmanship as exceeds all the skill of any Indians since the English came into this country, and became acquainted with them.— These were not only found when the town was first settled, but they are still found on the sides of Housatonic river."

Kilkenny, N. H.

Coos co. This place was granted in 1774, and contained, in 1830, but 27 inhabitants. They are poor, and for aught that appears to the contrary, must always remain so, as they may be deemed actual trespassers on that part of creation destined by its author for the residence of bears, wolves, moose, and other animals of the forest. An exception, however, may possibly be made in favor of a narrow strip of land along the S. boundary of the town. Pilot and Willard's mountains, so called from a dog and his master, cover a considerable part of this town. Willard, a hunter, had been lost two or three days on these mountains, on the east side of which his camp was situated. Each day he observed his dog Pilot left him, as he supposed in pursuit of game; but towards night he would constantly return. Willard being, on the second or third day, nearly exhausted with fatigue and hunger, put himself under the guidance of his dog, who in a short time conducted him in safety to his camp.

Killingly, Ct.

Windham co. This town lies 45 miles E. from Hartford, 25 W. from Providence, R. I., and 5 N. E. from Brooklyn. First settled in 1700. The first white person known to have been buried here was Mr. Nell Alexander's great-grand-mother. (See *Alexander's Lake*.) This town is rough and hilly, but there is a great deal of beauty about it, and its history is full of romantic stories relating to the first settlers and the red men. The town is well watered by the Quinnebaug and its branches. There are three villages, *Pleasant Valley*, *Daysville*, and *Danielsonville*, all pleasant and flourishing manufacturing places. They contain 14 cotton and 3 woolen mills, a furnace, an axe factory, and other mechanical operations. Killingly contains excellent quarries of freestone, and of a slate rock resembling granite, soft, and easily wrought; also of a slate rock composed of granular quartz, almost white. A rich bed of porcelain clay is found on Mashentuck hill, said to equal French or Chinese clay. Population, 1836, 4,000.

Killington Peak, Vt.

This noted elevation of the Green Mountain range, 3,924 feet above the ocean, lies in Sherburne, 10 miles E. from Rutland.

Killingworth, Ct.

Middlesex co. This town, the Indian *Hammonnasset*, was first settled in 1663. The central part of the town is 38 miles S. E. from Hartford, 27 W. from New London, and 17 S. by E. from Middletown. Population, 1830, 2,484. This town lies on Long Island

Sound with a harbor for small vessels. Many vessels are built at this place. There is 1,000 acres of good salt meadow in Killingworth, and the soil of the uplands, although hard and uneven, are rendered productive by industry and skillful management. The village is very pleasant, with a wide street a mile and a half in length, crossed about midway by Indian river, a small stream which enters the harbor. This was a great resort for the Indians. "Immense masses of mouldering shells still point out the places where they dwelt." Killingworth is a healthful, interesting place.

Kilmarnock, Me.

Piscataquis co. This town is well watered by Piscataquis river and the outlet of Scootum lake. It lies 103 miles N. E. from Augusta, and 22 N. N. E. from Dover. Incorporated, 1824. Population, 1830, 138; 1837, 313.

Kingfield, Me.

Franklin co. A fine farming township, east of Mount Abraham, and watered by Seven Mile brook and one of its tributaries. It lies 55 miles N. W. by N. from Augusta, and 25 N. from Farmington. Population, 1837, 614. Incorporated, 1808. Wheat crop of 1837, 3,877 bushels.

Kingsbury, Me.

Incorporated, 1836. See "Down East."

Kingston, N. H.

Rockingham co. This town is distant from Concord 37 miles S. E., from Exeter 6, and from Portsmouth 20. There are several ponds in this town. The largest is Great pond, which lies on the W. of the village, and contains upwards of 800 acres, with an island of 10 or 12 acres, covered with wood. There are no high hills in Kingston; those called the Great hill and Rockrimon are the highest. The soil of Kingston is generally loamy. The charter of Kingston was granted, 1694. The grant also comprehended what now forms the towns of East Kingston, Danville, and Sandown. This town suffered in common with others in the vicinity, from Indian depredations. Many Indian implements, with some ancient French coin, have been ploughed up in the vicinity of the ponds.

Maj. EBENEZER STEVENS, one of the early settlers, was a very distinguished and useful citizen.

This town was also the residence of the Hon. JOSIAH BARTLETT, one of the first worthies of the state, and an eminent physician. His public career commenced in 1765, and from that time to his death he was an unwearied advocate and supporter of the liberties of America. He was the first governor of the state under its free constitution. He died in 1795, aged 65. Population, 1830, 929.

Kingston, Vt.

Addison co. A mountainous township settled soon after the revolutionary war. Population, 1830, 403. White river is formed in Kingston by the union of several streams. Here is a beautiful water fall of 100 feet, 50 of which is perpendicular. At the bottom of the fall the water has worn a hole 10 feet in depth. Kingston lies 21 miles S. W. from Montpelier, and 14 E. from Middlebury.

Kingston, Mass.

Plymouth co. This town lies within Plymouth harbor, 4 miles N. W. from Plymouth, and 31 S. E. from Boston. Kingston has a good harbor, a considerable stream of water and some excellent land. There are a number of vessels engaged in the coasting trade, and some in foreign commerce. Many vessels are built here of the *south shore* white oak, noted for its strength and durability. During the year ending April 1, 1837, there were 19 vessels engaged in the cod and mackerel fishery. They took 14,214 quintals of cod fish, and 886 barrels of mackerel, the value of which amounted to $48,590. There is a cotton mill in Kingston, and manufactures of bar iron, nails, axes, cutlery, anchors, leather, shoes, palm-leaf hats, and shingles: total value in one year $105,302. Monk's hill presents an excellent view of Plymouth harbor. Kingston was incorporated in 1726. Population, 1837, 1,371.

Kirby, Vt.

Caledonia co. First settled, 1799. Population, 1830, 401. There are some tracts of good land in Kirby, but the township is generally either wet and cold, or too mountainous for cultivation. It has a number of springs, brooks, and a good fish pond. The town lies 36 miles N. E. from Montpelier, and 14 N. E. from Danville.

Kirkland, Me.

Penobscot co. Kirkland is finely watered by Dead stream, Pushaw lake and its principal tributary river. It lies 83 miles N. E. from Augusta, and 15 N. N. W. from Bangor. Incorporated, 1825. Population, 1837, 258.

Kittery, Me.

York co. A sea port town on the N. E. bank of the Piscataqua river, being the extreme southwestern boundary of the state on the Atlantic, adjoining York on the N. E. and Elliot on the N. W. It is one of the earliest settlements in the province, or state, and had its share of trial and suffering with others of their days, from repeated incursions of the Indians. The river or inlet, called Spruce creek, affords a convenient harbor for vessels usually employed in the coasting trade and fishery, and formerly considerable trade was carried on with the West Indies from this place;—but there is little or none at present.

Kittery point was the residence of Sir William Pepperell, who commanded the New England troops in the celebrated expedition to Cape Breton, in 1745, which resulted in the capture of Louisburg. It is divided from Portsmouth, N. H. by the Piscataqua. A bridge connects it with that place. Another bridge connects it with Badger's island, on which is the United States Navy Yard. Kittery lies 103 miles S. W. from Augusta, and 50 S. W. from Portland. Incorporated, 1653.— Population, 1837, 2,322.

Knox, Me.

Waldo co. A beautiful farming town, named in honor of Gen. HENRY KNOX, a patriot of the revolution, who died at Thomaston, 1806, aged 56. This is one of the many towns in Maine fast rising in wealth and respectability, by the fertility of the soil and industry of the people. It lies 32 miles N. E. by E. from Augusta, and 14 S. W. from Belfast. Incorporated, 1819. Population, 1837, 815. Wheat crop, same year, 4,037 bushels.

Lagrange, Me.

Population, 1837, 287. Wheat crop, same year, 1,749 bushels. See "Down East."

Lamoille County, Vt.

Hyde Park is the shire town.— This county was established in 1836. It is bounded N. by Franklin and Orleans counties, E. by Orleans and Caledonia counties, S. by Washington county, and W. by Chittenden and a part of Franklin counties. This county lies on the Green mountain range, and is the source of many streams. The river Lamoille passes nearly through its centre, and, with its tributaries, give the county a great hydraulic power. The elevation of the county renders the soil more adapted for grazing than for tillage, yet there are large tracts of excellent meadow bordering its streams. Manufactures flourish, and the exports of beef cattle and the products of the dairy are valuable, and annually increasing. In 1837, there were 28,677 sheep. Population, 1830, 8,930.

Lamoille River, Vt.

This river is formed in Greensborough. Its general course is N. W. It passes through Hardwick, Wolcott, Morriston, Johnston, Cambridge, Fairfax and Georgia, and falls into Lake Champlain at Milton, 12 miles N. from Burlington. This river has numerous tributaries: it has several falls, which produce a valuable water power. Its banks in many parts are very fertile. It was discovered by Champlain in 1609.

Lancaster, N. H.

Coos co. Shire town of the county, and situated on the southeastern bank of Connecticut river, which forms and washes its N. W. boundary, a distance of 10 miles. It lies distant 110 miles W. from Portland, 130 N. from Portsmouth, 95 N. from Concord, and 75 above Dartmouth College. Besides the Connecticut, which is deep and about 22 rods in width while it passes through Lancaster, the town is watered by Israel's river, and several considerable brooks. Across this river a bridge and several dams are thrown, forming a valuable water power. There are several ponds in Lancaster, the largest of which is called Martin-meadow pond, from Martin, a hunter. This communicates with Little pond.

Lancaster is situated near lofty mountains, but is not itself mountainous. There are three hills in the S. part of the town, called Martin meadow hills; and the land in the S. E. part lies too high up the mountains for cultivation. The soil along the Connecticut is alluvial, the meadows extending back nearly three-fourths of a mile; and at the mouth of Israel's river much farther.

The village, or most compact part of the town, lies on a street extending from the bridge across Israel's river northwardly:—it is pleasant, and is the site of some manufacturing establishments. Lancaster was granted and settled in 1763. The war of the revolution tended to retard the settlement of the town.— After the war closed, the town settled with considerable rapidity, and has since gradually increased in wealth and business. Population, 1830, 1,187.

Lancaster, Mass.

Worcester co. This town, the *Nasawogg* of the Indians, is the oldest town in the county; it was for many years a frontier settlement, and greatly harrassed by the natives. In 1676, the town was attacked by 1,500 Indians; many were killed on both sides; the town was destroyed, and a number carried into captivity, among whom was the celebrated Mrs. *Mary Rowlandson*. Lancaster lies on both sides of Nashua river, and has a remarkably fine, alluvial soil, in a high state of cultivation. Perhaps there is no inland town in New England that possesses more natural beauties, or that strikes the eye of the traveller more agreeably.— The village is very beautiful:—it is neatly built on an alluvial plain, surrounded by hills, and watered by a large and placid stream. There are 3 cotton and 1 woolen mills in the town, and manufactures of leather, boots, shoes, hats, forks, combs, palm-leaf hats, tenon machines, copper pumps, piano-fortes, chairs, and cabinet ware:—annual value about $100,000. Some mineral substances are found here. Lancaster was first settled, 1643. Incorporated, 1653. Population, 1837, 1,903. It lies 35 miles W. N. W. from Boston, and 15 N. N. E. from Worcester.

Landaff, N. H.

Grafton co. Its distance from Haverhill is about 12 miles N. E., and from Concord 90 N. by W. Wild Amonoosuck river runs from S. E. to N. W. through the S. part of the town. Through the northwesterly extremity passes the Great Amonoosuck river. Landaff mountain in the E. part, Cobble hill in the centre, and Bald hill in the W., are the principal elevations. The soil is fertile. Landaff was granted in 1764, to James Avery and others. Population, in 1830, 951.

Landgrove, Vt.

Bennington co. This town is on elevated land at the N. E. corner of the county, 33 miles N. E. from Bennington, and about 30 S. W. from Windsor. Some of the head branches of West river have their sources here. The lands are too rough and high for much improvement. First settled, 1769. Population, 1830, 385.

Lanesborough, Mass.

Berkshire co. This township lies on elevated ground, the sources of some of the head branches of Housatonick and Hoosack rivers. It is situated on two hills, with an intervening valley. The lands in the valley are very luxuriant, and the hilly parts are admirably adapted for grazing. Lanesborough is a beautiful town, under good cultivation, and very productive. The inhabitants are principally farmers, who make agriculture a *business*, and reap its rewards. In 1837 there were in this town 12,333 sheep, whose fleeces weighed 42,489 lbs., estimated at $26,100. Limestone abounds here; also beautiful marble, and graphic slate. There is a delightful pond partly in this town and partly in Pittsfield: it contains trout and other fine fish.— Lanesborough was incorporated, 1765. Population, 1837, 1,090. It lies 125 miles W. by N. from Boston, and 11 N. from Lenox.

Langdon, N. H.

Sullivan co. Langdon is 18 miles S. S. W. from Newport, and 50 W. by S. from Concord. The principal village it 3 miles E. from Connecticut river, and 6 from Bellows Falls. A considerable branch of Cold river passes S. W. through the whole extent of this town, and unites with the main branch near the S. line. Langdon, named in honor of Gov. Langdon, was incorporated 1787. Its settlement commenced in 1773. Population, 1830, 667.

Lebanon, Me.

York co. This town is bounded W. by Salmon Fall river, on the line of New Hampshire. It is a large agricultural township, with some trade and manufactures. It lies 99 miles S. W. from Augusta, 50 S. W. by W. from Portland, and 11 S. W. from Alfred. Incorporated, 1767. Population, in 1837, 2,240.

Lebanon, N. H.

Grafton co. This pleasant town on Connecticut river, is 4 miles S. from Dartmouth College, 49 N. W. from Concord, and 90 N. W. from Portsmouth. Besides the Connecticut on its W. border, this town is watered by Mascomy river, running from E. to W. through its centre, and affording many valuable mill seats and a constant supply of water. The soil here is alluvial, the intervales on the Connecticut extending back from the river about half a mile. There are meadows or intervales on Mascomy river. The principal village is situated on a plain near the central part, at the head of the falls of Mascomy river. There are falls in the Connecticut in this town, which have been ocked and canalled by a company, called the White River Company. Lyman's bridge connects this town with Hartford, Vt. A medicinal spring has been discovered. A lead mine has been opened, and there has been found on Enfield line, near the outlet of the Great pond, a vein of iron ore.

This is a place of considerable manufactures, and of extensive trade. Lebanon was granted 1761. It was the first town settled on Connecticut river to the N. of Charlestown. The first settlers were a hardy, brave people, tenacious of their principles: most of them were men of strong minds, good habits, correct principles, and good common education. Population, 1830, 1,868.

Lebanon, Ct.

New London co. Lebanon lies 30 miles S. E. from Hartford, and 10 N. W. from Norwich. First settled about 1700. Population, in 1830, 2,554. The surface of the town is uneven—moderately hilly. The soil is of a chocolate color;—a rich deep mould, very fertile, and well adapted for grass. Husbandry is the principal business of the inhabitants. The village is on a street more than a mile in length, wide, pleasant and interesting: it was the residence of the TRUMBULL family, celebrated for their genius and patriotism. On the family tomb, in the village, is the following inscription to the memory of the first governor Trumbull.

"Sacred to the memory of Jonathan Trumbull, Esq. who, unaided by birth or powerful connexions, but blessed with a noble and virtuous mind, arrived to the highest station in government. His patriotism and firmness during 50 years employment in public life, and particularly in the very important part he acted in the American Revolution, as Governor of Connecticut; the faithful page of History will record.

Full of years and honors, rich in benevolence, and firm in the faith and hopes of Christianity, he died August 9th, 1785, Ætatis 75."

This tomb contains the ashes of two governors, one commissary general, and a signer of the Declaration of Independence.

Ledyard, Ct.

New London co. This town was taken from Groton in 1836. It was formerly called North Groton. It is 7 miles N. by E. from New London, and 8 S. from Norwich. There is a pretty village, of some thirty houses, at Gale's ferry, on the Thames. The population of the town, in 1836, was about 2,000. About twenty of the Pequot tribe of Indians reside here: a miserable remnant of a great and powerful nation.

This town was named in honor of two brothers, natives of Groton: Col. LEDYARD, the brave defender of Groton Heights, in 1781;—and JOHN LEDYARD, the celebrated traveler, who died at Cairo, in Egypt, in 1789, aged 38. John Ledyard was probably as distinguished a traveler as can be found on record. "Endowed with an original and comprehensive genius, he beheld with interest, and described with energy, the scenes and objects around him; and by comparing them with what he had seen in other regions of the globe, he was enabled to give his narrative all the varied effect of contrast and resemblance."

This accurate observer of mankind pays the following tribute to female character.

"I have always remarked," says he, "that women in all countries are civil and obliging, tender and humane: that they are ever inclined to be gay and cheerful, timorous and modest; and that they do not hesitate, like men, to perform a generous action. Not haughty, nor arrogant, nor supercilious, they are full of courtesy, and fond of society; more liable in general to err than man, but in general also more virtuous, and performing more good actions, than he. To a woman, whether civilized or savage, I never addressed myself, in the language of decency and friendship, without receiving a decent and friendly answer. With man it has often been otherwise. In wandering over the barren plains of inhospitable Denmark, through honest Sweden and frozen Lapland, rude and churlish Finland, unprincipled Russia, and the wide spread regions of the wandering Tartar; if hungry, dry, cold, wet, or sick, the women have ever been friendly to me, and uniformly so. And add to this virtue, so worthy the appellation of benevolence, their actions have been performed in so free and kind a manner, that if I was dry, I drank the sweetest draught, and if hungry, I ate the coarsest morsel, with a double relish."

Lee, Me.

Wheat crop, 1837, 8,450 bushels: population, the same year, 536. It lies 125 miles from Augusta. See "Down East."

Lee, N. H.

Strafford co. In the N. part of the town lies Wheelwright's pond, containing about 165 acres, and forming the principal source of Oyster river.

This pond is memorable for the battle which was fought near it in 1690, between a scouting party of Indians, and two companies of rangers, under Capts. Floyd and Wiswall. The engagement lasted two hours. Wiswall, his lieutenant, sergeant, and 12 men were killed and several wounded. Floyd continued to fight till his men, wearied and wounded, drew off and obliged him to follow. The enemy also retreated. Lee is 28 miles E. S. E. from Concord, and 12 S. W. from Dover. From the N. E. extremity of Epping, Lamprey river enters Lee, and after a serpentine course of about 7 miles, it passes into Durham. Other parts of the town are watered by Little, North, and Oyster rivers. Lee was originally a part of Durham, and was incorporated, 1766. Population, in 1830, 1,009.

Lee, Mass.

Berkshire co. This is a pleasant town on the Housatonick river, admirably located for manufacturing purposes. It contains a cotton and a woolen mill, 12 paper mills, and various other manufactures by water power. The amount of manufactured goods for the year ending April 1, 1837, was $405,000. The paper manufactured, amounted to $274,500. The articles manufactured, besides paper, cotton and woolen goods, were leather, hats, boots, shoes, bar iron, iron castings, axes, shovels, spades, hoes, forks, ploughs, chairs, tin, cabinet and wooden ware, carriages, chair stuff, &c. The soil of the town is good, particularly for grazing. The wool of 2,000 sheep, in 1837, was valued at $4,500. There is an abundant supply of iron ore and marble of excellent qualities. Lee was incorporated in 1777. It lies 130 miles W. from Boston, and 5 S. E. from Lenox. Population, in 1830, 1,825; 1837, 2,095.

Leeds, Me.

Kennebec co. This is a large and flourishing agricultural town, finely watered by a large and beautiful pond. The outlet of this pond into the Androscoggin, gives the town a good water power, for saw mills and other manufactories.

The villages in Leeds are very neat and pleasant. The soil is fertile and productive. Wheat crop, 1837, 5,421 bushels. Leeds was incorporated in 1802. It lies 30 miles W. S. W. from Augusta.— Population, 1837, 1,743.

Leicester, Vt.

Addison co. Leicester is watered by a river of its own name, by Otter creek, and by a part of lake Dunmore. These waters are too sluggish to afford the town much water power. The soil is a sandy loam, interspersed with some flats of clay. Along the rivers the soil is rich and productive. The high lands are hard and fit for grazing. About 4,000 sheep are kept here. Leicester lies 36 miles S. W. from Montpelier, and 10 S. by E. from Middlebury. First settled, 1773. Population, 1830, 638.

Leicester, Mass.

Worcester co. This town is on the height of ground between Boston harbor and Connecticut river. It lies 46 miles W. from Boston, 6 W. S. W. from Worcester, 42 E. S. E. from Northampton, and 44 N. W. from Providence. It was first settled in 1713, and incorporated about the year 1721. Its Indian name was *Towtaid*. Population, 1837, 2,122. This town is well watered by French river, and branches of the Connecticut and Blackstone, which rise here, and afford mill sites for numerous manufactories.

Leicester Academy was founded in 1784. It has considerable funds, commodious buildings, and is highly respectable. It accommodates 100 pupils throughout the year.

The surface of the town is uneven with a strong, deep soil. There are 5 woolen mills in the town, and manufactures of machines, hand cards, machine cards, chairs, cabinet ware, scythes, leather, boots and shoes: total value the year ending April 1, 1837, $531,939.

A society of Jews built a synagogue, and resided here from 1777 to 1783. They were much esteemed. The families of Denny, Earle and Henshaw, have been numerous in Leicester, and highly respectable.

Lemmington, Vt.

Essex co. A mountainous township, on the W. side of Connecticut river, with a small portion of intervale. There are several brooks in the town, and a beautiful cascade of 50 feet. There is a mountain in the town called "the Monadnock of Vermont," from which may be discovered that this town, generally, is not fit for cultivation. It lies 64 miles N. E. from Montpelier, and 24 N. from Guildhall. Population, 1830, 183.

Lempster, N. H.

Sullivan co. It is 40 miles W. from Concord. The surface is, in general, uneven, and the eastern part is mountainous. The soil is moist, and better suited for grass than grain. The town is well watered, although its streams are small. One branch of Sugar river, and the S. and W. branches of Cold river afford conveniences for water machinery. Near the W. boundary line is a pond 320 rods long and 80 wide. Sand pond lies in this town and Marlow. Lempster was granted 1761. It was settled about 1770, by emigrants from Connecticut. Population, in 1830, 999.

Lenox, Me.

See "Down East."

Lenox, Mass.

Berkshire co. Shire town. This is an excellent township of land, watered by Housatonick river, and surrounded by beautiful mountain scenery. It lies 130 miles W. from Boston, 25 N. E. from Hudson, N. Y., and 55 N. W. from Hartford, Ct. Lenox is accommodated with a water power, and contains mines of rich iron ore, and quarries of beautiful marble. There are some manufactures of iron, leather, marble, &c., in the town, but agriculture is the chief pursuit of the inhabitants. Incorporated, 1767. Population, 1837, 1,277.

Leominster, Mass.

Worcester co. A beautiful town, of an excellent soil, and great water power, on both sides of a principal branch of Nashua river, 42 miles N. W. from Boston, and 20 N. from Worcester. This town was taken from Lancaster in 1740, and shared with that town in the sufferings occasioned by Indian hostility. The manufactures of Leominster, for the year ending April 1, 1837, exclusive of the product of 5 paper mills, was $111,505. The articles manufactured were leather, boots, shoes, hats, axes, chairs, cabinet ware, combs, tin ware, straw bonnets, palm-leaf hats, chaises, carriages, and harnesses. Population, 1037, 1,944.

A rich alum rock has been found in this town which is said to be a decomposed mica slate. It contains an abundance of beautiful plumose, or feather form alum, like that of Milo, one of the Grecian isles, mixed with the green crystals of copperas, or sulphate of iron.

Levant, Me.

Penobscot co. This town lies principally on the S. W. side of Kenduskeag stream, by which and its tributaries it is well watered. The soil is good and productive.—The wheat crop of 1837 was 3,432 bushels. Levant lies 78 miles N. E. from Augusta, and 10 N. W. from Bangor. Incorporated, 1813. Population, 1830, 747; 1837, 1,081.

Leverett, Mass.

Franklin co. A good grazing town, on high ground, 85 miles W. N. W. from Boston, and 10 S. E. from Greenfield. The town is watered by Roaring brook, a rapid stream, on which is a cascade, and some wild scenery, worthy of the traveler's notice. Incorporated, 1774. Population, 1837, 902.

Lewiston, Me.

Lincoln co. Lewiston lies on the E. side of Androscoggin river, at the falls. The waters of that river descend 47 feet in the distance of 12 to 15 rods, and produce a valuable hydraulic power. The town extends on the river about 13 miles, and is connected with Minot by a bridge, at the foot of the falls, of 1,000 feet in length. This is a township of good land, with some manufactures of woolen and cotton goods, and a number of saw mills. Wheat crop, 1837, 1,920 bushels. Incorporated, 1795. Population, 1830, 1,549; 1837, 1,737. Lewiston is 28 miles S. W. from Augusta, 34 N. by E. from Portland, and 25 N. W. from Bath.

Lexington, Me.

Somerset co. This town lies 57 miles from Augusta. Population, 1837, 457. Wheat crop, same year, 2,346 bushels. See "Down East."

Lexington, Mass.

Middlesex co. This pleasant town lies 10 miles N. W. from Boston, and 7 E. from Concord. Incorporated, 1712. Population, 1837, 1,622. There are some excellent farms in this town, large tracts of meadow on some of the branches of the Shawsheen, which rise here, and some valuable woodland. The manufactures consist of boots, shoes, caps, clocks, cabinet ware, and calico printing: annual value, about $100,000.

Lexington will ever be an interesting place, as here the first blood was shed in the cause of American Independence. "A detachment of British soldiers were sent at daylight on the morning of the 19th of April, 1775, to take or destroy a quantity of military stores collected at Concord. They were under the command of Col. Smith and Maj. Pitcairn. On reaching this place, a militia company were exercising on the common. A British officer rode up and ordered them to disperse, but not being instantly obeyed, he discharged his pistol and ordered his men to fire, which they did, and eight of the Americans fell dead on the spot! The militia retreated, and the British proceeded to Concord, and in part succeeded in destroying the stores, but were so harassed on their return, that they would inevitably have been cut off, had they not been met at this place by a strong detachment of artillery under Lord Percy. The party suffered extremely by the fire of the Americans, aimed with deadly effect from the buildings, trees, and fences; and left 65 killed, and had 180 wounded. The Americans had 50 killed and 34 wounded. There is a monument on the spot where the first victims fell, to perpetuate the memory of the slain, and of this event."

Leyden, Mass.

Franklin co. Leyden is watered by Green river and several small streams. It is 100 miles N. W. from Boston, and 7 N. by W. from Greenfield. It is a mountainous township, more fit for grazing than tillage. The number of sheep in the town, in 1837, was 3,142; their fleeces weighed 9,326 pounds; value of the wool, $5,129. The town was incorporated in 1809. Population, 1837, 656.

There is a romantic spot in Leyden, called "the Glen," a curious place, worth looking at.

Liberty, Me.

Waldo co. This town is 29 miles E. from Augusta, and 18 W. S. W. from Belfast. It is watered by large ponds and small streams. The soil is good and produced, in 1837, 2,022 bushels of wheat. Incorporated, 1827. Population, 1837, 804.

A short time since a pine tree was cut in Liberty, which measured 7 feet in diameter, at the stump. It had three branches. The tree was sound, and 10,610 feet of square edged boards were made from it.

Limerick, Me.

York co. Little Ossipee river waters this town. It lies 28 miles W. from Portland, 85 S. W. from Augusta, and 15 N. by W. from Alfred. This is a good farming town, with a pleasant village, and an academy, incorporated in 1812. The town was incorporated in 1787 Population, 1837, 1,484.

Limington, Me.

York co. This town is bounded on the S. by Limerick, and is watered by Saco river on the S. and W. The town has a good soil, very productive of hay, wheat and other grain. It lies 89 miles S. W. from Augusta, and 28 W. S. W. from Portland. Incorporated, 1762.— Population, 1837, 2,223.

Lincoln County, Me.

Wiscasset, Topsham and *Warren* are the county towns. Lincoln county is bounded N. by the counties of Kennebec and Waldo, E. by Waldo county and Penobscot bay, S. by the Atlantic ocean, and W. by Cumberland county and Casco bay. Area about 950 square miles. This county is bounded on the ocean nearly fifty miles, and like the county of Hancock in this state, comprises an almost innumerable number of bays, coves, inlets, commodious harbors and fertile islands. The waters of the Muscongus, Damariscotta and Sheepscot pierce its centre, and the noble Kennebec finds all its Atlantic harbors in the county of Lincoln.

Considerable attention is paid to agriculture, for the soil is generally fertile and well adapted to the pursuit; but this county is essentially a maritime section of New England, possessing every requisition for foreign commerce, the coasting trade and fisheries. The tonnage of the three districts, Bath, Wiscasset and Waldoborough, in 1837, was 93,347 tons. This county contained, in 1837, 84,000 sheep, and raised 37,963 bushels of wheat. Population, 1820, 53,189; 1830, 57,181; 1837, 60,226: 63 inhabitants to a square mile.

Lincoln, Me.

Penobscot co. This is a very large town, more than double the common size. It lies on the E. side of the Penobscot, at the mouth of Matanaucook river, where is a pleasant and flourishing village, 45 miles N. by E. from Bangor, and 114 N. E. from Augusta. Lincoln has recently been incorporated, and possesses a soil of remarkable fertility. Population, 1830, 414; 1837, 1,045. Wheat crop, 1837, 4,263 bushels.

Lincoln, N. H.,

Grafton co., a mountainous township 70 miles N. from Concord.—The middle branch of the Pemigewasset passes through nearly the centre of the town. It has its source in Ferrin's pond, in the S. part of Franconia. There are several ponds, viz: Bog, Fish and Loon ponds. There are many elevations, of which Kinsman's mountain is the most considerable. In the N. part of the town are two large gulfs, made by an extraordinary discharge of water from the clouds in 1774. The numerous "slips," as they are called, from the mountain are worthy of notice. They commence near the summit of the mountain, and proceed to its base, forcing a passage through all obstructions. The soil here is poor. Wild animals, such as bears, raccoons, foxes, sables, otters, deer, &c., are very numerous. Lincoln was granted in 1764, to James Avery and others. Population, 1830, 50.

Lincoln, Vt.

Addison co. Lincoln was first settled by a number of "Friends," in 1790. The town is on high ground with an uneven surface. It lies 21 miles S. W. from Montpelier, and 15 N. E. from Middlebury. Population, 1830, 639.

Lincoln, Mass.

Middlesex co. Lincoln is bounded W. by Sudbury river. It lies 16 miles N. W. by W. from Boston, and 3 S. from Concord. Incorporated, 1754. Population, 1837, 694. It has some good farms and a large fish pond. The manufactures of the town consist of clothing, leather, straw bonnets, boots and shoes.

Lincolnville, Me.

Waldo co. On the W. side of Penobscot bay, 10 miles S. from Belfast, 7 N. from Camden, and 51 E. from Augusta. Incorporated, 1802. Population, 1837, 1,999.—This township has a good soil for grass, grain and potatoes. Wheat crop of 1837, 4,212 bushels. The town is well located for any branch of navigation. Duck Trap is an excellent harbor, and a busy place in the coasting trade.

Linneus, Me.

Washington co. This town is the source of a branch of the Mattawamkeag; and of a branch of the Meduxnekeag, flowing into the St. John's. It lies 8 miles S. W. from Houlton. Population, 1837, 208. Wheat crop same year, 2,514 bushels. Incorporated, 1836.

Lisbon, Me.

Lincoln co. Lisbon lies on the E. side of Androscoggin river, and 6 miles below Lewiston Falls. There are falls in the river at this place, called the "Ten mile falls." Lisbon has some manufactures of cotton and wool, a number of saw mills, and is united with Durham by a bridge. Wheat crop 1837, 3,781 bushels. Population, same year, 2,660. It lies 30 miles S. S. W. from Augusta, and 22 W. by N. from Wiscasset.

Lisbon, N. H.

Grafton co. It is 20 miles N. E. from Haverhill, and 90 from Concord. It is watered by Amonoosuck river, running through the whole extent of the town, and by several smaller streams. There are several ponds, the most noted of which is called Mink pond, lying in the S. part of the town, affording mill seats at its outlet. The soil admits of three divisions; the meadows or intervales on Amonoosuck river, which are generally very productive; the plain land, of a light, thin soil, requiring considerable manure to make it productive; and the uplands, of a strong deep soil, which afford many good farms. Blueberry mountain is the principal elevation. Large quantities of iron ore and limestone are found here. Maple sugar is manufactured and clover seed is raised in considerable quantities. This town was called Concord until 1824. Population, 1830, 1,485.

Lisbon, Ct.

New London co. This town is 7 miles N. from Norwich, from which it was taken in 1786. It is watered by Quinnebaug and Shetucket rivers, which unite in the S. part of the town. The soil is a gravelly and sandy loam, with some alluvial meadow. This is an excellent farming town: the inhabitants are generally industrious and independent. In that part of the town called Hanover, is a woolen and silk factory. Lisbon is 45 miles S. E. from Hartford. Population, 1830, 1,161.

Litchfield, Me.

Kennebec co. An excellent township of land, pleasantly situated 10 miles S. W. from Gardiner, and the source of some of the Cobbesseecontee waters. Litchfield lies 16 miles S. S. W. from Augusta, and was formerly a part of Lincoln county. Incorporated, 1795. Population, 1837, 2,341. Wheat crop, same year, 5,123 bushels.

Litchfield, N. H.,

Hillsborough co., is a small fertile township on the E. bank of Merrimack river. It is 8 miles E. from Amherst, and 30 S. by E. from Concord. This town has an excellent soil. There are two ferries, Thornton's, near the meeting house, on the post road from Amherst to Portsmouth; and Read's, 3 miles above.

Litchfield was taken from Dunstable in 1734. It was originally known by the Indian name of *Natticott*, and by the English one of *Brenton's Farm*. The settlement commenced about 1720.

The Hon. WYSEMAN CLAGETT closed his life in this town. He was a native of England, came to this country before the revolution commenced, and sustained several important offices. He was attorney general under the provincial and state governments, and filled the office with dignity and honor. Population, 1830, 505.

Litchfield County, Ct.

Litchfield, county town. This is the largest and most elevated county in the state. The surface is hilly and in some parts mountainous. The soil is chiefly a gravelly loam, under good cultivation, and very productive of butter, cheese, beef and pork. It abounds in iron ore, which is extensively manufactured. This county contains an area of 835 square miles. Population, 1820, 41,267; 1830, 42,855; containing 48 inhabitants to a square mile. This county is watered by numerous ponds; by the beautiful Housatonick, and by many rivers rising in the high grounds. The streams give a valuable water power, and flourishing manufacturing establishments are found in almost every town. The number of sheep in this county, in 1837, was 72,832. Litchfield county was incorporated in 1751. It is bounded N. by Berkshire county, Mass., E. by Hartford and New Haven counties, S. by the counties of New Haven and Fairfield, and W. by the state of New York.

Litchfield, Ct.

Litchfield co., chief town. This town, the Indian *Bantam*, comprising, as it was supposed, ten miles square, was valued at £300 in the year 1718. Bantam was first settled in 1720, and incorporated by its present name in 1724. It was a frontier town for many years, and during the wars between England and France was much harassed by the Canadians and Indians. Litchfield is an elevated township, and its surface presents a diversity of hills and valleys. The soil is a gravelly loam, deep, strong, and admirably adapted for grazing. Great pond is a beautiful sheet of water; it comprises an area of 900 acres, and is the largest pond in the state.

The waters of the Naugatuck, Shepung and Bantam give the town a good water power, and manufactures of cotton, wool, iron, and other articles are in successful operation on their banks.

Litchfield village, on "Litchfield Hill," was incorporated in 1818. It is a delightful place. It is situated on an elevated plain, surrounded by interesting scenery, and affords extensive prospects. The two principal streets cross each other nearly at right angles; they are wide, well shaded, and built upon with great taste and elegance. It lies 30 miles W. from Hartford, and 35 N. W. from New Haven. Population of the town, 1830, 4,458.

In the W. part of the town Mount Tom rears a front of 700 feet above the Naugatuck, presenting a panoramic landscape of great beauty and vast extent. Near this mountain is a mineral spring "which is saturated with iron and sulphur. The water issues from the E. side of the mountain in considerable quantities. The mud from the bottom of the spring burns with a blue flame, and the principal part of it consumes."

A law school of great respectability was established in this town, by the Hon. TAPPING REEVE, in 1784. The Hon. JAMES GOULD was associated with Judge Reeve, as instructor, for some years. This institution continued nearly thirty years, and furnished instruction to many of our most eminent jurists.

OLIVER WOLCOTT, one of the signers of the Declaration of Independence, resided here. He was the son of the Hon. Roger Wolcott. He died December 1, 1797, aged 72. He was distinguished for integrity, decision of character, and for his love of order and religion.

OLIVER WOLCOTT, son of the preceding, was born in 1760.— When a lad of 17, he lent his aid to the cause of his country: he was present in the engagement with the British at the time of their invasion of Danbury. On the formation of the U. S. Government, in 1789, he was appointed first auditor of the treasury; and in 1794 he succeeded Gen. Hamilton as secretary of the treasury. In 1817 he was elected governor of Connecticut, which office he held till 1827. He was the last survivor of the administration of Washington. He died in New York, June 2d, 1833, aged 74.

BENJAMIN TALLMAGE, a colonel in the revolutionary army, was a resident of this town. He was an ardent patriot and sincere christian. He was honored with the confidence of Washington in several hazardous and important trusts. He died at Litchfield, March 7, 1835, aged 81.

ETHAN ALLEN, a brigadier-general in the American service, distinguished for his daring and intrepid spirit, was a native of this town. "While he was young, his parents emigrated to Vermont. At the commencement of the disturbances in this territory, about the year 1770, he took a most active part in favor of the Green Mountain boys, as the settlers were then called, in opposition to the government of New York. An act of outlawry against him was passed by that state, and 500 guineas were offered for his apprehension: but his party was too numerous and faithful to permit him to be disturbed by any apprehensions for his safety. In all the struggles of the day he was successful; and he not only proved a valuable friend to those whose cause he had espoused, but he was humane and generous towards those with whom he had to contend. When called to take the field, he showed himself an able leader and an intrepid soldier.

"The news of the battle of Lexington determined Col. Allen to engage on the side of his country, and inspired him with the desire of demonstrating his attachment to liberty by some bold exploit. While his mind was in this state, a plan for taking Ticonderoga and Crown Point by surprise, which was formed by several gentlemen in Connecticut, was communicated to him, and he readily engaged in the project. Receiving directions from the general assembly of Connecticut to raise the Green Mountain boys, and conduct the enterprise, he collected 230 of the hardy settlers and proceeded to Castleton. Here he was unexpectedly joined by Col. Arnold, who had been commissioned by the Massachusetts committee to raise 400 men, and effect the same object, which was now about to be accomplished. As he had not raised the men, he was admitted to act as an assistant to Col. Allen. They reached the lake opposite Ticonderoga on the evening of the 9th of May, 1775. With the utmost difficulty boats were procured, and 83 men were landed near the garrison. The approach of day rendering it dangerous to wait for the rear, it was determined immediately to proceed. The commander in chief now addressed his men, representing that they had been for a number of years a scourge to arbitrary power, and famed for their valor, and concluded with saying, 'I now propose to advance before you, and in person conduct you through the wicket gate; and you, who will go with me voluntarily in this desperate attempt, poise your firelocks.' At the head of the centre file he marched instantly to the gate, where a sentry snapped his gun at him, and retreated through the covered way: he pressed forward into the fort, and formed his men on the parade in such a manner as to face two opposite barracks. Three huzzas awaked the garrison. A sentry, who asked quarter, pointed out the apartments of the commanding officer; and Allen with a drawn sword over the head of Capt. De la Place, who was undressed, demanded the surrender of the fort. 'By what authority do you demand it?' inquired the astonished commander. 'I demand it (said Allen) in the name of the great Jehovah and of the continental congress.' The summons could not be disobeyed, and the fort, with its very valuable stores and 49 prisoners was immediately surrendered. Crown Point was taken the same day, and the capture of a sloop of war, soon afterwards, made Allen and his brave party complete masters of Lake Champlain."

Gen. Allen possessed strong powers of mind, but they never felt the influence of education. Though he was brave, humane and generous, yet his conduct does not seem to have been much influenced by considerations respecting that holy and merciful Being, whose character and whose commands are disclosed to us in the scriptures." Gen. Allen died at Colchester, Feb. 13, 1789, aged 52.

Little Androscoggin River,

In Maine, has its sources in ponds in the towns of Woodstock, Greenwood, and Norway: it passes in a southeasterly direction through Oxford, and falls into the Androscoggin between Minot and Danville, opposite to Lewiston.

Little Compton, R. I.

Newport co. This very pleasant town, the Indian *Seaconnet*, lies on the ocean, at the eastern entrance into Narraganset bay, 9 miles E. by N. from Newport, 30 S. S. E. from Providence, and 12 S. from Fall River, Mass. The soil of the town is uncommonly fertile, and being cultivated by an industrious class of men, is very productive of corn and other grain; beef, pork, butter, cheese, and wool.

Seaconnet Rocks, at the southeastern extremity of the town, where a break-water has been erected by government, is well known to sailors, and memorable as the place where a treaty was made between the English and the Queen of the powerful Seaconnet tribe, in 1674. That tribe is now extinct: *Seaconnet Rocks* is their only monument.

Little Compton is becoming celebrated as a place of resort, in summer months, for sea air and bathing; and very justly so, for very few parts of our coast exhibit a more interesting location.

Little Machias & Little Rivers.

See *Cutler.*

Littleton, N. H.

Grafton co. On Connecticut river. Its extent on Connecticut river is about 14 miles It is 30 miles N. by E. from Haverhill, and 80 N. N. W. from Concord. Connecticut river, in passing down the rapids called *Fifteen Mile Falls*, extending the whole length of Littleton, runs in foaming waves for miles together, which render it impossible to ascend or descend with boats in safety. There are three bridges over the Connecticut in Litteton. Amonoosuck river waters the S. part, having on its banks small tracts of excellent intervale. The principal village is on this river, in the S. part of the town, and is called *Glynville*. Raspberry, Black, Palmer's and Iron mountains are the most prominent elevations. Near Amonoosuck river, there is a mineral spring, the water of which is said to be similar to the Congress spring at Saratoga. The land comprehending Littleton was first granted in 1764, by the name of *Chiswick*. It was re-granted in 1770, by the name of *Apthorp*. In 1784, Apthorp was divided, and the towns of Littleton and Dalton incorporated. Population, 1830, 1,435.

Littleton, Mass.

Middlesex co. The Indians called this town *Nashabah*. It is 27 miles W. N. W. from Boston, and 10 N. W. from Concord. Incorporated, 1715. Population, 1837, 876. There are several beautiful ponds in the town, and limestone. The soil is tolerably good, and adapted for the growth of rye and hops. There are some manufactures of boots, shoes, and straw bonnets.

Livermore, Me.

Oxford co. An excellent township of land, on both sides of the Androscoggin river, 25 miles W. from Augusta, and 18 N. E. from Paris. Incorporated, 1795. Population, 1830, 2,456; 1837, 2,631. There are three pleasant villages in the town, fine falls on the river, saw mills and other manufactures.

Wheat crop of 1837, 8,472 bushels.

Londonderry, N. H.

Rockingham co. Adjoining the E. line of the county of Hillsborough. This town contains very little waste land, and it is believed, has as extensive a body of fertile soil as any town in the E. section of the state. It lies 25 miles S. S. E. from Concord, and 35 S. W. from Portsmouth. Population, in 1830, 1,469.

Londonderry, which formerly included the present town of Derry, was settled in 1719, by a colony of presbyterians, from the vicinity of the city of Londonderry, in the N. of Ireland, to which place their ancestors had emigrated about a century before from Scotland. They were a part of 120 families, chiefly from three parishes, who with their religious instructors came to New England in the summer of 1718. In October, 1718, they applied to the government of Massachusetts for the grant of a township, and received assurances that a grant should be made them when they should select a place for its location. After some time spent in viewing the country, they selected the tract afterwards composing the town of Londonderry, at first known by the name of *Nutfield*. In 1719, sixteen families, accompanied by Rev. James McGregore, one of the clergymen who had emigrated from Ireland with them, took possession of the tract, and on the day of their arrival attended religious services and a sermon under an oak on the east shore of Beaver pond. The inhabitants of Londonderry in 1720, purchased the Indian title, and although it was long a frontier town, were never molested by the Indians. They introduced the culture of the potatoe, a vegetable till then unknown in New England, and the manufacture of linen cloth, which, though long since declined, was for many years a considerable source of their early prosperity.

Rev. MATTHEW CLARK, second minister of Londonderry, was a native of Ireland, who had in early life been an officer in the army, and distinguished himself in the defence of the city of Londonderry, when besieged by the army of King James II. A. D., 1688-9. He afterwards relinquished a military life for the clerical profession. He possessed a strong mind, marked by a considerable degree of eccentricity. He died January 25, 1735, and was borne to the grave, at his particular request, by his former companions in arms, of whom there were a considerable number among the early settlers of this town; several of whom had been made free from taxes throughout the British dominions by King William, for their bravery in that memorable siege.

A company of 70 men from this town, under the command of Capt. George Reid, were in the battle of Breed's hill, and about the same number were in that at Bennington, in which Capt. David M'Clary, one of their citizens, a distinguished and brave officer, was killed. Major-general John Stark and Col. George Reid, officers of the army of the revolution, were natives of this town.

Londonderry, Vt.

Windham co. West river passes though this town and receives several tributaries in it. The land on the streams is rich and fertile; the uplands are good for grazing, except those parts that are mountainous. First settled, 1774. Population, 1830, 1,302. It lies 28 miles S. W. from Windsor, and 30 N. E. from Bennington.

Long Island Sound.

This inland sea washes the whole southern boundary of Connecticut, and is formed by Long Island, in the state of New York. This island extends from Montauk Point, off Stonington, to the harbor of New York. Its length is 120 miles. The widest part, 20 miles, is off New Haven; the narrowest parts, on the border of New England, are off the mouth of Connecticut river, about 8 miles, and off Greenwich, or *Saw Pits*, 7 miles.

This Sound, as far as Hurl Gate, is navigable for vessels of any burthen, and the passage to and from the sea round Montauk, is remarkably easy at any time of tide, and in all weather. See *Judith Point*.

Hurl Gate, sometimes called *Hell Gate*, but properly *Horll Gatt*, a Dutch term, signifying a whirlpool, is a narrow strait of difficult passage between Long and New York Islands. At half tide the current runs 7 or 8 miles an hour. It contains numerous whirlpools, is rocky and bears a threatening aspect; but good pilots navigate it with ease when the tide is favorable. Steam-boats press through at all times of tide. Through this passage a vast amount of the productions of Connecticut and Rhode Island pass to New York market.

A survey for a ship canal, uniting these waters and Narraganset bay with Boston harbor, was commenced by the government of the United States in 1827. From a tide lock at Braintree, in Boston harbor, to a tide lock at Somerset, Mass., on Taunton river, the distance is 36 miles. The summit level is at Randolph, Mass., 134 feet above high water mark at Boston. A ship canal in this direction, or one across Cape Cod, at Sandwich, would save many lives, and a vast amount of property.

Some of the distances from Providence, and along the northern coast of this Sound, to the city of New York, are here given.

From Providence to Newport, 30 miles:—to Judith Point, 11—41:—to the mouth of Stonington harbor, 27—68 :—to the mouth of **New** London harbor, 8--76:—to the mouth of Connecticut river, 13—89 :—to the mouth of New Haven harbor, 27—116:—to Stratford Point, 10—126:—to the mouth of Fairfield harbor, 6—132;—to Norwalk, 8—140 : —to Greenwich, or *Saw Pits*, 15—155:—to Throg's Point, 14—169:—to Hurl Gate, 6—175:—to New York, 8 miles, making the distance from Providence to New York, by water, 188 miles.

As the rail-road from Boston to Albany, although in good progress, is not completed; and as many of our friends at the north visiting the interior of the state of New York find it more agreeable to pass through the city of New York and up the Hudson river, rather than cross the country, we think it may be useful to give some of the distances on that noble river, from the city of New York to the city of Troy.

Note.—w. denotes *west side*, *e. east side*.

From New York to Hoboken, w. 2 miles :—to Manhattanville, e. 6—8 :—to Fort Lee, w. 2—10 :—to King's Bridge, 3—13:—(The Palisadoes, perpendicular cliffs of great elevation, on the west bank of the river, commence at Hoboken, and extend 20 miles to Tappan bay) to Fort Independence, e. 2—15:—to Tarrytown, e. 12—27 :—to Sing Sing, e. 5—32 :—to Stony Point light-house, w. 8—40 :—to Fort Fayette, Verplanck's Point, e. 1—41:—to Dunderburgh Mountain, w. and Peekskill, e. 2—43:—(Here we enter the justly celebrated Highlands, pronounced by every honest Yankee to be equal if not superior to any scenery of the kind in his own country) to St. Anthony's Nose, e. and Forts Montgomery and Clinton, w. 3—46:—to Buttermilk Falls, w. 4—50:—to West Point—Fort Putnam, w. 2—52:—to West Mountain, w. and Cold

NEW ENGLAND GAZETTEER.

Spring, e. 4—56:—to Newburgh, w. 5—61:—to Hamburgh, e. 7—68:—to Poughkeepsie, e. 4—72:—to Hyde Park, e. 9—81:—to Lewis' Landing, e. and Esopus, w. 5—86:—to Kingston Landing, w. and Rhinebeck Landing, e. 4—90:—to Upper Red Hook Landing, e. and Ulster, w. 11—101:—to Catskill Landing, w. 9—110:—to Hudson, e. and Athens, w. 6—116:—to Coxsackie Landing, w. 8—124:—to Kinderhook Landing, e.3—127:—to Cœmans, w. 5—132:—to the Overslaugh, (sand bars) 9—141:—to Albany, w. 3--144:—to Troy, e. 6—150. The whole distance from Boston to Troy, by this route, is 357 miles.

At *Catskill Landing*, visitors to the Catskill mountains stop. Pine Orchard Hotel, a splendid building, is 12 miles distant. This Mountain House is 2,274 feet above the tide of the Hudson. A few years ago this enchanting spot was a wilderness.

"From this lofty eminence all inequalities of surface are overlooked. A seemingly endless succession of woods and waters—farms and villages, towns and cities, are spread out as upon a boundless map. Far beyond rise the Tagkannuc mountains, and the highlands of Connecticut and Massachusetts. To the left, and at a still greater distance, the Green mountains of Vermont stretch away to the north, and their blue summits and the blue sky mingle together. The beautiful Hudson, studded with islands, appears narrowed in the distance, with steam-boats almost constantly in sight; while vessels of every description, spreading their white canvas to the breeze, are moving rapidly over its surface, or idly loitering in the calm. These may be traced to the distance of nearly seventy miles with the naked eye; and again at times all below is enveloped in dark clouds and rolling mist, which, driven about by the wind, is constantly assuming new, wild, and fantastic forms. From the Pine Orchard a ride or walk of a mile or two brings you to the Kauterskill falls. Here the outlet of two small lakes leaps down a perpendicular fall of 130 feet—then glides away through a channel worn in the rock, to a second fall of 80 feet. Below this it is lost in the dark ravine through which it finds its way to the valley of the Catskill."

Troy is a beautiful city. It lies on the east side of Hudson river, in the county of Rensselaer, New York, at the head of navigation, and at the junction of the northern and western canals with that noble river. The city is on an elevated plain, regularly laid out: the streets are wide and well shaded : the buildings are uniformly neat, and many of them in a style of superior elegance. St. Paul's church, and the new Presbyterian, are splendid edifices, and display great taste in their construction.

The city of Troy is abundantly supplied with excellent water from the neighboring hills, at an expense of $150,000. The source of the water is 75 feet above the level of the city. At the corner of every street are hydrants, and a hose placed on these sends the water up higher and with greater force than a fire engine.

The squares and private gardens are ornamented with perpetual water fountains.

In *Washington Square* is an Italian marble fountain, chaste and classic in its construction, in the centre of the city. It sends up the water ten or fifteen feet, and in its descent resembles the weeping willow.— This significant emblem of purity gives this beautiful square an additional charm.

Two streams, affording immense

water facilities, empty into the Hudson within the limits of the city, and one of them rolls down a beautiful cascade, a short distance from Washington square; an object worthy of a visit from the curious traveler. These streams move the machinery of numerous mills.

About a quarter of a mile from the centre of the city, *Mount Ida* rears its head three or four hundred feet in height, from whose summit every building in the city, the windings of the canals and river, the foaming of the Mohawk, and the neighboring towns of Albany, Waterford, and Lansingburgh, are distinctly seen.

Troy was incorporated as a village in 1801. It then had a population of 2,000. Population, 1810, 3,895. In 1816 it became a city. Population, 1820, 5,264; 1825, 7,875; 1830, 11,405; 1836, 18,000.

Troy has risen to its present state of opulence and population by its favorable position for trade, but more especially the enterprize and economical habits of its people.— Many of the first settlers of Troy came from New England in humble circumstances. Some of those who thus came have amassed princely fortunes, and acquired a name more valuable than gold. A recent Mayor of the city came from the east as a day laborer. The late chief magistrate of the justly styled "Empire State," a New Englander, was found in 1822 soliciting the patronage of the Trojans as an attorney at law. Troy was formerly called *Vanderheyden*, in honor of a worthy Dutchman whose farm comprised the most compact part of the city.

A notice of Mrs. WILLARD's Female Seminary must not be omitted in this brief account of the "Fountain City," as it is an institution of rare excellence, conducted by a lady of extraordinary attainments. This school was commenced at Troy in 1821, since which time a commodious building, on a pleasant site, has been erected, 130 feet by 40. The number of scholars varies from 200 to 275. They come from every state in the union, the Canadas, the West Indies, and even from Europe, but chiefly from the state of New York and New England. Mrs. Willard's plan of education has received the approbation of some of the wisest men in Europe. Dr. Combe quotes it, in his essay on education, with unqualified approbation. This institution is conducted almost entirely by females: it is, in fact, a female *college*, and many are the *degrees of usefulness* conferred by its learned principal on its numerous and lovely graduates.

The institution is incorporated, and it cannot fail of receiving the best wishes of the community.— May no event occur to mar its prosperity and usefulness.

The traveler will visit the "Fountain City" again, on his way from Champlain Lake. See *Burlington, Vt.*, in the *Register*.

Long Meadow, Mass.

Hampden co. This is a beautiful town with a fine soil, on the E. side of Connecticut river, 97 miles S. W. by W. from Boston, 5 S. from Springfield, and 22 N. from Hartford, Ct. Incorporated, 1783. Population, 1837, 1,251. There are several tanneries in the town, and some other manufactures, but the inhabitants are generally engaged in cultivating the soil. The Indian name of the place was *Massacsick*.

Long Lake, Me.

This is a sheet of water at the northern part of Piscataquis county, about 15 miles in length and 2 in width, which empties by Namjamskillecook river into Temiscouata lake, the head waters of Madawaska river. It lies about 210 miles N. by E. from Augusta.

Long Pond, Me.
See *Bridgeton.*

Loudon, N. H.
Merrimack co. Soucook river passes from Gilmanton S. through Loudon, furnishing valuable mill privileges. There is some good intervale on its borders. Loudon was originally a part of Canterbury; was incorporated, 1773. Loudon lies 7 miles N. E. from Concord. Population, 1830, 1,642.

Lovell, Me.
Oxford co. This town embraces Kezer pond, a large sheet of water, and other ponds whose outlet is into the Saco, at Fryeburgh. Lovell lies 10 miles N. from Fryeburgh, 20 W. S. W· from Paris, and 67 W. S. W. from Augusta. Incorporated, 1800. Population, 1837, 876.

"In this town are Lovell's Falls, which are an object of great natural curiosity. Where the water makes over into the tremendous basin below, it falls perpendicularly 40 feet. Above the falls, there is a chain of eight ponds, partly in Lovell and partly in Waterford, connected by small natural dams one or two rods in width, through which there are sluiceways, which will admit the passage of a common sail boat. The scenery of the mountains and ascending lands in the vicinity is rural and beautiful."

Lowell, Me.
Penobscot co. Formerly called *Huntressville.* Incorporated by its present name in 1833. "See Down East."

Lowell, Vt.
Orleans co. This town was first settled in 1806, and was called *Kelleyvale* for a number of years. It lies 36 miles N. from Montpelier, and 10 S. W. from Irasburgh. Population, 1830. 314. This township is mountainous, and the fountain head of Missisque river.

Lowell, Mass.
Middlesex co. County town.—This city, the American Manchester, is remarkable for the extent of its water power, its rapid growth, and the height to which it has raised the American character, by the perfection of its manufactures.

Lowell has risen to eminence by the remarkable energy and skill of a few individuals; among whom PATRICK T. JACKSON, Esq. of Boston, and the late KIRK BOOT, Esq. were distinguished.

It lies on the S. side of Merrimack river, below Pawtucket Falls, and at the union of Concord river with the Merrimack.

In 1815, the site where the city stands was a wilderness, with the exception of a few lonely dwellings. In 1824, Lowell, then a part of Chelmsford, was incorporated as a town. In 1835, it became a city. Lowell is situated 25 miles N. from Boston, 14 N. N. E. from Concord, 37 N. E. from Worcester, and 38 S. S. E. from Concord, N. H. Population, 1830, 6,474; 1837, 18,010.

The hydraulic power of this place is produced by a canal, of a mile and a half in length, 60 feet in width, and 8 feet in depth, extending from the head of Pawtucket Falls to Concord river. This canal has locks at its outlet into Concord river; it also serves for the passage of boats up and down the Merrimack. From this canal, the water is conveyed by lateral canals to various places where it is wanted for use, and then discharged, either into the Merrimack or Concord.

The canal is owned by "The Proprietors of the Locks and Canals on Merrimack river." This company was incorporated in 1792, and have a capital of $600,000. They dispose of lands and mill privileges, and own the machine shop, and carry on the manufacture of machinery. The first cotton mill at this place was erected in 1822.

The whole fall of the Merrimack

at this place is 30 feet, and the quantity of water never falls short of 2,000 cubic feet per second, and is very rarely so low as that. This quantity of water is estimated to carry 286,000 spindles, with all the preparatory machinery. There is therefore an unimproved water power at this place sufficient to carry eleven mills of the usual size, making the whole number of mills 39, when all the water is improved.

There are 10 corporations, with a capital stock of $8,250,000: 28 mills besides machine shops, print works, &c., all warmed in cold weather by hot air or steam.

There are 150,404 spindles, and 4,861 looms. There are 51,147,200 yards of cloth manufactured per annum; 12,220,000 yards dyed and printed, and 16,161,600 lbs. of cotton used annually, besides a large quantity of wool.

There are annually used in these manufactories, 11,000 tons of Anthracite coal, 4,810 cords of wood, 500,000 bushels of charcoal, 63,489 gallons of oil, 510,000 pounds of starch, and 3,800 barrels of flour for starch in the print works and bleachery.

The number of females employed in the mills, is 6,295: number of males, 2,047. Total number of hands, 8,342. The average wages of females per week, clear of board, is $1,75; of males, 80 cents per day, clear of board. The average amount of wages paid per month is $106,000.

The goods manufactured in these mills consist of sheetings, shirtings, drillings, calicoes, broadcloths, cassimeres, carpets, rugs, negro cloth; machinery for mills, and for engines and cars for rail-roads. The quality of these goods is generally superior to those imported. The annual amount of goods manufactured by these mills is about $8,000,000.

The mills are built of brick, and are about 157 feet in length, 45 in breadth, and from 4 to 7 stories in height.

The Locks and Canals Machine Shop, included among the 28 mills, can furnish machinery complete for a mill of 5,000 spindles in four months, and lumber and materials are always at command, with which to build or rebuild a mill in that time, if required. When building mills, the Locks and Canals Company employ directly and indirectly from a thousand to twelve hundred hands.

There are also in Lowell 10 powder mills, a flour mill, glass works, the Lowell bleachery, flannel mills, and manufactories of cards, whips, planing and reed machines, boots, shoes; brass, copper and tin wares, carriages, harnesses, iron castings, &c. &c.; the annual proceeds of which amount to about $500,000, employing about 200 hands.

Lowell is finely situated in regard to health: it is surrounded by pleasant hills and valleys, and seated on a rapid stream. We are enabled to state on good authority that 6 of the females out of 10 enjoy better health than before being employed in the mills, and that one half of the males derive the same advantage.

Lowell is very handsomely located: it is laid out into wide streets; all the buildings are of recent construction, and in a style of neatness and elegance.

With regard to the future prosperity of this interesting city, nothing need be said to those who know that it was founded, and is principally sustained, by the most eminent capitalists of Boston; a city renowned for its enterprize, wealth, and public spirit.

To strangers we would say—*visit it*. It is a pleasant ride of about an hour from Boston, by the rail-road. Foreigners view Lowell with admiration; and every American who sees it feels proud that such a city exists on this side of the Atlantic.

Lubec, Me.

Washington co. Lubec comprises a township of good land, lying at the northeasterly corner of the state, and contains a point of land extending easterly on which West Quoddy Head light-house is situated, at the western entrance into Passamaquoddy bay. This place possesses an admirable harbor for vessels of any draught of water; it is easy of access and never obstructed by ice. There are also within the town a number of bays, coves, and several islands. Grand Menan stretches off the mouth of the harbor on the E. 5 or 6 miles distant, and Campo Ballo, another English island, lies very near and protects the harbor on the north. This town was taken from Eastport in 1811, and contained 380 inhabitants. Population, 1820, 1430; 1830, 2,081; 1837, 4,161.

Lubec, in common with Eastport, enjoys a very extensive trade with the Bay of Fundy and the great waters of Passamaquoddy bay. The village, or principal place of business, is beautifully located on a point of land jutting out into the harbor; it makes a fine appearance, commands an active trade, and is flourishing in its navigation and fishery. It lies 3 miles S. from Eastport, 30 E. from Machias, 173 E. by N. from Augusta, and 31 S. E. from Calais, at the head of navigation on the St. Croix river.

Ludlow, Vt.

Windsor co. Black and Williams' rivers give this town a good water power. It is likewise watered by a number of large ponds well stored with fish. Ludlow was first settled in 1784. It lies 61 miles S. from Montpelier, and 18 S. W. from Windsor. Population, 1830, 1,227.

The town is mountainous, but contains good land for the grazing of sheep and other cattle. The village is very pleasant, and the centre of considerable trade with the surrounding country. Some valuable minerals have been discovered here.

Ludlow, Mass.

Hampden co. This town lies N. of Wilbraham, and is separated from it by Chickopee river. It is 84 miles W. by S. from Boston, and 10 N. E. from Springfield. Incorporated, 1774. The Chickopee here is a large stream, and adds much to the beauty of the place. There are two cotton mills in the town, and manufactures of palm-leaf hats and ploughs: total value, in one year, $160,850. Population, 1837, 1,329.

Lunenburgh, Vt.

Essex co. On the west side of Connecticut river, and watered by Neal's branch and pond, and Catbow branch;—good mill streams. Some of the land is very good, but the most of it is stony, appearently of diluvial formation, consisting of rounded masses of granite embedded in clay and gravel. This is a good grazing town, and produces some cattle, and butter and cheese for market. First settled about 1770. Population, in 1830, 1,054. Lunenburgh lies 45 miles E. N. E. from Montpelier, and 8 S. from Guildhall.

Lunenburgh, Mass.

Worcester co. The soil of this town is good, the surface uneven and watered by some branches of Nashua river. Considerable amount of books are printed and bound in this town, and there are some manufactures of palm-leaf hats, chairs, cabinet ware, leather, boots and shoes. Lunenburgh is a very pleasant town: 42 miles N. W. from Boston, and 24 N. from Worcester. Incorporated, 1728. Population, 1837, 1,250.

Lyman, Me.

York co. This is a pleasant

town, watered by several ponds which empty, some into the Saco, and others into the Kennebunk and Mousum. It lies 87 miles S. W. from Augusta, 5 E. from Alfred and 6 N. N. W. from Kennebunk. Population, 1837, 1,528.

Lyman, N. H.

Grafton co. On Connecticut river. This town is 13 miles above Haverhill, 90 miles N. N. W. from Concord. There is one considerable elevation, called Lyman's mountain. The N. W. branch of Burnham's river has its source from this mountain. There are several ponds in the E. part of Lyman, through the largest of which Burnham's river has its course. The lower bar of the Fifteen Mile falls is in this town. Carleton's falls are several miles below, and below these is Stevens' ferry, which communicates with Barnet. Lyman was granted in 1761. Population, in 1830, 1,321.

Lyme, N. H.

Grafton co. This town is 6 miles S. from Orford, and 54 N. W. from Concord. The soil here is similar to that of other towns on Connecticut river, with this difference, that there is a less proportion of intervale, and a less difference between that directly adjoining the river and the other parts of the town. There are three small streams passing through Lyme and emptying into Connecticut river. There are two small ponds, the largest of which is called Ports pond. There is a mountain, called Smart's mountain, lying in the N. E. part of the town.— Lyme was granted 1761. The town was settled 1764. Population, in 1830, 1,804.

Lyme, Ct.

New London co. Lyme is situated at the mouth of Connecticut river, on the east side, opposite to Saybrook. It is a pleasant town, generally of good soil, but greatly diversified in regard to surface: some parts are mountainous and rocky, while others are level, with large tracts of salt meadow. The town is watered by several streams and ponds, and the shores on the sound and river are indented by small bays and harbors, which afford the town some navigable privileges. There are several neat villages in the town, a cotton mill, 2 woolen factories, and about 6,000 sheep. Lyme was first settled in 1664. Incorporated, 1667. It lies 40 miles S. E. from Hartford, and 40 E. from New Haven. Population, 1830, 4,084. Its Indian name was *Nehantic.*

Among the first settlers was MATTHEW GRISWOLD, the ancestor of two governors, and of a numerous and highly respected family in the state.

A tract of land, once an Indian reservation, was for some time in dispute between the towns of Lyme and New London. It was finally agreed to settle their respective titles to the land in controversy, by a combat between two champions, to be chosen by each for that purpose. The combatants were chosen, and on a day mutually appointed, the champions appeared in the field, and fought with their fists till victory declared in favor of each of the Lyme combatants. Lyme then quietly took possession of the controverted tract, and has held it undisputed, to the present day.

Deacon Marvin, a large land holder and an exemplary man, was exceedingly eccentric in some of his notions. His courtship, it is said, was as follows:—Having one day mounted his horse, with only a sheep skin for a saddle, he rode in front of the house where Betty Lee lived, and without dismounting requested Betty to come to him; on her coming, he told her that the Lord had sent him there to marry her. Betty, without much hesitation, replied, The Lord's will be done.

The following is on the Deacon's monument in the grave yard, dated, October 18, 1737.

This Deacon aged 68:
Is freed on earth from serving
May for a crown no longer wait:
Lyme's Captain REYNOLD MARVIN.

Lyndeborough, N. H.

Hillsborough co. This town is 10 miles W. N. W. from Amherst, and 35 S. S. W. from Concord. It is an elevated township, having a considerable mountain which divides it from E. to W. There is, in the N. E. part of the town, below the mountain, a plain, where there is a small village, pleasantly situated near Piscataquog river. The soil of this town, though stony, is deep and strong. For grazing it is, perhaps, not exceeded by any town in the county. The streams are small, originating principally from sources in the town, and running N. and S. from the mountain.—Lyndeborough was originally granted in 1690. In 1753, Benjamin Lynde, Esq. of Salem, purchased a considerable part of the township, and adjoining lands. From him, the place, when it was incorporated in 1764, took the name of Lyndeborough. It was settled as early as 1750. On the 15th of Nov., 1809, three children were burnt in a barn, while their parents were attending an installation at Mont Vernon.—Population, in 1830, 1,147.

Lyndon, Vt.

Caledonia co. First settled, 1788. It lies 34 miles N. E. from Montpelier, and 10 N. N. E. from Danville. Population, 1830, 1,822. Lyndon is one of the best townships in the state: its surface is undulating, with a soil of rich loam, free from stone, easy to cultivate, and very productive of wool, cattle, pork, butter and cheese. It is admirably well watered by the Pas- sumpsic and some of its tributaries. Two important falls of that river are in the town, one of 65 feet in the distance of 30 rods; the other of 18 feet. These are called *Great* and *Little Falls*, and afford a water power of great extent. Agaric mineral, used for chalk, and a good substitute for spanish white, is found here. The principal village is very pleasant and the seat of considerable business. The scenery about the town is picturesque and interesting. There is probably no interior town in the state that contains more valuable water privileges than Lyndon.

Lynn, Mass.

Essex co. Lynn is one of the most flourishing and beautiful towns in the state. It lies on a plain, surrounded by rising ground, except on the east, where it opens to Lynn bay, embracing the romantic peninsula of *Nahant*, with its beautiful beach, and *Phillips' Point*, both highly esteemed resorts for all classes of people;—the sick, the serious, and the gay. The soil of the town is fertile and well cultivated. It is watered by the river *Saugus*, the Indian name of the place. The town is neatly built on wide and pleasant streets, and contains a population of about 10,000. It lies 9 miles N. E. from Boston, and 5 S. W. from Salem.

Lynn has risen to wealth and importance by the enterprise and industry of its people, in the manufacture of shoes, particularly for which, more than any other town in the country, it is justly celebrated. The manufacture of ladies' shoes was commenced here before the revolutionary war, and it is curious to observe the great changes that have occurred in the fashion and manufacture of that article.

"In olden times," says the Newburyport Herald, "ladies' shoes were made in Lynn of common woolen cloth, or coarse curried leather; afterwards of stuffs such as cassimere, everlasting, shalloon and russet; some of satin and damask, others of satin lasting and florentine. They were generally cut with straps, for large buckles, which were worn in those days by women as well as men. Ladies' shoes, 70 years ago, were made mostly with white and russet rands, and stitched very fine on the rand with white-waxed thread. Some were made turn pumps and channel pumps, all having wooden heels, called *cross-cut, 'common*, and *court heels.* Then the cork, plug, and wedge or spring heels, came into use. The sole-leather was all worked with the flesh side out.

"Previous to the war of the revolution, the market for Lynn shoes was principally confined to New England; some few, however, were exported to Philadelphia. Many individuals with small capital carried on the business in their own families. Fathers, sons, apprentices, and one or two journeymen, all in one small shop, with a chimney in one corner, formed the whole establishment.

"After the revolution, the business assumed a different aspect. Enterprising individuals embarked in the business in good earnest; hired a great number of journeymen; built large shops, took apprentices, and drove the business. Master workmen shipped their shoes to the south, so that Lynn shoes took the place of English and other imported shoes. Morocco and kid leather, suitable for shoes, began to be imported from England, which soon took the place of stuffs. Roan shoes were now little called for; and the improvement of working the sole-leather grain side out, was now generally adopted, making what is called *duff bottoms.* About the year 1794, wooden heels began to go out of use, by the introduction of leather spring heels. This improvement progressed gradually, until the heel making, which was once a good business, was totally ruined."

In the year ending April 1, 1837, there were manufactured in Lynn 2,543,929 pairs of shoes, and 2,220 pairs of boots, valued at $1,689,793. In this manufacture, 2,631 males and 2,554 females were employed; total number, 5,185. During that time the manufacture of vessels, cordage, tin ware, oil casks, morocco leather and shoe boxes amounted to $188,409. During the same period there were 5 vessels employed in the whale and 14 in the cod and mackerel fishery. Besides this, 4,608,000 pounds of cod, haddock, halibut and other fish were taken in boats and sold fresh. The total value of the fisheries amounted to $170,320. Total value of the manufactures and fisheries of Lynn, in one year, $2,048.522. Lynn was first settled in 1629 Incorporated, 1637.

Lynnfield, Mass.

Essex co. The surface of this town is uneven, and the soil rather hard and unproductive. It contains some good farms, a number of pleasant ponds, and is watered by Ipswich river on the north. There is a woolen mill in the town, and manufactures of bar iron, ploughs, boots and shoes; annual value about $50,000. Incorporated, 1782.—Population, 1837, 674. Lynnfield is 12 miles N. from Boston, and 9 W. by N. from Salem.

Machias Rivers and Bay, Me.

The river in Washington County is formed of two branches, which receive their head waters from several ponds, at the distance of about 40 miles, in a N. W. direction.—The eastern branch passes through East Machias. These branches unite near the line of Machias and Machias Port, and in their course produce a great and valuable hydraulic power.

Machias and *Little Machias rivers*, in Penobscot county, are important tributaries to the Aroostook. Their course is easterly, and their mouths meet near each other about 30 miles W. N. W. from Mars Hill. *Machias Bay* sets up from the sea about 10 miles and meets Machias Port. This bay is 4 or 5 miles in width at its mouth, and contains in its bosom several coves, harbors, and beautiful islands: Cross island lying at its mouth is the largest, being about 3 miles by 2.

Machias, Me.

Washington co. County town. This was a famous lodgement of the Indians. First settled, 1762. It was incorporated in 1784, and was the first corporate town between Penobscot and St. Croix rivers. It formerly comprised East Machias and Machias Port. The village is situated on the east side of the west branch, and near the mouth of Middle river. It contains the county building, numerous saw mills, and has an extensive trade, particularly in lumber. Machias lies 143 miles E. N. E. from Augusta. Population, 1837, 1,239. This is a pleasant and interesting town.

Machias Port, Me.

Washington co. Incorporated in 1826. It is the southern part of Old Machias, and extends northward to the union of the branches of Machias river. It has a great number of mills, and is very extensively engaged in the lumber trade. It is a port of entry:—it has an excellent harbor, and considerable navigation in the coasting and fishing business. The tonnage of the district in 1837, was 8,360 tons. In this part of Old Machias the Plymouth Colony established a trading house in 1630. It was subsequently occupied by the French for several years. Machias Port lies 146 miles E. N. E. from Augusta, and 3 S. from Machias. Population, 1837, 821.

Madamiscontis River, Me.,

Rises in a large pond, and empties, from the N. W. into Penobscot river, about 45 miles above Bangor.

Madawaska River, Me.

This river is in the county of Penobscot, and is the outlet of Temiscouata lake, and other large bodies of water in the northern part of the county bordering on the line of Lower Canada. This river and these lakes, with their numerous tributaries, water a country of great extent, and which is said to equal any country in the world in fertility, even the luxuriant prairies of the "boundless west." The course of these waters is N. W. and traverse a distance of more than 100 miles. From the mouth of Madawaska into the St. John's to Augusta is about 240 miles N. N. E.

Madawaska, Me.

Washington co. This town was incorporated in 1831, and comprises the territory marked F. and K. on Greenleaf's map. It is bounded E. by the British Province of New Brunswick, N. near the passage of St. John's, across the line of the state; and W. and S. by a vast and fertile territory between the Aroostook and St. John's rivers; at present but thinly inhabited. This town was the place where the land agents of Maine were taken, by order of the British government, and imprisoned at Fredrickton, N. B. In 1837, Madawaska was supposed to contain a population of 2,487. It lies about 220 miles N. E. by N. from Augusta, and 130 N. W. from Fredrickton, N. B.

Madbury, N. H.,

Strafford co., is bounded N. E. by Dover, S. W. by Durham and

Lee, N. W. by Barrington. The soil of this town is generally productive. In some parts of the town, bog iron ore has been dug up in considerable quantities, and in some instances red and yellow ochre.—Bellamay bank river is the only stream of any magnitude, and Barbadoes pond the only considerable body of water. This pond lies between Dover and Madbury, and is 120 rods long, 50 wide. Madbury formerly constituted a part of the ancient town of Dover; but was set off and incorporated May 31, 1755, by its present name. Population, in 1830, 510.

Madison, Me.

Somerset co. This township lies on the E. side of Kennebec river, 34 miles N. from Augusta and bounded S. by Norridgewock. It was incorporated in 1804. Population, 1830, 1,272; 1837, 1,608. It is watered by a beautiful pond, the outlet of which is at Skowhegan. There are three pleasant villages in the town:—the people are generally husbandmen. The best compliment that can be paid to the soil is, that it produced, without any extraordinary effort, 10,188 bushels of wheat, in 1837.

Madison, Ct.

New Haven co. This town was taken from Guilford in 1826. It lies on Long Island Sound, and embraces what is called Hammonasset Point. This town lies 18 miles E. by S. from New Haven, and 33 S. from Hartford. Population, 1830, 1,809. The soil of the town is stony, and naturally hard to cultivate; but it is made quite productive of corn, rye and potatoes by the use of *white fish*, ploughed in.—These fish appear in the sound about the 1st of June, and continue 3 or 4 months. They are taken in great quantities and are considered an excellent manure. They were first thus used about the year 1798.— About 10,000 of these fish are considered a good dressing for an acre of land.

This place has a small harbor and some navigation. Ship building is the most important mechanical pursuit.

The Hon. THOMAS CHITTENDEN, for many years governor of Vermont, and his brother EBENEZER CHITTENDEN, a gentleman of great mechanical genius, were natives of this town. The former was born in 1730, and died in 1797.

The following is the inscription on a monument in the grave yard, in memory of an old sea captain.

Though Boreas' blasts and Neptune's waves
  Have toss'd me to and fro,
In spite of both by God's decree
  I harbor here below,
Where I do at anchor ride
  With many of our fleet;
Yet once again I must set sail
  Our Admiral, Christ, to meet.

Mad Rivers.

Mad River in N. H., rises among the mountains in the N. E. part of Grafton county; it crosses the S. E. part of Thornton and falls into the Pemigewasset at Campton.

Mad River, Vt. A rapid stream, rises in the high lands S. of Warren, and after passing through Waitsfield, it falls into Onion river at Moretown.

Madrid, Me.

Franklin co. This township was incorporated in 1836. It is watered by some of the head branches of Sandy river and contains a part of Saddleback mountain. The soil is excellent and yielded, in 1837, 3,337 bushels of wheat. Population same year, 351. It lies 25 miles N. W. from Farmington and about 105 N. W. from Augusta.

Madunkeeunk River, Me.

Penobscot co. A tributary of

the Penobscot on the W. side, about 6 miles above the Madamiscontis.

Maidstone, Vt.

Essex co. This mountainous township lies on the W. side of Connecticut river: it is watered by a pleasant pond and by Paul's stream. It has some good land, but most of it is poor. First settled, 1770. Population, 1830, 236. It lies 54 miles N. E. from Montpelier, and 8 N. from Guildhall

MAINE.

This State was originally granted by James I. to the Plymouth Company, in 1606, by whom it was transferred to Mason and Gorges in 1624. This grant comprised all the territory between Merrimack river and Sagadahock. The territory was afterwards purchased by Massachusetts for £1,250, who obtained a confirmation of the charter in 1691, with the addition of the residue of Maine and Nova Scotia, including what is now called the Province of New Brunswick.

This state, formerly the District of Maine, became independent of Massachusetts in 1820. By the Constitution, the legislative power is vested in a Senate and House of Representatives, elected annually by the people, on the second Monday in September. The number of Senators cannot be less than 20, nor more than 31. The number of Representatives cannot be less than 100, nor more than 200. No town or city is entitled to more than seven Representatives.

The executive power is vested in a Governor, who is chosen annually by the people, on the second Monday in September :—His official term commences on the first Wednesday in January.

The Legislature meets at AUGUSTA, on the first Wednesday in January, annually, on which day seven Counsellors are elected, by joint ballot of both Houses, to advise the Governor in his executive duties.

The judicial power of the state is vested in a Supreme Judicial Court, and such other courts as the Legislature may, from time to time, establish. The Judges are appointed by the Governor and Council, and hold their offices during good behavior, but not beyond the age of 70 years.

The state of Maine is bounded northwest and north by Lower Canada, east by New Brunswick, south by the Atlantic ocean, and west by New Hampshire. It is situated between 43° 5′, and 48° 3′ N. lat. and 70° 55′, and 66° 47′ W. lon. It contains an area of about 33,000 square miles.

The surface of the state is diversified by hills and valleys. A tract on the west side east of the white mountains, and a part of the north boundary is mountainous, though not of extraordinary elevations. The highest mountains lie in detached groups, but they are not numerous.

The range of high land which crosses Vermont and New Hampshire, enters the northwest corner of Maine, passing round Chaudiere river and the head waters of Megantic lake, in Canada, and running nearly parallel with the St. Lawrence river, at the distance of about twenty miles, terminates on the gulph of St. Lawrence, near Cape Rosier.—This is the "Height of Land" or the "North East Ridge," spoken of in the treaty of 1783, between Great Britain and the United States, and which was never called in question until 1814, when the British plenipotentiaries at Ghent proposed to the American Commissioners to discuss and revise the boundary, so as to prevent future uncertainty and dispute. They stated that they desired a direct communication between Quebec and Halifax, and left it to the Americans to demand an equivalent. This proposition was refused by the Americans, on the ground that there was no question in regard to the limits of their territory. The "disputed territory," so called, includes most of the country north of latitude 46°, including a part of New Hampshire, and most of that large and valuable portion of Maine watered by the Madawaska, St. John's, Walloostook, Aroostook, and other rivers. This question involves nearly a third part of the territory of the state.

In the 2d article of that treaty are the following words :—"*And that all disputes which might arise in future, on the subject of boundaries of the United States, may be prevented*, it is hereby agreed and declared that the following are, and shall be, their boundaries, viz : *from the northwest angle of Nova Scotia*, (New Brunswick) viz: that angle which is formed by a line drawn due north from the source of St. Croix river to the highlands; along the said highlands which divide those rivers that empty themselves into the river St. Lawrence from those which fall into the Atlantic ocean, to the northwesternmost head of the Connecticut river."

"Our commissioners at Ghent, having successfully resisted every attempt for the dismemberment of Maine, agreed upon an article with the British commissioners, not to revise or to change the ancient treaty boundary, but to run and establish upon the ground that very boundary, without any alteration, and to ascertain " the northwest angle of Nova Scotia;" its place of beginning. This article is the fifth in the treaty. Under it, each party appointed a commissioner. These commissioners disagreed. According to the treaty, the question was then referred to the King of the Netherlands, as umpire, whose award was rejected by the United States, because it did not even profess to decide the controversy according to the terms of the submission, but proposed a compromise, by a division of the disputed territory between the parties. Great Britian has also since announced her abandonment of this award; and now, at the end of more than half a century after the conclusion of the treaty of 1783, the question not only remains unsettled, but threatens to involve the two nations in a dangerous dispute.

"The northwest angle of Nova Scotia was a well known point, capable of being easily ascertained, ever since the proclamation of 1763, by simply running a due north line from the source of the St. Croix, to intersect the southern line of the Province of Quebec, which consists of the highlands running from the western extremity of the bay of Chaleur, to the head of Connecticut river, and dividing those rivers that empty themselves into the river St. Lawrence from those which fall into the Atlantic ocean. It is certain as the laws of nature, that these highlands, from which we know that streams do flow in opposite directions, can be found on the face of the country.

"The whole argument of the British government rests upon the assumption that the St. John's is not a river falling into the Atlantic ocean, because it has its *mouth in the Bay of Fundy.* What is the Bay of Fundy, if it be not a part of the Atlantic ocean ? A bay is a mere opening of the main ocean into the land—a mere interruption of the uniformity of the sea coast by an indentation of water. These portions of the ocean have received the name of bays, solely to distinguish them from the remainder of the vast deep to which they belong. Would it not be the merest special pleading to contend that the bay of Naples was not a portion of the Mediterranean, or that the Bay of Biscay was not a part of the Atlantic ocean?

"Again, the description of the treaty is. "rivers which fall into the

Atlantic ocean." Can it be said, with any propriety, that a river does not fall into the Atlantic, because in reaching the main ocean it may pass through a bay? And yet this is the British argument. The Delaware does not fall into the Atlantic, because it flows into it through the bay of Delaware; and, for the same reason, the St. John's does not fall into the Atlantic, because it flows into it through the bay of Fundy."

It is ardently wished that this perplexing controversy may soon be amicably settled between two friendly powers, whose interests are so closely united. This will probably be the event. Maine is determined to vindicate her rights, and the whole country stands ready to sustain them.

Maine is divided into the twelve following counties: York, Cumberland, Lincoln, Kennebec, Waldo, Hancock, Oxford, Somerset, Penobscot, Washington, Franklin, and Piscataquis.

Succession of Governors.

William King, 1820. Albion K. Parris, 1821—1825. E. Lincoln, 1826—1829. Jonathan G. Hunton, 1830. Samuel E. Smith, 1831—1833. Robert P. Dunlap, 1834—1837. Edward Kent, 1838. John Fairfield, 1839—

Succession of Chief Justices.

Prentiss Mellen, 1820—1834. Nathan Weston, 1834—

The soil of Maine is various. For some miles from the sea coast it is rocky, sandy or clayey, with some fertile portions; generally this is the least productive part of the state. Advancing into the interior, the soil increases in fertility. The average quality of the soil is considered to be equal if not superior to any other portion of New England. In some parts it is not exceeded in fertility by any section of the Union. Some of the most fertile parts of Maine are now almost a wilderness.

The ability of the soil of Maine to furnish an ample supply of bread stuffs, was fully tested in 1837, by the production of more than a million bushels of wheat, besides vast quantities of rye and corn.

The natural productions in the state, already known to exist in exhaustless quantities, are pine and hemlock timber; granite, slate, lime, iron, and all the materials in the composition of glass. Of the first report of the learned and indefatigable Dr. Jackson, on the geology of Maine, the celebrated professor Silliman thus speaks:

"Maine is a country chiefly of primary rocks, with a large division of those of transition, and towards New Brunswick it has an important region of the lower secondary. Every where it has alluvial and diluvial deposits, and vast igneous formations, not only in the interior, but forming a barrier against the ocean surge along a considerable part of an immense sea coast, indented as it is by bays and estuaries almost beyond example. Among the mineral formations of Maine, are granite, gneiss, mica and talcose, and other slates, including roofing slate and alum slate; also, soapstone, limestone and marble, sandstones and brecciated rocks of many varieties; jasper, including the beautiful greenstone, trap and its varieties, and porphyry. The trap dykes are numerous and exceedingly distinct: They cut through most of the other rocks, and produce upon them, most distinctly, those peculiar effects, which to a demonstration prove their igneous origin. Scientific geology is greatly indebted to this survey for some of the most lucid and convincing facts on this head; while the diluvial deposits, the boulders and ruins, the diluvial furrows in the rocks, the sea shells now adhering to and inherent in rocks which once formed the sea coast, although elevated twenty-six feet above the sea board, a salt spring at Lubec, and many other topics equally illustrate other parts of scientific geology.

Dr. Jackson is entirely master of his subject, as well as of the kindred sciences of mineralogy and chemistry, and his report is remarkable for its lucid clearness and its attractive style."

The sea coast of Maine, extending more than 230 miles, indented by an almost countless number of bays, harbors and islands of romantic beauty, presents facilities for navigation unrivalled by any portion of the globe. The great rivers, St. Croix, Penobscot, Kennebec, Androscoggin, and Saco, with their numerous tributaries piercing the interior, give to the farmer and mechanic a cheap and easy mode of transportation. These rivers, and thousands of ponds and other streams, dispersed throughout the state, afford a water power of vast extent and usefulness.

The celebrated John Smith made an unsuccessful attempt to settle this part of the country as early as 1614. The first permanent lodgment of the whites in the state was made from the Plymouth colony, at York, in 1630.

The first settlers of Maine were a race of men of good minds, stout hearts and strong arms. By them and their sons the stately forests were converted into an article of commerce, of immense value; thus preparing the soil for its ultimate staples, WHEAT, BEEF, and WOOL. See *Register.*

Malden, Mass.

Middlesex co. A bridge over Mystic river, 2,420 feet in length, connects this town with Charlestown. It lies 5 miles N. from Boston, and 16 E. by S. from Concord. First settled, 1648. Incorporated, 1649. Population, 1830, 2,010; 1837, 2,303. It contains a large tract of salt meadow, and considerable timber. The uplands are rough and uneven. The manufactures of Malden consist of leather, boots, shoes, block tin, tin ware, twine, lasts, and manufactures of iron and dye-wood: total amount, the year ending April 1, 1837, $351,160.

Manchester, N. H.,

Hillsborough co., lies on the east side of Merrimack river, by which it is bounded on the W. for 8 miles; on the N. and E. it is bounded by Chester, S. by Londonderry and Litchfield. There are several streams which have their origin in this town, and which discharge themselves into the Merrimack.—Cohass brook, issuing from Massabesick pond, is the largest. It receives two other small streams from the S., and empties itself at the S. W. angle of the town. Massabesick is a large pond, at the E. side of the town, and partly within its limits. There are several smaller ponds.

The soil of a considerable part of the town is light and sandy. The intervales on the river are easy of cultivation, and productive.

The canal by Amoskeag falls is in this town, and was projected and constructed by the ingenuity and perseverance of the late Samuel Blodget, Esq. At these falls are the works of the Amoskeag Manufacturing Company, where the foundations of another Lowell are being laid. The water power is immense.

This town was formed of a part of Londonderry, a part of Chester, and a tract of land called Harrytown, and incorporated Sept. 3, 1751, by the name of *Derryfield*. This name it retained until 1810, when it was changed to Manchester, by an act of the legislature.

The venerable general JOHN STARK had his residence in this town, where he died May 8, 1822, at the great age of 93 years 8 months and 24 days. He was born at Londonderry, August 28, 1728; was taken prisoner by the Indians, while hunting near Baker's river, in Rumney, April 28, 1752. In 1775, he was appointed a colonel of one of the three regiments raised in New Hampshire; was engaged on the heights of Charlestown, June 17, 1775; was at the battle of Trenton, in 1776; captured Col. Baum and 1,000 of the British at Bennington, August 16, 1777. This event, in the language of president Jefferson, was "the first link in the chain of successes which issued in the surrender of Saratoga." He was soon after appointed a brigadier-general of the United States army, and, at the time of his death, was the only surviving American general officer of the revolution. Population, 1830, 887.

Manchester, Vt.

Bennington co. One of the county towns. Situated between the Green mountains on the E., and Equinox mountain on the W. The latter is 3,706 feet above the sea. There are two neat villages in this valley; the county buildings are in the south village. The scenery here is very beautiful. The town is watered by the Battenkill and its branches, and affords good mill sites. The soil along the water courses is good, but the principal part of the town is better for grazing than tillage. Here are large quarries of beautiful marble, some manufactures, a curious cavern, and about 6,000 sheep. Manchester lies 22 miles N. by E. from Bennington, and about 40 W. from Bellows Falls, across the mountains. First settled, 1764. Population, 1830, 1,525.

Manchester, Mass.

Essex co. This is a flourishing fishing town on Massachusetts bay, 26 miles N. E. from Boston, and 5 S. W. from Gloucester. It was taken from Salem in 1645. Population, 1837, 1,346. There are a number of vessels belonging to the town employed in the fishing and coasting business. The value of the fishery, the year ending April 1, 1837, amounted to $12,800. The value of the articles manufactured was $96,473. Those articles consisted of vessels, boots, shoes, leather, chairs, cabinet ware, palmleaf hats, and ships' wheels. The village is very pleasant, and commands fine prospects. Although Manchester is a rocky, rough township, it can boast a rare native production in this climate,—the magnolia, a beautiful flowering tree.

Manchester, Ct.

Hartford co. An important manufacturing town on the Hockanum, a valuable mill stream, 10 miles E. from Hartford. The first cotton mill in this state was built here in 1794. There are three pleasant villages, six or seven paper mills, two powder mills, woolen and other manufactures. The face of the town is uneven, but the soil, a sandy and gravelly loam, is quite productive. It was called Orford, a parish in East Hartford, until its incorporation, in 1823. Population, 1830, 1,576.

Manhegin Island, Me.

This island lies off Muscongus bay, Lincoln county. There is a light-house on it, the tower of which is 30 feet high. It bears S. from the mouth of St. George's river, about 12 miles.

Mansfield, Vt.

Lamoille co. There is some good land in this town, on Brown's river and the branches of Waterbury river, but in general it is too mountainous even for grazing. It lies 20 miles N. W. from Montpelier, 20 E. by N. from Burlington, and 13 S. W. from Hyde Park.— Population, 1830, 279. First settled, 1799.

Mansfield Mountains extend through the town of Mansfield from N. to S. They belong to the Green mountain range, and the *nose* and *chin*, so called, from their resemblance to the face of a man lying on his back, exhibits some of the loftiest summits in the state. The nose is 3,933 feet above tide water; the chin, 4,279.

Mansfield, Mass.

Bristol co. This town lies 26 miles S. S. W. from Boston, 18 N. E. from Providence, and 11 N. N. W. from Taunton. It was taken from Norton in 1770, and is watered by several branches of Taunton river. The soil is thin and the surface level. Population, 1837, 1,444. There are 6 cotton and 1 woolen mills in the town, and 2 nail factories. The manufactures consist of cotton and woolen goods, nails, straw bonnets, palm-leaf hats, and baskets: total annual amount, about $110,000.

A mine of anthracite coal was discovered in this town a few years since, near the Boston and Providence rail road, which promises to be of inestimable value to the community. It was discovered in digging a well. An incorporated company has purchased the right of mining on that and several adjoining farms. They sunk a shaft which struck a vein five feet in thickness, at the depth of 20 feet, running N.

E. and S.W., and dipping to the N. W. 52°. The shaft was continued 44 feet further, to another vein, which exceeded 5 feet in thickness, and which afforded coal of a better quality than that found above.— Subsequent operations have shown that the veins are numerous, and the quantity inexhaustible. The coal is of an excellent quality, more easily broken than the Pennsylvanian, and has less polish on its surface.

Mansfield, Ct.

Tolland co. Mansfield, the Indian *Nawbesetuck*, was taken from Windham in 1703. It lies 27 miles E. from Hartford, 12 S. E. from Tolland, and 19 N. N. W. from Norwich. Population, 1830, 2,661.— The face of the town is uneven, and some of the hills have considerable elevation. The town is watered by Willimantic river, and the Natchaug and its tributaries—Mount Hope and Fenton.

A larger quantity of silk is manufactured here than in any other place in the United States. This branch of industry was introduced into the country by Dr. Aspinwall, of this place, above seventy years since, who established the raising of silk worms in New Haven, Long Island and Philadelphia. At this period half an ounce of mulberry seed was sent to every parish in Connecticut, and the legislature for a time offered a bounty on mulberry trees and raw silk: 265 lbs. were raised in 1793, and the quantity has been increasing ever since. In 1830, 3,200 lbs. were raised. Two small silk factories have been established in this town by an English manufacturer, with swifts for winding hard silk; 32 spindles for doubling; seven dozens of spindles for throwing; 32 spindles for soft silk winding; and 2 broad and one fringe silk looms. There is machinery enough to keep 30 broad silk looms and fifty hands in operation. There are in the town two cotton factories. Screw augers and steelyards are manufactured here.

Marblehead, Mass.

Essex co. This is a noted fishing town, on a rocky point of land extending into Massachusetts bay, with a hardy and intrepid crew of fishermen and sailors. The harbor is commodious and easy of access. The quantity of fish exported from this place in 1794 amounted to $184,532. Since that time the fishing business has greatly increased, and this place has now become one of the largest fishing ports on the American coast. There belong to this place from 90 to 100 sail of fishing, coasting and merchant vessels. Tonnage of the district, in 1837, 10,037. First settled, 1631. Incorporated, 1649. Population, 1837, 5,549. It lies 14 miles N. E. from Boston, and 4 S. E. from Salem. The value of the cod and mackerel fishery the year ending April 1, 1837, was $153,487; employing 500 hands. The manufactures of Marblehead, the same year, amounted to $398,565. The articles manufactured consisted of boots, shoes, bar iron, chairs, cabinet and tin wares, vessels, soap, glue, cards and wheels. This is a romantic place; nearly allied to its neighbor, Nahant;—only 6 miles across the bay.

Margallaway River, N. H.,

Has its source among the highlands which separate Maine from Lower Canada, in the N. E. extremity of New Hampshire, about 30 miles N. from Errol. After a S. course of nearly 20 miles on the western border of Maine, it enters New Hampshire at the S. E. part of the 2d grant to Dartmouth college, where it forms a junction with the united streams of Dead and Diamond rivers. Thence, after a S. course of about 6 miles to Errol, it receives the waters of Umbagog lake. After this junction the main stream is the Androscoggin river.

Mariaville, Me.

Hancock co. This is a townsnip of good land, finely located on the E. side of Union river, 8 miles N. by E. from Ellsworth, and 89 E. N. E. from Augusta. This town has an extensive water power and many saw mills. It was incorporated in 1836. Population, 1837, 257.

Marion, Me.

Washington co. This township is bounded E. by Edmonds, and S. by Whiting. Population, 245.—Incorporated, 1834. See "Down East."

Marlborough, N. H.,

Cheshire co., is bounded N. by Roxbury, E. by Dublin and Jaffrey, S. by Troy, W. by Swanzey and part of Keene. It is 6 miles S. E. from Keene, and 55 S. W. from Concord. There are several ponds which are the sources of some of the branches of Ashuelot river.—The soil is rocky, but good for grazing. Marlborough was granted, 1751. The first settlement commenced about 1760. Incorporated Dec. 13, 1776. Population, in 1830, 822.

Marlborough, Vt.

Windham co. First settled, 1763. It lies 8 miles S. from Newfane, and 24 E. from Bennington. Population, 1830, 1,218. Mrs. Whittemore, the wife of one of the first settlers, spent the winter of 1764-5 in this then wilderness, alone, her husband being absent in the pursuit of his calling, as a tinker. During this winter she saw no human being, except her little daughter and some hunters who happened accidentally to pass that way. She cut down timber and furnished browse for their cattle, and thus kept them alive through the winter. Mrs. W. was very useful to the settlers, both as a nurse and a midwife. She possessed a vigorous constitution, and frequently travelled through the woods upon snow shoes from one part of the town to another, both by night and day, to relieve the distressed. She lived to the age of 87 years, officiated as midwife at more than 2,000 births, and never lost a patient.

The town is well watered by the W. branch of West river, Whetstone brook, and Green river. It has a good soil, and is very productive in wheat, rye, and other grain, fruit and potatoes. Here is a pleasant village, several fine trout ponds, various kinds of minerals and medicinal springs. Marlborough suffered some by the Indians, and did much for the cause of independence.

Marlborough, Mass.

Middlesex co. This is a large farming town, with a soil of great fertility and undulating surface.—The inhabitants are principally devoted to agricultural pursuits, and by their industry and skill, have acquired a great degree of independence. Among the productions of the town, are fat cattle, pork, fruit, and all the varieties of the dairy; a large amount of which is annually sent to Boston market. A branch of Concord river, and a number of beautiful ponds, water the town.—The manufactures consist of boots, shoes, straw bonnets, leather, chairs and cabinet ware: annual amount, about $75,000. Marlborough, the Indian *Okamakamesit*, was first settled in 1654. It was taken from Sudbury in 1660; it suffered much during the Indian wars, and was for many years the residence of a number of Indians who had embraced the christian religion. The villages are very pleasant: the richness of the soil, and surrounding scenery; its excellent roads and convenient access to Boston by the rail road, renders Marlborough a desirable residence. It is 28 miles W. from Boston, 14 S. W. from Concord, and 16 E. from Worcester.—Population, 1837, 2,089.

Marlborough Ct.

Hartford co. Marlborough was taken from three towns which belonged to three different counties, in 1803. It lies 14 miles S. E. from Hartford. The surface of the town is hilly and stony, and the lands best adapted for grazing. It has a cotton factory, a bed of black lead, and a good fish pond. *Dark hollow*, in the western part of the town, presents some wild scenery of more terror than beauty. Population, 1830, 704.

Marlow, N. H.

Cheshire co. It is 15 miles N. from Keene, and 45 W. by S. from Concord. Ashuelot river passes through almost the whole length of the town. There are no ponds of note, nor any mountains. Marlow was chartered, 1761. Population, 1830, 645.

Marshfield, Vt.

Washington co. This town, containing 23,040 acres, was granted to the Stockbridge Indians in 1782, and sold by them to Isaac Marsh, in 1789, for £140. A part of the soil is good and a part wet and stony. The town produces considerable wool, and some cattle are reared for market. It has a pleasant pond, and Onion river passes through it. It lies 12 miles N. E. from Montpelier. First settled, 1790. Population, 1830, 1,271.

Marshfield, Mass.

Plymouth co. A pleasant town on Massachusetts bay, 25 miles S. E. from Boston, and 15 N. by W. from Plymouth. It is watered by North and South rivers, has a tolerable harbor, and some navigation. Ship building is an important branch of business in the town. Here are two cotton mills, an air and cupola furnace, a nail factory, and manufactures of cotton and satinet warp.

Peregrine White, the first English child born in New England, died here in 1704, aged 83. Incorporated, 1640. Population, 1837, 1,660.

Mars Hill, Me.

This celebrated mountain is situated about a mile west from the east boundary of the United States;—200 miles N. N. E. from Augusta, and 80 N. W. from Frederickton, New Brunswick.

The British Queen seems desirous of annexing this portion of the territory of the United States to her wide and fair possessions. This notion of the pretty maiden is altogether preposterous: when she has maturely considered the treaty made by her grandfather and the United States, at Paris, in 1783, we trust her good sense will deter her from urging the claim.

The approach to this mountain is difficult: its sides are rugged, and its summit bold. It has two spurs; one of which is 1,506, the other 1,363 feet above the waters of Goosequill river, in New Brunswick.

Marshpee, Mass.

Barnstable co. An ancient Indian territory, and an incorporated district of 10,500 acres, or about 16 square miles. It lies 12 miles S. E. from Barnstable, 8 S. S. E. from Sandwich, and 8 E. from Falmouth. It is bounded on the S. by the ocean. There are 350 colored inhabitants on this territory, and some whites. There now remain only seven inhabitants, of pure blood of the fathers of the forest. Their land is good for grain of all sorts, and is well wooded. The territory is pleasant, and some parts of it afford beautiful scenery. The Marshpee and Quashmet are considerable streams, which, with numerous ponds and the ocean, afford an abundant supply of fish of various kinds. These people live by agricultural pursuits, the manufacture of various articles of Indian ware, by the sale of their wood, and by fishing, fowling, and taking deer. They are docile and hospitable; they appear to relish moral and religious instruction; and, under the superintendence of a humane and intelligent commissioner, appointed by the state, they are prosperous and happy. This is the largest remnant of all the tribes of red men west of Penobscot river, who, 218 years ago, were fee simple proprietors of the whole territory of New England!

Martha's Vineyard, Mass.

The principal of a cluster of islands lying off and S. of Barnstable county and Buzzard's bay, comprising the towns of Edgarton, Tisbury and Chilmark. See *Dukes county*.

Mason, N. H.

Hillsborough co. It is 15 miles S. W. from Amherst, 43 S. S. W. from Concord, and 50 N. W. from Boston. The surface is uneven; the hills are chiefly large swells, with narrow valleys between them. The streams are rapid. There are no natural ponds. The principal meadows were formerly beaver ponds. Souhegan is the principal stream, affording many fine mill seats. The small streams run into Nashua river, and into Tanapus, or Potanipo pond, in Brookline. The soil in the E. part is rather light. The W. part is mostly a strong deep soil, red or dark loam, but stony. It is good for grass and grain. In Mason village, on the Souhegan, are cotton and woolen manufactories, and other machinery. Mason was granted by charter, Aug. 26, 1768. It was formerly known by the name of *No. 1.* The first effort to settle this place was in 1751, and the next year a permanent settlement was made by Enoch Lawrence, from Pepperell, Mass. Population, in 1830, 1,433.

Massabesick Pond, N. H.

See *Chester*.

MASSACHUSETTS.

This ancient commonwealth, the mother of New England colonies, of free states, and of American liberty, was first permanently settled by Europeans, at Plymouth, on the 22d of December, 1620.

The history of this state is deeply interesting; it is interwoven with every political and moral event of important occurrence in the settlement and progress of the whole of North America, which preceded or was connected with the revolution of 1775.

The name of this state probably arose from the name of a tribe of Indians formerly at Barnstable; or from two Indian words—*Mos* and *Wetuset;* the former signifying an *Indian arrow's head,* the latter, *Hill.* It is stated that the Sachem who governed in this region about the time of the landing of our forefathers, lived on a hill in the form of an Indian arrow's head, a few miles south of Boston, and was called by the Indians —*Moswetuset.*

Massachusetts is bounded east, southeast, and south by the Atlantic ocean. It has, exclusive of the island counties of Dukes and Nantucket, a sea-coast of about 250 miles. It is bounded south and west by the state of Rhode Island, about 68 miles; south by the state of Connecticut, 87 miles; west by the state of New York, 50 miles; north by the state of Vermont, 42 miles; and north by the state of New Hampshire, 87 miles. It lies between 41° 31', and 42° 53' N. lat., and 69° 48', and 73° 17' W. lon. from Greenwich. Its area is about 7,800 square miles, or 4,992,000 acres.

NEW ENGLAND GAZETTEER.

The state comprises 14 counties, to wit: Barnstable, Berkshire, Bristol, Dukes, Essex, Franklin, Hampden, Hampshire, Middlesex, Norfolk, Nantucket, Plymouth, Suffolk, and Worcester.

The legislative power of this State is vested in a Senate and House of Representatives. The Senate consists of 40 members, and are chosen by districts.

The executive power is vested in a Governor, Lieutenant Governor, and a Council of 9 members. The Council is elected by the joint ballot of the Senators and Representatives, from the Senators; and in case the Council thus elected or any of them decline, the deficiency is supplied from among the people.

By the Constitution as amended in 1837, each town or city, having 300 ratable polls, at the last preceding decennial census of polls, may elect one representative; and for every 450 ratable polls, in addition to the first 300, one representative more.

Any town having less than 300 ratable polls, shall be represented thus:—The whole number of ratable polls, at the last preceding valuation census of polls, shall be multiplied by 10, and the product divided by 300, and such town may elect one representative, as many years within ten years, as 300 is contained in the product aforesaid.

Any city or town, having ratable polls enough to elect one or more representatives, with any number of polls beyond the necessary number, may be represented as to that surplus number, by multiplying such surplus number by 10, and dividing the product by 450; and such city or town may elect one additional representative, as many years within the ten years, as 450 is contained in the product aforesaid.

Representation.

Number of Representatives to which each town is entitled for 10 years, from 1837, according to the Constitution, as amended in 1837.

The column in the following table marked *tenths*, shows how many years in 10 the respective towns are entitled to an additional Representative.

Towns.	Repre.	Tenths.	Towns.	Repre.	Tenths.	Towns.	Repre.	Tenths.
BARNSTABLE.			Provincetown,	1	8	Alford,		4
Barnstable,	2	7	Sandwich,	2	4	Becket,		8
Brewster,	1	1	Truro,	1	4	Cheshire,		7
Chatham,	1	6	Wellfleet,	1	6	Clarksburgh,		3
Dennis,	1	9	Yarmouth,	1	8	Dalton,		7
Eastham,		8		—	—	Egremont,		8
Falmouth,	1	8		14	8|	Florida,		3
Harwich,	1	8	BERKSHIRE.			G. Barrington,	1	6
Orleans,	1	4	Adams,	2	6	Hancock,	1	

NEW ENGLAND GAZETTEER.

Towns.	Repre.	Tenths.	Towns.	Repre.	Tenths.	Towns.	Repre.	Tenths.
Hinsdale,		7	Danvers,	3	5	Chester,	1	1
Lanesborough,	1		Essex,	1	1	Granville,	1	2
Lee,	1	5	Georgetown,			Holland,		4
Lenox,	1		Gloucester,	6		Longmeadow,	1	
M't. Washington,		3	Hamilton,		6	Ludlow,		9
New Ashford,		2	Haverhill,	3	4	Monson,	1	3
New Marlboro'	1	1	Ipswich,	2		Montgomery,		4
Otis,		9	Lynn,	6	2	Palmer,	1	3
Peru,		6	Lynnfield,		5	Russell,		5
Pittsfield,	2	4	Manchester,	1	2	Southwick,	1	1
Richmond,		7	Marblehead,	3	5	Springfield,	5	7
Sandisfield,	1	2	Methuen,	1	9	Tolland,		5
Savoy,		7	Middleton,		6	Wales,		6
Sheffield,	1	6	Newbury,	2	4	Westfield,	2	1
Stockbridge,	1	5	Newburyport,	3	9	W. Springfield,	2	2
Tyringham,	1		Rowley,	2		Wilbraham,	1	5
Washington,		6	Salem,	8	5			
W. Stockbridge,	1	1	Salisbury,	1	9		18	60
Williamstown,	1	4	Saugus,	1				
Windsor,		7	Topsfield,	1		**HAMPSHIRE.**		
	16	134	Wenham,		7	Amherst,	1	7
			West Newbury,	1	3	Belchertown,	1	8
BRISTOL.						Chesterfield,		7
Attleborough,	2	1		53	116	Cummington,	1	
Berkley.		8	**FRANKLIN.**			Easthampton,		5
Dartmouth,	2	4	Ashfield,	1	3	Enfield,	1	
Dighton,	1		Bernardston,		7	Goshen,		5
Easton,	1	5	Buckland,		8	Granby,		8
Fairhaven,	2	6	Charlemont,		9	Greenwich,		7
Fall River,	3	6	Coleraine,	1	4	Hadley,	1	4
Freetown,	1	4	Conway,	1	1	Hatfield,		8
Mansfield,	1		Deerfield,	1	4	Middlefield,		6
New Bedford,	9		Erving,			Northampton,	2	4
Norton,	1	2	Gill,		5	Norwich,		5
Pawtucket,	1	5	Greenfield,	1	3	Pelham,		7
Raynham,	1	2	Hawley,		9	Plainfield,		7
Rehoboth,	1	5	Heath,		6	Prescott,		6
Seekonk,	1	5	Leverett,		7	S. Hadley,	1	1
Somerset,		9	Leyden,		5	Southampton,	1	
Swanzey,	1	2	Monroe,		1	Ware,	1	6
Taunton,	4	9	Montague,	1		Westhampton,		7
Westport,	1	8	New Salem,	1		Williamsburgh,	1	
			Northfield,	1	2	Worthington,		9
	33	81	Orange,	1	2			
DUKES.			Rowe,		6		11	117
Chilmark,		7	Shelburne,		8			
Edgartown,	1	4	Shutesbury,		7	**MIDDLESEX.**		
Tisbury,	1	1	Sunderland,		7	Acton,		9
			Warwick,		8	Ashby,	1	
	2	12	Wendell,		7	Bedford,		8
ESSEX.			Whately,		9	Billerica,	1	1
Amesbury,	1	8				Boxborough,		3
Andover,	3	2		9	128	Brighton,	1	2
Beverly,	3		**HAMPDEN.**			Burlington,		5
Boxford,		8	Blanford,	1	1	Cambridge,	5	
Bradford,	1	5	Brimfield,	1	1	Carlisle,		5

NEW ENGLAND GAZETTEER.

Towns.	Repre.	Tenths.	Towns.	Repre.	Tenths.	Towns.	Repre.	Tenths.
Charlestown,	6	3	Milton,	1	5	Berlin,		6
Chelmsford,	1	4	Needham,	1	1	Bolton,	1	
Concord,	1	4	Quincy,	2	5	Boylston,		7
Dracut,	1	3	Randolph,	2	3	Brookfield,	1	9
Dunstable,		5	Roxbury,	5		Charlton,	2	3
Framingham,	1	9	Sharon,		9	Dana,		5
Groton,	1	5	Stoughton,	1	6	Douglas,	1	3
Holliston,	1	5	Walpole,	1	2	Dudley,	1	2
Hopkinton,	1	7	Weymouth,	2	4	Fitchburgh,	1	9
Lexington,	1	3	Wrentham,	1	8	Gardner,	1	1
Lincoln,		6				Grafton,	2	1
Littleton,		8		28	91	Hardwick,	1	2
Lowell,	9					Harvard,	1	2
Malden,	1	9	NANTUCKET.			Holden,	1	3
Marlborough,	1	5	Nantucket,	6		Hubbardston,	1	4
Medford,	1	7				Lancaster,	1	3
Natick,	1			6		Leicester,	1	6
Newton,	2	2	PLYMOUTH.			Leominster,	1	4
Pepperell,	1	4	Abington,	2	2	Lunenburgh,		9
Reading,	1	8	Bridgewater,	1	6	Mendon,	2	5
Sherburne,	1		Carver,		9	Milford,	1	3
Shirley,		8	Duxbury,	2		Millbury,	1	8
South Reading,	1	3	E. Bridgewater,	1	5	New Braintree,		7
Stoneham,	1		Halifax,		7	Northborough,		9
Stow,	1		Hanover,	1	1	Northbridge,	1	1
Sudbury,	1	1	Hanson,		8	N. Brookfield,	1	3
Tewksbury,		7	Hingham,	2	4	Oakham,		9
Townsend,	1	2	Hull,		1	Oxford,	1	7
Tyngsborough,		8	Kingston,	1	1	Paxton,		6
Waltham,	1	6	Marshfield,	1	2	Petersham,	1	3
Watertown,	1	4	Middleborough,	3	4	Phillipston,		8
Wayland,		7	N. Bridgewater,	1	8	Princeton,	1	
W. Cambridge,	1	2	Pembroke,	1		Royalston,	1	2
Westford,	1		Plymouth,	3	3	Rutland,	1	
Weston,	1		Plympton,		7	Shrewsbury,	1	3
Wilmington,		7	Rochester,	2	3	Southborough,	1	
Woburn,	2	1	Scituate,	2	6	Southbridge,	1	4
			Wareham,	1	7	Spencer,	1	2
	52	187	W. Bridgewater,		9	Sterling,	1	2
						Sturbridge,	1	5
NORFOLK.				24	93	Sutton,	1	8
Bellingham,	1					Templeton,	1	4
Braintree,	1	8	SUFFOLK.			Upton,	1	2
Brookline,	1		Boston,	56	6	Uxbridge,	1	7
Canton,	1	7	Chelsea,	1	5	Warren,	1	
Cohasset,	1					Webster,		9
Dedham,	2	6		57	11	Westborough,	1	3
Dorchester,	2	7				W. Boylston,	1	1
Dover,		4	WORCESTER.			Westminster,	1	3
Foxborough,	1	1	Ashburnham,	1	4	Winchendon,	1	3
Franklin,	1	3	Athol,	1	2	Worcester,	5	2
Medfield,		7	Auburn,	1	5			
Medway,	1	5	Barre,	1	9		52	228

The whole number of towns in the state may send 375 Representatives every year, without counting the fractions. The fractions give an annual increase, on an average of 10 years of 133 and 9-10ths; making the average number of Representatives for the next 10 years, 508 9-10ths.

NEW ENGLAND GAZETTEER.

The Governor, Lieutenant Governor, Senators, and Representatives, are chosen annually by the people, on the 2d Monday of November, and meet at Boston on the 1st Wednesday of January. The Judiciary power is vested in a Supreme Court, a Court of Common Pleas, and such other courts as the Legislature may, from time to time, establish. The Judges are appointed by the Governor and Council, and hold their offices during good behavior.

Succession of Governors.

John Hancock, 1780—1784. James Bowdoin, 1785, 1786. John Hancock, 1787—1793. Samuel Adams, 1794—1796. Increase Sumner, 1797—1799. Caleb Strong, 1800, 1806. James Sullivan, 1807, 1808. Christopher Gore, 1809. Elbridge Gerry, 1810, 1811. Caleb Strong, 1812—1815. John Brooks, 1816—1822. William Eustis, 1823, 1824. Levi Lincoln, 1825—1833. John Davis, 1834, 1835. Edward Everett, 1835—

Succession of Chief Justices of the Supreme Judicial Court.

William Cushing, 1776—1789. Nathaniel Peaslee Sargent, 1789—1791. Francis Dana, 1791—1806. Theophilus Parsons, 1806—1814. Samuel Sewall, 1814. Isaac Parker, 1814—1830. Lemuel Shaw, 1830—

The foundation of a school fund was laid by legislative enactment, in 1834, by appropriating " all moneys remaining in the treasury on the 1st day of January, 1835, arising from the sale of public lands, and from payments made to this commonwealth by the United States, on account of the claim for military services and disbursements during the late war, together with one half of all future proceeds of the sales of public lands, as a permanent fund for the encouragement and support of common schools, which fund is never to exceed one million of dollars."

A trigonometrical and astronomical survey of the state, by order of the general court, for the purpose of a new map, was commenced in 1830, and will soon be completed. Surveys of the mineralogy, botany, zoology, and agriculture of the state have been commenced; some favorable reports have been made, and the researches of scientific men are continued, and promise great public usefulness.

The surface of the state is generally undulating. The most level parts are found in the counties of Plymouth, Barnstable, and Bristol. The Green and Taughkannic ranges of mountains pass through the western counties, but in few places are they remarkable for their elevation.

The soil of the state is well adapted to the growth of all the grasses, grains, fruits and vegetables common to a temperate climate. In no part of our country is agriculture more honored, or better understood and rewarded.

The resources of Massachusetts in its commerce, navigation, manufactures and fisheries are immense: they are stated under the counties and towns, and will be given summarily, with other statistics of New England, in the *Register*.

Although Massachusetts cannot boast of her navigable rivers and canals, to facilitate the commerce of her capital; yet she can boast of the most beautiful bay on the map of the western world; of her noble streams for water power; of her luxuriant vales, of her granite hills, of her ships, and the material for building them; and of her gallant sailors who traverse every sea, and who well understand the uses of the hook, harpoon and cannon.

Massachusetts Bay.

The whole of this bay is within the limits of Massachusetts. The exterior bounds of this celebrated bay are Capes Cod and Ann. The former is in N. lat. 42° 6', and W. long. 70° 7'. The latter in N. lat. 42° 45', and W. lon. 70° 17'. Cape Ann bears from Cape Cod, N. N. W., about 40 miles.

The length of this bay is about 62 miles, from N. W. to S. E.: its breadth is about 25 miles. Numerous bays and rivers of various sizes set in from this bay, and its whole coast is lined with commodious harbors, and pleasant commercial towns.

This bay is noted for its delightful scenery, and as containing the first settlements of the Pilgrim Fathers of New England.

Matawamkeag River, Me.

This is one of the most important tributaries to the Penobscot. It unites with that river at the Indian township from the E., about 60 miles N. by E. above Bangor.

Matawamkeag Plantation, on this river, lies 128 miles N. E. from Augusta.

Matinicus Islands, Me.

A cluster of islands at the entrance of Penobscot bay. The principal, or Marshall's island, is a plantation attached to the county of Hancock. The light on Matinicus bears about S. by E. from Thomaston, 15 miles.

Maxfield, Me.

Penobscot co. This town was incorporated in 1824. It is watered by Piscataquis river and Seboois stream. It lies 111 miles N. N. W. from Augusta, and 25 E. by N. from Dover. Population, 1837, 215. Wheat crop, same year, 1,304 bushels.

Mayfield, Me.

Somerset co. On the E. side of Kennebec river and about 10 miles from it. It is 58 miles N. from Augusta, and about 29 N. by E. from Norridgewock. Incorporated, 1836. Population, 1837, 224.

Medfield, Mass.

Norfolk co. This town is watered by Charles and Stop rivers. It is 17 miles S. S. W. from Boston, and 8 S. by W. from Dedham.

During the year ending April 1, 1837, there were manufactured at Medfield, 124,000 straw bonnets, the value of which was $135,000. There are also manufactures of boots, shoes, leather, cutlery, and brushes. Medfield was taken from Dedham, in 1651.

During king Philip's war, in 1765, the town was burnt, and many of the inhabitants murdered by the Narragansets. Philip rode on an elegant horse, and directed the massacre. Population, 1837, 899.

Medford, Mass.

Middlesex co. This beautiful town is situated at the head of navigation on Mystic river, 5 miles N. W. from Boston, and 14 E. by S. from Concord. The Boston and Lowell rail-road, and Middlesex canal pass through the town. The finest ships that float on the ocean, are built here: during the five years preceding April 1, 1837, sixty vessels were built, the tonnage of which was 24,195 tons: value $1,112,970. There are also manufactures of leather, spirits, linseed oil, bricks, boots, shoes, ploughs, hats and hat bodies. The soil of the town is very fertile, and in a high state of cultivation. The business of the town is much associated with the city, and many delightful country seats are scattered over and decorate the grounds improved as a farm by Governor Winthrop in 1633.

Winter Hill, memorable as the place of encampment of General Burgoyne and his army, after their capture at Saratoga, is in this town. It is 125 feet above tide water, and presents a view of great extent and beauty. Medford was incorporated in 1630. Population, 1830, 1,755; 1837, 2,072.

In the old burying ground, a beautiful granite monument is erected, bearing the following inscription:

Sacred to the memory of
JOHN BROOKS.
Who was born in Medford, in the month of May, 1752, and educated at the Town School. He took up arms for his country on the 19th April, 1775. He commanded the regiment which first entered the enemy's lines at Saratoga, and served with honor to the close of the war. He was appointed Marshal of the District of Massachusetts by President Washington, and after filling several important civil and military offices, he was in the year 1816, chosen Governor of the Commonwealth; and discharged the duties of that station for seven successive years, to general acceptance. He was a kind and skilful physician, a brave and prudent officer, a wise, firm, and impartial magistrate, a true patriot, a good citizen, and a faithful friend. In manners he was a gentleman, in morals pure, and in profession and practice a consistant Christian. He departed this life in peace on the first of March, 1825, aged 73. This monument to his honored memory was erected by several of his fellow citizens and friends in the year 1838.

Medway, Mass.

Norfolk co. Medway was taken from Medfield, in 1713. Charles river affords this town an excellent water power. There are 6 cotton, and 2 woolen mills in the town, 2 cotton wadding factories, and a bell foundry. The manufactures of cotton and woolen goods, boots, shoes, scythes, chairs, cabinet ware, ploughs, cotton wadding, and straw bonnets, the year ending April 1, 1837, amounted to $330,630. Population, 1837, 2,050. Medway lies 22 miles S. W. from Boston, and 12 S. W. from Dedham.

Megunticook River and Pond.

This river rises in a pond of the same name, in Lincolnville, Waldo county. The pond is about 9 miles in length, crooked and very handsome. It affords an excellent mill stream, which falls into Penobscot bay at Camden.

Memphremagog Lake, Vt.

This lake is about 30 miles in length, and two or three miles in width. About seven miles of it lies in the county of Orleans, the residue in Canada. It receives the waters of Barton, Black, Clyde and other smaller streams in Vermont, and discharges into the St. Francis, in Canada. On an island in this lake is a quarry of *Novaculite*, or the "Magog Oil Stone." This material is transported and manufactured. See *Burke, Vt.*

Menan Islands.

Grand Menan belongs to the British, and lies off the mouth of St. Croix river, and Passamaquoddy bay. It is 16 miles in length, and its average breadth is about 5. On the south side are a number of islands, and several small harbors. The inhabitants are principally fishermen.

Little Menan, or "Petit Menan," in Washington county, Me. lies off the harbors of Goldsborough and Steuben. It has a light house, with a tower 25 feet in height. It lies about 3 miles S. S. E. from Goldsborough harbor.

Mendon, Vt.

Rutland co. This was formerly called Parkerstown, and lies 47 miles S. S. W. from Montpelier, and 8 E. from Rutland. There is some good land in the town, but it is generally too high up the Green mountains for cultivation. Population, 1830, 432.

Mendon, Mass.

Worcester co. The Indian name of this town was *Quanshipauge.* It was first settled by people from Roxbury, about the year 1647. Incorporated, 1667. Mendon is a township of variegated surface, excellent soil, and in a good state of cultivation. The products of the dairy are large and valuable.— Blackstone river and canal pass its southwestern border, and Mill river traverses its whole extent. These streams afford an excellent hydraulic power. There are 8 cotton and 4 woolen mills in the town, and manufactures of boots, shoes, iron castings, scythes, ploughs, straw bonnets, palm-leaf hats, machinery, wagons and harnesses; total value, the year ending April 1, 1837,— $629,282. This very pleasant and flourishing town lies 32 miles S. W. from Boston, 18 S. E. from Worcester, and 22 N. from Providence. Population, 1830, 3,153; 1837, 3,657.

Mercer, Me.

Somerset co. Mercer has a fine soil, and is watered by a beautiful pond. It lies 32 miles N. N. W. from Augusta, and 6 S. W. from Norridgewock. Incorporated, 1804. The village near the pond is beautifully located. Wheat crop, 1837, 6,868 bushels. Population, same year, 1,525.

Meredith, N. H.,

Strafford co., is bounded N. by Centre Harbor and Winnepisiogee lake, N. E. and E. by said lake and river, S. E. by Great bay, S. and S. W. by Sanbornton, W. and N. W. by New Hampton and Centre Harbor. This town was incorporated, in 1767, and was first called *New Salem*. It lies 29 miles N. from Concord, and 8 N. W. from Gilford. There is in this town a pond adjoining Centre Harbor, about 2 miles long and one wide, emptying into the lake, near the village; besides this there are several smaller ponds. There is probably no town in the country more pleasantly and advantageously situated, or of a better soil, than Meredith. The waters of the Winnepisiogee washing the boundaries of a great part of the town, convey many heavy mercantile articles to and from almost the doors of several of the inhabitants in the summer; and in the winter, the ice serves as a level and easy road. Near the upper or N. W. part of the town, the traveler passing along the road, is presented with a very beautiful landscape. On the E. and S. E. the placid Winnepisiogee, the largest lake in New Hampshire, with its numerous islands, arrests the eye, and bounds the circle of vision in a S. E. direction. On the N. E., Ossipee mountain rises boldly to view. On the N., the prospect is intercepted by Red Hill, a pleasant and noted eminence in Moultonborough, only a few miles distant. At Meredith Bridge is a handsome and flourishing village, and the seat of much business. Here are 2 cotton mills, an extensive tannery, oil mill, &c., in another village are also some important manufactures. The water power of Meredith is immense. It is connected with the principal village of Gilford by a bridge over the Winnepisiogee.

Hon. EBENEZER SMITH, moved into this town at an early period of its settlement, and was as a father to the new settlers for many years. He died Aug. 22, 1807, aged 73. Population, in 1830, 2,683.

Meriden, Ct.

New Haven co. This hilly and somewhat mountainous township has, in general, a fertile soil, and is watered by Quinnepiac river. It lies 17 miles S. E. from Hartford, and 17 N. W. from New Haven. It was formerly a part of Wallingford, and incorporated in 1806.—Population, 1830, 1,708.

This is one of the most flourishing and enterprising manufacturing towns in the state. There is a considerable variety of manufactures here, forming the chief employment of the inhabitants. The following is a list of the manufactories, viz: 2 for patent augers and auger bits, 3 for ivory combs, 6 for tin ware, 4 for Britannia ware, 2 iron foundries, 1 manufactory for coffee mills, 1 for clocks, 1 for Norfolk door latches, 3 for block tin spoons, 1 for wood combs, 1 for skates and iron rakes, and 1 for gridirons. The value of articles manufactured yearly, has been estimated from 800,000 to 1,000,000 of dollars.

About thirty years since a road was constructed from the northwestern part of Meriden to Berlin, through a narrow and romantic glen, between two ridges of the Blue mountains; this pass, which is more than a mile in extent, is called the *Cat Hole*. In some parts of this glen there is but barely room for a path; small angular fragments of rocks rise on each side, at about an angle of forty five degrees: these rocks have been beaten down and covered with earth, which must have been brought here for the purpose. A few yards south of this place, elevated perpendicular rocks appear on the left, one of which has very much the appearance of a profile of the human face, and it is thought by some to resemble in a slight degree the profile of Washington. Following the foot of the mountain on the right, for about a mile, you will find large pieces of rocks lying upon each other in great disorder, which have evidently fallen from the precipitous heights above. Underneath these rocks ice may be found in almost every month in the year. A spring issues from between them, called the *Cold Spring*, and is a place of resort for parties in summer.

Merrimack River, N. H.,

One of the principal rivers of New England, is formed of two branches. The N. branch called Pemigewasset, rises near the Notch of the White mountains, and passes southwardly through the corner of Franconia, Lincoln, Peeling, Thornton and Campton, forming the boundary between Plymouth and Holderness, and also the boundary line between the counties of Strafford and Grafton from the S. corner of Holderness to near its junction with the Winnepisiogee. It receives several considerable branches in its course; Mad river in Campton, Baker's in Plymouth; and streams flowing from Squam and Newfound lakes, with numerous small tributaries.— The E. branch is the Winnepisiogee, through which pass the waters of the lake of that name. The descent of this branch from the lake to its junction with the Pemigewasset, is 232 feet. The confluent stream bears the name of Merrimack, and pursues a S. course, 78 miles, to Chelmsford, Mass.; thence an E. course, 35 miles, to the sea at Newburyport. On the N. line of Concord, the Contoocook discharges its waters into the Merrimack. The Soucook becomes a tributary in Pembroke, and the Suncook between Pembroke and Allenstown. The Piscataquog unites in Bedford; the Souhegan in Merrimack, and a beautiful river called Nashua in Nashua. The principal tributaries are on the W. side of the river, mostly rising in the highlands between the Connecticut and Merrimack. There are numerous falls in this river, the most noted of which are Garven's, in Concord, the falls in Hooksett, and Amoskeag in Goffstown and Manchester. These falls are all rendered passable by locks, and boat navigation has for several years been extended as far as Concord. There are several bridges over the Merrimack, and its principal branches, besides a number of ferries. The Merrimack, whose fountains are nearly on a level with the Connecticut, being much shorter in its course, has a far more rapid descent to the sea than the latter river. Hence the intervales on its borders are less extensive, and the scenery less beautiful, than on the Connecticut. It is, however, a majestic river; its waters are generally pure and healthy; and on its borders are situated some of the most flourishing towns in the state. The name of this river was originally written *Merramacke* and *Monnomake*, which in the Indian language signified a *sturgeon*. Its width varies from 50 to 120 rods; and at its mouth it presents a beautiful sheet of half a mile in width.

Merrimack County, N. H.

CONCORD is the county town. The county of Merrimack is bounded N. E. by the county of Strafford, S. E. by the county of Rockingham, S. W. by the county of Hillsborough, and N. W. by the counties of Sullivan and Grafton.

Its greatest length is 38 miles; its breadth at the broadest part is 26 miles. It contains an area of 506,000 acres. The surface is uneven, and in some parts rugged and mountainous; but its general fertility, is perhaps equal to either of the other counties in the state. In the towns of Hopkinton, Henniker, Boscawen, Salisbury, Canterbury, Concord, &c., are seen many extensive and well cultivated farms. The northerly part of the county is rough and mountainous. Kearsarge is the highest mountain, its summit being 2,461 feet above the level of the sea. It is composed of a range of hills, running north and south about six miles; its general aspect is rugged and craggy, excepting when its roughness is shaded by the woody covering that darkens its sides. The Ragged mountains, so called, from their appearance, lie northeast of Kearsarge, and between Andover and Hill. These are nearly 2,000 feet high at the north points of the range. Bear's Hill, in Northfield, Sunapee mountain, in Newbury, Catamount, in Pittsfield, and the peak in Hooksett, are the other most considerable elevations. A part of lake Sunapee lies in Newbury; and there are numerous ponds interspersed throughout the whole territory.

The Merrimack river meanders through nearly the centre of the county, and forms the boundary some distance at the northeastern part. It receives from the west the Blackwater and Contoocook rivers, and from the east, Soucook and Suncook, and other smaller streams.

This county was constituted by an act of the legislature, 1 July, 1823—being taken from the counties of Rockingham and Hillsborough, ten towns being separated from the former, and thirteen from the latter. Population, 1820, 32,843; 1830, 34,619. Twenty four towns, 44 inhabitants to a square mile. In 1837, there were 66,152 sheep in this county.

Merrimack, N. H.,

Hillsborough co., is bounded N. by Bedford, E. by Litchfield, S. by Nashua, and W. by Amherst.— It is 6 miles S. E. from Amherst, and 27 S. from Concord. Merrimack river waters its E. border through its whole extent, opening a communication by water from this place to Boston. Souhegan enters this town from Amherst, pursues a winding course to the Merrimack, where it discharges itself one mile above Thornton's ferry. There are fine water privileges on this stream. Babboosuck brook, issuing from Babboosuck pond in Amherst, empties into Souhegan river, and Penichook brook from a pond in Hollis, forms the southern boundary. The soil in various places is very fertile, but a considerable portion of the land is plain. There are some fine intervales on the Merrimack. Some of the best and most extensive water privileges the county affords, about 1 1-2 mile from the Merrimack, on Souhegan river, lie unimproved.

This town claims the first discovery in this region of making what are called leghorn bonnets. They were first made several years since, by the Misses Burnaps. Some of their bonnets were sold at auction in Boston for $50.

This town was formerly called *Souhegan East.* It was incorporated, 1746, having been settled about 13 years.

The first house in this town was erected on the margin of the river for a house of traffic with the Indians. For some time one Cromwell carried on a lucrative trade with the Indians, weighing their furs with his foot, till, enraged at his supposed or real deception, they formed the resolution to murder him. This intention was communicated to Cromwell, who buried his wealth and made his escape. Within a few hours after his flight, a party of the Penacook tribe arrived, and not finding the object of their resentment, they burnt his habitation.

Hon. MATTHEW THORNTON, one of the signers of the Declaration of American Independence, resided many years in this town. He died in 1803, at the age of 89. Population, 1830, 1,191.

Merrymeeting Bays.

Merrymeeting Bay, in Maine, is at the junction of the Androscoggin with the Kennebec, about 5 miles above Bath. It is a large expanse of water, and contains Swan and other islands. The passage through this bay, of 10 or 12 miles in length, is delightful.

Merrymeeting Bay, in New Hampshire, is an arm of Winnepisiogee lake, extending about 1,800 rods into the town of Alton, and is 27 miles from the navigable waters of Piscataqua river.

Methuen, Mass.

Essex co. In this town is a beautiful water fall of 30 feet, on Spicket river, which furnishes an excellent hydraulic power. Methuen lies on the N. bank of Merrimack river, and is 25 miles N. by W. from Boston, and 20 N. W. by N. from Salem. It was taken from Haverhill in 1725. Population, 1830, 2,011; 1837, 2,463. There are 2 cotton, and 2 paper mills in the town, and manufactures of leather, shoes, hats, ploughs, segars, essences, chaises, harnesses, chairs, tin and cabinet wares, and piano-forte frames: value, for the year ending April 1, 1837, $462,525. An excellent bed of peat has recently been discovered. It is 14 feet in depth, and very extensive. The soil of Methuen is very good, the village is pleasant, and the scenery around it, romantic and beautiful.

Mexico, Me.

Oxford co. This town lies on the north side of Androscoggin river, and is watered by two of its tributaries. It has a good soil and a good water power. It lies 47 miles W. N. W. from Augusta, and 20 N. from Paris. Incorporated, 1818. Population, 1837, 447. Wheat crop, same year, 1,552 bushels.

Middleborough, Mass.

Plymouth co. This is the Indian *Namasket;* formerly thickly populated by the people of that tribe, and governed by the noted sachem *Tispacan.* On the rocks, in this town, are the prints of naked hands and feet, supposed to be the work of the Indians. Here are numerous ponds, several kinds of fish, and large quantities of iron ore is found in the ponds. These ponds, of which the *Assawamset* and Long pond are the largest, empty into Taunton river, and produce an extensive water power.

This town lies 34 miles S. by E. from Boston, 14 S. S. W. from Plymouth, and 10 S. E. from Taunton. Incorporated, 1660. Population, 1837, 5,005. This is probably the largest town in the state: it is 15 miles in length, and about 9 average breadth : it has several pleasant villages. There are 2 cotton mills, 2 forges, an air and cupola furnace, a nail factory, and manufactures of leather, shovels, spades, forks, ploughs, wrought nails, chairs, cabinet ware, tacks, straw bonnets, and various other articles: total value, in one year, $200,000.

In 1763, Shubael Thompson found a land turtle, marked on the shell J. W., 1747. Thompson marked it and let it go. Elijah Clapp found it in 1773 ; William Shaw found it in 1775; Jonathan Soule found it in 1784; Joseph Soule found it in 1790, and Zenas Smith, in 1791: each marked it with his initials. Whether the *critter* is dead or gone to the west, we have no account.

Middlebury, Vt.

Addison co. Chief town. This is a large and flourishing town on both sides of Otter creek, 31 miles S. W. from Montpelier, and 33 S. S. E. from Burlington. The fathers of this town were Col. John Chipman and the Hon. Gamaliel Painter, who came here and settled in 1773. The settlement advanced but slowly until after the revolutionary war ; it then began to increase and is now one of the most important towns in the state. In 1791 it became the shire town of the county, and in 1800 Middlebury college was founded. The surface of the town is generally level. Chipman's hill, 439 feet above Otter creek, is the highest elevation. The soil is fertile and productive, and furnishes large quantities of wool, beef, pork, butter and cheese. The town is admirably watered by Otter creek and Middlebury river. At the falls on Otter creek, the site of the flourishing village, are extensive manufacturing establishments ; and large quantities of white and variegated marble, with which the town abounds, are sawed and polished for various uses and transported to market. Middlebury is a very beautiful town, and the mart of a large inland trade. Population, in 1830, 3,468. See *Register.*

Middlebury River rises in Hancock, and passing through Ripton falls into Otter creek at Middlebury. This mountain stream is about 14 miles in length, affords a fine water power, and is very romantic in its course. It passes some distance along the road from Windsor to Vergennes, and presents some delightful scenery.

Middlebury, Ct.

New Haven co. The surface of this town is hilly and rocky; the soil a coarse, gravelly loam, fit for grazing and the growth of rye. It lies 36 miles W. S. W. from Hartford, and 22 N. W. from New Haven. Incorporated, 1807. Population, 1830, 816. The town is watered by Quasepaug pond, which empties into the Housatonick, and furnishes a water power for a satinet factory, and other machinery.

Middlefield, Mass.

Hampshire co. This is an elevated agricultural township, watered by a branch of Westfield river. It lies 110 miles W. from Boston, 24 W. from Northampton, and 17 S. E. from Pittsfield. Incorporated, 1783. Population, 1837, 710. There are 2 woolen mills in the town, and 2 tanneries. Annual value of goods manufactured, about $75,000.— Among the productions of the soil, there were, in 1837, 9,724 fleeces of saxony wool, which weighed 26,741 pounds, value, $17,382.

Middlesex, Vt.

Washington co. Onion river and other streams give this town a good water power. It has considerable manufacturing concerns, and a very pleasant village. The soil along the streams is good, and that of the uplands, generally, is adapted for grazing. It lies 30 miles E. S. E. from Burlington, and is bounded by Montpelier on the S. E. First settled, in 1781. Population, 1830, 1,156.

There is a curious chasm in Middlesex, on Onion river, near Moretown. The river has worn a passage through rocks 30 feet in depth, 60 feet in width, and about 80 rods in length. The walls on each side are very smooth, over which a bridge is thrown. This place is worthy of a visit.

Middlesex County, Mass.

Concord, Cambridge, and Lowell, are the shire towns. The surface of this county is uneven and the soil various. It presents a great variety for the admiration of the patriot, scholar, farmer, mechanic, and the painter. It is bounded N. by New Hampshire; N. E. by the county of Essex; S. E. by Charles river, Boston harbor, and Norfolk county; and W. by the county of Worcester. Area, 800 square miles: population, in 1820, 61,476; 1830, 77,968; 1837, 98,565. Population to a square mile, 123. The principal rivers in this county, are the Merrimack, Charles, Mystic, Sudbury, Concord, and Nashua. The *Middlesex Canal* passes through its northeastern section. In 1837 there were 5,166 sheep in the county. The value of manufactures for the year ending April 1, 1837, amounted to $15,008,028. Fishery, same year, $33,000.

Middlesex County, Ct.

Shire towns—*Middletown* and *Haddam*. This county is bounded N. by Hartford county, E. by Hartford and New London counties, S. by Long Island Sound, and W. by New Haven county. The general surface of the county is uneven. The soil is generally good, particularly adjacent to Connecticut river. There are many small streams which afford mill privileges, fertilizing the soil and giving beauty to the county. The waters of the Connecticut afford it an important business in navigation, especially in the coasting trade. The tonnage of the district of Middletown, in 1837, was 13,133 tons. There are numerous manufacturing establishments in the county; large quantities of freestone are quarried and carried to market, and the shad fishery gives employment to many of its people.

Middlesex county contains an area of 342 square miles. Population, 1820, 22,405; 1830, 24,845; containing a population of 73 inhabitants to a square mile. Considerable amounts of the productions of the soil are exported, and in 1837, there were in the county 12,401 sheep.

Middleton, N. H.

Strafford co. This is a very level township, having no high ground except a part of Moose mountain, which separates it from Brookfield. There are no rivers nor ponds, and the soil is rocky. It lies 25 miles N. W. from Dover. Middleton was incorporated in 1778. Population, 1830, 562.

Middleton, Mass.

Essex co. A pleasant town on both sides of Ipswich river, 19 miles N. from Boston, and 7 N. W. from Salem. This place contains a large and expensive paper mill. This is the principal manufacturing concern in the town. Incorporated, 1728. Population, 1837, 671.

Middletown, Vt.

Rutland co. This town lies between two mountains, is watered by Poultney river, and has a good soil for grazing. It keeps, among other cattle, about 4,000 sheep. It lies 14 miles S. W. from Rutland. It has a neat and flourishing village, a woolen factory, marble factory, and other manufactures.—Population, 1830, 919.

Middletown, Ct.

Chief town of Middlesex co.— MIDDLETOWN CITY, and port of entry, lies on the W. bank of Connecticut river, 30 miles from its mouth, 15 S. from Hartford, 24 N. E. from New Haven, 35 N. W. from New London. Lat. 41° 34′ N., long. 72° 39′ W. The city is very pleasantly situated on ground rising gradually from the river. The principal street, called *Main street*, runs parallel with the river. This and other streets, are intersected by cross streets, leading to the river.

The wharves are commodious for shipping, there being ten feet of water for all vessels that can cross the bar at the mouth of the river. Two high wharves are appropriated for two lines of steam-boats, of a large class, which afford a daily communication with the cities of New York and Hartford.

The streets and side-walks are pleasantly shaded with trees, and the side-walks are remarkably well paved.

The population of the city, is about 3,500; of the town, above 7,000.

The public edifices are a court-house in the Grecian style of architecture, built in 1832; a custom-house handsomely built of Chatham freestone; 2 banks, and a savings bank, &c. The places of public worship in the city, and the principal houses and stores are of brick, many of which are built with great taste.

The WESLEYAN UNIVERSITY, under the patronage of the Methodist Episcopal church, was founded in 1831, and is very rapidly acquiring a high standing. It has now 160 students. Its officers are a president and 5 professors.

The college buildings command an extensive view of the surrounding country, as well as of the valley of the Connecticut, so justly famed for its beauty.

The college library, with those belonging to the societies, comprises about 10,000 volumes. It has many rare and choice works, an entire set of the Latin Classics, and most of the Greek, a set of the Philosophical Transactions, and all of the most important later scientific works of

France. There is also a collection of bibles and testaments in 81 languages and dialects, oriental, &c., into which the bible has been translated.

The philosophical and astronomical apparatus, has been lately increased at great expense. There is a telescope, with a six inch object glass, a splendid altitude and Azimuth instrument, so constructed as to be used for meridian transits. Russell's magnificent Orrery, an unrivalled instrument, and the only one of the kind. There is a noble Plate Electrical machine, with two plates 36 inches in diameter, &c.

The chemical department has a good laboratory and apparatus.—The cabinet of minerals is becoming extensive. In geology, besides specimens, there are several valuable charts to illustrate the different states, and many districts of England.

In botany, there are several of the best standard works, and for the preservation of the science, the richness in species of the native plants about Middletown, is not surpassed by any location in New England. The place is also remarkable for the variety and abundance of its rare minerals.

The rising reputation of its university, the great salubrity of its atmosphere, and the activity of its manufacturing capital, render Middletown equally attractive to the traveler, the man of science, or of business. There are besides in this city, several fine cabinets of shells, insects, minerals, &c., and an Herbarium of considerable extent, of North American as well as of European plants, also several choice private libraries.

The library of the Rev. Dr. Jarvis, contains 13,000 volumes of exceeding choice books, collected by him, during a residence of several years in Europe, and his gallery of about 120 paintings, is regarded as being very valuable.—About 70 of these pictures formed the gallery of the Archbishop of Tarento at Naples, and are of the old masters—Titian, Rubens, Tintoretto, Salvator Rosa, Carlo Dolce, Lueca, Giordano, Jordens, Spagnoletto, &c. There is also in another collection some very fine paintings of the old masters, and an exquisite piece of statuary by the Chevalier P. Marchesi of Milan, representing Christ when 12 years of age! This is the only work of the distinguished sculptor, that has yet arrived in this country.

The township from N. to S. is about 9 miles long, its breadth varying from 4 to 10 miles at its greatest area, or about 43,520 acres.—The Indian name of the town was *Mattabesett*. The town is divided into 4 societies or parishes.

There is in the city a preparatory school connected with the university, as well as several flourishing private schools.

The public records of this town commenced in 1654. The city was incorporated in 1784.

The burial grounds contain many curious, as well as antique monuments of its earliest settlers.

The burial ground at the N. part of the city, and by the river, was laid out in 1650.

Middletown meadows, north of the city, contain about 640 acres. The height of the base of the village is 160 feet above the river, and is from it, five eighths of a mile. Main street is from 40 to 50 feet above the river.

The Connecticut river is here generally closed with ice about the middle of December, and opens about the end of the third week in March.

The manufactures in this city, are 3 establishments on a large scale for the manufacture of arms, for the United States service; broadcloths and cotton goods, brittannia and tin wares, stoves, combs, tubs, machinery, steam engines, cotton machinery, paper, powder, jewelry, brass ware, steel pens, buttons, looking-glasses, carriages, carpenter's tools and locks, besides many manufactures of minor importance.

Geology. Middletown rests on secondary red sandstone: within 2 miles of the city, south, there is a granite ridge, here known by the name of the White rocks. It runs N. N. E., and forms the straits of the Connecticut river. This granite ridge is from 400 to 600 feet above the tide water. Here occurs an inexhaustible quantity of the finest *feldspar*, the material used for the glaze of porcelain. This was first brought into notice in 1833, at the recommendation of Dr. Barrett. A large quantity of it has been sent to Europe, as well as being used in this country, and it has been proved to be of the best quality.

The feldspar is often so pure at the quarry opened on the Haddam road, that masses of several hundred weight occur without any admixture of quartz and mica.

Middletown, R. I.

Newport co. This is the middle township on the island of Rhode Island. It lies 2 miles N. E. from Newport, and 28 S. by E. from Providence. The surface of the town is undulating, and affords many interesting and beautiful landscapes. The soil is a rich loam, very productive and under a high state of cultivation; the lands are highly valued and command a great price. The inhabitants of the town are principally farmers; they are distinguished for their habits of industry and economy, and for the uniformity, plainness, and simplicity of their manner of living. The products of the town consist of corn, barley, hay, and great varieties of fruits and vegetables for Newport market. Incorporated, 1743. Population, 1830, 915.

Milan, N. H.,

Coos co., is 139 miles N. by E. from Concord, and about 22 N. E. from Lancaster. This tract was granted in 1771, and was called *Paulsburgh*, until 1824. The Upper Amonoosuck and Androscoggin rivers pass through this town.— There are several ponds, and some considerable mountains. Population, 1830, 57.

Milford, Me.

Penobscot county. See "Down East."

Milford, N. H.,

Hillsborough co., is bounded E. by Amherst, and is 31 miles S. by W. from Concord. Milford lies on both sides of Souhegan river, which runs through the town from W. to E., forming a rich meadow or intervale, from 1-4 to 1-2 a mile wide. The banks of this river are annually overflowed, by which means, the soil, which is black and deep, is much enriched. This town has excellent water privileges, and there is a valuable factory in the village. Population, 1830, 1,303.

Milford, Mass.

Worcester co. This town, the Indian *Wopowage*, is well watered by Charles and Mill rivers. It lies 28 miles S. W. by W. from Boston, and 18 S. E. from Worcester. Incorporated, 1780. Population, 1837, 1,637. The soil is generally fertile, and the surface pleasantly diversified. The manufactures of the town, for the year ending April 1, 1837, amounted to $257,671. They consisted of cotton goods, leather, boots, shoes, chairs, tin and cabinet wares, straw bonnets, varnish, clothing, shoe pegs, wagon irons, and whips.

Milford, Ct.

New Haven co. This is one of the towns which composed the "Old Jurisdiction of New Haven."

The settlement commenced in 1639. The first purchase of land was made of the Indians, for the consideration of "6 coats, 10 blankets, 1 kettle, besides a number of hoes, knives, hatchets, and glasses." The Indians made a reservation of 20 acres in the town, which was sold by them, in 1661, for 6 coats, 2 blankets, and a pair of breeches.

Milford is bounded W. by Housatonick river, and S. E. by Long Island Sound. The Indian name of the place was *Wepawaug.* The town is generally level, and the soil productive. There is a quarry of beautiful serpentine marble in the town, and a harbor for small vessels.

Poconock or Milford point is a noted place, where are a number of huts on the beach, occupied by persons engaged in the oyster and clam business.

Milford village is very pleasant, and the scenery variegated and interesting. Population, 1837, about 2,800.

Millbury, Mass.

Worcester co. Millbury was taken from Sutton, in 1813. It lies 42 miles W. S. W. from Boston, and 6 S.E. from Worcester. Branches of the Blackstone river rise in the town, and the Blackstone canal passes through it. It is a very pleasant manufacturing place, with a valuable water power. There are 1 paper, 6 woolen, and 1 cotton mills; and manufactures of boots, shoes, leather, hats, scythes, spades, forks, hoes, ploughs, muskets,trying squares, levels, trowels, machinery, black lead, tin ware, sashes and blinds: total value, the year ending April 1, 1837, $566,150. Population, 1837, 2,153.

Miller's Rivers.

Miller's River, in Vermont, rises in Sheffield, Caledonia county, and passing through a part of Wheelock falls into the Passumpsick at Lyndon.

Miller's River, in Massachusetts, rises in ponds in Ashburnham, and Winchendon; it has many tributaries, and passes through Athol, Orange, and Wendell, and falls into the Connecticut at Erving. This is a noble mill stream.

Millinoket Lake, Me.

This is a large body of water in the county of Penobscot, the recipient of many rivers. It is an important source of the west branch of Penobscot river. Its outlet is a river of the same name, and unites with the waters of Pemadumcook lake, near the Great falls at the outlet of the Pemadumcook.

Mill River, Mass.

See *Springfield.*

Millsfield, N. H.,

Coos co., is 7 miles W. from Umbagog lake, and about 35 N.from the White mountains. Clear stream waters its N. extremity, and Phillip's river with several small streams the other parts. Here are several ponds, the largest is about 300 rods long, 140 wide. Millsfield was granted in 1774, and was named after Sir Thomas Mills, a grantee. It had but 33 inhabitants in 1830.

Milo, Me.

Piscataquis co. This is a beautiful township on the fertile banks of Sebec and Pleasant rivers, at their union with the Piscataquis. It lies 103 miles N. E. from Augusta, and 15 N. E. from Dover. Population, 1830, 381; 1837, 640.—Wheat crop, 1837, 4,514 bushels. Incorporated, 1823.

Milton, Me.

Piscataquis co. Population, 1837, 352. Wheat crop, same year, 1,323

Milton, N. H.

Strafford co. The Salmon Fall river washes its whole E. boundary, a distance of 13 miles; and a branch of the same river crosses from the S. part of Wakefield, and unites near the centre of the E. boundary. Teneriffe, a bold and rocky mountain, extends along the E. part of Milton, near which lies Milton pond, of considerable size, connecting with the Salmon Fall river. This town was formerly a part of Rochester, from which it was detached in 1802. It lies 40 miles N. E. from Concord, and 20 N. W. by N. from Dover. Population, 1830, 1,273.

Milton, Vt.

Chittenden co. Milton is bounded on the W. by lake Champlain, and is finely watered by the river Lamoille. It lies 12 miles N. from Burlington, and 40 N. W. from Montpelier. Population, 1830, 2,100. The soil of the town is generally good, and about 9,000 sheep graze in its pastures. There are some places in Milton worthy of the traveller's notice. A little distance from the neat and flourishing village are the Great falls, on the Lamoille. In the course of 50 rods the whole river falls 150 feet.— About the middle of the rapid is a small island, by which the water passes on each side, with great violence and loud roaring. The scenery on the banks of the river is wild and beautiful. There are some mills on the river, and considerable trade on the lake.

Milton, Mass.

Norfolk co. This interesting and pleasant town, the *Uncataquissit* of the Indians, lies 7 miles S. from Boston, and 6 E. from Dedham. Neponset river washes its northern border and affords numerous valuable mill sites. This town was taken from Dorchester, in 1662. Population, 1837, 1,772. A large part of the land is a gravelly loam, strong and very productive. The manufactures consist of paper, granite, leather, hats, chairs, cabinet ware, playing cards, &c.: total annual amount, about $100,000. The manufacture of paper from *beach grass* has recently been commenced, and promises to be a good substitute for rags, for the more common kinds.

The village called the "Mills," comprising a part of Dorchester, at the head of navigation, on the Neponset, is a wild, romantic place, and ever since the first settlement of the country, has been the seat of considerable trade and manufacture.

The village at the rail-road, near the granite quarry, in Quincy, about a mile S. E. of the "Mills," is very pleasant and flourishing.— By a new and beautiful bridge, called the "Granite bridge," across the Neponset, the distance to the city is reduced to 6 miles.

Milton contains some elegant country seats, and much delightful scenery. The views from "Milton Hill," near the head of the Neponset; and "Blue Hill," a celebrated land mark for sailors, 710 feet above the sea, in the south part of the town, 12 miles from Boston, are among the most admired in our country.

Minot, Me.

Cumberland co. Minot is a large and excellent township of land with three very pleasant villages. The Androscoggin passes its eastern border and Little Androscoggin separates it from Poland, on the S. This is one of the most flourishing towns in the state. Although agriculture is the chief business of the people of Minot, yet its water power is so valuable, that manufactures of various kinds are springing up with promising success. Minot is connected with Lewiston, across the Androscoggin, by a bridge. It lies 33 miles S. W. from Augusta, and 35 N. from Portland. Population, in 1830, 2,908; 1837, 3,326. Incorporated, 1802. Wheat crop, 1837, 7,266 bushels.

Missisque River, Vt.

This crooked river is about 75 miles in length. It rises in Orleans county, and passes N. into Canada, about 5 miles; it then returns to the state at the N. E. corner of Franklin county, and after meandering through the north part of that county, it falls into Missisque bay at Highgate. There are several falls on this river, which afford numerous mill sites; but it is generally sluggish in its course, and being wide, is rather shallow. Its waters fertilize a large portion of country, and it is navigable for small vessels, six miles from its mouth.

Molechunkamunk Lake, Me.

This is one of a number of large lakes extending northwest from Umbagog lake, and which empty through the Umbagog into the Androscoggin. These lakes lie in the counties of Oxford and Franklin: their borders are but little settled, but those who have visited them report that the soil is exceedingly fertile, and that the beauties of these little inland seas, equal that of the celebrated Winnepisiogee. The Molechunkamunk lies about 80 miles N. by W. from Portland.

Molumkus River,

A large tributary to the Matawamkeag from the north. It unites with that river about 8 miles above its mouth.

Monadnock Mountain, N. H.,

Usually called the *Grand Monadnock*, is situated in the towns of Jaffrey and Dublin, in Cheshire county, about 22 miles E. from Connecticut river, and 10 N. of the southern boundary of this state.— The direction of the ridge is N. E. and S. W. The mountain is about 5 miles long from N. to S., and 3 miles from E. to W. Its summit is 3,718 feet above the level of the sea. Thirty years since, Monadnock was nearly covered with evergreen wood of considerable growth. By the repeated ravages of fire, it now presents to the distant beholder, nothing but a barren and bald rock. But on ascending, we find plats of earth sufficient to give growth to the blueberry, cranberry, mountain ash, and a variety of shrubs. Some caves are discovered, which excite curiosity. They appear to have been formed by large fissures, and by extensive strata being thrown from their primitive state, and forming different angles with each other and with perpendicular precipices. The mountain is composed of talc, mica, slate, distinctly stratified.— Garnet, schorl, feldspar and quartz occur in various parts. On the E. side, plumbago is found in large quantities. Crucibles and pencils have been manufactured from it, but for the latter, it proves not very good. The summit, when seen at a distance of 4 or 5 miles, appears rounded and destitute of those high cliffs and mural precipices belonging to granitic mountains. The prospect from the pinnacle is very extensive; thirty ponds of fresh water, some of which are so large as to contain islands of 8 or 10 acres, may be seen from it, in the immediate vicinity. Near the base of the mountain, in Jaffrey, is the "Monadnock Mineral Spring."

Monkton, Vt.

Addison co. This town lies 27 miles W. from Montpelier, 16 N. from Middlebury, and 18 S. by E. from Burlington. This is a good farming town, and the products of wool, cattle, and of the dairy are considerable. Iron ore is found in abundance, and a bed of porcelain earth. By mixing this earth with common clay, in different proportions, various kinds of pottery are produced. This earth is very pure, and it is said might be manufactured into the best china ware. The bed is inexhaustible. The black oxide of manganese is also found here. There is also a curious cavern in the town: after descending about 16 feet, you arrive at a room 30 feet long, and 16 wide. From this is a passage leading to a second apartment, which is not quite so large, but more pleasant. Monkton is a pleasant town, 3 miles E. from Ferrisburgh, and is frequently visited by the curious. Population, 1830, 1,384.

Monmouth, Me.

Kennebec co. This is a fine township, and beautifully watered by some of the sources of the Cobbessecontee. It lies 15 miles S. W. from Augusta. The village is very pleasant, and is the seat of a flourishing academy. Wheat crop, 1837, 5,256 bushels. Population, same year, 1,847. Incorporated, 1792.

Monroe, Me.

Waldo co. This town is watered by Marsh river, a branch of the Penobscot. It lies 59 miles N. E. from Augusta, and 14 N. from Belfast. Population, 1837, 1,365. Wheat crop, same year, 5,897.

Monroe, Mass.

Franklin co. This is an elevated township, bounded E. by Deerfield river. It lies 105 miles W. N. W. from Boston, and 23 W. by N. from Greenfield. Incorporated, 1822.—Population, 1837, 232.

Monroe, Ct.

Fairfield co. This town was taken from Huntington in 1823. The soil is good, and well adapted for grazing, but the surface is rough and stony. Agriculture is the principal business of the inhabitants. There are excellent orchards of various kinds of fruit in the town, a pleasant village on elevated ground, and a classical school. It lies 15 miles W. by N. from New Haven, and 12 E. by S. from Danbury. Population, 1830, 1,522.

A rich variety of mineral substances have been discovered here. Among them, are tungsten, tellurium, native bismouth, native silver, magnetical and common iron pyrites, copper pyrites, galena, blende, tourmaline, &c.

Monson, Me.

Piscataquis co. This town is watered by Piscataquis river and Wilson's stream. Monson comprises a fine tract of land, and is settled by a worthy class of people. Incorporated, 1822. Population, in 1837, 565. Wheat crop, same year, 2,267 bushels. It lies 83 miles N. by E. from Augusta, and 20 N. W. from Dover. A stage runs between this town and Bangor, three times a week. Distance from Monson to Bangor, 60 miles; to Moosehead lake, 15.

Monson, Mass.

Hampden co. Monson was taken from Brimfield in 1760. It lies 73 miles S. W. by W. from Boston, and 13 E. from Springfield. Population, 1837, 2,179. This is a pleasant town of variegated surface, good soil and well watered by Chickopee river. It contains a flourishing academy. There are 3 cotton mills in Monson, and other manufactures. The value of cotton goods manufactured in the year ending April 1, 1837, was $67,500.

Montague, Mass.

Franklin co. This town is on the E. bank of Connecticut river, opposite to Deerfield, and united to that town by a bridge. *Turner's Falls*, at the northerly part of the town, are more interesting than any in the state, and probably as much so as any in New England. The canal for passing these falls, 3 miles in length and 75 feet lockage, with an immense dam across the river, greatly facilitates the navigation on Connecticut river. This place has a great water power, and promises peculiar advantages to the manufacturing interest. The scenery around this place is romantic and beautiful, and to the lovers of antiquarian lore, full of interesting associations. It lies 80 miles W. by N. from Boston, and 7 S. E. from Greenfield. Incorporated, 1753. Population, in 1837, 1,260.

Montgomery, Vt.

Franklin co. This town lies in a mountainous country, but it has a valuable tract of land on Trout river, a good mill stream, a branch of the Missisque. It lies 42 miles N. from Montpelier, and 27 E. N. E. from St. Albans. First settled, in 1793. Population, 1830, 460.

The Rev. Joel Clapp was the first child born in this town, September 14, 1793. He preached the first fast-day sermon, the first thanksgiving sermon, and the first mother's funeral sermon, which were preached in the town.

Montgomery, Mass.

Hampden co. This is a mountainous township on the N. side of Westfield river, and has a good water power. It lies 100 miles W. by S. from Boston, and 12 N. W. from Springfield. Incorporated, 1780. Population, 1837, 497. This is a good town for grazing, and it produces considerable wool and some beef cattle.

Montpelier, Vt.

The capital of the state and shire town of the county of Washington. It lies in N. lat. 44° 17′, and W. lon. 72° 36′. It is 182 miles W. from Augusta, Me.; 97 N. N. W. from Concord, N. H.; 160 N. W. by N. from Boston, Mass.; 200 N. by W. from Providence, R. I.; 205 N. from Hartford, Ct.; 148 N. E. from Albany N. Y.; and 524 miles from Washington. First settled, in 1786. Population, 1830, 2,985. Montpelier became the seat of government in 1805, and the shire town of the county, in 1811. It is finely watered by Onion river and by several branches of that stream. These streams afford a good water power, on which are manufacturing establishments of various kinds. The surface of the town is very uneven and hilly, but not mountainous. The soil is very good along the streams, and the highlands produce excellent pasturage. The agricultural products are various and valuable. In 1837 there were between 8,000 and 9,000 sheep in the town.

This township was granted October 21, 1780, and chartered to Timothy Bigelow and others, August 14, 1781, containing 23,040 acres. It was rechartered February 6, 1804. In the spring of 1786, Joel Frizzle erected a log house on the bank of Onion river, in the southwest corner of this township, and moved his family into it from Canada. This was the first family in town. Early in the month of May, 1787, Col. Jacob and Gen. Parley Davis, from Worcester county, Mass. began improvements near the place where the village now stands, and erected a log house, into which Col. Davis removed his family the winter following.

The *village* of Montpelier is surrounded by hills of considerable elevation; and although it is too low to command an extensive prospect, is very pleasant, and quite romantic in its appearance. It is located very near the centre of the state: it is a great thoroughfare from all directions, and commands a large and valuable interior trade. The buildings are in good style; some of which are very handsome.

VERMONT STATE HOUSE, MONTPELIER.

NEW ENGLAND GAZETTEER.

We take pleasure in presenting to the public a well executed engraving of the Vermont State House, at Montpelier; designed by A. B. YOUNG, Esq., a native of New England, and executed under his immediate superintendence.

The engraving represents a southeast front view of the building, which stands on an elevated site, about 325 feet from State street, on which it fronts, and is alike beautiful in design and execution. The yard and grounds pertaining to it are large and spacious, and, in the manner they are laid out, give great importance to the building. Through the whole design, a chaste architectural character is preserved, which, combined with the convenient arrangement of the interior and the stability of its construction, renders this edifice equal in every respect to any in New England, and probably to any in the United States. The building is in the form of a cross, showing in front a centre, 72 feet wide, and two wings, each 39 feet, making the whole length 150 feet. The centre, including the portico, is 100 feet deep; the wings are 50 feet deep. The six columns of the portico are 6 feet diameter at their base, and 36 feet high, supporting an entablature of classic proportions. The dome rises 36 feet above the ridge, making the whole height from the ground 100 feet. The order of architecture used is the Grecian Doric, and is made to conform to the peculiar arrangement necessary in this building. The walls, columns, cornices, &c., are of dark Barre granite, wrought in a superior manner: the dome and roofs are covered with copper.

In the interior, the lower story contains an Entrance Hall, rooms for the Secretary of State, Treasurer, Auditor, and numerous Committee rooms. The second or principal story, contains a Vestibule, and stairways, a Representatives Hall, 57 by 67 feet, with a Lobby, and Galleries for spectators; a Senate Chamber, 30 by 44 feet, with Lobby and Gallery; a Governor's room, 24 by 20 feet, with an ante-room, and a room for his Secretary adjoining; a Library room, 18 by 36 feet; rooms for the several officers of the Senate and House of Representatives, and several committee rooms. The cost of this building, including all expenses, was about $132,100; of which the inhabitants of Montpelier paid $15,000.

At the first session of the Legislature of Vermont, within this building, in October, 1838, the following resolution was unanimously adopted:

"Resolved, by the General Assembly of the State of Vermont, that the thanks of this Legislature be presented to AMMI B. YOUNG, Esq., as a testimonial of their approbation of the taste, ability, fidelity and perseverance which he has manifested in the design and execution of the new capitol of this state; which will abide as a lasting monument of the talents and taste of Mr. YOUNG as an Architect."

Montville, Me.

Waldo co. This is a beautiful and flourishing town, watered by some of the head branches of Sheepscot river, 26 miles E. N. E. from Augusta, and 15 W. from Belfast. Incorporated, 1807. Population, in 1830, 1,243; 1837, 1,987. Wheat crop, 1837, 8,088 bushels.

Montville, Ct.

New London co. Montville was taken from New London in 1786. The surface is hilly and stony; the soil a dry, gravelly loam, strong and fertile. It lies on the W. side of the river Thames, 35 miles S. E. from Hartford, 8 N. from New London, and 7 S. from Norwich. The town has a good water power and contains 3 cotton and 2 woolen factories, and an oil mill. Population, 1830, 1,964.

This, and a large tract of country lying north and east of it, formerly belonged to the Mohegans, a tribe of Indians once celebrated for their warlike prowess and friendship to the English. In Montville is a tract reserved by the state, for the maintenance of a remnant of that tribe, " on the land of their fathers."

The Mohegan reservation consists of about 2,700 acres. It was holden by them in common till the year 1790, when it was divided to each family by the legislature of Connecticut. The Mohegans are under the care of guardians, or overseers, appointed by the legislature. A part of the lands are occupied by the Indians themselves, and a part by white tenants, of which there are as many as Mohegans living on the reservation. The rents go into a common fund, from which the Mohegans derive, individually, a small sum annually.

In 1774, when a census of the inhabitants of Connecticut was taken, there were in the colony 1,363 Indians. The number in the township of New London was stated to be 206. Mohegan was then included in the limits of that town. At the same time there were in Stonington 237; in Groton 186; in Lyme 104; in Norwich 61, and in Preston 30: in all, 824. Most of these may be considered as descended from those who once owed some kind of allegiance to Uncas. Dr. Holmes, who visited Mohegan in 1803, says that " there were not more than 80 persons of this tribe remaining, and that John Cooper, the richest man in the tribe, possessing a yoke of oxen and two cows, was then their religious teacher." Four years after, they were reduced in number to sixty nine, these being for the most part aged persons, widows, and fatherless children.

Within the course of a few years past, an effort has been made to elevate and rescue the remnant of this tribe from extinction. A small house for divine worship has been erected, and also a house for a teacher; towards erecting this last building, the United States government appropriated 500 dollars; they have also allowed, recently, 400 dollars annually for the support of a teacher. The school, consisting of upwards of 20 scholars, at this time is under the care of Mr. Anson Gleason, who also officiates as a religious teacher at the Mohegan Chapel. Mr. Gleason commenced his labors among this people in 1832, and it is firmly believed that his efforts to promote the welfare of this people will be attended with lasting and beneficial effects. Mr. Gleason says, " that he can say for a certainty, that the native children are as apt to learn as any children he ever taught, and bid fair for intelligent men and women." He also says, " This tribe had well nigh run out by indulging in the use of ardent spirits; but of late there is a change for the better, a number of reformations having taken place. Most of the youth are opposed to strong drink, and are members of the temperance reform. The greater part of the working men follow the whale trade, and come home only now and then. . . . We are on the increase, and hope in the course of a few years, through the mercy of God, to rise in point of virtue and respectability."

The Mohegan church is between three and four miles from Norwich city, a few rods east of the public road from Norwich to New London. It is beautifully situated on an eminence commanding a fair view of Norwich at the north, and New London at the south. It was built in 1831, at an expense of between six and seven hundred dollars, contributed for the purpose mostly by benevolent ladies in the cities of Norwich, Hartford and New London. This house is designed for the use of the Mohegans, and the white inhabitants who reside on the reservation. The Mohegan schoolhouse is 40 or 50 rods south of the chapel, at the foot of the hill, near by which is the house for the teacher. About 100 rods west of the chapel, on the summit of a commanding eminence, was situated a Mohegan fort, some traces of which remain; they also had another fort near the river.

"Lo! where a savage fortress frown'd
Amid yon blood-cemented ground,
A hallowed dome, with peaceful claim,
Shall bear the meek Redeemer's name;
And forms like those that lingering stayed
Latest 'neath Calvary's awful shade,
And earliest pierc'd the gather'd gloom
To watch the Savior's lowly tomb—
Such gentle forms the Indian's ire
Have sooth'd and bade that dome aspire.
And now, where rose the murderous yell,
The tuneful hymn to God shall swell—
Where vengeance spread a fatal snare,
Shall breathe the red man's contrite prayer."

Moose Rivers.

Moose river, in Maine, is a large tributary to Moosehead lake. It rises in the western part of Somerset county, and after receiving the waters of several large ponds in that quarter, it passes through Brassua lake, 4 or 5 miles W. of the Moosehead.

Moose river, in New Hampshire, has its source on the N. side of the White Mountains, and unites with the Androscoggin in Shelburne.—Its source is very near that of Israel's river, which passes W. into the Connecticut.

Moose river, in Vermont, is a branch of the Passumpsic; it rises in Granby and East Haven, and falls into that river at St. Johnsbury. This, in many places, is a rapid stream, about 25 miles in length.

Moose Head Lake, Me.

This lake, the outlet of which is the source of Kennebec river, lies in the county of Piscataquis. Its form is very irregular. Its length is between 40 and 50 miles, and its breadth, in the widest part, about 12 miles. The tributaries are numerous, and flow from almost every direction. It contains a number of islands, the largest of which is Sugar island, containing 5,440 acres, and Deer island, containing 2,000 acres. These islands are fertile, as is the whole country surrounding the lake, except in some places where the banks are high and precipitous. The waters are deep and abound in trout of an extraordinary size.

It is remarkable that the territory surrounding this inland sea, possessing in rich abundance all the necessary requirements for the uses and comforts of man, and within three hundred miles of the capital of New England, should be left a wilderness garden, uninhabited and almost unexplored; while thousands of New England men are pressing to distant regions, less healthful, and *less productive*, when markets for surplus produce are considered.

The only settlement, of any consequence, on the borders of this beautiful lake, is *Haskell's Plantation*, at the southern boundary.—

This place lies 15 miles N. from Monson, from which town stages pass to Bangor, 60 miles. A steamboat plies up and down the lake, for the purpose of transporting passengers, more particularly those who are engaged in felling timber; and for the purpose of towing the timber down to the Kennebec outlet.

The lumber business on this lake is very extensive, and doubtless lucrative; but the time is not very distant when this and other sections of Maine, will be as much valued for the fruits of the soil; and, under the wise system of geological exploration, adopted by the legislature, for the quarries of slate, lime, granite, marble, and even coal, as they are now for their forests of timber.

This lake may be divided into two bays. A little above the centre of it, is a narrow pass of rather less than a mile across. At this place, on the western side, is Mount Keneo, an elevation of five or six hundred feet projecting over the water. From this height a picturesque view of the lake, its islands, and a boundless wilderness, is presented. When the wind blows fresh from the north, the waters of the north bay press through this strait with considerable force, and cause the south bay to rise two or three feet.

A dam has been erected at the outlet, for the purpose of raising the lake 3 or 4 feet, so as to let the the water off as occasion may require, to facilitate the passage of lumber on the river. We hope, for the benefit of our friends down stream, that the dam is of solid materials and well constructed.

Moosehillock Mountain, N. H.,

Is a noble and lofty eminence in the S. E. part of Coventry, and ranks among the highest mountains in New England. The altitude of the north peak above tide water, is 4,636 feet—that of the south peak, is 4,536 feet. Baker's river has its source on its eastern side.

Moosoluckmaguntic Lake, Me.

A large sheet of water which empties into the Molechunkamunk, about 2 miles south.

Moretown, Vt.

Washington co. Mad river, a branch of the Onion, waters this town and gives it good mill seats. The surface is mountainous, and a great part of the soil unfit for cultivation. First settled, 1790. Population, 1830, 816. It lies 8 miles S. W. from Montpelier.

Morgan, Vt.

Orleans co. First settled, 1800. It lies 50 miles N. E. from Montpelier, and 15 N. N. E. from Irasburgh. Population, 1830, 331. Knowlton's lake, a handsome sheet of water, containing a variety of fish, lies in this town. It is 4 miles in length, and 2 in breadth, and empties into Clyde river.

Morristown, Vt.

Lamoille co. This town lies 20 miles N. by W. from Montpelier, and 6 S. from Hyde Park. First settled, 1790. Population, 1830, 1,315. The surface of the town is diversified by hills and valleys; the soil is good, particularly on the banks of Lamoille river, which affords some water power. Here is a neat village, and considerable business. The people are generally farmers, and produce cattle, butter, cheese, and a large quantity of wool for market.

Moscow, Me.

Somerset co. Moscow is watered by a pond, and by a beautiful stream, a branch of the Kennebec, and lies on the east side of that river. It is 30 miles N. from Norridgewock, and 58 N. from Augusta. This town has a good soil and a pleasant village. It was incorporated in 1816. Population, 1837, 477. Wheat crop, same year, 4,273 bushels.

Moultonborough, N. H.,

Strafford co., is situated on the N. W. shore of Winnepisiogee lake. This interesting town lies 45 miles N. from Concord, and 20 E. from Plymouth. This town is broken by mountains and ponds. Red Hill, lying wholly within this town, commands notice from the east, south, and west; and extends about 3 miles from E. to W., between Red Hill river on the N., Great Squam on the W., Great Squam and Long pond on the S., terminating S. E. by a neck of fine land extending into the Winnepisiogee. Its summit is covered with the *uvæ ursi* and low blueberry bush, which in autumn give the hill a reddish hue, from which circumstance its name was probably derived. A number of oval bluffs rise on its summit, from each of which the prospect on either hand is extensive and delightful. The north bluff is supposed to consist of a body of iron ore. Bog ore is found in a brook descending from this bluff. Ossipee mountain extends its base into this town, and is a commanding elevation. On the south part of this mountain, in Moultonborough, is a mineral chalybeate spring, the waters strongly impregnated with iron and sulphur. and efficacious in cutaneous eruptions. About a mile north is a spring of pure cold water, 16 feet in diameter, through the centre of which the water, containing a small portion of fine white sand, is constantly thrown up to the height of two feet—the spring furnishing water sufficient for mills. On the stream nearly a mile below, is a beautiful waterfall of 70 feet perpendicular. Descending on the left of this fall, a cave is found, containing charcoal and other evidences of its having been a hiding place for the Indians. Red Hill river originates in Sandwich, and passes through this town into the Winnepisiogee. Long pond is a beautiful sheet of water, and connects with the lake by a channel sixty rods in length. Squam and Winnepisiogee lakes lie partly in Moultonborough. The soil of this town is fruitful, though in some parts rocky. Moultonborough was granted in 1763, to Col. Jonathan Moulton and others. Settlements commenced in 1764.

Many Indian implements and relics have been found indicating this to have been once their favorite residence. In 1820, on a small island in the Winnepisiogee, was found a curious gun barrel, much worn by age and rust, divested of its stock, enclosed in the body of a pitch pine tree 16 inches in diameter. Its butt rested on a flat rock, its muzzle elevated about 30°. In 1819, a small dirk, 1 1-2 feet in length from the point to the end of the hilt, round blade, was found in a new field, one foot under ground, bearing strong marks of antiquity.

On the line of Tuftonborough, on the shore of the lake, at the mouth of Melvin river, a gigantic skeleton was found about 30 years since, buried in a sandy soil, apparently that of a man more than seven feet high —the jaw bones easily passing over the face of a large man. A tumulus has been discovered on a piece of newly cleared land, of the length and appearance of a human grave, and handsomely rounded with small stones, not found in this part of the country; which stones are too closely placed to be separated by striking an ordinary blow with a crow-bar, and bear marks of being a composition. The Ossipee tribe of Indians once resided in this vicinity, and some years since a tree was standing in Moultonborough, on which was carved in hieroglyphics the history of their expeditions. Population, 1830, 1,422.

Mount Desert, Me.

Hancock co. This town comprised the whole island of the same name, lying between Frenchman's bay and the waters of Blue Hill bay, and Union river, until 1795, when the north part was set off and called Eden. It lies 110 miles E. from Augusta. Incorporated, 1789. Population, 1837, 1,783.

This town has an extensive coast, and a number of excellent harbors. The people of Mount Desert own considerable navigation employed in the coasting trade; and the shore fishery, is a lucrative branch of business. The soil of the town is good, and abundantly able to supply the inhabitants with bread stuffs. In 1837, the ocean towns of Mount Desert and Eden, produced 674 bushels of good wheat. We mention this fact, to show that there must be something, other than sea air, which causes that valuable grain to blight on the coast of Massachusetts.

Mount Holly, Vt.

Rutland co. A pleasant town lying 60 miles S. from Montpelier, and 17 S. E. from Rutland. First settled, 1781. Population, 1830, 1,318. The surface of the town is elevated, and in some parts mountainous, but the soil is well adapted for grazing, and produces considerable quantities of wool, beef, butter, and cheese.

Mounts Holyoke & Tom, Mass.

See *Northampton*.

Mount Hope,

And MOUNT HOPE BAY. See *Bristol, R. I.*

Mount Tabor, Vt.

Rutland co. Otter Creek rises in this town, by a branch on each side of a mountain. Most of the land is unfit for cultivation, it being so high on the Green mountain range. It lies 66 miles S. by W. from Montpelier, and 19 S. by E. from Rutland. Population, 1830, 210.

Mount Vernon, Me.

Kennebec co. This town lies W. of Belgrade, E. of Vienna, and 15 miles N. W. from Augusta. Incorporated, 1792. Population, 1837, 1,503. There are three pleasant villages in the town: the soil is remarkably good, and is watered by a number of beautiful ponds and small streams. Wheat crop, 1837, 5,888 bushels.

Mount Vernon, N. H.,

Hillsborough co., is 3 miles N. W. from Amherst, and 28 S. W. from Concord. There is but one stream of any note, and this was called by the Indians *Quohquinapassakessananagnog*. The situation is elevated, and towards the E. and S E. there is a considerable prospect. There is a flourishing village situated near the highest point of elevation. This town was originally a part of Amherst, from which it was detached in 1803.

Dr. DANIEL ADAMS, who commenced and conducted the Medical and Agricultural Register, and is author of a popular system of arithmetic, school geography, and a number of useful school books, has his residence in this place. Population, 1830, 763.

Mount Washington, Mass.

Berkshire co. This town lies in the S. W. corner of the state, bordering on Ct. and N. Y. It is 135 miles W. by S. from Boston, 22 S. W. from Lenox, and 26 S. E. from Hudson, N. Y. Incorporated, 1779. Population, 1837, 337.

These people seem to enjoy a more elevated situation than any of their neighbors: one of their *hills* is 3,150 feet above the sea. They keep 600 sheep, and manufacture about 100,000 bushels of charcoal, annually. A mountain stream affords them a water power for an axe factory and forge. These people, likewise, appear to be more independent of the common wants of mankind than other folks; for they have no minister, physician, lawyer, post office, or tavern, yet they are remarkably healthy; and as far as we can judge, intelligent and kind.

Muscongus River and Bay, Me.

Lincoln co. *Muscongus river*, rises in large ponds in the interior of the county, and on the border of Waldo county: it passes through Waldoborough, and separating Bremen and Friendship, it forms the head waters of *Muscongus bay*.— This bay has a number of islands and lies between St. George's islands off the town of St. George, on the E., and Pemmaquid point, in Bremen, on the W.

Nahant, Mass.

This celebrated watering place, is a part of the beautiful town of Lynn. It is a peninsula, jutting out about 5 miles into Massachusetts bay, and forms Lynn bay on the south. From Boston to Nahant hotel, on the eastern point of the peninsula, by land, is 14 miles; from the centre of Lynn, 5; and from Salem 9 miles. On the N. E. side of this peninsula is a beach of great length and smoothness. It is so hard that a horse's foot-steps are scarcely visible; and, from half-tide to low water, it affords a ride of superior excellence. Much may be said in praise of Nahant without exaggeration. Its formation, situation, and rugged shore, excites the curiosity of all, and many thousands annually visit it for health, or pleasure.

It is only 10 miles N. E. from Boston, by the steam-boats, continually plying in summer months: at this place are good fishing and fowling, excellent accommodations: the ocean scenery is exceedingly beautiful in fair weather, and truly sublime in a storm.

Nantasket, Mass.

See *Hull*.

Nantucket Co. Mass. and Town.

An island in the Atlantic ocean— town and county. It lies E. of Dukes county, and about 30 miles S. of Cape Cod, or Barnstable county. This island is about 15 miles in length, from east to west, and about 4 miles average breadth. It contains 50 square miles. The town, formerly called *Shelburne*, is in about the centre of the island, on the north side, in lat. 41° 16′ 42″, W. lon., 70° 7′ 42″. It is 100 miles S. E. by S. from Boston, 55 S. E. from New Bedford, 30 S. E. from Falmouth, and 500 from Washington. Population, 1837, 9,048.

Nantucket has a good harbor, with 7 1-2 feet of water, at low tide, on the bar at its mouth. This island was formerly well wooded, but for many years it has not had a single tree of natural growth. The soil is light and sandy; it however affords pasturage for about 7,000 sheep, 500 cows, and other cattle. In 1659, when this county was incorporated, the island contained 3,000 Indians, but now, not one.

The whale fishery commenced here in 1690; and this place is, perhaps, more celebrated than any other, for the enterprize and success of its people, in that species of nautical adventure. Indeed Nantucket is the mother of that great branch of wealth in America, if not in the world. In the year ending April 1, 1837, Nantucket employed 74 vessels in that fishery, the tonnage of which was 25,875 tons 1,277,009 gallons of sperm and whale oil was imported, the value of which was $1,114,012. The number of hands employed, was 1,897. The capital invested, was $2,520,000; this includes the ships and outfits only; yet many of the manufactories of the place, are appendages of the whale fishery; altogether, employing a capital of over five millions of dollars. There are manufactures on the island, of vessels, whale boats, bar iron, tin ware, boots, shoes, oil casks, and candle boxes. The whole amount of the manufactures, for that year, including oil and candles, was $2,524,907. Total tonnage of the district of Nantucket, in 1837, 29,960 tons.

Great attention is paid to education on this island. The men are noted for their sedateness and daring spirit, and the women for their intelligence and beauty. *Nantucket Shoals* is a dangerous place, where many a sailor has found a watery grave. They lie S. E. from the island, and cover an area of about 50 by 45 miles.

Naples, Me.

Cumberland co. This town was formed from Otisfield and Raymond, and incorporated in 1834. It is watered by Sebago and Songo ponds, and Crooked and Muddy rivers. It has good mill privileges, and a productive soil. Population, 1837, 722. Naples lies 63 miles W. S. W. from Augusta, and 27 N. N. W. from Portland.

Narraganset Bay, R. I.

This delightful bay lies wholly within the limits of Rhode Island: its entrance extends from Point Judith on the west, to Seaconnet Rocks on the east, and terminates at Bullock's point, about 6 miles below the city of Providence. The length of this bay is about 28 miles: its breadth varies from 3 to 12 miles. It receives the waters of the Taunton, Providence, Pawtuxet, and other rivers, and on its borders are Newport, Bristol, Warren, and other large and flourishing towns. It is decked with many islands of great fertility and beauty; the principal of which are Connanicut, Prudence, Patience, Block and Hope. This bay is near the ocean; is accessible at all seasons; is well protected by powerful forts, and affords some of the best harbors in the world. The board of naval commissioners have recently reported to Congress that the waters of Narraganset Bay afford greater advantages for a naval depot, than any other unoccupied position on the coast of the United States.

Narraguagus River & Bay, Me.

Washington co. The *river* rises in several ponds in Beddington, and passing in a southeastern direction, falls into a bay of the same name, between Harrington and Steuben. The *bay* contains a number of islands, between which is a good passage into Pleasant bay, on the east side.

Nashawn Island, Mass.,

And NASHAWENNA. See *Elizabeth Islands*.

Nashua River,

A beautiful stream on the S. part of Hillsborough co. N.H. has its source in Worcester county, Massachusetts. It is formed of two branches called the north and south branches. The north branch is formed of two streams, one from Ashburnham, the other from Wachuset ponds. The south branch is composed of Still river, issuing from the E. side of Wachuset mountain, and a small stream from Quinepoxet pond in Holden. These branches are united in Lancaster, from which the main river proceeds in a N. E. course to Harvard, Shirley, Groton, and Pepperell in Massachusetts; and from thence into New Hampshire through Hollis, and nearly the centre of the town of Nashua, where it falls into the Merrimack river.

Nashua, N. H.

Hillsborough co. This town originally embraced a large extent of territory, and was called Dunstable until 1836. It lies 34 miles S. by E. from Concord, 12 S. E. from Amherst, and 12 N. W. from Lowell. The population of Dunstable, in 1830, was 2,414. Population of Nashua, in 1836, 5,065; 1837, 5,613; 1838, 5,691.

In the N. E. part of the town, on Nashua river, is the flourishing *Village of Nashua*, the centre of a considerable trade, and the seat of important manufactures. This village contains 8 beautiful churches, a large number of elegant dwelling-houses, 50 stores, and 10 taverns.

The *Nashua Manufacturing Company* was incorporated in 1823. It has three cotton mills, 155 feet in length, 45 in breadth and six stories in height. They contain 22,000 spindles, 710 looms, and manufacture 9,390,000 yards of cloth per annum. Their canal is 3 miles long, 60 feet wide, and 8 feet deep. Head and fall, 33 feet. Capital, $750,000.

The *Jackson Manufacturing Company* was incorporated in 1824. Capital, $600,000. They have two cotton mills, 155 feet long, 47 wide, and 4 stories high. These mills contain 11,500 spindles, and 388 looms. They manufacture 5,634,-000, yards of cloth annually. Their canal is half a mile in length, and serves for transportation on the river. Head and fall, 20 feet.

The volume of water afforded by the Nashua river, at the *dryest* season of the year, is 180 cubic feet per second.

The number of operatives in all the mills at Nashua is 1,448:—females, 1,288; males, 160. The number of pounds of cotton used is 14,500 per day, or 4,533,500 lbs. per annum.

There are other valuable manufactures on Nashua river and the waters of Salmon brook.

The Nashua and Lowell railroad was opened for travel on the 8th of October, 1838.

The soil of Nashua has considerable variety. It is easy of cultivation, and is generally productive. The east part of the town, lying on the river, presents a very level surface. The west parts are divided into hills and valleys, but the whole township may be considered far from being hilly or mountainous. It is watered by the Nashua river, a fertilizing stream, which rises in the state of Massachusetts, and Salmon brook, a small stream which originates from several ponds in Groton. Both of these empty into Merrimack river, the former at Nashua village, the latter about one and a half mile below.

This was for a long time a frontier town, and the first settlers were many times annoyed by the Indians, in the successive wars in which this country was engaged with them. In the war with the famous Narraganset sachem, this town was much exposed, and some of the inhabitants fled to the older settlements. In Lovewell's war, the company in this town under the brave Capt. John Lovewell, acquired an imperishable name. Their successes at first, and misfortunes afterwards, have been often repeated and are generally known.

Dunstable belonged to Massachusetts till the divisional line between the two provinces of Massachusetts and New Hampshire was settled, in 1741. It was incorporated by New Hampshire, April 1, 1746, and the name was altered to Nashua in December, 1836.

Natchaug River, Ct.

This is the largest branch of the Shetucket. It rises in Union and Woodstock, and joins the Shetucket near the line of Chaplin and Mansfield.

Natick, Mass.

Middlesex co. Natick is a pleasant town, of good soil: it is watered by Charles river, and contains several delightful ponds, well stored with fish. This was a favorite resort of the Indians. There are some moderate elevations in the town: the Indians used to call it "the place of hills."

Under the advice and direction of the apostle Elliot, the first Indian church in New England was formed here in 1660, and comprised 40 communicants.

The manufactures of the town consist principally of shoes. During the year ending April 1, 1837, 250,650 pairs were made, valued at $213,053: employing 452 hands. This town was incorporated in 1781. Population, 1830, 890; 1837, 1,221. It lies 16 miles W. S. W. from Boston, and 12 S. from Concord.

Naugatuck River, Ct.

This important mill stream is about 50 miles in length. It rises in the north part of Litchfield county, and after traversing a S. course nearly the whole length of that county, it crosses the west part of New Haven county, and falls into the Housatonick at Derby.

Neal's Brook and Pond, Vt.

Neal's brook, or branch, rises in Lunenburgh and the border of Guildhall, and running south falls into a pond of the same name. It continues its course south and meets the Connecticut. This is a short stream, but valuable on account of its water power.

Neal's pond, a mile in length, and a half mile in width, is a handsome sheet of water, and contains a variety of fish.

Needham, Mass.

Norfolk co. This town is nearly surrounded by the waters of Charles river. It contains numerous valuable mill seats. There are in the town 6 paper mills, a cotton factory, and manufactures of shoes, hats, and window blind hinges:—annual value, about $150,000. Incorporated, 1711. Population, 1837, 1,492. Needham lies 4 miles N. W. from Dedham, and 12 W. S. W. from Boston, by the Boston and Worcester rail-road.

Neddock, Cape, Me.

A rocky, barren bluff, inhabited by a few fishermen, about 3 miles N. from York harbor.

Nelson, N. H.,

Cheshire co., is situated on the height of land between Connecticut and Merrimack rivers. The surface is hilly, but good for grazing. In the S. part, a branch of the Ashuelot river rises; and from Long pond in this town, and Hancock, issues a branch of Contoocook river. The best mill privileges are furnished by streams issuing from ponds in this town, of which there are four, containing a surface of 1,800 acres. There is a cotton and other manufactories. The inhabitants are principally farmers of industrious habits. It was chartered Feb. 22, 1774, by the name of *Packersfield*. In June, 1814, the name was altered to Nelson. The first settlements commenced in 1767. Nelson lies 40 miles S. W. from Concord, and 8 N. E. from Keene. Population, 1830, 875.

Neponset River, Mass.

Norfolk co. The sources of this river are in Canton, Stoughton, and Sharon. It receives a tributary from Charles river, Mother brook, so called, and meets the tide of Boston harbor at Milton Mills, 4 miles from Dorchester bay. This is a noble mill stream: on its navigable waters is the depository of the Quincy granite rail-road company, and at its mouth is Commercial Point, in Dorchester, a beautiful place, with an excellent harbor.

Newaggen, Cape, Me.

This cape is a part of the town of Boothbay. It extends about 5 miles into the sea, and forms the eastern boundary of Sheepscot's bay.

Newark, Vt.

Caledonia co. The Passumpsic river is formed in this town by a collection of streams issuing principally from ponds. The town is not mountainous, but the soil is cold and generally unproductive. It lies 44 miles N. E. from Montpelier, and 19 N. W. from Guildhall. First settled, 1800. Population, in 1830, 257.

New Ashford, Mass.

Berkshire co. This is a mountainous township, but the soil is good for grazing. In 1837, the value of 2,708 fleeces of wool, produced in this town, weighing 7,785 pounds, was worth $3,893. New Ashford produces fine white and variegated marble, and is the source of Green river. It lies 130 miles W. by N. from Boston, and 18 N. from Lenox. Incorporated, 1801. Population, 1837, 253.

New Bedford, Mass.

This is a half shire town of Bristol county, and port of entry, pleasantly situated on the W. side of the Acushnet, a river, or more properly an estuary, connected with Buzzard's bay. The ground on which the town stands rises rapidly from the river, and affords an interesting view from the opposite side.

The upper part of the town is laid out into beautiful streets, which contain many costly and superb dwellings.

This harbor, though not easy of access, is capacious and well secured from winds. A wooden bridge, near the centre of the town, connects it with the village of Fairhaven. A ferry has also been established, on which it is proposed to run a steam boat.

New Bedford was incorporated in 1787, previous to which it constituted a part of the town of Dartmouth. In 1812, the eastern part was set off as a separate township by the name of Fairhaven.

The almost exclusive business of the place is the whale fishery, which commenced before the war of the revolution, and has gradually grown to its present importance. The increase, however, within the last 12 years has been more rapid than during any former period.— The number of ships and brigs now employed is 169. Tonnage of the district, in 1837, 85,130 tons.

There are 16 oil manufactories, at which a large amount of oil and candles is made. A considerable quantity of the oil imported is, however, sold in the crude state to other places.

The manufactures of the town consist of leather, boots, shoes, hats, iron castings, axes, chairs, tin and cabinet wares, vessels, salt, cordage, soap, Prussian blue, paper hangings, carriages, looking-glass frames, and carpenter's tools: the total value, for the year ending April 1, 1837, including oil and candles, amounted to $690,800. There were imported, during that year, 2,472,735 gallons of oil, and 305,170 pounds of whale bone, the value of which was $1,750,832. The capital invested in the whale fishery was $4,210,000. The number of hands employed was 4,000.

Few places in Massachusetts have increased in population more rapidly than this. By the census of 1790, the population of the village was about 700. In 1830, the township contained 7,592; in 1833, 9,200, and in 1837, 14,304.

Within a few years, the inhabitants of this town have manifested a commendable liberality in providing the means of education. There is a flourishing academy in the town, and large sums are annually appropriated for the maintenance of public and private schools.

A rail-road will soon be constructed from this place, to meet the Boston and Providence, at Seekonk, by the way of Fall River; or to meet the Taunton rail-road at Taunton. By either of those routes, a trip to Boston or New York, would be very pleasant. A large and wealthy town, highly flourishing in its commerce and manufactures like this, with the neighboring islands of Nantucket and Martha's Vineyard, seem to require it.

New Bedford lies 52 miles S. from Boston, 52 N. W. from Nantucket, 14 E. by S. from Fall River, 20 S. S. E. from Taunton, and 214 N. E. by E. from New York.

New Boston, N. H.,

Hillsborough co., is 9 miles N. N. W. from Amherst, and 22 S. by W. from Concord. It is watered by several streams, the largest of which is the S. branch of Piscataquog river, having its source in Pleasant pond, in Francestown.—This town consists of fertile hills, productive vales, and some valuable meadows. The soil is favorable for all the various productions common to this section of the state, and there are many excellent farms, under good cultivation. In the S. part of New Boston, there is a considerable elevation, called Jo English hill, on one side of which it is nearly perpendicular. Its height is 572 feet. Beard's pond, and Jo English pond, are the only ponds of note. New Boston was granted, 1736, to inhabitants of Boston. It was incorporated, 1763. The first settlement commenced about the year 1733. The first minister was Rev. Solomon Moor, from Ireland, who received his education at Glasgow. In Feb. 1767, he arrived at New Boston, and was ordained Sept. 6, 1768; died May 28, 1803, aged 67. Population, 1830, 1,680.

New Braintree, Mass.

Worcester co. Ware river and other streams water this town, and afford it good mill privileges. The soil of the town is good, particularly for grazing: it has become celebrated for its good farmers, and for its excellent beef cattle, butter and cheese. There is a cotton mill in the town, and manufactures of leather, palm-leaf hats, &c. It lies 60 miles W. from Boston, and 18 W. N. W. from Worcester. Incorporated, 1751. Population, 1837, 780.

Newburgh, Me.

Penobscot co. This is a good township of land, 54 miles N. E. from Augusta, and 14 S. W. from Bangor. Incorporated, 1819. Population, 1830, 626; 1837, 867. Watered by a branch of the Sowadabscook. Wheat crop, 1837, 5,041 bushels.

Newbury, N. H.

Merrimack co. This town was originally called *Dantzick;* it was incorporated by the name of Fishersfield, in 1778, and took its present name, in 1837. It lies 40 miles N. W. by W. from Amherst, and 30 W. by N. from Concord. The S. part of Sunapee lake lies in the N. W. part. Todd pond, 500 rods in length, and 60 in width, affords a small branch to Warner river.—From Chalk pond issues a small stream communicating with Sunapee lake. The land is generally mountainous, and the soil hard and rocky. The first settlement in this town was made in the year 1762, by Zephaniah Clark, Esq. Population, 1830, 798.

Newbury, Vt.

Orange co. This is a beautiful town on the W. side of Connecticut river, and supplied with mill privileges by Wells river, and

Hariman's and Hill's brooks. These brooks have their sources in ponds of considerable size. Newbury comprises the tract commonly called the Great Oxbow, on a bend in Connecticut river. This tract is of great extent, and celebrated for its luxuriance and beauty. The agricultural productions of the town are very valuable, consisting of beef cattle, wool, and all the varieties of the dairy. The town contains a number of mineral springs, of some celebrity in scrofulous and cutaneous complaints.

The villages of *Newbury and Wells River* are very pleasant : they command a flourishing trade, and contain manufacturing establishments of various kinds. Some of the buildings are very handsome. The scenery of the windings of the river through this fine tract of alluvial meadow, contrasted with the abrupt acclivities in the north part of the town, is very striking and beautiful.

The town is connected with Haverhill, N. H., by two bridges. It lies 27 miles S. E. from Montpelier, and 20 N. E. from Chelsea. Population, 1830, 2,252. First settled, 1764. The first settlers endured many hardships. For some years they had to go to Charlestown to mill, 60 miles distant, carrying their grain in canoes down the river, or drawing it on the ice.

General BAILEY, a patriot of the revolution, distinguished himself in the settlement of the town.

The state legislature held their sessions in Newbury, in the years 1787, and 1801.

Newbury, Mass.

Essex co. This ancient and respectable town, lies on Merrimack river, opposite to Salisbury. It formerly comprised the territory of Newburyport and West Newbury. The soil is of an excellent quality, and in a high state of cultivation. Parker and Artichoke rivers are pleasant streams ; the former falls nearly 50 feet in the town, and affords it good mill seats. A part of Plum island, is attached to this town. This island, about nine miles in length and one in breadth, extending from Ipswich river to the mouth of the Merrimack, is comprised of sandy beach and salt meadow ; and is noted for the beach plum, which ripens in September.

A curious cavern, called the " Devil's Den," contains specimens of asbestos, limestone, marble, serpentine and amianthos. The scenery on the high grounds is rich, variegated and beautiful.

Dummer academy, founded in 1756, is a flourishing institution : it is situated in the parish of " Byfield."

The manufactures of Newbury consist of cotton goods, leather, boots, shoes, carriages, cordage, fishing nets, bed cords and cotton lines: annual value about $75,000. A large number of vessels are built in the town, and some navigation is owned and employed in the coasting trade and fishery.

This town is celebrated as the birth place of many distinguished men. THEOPHILUS PARSONS, LL. D., an eminent jurist, was born in Newbury, February 24, 1750. He died in Boston, October 6, 1813.

Newbury was first settled, in 1635. Its Indian name was *Quafcacunquen*. It lies 31 miles N. by E. from Boston, 17 N. from Salem, and 3 S. from Newburyport. Population, 1837, 3,771.

Newburyport, Mass.

One of the shire towns of Essex county. This is considered one of the most beautiful towns in New England. It lies on a gentle acclivity, on the south bank of the Merrimack, at the union of that river with the ocean. In point of territory, it is the smallest town in the commonwealth, being only one mile square. It was taken from Newbury in 1764. Population, in 1837, 6,741. This place has been and now is considerably noted for its commerce and ship building. Some of the old continental frigates were built here; and in 1790, the tonnage of the port was 11,870 tons. Of late years the foreign commerce of the place has diminished, in consequence of a sand bar at the mouth of the harbor. This place has considerable inland and foreign commerce. It has four whale ships, and a large amount of tonnage engaged in the freighting business and the cod and mackerel fisheries. Tonnage of the district, in 1837, 22,078 tons.

The manufactures of Newburyport consist of cotton goods, boots, shoes, hats, bar iron, iron castings, chairs, cabinet and tin wares, combs, spirits, vessels, snuff, segars, organs, soap and candles: annual amount about $350,000. The product of the whale fishery, the year ending April 1, 1837, was $142,982. During the same period, this town and Newbury had 128 vessels employed in the cod and mackerel fishery, employing 1,000 hands: product that year, $177,700.

Newburyport lies 34 miles N. by E. from Boston, 20 N. from Salem, 24 S. by W. from Portsmouth, N. H., and 2 miles S. E. from Essex bridge. Lat. 42° 47′ N.; lon. 70° 47′ W. From the mouth of this harbor, Plum Island, extends to the mouth of Ipswich river.

The Hon. WILLIAM BARTLETT and MOSES BROWN, ESQ., distinguished for their enterprise and integrity as merchants, were natives of this town.

The celebrated GEORGE WHITEFIELD, one of the founders of the sect of the Methodists, and one of its most eloquent preachers, died in this town, Sept. 21, 1770.

A handsome monument has been erected to his memory, by the Hon. WILLIAM BARTLETT, the following is a part of the inscription:

This Cenotaph
Is erected, with affectionate
veneration, to
The memory of the
Rev. GEORGE WHITEFIELD:
Born at Gloucester, England,
December 16, 1714.
Educated at Oxford University;
Ordained 1736.
In a ministry of thirty-four years,
He crossed the Atlantic thirteen times,
And preached more
Than eighteen thousand sermons.
As a Soldier of the
Cross, humble, devout, ardent,
He put on the
Whole armor of God; Preferring
The honour of Christ
To his own interest, repose,
Reputation, and life.

New Canaan, Ct.

Fairfield co. This town was taken from Norwalk and Stamford in 1801. It lies 5 miles N. W. from Norwalk, 37 W. S. W. from New Haven, and 50 N. E. from New York. Population, 1830, 1,826.— The surface of the town is rough and mountainous; the soil is a hard, gravelly loam, but generally productive. The manufacture of shoes is carried on to a considerable extent: the annual value is about $400,000.

An academy was established here in 1815, and has acquired a high reputation. It stands on an elevated and commanding situation, having a fine prospect of Long Island Sound and the intervening country. Pestles and other Indian implements have been found at the north part of the town, which probably was the resort of the natives. Excavations in solid rock, one large enough to contain eight gallons, are found: these were doubtless Indian mortars.

New Castle, Me.

Lincoln co. New Castle lies on the W. side of Damariscotta river, about 15 miles from its mouth. It is 36 miles S. E. from Augusta, and 8 N. E. from Wiscasset. Incorporated, 1753. Population, in 1837, 1,545. This is a pleasant town, and flourishing in its trade and navigation.

New Castle, N. H.,

Rockingham co., is a rough and rocky island, situated in Portsmouth harbor, and formerly called *Great Island*. A handsome bridge, built in 1821, connects this town with Portsmouth. Here is an ancient church. Rev. Samuel Moody preached here previous to the commencement of the 18th century. New Castle was incorporated in 1693, and contains 458 acres. This island was the seat of business, when ancient *Strawberry Bank* was the mere germ of the town of Portsmouth. Fishing is here pursued with success; and the soil among the rocks, being of good quality, is made to produce abundantly. Fort Constitution and the light-house stand on this island.— Population, 1830, 850.

New Fairfield, Ct.

Fairfield co. This is a small township, rough and hilly, with a hard and gravelly soil. It lies 64 miles S. W. from Hartford, and 7 N. from Danbury. Incorporated, in 1740. Population, 1830, 940.

New Durham, N. H.

Strafford co. The surface of this town is very uneven, a portion so rocky as to be unfit for cultivation. The soil is generally moist, and well adapted to grazing. There are 5 ponds in New Durham, the largest of which is Merrymeeting pond, about 10 miles in circumference, from which a copious and perpetual stream runs into Merrymeeting bay, in Alton. Ela's river flows from Coldrain pond into Farmington, on which is a fine waterfall. The Cocheco also has its source here. Mount Betty, Cropple-crown and Straw's mountains are the principal eminences. On the N. E. side of the latter is a remarkable cave, the entrance of which is about 3 feet wide and 10 feet high. The outer room is 20 feet square; the inner apartments become smaller, until at the distance of 50 feet they are too small to be investigated.— The sides, both of the galleries and the rooms are solid granite. They bear marks of having been once united, and were probably separated by some great convulsion of nature.

There is a fountain, over which a part of Ela's river passes, which is regarded as a curiosity. By sinking a small mouthed vessel into this fountain, water may be procured extremely cold and pure. Its depth has not been ascertained. Near the centre of the town is Rattlesnake hill, the S. side of which is almost 100 feet high, and nearly perpendicular. Several other hills in this town contain precipices and cavities, some of considerable extent. New Durham was granted in 1749. It was incorporated Dec. 7, 1762.

Elder BENJAMIN RANDALL, the founder of the sect of Freewill Baptists, commenced his labors here in 1780, and organized a church. He died in 1808, aged 60.

New Durham lies 30 miles N. E. from Concord, and 32 N. W. by N. from Dover. Population, in 1830, 1,162.

Newfane, Vt.

Windham co. County town.— Newfane lies about 100 miles S. from Montpelier, and 12 N. W. from Brattleborough. First settled, 1766. The town is watered by a branch of West river, and several other streams. The surface of the town is diversified by hills and valleys; the soil is good, and produces white oak and walnut in abundance. There is but little waste land in the town: the uplands are inferior to none for grazing, and the intervales afford excellent tillage. Newfane exhibits a great variety of minerals, among which are some of value. Perhaps no town in the state presents a more inviting field for the mineralogist than this.

There are two pleasant villages in the town. The centre village contains the county buildings: it is on elevated land, and commands a very extensive and delightful prospect. Population, 1830, 1,441.

Newfound Pond and River, N.H.
See *Bristol*.

Newfield, Me.

York co. This town is watered by Little Ossipee river, and lies 99 miles S. W. by W. from Augusta, and 15 N. W. from Alfred. It is a good farming town and produces considerable wheat and wool. It was incorporated in 1794. Population, 1837, 1,322.

New Gloucester, Me.

Cumberland co. This is a pleasant and flourishing farming town, 23 miles N. from Portland, and 38 S. W. from Augusta. Incorporated, 1774. Population, 1837, 1,861. It is well watered by Royal's river, on which are mills of various kinds. The soil of the town is very fertile, containing large tracts of intervale. The first settlers were compelled to build a block house for their protection against the Indians. In this building the people attended public worship for a number of years. This town has an abundant water power, a school fund of $4,000, and a society of about 300 of those neat and industrious people, "whose faith is one and whose practice is one." See *Canterbury, N. H.*

NEW HAMPSHIRE.

This state is bounded north by Lower Canada, east by Maine, southeast by the Atlantic and the State of Massachusetts, south by Massachusetts, and west and north-west by Vermont. Situated between 42° 40′ and 45° 16′ N. lat., and 72° 27′ and 70° 35′ W. lon. Its length is 168, and its greatest breadth about 90 miles, and it comprises an area of about 9,280 square miles.

The first discovery of New Hampshire was in 1614, and the first settlements made by Europeans were at Dover and Portsmouth, in 1623, only three years after the landing of the Pilgrims at Plymouth. The next settlements were at Exeter and Hampton, in 1638. The inhabitants of these and all the early settlements, until after the cession of Canada to England by France, were greatly annoyed by the Indians, who existed in large and powerful bodies in this then wilderness. In the repeated and general wars with the Indians, New Hampshire suffered more than any other of the colonies. This colony was twice united with that of Massachusetts, and the final separation did not take place until 1741, when the boundaries of the two colonies were settled. In the revolutionary contest, New Hampshire bore a distinguished and honorable part. The blood of her sons was freely shed on most of the battle fields of the revolution. As early as June 15, 1776, New Hampshire made a public DECLARATION OF INDEPENDENCE, and in December of that year, the delegates of the people adopted a temporary form of Government, which was continued until 1784, when the first constitution was adopted. This being found deficient in some of its provisions, a new constitution was adopted in 1792, which is now in force.

The executive power is vested in a Governor and five Counsellors, chosen annually by the people. The legislature consists of the Senate, comprising twelve members, chosen in twelve districts, and the House of Representatives, chosen annually in the month of March, every town having 150 rateable polls being entitled to send one, and an additional representative for every 300 additional polls. The legislature assembles annually at Concord, on the first Wednesday of June.

All male citizens, of 21 years and upwards, except paupers and persons excused from taxes, have a right to vote for state officers—a residence of at least three months within the town being required to entitle the person to vote.

The judiciary power is vested in a Superior Court of Judicature, and Courts of Common Pleas. The four Judges of the Superior Court, hold law terms once a year in each of the counties; and Judges of the Superior Court are *ex officio* Presiding Judges in the courts of Common Pleas, holden semi-annually in each county, by one of the Superior Judges with the two Associate Justices of the Common Pleas for each county. The Judges hold their offices during good behavior, until 70 years of age; but are subject to removal by impeachment, or by address of the two houses of the legislature.

Succession of Governors.

Meshech Weare,* 1776—1784. John Langdon, 1785. John Sullivan, 1786, 1787. John Langdon, 1788. John Sullivan, 1789. Josiah Bartlett, 1790—1793. John Taylor Gilman, 1794—1804. John Langdon, 1805—1808. Jeremiah Smith, 1809. John Langdon, 1810, 1811. William Plumer, 1812. John Taylor Gilman, 1813—1815. William Plumer, 1816—1818. Samuel Bell, 1819—1822. Levi Woodbury, 1823.— David Lawrence Morril, 1824—1826. Benjamin Pierce, 1827. John Bell, 1828. Benjamin Pierce, 1829. Matthew Harvey, 1830. Samuel Dinsmoor, 1831—1833. William Badger, 1834, 1835. Isaac Hill, 1836 —1838. John Page, 1839—

Succession of Chief Justices of the Superior Court.

Meshech Weare, 1776—1781. Samuel Livermore, 1782—1789. Josiah Bartlett, 1790. John Pickering, 1791—1794. Simeon Olcott, 1795 —1801. Jeremiah Smith, 1802—1808. Arthur Livermore, 1809—1812.

---

* The Chief Magistrates were styled *President*, until the adoption of the Constitution of 1792, when the title of Governor was substituted.

NEW ENGLAND GAZETTEER.

Jeremiah Smith, 1813—1815. William Merchant Richardson, 1816—1837. Joel Parker, 1838—

New Hampshire is divided into eight counties, as follows:—

Counties.	No. of towns.	Population in 1830.	Shire Towns.
Rockingham,	35	44,552	Portsmouth, Exeter.
Strafford,	33	58,916	Dover, Gilford, Rochester.
Merrimack,	24	34,619	Concord.
Hillsborough,	30	37,762	Amherst.
Cheshire,	23	27,016	Keene.
Sullivan,	15	19,687	Newport.
Grafton,	37	38,691	Haverhill, Plymouth.
Coos,	27	8,390	Lancaster.
	224	269,633	

New Hampshire is more mountainous than any of her sister states, yet she boasts of large quantities of luxuriant intervale. Her high lands produce food for cattle of peculiar sweetness; and no where can be found the necessaries, conveniences, and luxuries of life, united, in greater abundance: cattle and wool are its principal staples. This state may be said to be the mother of New England rivers. The Connecticut, Merrimack, Saco, Androscoggin and Piscataqua, receive most of their waters from the high lands of New Hampshire: while the former washes the western boundary of the state 168 miles, the Merrimack pierces its centre, and the Piscataqua forms the beautiful harbor of Portsmouth, a depot of the American navy.

These majestic rivers, with their tributary streams afford this state an immense water power, of which manufacturers, with large capitals, avail themselves.

The largest collection of water in the state is Lake Winnepisiogee, (pronounced Win-ne-pe-sok'-e.) It is one of the most varied and beautiful sheets of water on the American continent. Lakes Connecticut, Ossipee, Umbagog, Squam, Sunapee, and Massabesick, are large collections of water, and abound with fish and fowl.

New Hampshire is frequently called the *Granite State*, from the vast quantities of that rock found within its territory. The granite is of a superior quality, and much of it is quarried and transported to other states. The geological structure of the state is highly interesting. Iron and copper ore and plumbago, of excellent qualities, are found; and coal and other valuable minerals are supposed to exist.

This state is also called the *Switzerland of America*, on account of the salubrity of its climate; its wild and picturesque landscapes; its lakes and rapid streams. The celebrated White Mountains, in the northern part of the state, are of great elevation, and afford the grandest display of mountain scenery in our country. See *Winnepisiogee Lake*, and *White Mountains—also Register.*

New Hampton, N. H.,

Strafford co., lies 30 miles N. by W. from Concord, and about 20 N. W. from Gilmanton. Population, 1830, 1,904. Pemigewasset river, which washes the W. boundary, is the only stream of magnitude; and over it is thrown the bridge which unites the town with Bristol.

There is a remarkable spring on the W. side of Kelly's hill in this town, from which issues a stream sufficient to supply several mills. This stream is never affected by rains or droughts, and falls into the river after running about a mile. Pemigewasset pond lies on the border of Meredith. There are 4 other ponds in this town. The soil of New Hampton, though the surface is broken and uneven, is remarkably fertile, producing in abundance most kinds of grain and grass. The industry of the inhabitants has enabled them in years of scarcity to supply the wants of other towns. In the S. part of the town there is a high hill of a conical form which may be seen in almost any direction from 10 to 50 miles; the prospect from the summit of which is very pleasant.

In 1763, Gen. Jonathan Moulton, of Hampton, having an ox weighing 1,400 pounds, fattened for the purpose, hoisted a flag upon his horns and drove him to Portsmouth as a present to Gov. Wentworth. He refused to receive any compensation for the ox, but merely as a token of the governor's friendship and esteem, he would like to have a charter of a small gore of land he had discovered adjoining the town of Moultonborough, of which he was one of the principal proprietors. It was granted, and he called it *New Hampton*, in honor of his native town. This *small gore* of land contained 19,422 acres, a part of which now constitutes the town of Centre Harbor. It was incorporated Nov. 27, 1777.

New Hartford, Ct.

Litchfield co. This town was first settled in 1733. It lies 20 miles N. W. from Hartford, and 11 N. E. from Litchfield. Population, 1830, 1,766. The surface of the town is hilly and mountainous. The lands are best adapted for grazing. It is watered by Farmington river and other streams, on which are several mills.

"In the eastern part of this town there is a rough and mountainous district, formerly designated *Satan's Kingdom;* and the few inhabitants who lived here were in a measure shut out from the rest of mankind. An inhabitant of the town invited one of his neighbors, who lived within the limits of this district, to go and hear Mr. Marsh, the first minister who was settled in the town. He was prevailed upon to go to church in the forenoon. In the course of his prayer, Mr. Marsh, among other things, prayed that *Satan's kingdom might be destroyed.* It appears that the inhabitant of this district took the expression in a literal and tangible sense, having probably never heard the expression used but in reference to the district wherein he resided. Being asked to go to meeting in the afternoon, he refused, stating that Mr. Marsh had insulted him; 'for blast him,' said he, "when he prayed for the destruction of Satan's kingdom, he very well knew all my interests lay there."

New Haven, Vt.

Addison co. The soil of this town is various, consisting of marl, clay and loam, and is generally productive. The waters of Otter creek, Middlebury river, and Little Otter creek give the town a good water power. There are some manufactures in the town, but agriculture is the chief pursuit of the inhabitants. New Haven lies 30 miles W. S. W. from Montpelier, and 7 N. W. from Middlebury. First settled, 1769. Population, 1830, 1,834.

New Haven County, Ct.

Chief town, *New Haven*. New Haven county is bounded N. by Litchfield and Hartford counties, E. by Middlesex county, S. by Long Island Sound, and West by Litchfield county and the Housatonic river, which separates it from Fairfield county. Its average length from east to west is about 26 miles, and its width from north to south 21 miles; containing 540 square miles, or 345,600 acres. This county, lying on Long Island Sound, has a very extensive maritime border, but its foreign trade is chiefly confined to New Haven harbor. Its fisheries of oysters and clams, and other fish, are valuable. It is intersected by several streams, none of them of very large size, but of some value for their water power and fish. Of these the principal are the Pomperaug and Naugatuc, on the west: Quinnipiac, Menunkatuc, West and Mill rivers, on the east. The Quinnipiac is the largest, and passes through extensive meadows. The county is intersected centrally by the New Haven and Northampton canal, which passes through this county from north to south. There is a great variety of soil in this county, as well as of native vegetable and mineral productions. The range of secondary country which extends along Connecticut river as far as Middletown, there leaves that stream, crosses into this county, and terminates at New Haven. This intersection of the primitive formation, by a secondary ridge, affords a great variety of minerals, and materials for different soils.

The population of this county in 1820, was 39,616; 1830, 43,847:—81 inhabitants to a square mile. The manufacturing business is quite extensive in the county, and in 1837 it contained 23,895 sheep.

New Haven, Ct.

New Haven, city and town, the chief town of New Haven county, and the semi-capital of the state of Connecticut, is 76 miles N. E. from New York, and 300 from Washington city, in latitude (Yale College Observatory) 41° 18′ 30″ N., and W. longitude 72° 55′. It is situated on a large and pleasant plain, around the head of a bay which sets up four miles from Long Island Sound. This plain is nearly level, and is partially enclosed by an amphitheatre of lofty hills, and by two bold eminences called East and West rocks, which vary in height from 330 to 370 feet. These rocks, which consist of trap, terminate in naked precipitous fronts, and are conspicuous and beautiful objects in the landscape. On the west, the plain is limited by a small stream called West river, and on the east by the Quinnipiack, which is navigable for several miles. Another stream, called Mill river, passes through the eastern part of the city and enters the harbor in union with the Quinnipiack.

New Haven was planted in April, 1638, by a company from London, under the direction of Theophilus Eaton and John Davenport. These two men, in the language of Mather, were " the Moses and Aaron" of this new settlement; and whatever there was of good or evil, of wisdom or folly, in laying the foundations of civilized society in this part of New England, must be ascribed in a great measure to them. Though the government which was established was extremely popular in its form, these men without doubt were looked up to for devising and executing the most important measures. Their "company," as it was called, appear to have had entire confidence in their sound judgment, ability and integrity; and they did nothing to forfeit the good opinion of their followers. Their influence in all the concerns of the colony, especially in what respected the form of government, the means of education, and the institutions of religion, must have been constant and commanding.

In 1784, New Haven was incorporated as a city, the limits of which on the northwest fall within those of the town, so that Westville, a settlement on the foot of West Rock, is excluded from the former. About one half of the village of Fair Haven, in the eastern portion of the town, lies within the bounds of the city. The area of the town is about eight, and that of the city about six square miles. The harbor is well protected and spacious, but the water is shallow. A wharf extends into the harbor about three quarters of a mile.

The original town is a square, half a mile on each side, and subdivided by streets four rods in width, into nine squares, the central one of which is reserved for public uses. Most of the squares are further divided by intermediate streets. At the present day, this original plot comprises less than half of the inhabited part of the city. Streets and avenues have been opened on every side, and many of them have become thickly settled. The streets are in general, spacious and regular; very many of them adorned with lofty elms, which in the summer season contribute much to the beauty and comfort of the place. The number of shade trees throughout the city is uncommonly large, and they constitute one of its most attractive features. Most of the dwelling houses are distinguished for simplicity and neatness. Within a few years the style of building has greatly improved, and many private houses have been erected and are now going up, which display much elegance and architectural taste. The houses are commonly detached, and supplied with court yards and gardens ornamented with trees and shrubbery, and the eye is thus gratified with a delightful union of the country and the city.

There are two principal public squares. The first, commonly called *the Green*, is in the centre of the original town, and comprises in all a little more than sixteen acres. It is divided into two sections by Temple street, which is lined with ranges of stately and over-arching elms, and is considered one of the finest streets in the city. The eastern section of the Green is entirely free from buildings. On the western section, facing the S.E., stand 3 churches, two Congregational, built of brick, and one Episcopal, of stone: all of these buildings are of excellent appearance. In the rear of the centre church stands the state house. These four buildings, taken in connexion with the line of college edifices on the next square beyond, and with the surrounding scenery, constitute a group not often equalled in this country. The state house is a structure of great size and admirable proportions. The porticos are modelled from those of the temple of Theseus, at Athens, and the building, viewed at a short distance, has an air of uncommon beauty and majesty. On the northern corner of this section stands the methodist church.

Wooster Square, which lies in the eastern part of the city, comprises five acres, and has recently been planted with a large number of native ornamental trees of various kinds.

The *Public Cemetery* is situated opposite the northern angle of the original town plot, and encloses seventeen acres and two thirds. It is divided by avenues and alleys into family lots, 32 feet in length and 18 in breadth. There is a grave and silent grandeur in this place; but it would appear more beautiful were it shaded by *native* trees instead of *Lombardy poplars*.

The *State Hospital* is located at New Haven. It is a large and commodious building of stone, very favorably situated on elevated ground, in the western part of the city.

One daily and four weekly newspapers, and one religious weekly sheet, are published here. The Daily Herald was the earliest daily paper issued in this state, it having been commenced here November 26, 1832. The other periodical publications of the place, are the *Yale Literary Magazine*, edited by the students of Yale College; the *Quarterly Christian Spectator*, a work of established reputation, which began as a monthly in 1819, and after ten volumes of that series had been completed, adopted its present form, in which it has reached its tenth volume; and the *American Journal of Science and Arts*, edited by Professor Silliman. This important periodical was commenced in 1819, and has arrived at the 35th volume, having outlived many of its early European contemporaries. It is a work which has done much for the advancement of science, and reflects great honor on the nation and city of its birth, as well as on its distinguished editor.

The population of the town, including the city, was in 1820, 8,326; in 1830, 10,678; in December, 1833, 12,199, of whom 11,567 were within the city. The number of inhabitants in 1837, was estimated at 14,000.

As a seat of education, New Haven is justly celebrated. At a moderate estimate, one thousand persons from abroad are constantly here for the purposes of receiving instruction.

Yale College is one of the most ancient and celebrated institutions of learning in the country, and numbers among her academical graduates, 4,824 persons.

The *Mineral Collection*, well known as the most extensive in the country, occupies a spacious and well lighted apartment.

The *Telescope* belonging to the college was made by Dolland, and presented by Mr. Sheldon Clark, of Oxford. It is an achromatic of five inches aperture and ten feet focal length, and is considered an instrument of great excellence. See *Register*.

Besides the College libraries, there are in the city several libraries of considerable extent and importance. Among them, that belonging to Mr. Ithiel Town deserves to be particularized. This is a large and precious collection of books, principally on architecture and the other fine arts, together with many volumes of great antiquity and rarity. It is the most complete architectural library in the United States. It is placed beyond the reach of fire, in an elegant building on Hillhouse avenue. In 1837, there were in New Haven 43 well conducted academies and private schools, some of which were of an elevated character for females. The public schools are well sustained. The annual expenditure for schools is about $30,000. The whole number of pupils is about 2,500.

There are in New Haven several

institutions for the promotion of the science, industry and comfort of its inhabitants. The *Connecticut Academy of Arts and Sciences* was incorporated in 1799. It has published one volume of Memoirs, (8 vo. 1810—1813, pp. 412;) but since the establishment of Prof. Silliman's Journal of Science, their Memoirs have appeared in that work. The *American Geological Society* was incorporated in 1819.— Its collection of specimens is connected with the mineral cabinet of Yale College. The *Yale Natural History Society* has existed four years, and has a considerable collection of birds, shells, minerals, plants, &c. Its transactions have hitherto been made public through Prof. Silliman's Journal of Science. The *Mutual Aid Association* is an institution of great utility. The *New Haven Horticultural Society* and the *Orphan Asylum* are well supported and highly beneficial.

The mechanics of New Haven have long been distinguished for their industry, intelligence and love of knowledge. As early as 1807 they established the *Mechanics' Society*, for the promotion of the useful arts, and the encouragement of industry and merit. The society is in a prosperous condition. The young mechanics have, moreover, established for their mutual improvement, the *Young Mechanics' Institute*. The plan has been prosecuted with zeal and success. The Institute has a cabinet of minerals; a collection of philosophical apparatus, and several hundred volumes of books. The manufactures of New Haven are numerous; among which are boots, shoes, carpets, and rugs of a superior quality, stoves, locks, paper, books, hats, tin and cabinet wares, muskets, iron castings, machinery, sashes, window blinds, &c.

The manufacturing interest of New Haven employs an extensive capital, and a large number of persons.

The foreign commerce of New Haven is principally confined to the West India Islands, with which a considerable trade is carried on. Tonnage of the district, in 1837, 9,559 tons.

A line of packets plies between this and New York city, and an excellent line of steam-boats furnishes daily communication with that city.

The New Haven and Northampton Canal connects the waters of Connecticut river at the latter place, with the harbor of this city. This great work, having surmounted many difficulties and embarrassments, is now in a fair way to give a new impulse to the business of the city. A line of packet boats runs daily between Northampton and New Haven, and promises to be well sustained.

The New Haven and Hartford Rail-Road is now in the course of construction, and will probably be completed during the present year. When finished it must prove of great importance to the interests of the place.

The village of *Fair Haven* is built on both sides the Quinnipiack, and about one half of it lies within the limits of the city of New Haven. This village has grown to its present importance with great rapidity, and now carries on an extensive and thriving business. It has two churches, and a large and prosperous high school, known as the *Fair Haven Institute*.

The village of *Westville* contains about 700 inhabitants. Manufactures and agriculture constitute the chief business of the place.

New Haven may justly boast of many distinguished men who made that city their favorite residence. The names of DAVID WOOSTER, of NATHAN WHITING, of ROGER SHERMAN, of JAMES HILL-

HOUSE, and many others, will never be forgotten.

How large a part of the United States is indebted for its prosperity to the inventive genius of ELI WHITNEY, late a citizen of New Haven? "The commerce, the business of the world, has been essentially modified and increased through the operation of his principal invention, the *cotton gin;* and the substantial convenience and enjoyment of mankind have, by the same means, been extended and are extending, to a degree which no man can calculate."

This *City of Groves* is a very delightful place: it probably concentrates more charms than any city of its age and population in the world.

Newington, N. H.

Rockingham co. The soil is generally sandy and unproductive; excepting near the waters, where it yields good crops of grain and grass. At Fox point, in the N. W. part of the town, Piscataqua bridge is thrown over the river to Goat island, and thence to Durham shore. The bridge was erected in 1793, is 2,600 feet long, and 40 wide; cost $65,401. Newington was originally a part of Portsmouth and Dover, and was early settled. It was disannexed, and incorporated in July, 1764.

Newington was among the settlements early exposed to the ravages of the Indians. In May, 1690, a party of Indians, under a sagamore of the name of Hoophood, attacked Fox point, destroyed several houses, killed 14 persons, and took 6 prisoners. They were immediately pursued by the inhabitants, who recovered some of the captives and a part of the plunder, after a severe action, in which Hoophood was wounded.

Newington is 42 miles E. S. E. from Concord, and 5 W. from Portsmouth. Population, 1830, 549.

New Ipswich, N. H.

Hillsborough co. This town is 50 miles S. S. W. from Concord, 70 W. S. W. from Portsmouth, and 50 N. W. by W. from Boston. The town is watered by many rivulets, but principally by the Souhegan river, which is formed by the junction of two streams; the W. issuing from a small pond on the Pasture mountain, so called; the S. from two ponds in Ashburnham, Mass., near the base of Watatick hill. Over this river is a stone bridge, built in 1817. It is 156 feet long, 22 feet wide and 42 feet high, resting on a single arch of split stone; cost $3,500. The first cotton factory in the state was built in this town, in 1803. There are now 4 cotton factories, and in other respects New Ipswich has become an important manufacturing town.— Pratt's and Hoar's ponds contain about 50 acres each. Here is fine pasture land, and under cultivation, Indian corn, rye, oats, barley, potatoes, beans, turnips, &c., are produced in abundance.

The New Ipswich academy was incorporated June 18, 1789. Its funds are large.

The principal village is in the centre of the town, in a pleasant and fertile valley. Many of the dwelling-houses are of brick, and are elegant in appearance.

New Ipswich was first settled prior to 1749, and was incorporated by charter, Sept. 9, 1762.

The first minister was the Rev. Stephen Farrar, a native of Lincoln, Mass., where he was born Oct. 22, 1738. He was ordained Oct. 22, 1760; died June 23, 1809, aged 71.

New Ipswich has produced many who have become eminent as patriots, merchants, and men of science. Population, 1830, 1,673.

New Limerick, Me.

Washington co. In 1837, this

town was incorporated; it then had 124 inhabitants and produced 1,780 bushels of wheat. See "Down East."

New London, N. H.

Merrimack co. It is 30 miles W. N. W. from Concord, and 12 E. from Newport. Population, 1830, 913. Lake Sunapee separates this town from Wendell, and is the principal source of Sugar river.— There are three considerable ponds. Little Sunapee pond, 1 1-2 miles in length and 3-4 of a mile in width, lies in the W. part, and empties its waters into lake Sunapee. Harvey's and Messer's ponds, near the centre of the town, are the principal sources of Warner river. They are about a mile in length and 3-4 of a mile in breadth, and are separated by a bog, many parts of which rise and fall with the water. Pleasant pond, in the N. part of New London, is nearly 2 miles long and 1 wide. The settlements of New London are formed principally on three large swells of land. The soil is deep and generally good.— In the N. part are several elevations. In some parts the land is rocky, but there is little not capable of cultivation. New London was incorporated in 1779. Its first name was *Dantzick*.

The damage sustained by the inhabitants of this town, by the violent whirlwind of Sept. 9, 1821, was estimated at $9,000. A large rock lying out of the ground, 100 feet long, 50 wide and 20 high, was rent into two pieces, and thrown about 20 feet asunder.

New London County, Ct.

New London and *Norwich* are the county towns. New London county is bounded N. by Windham, Tolland and Hartford counties, E. by Windham county and the state of Rhode Island, S. by Long Island Sound, and W. by the county of Middlesex. Its average length from E. to W. averages about 26 miles, and it has a medium breadth of about 20 miles. This county possesses superior maritime advantages, having an extensive border on Long Island Sound, which affords numerous bays, inlets and harbors. Excepting a small section, principally in the town of Lyme, no portion of the county can be considered as mountainous, but it is generally hilly and elevated, and comprises a small proportion of alluvial. The hills and elevated tracts are considerably rough and stony. The lands in general are not adapted to grain culture, although upon the intervales and other tracts Indian corn is raised to advantage, and to a considerable extent. The principal agricultural interests depend very much upon grazing. The waters of the county are abundant and valuable. On the south it is washed more than thirty miles by Long Island Sound, part of its western border by Connecticut river, and the interior of the county is watered and fertilized by the Thames and its branches. The fishing business is more extensively carried on in this county than in any other section of the state, and is an important branch of industry. The manufacturing business is carried on to considerable extent in the northern part of the county, and is increasing.

In 1837, this county contained 41,387 sheep. Population, in 1820, 35,943; 1830, 42,201: 81 inhabitants to a square mile. The tonnage of the district of New London, in 1837, was 41,626 tons.

New London, Ct.

One of the shire towns of New London county. The first English settlement in New London commenced in 1646. It is situated on the west bank of the river Thames. In its territorial limits it is much the smallest of any town in the state, being about 4 miles in length from north to south, and averages about 3-4 of a mile in breadth.—

The city of New London is situated 3 miles from Long Island Sound, and is a port of entry. It is 42 miles southeast from Hartford, 13 south from Norwich, and 53 east from New Haven. Population, in 1830, 4,356. Lon. 72° 9′ W., lat. 41° 0′ 25″ N. The city is principally built on a declivity, which descends to the east and south. On the summit of the high ground, back of the most populous part of the city, the observer has a fine prospect of the surrounding country. The city is irregularly laid out, owing to the nature of the ground on which it is built, being much incumbered with granite rocks.— The houses are not so handsome in their outward appearance, as might be reasonably expected, considering the wealth of the inhabitants. In the course of a few years past, however, a spirit of improvement in this respect has taken place, and many buildings have been erected which are elegant in their appearance. Some of the streets have been straitened and leveled, by blasting the granite rocks with which they were disfigured. These rocks afford an excellent material for the construction of buildings, and it is believed that no city in this country has the advantages of New London, in this particular, where the materials for erecting houses can be found in their streets. The harbor is one of the best in the United States, being large, safe, and commodious, having five fathoms of water. It is 3 miles long, and rarely obstructed with ice. During the extreme cold in January, 1835, while the navigation of the harbor of New York was closed by the ice, the harbor of New London remained open and unobstructed.

From the excellent maritime location of New London, the navigation, commercial and fishing business, has ever been the principal pursuit of the inhabitants. Their fine harbor has served in a great degree as the port of Connecticut river, the impediments in which frequently prevent its being navigable for large vessels fully laden. The whale fishery and sealing business is an important branch of commerce. About a million of dollars is devoted to its prosecution. In 1834, upwards of thirty ships and 900 men and boys were employed in this business.

The city is defended by two forts, Fort Trumbull and Fort Griswold. Fort Trumbull stands on the New London side of the Thames, about a mile below the city. It is situated on the rocky extremity of a peninsula extending eastward into the river. This fort is a station for United States soldiers. Fort Griswold is on the E. side of the Thames, on a commanding eminence opposite the city, in the town of Groton.

New London has been rendered conspicuous for its sufferings during the revolutionary war, and the theatre of hostile operations. On the 6th of September, 1781, a large proportion of this town was laid in ashes by Benedict Arnold. The following account of this transaction is taken from the Connecticut Gazette, printed at New London, Sept. 7, 1781.

"About daybreak on Thursday morning last, 24 sail of the enemy's shipping appeared to the westward of this harbor, which by many were supposed to be a plundering party after stock; alarm guns were immediately fired, but the discharge of cannon in the harbor has become so frequent of late, that they answered little or no purpose. The defenceless state of the fortifications and the town are obvious to our readers; a few of the inhabitants, who were equipped, advanced towards the place where the enemy were thought likely to make their landing, and manœuvred on the heights adjacent, until the enemy about 9 o'clock landed in two divisions, and about 800 men each, one of them at Brown's farm, near the lighthouse, the other at Groton Point: the division that landed near the light-house marched up the road, keeping up large flanking parties, who were attacked in different places on their march by the inhabitants, who had spirit and resolution to oppose their progress. The main body of the enemy proceeded to the town, and set fire to the stores on the beach, and immediately after to the dwelling-houses lying on the Mill Cove. The scattered fire of our little parties, unsupported by our neighbors more distant, galled them so that they soon began to retire, setting fire promiscuously on their way. The fire from the stores communicated to the shipping that lay at the wharves, and a number were burnt; others swung to single fast, and remained unhurt.

"At 4 oclock, they began to quit the town with great precipitation, and were pursued by our brave citizens with the spirit and ardor of veterans, and driven on board their boats. Five of the enemy were killed, and about twenty wounded; among the latter is a Hessian captain, who is a prisoner, as are seven others. We lost four killed and ten or twelve wounded, some mortally.

"The most valuable part of the town is reduced to ashes, and all the stores. Fort Trumbull, not being tenable on the land side, was evacuated as the enemy advanced, and the few men in it crossed the river to Fort Griswold, on Groton Hill, which was soon after invested by the division that landed at the point. The fort having in it only about 120 men, chiefly militia hastily collected, they defended it with the greatest resolution and bravery, and once repulsed the enemy: but the fort being out of repair, could not be defended by such a handful of men, though brave and determined, against so superior a number; and after having a number of their party killed and wounded, they found that further resistance would be in vain, and resigned the fort." See *Groton, Ct.*

The following is the inscription on Bishop Seabury's monument:

Here lyeth the body of SAMUEL SEABURY, D. D. Bishop of Connecticut and Rhode Island, who departed from this transitory scene, February 25th, Anno Domini, 1796, in the 68th year of his age, and the 12th of his Episcopal consecration.

Ingenious without pride, learned without pedantry, good without severity, he was duly qualified to discharge the duties of the Christian and the Bishop. In the pulpit he enforced Religion; in his conduct he exemplified it. The poor he assisted with his charity; the ignorant he blessed with his instruction. The friend of men, he ever designed their good; the enemy of vice, he ever opposed it. Christian! dost thou aspire to happiness? Seabury has shown the way that leads to it.

"An epitaph on Captaine Richard Lord, deceased May 17, 1662.—Ætatis svæ 51.

.... Bright starre of ovr chivallrie lies here
To the state a covnsillovr fvll deare
And to ye trvth a friend of sweete content
To Hartford towne a silver ornament
Who can deny to poore he was releife
And in composing paroxyies he was cheife
To marchantes as a patterne he might stand
Adventring dangers new by sea and land."

New Market, N. H.

Rockingham co. It lies 36 miles S. E. from Concord, and 12 W. by S. from Portsmouth. Population, 1830, 2,013.

Piscassick river passes through this town into Durham. The Lamprey river washes its N. E. boundary, as does the Swamscot the S. E. The soil is good, and agricultural pursuits are here crowned with much success. There are several pleasant and thriving villages, in which are large and valuable manufactures.

New Market was originally a part of Exeter, and was detached and incorporated, 1727.

Mrs. Fanny Shute, who died in this town September, 1819, was respected not only for her excellent qualities, but the adventures of her youth. When 13 months old, she was taken by a party of Indians, carried to Canada, and disposed of to the French—educated in a nunnery, and after remaining 13 years in captivity, was redeemed and restored to her friends.

Daniel Brackett recently died in this town. He weighed 560 lbs.

New Marlborough, Mass.

Berkshire co. There is a large pond in this town, and a branch of Housatonick river. The surface is uneven, and the soil best adapted for grazing. It was incorporated in 1759, and lies 135 miles S. W. by W. from Boston, and 20 S. by E. from Lenox. Population, in 1837, 1,570.

There are two caverns in this town, containing stalactites. The manufactures consist of leather, boots, shoes, chairs, cabinet ware, and a variety of sawed lumber.—The products of the dairy are considerable, and about 1,600 sheep are pastured.

New Milford, Ct.

Litchfield co. This township is hilly and broken, several mountainous ridges extending through it. The soil is much diversified, and where susceptible of cultivation, it is generally good; but on the whole more distinguished for grain than grass. There are, however, large quantities of excellent meadow ground, but the pasturage is, on the whole, not abundant. It is essentially a farming town. For some time after the white people come here, an Indian chief, or sachem, named *Werauhamaug*, had a palace standing near the Great falls, where he resided. On the inner walls of this palace, (which were of bark with the smooth side inwards,) were pictured every known species of beast, bird, fish and insect, from the largest to the smallest. This was said to have been done by artists whom a friendly prince at a great distance sent to him for that purpose, as Hiram did to Solomon. The town of New Milford was purchased of the Colony of Connecticut by a company of individuals chiefly belonging to Milford, and was first settled in 1707. The first bridge that was ever built over the Housatonick river, from the sea to its source was built in this town in 1737. The village of New Milford is very handsome; the streets are wide and well shaded. It lies 36 miles N. W. from New Haven, and 18 S. W. from Litchfield. Population, 1830, 3,979. The territory of this town is larger than any other in the state: it is 13 by 6 1-2 miles. The town is well watered, and has some manufactures. There are large quantities of granite and marble, and the town produces large quantities of grain and wool for market.

Newport, Me.

Penobscot co. This is a fine farming town, and watered by a large and beautiful pond which empties into Sebasticook river. It lies 56 miles N. E. from Augusta and 24 W. from Bangor. Population, 1837, 1,088. Wheat crop same year, 5,173 bushels. This town contains a pleasant village and some mills.

Newport, N. H.

Shire town, Sullivan county. Its central situation and its water power, together with the enterprising spirit of its inhabitants, has rendered Newport a place of considerable business. It is 40 miles W. by N. from Concord, about 35 N. from Keene, and 14 E. S. E. from Windsor, Vt. Near the centre of the town, and the confluence of the E. and S. branches of Sugar river and the Croydon turnpike, is a handsome village. In general the soil is rich and productive. Sugar river flows through this town, and its three branches unite near the village, whence it passes through Claremont into the Connecticut. On the eastern branch are situated, principally near the village, large and valuable manufacturing establishments.— There are other mills in different parts of the town. There are a few eminences, designated as Bald, Coit and East mountains, and Blueberry hill. Newport was granted by charter in 1761. The first effort towards a settlement was made in the fall of 1763. The first settlers were principally from Killingworth, Ct. This town is noted for its good schools and its various charitable societies. Population, 1830, 1,913.

Newport, Vt.

Orleans co. This town is separated from Derby by Memphremagog lake, and is watered by a branch of Missisque river. It lies 48 miles N. by E. from Montpelier, and 10 N. from Irasburgh. Population, 1830, 284.

Newport County, R. I.

Newport is the chief town. This county comprises seven towns and a number of islands; but the most interesting section of it is the island of Rhode Island, from which the state derives its name. This island is about 15 miles in length, and has a mean breadth of two miles and a half.

The surface presents an interesting variety of moderate eminences and declivities, which render the scenery very pleasing. Valuable minerals are found on the island, and fossil coal, difficult of ignition, is found in large quantities. The soil of the island is very rich, and under the management of skilful farmers is made to produce in great abundance all the varieties of grains, grasses, vegetables, fruits and flowers common to its latitude.

It is remarkable that not only this island, but the county generally, should be so fertile. The poorest lands in New England are generally on the sea board; but as it regards this county, few sections of the interior present a better soil.

From the earliest settlement of the country, this county has been engaged in commerce and the fishery. These interests are now in a flourishing condition; and manufacturing establishments are increasing, by the aid of steam power. In 1837 there were 37,340 sheep in the county.

Newport county is bound N. by Mount Hope bay, and Bristol county, Mass.; E. by said county of Bristol; S. by the Atlantic ocean, and W. by Narraganset bay. Area, 136 square miles. Population, 1820, 15,771; 1830, 16,535. Population to a square mile, 122.

Newport, R. I.

Chief town of Newport county, and one of the seats of the state legislature. It is in N. latitude 41° 28' 20", and W. longitude 71° 21' 14": 5 miles from the sea, 30 miles S. by E. from Providence, 70 S. S. W. from Boston, and 153 from New York, by water. The township lies in an irregular and somewhat of a semicircular form, about 6 miles in length and 1 in breadth. In common with the whole island of Rhode Island, on which Newport is situated, the soil is remarkably fertile and under good cultivation. The surface is undulating, presenting a great variety of delightful scenery. The waters of Narraganset bay at this place are unrivalled for beauty and convenience. The harbor of Newport is considered one of the best on the coast of America: it has sufficient depth of water for the largest class of vessels, is exceedingly easy of access from the ocean, and sufficiently capacious to contain whole fleets. This harbor is admirably defended by forts Wolcott, Green and Adams, and will probably soon become a naval depot. Newport was first settled by William Codington and his associates in 1638. The growth of the town was so rapid for the first hundred years, that in 1738 there were 7 worshipping assemblies, and 100 sail of vessels belonged to the port.

Newport suffered severely during the revolutionary war, and was for a long time in possession of the enemy. After the war it revived again, but the more favorable location of Providence for an interior commerce, deprived it of a large portion of its original business.

Newport however retains its former character for foreign commerce and the fishery. A number of vessels are now engaged in the whaling business, and manufacturing establishments have recently been put into operation by steam power, which promise success.— Ship and boat building and the manufacture of cordage are carried on extensively. The domestic fishery is to Newport an important resourse. There is probably no place in the world where a greater variety of fish, or of a better quality, are found. About sixty different kinds, comprising almost every species of fin and shell fish, fit for the table, are taken in great abundance around the shores of Narraganset. The tonnage of the district of Newport, in 1837, was 11,498 tons.

The compact part of the town is built on a beautiful site, facing the harbor in a southeasterly direction. The main street extends more than a mile in length. The buildings on this and other streets and on Washington square are neatly built, and some of them are very handsome The marks of age which some of these buildings bear, with the excellent state of preservation in which they appear, give them a grace not found in many of those of more modern construction.

Although this ancient town has passed through many vicissitudes and changes of fortune, still it continues to advance in the number of its people. Population, in 1820, 7,319; 1830, 8,010.

Newport is celebrated for its beauty and the salubrity of its climate. From these circumstances, and from the numerous inviting objects which surround it, it has become a favorite resort for visitors from warmer climates; and in no place can the summer season be more enjoyed than amid the charms of Newport.

OLIVER HAZZARD PERRY, the victor on Lake Erie, Sept. 10, 1813, was born at Newport, in 1785.— He died in the West Indies, in 1820. A monument is erected to his memory.

New Portland, Me.

Franklin co. This town is finely watered by two branches of Seven Mile brook. This is one of the finest farming towns in the county. It produced, in 1837, 10,451 bushels of wheat. Population, same year, 1,476. This town has a pleasant village, a number of saw mills and other manufactories. It lies 48 miles N. N. W. from Augusta, and 18 N. by E. from Farmington. Incorporated, 1808.

Newry, Me.

Oxford co. A branch of Androscoggin river waters this town, and affords it good mill privileges. It lies 63 miles W. from Augusta, and 25 N. W. from Paris. Population, 1837, 412. Incorporated, 1805.

New Salem, Mass.

Franklin co. This town is bounded N. by Miller's river, and has a good water power. It lies 74 miles

W. N. W. from Boston, and 17 E. S. E. from Greenfield. This is a pleasant town of elevated surface, and good soil for grazing. Population, 1837, 1,255. The manufactures of the town, consist of palm-leaf hats, boots, shoes, leather, straw bonnets, and ploughs. Incorporated, 1753.

New Sharon, Me.

Franklin. co. This town is watered on the northwest side by Sandy river, and is bounded south by Vienna. The soil is admirably adapted to agricultural purposes. Population, 1837, 1,771. Wheat crop, same year, 8,132 bushels. It lies 26 miles N. W. from Augusta. Incorporated, 1794.

New Shoreham, R. I.

Newport co. This town comprises the island of *Block Island.* The island lies in the open sea, about 14 miles S. S. W. from Judith Point, and 13 N. E. from Montauk Point, on Long Island, N. Y. It is about 8 miles in length, and varies from 2 to 4 miles in width. It has several ponds, which cover about a seventh part of the island. The surface of the town is uneven; in some parts elevated. The soil is a sandy, gravelly loam, and quite productive. This island was once famous for its cattle and good dairies. The people are mostly fishermen: they have no harbor, and peat is their only fuel. Population, 1830, 1,185. Incorporated, 1672. Its Indian name was *Manisses.*

Newton, Mass.

Middlesex co. A very beautiful, agricultural and manufacturing town, the *Nonantum* of the Indians, 7 miles W. by S. from Boston, 12 S. E. from Concord, and 7 N. from Dedham. Charles river washes the borders of this town 15 miles, and, by two falls of considerable extent, affords it a great and valuable water power. Nine bridges cross Charles river in this town. The soil is generally very good, and highly cultivated. There are 2 cotton, 1 woolen, and 5 paper mills in the town, and manufactures of nails, rolled iron, candles, vitriol, barilla, chaises, harnesses, morocco, leather, boots, shoes, machinery, chairs, and cabinet ware; the value of which, the year ending April 1, 1837, amounted to $815,872. Newton was incorporated in 1691; it formerly comprised the town of Cambridge, and is noted as the birth place and residence of many distinguished men. Population, 1830, 2,377; 1837, 3,037. A *Theological Seminary* was established in this town, in 1825. See *Register.*

Newtown, N. H.,

Rockingham co., lies 40 miles S. E. from Concord, and 27 S. S. W. from Portsmouth. Country pond lies in Newtown and Kingston, and two other small ponds connect by outlets with its waters. The soil produces good crops of grain or grass. Joseph Bartlett first settled in this town, in 1720. Bartlett was taken prisoner by the Indians at Haverhill, in 1708, and remained a captive in Canada about 4 years. Population, 1830, 510.

Newtown, Ct.

Fairfield co. This town was incorporated in 1708. It is watered by *Patatuck* river, the Indian name of the place. It lies 25 miles W. N. W. from New Haven, 10 E. from Danbury, and 22 N. from Fairfield. Population, 1830, 3,100.—The surface of the town is hilly; many of the eminences are extensive and continuous. The soil is principally a gravelly loam, generally fertile and productive. It is well adapted to the culture of grain, and is also favorable for fruit, there being many valuable orchards in the town. The borough of Newtown is beautifully situated on high ground; it commands an extensive prospect, and contains some handsome buildings.

The flourishing village of *Sandy Hook* is situated about 1 1-2 miles N. E. of the central part of Newtown, at the foot of a rocky eminence or bluff, from the top of which is a fine prospect of the surrounding country. A fine mill stream (the Patatuck) runs in a northerly course through the village, at the base of the cliff, which rises almost perpendicular to the height of 160 feet. Near a cotton factory, at the northern extremity of the village, some traces of coal have been discovered. The village contained, in 1834, 1 cotton, 1 hat, 1 comb and 2 woolen factories. There was also 1 machine shop, and 1 establishment for working brass.

New Vineyard, Me.

Franklin co. This town is watered by a branch of Seven Mile brook. The surface of the town is uneven, but the soil, generally, is productive. It produced, in 1837, 7,063 bushels of wheat. Population, same year, 870. Incorporated, 1802. It lies 40 miles N. W. from Augusta, and 8 N. by E. from Farmington.

Nobleborough, Me.

Lincoln co. This town lies on the east side of the upper waters of Damariscotta river. It is a place of considerable trade. Many ships are built here, and a large number of vessels are employed in the coasting trade. The soil of the town is generally good, and considerable attention is paid by the inhabitants to agricultural pursuits. It lies 38 miles S. E. from Augusta, and 11 E. from Wiscasset. Population, 1837, 1,999. Incor., 1788.

No-Mans-Land, Mass.

Dukes co. A ledge of rocks, the most southern part of the state. It lies 7 miles S. from Gay Head.

Norfolk County, Mass.

Chief town, *Dedham*. This county is bounded N. E. by Boston harbor, N. by Suffolk county, W. by the S. E. corner of Worcester county, S. by the N. E. corner of the state of Rhode Island, and S. S. E. and E. by the counties of Bristol and Plymouth. Area, about 400 square miles. Population, in 1820, 36,452; in 1830, 41,901; in 1837, 50,399. Taken from Suffolk county in 1793.

This county has a maritime coast on Boston harbor of about 12 miles, which is indented with many small bays and navigable rivers. Its surface is uneven, and in some parts hilly. Its soil is generally strong and rocky. Much of the dark colored granite, or sienite, is found here. A large part of Norfolk county, particularly those towns near Boston, is under a high state of cultivation, and affords fruits and vegetables in great abundance.— The proximity of this county to the capital gives it many facilities; and the towns in this, and in the county of Middlesex, that border on Boston harbor, may be called the *Gardens of Boston*. It contains 22 towns, and 126 inhabitants to a square mile. The Charles, Neponset, and Manatiquot are its chief rivers.

In 1837, this county contained 2,054 sheep. The value of the manufactures in the county, the year ending April 1, 1837, was $6,466,010. The value of the fishery, the same year, was $244,927.

Norfolk, Ct.

Litchfield co. The settlement of Norfolk began in 1744. It lies 35 miles W. N. W. from Hartford, and 17 N. from Litchfield. Population, 1830, 1,485.

This town is elevated and mountainous. The soil is a primitive, gravelly loam, generally cold and stony, but has considerable depth, and affords good grazing. Formerly large quantities of sugar were made from the maple: more than 20,000 lbs. have been manufactured in a single season; but since the land has been cleared by progressive settlements, and in consequence of the destruction of the maple trees by some tornadoes, the business has greatly declined. The dairy business comprises the principal interests of the town. A stream, called Blackberry river, runs near the centre of the place, and a little westward of the congregational church falls over a ledge of rocks 30 feet in height. This is an excellent site for mills, of which there are several near this spot.

There is a handsome village, with an open square or green in front of the church, which is uncommonly neat and beautiful in its appearance. About half a mile north is another village, in which are two woolen and three scythe factories.

Norridgewock, Me.

Chief town of Somerset co. This town is situated on both sides of the Kennebec river, 28 miles N. from Augusta. Incorporated, 1788. Population, 1837, 1,955. Its surface is diversified with hills of a moderate elevation, the soil various, but generally good and well cultivated. Wheat crop, 1837, 10,299 bushels. This town was formerly the site of the celebrated tribe of Norridgewock Indians. Their village was situated at the foot of Norridgewock falls. in the N. W. part of the town, and the border of Madison. The tribe had a church, the bell of which was dug up a few years since, and placed in the cabinet at Bowdoin college. The tribe was destroyed by a party of 168 men, sent out from Massachusetts for that purpose, commanded by Capt. Moulton, on the afternoon of August 23, 1724. Among the killed was the noted Jesuit missionary, Ralle. A monument was erected the 23d of August, 1833, by Bishop Fenwick, to his memory.— It is a plain granite pyramidal shaft, standing on a square base of the same material, having the following inscription :—

Sebastianus Rasles natione Galluse Societate Jesu missionius, per aliquot annos Illinois et Huronibus primum evangelanus, deinde per 34 annos Abenaquis, fide et charitate Christi verus Apostolus, periculus armorum intenitus se pro suis oribus mori paratum soepius testificans, inter arma et cocdes ac Pagi Nanarantsouak Norridgewock, et Ecclesiae suae minas, hoc in ipso loco, cecidit tandem optimus pastor, die 23 Augusti, A. D. 1724, ipsi et filius in Christo defunctis Monumentum hoc posuit Benidictus Fenwick, Espiscopus Bostoniensis dedicavitque 23 Augusti, A. D. 1833. A. M. D. G.

Norridgewock village is situated on the north side of the river, directly in the bend, five miles west of Skowhegan falls. It is one of the most pleasant and delightful villages, especially in the summer, in the state. The main street is lined with ornamental trees, some of them venerable for age and magnitude, extending their long arms quite across the street, forming a beautiful avenue from east to west. On the south side of the river, connected by a bridge, is a pleasant and rapidly increasing village.

The public buildings consist of a church and court house, on the north side of the river, and on the south, a female academy, and a free church at "Oak Hill," about 5 miles from the village.

This section of country is remarkable for its luxuriant growth of the white pine. A few years since, one of these trees was cut for a canoe Its length was 154 feet and measured 4 1-2 feet in diameter.

North Hampton, N. H.,

Rockingham co., formerly constituting the parish called *North Hill*, in Hampton, lies on the sea coast 50 miles S. E. by E. from Concord, and 9 S. by W. from Portsmouth. Little river rises in the low grounds in the north part of the town, and after running southeast one or two miles, takes an east course, falling into the sea between Little Boar's head, in this town and Great Boar's head, in Hampton. Winnicut river rises near the centre of the town, and passes northwest into Great bay. In 1742, the town was incorporated. Population, 1830, 767.

Northampton, Mass.

Chief town of Hampshire co. This is a very beautiful town, delightfully situated on the west bank of Connecticut river, and united to Hadley by a bridge. Since the first settlements on the Connecticut basin, this town has been an important point of attraction. This was the third town settled on Connecticut river in this state. Its Indian name was *Nonatuck*. The soil of the town is alluvial and its products exuberant. Both before and since the division of the old county into three, this place has been the seat of justice. The buildings are handsome, and the most important county offices are *fire proof*. A fine stream passes through the centre of the town, possessing a good water power, on which are manufactories and mills of various kinds.

The manufactures of Northampton consist of woolen and silk goods, boots, shoes, leather, paper, brooms, chairs, iron, tin, and cabinet wares, &c.; total value the year ending April 1, 1837, about $350,000. The manufacture of sewing silk, ribbons, &c., is on a large scale, and the most flourishing establishment of the kind in this country. In 1837, there were 3750 sheep sheared in the town; the value of the wool was $7,075.

This place has considerable river and inland commerce, which will be increased by the Hampshire and Hampden canal, which meets the Connecticut river here and terminates at New Haven.

This town was incorporated, in 1654; population, 1820, 2,854, and in 1837, 3,576. It is 91 miles W. from Boston, 67 E. from Albany, 39 N. from Hartford, 22 S. from Greenfield, 17 N. by W. from Springfield, and 376 from Washington.

There are many institutions of a literary and religious character in this town, and its schools are of the first order. The country around the town is enchanting, and those who visit Mount Holyoke, 830 feet above the river, on the east side, or Mount Tom, 1,200 feet above the river, on the west side, will find a wonderful variety of landscape scenery, probably unsurpassed in beauty by any in the New England States.

North Berwick, Me.

York co. This town was incorporated in 1831, and was taken from the east side of Berwick. It comprises a fine tract of land; it is well watered and very pleasant. Population, 1837, 1,493. It lies 91 miles S. W. from Augusta, and 13 N. W. from York.

Northborough, Mass.

Worcester co. This is a pleasant farming town, of good soil, and watered by Assabet river. It was incorporated in 1766, and lies 32 miles W. from Boston, and 10 N. E. from Worcester. Population, 1830, 994 —1837, 1,224.

The manufactures of the town consist of cotton goods, boots, shoes, leather, children's wagons, &c.; annual amount about $75,000.

North Branford, Ct.

New Haven co. This town was incorporated in 1831, and was taken from Branford. A range of mountains from the southwest to northeast passes through the central part of the town. The inhabitants are generally substantial farmers, and property is very equally distributed. The face of the township is generally hilly, but the soil is strong and fertile. It lies 9 miles E. from New Haven. Population, 1832, 1,100

About a mile southeast of the Northford church, on *Tetoket* mountain, there is the appearance of having been, at some remote period, some violent convulsions in nature; the rocks appear to have been rent asunder, and are thrown about in great disorder. Lead is said to have been found near this spot, a mass of it being discovered by a person who was hunting, at the time of the first settlement of the parish: he hung up a pair of buck's horns to designate the spot, but the place could not be found afterwards.

Northbridge, Mass.

Worcester co. The Blackstone river and canal pass through this pleasant manufacturing and agricultural town. It has some excellent intervale land, and the soil of the uplands produces grass, grain, and vegetables in abundance. The river here is beautiful, and produces a great hydraulic power. The manufactures of the town consist of cotton and woolen goods, cotton machinery, boots, shoes, &c.: value, the year ending April 1, 1837, $231,000.

Northbridge lies 35 miles S. W. by W. from Boston, and 13 S. E. from Worcester. Incorporated, 1772. Population, 1830, 1,053; 1837, 1,409.

North Bridgewater, Mass.

Plymouth co. This town lies 20 miles S. from Boston, 24 N. W. from Plymouth, and 10 S. S. W. from Weymouth Landing. Population, 1830, 1,953; 1837, 2,701. It is well watered by Salisbury river and other small streams which empty into the Taunton. The surface of the town is uneven, but the soil is of a good quality, particularly for grazing. Incorporated, 1821.

The manufactures of the town consist of cotton goods, boots, shoes, hats, chairs, shoe tools, forks, hoes, cabinet and wooden wares, &c.: total amount, the year ending April 1, 1837, $236,700.

We regret that this very pleasant town was not called *Titicut* or *Nunketest;* one of the Indian names of the ancient territory.

This town was the first of the three Bridgewaters that have sprung from Old Bridgewater, named after a celebrated English Duke. We can see no good cause for attaching a cardinal point of the compass to the name of any town, particularly one of foreign derivation, when some beautiful Indian name meets the ear on the bank of almost every stream. Had the noble Duke bequeathed to good old mother Bridgewater and her three handsome daughters, (as he did to the city of Manchester,) the perpetual privilege of obtaining 140 pounds of coal for *four pence*, there would appear some reason for perpetuating and extending the name.

Some just remarks on the names of towns appeared in the *Providence Journal*, which are worthy of repetition.

"INDIAN NAMES. The new state of Michigan has passed one of the most sensible laws that was ever enacted. Its object is to preserve the noble and harmonious old Indian names, which have been given to every river and lake and forest and mountain in our country, and which, by a bad taste, have in many instances, been displaced by the hackneyed names of European cities, or of distinguished men. The law provides that no town shall be named after any other place or after any man, without first obtaining the consent of the Legislature. The consequence is, that

Michigan is destitute of London, Paris and Amsterdam; unlike her sister states, she boasts neither Thebes, Palmyra, Carthage or Troy. No collection of log huts, with half a dozen grocery stores, has been honored with the appellation of Liverpool, nor has any embryo city, with a college or an academy, received the appropriate name of Athens. She has no Moscow and Morocco, in the same latitude; and noEdinburgh and Alexandria within thirty miles of each other. Babylon, Sparta and Corinth, though they have been transplanted to other parts of the Union, are destined never to flourish on the soil of Michigan. No Franklin or Greene or Jefferson, no Washington, is to be found in her borders. On the contrary, her rivers and lakes still retain the full, rich, swelling names which were bestowed upon them by the red men of the forests, and her towns bear the names of the sturdy chiefs who once battled or hunted in their streets. Strange, when we have such a noble nomenclature as the Indians have left us, that we should copy from the worn out names of ancient cities, and which awake no feelings but ridicule, by the contrast between the old and the new. Mohawk, Seneca, Massasoit, Ontario, Erie, how infinitely superior to Paris, London, Fishville, Buttertown, Bungtown, &c. The feeling which prompts us to perpetuate the names of our revolutionary heroes by naming towns after them, is highly honorable; but it should not be forgotten that frequent repetition (especially in cases where the town is utterly unworthy of its namesake) renders the name vulgar and ridiculous. It seems, that not content with driving the Indians from the soil, we are anxious to obliterate every trace of their existence.

We are glad to see a better taste beginning to prevail upon this subject, and we hope that the example of Michigan will be followed, if not by legal enactments, at least by the force of public opinion."

North Brookfield, Mass.

Worcester co. This town is on elevated ground: it is of good soil, well cultivated, well watered and very pleasant. It has a fine fish pond, and lies 68 miles W. from Boston, and 18 W. from Worcester: taken from Brookfield in 1802. Population, 1830, 1,241; 1837, 1,509. The agricultural products sent to market are very considerable. The manufactures of the town consist of boots and shoes, woolen cloth, leather, &c., the value of which for the year ending April 1, 1837, was $525,224; of which $470,316 was for boots and shoes.

Northfield, Vt.

Washington co. This town lies 10 miles S. S. W. from Montpelier, and 35 E from Burlington. Population in 1830, 1,412. First settled, 1785. The principal stream in this town is Dog river, which runs through it in a northerly direction, and affords a great number of valuable mill privileges. The surface is uneven, but the soil is generally good and easily cultivated. In the centre of the town is a neat, pleasant and flourishing village, containing a number of saw mills and other mechanical operations by water.

Northfield, Me.

Incorporated 1838. See "Down East."

Northfield, N. H.,

Merrimack co., is bounded N. by Winnepisiogee river, and W. by the Merrimack. It is 14 miles N. from Concord, and 10 W. by S. of Gilmanton. The soil here is in some parts good—that of the best quality lies on the two ridges extending through the town. Chesnut pond lies in the east part of the town, and its waters flow into the

Winnepisiogee three miles from its junction with the Pemigewasset.—Sondogardy pond flows into the Merrimack. Near Webster's falls, the Winnepisiogee falls into the Pemigewasset, and the united streams form the Merrimack river. The principal elevation, called Bean hill, separates the town from Canterbury. Northfield formerly possessed valuable water privileges on the Winnepisiogee river, but this portion of its territory is embraced by the new town of Franklin.—The first settlement was made here in 1760, by Benjamin Blanchard and others. A methodist church was formed here in 1806. Incorporated June 19, 1780. Population, 1830, 1,169.

Northfield, Mass.

Franklin co. This is an interesting town, on both sides of Connecticut river. It was incorporated in 1673, and some years after desolated by the Indians. The inhabitants returned again in 1685, but it was soon after destroyed a second time. In 1713, it was again rebuilt. Fort Dummer was in the vicinity. This town was purchased of the Indians in 1687, for 200 fathoms of wampum and £57 value of goods. Its Indian name was *Squawkeag*. Most of the land in this town is excellent, and the village very pleasant: 28 miles below Walpole, N. H., 11 N. E. from Greenfield, and 83 N. W. by W. from Boston. Northfield produces fine cattle, and considerable wool. The manufactures of the town consist of leather, boots, shoes, ploughs, chairs and cabinet ware. Population, 1837, 1,605.

North Haven, Ct.

New Haven co. North Haven was taken from New Haven in 1786. The town lies on both sides of the Wallingford, or Quinnipiac river, and comprises the valley and a part of the bordering hills. The valley is partly rich intervale land, and more extensively sand; covered with a thin stratum of loam; light but warm. Near the northern line of the town it is so light as, in two or three places of small extent, to be blown into drifts. The soil of the hills is good, being a reddish loam. From the vicinity of this town to New Haven, and from its light and warm soil, which is favorable for early vegetation, there are various culinary vegetables, particularly peas, cultivated for the New Haven market. But the most striking feature in the township, is the large and beautiful tract of salt meadows on both sides of the Quinnipiac.—These meadows produce large quantities of grass, which is mowed and stacked upon the land, from whence, when the ground is frozen sufficiently solid in the winter, it is removed. Upon the salt marsh the hay is salt; but on those meadows which are protected from the salt water by means of dikes, the grass is fresh and of a better quality.—These are called dike marshes or meadows. The making of brick receives considerable attention in this town. Four and a half millions of them are manufactured annually, and principally sold in New Haven.

The village is very pleasant, and was, for more than half a century, the residence of Dr. TRUMBULL, the celebrated historian of Connecticut.

EZRA STILES, D. D., president of Yale college, was born in this town, in 1727, and died in 1795. He delighted in preaching the gospel to the poor. Among the members of his church at Newport were seven negroes. These occasionally met in his study, when he instructed them, and falling on their knees together he implored for them and for himself the blessing of that God with whom all distinction excepting that of Christian excellence is as nothing. In the cause of civil and religious liberty, Dr. Stiles was an enthusiast. He contended, that the right of conscience and private judgment was unalienable; and that no exigencies of the Christian church could render it lawful to erect any body of men into a standing judicatory over the churches. He engaged with zeal in the cause of his country. He thought, that the thirtieth of January, which was observed by the Episcopalians in commemoration of the martyrdom of Charles I, " ought to be celebrated as an anniversary thanksgiving, that one nation on earth had so much fortitude and public justice, as to make a royal tyrant bow to the sovereignty of the people." He was catholic in his sentiments, for his heart was open to receive all who loved the Lord Jesus in sincerity. He was conspicuous for his benevolence, as well as for his learning and piety. He was a man of low stature, and of a small, though well proportioned form. His voice was clear and energetic. His countenance, especially in conversation, was expressive of benignity and mildness; but if occasion required, it became the index of majesty and authority.

North Hero, Vt.

Chief town, Grand Isle co. This town was granted to Ethan Allen and others in 1779, and the settlement commenced in 1733. The British erected a block house here, at a place called Dutchman's Point, which was garrisoned and not given up till 1796. The soil of the township is of an excellent quality, and produces grain of all kinds in abundance. The county buildings are well situated, and the scenery about the village is very pleasant. It lies 57 miles N. W. from Montpelier, and 28 N. N. W. from Burlington. Population, 1830, 638.

North Kingston, R. I.

Washington co. This is a wealthy township on the west side of Narraganset bay, 21 miles S. from Providence, 10 N. W. from Newport, and 8 N. from South Kingston.— The surface of the town is uneven; the soil is a gravelly loam, well adapted for the culture of grain and vegetables, and the productions of the dairy. There are some forests in the town of good ship timber.— It is watered by several small streams which produce a good water power, on which are numerous manufacturing establishments. These streams afford bass and other fish in abundance. There is considerable navigation owned at North Kingston, which is employed in the coasting trade and fishery.

Wickford village, in this town, is very pleasant and flourishing: it has a good harbor, and is a place of considerable trade. It lies about 2 miles east of the Stonington railroad. Pop. of the town, 1830, 3,037.

Northport, Me.

Waldo co. This town is bounded on the east by Penobscot and Belfast bays. It is well watered by several ponds and small streams: the soil is good and productive. The navigable advantages of the place are great. Considerable ship building is carried on here, and there is considerable trade in the lumber and coasting business. It lies 46 miles E. from Augusta and 6 S. from Belfast. Population, 1837, 1,107.

North Providence, R. I.

Providence co. This ancient and wealthy town was a part of Providence until 1767. Population, in 1810, 1,758; 1820, 2,420; 1830, 3,503.

The surface of this town is uneven, consisting of moderate elevations and gentle declivities. The rocks are primitive and transition: some limestone is found.

The prevailing soil is a gravelly loam, which is interspersed with tracts of sandy loam, and some of calcareous. The forests consist of oak, walnut and some pine; and the agricultural productions, of grass, hay, corn, some rye, potatoes, vegetables and fruits, many of which are sent to Providence.

The waters of the town consist of the Seekonk river, which washes its eastern border; the Wanasquatucket, which forms its western boundary; and the Mashasuck, which intersects the interior of the township. These streams afford numerous sites for hydraulic works, some of which are almost unrivalled. There are some valuable shad and herring fisheries in the Seekonk.

This town is distinguished for its manufactures, particularly those of cotton, which form an important interest. The extent of this business, having concentrated a large capital, and an immense aggregate of industry, has, within the last fifty years, given rise to a large and flourishing village. The village of Pawtucket is situated in the northeast section of the town, four miles northeast from Providence, on the border of the Seekonk river; its site being principally the declivity of a hill, and it is highly romantic and picturesque. The river here affords numerous natural sites for manufacturing establishments, mills and hydraulic works of almost every description, which are scarcely rivalled, and which are occupied to a great extent. The rapid march of manufacturing and mechanical industry, which the short annals of this place disclose, has few examples in our country, and has produced one of the most considerable and flourishing manufacturing villages in the United States. The river here forms the boundary line between Massachusetts and Rhode Island, and the village is built upon both sides of it; being partly in each state. That part of the village which is in this state is principally built on four streets; and comprises a large number of handsome buildings.

Besides the cotton business, there are in the town furnaces for casting, slitting mills, anchor shops, cut nail factories, screw manufactories, &c. &c. See *Pawtucket, Mass.*

North Stonington, Ct.

New London co. This town was taken from Stonington in 1808. It is watered by the Pawcatuck and its branches, which afford good mill sites. The surface is uneven, hilly and abounding in granitic rocks. The soil is a gravelly loam, and generally productive of good pasturage. Agriculture is the principal employment of the inhabitants.

Milltown is a pretty village with some trade: it lies 50 miles S. E. from Hartford, 13 N. E. from New London, and 7 N. by E. from Stonington Borough. Population of the town in 1830, 2,840.

Northumberland, N. H.,

In Coos county, on Connecticut river, is 130 miles N. from Concord, and 7 N. E. from Lancaster. The soil along the Connecticut is very productive, perfectly free from stone and gravel, and originally covered with a growth of butternut. A portion of the upland is also good, and covered with pine, spruce, fir, ash, maple, &c. Cape Horn, an abrupt mountain of 1,000 feet in height, lies near the centre of the town. Its north base is separated from the Connecticut by a narrow plain, and the upper Amonoosuck passes near its east base, as it falls into the Connecticut. Here the meadows are extensive, and are annually covered by the spring floods, presenting the appearance of an inland sea. At the falls in the Connecticut, below the mouth of the Amonoosuck, a handsome bridge connects Northumberland with Guildhall, in Vermont. A dam is also thrown across the river at this place, at both ends of which are

NEW ENGLAND GAZETTEER.

pleasant villages and mills of various kinds are erected. Northumberland was incorporated in 1779. First settled, 1767. Population, 1830, 352.

Near the river a small fort was erected during the revolutionary war, and placed in the command of Capt. Jeremiah Eames, afterwards well known for his usefulness, wit and pleasantry.

Northwood, N. H.

Rockingham co. There are a number of ponds in this town, and excellent fishing. Suncook pond, 750 rods long, 100 wide; Jenness' pond, 300 rods long, 150 wide; Long pond, about 300 rods long, 50 wide; Harvey's pond, 200 rods long, from 40 to 80 wide; a part of Great Bow pond is also in this town, and a part of North river pond; Pleasant pond, and Little Bow pond. The north branch of Lamprey river has its rise in this town near Saddleback mountain, a high ridge between this town and Deerfield. On the E. side of this ridge are found crystals and crystalline spars of various colors and sizes. This town has an elevated site, and commands a distant and varied prospect. The waters flowing from the farm of the late Jonathan Clarke, Esq., one of the first settlers, fall into three different rivers, the Suncook, Lamprey and Isinglass. The soil of this town is generally moist, and well suited to grazing. Northwood was originally a part of Nottingham, and was settled in 1763. Northwood is 20 miles E. from Concord, 20 N. W. from Exeter, and about the same distance W. from Dover. Population, 1830, 1,342.

North Yarmouth, Me.

Cumberland co. This is a pleasant town on Casco bay, 10 miles N. from Portland, and 42 S. E. from Augusta. Population, 1837, 2,782. The town was first settled in 1640. In 1687 it was attacked by the Indians, and deserted by the whites; and was not re-settled by them until 1725. It was incorporated in 1713. About 4000 tons of navigation is owned here, employed in the transportation of lumber and the fishery. There is a fine stream of water in the town, on which are a paper and saw mills, and other manufactories. The academy in North Yarmouth is well founded and is in a flourishing condition. See *Register*.

Norton, Mass.

Bristol co. Norton was taken from Taunton in 1771. It lies 30 miles S. from Boston, 17 N. E. from Providence, and 8 N. W. from Taunton. Population, 1837, 1,530. It is well watered by Rumford, Cocasset and Canoe rivers, which empty into the Taunton. The manufactures of the town consist of sheet copper and copper bolts, cotton goods, boots, shoes, leather, iron castings, ploughs, shuttles, straw bonnets and baskets:—total value, the year ending April 1, 1837, $397,763.

Winnicunnit pond, in this town, was a great resort for the Indians, some of whom resided in natural caves, on its shores, and lived on fish and clams.

Norwalk, Ct.

Fairfield co. This pleasant town lies on Long Island Sound, 32 miles W. S. W. from New Haven, 22 S. from Danbury, and 48 N. E. from New York. Population, 1830, 3,792.

Norwalk originally included part of the present towns of New Canaan and Wilton, and part of Westport. In the ancient record, the bounds are stated to be "from Norwalk river to Sauhatuck river, from sea, Indian one day walk into the country." For this tract the following articles were given, viz; "8 fathom wampum, 6 coats, 10 hatchets, 10 hoes, 10 knives, 10 scissors, 10 jewsharps, 10 fathom tobacco, 8 kettles, 3 hauds-about, and 10 looking glasses." The following articles were given to the Indians for the tract " from Norwalk river to Five mile river, from sea, Indian one day in country," viz. " 10 fathom wampum, 3 hatchets, 3 hoes when ships come, 6 glasses, 12 tobacco pipes, 3 knives, 10 drillers, 10 needles." The name of Norwalk is derived from the above bargain, viz ; the northern bounds of the lands purchased were to extend from the sea one day's *"north walk"* into the country,

The soil in this town is excellent. The surface is uneven, being pleasantly diversified with hills and valleys. On the border of the Sound the hills are generally moderate, and in the interior more elevated.

"The valley which lies along Norwalk river, and in which the town is built, is beautiful. Few richer prospects of the same extent can be found than that which is presented from the neighboring eminences of this ground : the town built in its bosom, with its cheerful spires ; the river flowing through the middle ; the farms on the bordering hills; the rich plain that skirts the Sound, and a train of islands fronting the mouth of the river, and extending eastward five or six miles ; together with an unlimited view of the Sound, and the Long Island shore."

Norwalk contains two considerable and flourishing villages, Norwalk Borough, and the village of Old Well. Norwalk Borough, (constituted as such in 1836,) is a village of upwards of 130 handsome buildings, and an extensive pottery. Norwalk is a place of considerable activity and business, being a commercial depot and market for the northern part of the county ; a considerable proportion of the staple products being brought here for sale, or to be freighted for New York.

The village is built on both sides of a small river or creek, which is much contracted in width at the bridge which connects the two parts of the village, and the buildings on each side of the stream are so near each other, that the passage of the river from the north is not readily perceived at a short distance. Vessels drawing six feet of water can get up to the bridge in the most compact part of the village.

The flourishing village of Old Well is situated about 1 1-2 miles south of the central part of Norwalk Borough, on the west side of the creek.

There are at present in this village six or seven hat factories, three potteries, and a carriage making establishment. This is the principal landing place for steam-boats for Norwalk and the vicinity, there being a daily line from and to New York. A boat every other day leaves Norwalk bridge for New York.

There is a cotton factory and a factory for manufacturing carpets in the town. This establishment, called the " Patent Carpet Company," was commenced in 1834.— Their carpeting, of which they manufacture at this time about 200 yards daily, is made *without* spinning or weaving, being made of felting, the material of which hats are composed.

This town was burnt by the British, under Tryon, on the 17th July, 1779. Eighty dwelling houses, 2 churches, 87 barns, 17 shops, 4 mills, and 5 vessels were destroyed.

Norway, Me.

Oxford co. This is a fine township, well watered by several streams and ponds. One of the ponds is large,—very handsome, and discharges its waters into Little Androscoggin river. Norway lies 47 miles W. by S. from Augusta, and is bounded on the E. by Paris. Incorporated, 1797. Population,

1837, 1,791. Wheat crop, same year, 7,272 bushels.

Norwich, Vt.

Windsor co. This town lies on the west side of Connecticut river, and is connected with Hanover, N. H. by a bridge. The surface of the town is uneven, but the soil is good for grain, pasturage and fruit. Ompomponoosuck river and other streams water the town and afford it good mill seats. First settled, 1763. Population, 1830, 2,316.—It lies 40 miles S. S. E. from Montpelier and 19 N. from Windsor.

Norwich village is pleasantly situated on a plain, near Connecticut river, and contains a university and a number of handsome buildings. See *Register*.

Norwich, Mass.

Hampshire co. This mountainous town is watered by Westfield river. The soil in many parts is good for grazing, and many sheep are kept here. There is a cotton mill in the town, and manufactures of leather, boots, shoes, axes, and spirits. It lies 108 miles W. from Boston, and 12 W. by S. from Northampton. Incorporated, 1773. Population, 1837, 714.

Norwich, Ct.

One of the chief towns of New London county. Norwich city is situated at the head of navigation of Thames river, at the point of land formed by the junction of the Shetucket and Yantic rivers, whose united waters constitute the Thames. The main part of the city is built on the southern declivity of a high and rocky hill: the houses are built in tiers, rising one above another. The city, as it is approached from the south, presents one of the most beautiful, interesting and romantic prospects in the state. The buildings, which are mostly painted white, appear in full view for a considerable distance down the river; these contrasted with the deep green foliage covering the rocky and elevated banks of the river, give a picturesque variety to the scene, forming on the water a delightful avenue to the city. There are in this city, (or as it was formerly called, Chelsea or Norwich Landing,) a court house and town hall. A high school for boys, and a female academy, in which the higher branches of education are taught, have been in operation for a considerable time, and are in flourishing circumstances. About a mile eastward of the landing is situated the flourishing village of Greenville, at the eastern extremity of which a dam has been constructed across the Shetucket,which will, it is calculated furnish sufficient water power to carry 60,000 spindles: four or five large factories, and perhaps 40 or 50 dwelling houses, are, or are about to be built. Among the factories there is perhaps the most extensive paper mill in the state, owned, by the Chelsea Manufacturing Company. There are also two other paper mills near the falls, which do an extensive business. The first paper manufactured in Connecticut was made in this town by Col. Christopher Leffingwell. There are at, and near the falls, 9 or 10 establishments for manufacturing purposes. Besides these, and those at Greenville, there are some more in other parts of the town. The principal manufactures are those of cotton, paper and woolens. Norwich city is 13 miles N. from New London, 38 S. E. from Hartford, 38 S. W. from Providence, and 50 N. E. from New Haven. Population of Norwich, in 1830, was 5,179; of which 3,144 were in the city limits.

Above the cove, which sets up about a mile from the river, "the bed of the river consists of a solid rock, having a perpendicular height of ten or twelve feet, over which the whole body of water falls in an entire sheet upon a bed of rocks below. The river here is compressed into a very narrow channel, the banks consisting of solid rocks, and being bold and elevated. For a distance of 15 or 20 rods, the channel or bed of the river has a gradual descent, is crooked and covered with pointed rocks. The rock, forming the bed of the river at the bottom of the perpendicular falls, is curiously excavated, some of the cavities being five or six feet deep, from the constant pouring of the sheet of water for a succession of ages." At the bottom of the falls there is the broad basin of the cove, where the enraged and agitated element resumes its usual smoothness and placidity, and the whole scenery about these falls is uncommonly beautiful and picturesque.

During the wars between Uncas and the Narragansets, Uncas was closely besieged in his fort near the Thames, until his provisions became nearly exhausted, and he with his men were on the point of perishing by famine or sword. Fortunately he found means of giving intelligence to the scouts who had been sent out from Saybrook fort.— By his messengers, he represented the great danger the English would be in, were the Narragansets suffered to overpower the Mohegans.

"Upon this intelligence, one Thomas Leffingwell, an ensign at Saybrook, an enterprising, bold man, loaded a canoe with beef, corn and peas, and under the cover of night paddled from Saybrook into the Thames, and had the address to get the whole into the fort. The enemy soon perceiving that Uncas was relieved, raised the siege.— For this service, Uncas gave Leffingwell a deed of a great part, if not the whole town of Norwich.— In June, 1659, Uncas with his two sons, Owaneko and Attawanhood, by a more formal and authentic deed, made over to said Leffingwell, John Mason, Esq., the Rev. James Fitch and others, consisting of thirty-five proprietors, the whole of Norwich, which is about nine miles square. The company at this time gave Uncas and his sons about £70, as a further compensation for so large and fine a tract."

Nottingham, N. H.,

Rockingham co., is 25 miles E. S. E. from Concord, and 20 W. from Portsmouth. Population, in 1830, 1,157. There are several ponds in this town, mostly of small size. Little river and several other streams rise here; and North river passes through the town. The soil is in many parts good, though the surface is rough and broken. Several mountains extend along the W. part of the town, forming parts of the range called Blue Hills.

Nottingham Square is a pleasant village on an elevated site. Bog iron ore is found here in great quantities; and it is said inexhaustible masses of mountain ore exist in the mountains. Crystals and crystalline spars are found here; and also ochres in small quantities. Nottingham was incorporated in 1722, and settled in 1727.

Gen. JOSEPH CILLEY entered the army of the revolution at its commencement and commanded the 1st N. H. regiment. He was distinguished for bravery and patriotism during the whole contest.

Hon. THOMAS BARTLETT was an active revolutionary patriot; one of the committee of safety; Lt. Col. under Stark at the capture of Burgoyne, and commanded a regiment at West Point in 1780, when the treachery of Arnold betrayed that post.

Gen. HENRY BUTLER was an officer in the army of the revolution, and Major General of militia. Descendants of these revolutionary worthies now live in the town.

Nulhegan River, Vt.

This river rises by several branches in the highlands, at the north part of Essex county. These branches unite and fall into the Connecticut at Brunswick. This river is in some parts rapid; in others, deep and sluggish. It waters about 120 square miles, and is fifty feet wide at its mouth. The head waters of this and of the river Clyde, pass N. into Memphremagog lake, and are near each other. This was formerly an Indian route between Connecticut river and Canada.

Oakham, Mass.

Worcester co. The surface of this town is uneven; some of the lands which border on the streams that fall into Chickopee river are fertile. The highlands are not very good. There is a satinet factory in the town, and manufactures of straw bonnets, palm-leaf hats, leather, ploughs, boots and shoes. Oakham lies 60 miles W. from Boston, and 15 N. W. from Worcester. It was taken from Rutland in 1762. Population, 1837, 1,109.

Oldtown, Me.
Penobscot co. See *Orono.*

Oldtown Harbor, Mass.
See *Edgartown.*

Olammon, Me.
Penobscot co. See *Greenbush.*

Ompomponoosuc River, Vt.

This good mill stream is about 20 miles in length:—it rises near the centre of the county of Orange, and falls into Connecticut river at Norwich.

Onion River, Vt.

This is one of the largest and most valuable rivers in the state.— It is about 70 miles in length, and in its course fertilizes large tracts of land and produces a great hydraulic power. This stream rises in Caledonia county: it passes nearly through the centre of the counties of Washington and Chittenden, and after passing " Winooski city" it falls into Champlain lake, five miles N. from Burlington village.

Winooski is the beautiful Indian name of this river, and had the good people of Winooski possessed the *exquisite taste* of their predecessors they would probably have called their charming little city *cabbage town.*

Onion river, so called, has numerous tributaries, and is one of the most romantic streams in the country. The channels which have been worn in the rocks, by its ceaseless current, are objects of great admiration. In its passage through the mountains are found fissures through solid rocks from 30 to 100 feet in depth, with smooth perpendicular sides, 60 or 70 feet in width. In many places on this stream are natural bridges, curious caverns, and delightful water-falls.

The road near the banks of this stream, from Connecticut river to Burlington, is said to be the best passage across the mountains, in that direction: it is certainly highly picturesque and delightful.

Oquossak Lake, Me.

Oxford co. This large lake lies a few miles N. E. of the Mooseluckmaguntic. It is very irregular in its form, and contains many islands.

Orange, N. H.,

Grafton co., is 16 miles E. from Dartmouth college, 10 S. W. from Plymouth, and 40 N. W. from Concord. Population, 1830, 405. In this town are found many mineral substances, such as lead ore, iron ore, &c. There is in the S. E. part a small pond, in which is found a species of paint resembling spruce yellow. Chalk, intermixed with magnesia, is said to be procured from the same pond. In 1810, a valuable species of ochre was discovered. It is found in great abundance, deposited in veins, and of a quality superior to the imported.—

Large quantities of it are annually prepared for market. The surface of Orange is uneven, but the soil in many parts of it is productive.—Cardigan mountain lies in the E. part of the town. Orange was granted by the name of *Cardigan*, Feb. 6, 1769. Its settlement commenced in 1773.

Orange County, Vt.

Chelsea, chief town. This county is bounded N. by Washington and Caledonia counties, E. by Connecticut river, S. by Windsor county, and W. by Addison and Washington counties. Area, 650 square miles. Population, 1820, 24,169; 1830, 27,285. Population to a square mile, 42. Incorporated, 1781. The eastern range of the Green mountains extends along the northwestern part of the county. The principal rivers, besides the Connecticut, are the Ompomponoosuc, Wait's, branches of the White, and Stevens' branch of the Onion. The lands in Orange county are generally good for grazing, and supply many cattle and all the varieties of the dairy, of which a large amount is annually sent to market. In 1837 there were 99,346 sheep within its limits. This county contains some excellent tracts of land on the banks of the Connecticut. Iron and lead ores, slate and granite, are abundant.

Orange, Vt.

Orange co. This town lies 12 miles S. E. from Montpelier, and 12 N. from Chelsea. First settled, 1793. Population, 1830, 1,016.—The soil is cold, and better suited for grazing than grain. Knox's mountain lies in this town:—it is quite an elevation, and is composed principally of granite. Some of the quarries in the town produce excellent granite for building, and here are found plates of beautiful white mica, several inches square. The products of the town in cattle and wool are considerable.

Orange, Mass.

Franklin co. Orange lies 72 miles W. from Boston, and 20 E. from Greenfield. Incorporated, 1783. Population, 1830, 880; 1837, 1,543. The manufactures of the town consist of iron castings, boots, shoes, palm-leaf hats, card boards, shoe pegs, chairs and cabinet ware : annual amount about $40,000. Miller's river affords the town a good water power, and Tully hill a fine prospect. The soil is uneven, and better fitted for grazing than tillage. There is a pleasant village in the town, and a good fish pond.

Orange, Ct.

New Haven co. This town was taken from New Haven and Milford in 1822. The name was adopted in honor of William, Prince of Orange, in commemoration of the benefits received from him by the colony of Connecticut; particularly for the restoration of their charter after the usurpation and tyranny of Edmund Andros.

Orange lies about 4 miles S. W. from New Haven and is a pleasant town with a productive soil. The inhabitants are principally farmers. *Savin Rock* in this town is a romantic spot, and a place of resort in the summer. There are mines of silver and copper in the town, and asbestos is found in abundance in serpentine rocks. Population, 1830, 1,341.

Orford, N. H.

Grafton co. It lies on Connecticut river, over which is a bridge, connecting with Fairlee. Orford is 11 miles below Haverhill, 17 N. of Hanover, and 64 N. W. from Concord. The soil is generally of a fertile character. The large intervale farms, watered by the Connecticut, are particularly distinguished for their beauty and fertility. There are two considerable elevations, called Mount Cuba and Mount Sunday, lying near the centre of the town. There are four or five ponds of considerable size, one of which, called Baker's upper pond, lies within 3 or 4 miles of Connecticut river. This pond discharges its waters into another pond, lying partly in Wentworth, and the waters of both empty into Baker's river. Indian pond lies about 1 mile west from Baker's upper pond. Limestone is found in great abundance. It is of the primitive kind, coarse grained, and forms a strong and hard cement. It is found at the foot of a mountain, about 400 or 500 feet above Connecticut river. Soap stone is also found here in great abundance. A light grey granite rock, much used for mill stones and for building, is found in various places. Galena, or lead ore, of a very fine texture, containing needles of crystallized quartz, or lead, has been found, in considerable quantities in sinking a well. Orford contains a pleasant village, situated on the main road. "It is built on a beautiful plain bordered by intervale on the W. The hills on both sides of the river, near the centre of the expansion, approach each other so as to form a kind of neck; and with a similar approximation at the two ends give the whole the appearance of a double amphitheatre, or of the numerical figure 8. The greatest breadth of each division is about 1 1-2 miles; and the length of each between 2 and 3 miles." The buildings stand principally on a single street, of 2 or 3 miles in extent. Orford was granted Sept. 25, 1761. In June, 1765, a Mr. Cross with his family, from Lebanon, first settled in this town. A congregational church was gathered Aug. 27, 1770. Rev. Oliver Noble was ordained Nov. 5, 1771. Population, 1830, 1,829.

Orland, Me.

Hancock co. This town lies on the east side of Penobscot river, opposite to Orphan's Island. It lies 64 miles E. from Augusta and 12 W. from Ellsworth. Orland is finely watered by ponds and streams: it has a good soil, a pleasant village and great navigable facilities. Incorporated, 1800. Population, 1830, 975; 1837, 1,244.

Orleans County, Vt.

Irasburgh, chief town. This county is bounded N. by Lower Canada, E. by Essex and Caledonia counties, S. by Caledonia county, and W. by Franklin and Lamoille counties. This county lies between the eastern and western ranges of the Green mountains. The surface is generally handsome and the soil well adapted for wheat, rye and grass: the climate is rather too cold for corn, and some parts of the county is low and marshy. Orleans county is watered by Missisque, Black, Barton and other rivers. It contains more ponds than any county in the state. Much of its trade goes to Canada by the way of Memphremagog lake, which lies in this county and Canada. In 1837 there were 30,657 sheep in the county. Incorporated, 1792. Population, 1830, 11,375.

Orleans, Mass.

Barnstable co. Orleans was taken from Eastham, in 1797. It extends across a narrow part of Cape Cod, and is indented with coves and creeks on both sides. Stage harbor opens on the east through Chatham and Nauset beaches, which extend along the coast:—between which and the town is Pleasant bay, with several islands. In 1837, there were 33 vessels belonging to Orleans engaged in the cod and mackerel fishery, the tonnage of which was 2,310 tons. They took 20,000 quintals of cod fish and 600 barrels of mackerel. There were 31,000 bushels of salt used, and 264 men and boys were employed. The value of fish taken, when cured and packed, was $91,100 :—capital invested, $33,000. There are 50 establishments for the manufacture of salt in the town ; during the year ending April 1, 1837, there were 21,780 bushels made. There are also manufactures of palm-leaf hats, leather, boots, shoes and tin ware. Orleans lies 20 miles E. from Barnstable. Population, 1830, 1,799 ; 1837, 1,936.

Orono, Me.

Penobscot co. This town lies on the west side of Penobscot river, and is watered by Dead stream and a large part of Pushaw lake. It is 74 miles N. E. from Augusta. Incorporated, 1806. Population, 1830, 1,473 ; 1837, 3,961. The soil of the town is good, and produced, in 1837, 1,744 bushels of wheat. This town borders on the Great Falls in Penobscot river, and contains a great number of saw mills, which manufacture a vast amount of lumber annually for the Bangor market. Orono is pleasant and uncommonly flourishing.

A rail-road between Bangor and the villages of *Stillwater* and *Oldtown*, in Orono, was opened for travel in 1836. It is 12 miles in length, and cost $350,000. The Penobscot river at Oldtown, above the falls, is 40 feet higher than at Bangor. The village of Stillwater is 4 miles below Oldtown.

Above the falls, and about a mile above the village of Oldtown, near the mouth of Dead stream, on " Oldtown Island," is the *Indian Settlement*. This settlement is very pleasantly located, and secure from approach except by boats or canoes. It contains a number of framed houses, and a neat chapel with a bell.

In 1837, John Neptune, the lieutenant Governor, and other officers of the Penobscot tribe of Indians, finished taking by families a very particular census of all who belong to the tribe, for the purpose of a just and equal distribution of the annuities and other monies paid to them. It was found that the families in all were ninety five—the list exhibiting the head of each family by name, and the number of individuals each one contains, annexed thereto. The whole number of souls in the tribe was three hundred and sixty-two. Their officers are, a governor, lieutenant governor, a colonel, four captains, one 'squire, and one deacon. In religion they are catholics. Several of them can read, and a few can write, though in a poor hand.

The whole tribe is divided in politics, and on some occasions party spirit rages with almost as much warmth as among the pale faces, though generally better tempered. No affair of *honor*, or rather of *murder*, has ever been known to disgrace these savages.

The tribe own, collectively, all the islands in the Penobscot river, beginning with that of Oldtown, where their village is, and including all up as far as the forks, several miles above the Matawamkeag, many of which are exceedingly pleasant and fertile.

The Indians are not poor, having sold some of their lands for large sums. To such a remnant, however, is this tribe reduced—a tribe anciently and uniformly called the Tarratines, who could bring into the field more than two thousand warriors, and who claimed the lands on both sides of the Penobscot river from its sources to its mouth.

Orphan's Island, Me.

Penobscot co. This island, containing about 5,000 acres of excellent land, at the mouth of Penobscot river, is 4 miles in length. It is attached to the town of Bucksport ; the head or north part of it lies opposite to the beautiful village in that town. This island divides the Penobscot into two branches: the western or main branch is called the "Narrows," on which side a fort is about to be constructed by the U. S. government for the protection of the river. The other branch is called " Eastern river."

This beautiful island derived its name from its having been the property of an orphan heiress who inherited it as her part of the Waldo Patent.

Orrington, Me.

Penobscot co. This is a fine township of land with a handsome village on the east side of Penobscot river, opposite to Hampden. The town has a good mill stream and enjoys great navigable facilities. Population, 1837, 1,426. Wheat crop, same year, 2,340 bushels.

Orwell, Vt.

Rutland co. This town lies on Champlain lake opposite to Ticonderoga, N. Y. and contains Mount Independence, celebrated in the annals of the revolutionary war. The lake here is about a mile wide, and from the Mount a delightful prospect is presented. Orwell was first permanently settled in 1783. The soil of the town is generally good and productive. In 1837 it contained 21,512 sheep. There is a spring in the town from the waters of which Epsom salts have been made, and shells of animals have been found supposed to have pertained to the ocean. There are good mill streams in Orwell and a pleasant village. Population, 1830, 1,598.

Ossipee, N. H.,

Strafford co. is 60 miles N. N. E. from Concord, and about 15 N. E. from Gilford, across Winnepisiogee lake. Ossipee mountain, a rough and broken range, lies in the N. W. part of Ossipee, extending into the adjoining towns. It is 6 or 8 miles in length, and is so elevated that in easterly storms the winds break over the summits, frequently causing much injury to the farms, and buildings at its base. Ossipee lake is in this town, and Freedom: it is a fine body of water, of an oval form, covering about 7,000 acres, having no island, and its waters clear and beautiful. Ossipee river flows from this lake, from whence it passes through Freedom into the Saco, in Maine. Pine river passes through the E. part of Ossipee, and Bearcamp river falls into the lake on the N. W. There are several ponds in Ossipee, the largest of which lies partly in Tuftonborough, and is about 400 rods long. Bear pond in the S. E. part, has no visible outlet. Near the W. shore of Ossipee lake, is a mound of earth 45 or 50 feet in diameter, of a circular form, and about 10 feet high, from which have been taken several entire skeletons, and also tomahawks, &c. exhibiting the strongest evidence that the tribe once so powerful in this vicinity had their principal residence here. Ossipee was incorporated, Feb. 22, 1785. Population, 1830, 1,935.

Otis, Me.

Hancock co. Otis was incorporated in 1835. It is bounded on the west by Ellsworth. It is the source of some of the rivers which flow into Frenchman's bay, and Union river, passes its N. W. corner. Population, 1837, 92.

Otis, Mass.

Berkshire co. This township is on high ground, and is the source of some of the head waters of Farmington and Westfield rivers. These streams flow from several very handsome ponds. The surface of the town is uneven but the soil is productive, particularly of good pasturage. The manufactures consist of leather, boots, shoes, chairs, cabinet ware, lumber, &c. It lies 130 miles W. by S. from Boston, and 15

S. E. from Lenox. Population, 1837, 1,077. Incorporated, 1793.

Otisfield, Me.

Cumberland co. This town is watered by Crooked river, which empties into Sebago lake. The soil is very good, and produced, in 1837, 4,525 bushels of wheat. It lies 82 miles S. S. W. from Augusta and 32 N. N. W. from Portland. Population 1830, 1,257.

Otter Creek, Vt.

This stream rises on the south part of Rutland county :—it traverses, in a northern course, nearly through the centre of that county, and waters Clarendon, Rutland, Pittsford, Brandon and other towns; it then enters Addison county, and passes to Middlebury, where it falls very considerably, affording that pleasant town an admirable water power;— it then passes Weybridge, New Haven and Vergennes, and falls into Champlain lake at Ferrisburgh. From Vergennes it is navigable for the largest lake vessels, 8 miles. There are no considerable falls on this stream except at Middlebury, Weybridge and Vergennes. In many parts of its course it is sluggish. From Middlebury to Pittsford, a distance of 25 miles, it is navigable for boats. Otter Creek has many tributaries which afford a great water power. Its length is about 90 miles, and on its banks are large tracts of alluvial meadows, some of the best in the state. It receives the waters of a basin of about 900 square miles.

Owl's Head, Me.

Lincoln co. This noted place on our eastern waters is a point of land attached to the town of Thomaston, running out three or four miles into Penobscot bay, opposite to the island town of Vinalhaven. Owl's Head forms the western entrance into the mouth of Penobscot river, and has a light house to guide the wary mariner on his way. A breakwater is about being erected, which will render the harbor at this place one of the most commodious, as it is one of the most important, on the coast. An almost countless number of vessels pass this place annually. Frequently five hundred pass in a day. From March 15th to June 15th, 1838, 5019 sail were seen to pass in the day time. Owl's Head is not only a stopping place in a storm, but a resort for great numbers of people, for many miles around, to take passages on board of steamers and other vessels. It is a delightful place in summer, and has justly acquired a reputation for possessing all the various enjoyments which induce thousands to visit the sea coast at other places. It lies 4 miles E. from Thomaston, 55 S. from Bangor, 40 S. E. from Augusta, and 79 E. N. E. from Portland.

Oxford County, Me.

Paris, chief town. This county is bounded N. by Lower Canada, E. by Franklin and Kennebec counties, S. by Cumberland and York counties, and W. by New Hampshire. It is watered by the Margallaway, Androscoggin, Saco, and numerous other rivers. In the northern part of the county lies a collection of large lakes whose waters empty into the Umbagog, and pass to the ocean by the Androscoggin and Kennebec rivers. Although some parts of the county are rough and mountainous, yet a very large part of it is exceedingly fertile, particularly on the borders of its numerous rivers, lakes and ponds. This county contained an area of 2,684 square miles previous to the formation of Franklin county, in 1838, which was formed partly from Oxford county. The population of Oxford county, in 1820, was 17,630; 1830, 35,211; 1837, 40,640. Population to a square mile, 15. The number of sheep in this county, in 1837, was 76,028.

Oxford, Me.

Oxford co. This town is watered by little Androscoggin river and several ponds. It contains some excellent land and two flourishing villages. It produced, in 1837, 3,226 bushels of wheat. Population, same year, 1,124. Oxford lies 52 miles S. W. from Augusta, and 8 S. from Paris.

Oxford, Mass.

Worcester co. This is an important manufacturing town, of uneven surface, strong, gravelly soil; 45 miles W. from Boston and 10 S. from Worcester. Incorporated, 1773. Population, 1837, 2,047. There are in the town 5 woolen and 4 cotton mills, and manufactures of boots and shoes:—total value, the year ending April 1, 1837, $501,394. Oxford is a pleasant town, and finely watered by French river, which passes to the ocean by the Quinnebaug and Thames.

The original township of Oxford was eight miles square, and was granted to Joseph Dudley and others, in 1680, for the accommodation of about 30 French protestant families, who had escaped from France after the revocation of the Edict of Nantz, when they became exposed to every cruelty and hardship that catholic intolerance and religious bigotry could invent. They were assisted in their emigration to this country by the proprietors of the grant, and settled here about 1686. They built a fort on a hill in the eastern part of the town, now called Mayo's, or Fort Hill, where its remains are still visible. It was constructed by the rules of art, with bastions, and had a well within its enclosure. They had another fort, and a meeting house. The grapes, currants, and asparagus of their planting, still grow here, and the last of the peach trees was destroyed by the gale of 1815. They had a minister while resident here, whose name was Bondet. These people remained here till 1696, when the Indians attacked the place and murdered some of the people. This so terrified the inhabitants that they left the place, and most of them settled in Boston, where a French church was maintained by them several years.

Oxford, Ct.

New Haven co. Oxford was taken from Derby in 1798. It lies 14 miles N. W. from New Haven and 40 S. W. from Hartford. It is watered by Housatonick and Naugatuck rivers. The surface of the town is diversified with hills and valleys;—the soil is generally a gravelly loam, fertile and productive.

There are large manufacturing establishments in Oxford, among which are three satinet factories and an extensive hat manufactory. The water power at this place is excellent. Population, 1830, 1,763. From "Governor's Hill" a fine view of the neat village of "Quaker Farms," and the surrounding country is presented.

About one mile south of the central part of the town is a remarkable mineral spring, called "The Pool," from the circumstance of its waters being efficacious, and much used for the cure of the salt rheum and other complaints. "Once in a month a yellowish scum will collect upon the surface of the water, which in a few days runs off, and leaves the pool perfectly clear. In the coldest weather, this spring never freezes; in the dryest season it is as full as at other times."

Palermo, Me.

Waldo co. This town is watered by several beautiful ponds, which form the head waters of Sheepscot river. This is a farming town of good soil and undulating surface,—it produced, in 1837, 5,326 bushels of wheat. Population, same year, 1,538. It lies 16 miles E. N. E. from Augusta, and 24 W. from Belfast. Incorporated, 1804.

Palmer, Mass.

Hampden co. This town was originally settled by a colony from Ireland. It was incorporated in 1752. The surface of Palmer is hilly, but the soil is good, particularly along the banks of Ware and Swift rivers, by which it is finely watered, and supplied with water power. There are 1 woolen and 2 cotton mills in the town, and manufactures of boots, shoes, scythes, palm-leaf hats and wagons;—total amount, the year ending April 1, 1837, $178,556. The value of 2,652 fleeces of wool sheared in this town, that year, was $4,243.—Palmer lies 70 miles W. by S. from Boston, and 16 E. N. E. from Springfield. Population, 1830, 1,237; 1837, 1,810.

Palmyra, Me.

Somerset co. Sebasticook river passes through this town, and affords it a good water power. The soil is rich, and the surface undulating. There are some mills in the town, and considerable attention is paid to its agricultural interests. It lies 51 miles N. N. E. from Augusta, and 25 E. N. E. from Norridgewock. Incorporated, 1807. Population, in 1837, 1,328. Wheat crop, same year, 8,523 bushels.

Panton, Vt.

Addison co. This town is bounded W. by Champlain lake, and E. by Otter creek. A sluggish stream passes through it; yet, although thus watered, it does not possess a good mill site, the country being exceedingly level. It lies 40 miles W. S. W. from Montpelier, 13 N. W. from Middlebury, 25 S. by W. from Burlington, and is 4 miles from Elizabethtown, N. Y., across the lake. Population, 1830, 605.

Paris, Me.

Chief town, Oxford co. Paris is well watered, and supplied with mill privileges by Little Androscoggin river, on which are several mills in the town. The soil is excellent, although in some parts uneven and mountainous. The principal village is well built, pleasantly located, and the seat of considerable business. The town was incorporated in 1793. Population, 1837, 2,352. Wheat crop, same year, 10,453 bushels. Paris lies 42 miles W. by S. from Augusta, and 40 N. by W. from Portland.

Parkman, Me.

Piscataquis co. This town is watered by a branch of Piscataquis river, and has an excellent soil for agricultural purposes. It lies 64 miles N. by E. from Augusta, and 14 W. from Dover. Incorporated, 1822. Population, 1830, 803; 1837, 1,125. Wheat crop, 1837, 6,018 bushels.

Parsonsfield, Me.

York co. This town lies at the N. W. corner of the county, and is bounded W. by the state of New Hampshire, and N. by Ossipee river. It is 36 miles W. by N. from Portland, 21 N. by W. from Alfred, and 93 W. S. W. from Augusta.—First settled, 1774. Incorporated, 1785. Population, 1837, 2,510.—The surface of the town is rough and hilly, but the soil, though hard, is productive of good crops of grain and hay. Wheat crop, 1837, 3,929 bushels.

There are many good farmers in this town, and good specimens of iron ore, zinc and crystalized quartz are found here. In this place is an incorporated seminary, for the education of males and females. The institution is under the direction of the Free Will Baptists, and is in a flourishing condition.

Passadumkeag, Me.

Penobscot co. This town lies on the east side of Penobscot river, 98 miles N. E. from Augusta, and 30 N. by E. from Bangor. The soil of the town is fertile, and promises a rich reward to the industrious farmer. Population, 1837, 422. Wheat crop, same year, 1,070 bushels.

The *village of Passadumkeag* is admirable located, and will doubtless become an important mart of the trade of a large section of country. This flourishing village lies at the junction of Passadumkeag river with the Penobscot. This delightful stream is about 25 miles in length. It rises in the north eastern part of this county, and waters the northern part of Hancock county. It re-enters Penobscot county, and receives the Cold stream, two miles from Passadumkeag village. Both the Passadumkeag and Cold stream afford excellent mill privileges.

Passamaquoddy Bay, Me.

This bay lies partly in Maine, and partly in the British Province of New Brunswick. The boundary line between the state of Maine and New Brunswick passes through the western part of this bay up the river St. Croix. Campo Bello, Deer, and other English islands almost enclose this bay from the ocean. At its mouth it is about 9 miles in width, and extends from West Quoddy Head, in Lubec, due north into New Brunswick, about 25 miles.—This bay contains a great number of excellent harbors; it is never frozen over, and abounds with cod, herring and other fishes. The most important English town on this bay is St. Andrews, a very flourishing place, 15 miles N. from Eastport.—The *Passamaquoddy Indians* reside at Perry, Me.

Passumpsick River, Vt.

This river rises in Caledonia, and on the south border of Essex counties. It passes south about 35 miles, and falls into the Connecticut at Barnet, about a mile below the foot of Fifteen Mile Falls. It has a number of tributaries. This is a valuable stream, both on account of the numerous mill sites it affords, and the large tracts of choice intervale it forms on its borders.—It is generally deep, but in many places it is very rapid, and forms beautiful cascades.

Patricktown, Me.

Lincoln co. This *plantation* contains the principal part of a large pond, and is watered by streams which flow into the Sheepscot and Damariscotta. This is a large plantation, of good soil. Population, 1837, 465. It lies 17 miles E. from Augusta, and 20 N. W. from Warren.

Pawcatuck River.

This river rises in the western part of Rhode Island, and empties into Long Island Sound, separating, at its mouth, the towns of Westerly, R. I., and Stonington, Ct. It is navigable about 6 miles from its mouth, and Wood and Charles rivers, two of its principals tributaries, are good mill streams.

Pawcatuck village. See *Westerly.*

Pawlet, Vt.

Rutland co. First settled, 1761. Population, 1830, 1,965. Pawlet lies 21 miles S. W. from Rutland, and 27 S. E. from Whitehall, N. Y. The town is watered by Pawlet river, which falls into Champlain lake at Whitehall, and by Indian river, which rises from a spring sufficiently large to carry a mill.—The latter river was formerly a great resort of the natives, who frequented it for trout and other fish with which it abounds. The territory of Pawlet is nearly divided by a range of mountains, the highest summit of which is known by the name of "Haystack." This is a pleasant town, with some manufactures. The soil is dry and warm, and produces good crops of corn and hay. It feeds about 14,000 sheep.

Pawtucket, Mass.

Bristol co. The *town* of Pawtucket lies on the east side of the river of the same name. It is two miles square, and was taken from Seekonk in 1828. The population of the town, in 1830, was 1,458; 1837, 1,881.

The *village of Pawtucket* is very pleasant;—it is an important manufacturing place, commanding a considerable trade, and contains a population of about 8,000. It lies on both sides of the river, and includes a part of the town of North Providence, in R. I.

The first manufacture of cotton cloth in this country, by water power machinery, was commenced at this place. The water power is immense, and the fall of the river within a short distance, is 50 feet. The river is navigable to the village for vessels of considerable burthen. It runs 4 miles S. by W. to Providence river, at India Point, near the depot of the Boston and Providence rail-road, one mile below the centre of the city of Providence. The river, *above* Pawtucket, in Massachusetts, takes the name of *Blackstone;* below the falls it takes the name of *Seekonk*. This place is 4 miles N. from Providence, 36 S. from Boston, 16 W. by S. from Taunton, and 38 S. E. from Worcester. At this place are 12 or more cotton mills and print works, and manufactures of cotton machinery, bobbins, spools, &c. ; of boots, shoes, carriages, vessels, chairs, cabinet wares, &c. ; total annual value, about two millions of dollars.

The turnpike road from this place to Providence is probably the best road of the kind in the world. It is very straight, wide, level, smooth, and shaded on each side by beautiful trees.

SAMUEL SLATER, Esq., the father of cotton manufactures in America, resided in this village many years. He died at Webster, Mass., greatly respected, April 20, 1835, aged 67.

Pawtuxet River, R. I.

This celebrated river rises in the western part of the State. It has numerous tributaries, and mingles with the waters of the Narraganset, five miles below Providence. This river is distinguished for its valuable mill sites, and for the numerous manufacturing establishments erected on its banks. Pawtuxet and its branches fertilize a large portion of the state. See *Warwick*.

Paxton, Mass.

Worcester co. Paxton was taken from Leicester and Rutland, in 1765. It is on high ground; its waters descend both to the Connecticut and Merrimack. It lies 50 miles W. from Boston, and 7 N. W. from Worcester. Population, 1837, 619. This is a pleasant town, with manufactures of palm-leaf hats, boots, shoes, leather, carriages, &c. The surface of the town is uneven, but the soil is good, and well cultivated by its proprietors.

Peacham, Vt.

Caledonia co. As no town can be considered properly peopled without some of the fair sex, the date of the first settlement of Peacham must have been near 1777, when Henry Elkins, the first child in town, was born. The first mill was erected in 1781. The town is well watered by several ponds and streams; the surface is pleasantly diversified; the soil fertile and well cultivated by independent farmers. The agricultural products are considerable. About 6,000 sheep are kept. Peacham lies 20 miles E. by N. from Montpelier, and 8 S. by W. from Danville. Population, 1830, 1,351.

Peeling, N. H.

Grafton co. This town is 20 miles N. from Plymouth, and 60 N. from Concord. The Pemigewasset passes through its E. section. The three branches of this river unite in the N. part of Peeling. There are several brooks and rivulets which supply this place with a number of mill privileges. The ponds are numerous. Cushman's mountain, in the S. W., Black mountain in the N. W., and Blue mountain in the W. are the highest elevations. Among these mountains, branches of the Wild Amonoosuck and Baker's rivers, and Moosehillock brook, have their sources. On the last stream there is a beautiful cascade. There are here two springs which have been termed medicinal. Peeling was settled about 1773. Population, 1830, 291.

Pelham, N. H.

Hillsborough co. This town is distant 37 miles S. from Concord, and 19 S.E. from Amherst. Here are three ponds, called Gumpas, Island, and North ponds. Beaver river passes through the town. On this river and the tributary streams there is much valuable meadow.— The inhabitants depend principally on agriculture for the means of support. Much timber and cord wood are carried annually to the banks of the Merrimack, and thence conveyed to Newburyport, or to Boston through Middlesex canal. The first settlements were made in 1722. The town was incorporated in 1746, about 5 years after the state line was established, by which a part was separated from Dracut, Mass. Population in 1830, 1,075.

Pelham, Mass.

Hampshire co. This town lies 80 miles W. from Boston, and 13 N. E. from Northampton. It was incorporated in 1742. Population, in 1837, 957. The surface of the town is elevated and uneven; the soil is hard but productive. Swift and Fort rivers afford it mill privileges. Some palm-leaf hats are made here.

Some years ago the notorious Stephen Burroughs profaned the christian sabbath, by imposing himself on the innocent people of Pelham as a minister of the gospel.

Pemadumcook Lake, Me.,

Or the *Bamedumpkok*. This large lake is of very irregular form, containing a great number of islands, and lies a few miles N. from Baker's mountain. It receives the waters of numerous lakes, or collections of water, lying between it and the eastern sources of the Moose Head. The soil on the borders of the Pemadumcook, and the lakes connected with it, is remarkably fertile. The Jo Mary lakes are beautiful sheets of water, and are surrounded by some of the best timbered land in the state. They lie near the Pemadumcook; and the facilities afforded for rafting lumber down the Penobscot, through that lake, render that section of country very valuable.

Pembroke, Me.

Washington co. Population, in 1837, 866. Wheat crop, same year, 1,216 bushels. It lies 178 miles from Augusta.
See "Down East."

Pembroke, N. H.,

Merrimack co., lies 60 miles N. W. from Boston, and 6 S. E. from Concord. This town is generally well watered. The Suncook, on the S. E. boundary, furnishes many valuable water privileges. The main street extends nearly on a parallel with Merrimack river in a straight course about three miles, and is very pleasant. On this are situated the academy and the principal village. Pembroke has a variety of soils, mostly very productive. On the rivers are small but valuable tracts of intervale, and from these the land rises in extensive and beautiful swells, yielding in abundance when properly cultivated. Pembroke is the ancient *Suncook* of the Indians. It was granted by this name in 1727, by the government of Massachusetts, to Capt. John Lovewell, and his brave associates, in consideration of their services against the Indians. The whole number of grantees was 60; 46 of whom accompanied Lovewell in his last march to Pequawkett. The first survey was made in 1728; and in the following year settlements were commenced. The settlements increased slowly, in consequence of the frequent alarms from the Indians, who committed many depredations upon their property. Population, 1830, 1,312.

Pembroke, Mass.

Plymouth co. This town was taken from Duxbury in 1711. Population, 1837, 1,258. It lies 27 miles S. E. from Boston, and 12 N. N. W. from Plymouth. North river separates this town from Hanover; and some branches of that stream, rising from ponds in Pembroke, give it a good water power. For more than 40 years after the settlement at Plymouth, this town contained the only saw-mill in the colony. Pembroke is at the head of navigation on the North river, and possesses superior advantages for ship building; and many noble vessels, constructed of native white oak, are annually launched. The manufactures of the town consist of vessels, cotton goods, tacks, iron ware, chairs, cabinet ware, &c.

The North river is very deep and narrow, and so exceedingly crooked that it meanders 18 miles in its course from Pembroke to Scituate harbor, when the distance by land is less than 6 miles.

Pemigewasset River, N. H.

This stream and the Winnepisiogee constitute the Merrimack. It is formed of three principal branches, having their sources in Peeling, Franconia, and the ungranted lands S. W. of the White Mountains.— These branches unite in Peeling, from whence the main stream passes in a S. direction through Thornton, Campton, between Plymouth and Holderness; Bridgewater, Bristol and New Hampton; Hill and Franklin, where it unites with Winnepisiogee river, and the main stream becomes the Merrimack.

Pemmaquid Point, Me.

Lincoln co. This is an important point of land, extending into the sea between Muscongus bay on the east, and Pemmaquid river and the waters of Damariscotta on the west. There is a light house on this point, which bears W. 10 miles from St. George's island, and about N. E. 9 miles from Bantam Ledge.

Penobscot River and Bay, Me.

This large and important river, with its numerous and extensive branches water a large portion of the state. It pierces the county which bears its name and receives tributaries from Washington, Hancock, Waldo, Piscataquis and Somerset counties. Below the union of the eastern and western branches the Piscataquis and Matawamkeag are its largest tributaries. From the junction of the two branches, or "the Forks," to tide water at Bangor is about 76 miles.

The east branch rises at the north, in the Seboois lakes, near Aroostook river, and on its passage to the junction, a distance of about 50 miles, it is properly called Seboois river.

The western branch of the Penobscot rises in the high lands on the border of Lower Canada and the western frontier of Maine. It passes through the counties of Somerset and Piscataquis in an eastern direction, to its junction with the eastern branch, receiving in its course the waters of lakes Chesuncook, Pemadumcook, Millinoket, and other large collections of water. This branch passes within 3 miles of the northern border of Moose Head lake, the source of Kennebec river. The length of this branch of the Penobscot, from its source to its union with the east branch or Seboois river, may be stated at about 140 miles; and the greatest length of the river to Bangor, 215, and to the ocean, 275 miles.

Some of the most important tributaries of this majestic river, are noted under their distinctive names; a description of them all with their hydraulic powers and boatable capabilities, their rapid courses and beautiful cataracts, their fertilizing qualities, and other peculiarities, would fill a volume. Indeed, these streams and the immense basin which they drain, are so little known, that some years must elapse before any thing like a fair delineation of the value and beauty of this interesting section of New England can be given.

Penobscot Bay. The waters of this bay extend from *Owl's Head* on the west, to *Burnt Coat Island* on the E.; a distance of about 30 miles. At its mouth are Fox Islands, Deer Isle, Isle of Haut, and a number of smaller islands. It extends to Belfast bay, at the mouth of Penobscot river, a distance of 20 miles N. from Owl's Head. This bay contains a great number of commodious harbors, and on its borders are many large and flourishing commercial towns. It affords a great variety of fish, and the scenery among the islands is delightful.

Penobscot County, Me.

Bangor, chief town. This section of country constituting a county, is rather a district within the state, to be divided into counties as exigencies may require. Not more than a fourth part of the territory is settled, incorporated into towns, or even granted. With the exception of a small portion at its southern boundary, it comprises a fertile wilderness, densely wooded, pierced in every direction with mill streams, and adorned with beautiful lakes. It contains a larger extent of territory than the whole agricultural state of Vermont, with its 14 large and flourishing counties; of no better soil, at a greater distance from the ocean, in nearly the same latitude, and, in 1837, with a population of no less than 31 to a square mile.

In 1837, before a part of this territory was set off to form Piscataquis county, it comprised an area of 10,578 square miles. It was incorporated as a county in 1816. In 1790, it contained a population of only 1,154. In 1820, the population was 13,870; 1830, 31,530, and in 1837, 54,961. Population to a square mile, 5 and a fraction. Increase of population, in 7 years, 74 per cent.

There are some mountains in this county, but the surface is generally undulating, containing as small a portion of waste land as any county in the state, in proportion to its size.

With regard to its soil, it is conceded by all who have traveled through the territory and examined it, that its quality, for the production of all the commodities necessary for the wants and comforts of man, is better than the soil of New-England generally.

The manufactures of this county consist principally of lumber, of which an immense amount is annually transported. Other manufactures, however, are rising on the banks of its rivers, and will doubtless increase with its population. In 1837, there were 39,154 sheep in the county of Penobscot, and its wheat crop, the same year, amounted to 202,143 bushels.

Large portions of the soil of this almost wilderness county are stated to be exceedingly luxuriant, equalling in quality the famed lands of the Ohio valley. There are doubtless large tracts of land in the valleys of the Mattawamkeag, Aroostook, St. Johns, and Madawaska, as fertile, and which will ultimately become as valuable for their agricultural productions, as any in our country.

The water power of this county is unrivalled by any section of country of its extent in the world, and the noble Penobscot furnishes it with a cheap and convenient passage for the wants of its people from abroad, and for the surplus productions of the soil at home.

When the resources of this county are more fully developed and better understood; when the healthfulness of the climate, the purity of its air and water, are fairly compared with those of the western and southern prairies, and when the value of a surplus bushel of wheat, or a fat ox on the banks of the Ohio, is compared with the value of the same productions on the banks of the Penobscot, we trust there will be less complaint against the soil of New England, for the want of patronage it affords to the enterprize, comfort, and wealth of her children.

Penobscot, Me.

Hancock co. A maritime town, on the E. side of Penobscot bay, nearly opposite to Belfast, and 12 miles E. by N. from it. It is 75 miles E. by N. from Augusta, 8 N. by E. from Castine, and 17 S. W. from Ellsworth. An arm of Penobscot bay sets up from the S. W., and gives the town great navigable facilities. It has a great water power, and its manufacture of lumber, its ship building, and coasting trade, render it an important and flourishing sea port. The surface of the town is pleasant, and the soil good. Population, 1837, 1,496. Wheat crop, same year, 2,074 bushels.—Incorporated, 1787.

Pepperell, Mass.

Middlesex co. This is a very pleasant town, with a good soil and handsome orchards. It is watered by the Nashua river, which gives it a good water power. There are three paper mills in the town, and manufactures of palm-leaf hats, boots, shoes, &c. Annual amount about $80,000. Incorporated, 1753. Population, 1837, 1,586. It lies 33 miles N. W. from Boston, and 17 N. N. W. from Concord.

Col. WILLIAM PRESCOTT, the brave defender of Charlestown heights, was a native of this town. He died in 1795, aged 70.

This town derived its name from Sir WILLIAM PEPPERELL, who about the year 1727, was chosen one of his majesty's council, and was annually re-elected 32 years, till his death. Living in a country exposed to a ferocious enemy, he was well fitted for the situation, in which he was placed, for it pleased God to give him a vigorous frame, and a mind of firm texture, and of great calmness in danger. He rose to the highest military honors which his country could bestow upon him. When the expedition against Louisbourg was contemplated, he was commissioned by the governors of New England to command the troops. He invested the city in 1745. There was a remarkable series of providences in the whole affair, and Mr. Pepperell ascribed his unparalleled success to the God of armies. The king, in reward for his services, conferred upon him the dignity of a baronet of Great Britain, an honor never before conferred on a native of New England. He died at his seat in Kittery, Maine, July 6, 1759, aged 63 years, leaving but one daughter, the wife of Col. Nathaniel Sparhawk. The last Sir William (son of Col. Sparhawk,) died in London in 1817. The name and title are extinct.

Lady Mary Pepperell, relict of Sir William Pepperell, died at her seat in Kittery, Nov. 25, 1789. She was daughter of Grove Hirst, Esq. and grand-daughter of Hon. Judge Sewall. Her natural and acquired powers were said to be very respectable, and she was much admired for her wit and sweetness of manners.

WILLIAM PEPPERELL, the father of the first Sir William, was a native of Cornwall, England, and emigrated to this country about the year 1676, and settled at the Isles of Shoals, as a fisherman. It is said, he was so poor for some time after his arrival, that the lady to whom he paid his addresses at the Shoals would not hearken to him. However, in a few years, by his industry and frugality, he got enough to send out a brig, which he loaded to Hull. The lady now gave her consent. After his marriage, he removed to Kittery, where he became a very wealthy merchant, and died in 1734.

Pequawkett River, N. H.

Pequawkett, written by Belknap *Pigwacket*, and by Sullivan *Pickwocket*, but the true orthography is found to be Pe-quaw-kett; an Indian name applied to a considerable tract of country, now including Conway, N. H., Fryeburgh, Me., and some of the adjacent towns.— It is also the name of a river flowing into the Saco, from two ponds in Eaton; and of a mountain between Bartlett and Chatham, formerly called Kearsarge.

Perry, Me.

Washington co. This town lies on the W. side of St. Croix river, and 5 miles N. W. from Eastport, to which it is connected by a bridge. It is favored with good navigable waters, and is a place of considerable enterprise in the fishing business, ship building, and the coasting and lumber trade. It is 184 miles E. by N. from Augusta, and 25 E. N. E. from Machias. Incorporated, 1818. Population, 1837, 929.

At *Pleasant Point*, in this town, on the margin of the river, is an Indian reservation, the residence of the remnant of the *Openangos*, or *Passamaquoddy* tribe. The village contains a Roman Catholic church, about 20 cottages, and 120 souls.— The reservation comprises about 27,000 acres.

Peru, Me.

Oxford co. Peru is bounded on the N. by Androscoggin river, and contains some pleasant ponds and mill streams. It has a good soil and produced, in 1837, 3,457 bushels of wheat. Population, same year, 854. Incorporated, 1821. Peru lies 38 miles W. by N. from Augusta, and 17 N. by E. from Paris.

Peru, Vt.

Bennington co. This is a Green Mountain township, high and broken. It contains two large fish ponds from which issue beautiful mountain streams. First settled, 1773. Population, 1830, 455. It lies 30 miles N. N. E. from Bennington, and 30 S. W. from Windsor.

Peru, Mass.

Berkshire co. This is a rough and mountainous town, wherein branches of Housatonick and Westfield rivers rise. It was formerly called Partridgefield, and incorporated by that name in 1771. The soil is cold but adapted for grazing. The inhabitants are chiefly farmers. Population, 1837, 656. In that year 6,127 sheep were sheared in this town; the value of the wool, which weighed 18,381 lbs., was $11,948. Peru lies 111 miles W. from Boston, 18 N. E. from Lenox, and 47 E. from Albany, N. Y. It is the highest land between the Connecticut and Hudson rivers.

Peterborough, N. H.

Hillsborough co. This town lies midway between Amherst and Keene, being 20 miles from each. It is 75 miles W. S. W. from Portsmouth, 60 N. W. from Boston, and 40 S. W. from Concord. Peterborough lies in a N. E. direction from the Grand Monadnock, and is bounded on the E. by a chain of hills called *Pack Monadnock.* Contoocook river runs in a N. E. and N. direction through the centre of the town, affording several good privileges for mills and factories. The N. branch, from Dublin, originating partly from waters near the Monadnock, and partly from Long, or Hunt's pond, lying in Nelson and Hancock, affords a never-failing supply of water, and furnishes those noble falls, on which are situated several factories. There are extensive and valuable meadows on this branch, above these falls; and the soil generally throughout the town is excellent. In the centre of the town is a high hill, on which is situated the meeting house, at an elevation of 200 feet above the river. The chain of hills on the E. is distinguished by two principal summits. Between these summits is a depression of a quarter part of the mountain's height. About 60 rods W. of the ridge, or summit of this depression, on an *embenchment* of the mountain, is a pond of about 9 acres extent, very deep and replenished with fish, at an elevation of 200 feet above the site of the meeting house. There are rocks in several places which afford indications of sulphur, and crumble on exposure to the sun and air. Iron ore of an excellent quality has been discovered, but as yet in small quantities. Peterborough was granted in 1738, by the government of Massachusetts to Samuel Heywood and others. The first settlement took place in 1739. In 1759 there were 45 families, and on the 17th Jan., the next year, the town was incorporated. The first settlers of Peterborough were Scotch Presbyterians, from Ireland, or their immediate descendants. Wholly unused to clearing and cultivating of wild lands, they endured great hardships. Their nearest gristmill was at Townsend, 25 miles distant—their road, a line of marked trees. The first male child born here, was John Richie; he was born Feb 22, 1751, and died in the service of his country at Cambridge, in 1776.—Population, 1830, 1,934.

Petersham, Mass.

Worcester co. Petersham is a very pleasant town, elevated on a swell of fertile land, and presenting a fine prospect of many of the neighboring towns. It was first settled about the year 1732, and was called by the Indians *Nashawang.* Swift river waters a part of the town, and affords a water power. There is a woolen mill in the town; and manufactures of palm-leaf hats, leather, boots, shoes, chairs, and cabinet ware: total annual value, about $60,000. It lies 62 miles W. by N. from Boston, and 27 N. W. from Worcester. Population, 1837, 1,731. Incorporated, 1754.

Phillips, Me.

Franklin co. This town is watered by Sandy river. It lies 53 miles N. W. from Augusta, and 15 N. W. from Farmington. Incorporated, 1812. Pop. 1830, 954; 1837, 1,283. Wheat crop, in 1837, 6,238 bushels.

Phillipston, Mass.

Worcester co. There is a large pond in this town, the source of Burnshint river. This pleasant town was taken from Athol and Templeton, in 1786. It was called Gerry until 1812. The manufactures of the town consist of cotton and woolen goods, palm-leaf hats, leather, boots and shoes; annual value, about $75,000. It lies 58 miles N. W. by W. from Boston, and 25 N. W. from Worcester. Population, 1837, 887.

Phipsburgh, Me.

Lincoln co. This is a maritime town at the mouth of Kennebec river, on the west side, 40 miles S. from Augusta, and 18 S. W. from Wiscasset. Population, 1837, 1,430. It consists of a peninsula of land, of about 15 miles in length, and from two to four miles in width, lying between Kennebec river, on the east, and New Meadows, or Stevens' river, on the west, extending from Small Point, the eastern boundary of Casco bay, to the town of Bath on the north. It contains a U. S. fort, and Seguin and Pond islands, on which are light houses.

Phipsburgh was taken from the ancient town of Bristol, in 1816, and named in honor of Governor Phips, who was born in Bristol.

Governor Phips lived in the wilderness of Maine till he was eighteen years of age, and was then an apprentice to a ship-carpenter four years. He went to Boston, and learned to read and write. He chose to seek his fortune on the sea, and had the good luck to discover the wreck of a very valuable Spanish vessel on the coast of Hispaniola, and by the aid of the British government succeeded in fishing up plate, pearls and jewels, amounting in value to three hundred thousand pounds sterling, with which he sailed to England in 1687. He obtained by his enterprise sixteen thousand pounds, and the honor of knighthood. He returned to Boston in 1690, and commanded the expedition against Port Royal, which place he captured. When the new charter of Massachusetts was obtained he was appointed the first governor under it. He arrived at Boston, as governor, in 1692. In 1694, in a dispute with the collector of the port, Sir William so far forgot his dignity as to descend to blows. He was removed from office, and returned to England. He received assurance of being restored, but before that event happened he died, in 1695, aged 44.

Phipsburgh has considerable trade and navigation. Ship building is pursued, and fishing is a source of profit. There is no better site for fishing establishments on the coast. It is a very pleasant town, and an agreeable location to court the sea breezes in summer.

Piermont, N. H.,

Grafton co., is bounded N. by Haverhill. It is 65 miles N. N. W. from Concord. The soil, especially on the Connecticut, is good. The meadows, or intervales, are extensive, and in some instances highly cultivated. The meadows are composed of sandy loam, in some places inclined to marle, and are favorable to the growth of wheat, corn and every kind of grain. Back from the river the town is made up of swells of fine grazing and mowing land, well watered with brooks and springs. In the N. E. part of the town are three considerable ponds, called Eastman's ponds. From these ponds issues Eastman's brook, which, passing in a S. E. direction, falls into Connecticut river, forming a number of excellent mill seats. Indian brook, on which mills are erected, is in the S. part. The settlement commenced in 1770. Population, in 1830, 1,042.

Pilot Mountain, N. H.

See *Kilkenny*.

Piscataqua River, N. H.

The only large river whose entire course is in New Hampshire, is formed by the junction of several small streams in a wide and deep bed; hollowed out partly by them, and partly by the tide. The names of these streams, beginning at the northeast, are Salmon Fall, Cocheco, Bellamy bank, Oyster, Lamprey, Squamscot, and Winnicut rivers. The five last unite their waters in a large and irregular bay between Durham and Greenland, more resembling a lake than a river. The waters of this bay meet those of Salmon Fall and Cocheco rivers, coming from the northwest at Hilton's point, a few miles below Dover. After this junction, they proceed in a direct line to the southeast; and join the ocean 2 or 3 miles below Portsmouth; embosoming several islands, and forming one of the best harbors on the continent. Few rivers make a more magnificent appearance than this; yet the streams by which it is supplied are small. Salmon Fall furnishes more than all the rest. This stream is called *Newichawannock* from the falls in Berwick till it receives the waters of the Cocheco; but the name of Piscataqua ought to be applied to the whole of Salmon Fall river.

Piscataquis River, Me.

The head waters of this river are found in the high lands which separate the waters of Penobscot and Kennebec rivers. Its length is about 65 miles, passing in a course nearly east. It has many tributaries, of which Sebec and Pleasant rivers, and Seboois stream, from the north, are the largest. In its course it fertilizes large tracts of country, and gives to the towns through which it passes a good hydraulic power.

Piscataquis County, Me.

Dover, chief town. This county was incorporated, March 23, 1838. Its territory is thus described in the act of incorporation, to wit:

"That from and after the last day of April next, all that portion of territory lying north of the south lines of Parkman and Wellington, in the county of Somerset, and lying north of the north lines of the towns of Dexter, Garland, Charleston, Bradford, and south line of Kilmarnock, in the county of Penobscot; and bounded east by the east lines of Milton, Kilmarnock and townships numbered four in the eighth and ninth ranges; and thence bounded east by a line running north from the northeast corner of said township numbered four, in the ninth range, to the north line of the state; and bounded on the west by the west lines of Wellington, Kingsbury, Shirley, and township number two in the fifth range; and thence bounded west by a line running north from the northwest corner of said township number two, to the Kennebec river; thence up and by the southerly bank of said river to Moose Head lake; thence bounded westerly by the westerly margin of said lake, to the northwest angle of said lake—and thence bounded west by a line running north, to the north line of the state—be and the same is hereby constituted and made a county by the name of," &c.

This county is therefore bounded N. W. and N. by the British possessions in Lower Canada, E. by the county of Penobscot, S. by the counties of Penobscot and Somerset, and W. by Somerset county. There are numerous lakes and ponds in the county, the largest of which are the Moose Head, Chesuncook and Pemadumcook. The county is crossed by the Piscataquis, Penobscot and Walloomstook rivers, but most of its excellent mill streams, of which there are many, rise within the county, from its own natural sources. There are some considerable elevations, the largest of which is *Katahdin* Mountain. The character of the surface and soil of Piscataquis county is generally that of

Penobscot and Somerset counties, from which it was taken.

Piscataquog River, N. H.,

Is formed of two principal branches, one from Francestown, the other from Henniker and Deering, which unite and form the main stream near the W. line of Goffstown. It pursues a southeasterly course through Goffstown and the N. E. corner of Bedford, where it falls into Merrimack river.

PISCATAQUOG VILLAGE, on this river and near its mouth, is a thriving and pleasant village, situate in the N. E. part of Bedford. A handsome bridge is constructed over the Piscataquog, in this village, 60 feet in length. Since the Union Canal commenced operation, the boating business to this place has been carried on with much success. On the S. side of the river, below this village, is a public landing place, extending to the Merrimack, and from this place lumber of all descriptions from the circumjacent country, is conveyed down the river to market by rafts and boats to Newburyport, and through the Middlesex canal to Charlestown and Boston. The rise and present flourishing appearance of this village is owing in a great measure to the enterprise and industry of William Parker and Isaac Riddle, esquires, who were the first to commence the mercantile business in this place.

Pittsfield, Me.

Somerset co. This is a town of excellent soil, and a branch of Sebasticook river rises in the S. E. corner. The inhabitants are generally good and thriving farmers. Pittsfield was incorporated in 1819. Wheat crop, 1837, 4,869 bushels. Population, 1830, 609; 1837, 836. It lies 38 miles N. N. E. from Augusta, and 20 E. from Norridgewock.

Pittsfield, N. H.

Merrimack co. The surface of Pittsfield is pleasantly varied, with a good soil. Suncook river passes through the town, affording good mill privileges. Catamount mountain stretches across the S. E. part of the town, from the summit of which delightful views are obtained. There are a number of ponds in the town; west of which the magnetic-needle varies materially. Berry's pond is on the mountain:—it is half a mile in length, and is supplied by mountain springs. There is a neat and flourishing village in Pittsfield; a large cotton mill, a scythe factory, and an academy.

This town was first settled in 1734. Population, 1830, 1,271. It is 16 miles N. E. from Concord.

Pittsfield, Vt.

Rutland co. Tweed river is formed in this town, by two branches, which afford mill seats: it empties into White river, which passes through the N. E. corner. The surface of the town is mountainous, and the soil hard. Pittsfield was first settled in 1786. Population, 1830, 505. It lies 35 miles S. S. W. from Montpelier, and 17 N. E. from Rutland.

Pittsfield, Mass.

Berkshire co. This large manufacturing and agricultural town, a mart of trade for a large section of country, lies 125 miles W. from Boston, 5 N. from Lenox, and 33 E. from Albany, N. Y. Population, 1837, 3,575. The settlement of this place, the Indian *Pontoosuck*, was commenced in 1736. It was incorporated in 1761. It was a frontier town for some years, and garrisons were erected for the protection of the inhabitants against the inroads of the savages. The town is finely watered by two branches of the Housatonick, which unite near its centre. There are in Pittsfield

6 woolen and 2 cotton mills, and manufactures of muskets, iron castings, tin ware, leather, hats, carriages, prunella buttons, chairs, corn brooms, cabinet ware, &c.; total amount, the year ending April 1, 1837, $688,716. The value of 12,962 fleeces of wool sheared in the town the same year, was $19,443. Pittsfield is one of the pleasantest towns in New England: it lies 1,000 feet above the level of the sea, in a fertile valley between the Taughkannick and Green mountain ranges. The village is well located, and contains many beautiful buildings, which, with the fine scenery and well cultivated farms that surround it, presents a great variety to charm the eye and to gratify the taste of the intelligent agriculturalist.

There are in Pittsfield a medical institution, a female academy, &c., which will be noticed in the *Register*.

Pittsford, Vt.

Rutland co. Otter creek meanders through this very pleasant and flourishing town, nearly in its centre, and fertilizes a large part of its territory. Furness river affords the town good privileges, on which are large iron works and other manufactories. Iron ore of a very fine quality, and elastic marble, are abundant; also, the oxide of manganese. The agricultural productions are valuable. In 1837 there were in the town 12,368 sheep. A female child was born here in 1784, who died at the age of 9 years, and weighed 200 pounds. Pittsford was first settled about the year 1770.— It was a frontier town for a number of years. The remains of Fort Vengence are still visible. This town lies 44 miles S. W. from Montpelier, and 8 N. from Rutland.— Population, 1830, 2,005.

Pittston, Me.

Kennebec co. Pittston is a pleasant town, on the east side of Kennebec river, opposite to Gardiner; 7 miles S. by E. from Augusta. It is a flourishing town, of good soil, and has several ponds and mill streams, and a considerable business in the lumber trade. Incorporated, 1779. Population, 1837, 2,121.— Wheat crop, same year, 2,231 bushels.

Plainfield, N. H.,

Sullivan co., lies on Connecticut river. It is 12 miles S. from Dartmouth college, and N. W. 55 from Concord. There is considerable valuable intervale, on Connecticut river, and in other parts are excellent meadows. There are two ponds. At the S. W. part of this town, in Connecticut river, is Hart's island, which contains 19 acres.— Waterqueechy falls are in this town. A bridge was erected here in 1807. A small stream, flowing from Croydon mountains, waters the town.— Plainfield has a pleasant village, situated on a handsome plain, through the centre of which the street passes N. and S. On a pleasant eminence in Meriden parish is located "The Union Academy," incorporated June 16, 1813. It is endowed with a permanent fund of $40,000, the liberal bequest of the late Hon. DANIEL KIMBALL, the interest of which, as directed by his last will, is to be applied as follows, viz: $150 annually to the support of a Calvinistic preacher, and the remainder for the instruction of pious young men for the ministry. This seminary is in a flourishing condition. Plainfield was granted in 1761, and was settled in 1764. Population, 1830, 1,581.

Plainfield, Vt.

Washington co. First settled, 1794. Population, 1830, 874. It lies 8 miles E. from Montpelier, and 21 from Newbury. At the junction of Onion river and Great brook, in this town, is a neat village with some manufacturing operations by water. There is a mineral spring in the town of some note, and a fine trout pond. The soil is generally of a good quality, and feeds about 3,000 sheep.

Plainfield, Mass.

Hampshire co. This town is elevated on the Green mountain range, at the N. W. corner of the county, and watered by the upper branches of Westfield river.— Although the surface is rough and mountainous, yet the soil is excellent for pasturage, and produces some fine cattle. In 1837, the fleeces of 3,772 sheep, sheared in this town, were valued at $5,379. There are 2 woolen mills, and manufactures of boots, shoes, leather, palm-leaf hats, chairs, cabinet ware, &c; total annual value about $40,000. Plainfield lies 110 miles W. by N. from Boston, and 20 N. W. from Northampton. Incorporated, 1785. Population, 1837, 865.

Plainfield, Ct.

Windham co. Mooseup river affords this town a good water power, on which, in the pleasant villages of Unionville and Centreville, are considerable manufactures of cotton and woolen goods. This town was incorporated in 1700: a part of the land is broken and stony, but in the western section there is an extensive plain, of a light sandy loam, noted for its adaptation to the growth of corn and other grain.— In olden times this plain was called the *Egypt* of the surrounding country. The village is on a commanding eminence, from which there is an extensive prospect, and in which is one of the best academies in the state; incorporated in 1783. It lies 41 E. from Hartford, and 8 S. by E. from Brooklyn. Population, 1830, 2,290.

Plaistow, N. H.

Rockingham co. It lies 36 miles S. S. E. from Concord, and 30 S. W. from Portsmouth. Plaistow was orriginally a part of Haverhill, Mass., and included in the purchase of the Indians in 1642. Among the first settlers were Capt. Charles Bartlett, Nicholas White, Esq., Dea. Benjamin Kimball and J. Harriman.— Their posterity now inhabit the town. After it became annexed to New Hampshire, a charter was granted in 1749. The soil of this town is good, being a mixture of black loam, clay and gravel. Population, in 1830, 591.

Platt River, Vt.

This small but good mill stream rises in a pond in Richmond; passes through Hinesburgh, and a corner of Charlotte, and falls into Shelburne bay.

Pleasant Rivers, Me.

Pleasant River, in Washington county, rises from a pond in Beddington, and passing in a N. E. direction falls into *Pleasant river bay*, which lies E. from Naraguagus bay, and is connected with that bay, at its mouth.

Pleasant River, Piscataquis county, is an important mill stream; a tributary of the Piscataquis, from the north. It receives the two Ebeeme branches, as they are called, about 15 miles from its mouth, in Milo.

Plum Island, Mass.

See *Newbury*.

Plymouth, Me.

Penobscot co. This is a fine township of land, watered by beautiful ponds, and a valuable branch of Sebasticook river. It lies 45 miles N. E. from Augusta, and 23 W. from Bangor. Wheat crop, 1837,

NEW ENGLAND GAZETTEER.

4,530 bushels. Population, same year, 791. Incorporated, 1826.

Plymouth, N. H.,

The half shire of Grafton county, is 75 miles N. W. from Portsmouth, 31 S. E. from Haverhill, and 40 N. from Concord. This town is well watered. Besides numerous smaller streams, there are two rivers, Pemigewasset and Baker's, both of which are of considerable importance. They take their rise in the height of land between the Connecticut and Merrimack, called the eastern ridge. Baker's river is 30 miles in length. The soil is tolerably good, and in general is well cultivated. Holmes' academy is situated in this town, and is a very flourishing school. Plymouth was granted in 1763. The first settlement commenced in 1764. The intervales in this town were formerly the resort of Indians for hunting. At the mouth of Baker's river they had a settlement, where Indian graves, bones, &c., have been found: also gun barrels, stone mortars, pestles, and other utensils. Here, it is said, the Indians were attacked by Capt. Baker and a party from Haverhill, Mass., who defeated them, killed a number and destroyed a large quantity of fur.—From him, Baker's river derives its name. Population, in 1830, 1,175.

Plymouth, Vt.

Windsor co. Two mountains in this town rise to a considerable elevation, one of which, Mount Tom, is quite abrupt. The soil is generally good for grazing, and considerable products of the dairy are sent to market. Black and Queechy rivers take their rise here, and afford mill privileges. There are a number of natural ponds in the town, which furnish a great supply of trout and other fish. Among the lime stone rocks which abound in this town are numerous caves, some of which are very large, and curious. Extensive beds of soapstone are found here.

Plymouth lies 52 miles S. from Montpelier, and 15 W. by N. from Windsor. Population, 1830, 1,237. First settled, 1776.

Plymouth County, Mass.

Plymouth, chief town. The soil of this most ancient county in New England, is not so productive as that of many others in Massachusetts; yet there is considerable good land within its limits. It has a great water power, which is more particularly applied to the manufacture of iron ware, of all sorts, both wrought and cast. It has an abundant supply of iron ore, of a superior quality. This county has a sea coast on Massachusetts bay, of between 30 and 40 miles, and many ships are built in its numerous ports of native white oak. This county has considerable foreign commerce; but its shipping is principally engaged in the fishing business and coasting trade. It is bounded N. E. by Massachusetts bay, N. by Norfolk county, and Boston harbor, W. and N. W. by Norfolk county, S. W. by Bristol county, and S. E. by Buzzard's bay, and Barnstable county. Area, about 600 square miles. This county was incorporated in 1635. Population, 1820, 38,136; 1830, 42,993; 1837, 46,253. Population, to a square mile, 77.—The North river, emptying into Massachusetts bay, and numerous branches of the Taunton, are its chief rivers.

In 1837, there were in this county 11,410 sheep. The value of the manufactures, the year ending April 1, 1837, was $4,896,907.—The value of the fishery, during the same period, was $582,419.

Plymouth, Mass.

Plymouth co. Chief town. This place is full of interest, it being the oldest settlement by Europeans in New England, and the landing place of our forefathers on the 22d of December. 1620. Its Indian name was *Patuxet*. Plymouth lies 35 miles S. E. by S. from Boston : N. lat. 41° 57' 30". W. lon. 70° 40' 45". Population, 1830, 4,384; 1837, 5,034. Incorporated, 1620.

"Plymouth was the first town built in New England by civilized man; and those by whom it was built were inferior in worth to no body of men, whose names are recorded in history, during the last seventeen hundred years. A kind of venerableness, arising from these facts, attaches to this town, which may be termed a prejudice. Still, it has its foundation in the nature of man, and will never be eradicated either by philosophy or ridicule. No New Englander, who is willing to indulge his native feelings, can stand upon the rock, where our ancestors set the first foot after their arrival on the American shore, without experiencing emotions very different from those which are excited by any common object of the same nature. No New Englander could be willing to have that rock buried and forgotten. Let him reason as much, as coldly, and as ingeniously as he pleases, he will still regard that spot with emotions wholly different from those which are excited by other places of equal or even superior importance. We cannot wish this trait in the human character obliterated. In a higher state of being, where truth is universally as well as cordially embraced, and virtue controls without a rival, this prejudice, if it must be called by that name, will become useless, and may, therefore, be safely discarded. But in our present condition, every attachment, which is innocent, has its use, and contributes both to fix and to soften man. When we call to mind the history of their sufferings on both sides of the Atlantic, when we remember their pre-eminent patience, their unspotted piety, their immovable fortitude, their undaunted resolution, their love to each other, their justice and humanity to the savages, and there freedom from all those stains which elsewhere spotted the character even of their companions in affliction, we cannot but view them as illustrious brothers, claiming the veneration and applause of all their posterity.

The institutions, civil, literary, and religious, by which New England is distinguished on this side the Atlantic, began here. Here the manner of holding lands in free soccage, now universal in this country, commenced. Here the right of sufferage was imparted to every citizen, to every inhabitant not disqualified by poverty or vice. Here was formed the first establishment of towns, of the local legislature, which is called a town meeting, and of the peculiar town executive, styled the selectmen. Here the first parochial school was set up, and the system originated for communicating to every child in the community the knowledge of reading, writing, and arithmetic. Here, also, the first building was erected for the worship of God; the first religious assembly gathered; and the first minister called and settled, by the voice of the church and congregation. On these simple foundations has since been erected a structure of good order, peace, liberty, knowledge, morals and religion, with which nothing on this side the Atlantic can bear a remote comparison."

The land in this town is generally hilly, and sandy; but there is a border of considerable extent on the sea board, having been well cultivated, consisting of a rich loamy soil, and capable of yielding large crops.

The town is watered by Eel and Wonkinqua rivers, Town, Willingsly and Double brooks, and more than 200 ponds, the largest of which is called *Billington Sea*. "This was formerly called *Fresh Lake.* It was discovered about the 1st of January, 1621, by Francis Billington, while mounted on a tree standing on a hill. It was in the midst of a thick forest, and when seen at a distance, Billington supposed it to be another sea. On the 8th of January, he went with one of the master's mates, to view the place. They found two lakes contiguous, separated by a narrow space; the largest is about six miles in circumference, and is the far famed *Billington Sea.* It is about two miles southwest from the town, and from it issues the Town brook. In this pond there are two small islands. The largest, containing about two acres, having been planted with apple-trees, produces excellent fruit. This pond is well stocked with pickerel and perch. The majestic eagle is frequently seen cowering over this pond, and has for ages built its nest in the branches of the trees, visiting the flats in the harbor at low tide in pursuit of fish and birds. Loons, and the beautiful wood-duck produce their young in sequestered retreats about this pond, annually.

The fallow deer, tenacious of their ancient place of rendezvous, continue to visit this pond for drink, and to browse on its margin. For many years this beautiful pond was a favorite resort for social parties. A house was erected on the bank, a pleasure-boat was in the pond, and tea-parties and fishing-parties united in the happiest enjoyments.

There are on the road to Sandwich, in the woods, two rocks called Sacrifice rocks. They are covered with sticks and stones, which have been accumulating for centuries. It was the constant practice among the aboriginals, to throw a stone, or stick on the rock in passing. The late Rev. Mr. Hawley, who spent many years among the natives at Marshpee, endeavored to learn from them the design of this singular rite, but could only conjecture that it was an acknowledgment of an invisible Being, the unknown God whom this people worshipped. This pile was their altar.

Burying Hill, formerly *Fort Hill.* Immediately in the rear of the town is a hill, rising 165 feet above the sea level, embracing about eight acres. On the summit of the southwest side, the pilgrims erected first some temporary defence, but, in 1675, on the approach of Philip's war they erected a strong fort, 100 feet square, strongly palisadoed, ten and a half feet high.— No other place could have been so well chosen, either for discovering the approach of savages, or for defending the town against their attacks. The settlement was rendered perfectly secure, and springs of water were at their command. The whole circuit of the fort is still distinctly visible, a watch-house of brick was also built near the fort.

The view presented from this eminence, embracing the harbor and the shores of the bay for miles around, is not, perhaps, inferior to any in the country. Let the antiquarian come at full tide and when the billows are calmed, and seat himself on this mount, that he may survey the incomparable landscape, and enjoy the interesting associations with which he will be inspired. Immediately beneath the hill lies the town in full view, and beyond this the harbor and shipping. The harbor is a beautiful expanse of water, bounded on the S. by Manomet point, and near which commences a beach three miles in length, breasting the rolling billows of the bay, and serving as a barrier to the wharves; and on the N. E. by a promontory extending from Marshfield, called the Gurnet, on the point of which stands the light-house.

These several points, together with the opposite shores, completely enclose the harbor, having

Clark's Island and Saquish in its bosom. Beyond these points opens the great bay of Massachusetts, bounded at the southern extremity by the peninsula of Cape Cod, which is distinctly visible, and spreading boundless to the northeast. On the N. appears the flourishing village of Duxbury, shooting into the bay, and exhibiting a handsome conical hill, ever to be remembered as once the property and residence of the gallant Standish. Between Duxbury and Plymouth, is the harbor and pleasant village of Kingston. Having taken a survey of this magnificent group, so exceedingly endeared to the New England antiquarian, and enjoyed a spiritual vision of the Mayflower, laden with men, women and children, come as founders of a mighty empire, we are next led to view a scene of more solemn contemplation. The whole extent of the hill is covered with the symbols of mortality, the sepulchres of our venerated fathers. We tread on the ashes of some of those to whom we are indebted, under Providence, for our most precious earthly enjoyments, all that is valuable in life, much of principle and example which are consoling in death. With what solicitude do we search for a sepulchral stone bearing the names of Carver, Bradford, and their glorious associates.

The following are the most ancient monuments which can be traced within this enclosure:—

Here lies the body of Edward Gray, Gent., aged about fifty-two years, and departed this life the last of June, 1681.

Here Ives ye body of ye Honorable Major William Bradford, who expired February ye 20, 1703-4, aged 79 years.

He lived long, but still was
    doing good,
And in his country's service lost
    much blood.
After a life well spent he's now
    at rest—
His very name and memory is blest.

There are in Plymouth 3 cotton mills, 3 nail factories, and manufactures of vessels, cordage, boots, shoes, leather, hats, straw bonnets, chairs, tin and cabinet wares:—the value of which for the year ending April 1, 1837, was $508,932. During that year there were 4 vessels engaged in the whale fishery, 45 in the cod and mackerel fishery, and a large number of vessels employed in the merchant service and coasting trade. Tonnage of the district, in 1837, 26,635 tons. The product of the fishery, the same year, was $154,636.

The corner stone of PILGRIM HALL was laid in this town on the 1st of September, 1824. This edifice is 70 by 40 feet, with walls of unwrought split granite; the height from the top of the foundation to the eave cornice being about 33 feet, forms two stories. The lower room is about 10 feet in the clear of the ceiling; and the upper to the impost moulding about 20 feet, to which being added the curve of the ceiling is about 23 feet. It is intended, as soon as the state of the funds will justify, to form the front by an addition of about 20 feet, with a double tier of steps, having entrance to the upper room and by descent to the lower. The front to be finished with a Doric portico on 4 columns, of about 20 feet in height, the base of which to be from 3 to 4 feet above the level of the street. The situation presents a full view of the river and outer harbor.

An *Anniversary Commemoration* of the landing of the pilgrims commenced in Plymouth on the 22d of December, 1769, and will, we trust, be continued in *Pilgrim Hall*, so long as the virtues, unparalleled sufferings, and the conscientious performance of the duties of piety and benevolence of our pilgrim fathers are held in veneration by a grateful posterity. See *Reg-*

ister, and Thachers History of Plymouth.

Plymouth, Ct.

Litchfield co. Plymouth lies 22 miles W. S. W. from Hartford, 31 N. by W. from New Haven, and 12 S. E. from Litchfield. Taken from Waterbury in 1795. Population, 1830, 2,064. The surface of the town is rough and hilly, with a strong, gravelly soil, well adapted for grazing. The Naugatuck affords an ample water power, which is improved for the manufacture of cotton goods, clocks, &c.

The manufacture of small wooden clocks, it is believed, originated with Mr. Terry, of this town, about 20 years ago; since that period, the manufacture of wooden clocks has been widely extended, and forms a very important branch of the manufactures in this part of the state.

Plympton, Mass.

Plymouth co. This town is watered by a branch of Taunton river. It lies 32 miles S. E. by S. from Boston, and 8 W. from Plymouth. Incorporated, 1707. Population, 1837, 835. The manufactures of the town consist of cotton and woolen goods, nails, shovels, spades, hoes, forks, hoop rivets, shoes, leather, palm-leaf hats, chairs and cabinet ware; annual amount about $100,000. The Indian name of Plympton was *Wanatuxet.*

A noble white oak was cut in this town a few years ago. It contained seven tons and seven feet of ship timber, and two cords of fire wood.

Poge, Cape, Mass.

This cape forms the northern extremity of Chappequiddic island, a part of *Dukes county.*

Poland, Me.

Cumberland co. Poland is situated on Little Androscoggin river, 6 miles above Lewiston falls. It is 44 miles S. W. from Augusta, and 26 N. from Portland. Incorporated, 1795. Population, 1837, 2,251.—Wheat crop, same year, 3,965 bushels. This is an excellent farming town with good mill privileges, several ponds, and a pleasant village.

A family consisting of about 70 of that curious people denominated " Shakers," reside in Poland. They possess about 600 acres of choice land. They are attached to the society at New Gloucester, about a mile distant. Their village is on a beautiful eminence. To say that their village is neat and handsome, and that their lands and gardens are well improved, would be superfluous. See *Canterbury, N. H.*

Pomfret, Vt.

Windsor co. First settled, 1770. Population, 1830, 1,867. Pomfret lies 45 miles N. by E. from Montpelier and 20 N. N. W. from Windsor. The town is watered by White and Queechy rivers. The surface is hilly, but the soil is generally good, particularly for grazing :—it pastures about 8000 sheep. Pomfret contains a mineral substance, said to prove a good substitute for paint.

Pomfret, Ct.

Windham co. Pomfret was first settled in 1686. Incorporated, 1713. Its Indian name was *Mushamoquet.* The surface of the town is pleasantly diversified by hills and valleys: from some of the elevations, delightful views are obtained. The soil is deep, strong and fertile, and, although somewhat stony, is very productive, and exceedingly well adapted for grazing. A considerable amount of the productions of the dairy are sent to market. The Quinnebaug and several of its branches water the town, and flourishing manufacturing establishments of cotton and other materials are springing up within its borders. Pomfret lies 40 miles E. by N. from

Hartford, 7 N. from Brooklyn and 30 W. from Providence, R. I. Population, 1830, 1,981.

Pomfret contains the "Wolf Den," celebrated for the bold exploit of the gallant Putnam, who resided here some years. He died at Brooklyn, in this state. in 1790.

The aperture to this den or cave, which is situated under a high ledge of rocks, is about two feet square. It is about forty feet in length, narrow, of uneven surface, and in no part of it can a man stand upright. The sides of this cave are of smooth rock, which appear to have been rent asunder by an earthquake. After making the necessary preparations for his venturous expedition, Putnam entered the den, and "having groped his passage in the horizontal part of it, the most terrifying darkness appeared in front of the dim circle of light afforded by his torch. It was silent as the house of death. None but monsters of the desert had ever before explored this solitary mansion of horror. He cautiously proceeding onward came to the ascent; which he slowly mounted on his hands and knees until he discovered the glaring eye-balls of the wolf, who was sitting at the extremity of the cavern. Started at the sight of fire, she gnashed her teeth, and gave a sudden growl. As soon as he had made the necessary discovery, he kicked the rope as a signal for pulling him out. The people at the mouth of the den, who had listened with painful anxiety, hearing the growl of the wolf, and supposing their friend to be in the most imminent danger, drew him forth with such celerity that his shirt was stripped over his head and his skin severely lacerated. After he had adjusted his clothes, and loaded his gun with nine buck-shot, holding a torch in one hand and the musket in the other, he descended the second time. When he drew nearer than before, the wolf assuming a still more fierce and terrible appearance, howling, rolling her eyes, snapping her teeth, and dropping her head between her legs, was evidently in the attitude and on the point of springing at him. At this critical instant he leveled and fired at her head. Stunned by the shock, and suffocated with the smoke, he immediately found himself drawn out of the cave. But having refreshed himself, and permitted the smoke to dissipate, he went down the third time. Once more he came in sight of the wolf, who appearing very passive, he applied the torch to her nose, and perceiving her dead, he took hold of her ears, and then kicking the rope, (still round his legs,) the people above, with no small exultation, dragged them both out together."

Poplin, N. H.,

Rockingham co., is 24 miles W. S. W. from Portsmouth, and 33 S. S. E. from Concord. There is a small pond in the N. part of the town called Loon pond; and the town is watered by Squamscot, or Exeter river, beside several small streams. The soil is generally of a good quality, and the surface of the town is not broken by high hills. Poplin was incorporated, in 1764. The inhabitants are principally industrious farmers. Population, in 1830, 429.

Porpoise, Cape, Me.

This cape lies in the county of York, and forms the N. E. boundary of Kennebunk Harbor. N. lat. 43° 22′, W. lon. 70° 23′.

Porter, Me.

Oxford co. Porter is bounded W. by New Hampshire, and Ossipee river separates it from the county of York. It lies 99 miles S. W. from Augusta, 42 W. N. W. from Portland, and 37 S. W. from Paris. Population, 1837, 1,087. Incorporated, 1807.

Portland, Me.

Chief town, Cumberland co. This beautiful city lies upon a peninsula at the western extremity of Casco bay; its length is three miles from east to west, and the average width is three quarters of a mile; containing about two thousand two hundred acres of land. The settlement of this neck of land was commenced as early as 1632, by two individuals from England, George Cleaves and Richard Tucker, who purchased the whole tract in 1637, of Gorges, the proprietor. For the first 40 years the settlement made but little progress, and it was entirely destroyed in the Indian war of 1675. In 1680, it was revived under more favorable auspices, the government of Massachusetts having some years previous to that time extended her sovereignty over this part of Maine. It had scarcely begun to gather the fruits of prosperity, before it was again doomed to a second entire overthrow in 1690, by the remorseless enemy, who spared neither dwellings nor their inhabitants.

The territory lay waste after this, until about 1715, when a new attempt was made, and the foundations of the present city were laid. The inhabitants in the early period of the settlement, suffered much from the privations which awaited them in this their remote wilderness. The Indians were still hanging about them in an unquiet state, and occasionally visiting them with rapine and blood.

After supplying the first necessities of their condition, the people turned their attention to the lumber business, the materials and the facilities of which, were abundant about them. In about 20 years from the re-settlement, it became the principal port on the coast from which the English navy was supplied with masts and spars. They were transported in large ships owned abroad. Manufactured lumber was sent to the West Indies and to the colonies on the continent.

At the commencement of the revolutionary war, there were owned in Portland, 2,535 tons of shipping. The population was about 1,900, occupying 230 houses: there were two religious societies, one congregational, the other episcopalian, and the place was marked by enterprise and prosperity. But it was destined a third time to be prostrated by the ravages of war. In 1775 it was bombarded by a British fleet, by which catastrophe 136 of the principal houses were destroyed, together with a new court house, the episcopal church, and the town house, to the loss of the inhabitants of over £54,000.

From the close of the revolutionary war, to the year 1807, the growth of the town was almost unexampled. The amount of tonnage, which in 1789 was but 5,000 tons, had increased in 1807 to 39,000, and the amount received for duties had advanced from $8,000 to $346,000. During the restrictions and war, the town suffered severely. It had been sustained principally by foreign commerce, which those disastrous times wholly prostrated. After the peace of 1815, the old channels of trade were revisited, and new ones opened with still increasing success. Portland probably enjoys a larger commerce with the West Indies, than any other port in the union. In 1830, the quantity of shipping was 43,071 tons; in 1832, there were owred in this port 412 vessels, employing 2,700 seamen; in 1834 the tonnage of vessels belonging to the port was 51,433 tons, and in 1837, 53,081 tons. There arrived in one year 484 vessels exclusive of coastwise arrivals from ports north of Cape Cod, of which 163 were from foreign ports, and 321 were coastwise. The importations were as follows, molasses, 30,425 hhds; flour, 65,471 barrels; corn, 76,118 bushels; salt, 24,267 hhds; coal, 1,758 tons, &c. The principal exports are lumber, fish, beef, pork, pot and pearl ashes, hay, potatoes, &c.

The population has advanced in a similar ratio; in 1790 it was 2,240; 1800, 3,704; 1810, 7,169; 1820, 8,521; 1830, 12,601; 1834, 13,289; and in 1837, 15,637, exclusive of foreigners.

Portland was connected with Falmouth until 1786, and commonly went by the name of Falmouth Neck. In that year it was incorporated and received its present name.

In 1832 a charter for a city was obtained, and a government, consisting of a mayor, seven aldermen and twenty-one common councilmen was duly organized under it in April, of the same year.

There are in the city 16 houses of public worship, many of which are very elegant. There is also in the city a beautiful court house, a spacious city hall, and a substantial stone jail. An athenæum was founded here in 1826, embracing a large reading room and library; the library at this time contains between 3,000 and 4,000 volumes of well selected books.

The public press is as flourishing in Portland as in other parts of the United States. There were published in that city, in 1837, 3 daily papers, 2 tri-weekly, 1 semi-weekly and 12 weekly, embracing all the subjects of politics, literature, agriculture, religion and morals.

Portland is 110 miles N. N. E. from Boston, 54 S. W. from Augusta, and 554 from Washington. Lat. 43° 39' 26" N., lon. 70° 20' 30" W.

It is pleasantly situated between Fore or Casco river, and Back cove. The location is calculated to exhibit the city very favorably on approaching it from the sea, as the buildings rise between two hills in the form of an amphitheatre. On the site of old fort Sumner is an observatory about 70 feet in height, commanding a delightful view of the city, the harbor, the islands in Casco bay; and, extending northwest to the elevated peaks of the White mountains.

The access to Portland by sea is easy, its harbor spacious and safe, and rarely obstructed by ice. It has a water communication with the country to a distance of nearly 50 miles, by the Cumberland and Oxford Canal, which was finished in 1830; and it is the nearest seaboard market for the rich and beautiful country on the upper waters of Connecticut river, through the Franconia and White mountain passes; and with the White mountains over a level road to Lancaster in N. H.

The rail-road from Boston will soon reach this place, and a rail-road from Portland to the upper waters of the Connecticut is in contemplation.

There are numerous resources in the interior not yet brought into activity, which will give to this place continually increasing importance, and reward the exertions of its intelligent and enterprising inhabitants.

Portsmouth, N. H.,

Rockingham co., is the principal town in the state, and the only seaport which it contains. It is situated in N. lat. 43° 4' 54", W. lon. 70° 45'. Portsmouth is built on a beautiful peninsula, on the south side of the river; and, as seen from the towers of the steeples, the river, harbor, points, islands and adjacent country, presents a delightful assemblage of objects. In many parts of the town are beautiful gardens. It was settled under the auspices of Sir Ferdinando Gorges and Capt. John Mason, in 1623, and was incorporated by charter in 1633. That part of it which lies round Church hill, extending N. and W., was originally called *Strawberry*

Bank. The first house of which we have any account, erected in what is now the compact part of the town, was built by Humphrey Chadbourne, and according to tradition, stood near the corner of Court and Pond streets. It was called the "Great house," and is frequently referred to in early histories. Within the memory of the present generation, a garrison house stood in Water street, another in Fore street, and a third at the Ferry-ways. These were probably the principal houses on " the Bank." The first meeting house stood on Pleasant street. Except the garrison houses above mentioned, the earliest settlements were probably on the south road. From the peculiar advantages of its situation, Portsmouth appears almost wholly to have escaped the ravages of the Indians. Secured on three sides by the Piscataqua, the ocean, and an inlet, it was accessible to the savages only by the isthmus which connects it with the main ; and across that a stockade fence was extended for defence. The settlements were also compact, and the number of inhabitants at an early date considerable. In 1822, the wealthy and enterprising citizens of this town connected Portsmouth with Kittery, in Maine, by two bridges, one 480 feet in length, supported by 20 piers; the other 1750 feet, supported by 70 piers. Under the long bridge, for 900 feet, the water varies from 45 to 53 feet in depth at low water. The draw is 1336 feet from the island, and the water is 21 feet deep at low tide. This bridge greatly increases and facilitates the travel from Portland and its vicinity to this town and Boston. The town is also connected with New Castle by a bridge built in 1821. The streets, though not laid out with much regularity, are neat and pleasant, and contain many beautiful buildings. Portsmouth Aqueduct Company was incorporated 1797, and commenced its operations in 1799. Water of excellent quality is brought from a fountain about 3 miles distant, and conducted into all the principal streets. Portsmouth pier, 340 feet in length, and about 60 feet wide, was incorporated 1795. Portsmouth Athenæum was incorporated, 1817, and has a library of about 5,000 volumes ; and cabinets of mineralogy, natural history, &c. The institution is rapidly increasing in value. The people of this town were at an early period friendly to literature, and their institutions for learning are highly respectable. Portsmouth is the centre of a considerable trade directed by wealthy and enterprising citizens. The Piscataqua, as it passes this town, is from 1-2 to 3-4 of a mile wide; and although the current is so swift as to prevent the river from freezing, yet it forms one of the most secure and commodious harbors in the United States, into which ships of any size or burthen may enter with perfect safety. It is protected by nature from the ravages of the N. E. storms, and can very easily be rendered inaccessible to enemies. The main entrance to the harbor, which is well protected by forts, is on the N. E., between New Castle and Kittery; the other entrance, on the S. of New Castle, is called *Little Harbor,* where the water is shoal, and the bottom sandy. At this place, in the spring of 1623, the first settlers of this state made their landing, and in the same year commenced settlements here and at Dover.

About one mile below the town the navigation is rendered somewhat difficult by the rapidity of the current ; the main body of the river being forced through a channel only about 45 rods wide.

There are in the harbor a number of islands, the most considerable of which is Great island. The others are Continental island, on which is the Navy yard, one of the safest and most convenient on the coast; Badger's island, on which the *North America*, (the first line of battle ship launched in the western hemisphere) was built during the revolutionary war.

Few towns in New England have suffered so much from fires as Portsmouth. On Dec. 26, 1802, 102 buildings were burnt. Dec. 24, 1806, 14 buildings, including St. John's church, were destroyed. But the most calamitous fire broke out Dec. 22, 1813, when 397 buildings were burnt, of which more than 100 were dwelling houses. The ravages extended over about 15 acres.

The United States navy yard is admirably located for its object. There are at present three ship houses in the yard, in which are a 74 and a 40 gun ship. One of the houses is 240 feet long and 131 feet wide:—the roof is covered with 130 tons of slate. In this building the keel of the frigate Congress was laid in 1837. The government of the U. S. has been liberal in its appropriations for this excellent naval depot, at which a dry dock will soon be constructed. Portsmouth has ever been celebrated for its fine white oak timber and its naval architects.

Ship building for the merchant service is extensively pursued, and other manufactures flourish. There are 35 ships belonging to this port regularly engaged in the freighting business; 100 vessels in the cod and mackerel fisheries, 52 in the coasting trade, 3 in the West India business, and 1 employed in whaling. The number of men and boys employed in navigation, in 1837, was 750. The tonnage of the district, the same year, was 25,114 tons. As much of the capital of this wealthy town is employed abroad, and much of the inland trade passes on the river, there is but little show of business in the streets, compared with some other commercial places.

Portsmouth lies 45 miles E. S. E. from Concord, 56 N. E. from Boston, and 54 S. W. from Portland. Population, 1820, 7,327; 1830, 8,082. The present population is about 9,000. The rail-road from Boston to Maine will probably pass through this town. The proximity of Portsmouth to the ocean, its neatness, quietude and beauty, render it an agreeable residence, and a fashionable resort in the summer.

Among the citizens of Portsmouth distinguished for their talents or public services, we may mention WILLIAM VAUGHAN, the original projector of the expedition against Louisbourg, was born at Portsmouth, Sept. 12, 1703, and died in London, in Dec. 1746.

JOHN WENTWORTH, the first governor of that name in N. H. He died Dec. 12, 1730, aged 59.

BENNING WENTWORTH, who died Oct. 14, 1770, aged 75.

Dr. JOSHUA BRACKETT, a distinguished physician and founder of the N. H. Medical Society, died July 17, 1802, aged 69.

Hon. SAMUEL HALE, a native of Newbury, Mass., who for more than 30 years, taught a public school in Portsmouth. He died July 10, 1807, aged 89.

Rev. SAMUEL HAVEN, D. D. was born at Framingham, Mass. Aug. 4, 1727; settled at Portsmouth in 1752; received the degree of D. D. from the University of Edinburgh in 1772; and died March 3, 1806, aged 79. He was eminently useful.

Dr. AMMI R. CUTTER, was born at North Yarmouth, Me. in March 1735. For 60 years he was an eminent practitioner, and during life a firm supporter of his country. He died Dec. 8, 1820, aged 86.

Hon. JOHN PICKERING, LL. D., was a native of Newington. He was appointed chief justice of the superior court in 1790, and continued in office five years. He was afterwards district judge of the U. S., and died April 11, 1805, aged 67. Hon. JOHN LANGDON, LL.D. was born at Portsmouth in 1740. In 1785 he was chosen president of the state. He was elected to the same office in 1788, and after the adoption of the constitution was governor six years. He ever discharged the duties of the offices to which he was elected faithfully and acceptably. Unlike many elevated to office, he remembered that the people clothed him with authority, and his only study was to serve them honestly and faithfully. He died Sept. 18, 1819, aged 79.

Hon. WOODBURY LANGDON, a firm patriot and useful citizen.

Hon. RICHARD EVANS was born at Portsmouth, May 13, 1777. He died July 18, 1816, aged 39.

JONATHAN M. SEWALL, Esq., counsellor at law, and a respectable poet, was born at Salem, Mass., in 1748, and died at Portsmouth, March 29, 1808.

Rev. JOSEPH BUCKMINSTER, D. D. a native of Rutland, Mass., settled at Portsmouth, 1779, and died at Reedsborough, Vt. June 10, 1812, aged 61. Dr. B. was a distinguished scholar and an eminent divine.

Portsmouth, R. I.

Newport co. The soil of this town, in common with all the lands on the island of R. I., is uncommonly fertile, well cultivated and productive. It is bounded N. by Mount Hope bay, E. by the Seaconnet passage from the sea to said bay, S. by the ocean, and W. by Middletown. The maritime situation of the town affords the people great facilities for the fisheries, which, with a fine soil, and industry, give them a great degree of independence. A number one called are attached to this town, of which the beautiful and fertile island of Prudence is the largest. It is six miles in length, and about three quarters of a mile average width. In this town are the Rhode Island coal mines, which are not worked at the present time. A fine bed of plumbago has recently been discovered. Portsmouth furnishes considerable quantities of wool, hay, grain, vegetables, and productions of the dairy. In 1837 there were 16,000 sheep in the town. Population, 1830, 1,727. Portsmouth lies 6 miles N. N. E. from Newport. A stone bridge, 1,000 feet in length, connects it with Tiverton. It received its charter from Charles II., in 1663.

Poultney, Vt.

Rutland co. The surface of this town is pleasantly diversified; the soil is warm and productive, particularly on the borders of the river. First settled, 1771. Population, 1830, 1,909. There are two flourishing villages in the town, and manufactures of various sorts. The productions of the soil are considerable, and 12,000 sheep are kept. It lies 60 miles S. W. from Montpelier, and 13 S. W. from Rutland.

Poultney river, rising in the high lands near Middletown, and emptying into East bay, an arm of Champlain lake, is about 25 miles in length, and in its course affords numerous valuable mill sites. This stream changed its course in 1783, by cutting a channel of 100 feet in depth through a ridge of land near the bay, and destroying the navigation of the bay for a time, by nearly filling it with earth. This obstruction has been removed.

Pownal, Me.

Cumberland co. This is a small town, of good soil, and bounded N. by Durham. It lies 35 miles S. W. from Augusta, and 19 N. from Portland. Incorporated, 1808. Population, 1837, 1,232.

Pownal, Vt.

Bennington co. First settled, 1761. Population, in 1830 1,835.

NEW ENGLAND GAZETTEER.

Pownal lies 30 miles W. by S. from Brattleborough, and 8 S. from Bennington. The surface is broken and hilly, but the soil is strong and remarkably well adapted for grass, producing all the varieties of the dairy in great abundance and of an excellent quality. The number of sheep kept in this town is about 8,000. Pownal is watered by Hoosack and Walloomsac rivers, which produce a good water power. The village is very pleasant.

Powow River.

Powow river has its principal source in Great and Country ponds in Kingston, N. H., and passes over the S. W. part of East Kingston into South Hampton; thence into Amesbury, Mass., where it turns E. into South Hampton again, and returns into Amesbury, falling into the Merrimack between Salisbury and Amesbury. There are several falls in this river; those in Amesbury being the most remarkable, the water falling 100 feet in the distance of 50 rods, and presenting, with the variety of machinery and dams, houses and scenery on the falls, one of the most interesting views in the country.

Prescott, Mass.

Hampshire co. The surface of this town is rough and hilly. The principal manufacture consists of palm-leaf hats, of which about 50,000 are annually made. The soil is better for grazing than tillage. Prescott lies 76 miles W. from Boston, and 16 N. E. from Northampton. Taken from Pelham in 1822. Population, 1837, 788.

Preston, Ct.

New London co. This is an irregular, uneven, rocky town, of a pretty good soil for corn and grazing. It is bounded W. and N. by the Thames and Quinnebaug rivers: 44 miles E. S. E. from Hartford. First settled, 1686. Population, 1830, 1,935. *Poquetannuck*, an ancient village, lies partly in Preston and partly in Ledyard. It has a water power, and small vessels pass within a short distance of it. Many of the inhabitants are employed in navigation, and considerable ship timber is taken from there down the river. *Preston City* lies in the eastern part of the town, 5 miles E. from Poquetannuck, and 6 E. from Norwich. Near this village is "Amos lake," a handsome sheet of water, and a place of resort for parties of pleasure.

Presumpscut River, Me.

This is the outlet of Sebago lake. It passes through parts of Gorham and Westbrook, and falls into Casco bay at Falmouth, 6 miles N. from Portland.

Princeton, Me.

Washington co. Population, in 1837, 207. See "Down East."

Princeton, Mass.

Worcester co. This town, the Indian *Wachusett*, is pleasantly situated at the base of the mountain of that name, 45 miles W. by N. from Boston, and 16 N. by W. from Worcester. Incorporated,1759. Population, 1837, 1,267. This is a township of good land, and produces considerable quantities of beef, butter, cheese, &c. It is watered by a branch of the Nashua, and has some manufactures. Wachusett is 2,990 feet in height; it is the highest land in the county, and presents a landscape exceedingly variegated and beautiful. It is a place much frequented in summer months. The manufactures of the town consist of shoes, leather, palm-leaf hats, chairs, and cabinet ware: annual amount, about $50,000.

Prospect, Me.

Waldo co. This is a beautiful town, of good soil, on the west side of Penobscot river. It is bounded on the S. by Belfast bay; 52 miles E. by N. from Augusta, 12 N. N. E. from Belfast, and 18 S. from Bangor. Prospect is very flourishing in its commercial and agricultural pursuits. Population, 1830, 2,381; 1837, 3,198. Incorporated, 1794. Wheat crop, 1837, 4,416 bushels.

Prospect, Ct.

New Haven co. This stony and mountainous town was taken from Cheshire and Waterbury, in 1827. It derived its name from its elevated situation. There is a pretty village in the town. The inhabitants are chiefly farmers. It lies 17 miles N. by W. from New Haven. Population, 1830, 651.

Some difficulty arose in the congregational society in this town a few years since, in consequence of the minister and a number of the influential members of the church having adopted the sentiments of the *Perfectionists*. The stray sheep, however, soon returned to the fold again. See *Religious Creeds and Statistics*.

Providence County, R. I.

Providence, chief town. This ancient and respectable county is bounded N. and E. by Massachusetts, S. by the county of Kent, and W. by Connecticut. It contains an area of 381 square miles. Population, 1820, 35,736; 1830, 47,018. Population to a square mile, 124. The surface of the county is generally uneven; some sections of it presents rugged features, but no part of it is mountainous. The soil is various: some portions of the county are alluvial, some calcareous loam, and some of sileceous sand; but a strong gravelly loam generally prevails.

More attention is paid to agriculture in this county than formerly; good crops of corn, barley and rye are obtained, and all the varieties of the dairy, of fruits and vegetables are abundant for the supply of its numerous villages and the city. The commercial interests of the county are important, but are principally confined to the flourishing city of Providence; but the manufacturing interests, particularly of cotton, are extended throughout the county, and engrosses a large share of its enterprize and capital. While the Pawtucket, Pawtuxet, Mashanticut, Pochasset, Wonasquatucket, and other streams, give those interests a constant operative power, the numerous beautiful villages erected on their borders testify that Providence county is one of the most important manufacturing districts in the new world.

A statistical account of the resources of this county, and of all the counties and towns in Rhode Island, is in preparation, and will appear in the *Register*.

Providence, R. I.

Chief town, Providence co. Roger Williams was the founder of this beautiful city. He was banished from the Massachusetts colony for maintaining that all denominations of christians were equally entitled to the protection of the civil magistrate; that the church of England was no true church, and that a patent from the king conveyed no title to the soil.

In 1636, Mr. Williams, accompanied by William Harris, John Smith, Joshua Virrin, Thomas Angell, and Francis Wickes, commenced a settlement and called it Providence; regarding his preservation as a favorable interposition of heaven. Mr. Williams sustained the two-fold character of a minister of the gospel and governor of the colony; he formed a constitution on the broad principle of civil and religious liberty, and thus established the first free government on the continent of America. Mr. Williams was a man of learning, and set a bright example of that toleration which he demanded from others. He was born in Wales, in 1599, and died in 1683.

Providence suffered great losses in king Philip's war, and during the revolutionary contest it furnished its full proportion of troops, and partook largely of the sufferings as well as of the glory of that struggle.

On the 9th of June, 1772, the king's ship Gaspee was taken possession of and burned, and the commander, Lieutenant Duddingston, wounded with a musket ball, in the thigh. Only one of the persons engaged in taking the Gaspee is now living—Col. Ephraim Bowen, of Providence.

Thus it appears, that in that contest, the first *blood* was shed at Providence; but the first *American blood* and *life* was sacrificed at Lexington, Mass., on the 19th of April, 1775, and the first *British life*, on the same day, a few hours after, at Concord, Massachusetts.

Providence formerly comprised the territory of a number of the neighboring towns. Its present limits contain an area of about nine square miles. It was incorporated as a town in 1649, and as a city in 1831. Population, in 1820, 11,767; 1830, 16,832; 1836, 19,277. The most compact part of the city is divided into two nearly equal parts, on both sides of Providence river, and are connected by wide and substantial bridges. The two principal streets are long and irregular, and comprise the business portion of the city, with the exception of a long range of large and handsome brick ware houses on the east side of the river. The buildings in other parts of the city are constructed with taste, and many of them in a style of superior elegance. On the east side of the river the land rises abruptly. On this elevation are a number of streets running parallel with the river, on the summit of which is located Brown University, established here in 1770. From the beautiful buildings on these streets, delightful views are obtained of a great extent of country, of the city, the shipping in the river, and of Providence and Narraganset bays.

There are in Providence a large number of handsome churches, and other public buildings. The Arcade is one of the most beautiful buildings in the country. It is situated on the west side of the river, and fronts on two streets. It is built of stone, 222 feet in length, and 72 feet in width. The fronts are ornamented, each with six massive columns, 25 feet high, the shafts of which are single blocks, 22 feet in length. The lower part of this building is improved for dry goods shops, &c.; the upper stories for offices, library rooms, &c. It was completed in 1828, and cost $130,000. The architecture of this building is exceedingly chaste.

Providence has long been celebrated for the commercial spirit of its citizens, and for their large investments of capital in foreign commerce, particularly with India. It is still a flourishing mart of foreign trade; the tonnage of the port, in 1837, was 17,526 tons. Much of the capital of the city has, however, of late years, been diverted to the pursuit of domestic manufactures; a pursuit probable of greater profit, and no less patriotic.

Besides the large capital employed by the citizens of Providence in manufacturing establishments without the city, the capital thus employed within it is very great. Those manufactures consist of cotton goods, (by steam power,) machinery, steam engines, vessels, jewelry, copper, brass, iron and tin wares, glass, combs, oil, soap, candles, hats, leather, boots, shoes, and numerous other articles. About 4,000 of the people of Providence are engaged in these manufactures.

The public schools in Providence are well sustained. The sum of about $10,000 is annually appropriated to this object. The number of scholars, in 1837, was 1626. A high school has recently been established, and $40,000 appropriated for the erection of new school houses. The athenæum library contains 7,000 volumes. It was incorporated in 1836. See *Register.*

Providence is approached with great ease from almost every direction. The roads are generally excellent: that to Pawtucket is unequalled by any in New England. The Blackstone canal, after winding its course through a fertile and manufacturing country, from Worcester, Mass., terminates at tide water in the centre of the city. Steam boats, of superior construction and elegant accommodations, ply between this city and New York, daily. Rail road cars between Boston and Stonington cross the lower part of the city several times a day, and steam boats and packets are continually passing to and from the several inportant towns on the shores of Narraganset and Mount Hope bays.

Providence has frequently sustained heavy losses by fire, and once by water. In 1815, during the memorable gale of September 23d, the tide rose 12 feet higher than the common high tides, and spread ruin to the buildings, navigation, wharves and bridges in every direction. The loss sustained by this flood was estimated at a million and a half of dollars.

Providence lies at the head of ship navigation on Providence river, the most northern waters of Narraganset bay; 35 miles from the sea, 40 S. W. from Boston, 169 N. E. by E. from New York, and 396 N. E. from Washington. N. lat. 41° 49′ 32″, W. lon. 71° 24′ 45″.

Provincetown, Mass.

Barnstable co. A noted fishing town on the extreme point of Cape Cod; including Race point, which lies 3 miles N. W. from Provincetown village. It comprises Cape Cod, or Provincetown harbor, which opens on the S. This ocean harbor is very large, exceedingly easy of access, and has sufficient depth of water for the largest ships of war. This is the first harbor the "Mayflower" touched at on her passage to Plymouth in 1620.

An elaborate and highly interesting report of a survey of this harbor and the extremity of Cape Cod, by Major J. D. Graham, has recently been printed by order of congress.

The report is accompanied by a series of tables, showing the result of a long course of observations on the tide, which are not only curious, but may be useful to those who are in a situation for pursuing their speculations on this subject, by comparing them with the results of similar observations in other places. The fullness and precision of these tables indicate the care and labor with which the work has been prosecuted. The result is of a nature to show the great importance of this position, both as a naval and commercial station.

The value of Cape Cod harbor to our naval and mercantile marine in time of war is inappreciable. In possession of an enemy, it would afford facilities for annoying our commerce, without exposure to the gales that so often sweep along the coast. Fortified, and in the occupancy of a portion of our navy, it offers a secure retreat, accessible at all seasons, and sheltered from every storm.

The soil of this town, in common with many others on Cape Cod, is very sandy; indeed, it may be said to possess no soil, for its vegetable qualities are very deficient.

During the year ending April 1st, 1837, there were belonging to Provincetown, 2 vessels employed in the whale, and 98 in the cod and mackerel fishery, besides a large number in the freighting business.

The value of fish and oil taken was $298,407. Hands employed, 1,113. During that year 48,960 bushels of salt were made, employing 156 hands, the value of which was $18,360. Provincetown lies 50 miles N. E. from Barnstable, by land, and 50 E. S. E. from Boston, by water. Incorporated, 1727. Population, 1830, 1,710; 1837, 2,049.

Putney, Vt.

Windham co. This town is finely located on the west side of Connecticut river, and embosoms a large tract of excellent intervale land, called the "Great Meadows." There is also a good tract of intervale on Sacket's brook, a fine mill stream, with beautiful falls, on which are erected valuable mills for the manufacture of woolen goods, paper, and various other articles. Sacket's brook is a large and constant stream: it falls 150 feet in the course of 100 rods. Some of the mill sites are unoccupied. There are various mineral substances in the town, worthy of the notice of the geologist. The village is pleasant, and bears the marks of taste and prosperity. It lies 9 miles E. from Newfane, and 9 N. from Brattleborough. First settled, 1754. Population, 1830, 1,510.

Pushaw Lake, Me.

This lake lies in the towns of Orono, Dutton and Kirkland, Penobscot county. It is about 8 miles long, and one mile wide. It empties into Dead stream, which meets the Penobscot at Orono.

Queechy River, Vt.,

Sometimes called Waterqueechy, rises in Sherburne, runs nearly east to the south part of Bridgewater; thence through Woodstock in to the south part of Hartford, and thence southeast through the northeast corner of Hartland into Connecticut river, about two miles above Queechy falls. In Bridgewater it receives two considerable branches, namely, north branch, which rises in the north part of this township from the north, and south branch, which rises in Plymouth, from the south, both considerable mill streams. In Woodstock it receives two other branches of considerable size; one rising in the northeast corner of Bridgewater and southeast corner of Barnard, falls into Queechy river from the north just below the north village in Woodstock, or "Woodstock Green," the other rising in the south part of Woodstock, passes through both the villages in that town, and empties into it from the south just above the mouth of the last mentioned stream. Both these streams afford excellent mill seats. Queechy river in its course receives numerous other tributaries of less note. It is a clear and lively stream, with a gravel or stony bottom. This stream is about 35 miles in length, and waters about 212 square miles.

Quincy, Mass.

Norfolk co. The territory of Quincy was a part of ancient Braintree, until 1792. It lies on Braintree or Quincy bay, in Boston harbor, and is bounded on the N. W. by Neponset river and the town of Milton. It is 8 miles S. by E. from Boston, and 10 E. by S. from Dedham. Population, 1820, 1,623; 1830, 2,192; 1837, 3,049.

The surface of the town is diversified by hills, valleys and plains. Back from the bay about 3 miles is a range of elevated land, in some parts more than 600 feet above the sea, containing an inexhaustible supply of granite. This is the source of the "Quincy Granite," a building material justly celebrated in all our cities for its durability and beauty. Vast quantities of this admirable stone are annually quarried and wrought in this vicinity by the most skillful workmen, into all dimensions, both plain and ornamental; and it is fortunate for the public that the supply is abundant, for the demand for it from various parts of the United States is constant and increasing.

By means of a rail-road from these quarries to the tide waters of Neponset river, and of a canal to the centre of the town, this stone is transported with great expedition and little cost. There are large quantities of slate stone near Neponset river; much of which is quarried. These slate quarries bear indications of coal in their vicinity.

In this town, between Quincy and Dorchester bays, is a point of land called *Squantum*, celebrated as having been the residence of the famous Indian Sachem, *Chickatabut*. This place is the *Mos-wetuset*, " a few miles south of Boston," supposed by some to have originated the name of the state. Squantum is a rocky, romantic place, six miles south of Boston, and a pleasant resort for fishing and bathing.

The soil of Quincy is generally of an excellent quality and under good cultivation. There are large tracts of salt meadow in the town, and many large and beautiful farms, which, in respect to soil and skillful management, may vie with any in the state.

The *Mount Wallaston* farm is noted as the site of an early settlement (1625,) and as the *Merry Mount* of Thomas Morton and his associates. This farm, with that of his venerated father, now belong to the Hon. Mr. Adams, representative to Congress. The ancestral estate of the Quincy family comprises one of the most beautiful and well cultivated farms in New England. It is the property of Josiah Quincy, LL. D., an eminent agriculturist, and president of Harvard University.

The village, in the centre of the town, is situated on an elevated plain, and is remarkable for its neatness and beauty. In this village is a stone church, designated the "Adams Temple." This building was dedicated, 1828, and cost $40,000. Within its walls is a beautiful marble monument to the memory of the Hon. John Adams and his wife.

About two miles east from the village is *Quincy Point*, at the junction of Town and Weymouth Fore rivers. This is a delightful spot, and contains some handsome buildings. This point of land, with a peninsula near it called *Germantown*, are admirably located for ship building, and for all the purposes of navigation and the fishery. Here is a fine harbor, a bold shore and a beautiful country, within 10 miles of the capital of New England.

The manufactures of Quincy consist of stone, slate, vessels, salt, leather, boots, shoes, hats, coach lace, carriages, harnesses, bleached bees wax, &c. Total value, the year ending April 1, 1837, $470,222. During that period there were 10 vessels engaged in the cod and mackerel fishery; the product of which was $31,042. Quincy is a place of considerable trade. Large quantities of lumber, bread stuffs, &c., are annually sold.

The proximity of Quincy to Boston, the excellent roads and bridges connecting it with the city and surrounding country, the beauty of the town, with the delightful scenery around it, render it a desirable residence in summer, and a pleasant home.

Quincy was named in honor of Col. JOHN QUINCY, a native of the place, who for forty successive years was a member of the executive council of the colony, and discharged many other public trusts with zeal and fidelity. He died July 13, 1767, aged 78.

This has been the birth place and residence of some of the most distinguished sons of America.—

The names of the patriots, JOHN HANCOCK and JOSIAH QUINCY, JR., will live until the death of liberty.

Two presidents of the United States, father and son, were natives of this place. JOHN ADAMS, born October 19, 1735. JOHN QUINCY ADAMS, born July 11, 1767. The senior Mr. Adams graduated at Harvard University in 1755, and was distinguished for his diligence and genius. He studied law at Worcester, and was admitted to practice in 1758. He commenced the labors of his profession in Braintree, his native town, and soon obtained business and reputation. In 1764, Mr. Adams married Miss Abigail Smith, a grand daughter of Col. Quincy, a lady as distinguished for her accomplishments and virtues as for the elevated station in society which Providence had destined her to fill. Mrs. Adams died at Quincy, Dec. 28, 1818, aged 74. In 1765, Mr. Adams removed to Boston; here he obtained an extensive legal practice, and, refusing all offers of patronage from the British government, espoused the cause of his native country with an ardor peculiar to himself, firmly resolved to sink or swim with its liberties. He was elected a member of Congress, and was among the foremost in recommending the adoption of an independent government. In 1777 Mr. Adams was chosen commissioner to the Court of Versailles. In 1779 he was appointed minister plenipotentiary to negotiate a peace and a commercial treaty with Great Britain. In 1780 he went embassador to Holland, and in 1782 to Paris, to negotiate a treaty of peace with Great Britain, having received the assurance that that power would recognize the independence of the United States. In 1785 Mr. Adams was appointed first minister to the court of St. James. After remaining in Europe nine years, he returned to his native country, and in 1789 was elected first Vice President of the United States, which office he held during the whole of Washington's administration. On the resignation of Washington, in 1797, Mr. Adams became President of the United States, which office he sustained until the election of Mr. Jefferson, in 1801. Soon after this, Mr. Adams retired to his farm at Quincy, and spent the remainder of an eventful life in rural occupations, the pleasures of domestic retirement, and those enjoyments which a great and good mind always has in store.

The account that Mr. Adams gives in a letter to a friend, of his introduction to George III., at the court of St. James, as the first minister from the *rebel colonies*, is very interesting. The scene would form a noble picture, highly honorable both to his majesty and the republican minister.

Here stood the stern monarch, who had expended more than six hundred millions of dollars, and the lives of two hundred thousand of his subjects in a vain attempt to subjugate freemen; and by his side stood the man, who, in the language of Jefferson, " was the great pillar of support to the declaration of independence, and its ablest advocate and champion on the floor of Congress."

Mr. Adams says, " At one o'clock on Wednesday, the first of June, 1785, the master of ceremonies called at my house, and went with me to the secretary of state's office, in Cleaveland row, where the marquis of Carmarthen received and introduced me to Mr. Frazier, his under secretary, who had been, as his lordship said, uninterruptedly in that office through all the changes in administration for thirty years. After a short conversation, Lord Carmarthen invited me to go with him in his coach to court. When we arrived in the antechamber the master of the ceremonies introduced him and attended me while the secretary of state went to take the commands of the king. While I stood in this place, where it seems all ministers stand upon such occasions, always attended by the master of ceremonies, the room was very full of ministers of state, bishops and all other sorts of courtiers, as well as the next room, which is the king's bed chamber. You may well suppose I was the focus of all eyes. I was relieved, however, from the embarrassment of it, by the Swedish and Dutch ministers, who came to me and entertained me with a very agreeble conversation during the whole time. Some other gentlemen whom I had seen before, came to make their compliments to me until the marquis of Carmarthen returned, and desired me to go with him to his majesty. I went with his lordship through the levee room into the king's closet. The door was shut, and I was left with his majesty and the secretary of state alone. I made the three reverences:—one at the door, another about half way, and another before the presence, according to the usage established at this and all the northern courts of Europe, and then I addressed myself to his majesty in the following words:

'Sire: The United States have appointed me minister plenipotentiary to your majesty, and have directed me to deliver to your majesty this letter, which contains the evidence of it. It is in obedienc to their express commands, that I have the honor to assure your majesty of their unanimous disposition and desire to cultivate the most friendly and liberal intercourse between your majesty's subjects and their citizens, and of their best wishes for your majesty's health and happiness, and for that of your family.

'The appointment of a minister from the United States to your majesty's court will form an epoch in the history of England and America. I think myself more fortunate than all my fellow citizens, in having the distinguished honor to be the first to stand in your majesty's royal presence in a diplomatic character; and I shall esteem myself the happiest of men if I can be instrumental in recommending my country more and more to your majesty's royal benevolence, and of restoring an entire esteem, confidence and affection; or, in better words, ' the old good nature and the good old humor,' between people who, though separated by an ocean, and under different governments, have the same language, a similar religion, a kindred blood. I beg your majesty's permission to add, that although I have sometimes before been instructed by my country, it was never in my whole life in a manner so agreeable to myself.'

The king listened to every word I said, with dignity, it is true, but with apparent emotion. Whether it was my visible agitation, for I felt more than I could express, that touched him, I cannot say; but he was much affected, and answered me with more tremor than I had spoken with, and said:—

"Sir: The circumstances of this audience are so extraordinary, the language you have now held is so extremely proper, and the feelings you have discovered so justly adapted to the occasion that I not only receive with pleasure the assurance of the friendly disposition of the United States, but that I am glad the choice has fallen upon you to be their minister. I wish you, sir, to believe and that it may be understood in America, that I have done nothing in the late contest but what I thought myself indespensibly bound to do, by the duty which I owed my people. I will be frank with you. I was the last to conform to the separation; but the separation having become inevitable, I have always said, as I now say, that

I would be the first to meet the friendship of the United States as an independent power. The moment I see such sentiments and language as yours prevail, and a disposition to give this country the preference, that moment I shall say —let the circumstances of language, religion, and blood have their natural full effect."

I dare not say that these were the king's precise words; and it is even possible that I may have, in some particulars, mistaken his meaning; for although his pronunciation is as distinct as I ever heard, he hesitated sometimes between members of the same period. He was, indeed, much affected, and I was not less so, and therefore I cannot be certain that I was so attentive, heard so clearly, and understood so perfectly, as to be confident of all his words, or sense. This I do say, that the foregoing is his majesty's meaning, as I then understood it, and his own words, as nearly as I can recollect them.

The king then asked me whether I came last from France; and upon my answering in the affirmative, he put on an air of familiarity, and, smiling, or rather laughing, said, 'There is an opinion among some people that you are not the most attached of all your countrymen to the manners of France.' I was surprised at this, because I thought it an indiscretion, and a descent from his dignity. I was a little embarrassed; but determined not to deny truth on the one hand, nor lead him to infer from it any attachment to England, on the other, I threw off as much gravity as I could, and assumed an air of gaiety, and a tone of decision, as far as was decent, and said, 'That opinion, sir, is not mistaken: I must avow to your majesty, I have no attachment but to my own country.' The king replied as quick as lightning, 'An honest man will never have any other.'

The king then said a word or two to the secretary of state, which being between them I did not hear, and then turned round and bowed to me, as is customary with all kings and princes when they give the signal to retire. I retreated, stepping backwards, as is the etiquette; and making my last reverence at the door of the chamber, I went to my carriage."

Mr. Adams died on the 4th of July, 1826, with the same words on his lips which fifty years before, on that day, he had uttered on the floor of Congress, "Independence forever."

Quinebaug River.

This beautiful stream rises in Mashapaug pond, in Union, Ct. It passes N. to Brimfield, Mass., then a S. E. course to Thompson, Ct., where it receives French river from the north. It then traverses a S. direction about 30 miles, affording fertility and a great hydraulic power in its course, when it joins the Shetucket, near the city of Norwich, and takes the name of that river to the Yantic. These three streams form the Thames.

Quinepiack River, Ct.

This river rises in Bristol and Farmington, and passes through Southington, Cheshire, Meriden, Wallingford, and falls into Long Island Sound at New Haven. This is a pleasant mountain stream, of considerable power, and about 30 miles in length.

Quoddy Head, Me.,

Or West Quoddy Head, the western entrance into Passamaquoddy bay. It is in N. lat. 44° 55', W. lon. 66° 49'. It has a light house 45 feet in height. See *Lubec* and *Eastport*.

Race Point, Mass.

The N. W. extremity of Cape

Cod. N. lat. 42° 6′, W. lon. 70° 7′. See *Provincetown.*

Ragged Mountains, N. H.,

So called from their rough appearance, lie between Andover and Hill, extending in a chain about 10 miles from the Pemigewasset to the vicinity of Kearsarge. It is a bleak and precipitous range, and is nearly 2,000 feet high, in its northern points.

Rail Roads in New England.

See *Register.*

Randolph, N. H.

Coos co. Until 1824 this town was called Durand. It is situated directly under the north end of the White mountains, its southeast corner bounding on the base of Mount Madison, the east peak of the range. Branches of Israel's and Moose rivers pass through it. The soil is in some parts good, but the town increases slowly in its settlements. It was granted August 20, 1772, to John Durand and others, of London. Joseph Wilder and Stephen Jillson were the first settlers. Population, 1830, 78.

Randolph, Vt.

Orange co. This is an elevated township of good soil, particularly for grazing. It is generally well improved, and produces good butter, cheese and mutton. Between twelve and thirteen thousand sheep graze in its pastures.

It is well watered by branches of White river, on which are two woolen mills and other manufactures. There are a number of flourishing business locations in the town: the centre village is very pleasant, and contains an academy of excellent reputation. This town was first settled about the year 1778. Population, 1830, 2,743.

Randolph lies 23 miles S. from Montpelier, 9 S. W. from Chelsea, and 34 N. N. W. from Windsor.

Randolph, Mass.

Norfolk co. Randolph constituted a part of ancient Braintree until 1793, when it was incorporated. It lies 14 miles S. from Boston, 12 S. E. from Dedham, and 7 S. S. W. from Braintree landing. Population, 1820, 1,546; 1830, 2,200; 1837, 3,041. Manatiquot river rises in the town, which, with other small streams, afford it a water power. Punkapog pond lies in this town and Canton. The land is elevated between the waters of Massachusetts bay and Taunton river; the surface is generally undulating and the soil strong and productive. There are two very pleasant and flourishing villages in the town, *East* and *West*, surrounded by fertile and well cultivated fields. Randolph has long been noted for the industry of its people, in the manufacture of boots and shoes. During the year ending April 1st, 1837, there were made in the town 200,175 pairs of boots, and 470,620 pairs of shoes, valued at $944,715, employing 1,475 hands. There are manufactures of leather, &c. in the town, but that of boots and shoes is the principal.

Rangely, Me.

Franklin co. This town lies on the Androscoggin river, and at the outlet of Oquossack lake. It is about 40 miles N. W. from Farmington. See *"Down East."*

Raymond, Me.

Cumberland co. Raymond is watered by Crooked river, and several ponds. This is a good farming town, with two villages, and some trade. The inhabitants are principally devoted to agricultural pursuits. In 1837 the population was 1,802; wheat crop 3,203 bushels. Incorporated, 1803. It lies 75 miles S. W. from Augusta and 22 N. N. W. from Portland.

Raymond, N. H.

Rockingham co. This town lies 25 miles W. by S. from Portsmouth, 25 S. E. from Concord, 13 W. by N. from Exeter. Two branches of the Lamprey river, from Deerfield and Candia, unite in Raymond; and the waters of two ponds also fall into this river as it passes through the town. The Patuckaway, from Nottingham, crosses the N. E. corner into Epping. The soil is various: that of the meadows bordering on the river is productive. In the N. part of the town, about 100 rods from the principal road leading to Deerfield, near the summit of a hill about 100 feet high, is a natural excavation in a ledge, called the *Oven*, from the appearance of its mouth. It is a regular arch about 5 feet high and of the same width, extending into the hill about 15 feet, and terminating in a number of fissures. Raymond was originally that part of Chester called *Charming-fare*. It was incorporated in 1765, by its present name. The names of 24 inhabitants of Raymond are found enrolled among the soldiers of the revolution, beside numbers of the militia engaged for short periods. Four were killed or died in service. Hon. JOHN DUDLEY, a distinguished patriot of the revolution, member of the committee of safety, speaker of the house, and judge of the superior court, died here May 21, 1805, aged 80. Population, in 1830, 1,000.

Raynham, Mass.

Bristol co. This town lies on Taunton river, and was taken from Taunton in 1731. Population, 1837, 1,379. It is 30 miles S. from Boston, 3 N. E. from Taunton, and 24 E. from Providence.

There are a number of large ponds in this town producing a good water power, and to which vast quantities of herring (alewives) resort. On the banks of one of these ponds, the celebrated King Philip had a hunting house. The first forge in America was erected in this town, by James and Henry Leonard, in 1652. The house of the Leonards, an old Gothic building, is now standing, and owned by the 7th generation.

The manufactures of Raynham consist of bar iron, nails, iron castings, anchors, shovels, forks, coffee mills, and straw bonnets: total value the year ending April 1, 1837, $360,650; of which $300,000 was for nails.

Readfield, Me.

Kennebec co. This is an excellent township of land, and finely watered by ponds and small streams. The people are generally industrious farmers, who find the cultivation of the earth the best source of independence. Readfield is a very pleasant town, and its vicinity to the Kennebec gives it many advantages. It lies 11 miles W. from Augusta. Population, 1837, 2,019. Wheat crop, same year, 6,391 bushels.

Reading, Vt.

Windsor co. First settled, 1772. This is an elevated township, uneven and mountainous. Several small streams rise here and pass to the Queechy and Black rivers. This town affords excellent pasturage, in which about 6,000 sheep are kept. Reading lies 53 miles S. from Montpelier, and 10 W. from Windsor. Population, 1830, 1,409.

Reading, Mass.

Middlesex co. Reading is an ancient town, 13 miles N. from Boston, 10 W. from Salem, and 17 N. E. from Concord.

The surface of the town is uneven, but the soil is generally of a good quality. The village is pleasant and flourishing. During the year ending April 1, 1837, the value of $184,583 of boots and shoes were made in Reading, and $91,360 of chairs and cabinet ware. First settled, 1640. Population, 1837, 2,144.

Reading, Ct.

Fairfield co. This town was incorporated in 1767, and derived its name from Col. John Read, one of its first settlers. The soil of the town is good, but the surface is rough and hilly. The business of the people is chiefly agricultural, who live scattered about on their farms. Considerable attention is paid in Reading to the growing of wool. It lies 15 miles N. W. from Bridgeport, 60 S. W. from Hartford, and 9 S. from Danbury. Population, 1830, 1,686. It is watered by Saugatuck and Norwalk rivers.

JOEL BARLOW, LL. D., was born in this town, 1755. He died in Poland, 1812.

America has produced few men, more justly deserving of immortality than Barlow; and none, it is believed, who have made their title to it more sure. He lived in an eventful period, and acted a conspicuous part in both hemispheres; and as a poet, a man of science, a politician, a philosopher and a philanthropist, his name will long be revered by the friends of civil liberty, and of science, throughout the civilized world.

Red Hill, N. H.

See *Moultonborough*.

Readsborough, Vt.

Bennington co. A mountainous township, at the S. E. corner of the county, watered by Deerfield river, 12 miles S. E. from Bennington, and 18 W. by S. from Brattleborough. Much of the land in the town is too elevated to admit of cultivation. Population, 1830, 662.

Rehoboth, Mass.

Bristol co. This town was first settled in 1643, by the Rev. Samuel Newman and others from Weymouth. Rehoboth formerly comprised the towns of Seekonk and Pawtucket. This ancient town suffered greatly by Indian depredations. The surface of the town is pleasant, and the soil generally good for tillage. Its manufactures consist of cotton goods, leather, shoes, cutlery, ploughs, straw bonnets, carpenters' and joiners' tools, wagons, ox yokes, bobbins, cotton batting, wooden ware, &c.: annual value, about $60,000. Rehoboth is watered by Palmer's river. It lies 40 miles S. by W. from Boston, 10 S. W. from Taunton, and 7 E. from Providence, R. I. Population, 1837, 2,202. Its Indian name was *Saconet*.

RHODE ISLAND.

The State of Rhode Island and Providence Plantations was settled by Roger Williams in 1636, a man remarkable for his benevolence, justice, and pacific policy. It derived its name from that of a beautiful island at the mouth of Narraganset bay. Its government commenced under the charter of Charles II., in 1663, which charter is the present Constitution of the State. It became a member of the Union May 29th, 1790.

The Legislative power is vested in a Senate and House of Representatives. The number of Senators cannot be more nor less than 10, 2 from each county, and are chosen annually by the people on the 3d Wednesday in April. The Representatives are in number 72. No town has less than 2, and but 4 towns have more than 2, viz.—Newport 6, Providence 4, Portsmouth 4, and Warwick 4: the number for each town having been determined by law without reference to the present ratio of population. They are elected semi-annually by the people, on the 3d Wednesday of April, and last Tuesday of August.

The Legislature meet at Newport on the 1st Wednesday of May, and at Providence and South Kingston, alternately, on the last Monday of October annually.

The executive power is vested in a Governor and Lieut. Governor, elected annually by the people on the 3d Wednesday of April. Their official term commences on the 1st Wednesday in May

NEW ENGLAND GAZETTEER.

Succession of Governors.

Nicholas Cooke, 1776—1778. William Greene, 1778—1786. John Collins, 1786—1789. Arthur Fenner, 1789—1805. Henry Smith, (Act. Gov.) 1805. Isaac Wilborn, (Lieut. Gov.) 1806. James Fenner, 1807—1811. William Jones, 1811—1817. Nehemiah R. Knight, 1817—1821. William C. Gibbs, 1821—1824. James Fenner, 1824—1831. Lemuel H. Arnold, 1831—1833. John Brown Francis, 1833—

The judicial power is vested in the Supreme Judicial Court and Court of Common Pleas.

The Judges of all the Courts, Sheriffs, Notaries, Justices of the Peace, and Clerks of the Courts are *chosen annually* by the Legislature in Grand Committee. In all the towns (except Providence) the town councils are, *ex officio*, Courts of Probate, and the town Clerks, Registers of Deeds and Probate. The Municipal Court in the city of Providence exercise probate jurisdiction, and the Clerk is Register of Probate. The city Clerk is Register of Deeds.

This state annually appropriates $10,000, to be divided among the towns for the support of free schools.

Rhode Island comprises five counties : Providence, Newport, Bristol, Kent and Washington. It is bounded N. and E. by the state of Massachusetts, S. by the Atlantic ocean, and W. by the state of Connecticut. It lies between 41° and 42° N. lat., and between 71° and 72° W. long.; and comprises an area of 1350 square miles. Population, 1755, 40,414; 1774, 59,678; 1790, 68,825; 1800, 69,122; 1810, 75,188; 1820, 83,059; 1830, 97,196. Population to square a mile, 71.

The natural features of this state are somewhat peculiar. About a tenth part of it is water, and of the residue of land a considerable portion is island territory. The interior of the state, with the exception of the intervales along the streams, is generally rough and hilly.

The most considerable eminences are Mount Hope, in Bristol, Hopkins' Hill, in West Greenwich, and Woonsocket Hill, in Smithfield. There are also some hills of considerable elevation in Exeter. Rhode Island, and most of the other islands in Narraganset bay, disclose a geological structure, of the transition character, and present a surface generally undulating, and often highly picturesque and beautiful.

The mineral treasures of the State have not been explored: but so far as they are known, they are not extensive or valuable. Iron ore is the most important mineral. Mineral coal is found upon Rhode Island. Limestone abounds in the northeastern section of the state; and in these calcareous strata there are some excellent quarries of marble. Serpentine marble is also found, and there are in various places extensive quarries of freestone.

The navigable waters of Rhode Island are abundant, and mill streams are found in every section of the continental part of the state. Rhode Island claims a conspicuous rank for its enterprise in foreign commerce, domestic trade, and the fishery. The tonnage of the state in 1837, was 45,651 tons. During the war with the Indian Sachem, Philip, and the war of the revolution, Rhode Island was always found at its post. In these wars her soldiers were conspicuous for bravery; among whom were found some of the most distinguished officers of the age. The rise and progress of this state to wealth and reputation is very interesting. It is the smallest republican state in the world, and the most important manufacturing district of its size in America. An impartial history of Rhode Island will soon be published by one of its distinguished sons :— that history will contain a merited eulogium on the character of its people.

Rhode Island is celebrated for its mild and salubrious climate, which is thought peculiarly favorable to female beauty. See *Register*.

Richford, Vt.

Franklin co. This is a mountainous township at the N. E. corner of the county, on the line of Canada, and watered by Missisque river and its branches. It lies 50 miles N. by W. from Montpelier, and 24 N. E. from St. Albans. There is some good land along the river; and the upland, though rough, affords good grazing. Population, 1830, 704. First settled, about 1790.

Richmond, Me.

Lincoln co. Within these limits, on the west bank of Kennebec river, stood an ancient fortress called Richmond; hence the name of the town. It lies between Bowdoinham and Gardiner, and is the site of some ship building and navigation. The town has mill privileges on a stream which empties into Merrymeeting bay: its soil is productive, and its location pleasant. Richmond lies 15 miles S. from Augusta and 15 N. from Topsham. Incorporated, 1823. Population, 1837, 1,526. Wheat crop, same year, 1,656 bushels.

Richmond, N. H.

Cheshire co. This town is 12 miles S. from Keene, and 70 S. W. from Concord. It is watered by branches of Ashuelot and Miller's rivers, which fall into the Connecticut. The ponds are three in number, one of which is one of the sources of Miller's river. The soil here is favorable for yielding rye, wheat, Indian corn, and most of the productions found in this section of New England. The land is generally level. There are no remarkable elevations. Richmond was granted in 1752, and was settled within 5 or 6 years afterwards, by people from Massachusetts and

Richmond, Vt.

Chittenden co. Richmond is 24 miles N. W. from Montpelier, and 13 S. E. from Burlington. Population, 1830, 1,109. First settled, 1784. The town is finely watered by Onion and Huntington rivers, on the banks of which are good mill seats and large tracts of beautiful meadow. The village is neat, and the centre of considerable travel. The several religious denominations united here in building a curious looking meeting house; it has sixteen sides. This is a healthy place, and noted for the longevity of its inhabitants.

Richmond, Mass.

Berkshire co. This town is situated in a deep valley of excellent soil, surrounded by elevated lands, and watered by Williams' river. This is an excellent farming town; the farmers' houses, extending some miles on one street, are neatly built and make a beautiful appearance. Iron ore of a good quality is found here in abundance, also marble and lime. The manufactures of the town consist of pig iron, shovels, spades, forks, hoes, leather, boots and shoes. Annual value, about $50,000. In 1836, there were 4,835 merino sheep in Richmond. They produced 14,505 pounds of wool, valued at $8,703. It lies 135 miles W. from Boston, and 5 W. from Lenox. Incorporated, 1765. Population, 1837, 820.

Richmond, R. I.

Washington co. Richmond is bounded on the west by Wood river, and on the east by the river Charles. Other streams water the town, which, with the Wood and Charles give it an excellent water power. Manufacturing establishments of various kinds flourish on its streams, particularly those of cotton. The soil is a gravelly loam, with an uneven surface. The agricultural productions of the town are very considerable.

This is an excellent township for grazing; a large amount of wool and of the productions of the dairy is annually transported. Richmond was incorporated in 1742. It lies 30 miles S. S. W. from Providence and is bounded E. by South Kingston. The Providence and Stonington rail-road passes through the S. E. corner of the town. Population, in 1830, 1,363.

Ridgefield, Ct.

Fairfield co. Ridgefield, or, as the Indians called it, *Caudatowa*, a word signifying *high land*, is bounded W. by New Salem, N. Y. and lies 31 miles W. by N. from New Haven, and 9 S. by W. from Danbury. This township is very elevated, and commands extensive views of Long Island Sound and of the surrounding country. The soil is a strong gravelly loam, and productive of grass and grain. It is watered by Saugatuck and Norwalk rivers, and by a branch of the Croton. It comprises a very handsome village, in which are manufactures of carriages, cabinet furniture, &c. Limestone is abundant. Population, 1830, 2,323. Incorporated, 1709.

The celebrated hermitess, Sarah Bishop, lived on the western border of Ridgefield. She lived on Long Island at the time of the Revolutionary war. Her father's house was burnt by the British, and she was cruelly treated by a British officer. She then left society and wandered among the mountains near this part of the state: she found a kind of cave near Ridgefield, where she resided till about the time of her death, which took place in 1810. It is said that the wild animals were so accustomed to see her, that they were not afraid of her presence.

The following account of a visit to this hermitess, is taken from a Poughkeepsie paper.

"Yesterday I went to visit the hermitage. As you pass the southern and elevated ridge of the mountain, and begin to descend the southern steep, you meet with a perpendicular descent of a rock, in the front of which is this cave. At the foot of this rock is a gentle descent of rich and fertile ground, extending about ten rods, when it instantly forms a frightful precipice, descending half a mile to the pond called Long pond. In the front of the rock, on the north, where the cave is, and level with the ground, there appears a large frustrum of the rock, of a double fathom in size, thrown out by some unknown convulsion of nature, and lying in the front of the cavity from which it was rent, partly enclosing the mouth, and forming a room: the rock is left entire above, and forms the roof of this humble mansion. This cavity is the habitation of the hermitess, in which she has passed the best of her years, excluded from all society; she keeps no domestic animal, not even fowl, cat, or dog. Her little plantation, consisting of half an acre, is cleared of its wood, and reduced to grass, where she has raised a few peach trees, and yearly plants, a few hills of beans, cucumbers, and potatoes; the whole is surrounded with a luxuriant grape vine, which overspreads the surrounding wood, and is very productive. On the opposite side of this little tenement, is a fine fountain of excellent water; at this fountain we found the wonderful woman, whose appearance it is a little difficult to describe: indeed, like nature in its first state, she was without form. Her dress appeared little else than one confused and shapeless mass of rags, patched together without any order, which obscured all human shape, excepting her head, which was clothed with a luxuriancy of lank grey hair depending on every side, as time had formed it, without any covering or ornament. When she discovered our approach, she exhibited the appearance of a wild and timid animal; and started and hastened to her cave, which she entered, and barricaded the entrance with old shells, pulled from the decayed trees. We approached this humble habitation, and after some conversation with its inmate, obtained liberty to remove the palisadoes and look in; for we were not able to enter, the room being only sufficient to accommodate one person. We saw no utensil, either for labor or cookery, save an old pewter basin and a gourd shell, no bed but the solid rock, unless it were a few old rags, scattered here and there; no bed clothes of any kind, not the least appearance of food or fire. She had, indeed, a place in one corner of her cell, where a fire had at some time been kindled, but it did not appear there had been one for some months. To confirm this, a gentleman says he passed her cell five or six days after the great fall of snow in the beginning of March, that she had no fire then, and had not been out of her cave since the snow had fallen. How she subsists during the severe season, is yet a mystery; she says she eats but little flesh of any kind; in the summer she lives on berries, nuts, and roots. We conversed with her for some time, found her to be of a sound mind, a religious turn of thought, and entirely happy in her situation; of this she has given repeated proofs by refusing to quit this dreary abode. She keeps a Bible with her, and says she takes much satisfaction, and spent much time in reading it."

Riley, Me.

Oxford co. This is a township of rough and unprofitable land, with few inhabitants; near to, and south of Speekled mountain, on the line of New Hampshire. It lies 30 miles N. W. from Paris.

Rindge, N. H.

Cheshire co. This town is 20 miles S. E. from Keene, 50 S. W. from Concord, and 55 W. N. W. from Boston. The soil is productive, lying on swells of land for the most part inclining to the south. There are 13 ponds, the largest of which are called Manomonack, Emerson, Perley, Long, Grassy, and Bullet. The 3 first discharge their waters into Miller's river in Mass., thence communicating with the Connecticut; the 3 last discharge themselves into Contoocook river, and from thence into the Merrimack. These ponds abound with fish, and were much frequented by the Indians for procuring fur, &c. There is a small elevation of land in Rindge, from which the waters that issue on one side descend into the Merrimack, and those on the other side, into the Connecticut. Iron is found here; also a species of paint nearly equal to the best quality of Spanish brown. Rindge was originally called *Rowley Canada*, or *Monadnock* No. 1. It received its present name from one of the proprietors, when it was incorporated, in 1768. The settlement commenced, 1752, by Jonathan Stanley, George Hewitt and Abel Platts. Population, in 1830, 1,269.

Ripley, Me.

Somerset co. A good farming town, 60 miles N. by E. from Augusta, and 30 N. E. from Norridgewock. Incorporated, 1816. Population, 1837, 555. Wheat crop, same year, 3,512 bushels. A branch of Sebasticook river passes through the town.

Ripton, Vt.

Addison co. This is a mountainous township, the surface and soil of which are too broken and cold for much cultivation. Middlebury river and the turnpike from Royalton to Vergennes pass through it. Ripton lies 26 miles S. W. from Montpelier, and 9 E. from Middlebury. Population, 1830, 278.

Robbinston, Me.

Washington co. This town lies on the Schoodic or St. Croix river, opposite to St. Andrews, in New Brunswick. It is 16 miles N. N. W. from Eastport, 30 N. E. from Machias and 192 E. N. E. from Augusta. This place enjoys great navigable privileges, and is the site of considerable ship building, and commerce in lumber. Incorporated, 1811. Population, 1837, 702. This town was settled soon after the revolutionary war. The first mail came to this place in 1796. A mail stage now arrives three times a week, and crosses the river to New Brunswick. Robbinston was named in compliment to the Hon. Edward H. Robbins, formerly Lieut. Governor of Massachusetts, and for many years speaker of the House of Representatives of that state.

Rochester, N. H.,

One of the county towns of Strafford co., is 10 miles N. W. from Dover, 22 N. W. from Portsmouth, 34 E. from Concord. Besides Salmon fall river, which divides this town from Berwick and Lebanon, in the state of Maine, the Cocheco river runs the whole length of the town, and nearly in the middle, and the Isinglass river crosses the southerly corner of the town just before its junction with Cocheco river, at a place called Blind Will's Neck. Both Salmon fall and Cocheco rivers afford valuable mill-seats; on the latter of which, near the centre of the town, stands the principal village, called *Norway Plains*. It is a place of considerable trade, and a great thoroughfare from the upper towns in the county to Dover and Portsmouth.

There is another village about 2 miles S. W. from this, called *Squamanagonnick*, the Indian name of the falls in the Cocheco at that place. Much of the soil in Rochester is good; the surface is uneven, with several swells, the principal of which is Squamanagonnick hill, which constitutes a considerable part of several valuable farms. In the W. part of the town, is a large tract of oak land, which is hard and stony; has a deep rich soil, and is very productive when well cultivated. The town was incorporated, in 1722. The first permanent settlement was made in 1728. Until Canada was taken by the British and American troops in 1760, it remained a frontier town; the people were poor and distressed, but not discouraged. Their men were bold, hardy and industrious; and their sons were trained to the use of arms. They early became a terror to their foes. In 1748, the wife of Jonathan Hodgdon was killed on a Sunday morning by the Indians, on refusing to be taken to Canada with the party. Her husband married again, had 21 children in all, and died in 1815, aged 90 years. In the revolutionary war, many of the inhabitants bore a part. Captains David Place and John Brewster led companies to Ticonderoga, and suffered much in their retreat from that place in 1777. Of the soldiers from Rochester, 29 were killed or died in that contest. Pop. 1830, 2,155.

Rochester, Vt.

Windsor co. Rochester lies 30 miles S. S. W. from Montpelier, 37 N. W. from Windsor, and 20 S. E. from Middlebury. It is watered by White river, which supplies it with mill seats. A large part of the surface of the township is broken and mountainous, but it contains much good land for grazing and some tracts of excellent meadow. It has a pleasant village with some trade. In 1837, there were 9,000 sheep in the town.

First settled, 1783. Population, 1830, 1,392.

Rochester, Mass.

Plymouth co. A large maritime town on Buzzard's bay, 9 miles E. from New Bedford, and 48 S. S. E. from Boston. Incorporated, 1686. Population, 1837, 3,570. The face of the town is uneven and the soil light. Mattepoiset and Sipican rivers, rising in large ponds in the town, empty into the bay and form good harbors. The manufactures of Rochester consist of vessels, salt, bar iron, boots, shoes, &c.; value, the year ending April 1, 1837, $101,811. During that period there were 9 vessels engaged in the whale fishery, and brought into port 116,928 gallons of oil, valued at $71,658. A number of merchant vessels belong to this place, and numerous coasting and fishing vessels.

Rockingham County, N. H.

Portsmouth and *Exeter* are the chief towns. The county of Rockingham is bounded N. and N. E. by Strafford county; E. by the Atlantic, from the mouth of Piscataqua river to the line of Massachusetts; W. by the counties of Merrimack and Hillsborough. Its greatest length is about 34 miles; its greatest breadth, from the west corner of Chester to the extremity of Rye, is about 30 miles. It comprises an area of 695 square miles. There are no remarkable elevations in this county; the surface, however, is uneven, and in the north part, from the higher eminences, there are some very fine views of the surrounding country. The highest point is Saddleback mountain, in Northwood and Deerfield. The rivers are the Lamprey, Exeter, Beaver, and Spiggot, which water the east and southeast parts of the county. Great Bay, between Newington and New Market, and connecting with the Piscataqua, is the largest collection of water. Massabesick pond or lake is principally in Chester, and is picturesque from its numerous islands and the surrounding elevations. The other principal ponds are Islandy, in Hampstead, Country, in Kingston, and Pleasant in Deerfield.

The soil of this county having been longer cultivated than that of any other county in the state, is very productive; and agricultural pursuits have been very successful. In 1837, there were 23,333 sheep in the county. The population, in 1820, was 40,526; and in in 1830, 44,552. Population to a square mile, 64.

Rockingham, Vt.

Windham co. This town is beautifully situated on the west side of Connecticut river, and at the celebrated "Bellows Falls," noted under *Walpole* N. H. The water power afforded by these falls, with that of Williams and Saxton's rivers, which pass through the town, are of vast extent; it cannot fail of becoming exceedingly useful, and of rendering this town and vicinity the site of immense manufacturing operations. Large and expensive manufacturing establishments have recently been commenced; an account of which may be expected in the *Register*.

This place lies on a navigable river, 65 miles above Northampton, and 85 above Springfield, Mass., 111 above Hartford, Ct., and 23 below Windsor, Vt. It is 85 miles S. from Montpelier, and 18 N. E. from Newfane. First settled in 1753. Population, 1830, 2,272.

The surface of the town is uneven; but the soil is generally strong, warm and productive. Its agricultural products are considerable: in 1837, it pastured 12,600 sheep.

The location of Rockingham renders it a mart of much interior trade, and has caused the erection of a number of pleasant villages. The scenery around the falls, in Rockingham, is of a sublime character, and perhaps no section of New England possesses a greater variety of minerals than are found in this vicinity.

Rome, Me.

Franklin co. This is a beautiful farming town, watered by several large ponds. It lies 19 miles N. N. W. from Augusta, and 13 E. S. E. from Farmington. It contains a pleasant and flourishing village. Incorporated in 1804. Population, 1837, 1,074. Wheat crop, same year, 4,177 bushels.

Rowe, Mass.

Franklin co. This town contains the site of old fort Pelham, erected in 1744. The township is elevated, and in some parts mountainous, but the soil is adapted for grazing. Considerable wool is produced; and there are manufactures in the town of woolen goods, boots, shoes, leather, and wooden ware.

Rowe is the source of a branch of Deerfield river, and lies 130 miles N. W. from Boston, and 22 W. by N. from Greenfield. Incorporated, 1785. Population, 1837, 633.

Rowley, Mass.

Essex co. This town was first settled by a party of industrious and pious persons from Yorkshire, Eng. in 1639. They erected the first fulling mill in New England, and manufactured the first cloth in North America. There are a great variety of soils in the town; a large part is salt meadow, and the residue is fertile and productive. It comprises a part of Plum island, and large tracts of wood land. It is watered by Rowley river, which rises from several ponds in Boxford. This river affords a water power, and before its junction with Plum Island Sound, forms a harbor for vessels of moderate draught of water, and in which many vessels have been built.

Ancient Rowley was divided in 1838: its western part was detached and incorporated by the name of Georgetown. Since this division Rowley possesses but little manufacturing interest, but a valuable agricultural one, to which its inhabitants are principally devoted.

This ancient town is very pleasant, and has been the birth place of many learned men. It lies 30 miles N. from Boston, 16 N. by W. from Salem, and 25 E. N. E. from Lowell. Population, 1838, about 1,000.

Roxbury, Me.

Oxford co. The surface of this town is elevated, and well timbered, with some good soil. Roxbury is watered by a branch of Androscoggin river. It lies 30 miles N. from Paris, and is bounded S. by Rumford. Incorporated, 1835.— Population, 1837, 182.

Roxbury, N. H.,

Cheshire co., is 5 miles E. from Keene, and 50 S. W. from Concord. The N. branch of Ashuelot river forms the boundary between this town and Keene. Roaring Brook, on which are several small meadows, waters the S. part, and empties into the Ashuelot at the S. W. corner. On the E. side of the township is a pond, called Roaring Brook pond, at the outlet of which are mills.

Roxbury presents a rough and uneven surface, rising into considerable swells, affording excellent grazing land.

This town was formed of a part of Nelson, Marlborough and Keene, and incorporated in 1812. Population, 1830, 322.

Roxbury, Vt.

Washington co. This town is elevated between the waters of Onion and White rivers. It lies 15 miles S. S. W. from Montpelier. First settled, 1789. Population, 1830, 737.

Roxbury, Mass.

Norfolk co. This town is joined to Boston by a neck of land, over which are broad and pleasant avenues. Between the centre of each town is about 3 miles. The surface is rocky and uneven, with a strong soil in a high state of cultivation. It displays a great degree of agricultural taste and skill, and abounds in country seats and pleasure grounds. That part of this town bordering on Jamaica pond, 4 miles S. W. from Boston, is exceedingly pleasant. This town and Boston were incorporated the same year, (1630;) and nothing but municipal regulations divide their interests and feelings. Population, 1810, 3,669; 1820, 4,135; 1830, 5,247; 1837, 7,493.

The first hourly coach from Boston commenced running to this town in 1827. There are now a large number continually running between the two places, and not less than 250,000 persons pass annually. Since that time, others of a similar kind have been established to Charlestown, Cambridge, Dorchester, &c., and tend greatly to promote the public convenience.

The manufactures of Roxbury consist of leather, nails, hats, chairs, cabinet ware, pig iron, spirits, &c.: annual value, about $300,000.

The Rev. JOHN ELIOT, the justly celebrated "Apostle of the Indians," was settled in Roxbury in 1632. Mr. Eliot imbibed the true spirit of the gospel, and his heart was touched with the wretched condition of the Indians. He learned their language, and translated the scriptures into it. This would seem the business of a life, when the sense of the simple expression, "Kneeling down to him," is conveyed in the Indian language by *Wutappessttukqussunnooweh-tunkquoh,* a word that would puzzle a Demosthenes to pronounce, without an extra pebble stone in his mouth. Mr. Eliot was remarkable for his indefatigable labors and charities; he endured hardship as a good soldier of Jesus Christ, and went to his reward in 1690, aged 86.

This was the birth place and residence of the patriot JOSEPH WARREN. Dr. Warren was born in 1740. He graduated at Harvard college in 1759. He was an ardent lover of his country, and sensibly felt the weight of her oppressions. Four days previous to the battle of "Bunker Hill," he received a commission in the army of Major General. He was within the entrenchment, and was slain on that hallowed spot, just at the commencement of the retreat. Dr. Warren was an able statesman, an eloquent orator, a man of uncompromising integrity and undaunted bravery. General Warren was the first officer of rank that fell in that glorious contest for liberty. His death shed a gloom throughout the country: he was exceedingly beloved for the mildness and affability of his deportment, and for the virtues of his private life.

Roxbury, Ct.

Litchfield co. Roxbury was taken from Woodbury and incorporated in 1801. It lies 32 miles N. W. from New Haven, 46 W. S. W. from Hartford, and 15 S. by W. from Litchfield. Population, 1830, 1,122.

The town is diversified with hills and vales. The soil is a gravelly loam, interspersed with some small tracts of sandy loam. It is watered by the Shepaug, a branch of the Housatonick. In digging for silver, a species of iron ore, called steel ore, was discovered.

Royalston, Mass.

Worcester co. Royalston is a pleasant town, and is well watered by Miller's river, a beautiful mill stream. The surface of the town is uneven, but the soil is generally rich and productive. There are two woolen mills, and manufactures of boots, shoes, leather, chairs, cabinet ware, palm-leaf hats and mats, wooden ware. &c. First settled, 1762. Incorporated, 1765. It lies 70 miles W. N. W. from Boston, and 38 N. W. from Worcester. Population, 1837, 1,629.

Royalton, Vt.

Windsor co. The surface of this town is somewhat rough and mountainous, but the soil is good, particularly on the banks of White river, by which it is watered.

This town was first settled in 1771, and for many years endured great suffering from Indian hostility. This is an excellent township for grazing, and its agricultural products are considerable. It has a pleasant village and an academy.

Royalton is 30 miles S. from Montpelier, and 25 N. N. W. from Windsor. Population, in 1830, 1,893.

Rumford, Me.

Oxford co. Rumford is a township of valuable land, 51 miles W. N. W. from Augusta, and 20 N. by W. from Paris. It lies on the northwestern bank of the Androscoggin, and enjoys a great water power. Mills of various kinds are already erected, and manufactures on a large scale are contemplated. White Cap mountain, rising 500 feet above the level of the surrounding country, and Glass-face, about 400 feet, present beautiful views from their summits. Population, 1837, 1,382. Wheat crop, same year, 4,385 bushels. Incorporated, 1800.

Rumney, N. H.

Grafton co. Rumney is 8 miles N. N. W. from Plymouth, 47 N. by

W. from Concord. It is watered by Baker's river, of which a considerable branch flows from Stinson's pond, and is called Stinson's brook. The pond is 400 rods long and 280 rods wide. Part of Loon pond is on the E. line of this town. The principal elevations are Stinson's and Webber's mountains in the E. part, and a small part of Carr's mountain, which here obtains the name of Rattlesnake mountain, on its N. W. border. Rumney was granted in 1767, and was first settled in 1765. It was in this town, on the 28th of April, 1752, that the late General STARK, while on a hunting expedition, was captured by a party of 10 Indians, commanded by Francis Titigaw. He was in company with Amos Eastman of Concord, David Stinson of Londonderry, and his brother William. Stinson was slain. Population, in 1830, 993.

Rupert, Vt.

Bennington co. A part of this township is mountainous, but the soil is generally good for grazing. Rupert produces some fine cattle, and keeps about 10,000 sheep. It is watered by Pawlet river, and a branch of the Battenkill, on which streams, are mills of various kinds. Rupert is 78 miles S. W. from Montpelier, and 25 N. from Bennington. Population, 1830, 1,313.

Russell, Mass.

Hampden co. Westfield river waters this town, and affords it good mill privileges. There is a cotton mill in the town and other manufactures. Russell lies 100 miles W. by S. from Boston, and 14 W. by N. from Springfield. Incorporated, 1792. Population, 1837, 475.

Rutland County, Vt.

Rutland, chief town. This county is bounded N. by Addison county, E. by Windsor county, S. by Bennington county, and W. by the state of New York. Incorporated, 1781. Population, 1820, 29,983; 1830, 31,294. This county contains an area of 958 square miles. Inhabitants to a square mile, 33. The principal streams are Otter Creek, Black, White, Queechy and Pawlet rivers. There is some fine land in this county along Otter Creek, but a large portion of it is elevated, and some parts mountainous. The soil, however, is generally warm and well suited for grazing. Many cattle are annually taken to market, and in 1837, there were 180,984 sheep in Rutland county. Excellent iron ore is found at the base of the mountains, and a range of marble quarries extends the whole length of the county from north to south. This marble is of a fine quality: much of it is wrought and transported.

Rutland, Vt.

Chief town, Rutland co. This town was settled about the year 1770, and for some time during the revolutionary war was a frontier town. The *Green mountain boys* erected here two small picket forts, which were found very useful. The soil of the town is various, but generally of an excellent quality. Iron ore of a good quality is found; clay, lime, and a great abundance of beautifully variegated marble.

The village of Rutland is neat, well built and handsomely located: it is the centre of trade for a large section of fertile country. The agricultural productions of Rutland are large and valuable:—in 1837, there were within its limits 20,981 sheep. Otter Creek and its tributaries give the town a good water power, and manufacturing establishments are springing up along their banks. Rutland lies 50 miles S. W. from Montpelier, 52 N. by E. from Bennington, 60 S. S. E. from Burlington, and 34 W. N. W. from Windsor. Population, 1830, 2,753.

Rutland, Mass.

Worcester co. Rutland was formerly twelve miles square, and was sold by the Indians, in 1686, for £23 lawful money. It was first settled about the year 1720, and incorporated, in 1722. It lies 51 miles W. by N. from Boston and 12 N. W. from Worcester. A branch of Ware river waters the town, and gives it mill privileges. The manufactures consist of woolen goods, leather, boots, shoes, chairs, cabinet and wooden wares; annual value about $50,000. Rutland is a very pleasant town, of good soil and well cultivated. Its exports of beef, butter and cheese are considerable. It contains some fine fish ponds. Population, 1837, 1,265.

Rye, N. H.,

Rockingham co., is pleasantly situated on the sea coast, 6 1-2 miles S. from Portsmouth. It was originally taken from Portsmouth, Greenland, Hampton and New Castle, chiefly the latter; and though it began to be settled as early as the year 1635, it was not incorporated till 1719. The sea coast here is about 6 miles in extent, being nearly one third of the coast in the state. On the shore, there are three considerable and very pleasant beaches, viz. Sandy, Jenness' and Wallis', to which many persons resort in the summer season from neighboring towns and the country, both for health and for pleasure. There is here a small harbor, near Goss' mill, into which vessels of 70 or 80 tons burden may conveniently enter, at high water. The boat fishery is carried on to considerable advantage, particularly in the fall and winter seasons. There was formerly a large fresh water pond, lying contiguous to the sand bank or bounds of the sea, covering a surface of about 300 acres. Between this and the sea, a communication was opened by the inhabitants about a century since. The waters were discharged into the sea, leaving a tract of marsh, which, being watered by the regular flowing of the tide, yields annually large quantities of salt hay. Breakfast Hill, between this town and Greenland, is distinguished as the place where a party of Indians were surprised at breakfast, at the time of their incursion in 1696. There are small circular holes in the rocks of which this hill is principally composed, supposed to have been made use of by the natives. This town has suffered considerably in times of war and danger. In the American or revolutionary war, 38 of its inhabitants lost their lives, by sea or land; most of them young men. Population, in 1830, 1,172.

Ryegate, Vt.

Caledonia co. This town is situated on the west bank of Connecticut river, opposite to Bath, N. H. It is 33 miles E. by S. from Montpelier, and 14 S. by E. from Danville. Ryegate is watered by Wells river, some smaller streams and several ponds. There is not much intervale land on the river, in the town, but the soil is generally rich and very productive of all kinds of vegetables and grain; but more particularly of grass. About 3,000 sheep are kept, and the products of the soil, annually transported to market, are very considerable. This town was first settled by emigrants from Scotland, in the year 1774. A large part of the present population of Ryegate are of Scotch descent, and are said to follow, in a great degree, the peculiar habits, in regard to diet, which Scotchmen are accustomed to in their own country. They annually prepare large quantities of oat meal for cakes, and lay in a good stock of hulled barley for broths, soups and puddings. The people of Ryegate are generally frugal and industrious; good farmers, and good livers. They manufacture their own apparel and some for their neighbors. Population, 1830, 1,119.

Sachem's Head, Ct.
See *Guilford*.

Saco River,

Is one of the largest in New England; yet being much broken in its course by falls, is not navigable to any considerable extent. It springs from three sources in the White mountains; the branch issuing from the southwest side of the mountains, near the Notch, is considered the main stream; next to this is the middle branch, which is the smallest; and beyond is the branch called Ellis's river, which rises on the northeast side of the mountains, and after a course of about eighteen miles, unites with the main branch in the town of Bartlett. Cutler's and New rivers are mountain torrents that discharge into the Ellis. The Ammonoosuck, a branch of the Connecticut, rises within about two rods of the Saco, flowing in an opposite direction. The whole length of Saco river is estimated to be 160 miles; running in its general course S. S. E., and discharging into the sea in N. latitude 43° 31′, W. longitude 70° 26′. The principal falls are, the Great Falls, at Hiram, where the water descends 72 feet; Steep Falls, at Limington, 20 feet; Salmon Falls, at Hollis and Buxton, 30 feet; and Saco Falls, 42 feet. The latter are about 4 miles from the mouth of the river. The ordinary rise of the water, in the spring, is from 10 to 15 feet, but in great freshets it has been known greatly to exceed that number. A long storm which occurred in October, 1785, raised the river to an immense height, sweeping away mills and bridges, and inundating houses that stood in its vicinity. In 1814, there was the greatest freshet known since that of 1785. At such seasons the appearance of Saco Falls is truly sublime.

Saco, Me.

York co. Saco is situated on the east side of the river of that name. It is 71 miles S. S. W. from Augusta, 15 S. W. from Portland, and 29 N. E. from York.

Saco is a port of entry, a place of some ship building, and commands a flourishing trade. Population, 1830, 3,219; 1837, 4,229.

Saco enjoys the rare privilege of possessing a great hydraulic power united with navigable accommodations. The Saco river terminates its fantastic course at this place, by leaping, within a short distance, 42 feet, and mingling with the ocean. This water power is very valuable, and cannot fail of becoming the site of large manufacturing operations.

From the mouth of the river a fine beach extends to the east about 5 miles, called Old Orchard beach. This name arose from a growth of apple trees formerly near the beach, planted at a very early period; some of them remained as late as 1770. Another beach of less extent, but not inferior in other respects, is found at the Pool, connecting Fletcher's Neck with the main, and forming the south shore of that peninsula. Its distance from the Falls is about 9 miles.

The small streams by which different parts of Saco are watered, generally derive their origin from an immense bog, commonly called the Heath, and flow into the river and sea. On one of these, Foxwell's brook, there is a fine waterfall, with a descent of about sixty feet, surrounded by scenery of a wild and striking character.

The lumber trade has long been the principal branch of business on Saco river. In early times, the mills were supplied with logs from the forests in the vicinity of the Falls: in the former part of the last century, they were procured at the distance of a few miles above the mills. In the winter of 1772, it is said, a few persons for the first time ascended the river as far as Fryeburg, in quest of timber, and finding an abundance, turned the attention of millmen to that region for their future supplies. After the war the number of mills was increased. Before the year 1800, seventeen saws were in operation about the Falls. There were others on the small streams in different parts of Saco and Biddeford. The quantity of boards sawed per day, (24 hours) has been estimated at fifty thousand feet.

There is considerable navigation owned at Saco, employed in foreign and domestic commerce and the fishery. The tonnage of the district, in 1837, was 3,666 tons.

There are at present a large cotton mill, a rolling mill, a nail factory, and numerous saw mills; but a great portion of the water power remains unimproved.

The village of Saco contains many handsome buildings, and the scenery around it is romantic and beautiful.

Saco and Biddeford were formerly united. The former was first settled in 1631, the latter in 1630.

We make a few extracts from Mr. Folsom's valuable history of those towns, as they contain some interesting information in relation to the first settlement of this part of New England.

"The unfortunate termination of Sir Walter Raleigh's attempts to colonize Virginia during the reign of Queen Elizabeth, had effectually checked the spirit of enterprise in England in relation to the settlement of America. The discoveries of Gosnold and Pring, and the shortness of their voyages, now caused the subject to be revived, and to excite more general interest than had before existed. On the petition of a number of gentlemen, a charter was granted by king James in the year 1606, dividing the country into two districts, called North and South Virginia, and authorizing the establishment of separate colonies in each district by two distinct companies. A right of property in the land fifty miles on each side of their first plantations, and extending 100 miles into the interior, was granted by this patent. The first or Southern colony were allowed to settle any part of the country within the degrees of 34 and 41 north latitude; the second, consisting chiefly of persons resident at Plymouth and other towns in the west of England, and thence denominated the Plymouth Company, were allowed to choose a place of settlement between 38 and 45 degrees north latitude. As a considerable portion of the territory thus allotted was common to the two districts, a provision was added, that the colony last planted should not approach within one hundred miles of that already established.

"The next year colonies were sent out by the two companies. One was fixed at Jamestown, of which Gosnold ' was the prime mover,' and Capt. Smith an active member; the other was established at Sagadahock, or the mouth of the Kennebec, led by Captains George Popham, brother to the Chief Justice, and Raleigh Gilbert. This colony consisted of 108 men;—whether accompanied by their families, we are not informed. They arrived on the coast near the island of Monheagan, a few leagues east of the Kennebec, in the month of August, and soon after entered the mouth of that river, where, on the eastern side, on an island now forming a part of Georgetown, they commenced preparations for a permanent settlement without delay. Monheagan was agreed upon as a place of rendezvous for the ships before leaving England, and although we are not directly told that the destination of the colony was determined before their arrival, there is no doubt of the fact. The great patron of the enterprise, Chief Justice Popham, obtained an accurate survey of the coast the year before, and doubtless selected the mouth of that " fair and navigable river," as the Kennebec is styled by Smith, as a favorable location for the seat of the colony.

"The lateness of the season scarcely allowed the colonists time to erect a fort and the necessary places of shelter before the approach of winter, which proved excessively rigorous. More than half their number returned with the ships to England in December, in consequence of the severity of the cold and the scantiness of their supplies. Soon after those who had remained had the misfortune to lose the greater part of their buildings and stores by fire. Capt. Popham died in the course of the winter, and an arrival in the spring brought news of the death of the Chief Justice. Raleigh Gilbert, who succeeded Popham as president of the Colony, was under the necessity of returning to England on account of the decease of his brother, of which intelligence was received by another arrival, and the colonists, discouraged by so many adverse circumstances, resolved to abandon the country and return with him. Thus in less than one year from the time the settlement was commenced, the northern colony was broken up; the country was denounced as uninhabitable, and no further attempts were made for many years to promote its settlement by the Company to whom it was assigned by the patent of King James.

"Sir Ferdinando Gorges, a conspicuous member of the Plymouth Company, alone remained undiscouraged. The attention of this gentleman appears to have been first turned to this part of America in the year 1605, when Capt. Weymouth arrived in the harbor of Plymouth where he resided, on his return from a voyage for the discovery of the northwest passage. Falling short of his course, Weymouth had accidentally discovered the river Penobscot, from whence he carried to England five of the natives, "three of whom," says Gorges, " I seized upon ; they were all of one nation, but of several parts and several families. This accident must be acknowledged the means under God of putting on foot and giving life to all our plantations." He retained these Indians in his family three years, and obtained from them much information respecting their native shores: they were afterwards sent back. Gorges henceforth took a deep interest in schemes for the settlement of North Virginia, and was rather chagrined than discouraged by the return of the Sagadahock colonists, and the unfavorable reports which they spread concerning the country. "He had too much experience in the world," he said, " to be frighted with such a blast, as knowing many great kingdoms and large territories more northerly seated and by many degrees colder, were plentifully inhabited, and divers of them stored with no better commodities than these afforded, if like industry, art and labor be used." Unable, however, to persuade the company to undertake the planting of a second colony, Gorges engaged in private enterprises to this coast, which began to be much resorted to by English ships for purposes of trade with the natives, and of fishing. In the year 1616, he sent hither a party commanded by Richard Vines, for the express object of exploring the country with a view to form a settlement. He contracted with them to remain during the winter, with the hope of removing the prejudice excited by the

Sagadahock colonists against the character of the climate.

"They arrived during the prevalence of a destructive disease among the natives, which spread throughout New England, commencing its ravages in the west. This pestilence is noticed by all the writers on the early history of New England, with some difference of opinion as to the precise year of its occurrence. A late and highly respectable writer supposes it to have prevailed in different places at different times, but a few years previous to the arrival of the Plymouth pilgrims. It was regarded by those pious colonists as a special interposition of divine providence in their favor, so great was the havoc it made among the tribes in that quarter. 'Thus,' says old Morton, 'God made way for his people by removing the heathen and planting them in the land.'

"Mr. Vines and his companions penetrated into the interior, visiting the Indians in their villages and wigwams, who received them with great kindness and hospitality. Beside the ravages of sickness, they were at this time thrown into confusion by the death of the Bashaba or chief sachem, whom the Tarrantines, living east of the Penobscot, had attacked by surprise and destroyed with his family the preceding year. Great dissensions had immediately followed among the different tribes, who were engaged in a destructive war with each other when the pestilence made its appearance. In the midst of these evils, the Englishmen passed with safety among them, and slept in their cabins without suffering from the contagion. They were in particular welcomed by the savages whom they had seen in the family of Gorges at Plymouth, and now met in their native homes. Having visited different parts of the coast, this little party prepared to establish themselves for the winter.

The spot which they selected for their abode, we have reason to suppose, was at the mouth of Saco river, on the western side, near the capacious and sheltered basin now called the Pool, but in early times known as Winter harbor.

"Vines performed several voyages to our coast in the service of Gorges, and it is probable made Winter Harbor his principal resort. While he was occupied in exploring the country and trading with the natives, his men were engaged in fishing. How long he pursued this course, we are not informed, nor do we find him mentioned again until several years after his early residence at Winter Harbor.

"The employments of the colonists were chiefly agriculture, fishing, and trade with the natives. Most of them combined these pursuits, and were styled husbandmen or planters.

"The husbandmen took up tracts of 100 acres, of which they received leases on nominal or small rents, from Mr. Vines. Some of these are now on record. An estate that had been in the possession of Thomas Cole, including 'a mansion or dwellinghouse,' was leased by Mr. Vines to John West for the term of 1000 years, for the annual rent of two shillings and one capon, a previous consideration having been paid by West. The lease which is partly in the latin language, was executed, 1638. Another deed from Vines requires the lessee to yield and pay an acknowledgement and rent-charge of 5s., two days work, and one fat goose yearly. In this manner were all the planters rendered tenants to the proprietor, none of them holding their estates in fee simple.

Fishing was the most common occupation, as it was both easy and profitable to barter the products of this business for corn from Virginia, and other stores from England. The trade with the planters of Massachusetts soon became considerable. In 1636, Mr. Vines had a consignment of bread and beef from that quarter. Jocelyn remarks that 'Winter Harbor is a noted place for fishers.' He describes the mode of pursuing this business in the following manner: 'The fishermen take yearly on the coast many hundred quintals of cod, hake, haddock, pollock, &c. and dry them at their stages, making three voyages in a year. They make merchantable and refuse fish, which they sell to Massachusetts merchants; the first for 32 ryals ($4) per quintal; the refuse for 9 and 10 shillings ($2, and 2,25.) The merchant sends the first to Lisbon, Bilboa, Marseilles, Bordeaux, Toulon, and other cities of France; to Canaries, pipe-staves and clapboards; the refuse fish to the W. Indies for the negroes. To every shallop belong four fishermen, a master or steersman, a midshipman, and a shore man, who washes it out of the salt, and dries it upon hurdles pitched upon stakes breast high, and tends their cookery. They often get in one voyage 8 or 9 barrels a share per man. The merchant buys of the planters beef, pork, peas, wheat, indian corn, and sells it to the fishermen.'

"The expense of each planter to provision himself was quite small, if we may judge from an estimate furnished by Mr. Jocelyn for the information of proposed emigrants. A similar estimate had been previously made by Capt. Smith with reference to Virginia. ' Victuals to last one man a year; 8 bushels of meal, £2: two bushels of peas, 6 shillings: two bushels of oatmeal, 9 shillings: one gallon of aqua vitæ, (brandy,) 2s. 6d.: one gallon of oil, 3s. 6d.: two gallons of vinegar, 2s.:' total, £3 3s., equal to $14.

"A considerable traffic was carried on with the natives by many of the planters, some of them visiting remote parts of the coast, or travelling into the interior for this purpose. English and French goods were bartered for valuable furs, particularly beaver."

Saddle Mountain, Mass.

See *Adams*.

Saddleback Mountain, Me.

Franklin co. This mountain is a few miles south of Mount Abraham. It is 25 miles N. W. from Farmington, and about 4,000 feet above the level of the sea.

Sagadahock, Me.

The ancient name of a section of country, at and east of the mouth of Kennebec river. See *Saco*.

St. Albans, Me.

Somerset co. This is a valuable township of land, 46 miles N. N. E. from Augusta, and 26 N. E. by E. from Norridgewock. Incorporated, 1813. Population, 1830, 911; 1837, 1,393. This town contains a large and beautiful pond; the outlet of which forms a good mill stream, a branch of Sebasticook river. There are two pleasant and flourishing villages in St. Albans. Wheat crop, 1837, 10,294 bushels

St. Albans, Vt.

Shire town of Franklin co. This town is bounded on the west by Champlain lake. It lies 46 miles N. W. by N. from Montpelier, and 25 N. from Burlington. First settled about the year 1785. Population 1830, 2,395. The soil of this town is fertile, and under the management of good farmers, is rendered very productive. In 1837, there were 8,459 sheep in the town, and the exports of wool and other productions of the soil are large and valuable. The water communications by the lake to New-York and Canada, render St. Albans a mart of considerable trade from the surrounding country. The first vessel from Lake Champlain, that arrived at New York, by the northern canal, was from, built and owned at St. Albans.

The Village of St. Albans is beautifully situated on elevated ground, and commands a fine prospect. It contains many handsome buildings, and is a busy place in the manufacture of various articles. It lies three miles from the lake, and twelve miles from the line of Canada.

St. Croix River.

This river forms the boundary line between the United States and the British Province of New Brunswick, from the ocean to Grand Lake. It is sometimes called *Passamaquoddy*, *Schoodic* and *Cheputnetecook*. This river rises in Grand Lake and passes to the ocean in a S. E. course. The distances on this important river are as follows: from Eastport to Calais, at the head of navigation, is 28 miles: from Calais to the mouth of Schoodic river, 21 miles, and from thence to Grand Lake is 33 miles: total distance from Eastport to Grand Lake, 82 miles. There are many elevations in this river, and consequently many falls and rapids, producing a great hydraulic power. The mouth of the western branch of the St. Croix, or Schoodic river, is 166 feet above tide water, at Calais; and the whole fall from Grand Lake to sea level is 444 feet.

St. Francois River, Me.

Or the *Pecheenegamook*, rises in the county of Piscataquis, on the border of Canada. It has a number of tributaries and receives the waters of several lakes. It is about 50 miles in length, and, passing nearly south falls into the river St. John, on the line of Penobscot county.

St. George, Me.

Lincoln co. This township is nearly surrounded by water It is bounded northerly by a neck of land adjoining Thomaston, E. by the western waters of Penobscot bay, S. by the Atlantic, and W. by the waters of Muscongus bay and St. George's river. This town possesses, in an eminent degree, every navigable facility. It is a place of considerable ship building, and the people are engaged in the lumber trade, coasting and fishing. There are a number of islands on the coast of this town: a cluster of islands called *St. Georges*, are the most considerable. They lie off the town S. by W. about 5 miles. St. George was incorporated in 1803. Population, 1837, 1,883. It lies 57 miles S. E. from Augusta, and 10 S. from Warren.

St. George River is a valuable stream, both on account of its hydraulic power and navigable accommodations. It receives its most distant waters from ponds in Montville, Searsmont and Belmont in the county of Waldo, and, in a southerly course, passes to Union, where it receives the waters of several ponds, and meets the tide at Warren. The length of this river is about 40 miles: it is navigable to Warren, 15 miles from the sea.

St. George, Vt.

Chittenden co. A small town bounded W. by Shelburne, 28 miles W. by N. from Montpelier, and 8 S. E. from Burlington. First settled, 1784. Population, 1830, 135. The surface is high and uneven: the soil is composed of loam, clay and gravel.

St. John's River.

See *Fundy, Bay.*

St. Johnsbury, Vt.

Caledonia co. This pleasant and flourishing town is 35 miles N. E. from Montpelier, 57 N. from Hanover, N. H., and 7 E. from Danville. The town was organized in 1790. Population, 1830, 1,592; 1838, about

NEW ENGLAND GAZETTEER.

2,000. The surface is uneven, but the soil is generally strong and fertile. In 1837, there were 4,546 sheep in the town. The amount of available water power in St. Johnsbury is great and valuable, indicating its future importance as a site for large manufactories. The Passumpsic river, a considerable stream, which falls into Connecticut river at the foot of Fifteen Mile Falls, passes through the central part of the town from north to south. Moose and Sleeper's rivers unite with the Passumpsic and afford a succession of excellent mill seats seldom seen so closely combined.

On Sleeper's river is the establishment of E. and I. Fairbanks, for the manufacture of their improved platform balances, on an extensive scale; also iron works of various kinds, on the other streams.

There are three handsome villages in the town: that called the *Plain*, is on elevated ground and near the junction of the streams. This town commands the trade of a considerable portion of country, and these villages, which are neatly built, enjoy an active business.

Salem, Me.

Somerset co. This town is watered by a branch of Seven Mile Brook, and lies 52 miles N. N. W. from Augusta, and 28 N. W. from Norridgewock. Incorporated, 1823. Population, 1837, 496. This is a good farming town; it produced in 1837, 4,216 bushels of wheat.

Salem, N. H.,

Rockingham co., is 30 miles S. from Concord, and 40 S. W. from Portsmouth. Policy pond, partly in this town, and partly in Windham, is the largest collection of water: World's end pond and Captain pond are in the S. E. and E. parts of the town; and there are other small ponds. The Spiggot river, passing from N. to S. through the town, receives in its course numerous branches, and waters the different portions of the town, furnishing also excellent mill privileges. The soil is generally fertile, and the surface uneven. Salem was incorporated by charter, May 11, 1750. Population, in 1830, 1,310.

Salem, Vt.

Orleans co. This is a township of level surface, and tolerable soil; 50 miles N. N. E. from Montpelier and 10 N. E. from Irasburgh. First settled, 1798. Population, 1830, 230. Clyde river passes through the N. E. part of the town and a part of the south bay of Memphremagog lake lies in the N. W. corner.

Salem, Mass.,

One of the shire towns in Essex co. This is the oldest and largest seaport but one in old Massachusetts. Its Indian name was *Naumkeag*. It is 14 miles N. N. E. from Boston, and lies in lat. 42° 31′ 19″ N., and lon. 70° 54′ W. Population, 1836, 15,002. Salem is nearly surrounded by water, being situated between two inlets of the sea, called the north and south rivers. To the main, and now inhabited part of the town, is attached a peninsular portion of land, called the Neck. This was the first inhabited land, and was formerly used for fishing and other purposes. It ultimately became the property of the town, and was, for a long time, used as a public pasture. In 1816, when the present Alms House was built, a large portion of it was enclosed, and has since been cultivated as the Alms House farm. The finest and most comprehensive view of Salem may be had from "Gallows Hill." Its situation is low, but pleasant and healthy. Its streets are quite irregular. Essex is the only street which runs through the town and is very angular and crooked. Federal and Bridge streets are broad, straight and regular. Chesnut is esteemed the handsomest, though it is not the most public street. It has rows of elms on either side. Winter and Broad streets are the widest. The first pavement was made in Essex street, between Court and North streets, in 1773, and is still in use. The south church has great architectural beauty, and the north church is built of stone, with a beautiful front of the gothic order. There is a Custom House at the head of Derby wharf. Salem has always been a commercial place. It has a convenient harbor and good anchorage. In point of wealth and commerce, it has always ranked as the second town in New England.

Its history is identified with that of Massachusetts, and there is much in it to interest and instruct. Its rank, the character and number of its population, its facilities for commerce, and the advantage of being the chosen residence of many of the first and most distinguished settlers, made it early and seriously thought of as the Capital, instead of Boston. It was first settled in 1626, by Roger Conant, Peter Palfray and others, who had failed in an attempt to plant themselves at Cape Ann. In 1628, a cession of Massachusetts was made to Sir Henry Roswell and others, with a view to establish a colony there. Of this company, Matthew Cradock was President, and in 1628, John Endicott was sent over to reside at Salem as the company's agent. In the same year, the first church was formed. It has ever been remarkable for its succession of eminent, independent and useful Divines; among whom, are the Higginsons, Skelton, Roger Williams, Hugh Peters, Noyes, Fiske, Dr. Prince, &c. In 1634, the first general court met at Newton. Roger Conant was one of the first deputies from Salem.

In 1643, Massachusetts was divided into 4 counties; Essex, Middlesex, Suffolk and Norfolk. In 1644, there was a strong party to make Salem the seat of government, but in this attempt, the deputies were defeated.

In 1675, Capt. Thomas Lathrop and his company were killed by the Indians, at Bloody Brook. He, with Roger Conant, had removed from Salem to Beverly, in 1668. His company were called the "Flower of Essex," and many of them were from Salem.

In 1681, Major William Hawthorne died. He was a leading and influential character in his time, having been speaker, assistant, judge, commissioner of the united colonies, &c., and having ever showed himself able, faithful, and worthy of confidence.

In 1687, William Brown gave a farm for the benefit of the schools of Salem. The Brown family were ever great friends and liberal patrons of learning. They not only made donations to the Salem schools, but also to Harvard College for the benefit of poor scholars.

In 1692, the witchcraft delusion prevailed in Salem, and nineteen persons were tried and hanged as witches. Though designated "the Salem witchcraft," it had pervaded other places, previously to its appearance here. In England, laws had been enacted against it, and Sir Matthew Hale, gave to those laws his sanction. In 1648, Margaret Jones was condemned and hanged at Charlestown, and in 1655, Ann Hibbins, at Boston. The imputation for a time induced a belief of the reality of the imposition; but time finally detected and exposed the error. The house, in which the accused were tried, is still standing at the western corner of Essex and North streets, and the place of their execution is now known as "Gallows Hill." A full and interesting account of this delusion of the imagination has been written and published by Rev. C. W. Upham.

In 1698, a great fire broke out, and destroyed several dwelling houses. In 1718, the second or east church was built and is still standing. The celebrated Dr. Bentley was pastor of this church. He wrote a "Description of Salem," which is published in the "Collections of the Mass. Hist. Society."

In 1774, General Gage ordered the removal of the general court to Salem. At that time, Boston was a closed port. The merchants and citizens of Salem called a town meeting, at which, resolutions denouncing, in very strong terms, the Boston port bill, were passed unanimously. The meeting was very full, and a copy of their doings was communicated to their neighbors of Boston. On the 11th of June, when Gov. Gage was at Salem, an address, numerously signed, was presented to him, which reflects high honor on the sense of justice and patriotism of this ancient town. Among other things it said, "By shutting up the port of Boston, some imagine that the course of trade might be turned hither and to our benefit: but nature in the formation of our harbor forbids our becoming rivals in commerce to that convenient mart. And were it otherwise, *we must be dead to every idea of justice—lost to all feelings of humanity—could we indulge one thought to seize on wealth and raise our fortunes on the ruin of our suffering neighbors.*"

In 1776, Feb. 26, Col. Leslie, with a British regiment from Boston Castle, landed privately at Salem and proceeded to the North bridge, with a view to seize on some military stores beyond it. The citizens were, at the time, in meeting; but Col. Timothy Pickering, with 30 or 40 men, got there in season to raise the draw, and thus prevent Leslie and his regiment from passing further. The British attempted to cross the river in a gondola, but the Americans scuttled the boat. Finally, Col. Leslie proposed that if he should be permitted to pass 30 rods beyond the bridge, he would return. Having been permitted, the gallant colonel returned peaceably to Boston.

During the revolution, there were about 60 armed vessels fitted out from Salem, manned by 4,000 men; and many unrecorded deeds of high daring and chivalrous adventure were performed on the sea by citizens of Salem, during that eventful period. Indeed, in her naval achievements consists principally the part which Salem bore in the revolutionary struggle.

This seaport has been more known for its East India trade than any other in the United States. The first ship from Salem engaged in this trade was the Grand Turk, owned by E. H. Derby. She was at the Cape of Good Hope in 1784, commanded by Capt. Jonathan Ingersoll, and at Canton in 1786, commanded by Ebenezer West. A model of her, completely rigged, is in the Museum. In 1818, there were 53 vessels employed in this trade belonging to Salem, the tonnage of which was 14,272 tons.

Salem became a city in 1836. Its government consists of a mayor and six aldermen, and twenty-four common council men. Its *public schools* are nineteen. The number of scholars in 1837, was 1,534, and the amount paid for instruction $8,877.

The *Athenæum* was incorporated in 1810. Edward A. Holyoke, William Orne, Nathaniel Silsbee and Samuel Putnam were authorised to call the first meeting of the proprietors. The stock is divided into 90 or 100 shares. Its library contains about 9,000 volumes. The institution, though at present rather private, may ultimately become more public.

The *Museum* is remarkable for the extent and variety of its natural and artificial curiosities, collected from almost every part of the world.

There are 4,724 names of different articles on the catalogue: they are kept in a spacious hall built for that purpose, and belong to the East India Marine society. This society consists of such only as have actually navigated the seas near the Cape of Good Hope or Cape Horn, as master or factor. In 1823, there were 160 of these enterprising men living in Salem. The hall is open daily for the reception of visitors, and vast numbers of strangers throng there. All come with an eager and excited curiosity, and leave with that curiosity at least gratified, if not satisfied.

The commerce of Salem is very extended. There is hardly any part of the world which her ships have not visited. The number of vessels, engaged in foreign commerce, is 100 or more, and 18 in the whaling business, beside the vessels employed in the coasting trade and fishery. Tonnage of the district in 1837, 32,800 tons.

Many of the wharves bear the names of their builders and owners: as the Allen, Derby, Peabody, Forester and Phillips' wharf. This last was recently re-built by Stephen C. Phillips, on the ruins of the old Crowninshield wharf, which had become dilapidated and useless. It is an admirable piece of work.

Although Salem is without any important water power, and has ever been almost exclusively devoted to maritime pursuits, yet its manufacturing interests are by no means small. During the year ending April 1, 1837, the value of its manufactures amounted to $1,471,889. They consisted of vessels, cordage, leather, boots, shoes, hats, tin and cabinet wares, chairs, spirits; white, sheet and pipe lead, carriages, straw bonnets, sperm candles, tobacco, alum, saltpetre refined, aquafortis, muriatic acid, oil of vitriol, &c. The value of its whale, cod and mackerel fisheries, the same year, amounted to $210,843.

The *Aqueduct* furnishes the city with a constant supply of fresh and soft spring water.

The fire department is under good regulations. Some of the societies in the city are the " East India Marine society," incorporated in 1801; the " E. I. M. Hall Corporation," in 1824; the " Salem Charitable Mechanic Association," instituted in 1817, and incorporated, in 1822; the " Essex Historical Society," in 1821, and the " Salem Lyceum," which was formed in 1830.

The Common was reserved " as a training field for the use of Salem," in 1713. It is a beautiful, level spot of ground, surrounded by a double row of elm and other ornamental trees, and is designed to have a gravel walk around it. The alms house formerly stood upon it, but it is now entirely unencumbered.

The *City Hall* was built in 1837. It has a beautiful granite front, and is handsomely finished and furnished within.

The *Rail-Road* from Salem to Boston, was opened for travel, August 28, 1838; thus making Salem, as it were, a part of Boston. The first stage between these cities was run by Ezra Burrill, in 1782. It went to Boston one day and returned to Salem the next. Now the distance can be easily passed over in 50 minutes; and at the same time, the traveller will ride rapidly through a beautiful and picturesque country. See *Register.*

Among the distinguished men, in almost every profession, which Salem claims as among its sons, the name of NATHANIEL BOWDITCH, LL. D., F. R. S., author of the *Practical Navigator*, is identified with its fame and nautical achievements. Dr. Bowditch was born at Salem, March 26, 1773. He was taken from school at the age of 10 years and placed as an apprentice to a ship chandler. At the age of 22 he went to sea and spent nine years in the capacity of captain's clerk, supercargo, and finally as master of a ship. In 1804, he became president of a Marine Insurance Company, in Salem, which office he held until 1823, when his superior talents called him to become Actuary of the Massachusetts Hospital Life Insurance Company, in Boston; the responsible and laborious duties of which office he faithfully discharged until his death, March 16, 1838. Notwithstanding his limited means of education, Dr. Bowditch acquired, by his extraordinary genius and economy of time, a perfect knowledge of all the modern languages, and became the most eminent mathematician and astronomer in America. The *Practical Navigator*, has been translated into every European language, and its use is co-extensive with maritime adventures.

Another work of Dr. Bowditch, places his name, as a man of science, still higher on the roll of fame. It is his translation of the *Mecanique Celeste* of La Place, with an elaborate and copious commentary on that work, in four large quarto volumes. This work was completed just before his death.

The last hours of such a man as Dr. Bowditch, cannot fail to be interesting, as they mark his character through life. A friend of his who was present, says, " He did not like to see those about him look sad and gloomy; and he remarked, on one occasion, 'I feel no gloom within me; why should you wear it in your faces?' On the morning of his death, when his sight was very dim and his voice almost gone, he called his children to his bed side, and, arranging them in the order of age, pointed to and addressed each by name, ' You see I can distinguish you all; and now I give you my parting blessing. The time is come. ' Lord, now lettest thou thy servant depart in peace, according to thy word?' These were his last words."

Salem, Ct.

New London co. This town was taken from the towns of Colchester, Lyme and Montville; but the principal part from Colchester, and incorporated in 1819. It comprises an area of six by five miles of fertile and productive land. The inhabitants are generally good farmers, who live scattered about on their farms. Population, 1830, 958. Salem is well watered by small streams, and is bounded on the N. E. by a large and beautiful pond. It lies 29 miles S. E. from Hartford, and 13 N. W. from New London.

Salisbury, N. H.,

Merrimack co., lies 15 miles N. from Concord. Black water river passes through the W. part of Salisbury. There are 5 bridges across this stream in this town. The soil of the upland is strong, deep and loamy; the hilly land affords some fine tracts of tillage, but chiefly abounds in excellent pasturage. On Blackwater river, there is some very fertile intervale, which united with the adjacent hilly land, composes several very valuable farms. A considerable portion of Kearsarge mountain ranges within the bounds of Salisbury, the N. W. corner bound of which extends nearly to the summit. There are two very pleasant villages in this town, situated on the 4th N. H. turnpike about 1 1-2 miles apart.

Salisbury was incorporated by charter from the government of N. H., March 1, 1768, when it took the name of Salisbury. It was settled as early as 1750. The first settlers were Philip Call, Nathaniel Meloon, Benjamin Pettengill, John and Ebenezer Webster, Andrew Bohonnon, Edward Eastman, and others. The first inhabitants experienced the inroads of the Indians. On the

16th of May, 1753, Nathaniel Meloon, living in the W. part of the town, was captured, together with his wife, and three children, viz: Sarah, Rachel, and Daniel. They were carried to Canada, where he and his wife were sold to the French in Montreal. The three children were kept by the Indians. After the parents had resided in Montreal about a year and a half, they had a son born, who was baptized by a French friar by the name of Joseph Mary. Mr. Meloon returned from captivity after four years and a half, to his farm in Salisbury. Sarah died with the Indians. Rachel, who was 9 years old when captured, returned after 9 years. She had become much attached to the Indians, was about to be married to Peter Louis, son of Col. Louis, of Cognawaga. She had the habits, and acted like an Indian, understood the Indian language and could sing their songs. Hon. EBENEZER WEBSTER was one of the early settlers; a patriot of the revolution; an officer of the militia; for several years a senator in the legislature, and a judge of the court of common pleas till his death in 1806. He was the father of the Hon. EZEKIEL and DANIEL WEBSTER, names well known throughout the country. Population, in 1830, 1,379.

Salisbury, Vt.

Addison co. The widow of Amos Story, with 8 or 10 small children, was the first family that made Salisbury a permanent residence. She came here in 1775, and endured every hardship incident to the life of a pioneer; chopping down timber, clearing the land, laboring in the field, and sleeping in a cavern. Mr. Story, was killed by the falling of a tree previous to the removal of his family. The proprietors gave Mrs. Story 100 acres of land for her *manly* conduct. The soil of the town is generally good; it contains some rough land, and some excellent meadows. It is watered by Otter Creek, Middlebury and Leicester rivers. The latter river affords a good water power, which propels a number of valuable manufacturing establishments. Leicester river is the outlet of *Lake Dunmore*, a fine sheet of water, about four miles in length, and three fourths of a mile in width. This lake lies in Leicester and Salisbury. There is a pleasant and flourishing village in the town, and a large cavern supposed to have been an Indian lodging place. Salisbury lies 34 miles S. W. from Montpelier, and is bounded N. by Middlebury. Population, 1830, 907.

Salisbury, Mass.

Essex co. In 1638, this town was granted, by the name of Merrimack, to be a plantation, unto Simon Bradstreet, Daniel Dennison, and others. The year following it was incorporated by the name of Colchester, and in 1640 assumed, by direction of the then general court, the name of Salisbury. It is seven by three miles in extent, and is bounded southerly by the river Merrimack, westerly by Powow river, which divides it from the town of Amesbury, northerly by the New Hampshire line, which separates it from the towns of South Hampton and Seabrook, and easterly by the sea.

In 1643, the plantation in New Hampshire, viz. Hampton, Exeter, Portsmouth and Dover, were united to Massachusetts, and, together with Salisbury and Haverhill, formed into a new and distinct county, called Norfolk, of which Salisbury was the shire town, and so continued to the year 1679, when New Hampshire was again separated and formed into a royal government. In August, 1737, commissioners, appointed by the crown, met at Hampton falls, for the purpose of settling a controversy, respecting the boundary line, which had long subsisted between the two governments of Massachusetts and New Hampshire. On this occasion the general court of New Hampshire convened at Hampton, and that of Massachusetts at Salisbury. Salisbury is distant from Newburyport, 4 miles, from Haverhill 12, from Exeter, N. H. 10, and from Portsmouth 20. Population, in 1837, 2,675.

There are two considerable villages in Salisbury; the largest is at the westerly part of the town, upon Powow river at the head of tide water. The village is divided by said river into two pretty equal parts, one in Salisbury, the other in Amesbury. In that part of the village that lies in Salisbury, are two flannel factories, one 200 feet long and 50 feet wide, the other 100 feet by 40 feet. The establishment is called, the Salisbury Manufacturing Corporation. Capital $500,000. There is also in this village a large tannery, and manufactures of cotton goods, shoes, combs, boats, wherries and molasses casks.

The other village is pleasantly situated on the bank of the Merrimack, on a point of land formed by the junction of that river with the Powow; and is generally known by the distinctive name of *Webster's Point*. Ship building long has been, and still is, a principal branch of business in this place; and its character is well established for building excellent vessels. There are now nine sail of vessels owned in this village and employed partly in the coasting trade, and partly in the cod and mackerel fishery.

The annual product of the manufactures of Salisbury, including vessels, and of the fishery, is about $500,000.

Salisbury and Amesbury are finely located for business; the villages are neat and the scenery around them very pleasant. *Salisbury Beach* is noted for its beauty, and is much frequented.

Salisbury, Ct.

Litchfield co. The Housatonick and Salmon rivers give this town a great and constant water power. The surface of Salisbury is formed of lofty elevations and deep valleys; but the soil is excellent for all sorts of grain and pasturage. The valleys are generally limestone, and the hills granite. The number of sheep kept here in 1837, was 8,999.

"Salisbury Centre," a pleasant village, is 58 miles N. W. from New Haven, 50 W. N. W. from Hartford, 22 N. W. from Litchfield, and 34 N. W. by W. from Hudson, N. Y. Population, 1830, 2,580. The Indian name of the town was *Weatog*. It was first settled by the whites in 1720.

Salisbury has long been celebrated for its excellent iron ore and iron manufactures. The guns on board our favorite frigate, "Old Iron Sides," used by Truxton in the capture of the L'Insurgente, were made at the old furnace in Salisbury.

The "Old Ore Hill," two miles west of *Wanscopommuc* lake, has been worked since the year 1732. Within the last 10 or 15 years, from five to six thousand tons of ore have been dug annually. The ore is sold at the mine for $3 a ton. One dollar and twenty-five cents is paid to the proprietor of the mine, and the residue to the miner. The first furnace in Salisbury was erected in 1762, at the outlet of Wanscopommuc, by S. and E. Forbes, Mr. Hazeltine, and Ethan Allen, the hero of Ticonderoga. A large amount of cannon, balls, and bombshells were manufactured here during the revolutionary war.

The large and inexhaustible quantities of iron ore found in Salisbury, and the abundant supply of wood for charcoal, and other materials necessary for smelting the ore, together with the superior quality

NEW ENGLAND GAZETTEER.

of iron, introduced other manufactures; and iron has continued from that time the staple commodity of the town. There are at present in Salisbury, 4 blast furnaces, 5 forges, with 20 fires, 2 puddling establishments, 1 screw shop, 1 anchor shop, 2 scythe manufactories, 1 hoe manufactory, 2 trip hammers, 2 cupola or pocket furnaces, for small castings.

From five to six hundred thousand bushels of charcoal are annually consumed at the different establishments. The puddling furnaces require from two to three thousand cords of wood annually. The number of workmen employed in the different processes of preparing the material and manufacturing the iron, amount in all to about five hundred men. The furnaces produce annually from two thousand to two thousand five hundred tons of pig iron. The forges and puddling establishments annually produce from one thousand two hundred to one thousand five hundred tons of wrought iron, which is used for anchors, car axletrees, musket barrels, and various other kinds of drafts. The Salisbury iron ore is the brown hematite, and yields about forty per cent of pig iron. It is well known to manufacturers, and stands as fair in the market as any other iron in the country.

Salmon Rivers.

Salmon river, in *Maine*, is a tributary to the Penobscot, of about 30 miles in length. Its course is S., and falls into the Penobscot about 4 miles below the union of the eastern and western branches of that river.

Salmon Fall river, *Maine* and *New Hampshire*. See *Piscataqua*. This river, between Rochester and Lebanon, Maine, is a fall, which from its singularity, deserves notice. The river is confined between two rocks, about 25 feet high, the breadth at the top of the bank not more than three rods. It is called the *flume*, and is about four rods in length, its breadth varying from two and one half feet to less than one foot; but here the water has a subterraneous passage. In the rocks are many cavities from one to seven feet in diameter, mostly cylindrical, and from one to four feet in depth.

Salmon Brook. See *Nashua, N. H.*

Salmon river, *Connecticut*. This beautiful mill stream has its source in the high lands in Tolland county, and passing south, receiving in its course many valuable tributaries, it meets the Connecticut at East Haddam, producing a beautiful cataract. There is a river of this name in *Salisbury, Ct.*

Sanbornton, N. H.,

Strafford co., has New Hampton and Meredith on the N., Gilmanton E. and S. E., Franklin S. and W., and is 20 miles N. from Concord, 60 N. W. from Portsmouth, and 9 W. from Gilford.

The bay between Sanbornton and Meredith is 3 miles in width. There are no rivers or ponds of magnitude in this town. Salmon Brook pond, in the N. part, and a brook of the same name, its outlet, are the only ones worth mentioning. This brook passes through the N. W. part of the town, and affords several mill sites.

Sanbornton presents an uneven surface, but contains no mountains. The highest hills, with one or two exceptions, admit of cultivation. The soil is almost universally good, and well rewards the labor of patient industry. There is a gulf in this town extending nearly a mile through very hard rocky ground, 38 feet in depth, the walls from 80 to 100 feet asunder, and the sides so nearly corresponding as to favor an opinion that they were once united. There is also a cavern in the declivity of a hill, which may be entered in a horizontal direction to the distance of 20 feet. This town was once the residence of a powerful tribe of Indians, or at least a place where they resorted for defence. On the Winnepisiogee, at the head of Little bay, are found the remains of an ancient fortification. It consisted of six walls, one extending along the river, and across a point of land into the bay, and the others in right angles, connected by a circular wall in the rear. Traces of these walls are yet to be seen, though most of the stones, &c. of which they were composed have been removed to the dam thrown across the river at this place. Within the fort have been found numbers of Indian relics, implements, &c., and also on an island in the bay. When the first settlers of Sanbornton arrived, these walls were breast high, and large oaks were growing within their enclosure.

This town was settled in 1765 and 1766, by John Sanborn, David Duston, Andrew Rowen and others. It was incorporated in 1770. Population, 1830, 2,866.

Sandgate, Vt.

Bennington co. The people of this town are favored with mountain air, and with crystal streams which even the Bostonians might relish. Shettarack and Bald mountains are in the N. W. part of the town; Spruce and Equinox are in the N. E.; Red mountain is in the S. E., and Swearing hill in the S. W. Between these elevations is some good land, which produces grass and grain; and which, with the mountain browse, affords feed for more than 7,000 sheep. Sandgate was chartered in 1761. It is 20 miles N. from Bennington, and 31 S. by W. from Rutland. Population, 1830, 933.

Sandisfield, Mass.

Berkshire co. This is an elevated township at the S. E. corner of the county, on the line of Connecticut. It is watered by a pleasant stream, a branch of Farmington river. The soil is generally good, particularly for pasturage. Considerble wool is grown in this town, and a large amount of leather tanned. Sandisfield is 124 miles W. by S. from Boston, 18 S. E. by S. from Lenox, and 38 E. from Hudson, N. Y. Incorporated, 1762. Population, 1837, 1,493.

Sandown, N. H.,

Rockingham co., is bounded N. by Chester and Poplin, E. by Danville, S. by Hampstead, W. by Chester and Londonderry. It is 31 miles S. E. from Concord, and 26 S. W. from Portsmouth. The surface of this town is rather uneven, but the soil in general is well adapted to the production of grain and grass. Phillip's pond, lying in the S. part of the town, is the largest, being about 340 rods long, 200 wide. Angle pond, in the S. E. part of this town, is about 200 rods long, and 90 or 100 wide. There are several other smaller ponds. Squamscot river flows from Phillip's pond, and pursues a nearly level course for 1 1-2 miles, where another stream unites with it: from this junction, whenever the waters are high, the current passes back with considerable force towards the pond. The settlement of Sandown was commenced about the year 1736, by Moses Tucker, and others.— The town was originally a part of Kingston, and was incorporated, 1756. Population, in 1830, 553.

Sandwich, N. H.

Strafford co. Sandwich is 70 miles N. N. W. from Portsmouth, and about 50 N. from Concord. This town was originally granted by Gov. Benning Wentworth, in 1763, and comprised 6 miles square. On the 5th Sept. 1764, upon the representation of the grantees that the

N. and W. sides thereof were "so loaded with inaccessible mountains and shelves of rocks as to be uninhabitable"—an additional grant was made of territory on the E. and S., called *Sandwich Addition*. Sandwich mountains are a lofty range extending N. E. and terminating in Chocorua Peak in Albany. Squam mountain, extending from Holderness through a corner of Campton into Sandwich, is of considerable height. There are other mountains. The Bearcamp river, its branches rising in the mountains N. and W., passes E. into Tamworth. The W. branch passes through Bearcamp pond. There is another pond not far distant from this, from which issues Red Hill river, passing S. into the Winnepisiogee lake. A small stream passes W. into the Pemigewasset river. About one fourth of Squam lake lies in the S. W. corner of Sandwich. This is a flourishing town with a number of mills. Thirty thousand pounds of maple sugar was made here in the spring of 1838. Population, 1830, 2,744.

Sandwich, Mass.

Barnstable co. This town is very pleasantly situated on the shoulder of Cape Cod, 12 miles S. W. from Barnstable, 30 E. from New Bedford, and 53 S. E. from Boston. Incorporated, 1639. Population, 1830, 3,367; 1837, 3,579. Sandwich is watered by a number of streams which afford a good water power; and by numerous ponds, some of which are large, affording a variety of excellent fish. The forests afford an abundance of deer, and to the lovers of rural sports, Sandwich and the neighboring towns of Barnstable and Falmouth have justly become favorite resorts. The value of the manufactures of the town for the year ending April 1, 1837, amounted to $382,248. They consisted of glass, ($300,000) leather, nails, vessels, salt, iron castings, stoves, &c. The value of the New England crown glass has been fully tested and found to be as clear and stronger than any other now in use. Sandwich has a good harbor, and about 20 sail of coasting and fishing vessels.

It is proposed to unite Massachusetts and Buzzard's bays by a ship canal through this town. The distance is five miles and the route level. A glance at Mr. Hale's excellent map of New England, shows most conclusively, the immense advantages to be derived by such a work.

Sandy Bay, Mass.

See *Gloucester*.

Sandy Point, Mass.

The most northern extremity of Nantucket Island, on which is a light, 60 feet in height.

Sandy River, Me.

This valuable mill stream receives its head waters in the county of Franklin, near Saddleback mountain, and in a winding course through the southern part of that county it enters Somerset county and mingles with the Kennebec at Starks, 37 miles above Augusta. Sandy river is a fertilizing stream; it receives a number of tributaries, and waters a beautiful portion of the state. Its length is about 45 miles.

Sanford, Me.

York co. Sanford is watered by Mousum river; it has a good water power, and an establishment for the manufacture and printing of cotton goods. Incorporated, 1768. Population, 1837, 2,324. It is 94 miles S. W. from Augusta, 35 W. S. W. from Portland, and is bounded S. W. by Alfred

Sangerville, Me.

Piscataquis co. This beautiful and thriving town is not mountainous, but it is so elevated between Penobscot and Kennebec rivers that

NEW ENGLAND GAZETTEER.

the waters of its ponds meet the ocean by both of those streams. Sangerville is 70 miles N. W. from Augusta, and is bounded by Dover on the W. Incorporated, 1814.—Population, 1837, 1,115. Wheat crop, same year, 10,792 bushels.

Saugatuck River, Ct.

See *Westport.*

Saugus, Mass.

Essex co. Saugus was taken from Lynn in 1815, and derives its name from the Indian name of the river which passes through it. That river is exceedingly crooked in its course, and forms large tracts of meadow. The uplands are uneven and rocky. It lies 10 miles S. W. from Salem, and 9 N. by E. from Boston. Population, 1837, 1,123.

The value of the manufactures of Saugus, the year ending April 1, 1837, was about $200,000. They consisted of shoes,($150,000) chocolate, morocco leather, snuff, cigars, bricks, wool cleaning, and silk and woolen dyeing.

Savoy, Mass.

Berkshire co. Savoy is an elevated township, and gives rise to branches of Deerfield and Hoosack rivers. The land is generally good, and pastures a considerable number of sheep. It lies 125 miles W. N. W. from Boston, and 20 N. N. E. from Lenox. Incorporated, 1797. Population, 1837, 917.

Saybrook, Ct.

Middlesex co. This is one of the most ancient towns in the state. Lord Say and Seal, Lord Brook and other gentlemen in England, dissatisfied with the government of Charles I., contemplating a removal to this country, procured, in 1632, of Robert, Earl of Warwick, a patent of all the country "which lies west from Narraganset river, a hundred and twenty miles on the sea coast; and from thence in latitude and breadth aforesaid, to the South Sea." In 1635, they appointed Mr. John Winthrop, a son of the governor of Massachusetts, to build a fort on Connecticut river, and appointed him governor for one year.

In the summer of 1639, Colonel George Fenwick, one of the patentees, arrived from England, and in honor of Lord Say and Seal, and Lord Brook, gave the tract about the mouth of Connecticut river, the name of Saybrook. Colonel Fenwick superintended the affairs of the colony until 1644, when, his associates having relinquished the design of removal to America, sold the jurisdiction of Saybrook to the Connecticut colony.

The original limits of the town extended upon the east side of the river for several miles, and included a part of the town of Lyme. The township now comprises three parishes, viz: Saybrook, Westbrook, and Essex. Saybrook parish is the southeast section of the town. The Indian name for this place was *Pattaquasset.* West of this is Westbrook parish, which was called by its Indian name *Pochaug,* until October, 1810. North of these two parishes is *Pautapoug* or Essex.

Saybrook is upwards of 7 miles in length from north to south, and averages more than 6 in breadth. The greater part of the township is uneven and stony. There are, however, some extensive levels, and tracts of rich soil, particularly in the vicinity of Saybrook village, in the southern part of the town. Some of the hills, near Connecticut river, have good granite quarries. There are several small harbors on the Sound, and on Connecticut river, at Saybrook point and Pautapoug. The bar at the mouth of the Connecticut is an impediment to navigation; vessels of a moderate draught are often obliged to pass it with part of their cargoes. The depth of water at the bar, at spring tides, is about twelve feet. Saybrook harbor is at the mouth of a handsome cove, making up from Connecticut river, and extending west almost to Saybrook village. It is often resorted to by coasters in bad weather. To this place the river is open through the winter, and it is here that vessels are frequently laid up, and goods deposited, while the river is frozen over above. Large quantities of fish are taken in this town. The shad fisheries are numerous, and a source of considerable wealth. Connecticut river shad are considered superior to any other in this country. White fish are taken upon the shores of the Sound, and are very valuable for the purposes of manure. They are afforded at a cheap rate; the lightest soils, enriched by them, have produced forty bushels of rye to the acre, and they have an equally advantageous effect upon the growth of corn and potatoes.

Saybrook village is 40 miles S. S. E. from Hartford, 34 E. from New Haven, and 18 W. from New London. Population, 1830, 5,018.

Besides the business in navigation, the fishery, ship building and quarrying of stone, there are many manufacturing establishments in the several villages in this town. Among the articles manufactured, are augers, gimlets, hammers, steel carriage springs, ivory and iron combs, ink stands, sand boxes, &c.

The Borough of *Essex* is about 7 miles from the mouth of Connecticut river, on the west side. It is a place of considerable commerce, navigation and ship building, with a population of about 1,000.

Ship building was commenced in 1740, on the Pochaug, and is still a leading branch of business in the place. There are at present about 15 vessels owned here, principally coasters. It is estimated that there are 1,200 inhabitants in its limits.

Saybrook point is a peninsula, circular in its form, and connected with the main land by a narrow neck, over which the tide sometimes flows. From this place to the fort, on the eastern extremity of the peninsula, the distance is about one mile. On the neck, a palisado was anciently formed from the river to the cove, to secure Saybrook point from any sudden incursion of the Indians. The soil on the peninsula is light and sandy, and the elevation of the highest part is about twenty feet. Being nearly destitute of trees and shrubbery, it presents to the beholder a bleak and naked aspect.

The land on the point was laid out with care, as it was expected to become the residence of great men, and the centre of great business and wealth. It is said that Oliver Cromwell, with other men then equally distinguished, actually embarked in the Thames, to occupy this ground. Westward of the fort a square was laid out, on which it was intended houses should be erected for Cromwell, Pymm, Hasselrig, and Hampden, the most illustrious Commoners in the English annals, who were expected from Europe; while a square still further west was reserved for public uses.

About half way between the palisado was erected the first building designed for the collegiate school, since named Yale College. This institution was founded in 1700, and remained at Saybrook 17 years. The building was one story in height, and about eighty feet in length. Some remains of the cellar, "over which the ploughshare has passed," are still visible. Fifteen commencements were held at Saybrook. More than sixty young men were graduated, most of whom entered the ministry, and some of them became characters of distinguished usefulness and excellence. To educate young men of piety and talents for the ministry, was the leading design of this institution. It was desired by the founders and others, that the churches should have a public standard or confession of faith, agreeable to which the instruction of the college should be conducted. This led to the adoption of the *Saybrook Platform,* after the commencement in 1708.

David Gardiner, was the *first white child* born in Connecticut. The following was written upon a blank leaf of an old bible, in possession of John G. Gardiner, Esqr., of Gardiner's Island, N. Y.

"In the year of our Lord, 1635, the 10th of July, came I, Lion Gardiner and Mary my wife from Worden, a town in Holland, where my wife was born, being the daughter of one Diricke Willemson deureant; her mother's name was Hachir, and her aunt, sister of her mother, was the wife of Wouter Leanerdson, old burger Muster, dwelling in the hostrade, over against the Bruser in the Unicorne's head; her brother's name was Punce Garretson, also old burger Muster. We came from Worden to London, and from thence to New England, and dwelt at Saybrook fort four years—it is at the mouth of Connecticut river—of which I was commander, and there was born unto me a son, named David, 1635, the 29th of April, the first born in that place, and 1638 a daughter was born, named Mary, 30th of August, and then I went to an island of my own, which I had bought and purchased of the Indians, called by them Monchouack, by us Isle of Wight, and there was born another daughter, named Elizabeth, the 14th September, 1641, she being the first child of English parents that was born there."

Saybrook is a very pleasant town, and full of interesting associations.

Saxton's River, Vt.,

Is formed in Grafton, Windham county, traverses an eastern course about 10 miles, and falls into the Connecticut at Rockingham. It is an excellent mill stream, and derived its name from a Mr. *Saxton*, who was drowned near its mouth.

Scantic River, Ct.

See *East Windsor.*

Scarborough, Me.

Cumberland co. This town lies 105 miles N. E. from Boston, and 60 S. W. from Augusta. It contains 30,634 acres of land, and a population of 2,244.

A part of this town, called Black point, lying upon the sea, was granted by the council of Plymouth to Thomas Cammock, in 1631; this was soon after settled, and became of considerable importance on the coast in the fisheries and trade. The land is held under that ancient grant at the present day. Another settlement was early made by a family of Algers, from England, near the centre of the town, and called Duastan corner, which name it still bears. This was wholly destroyed in the Indian war of 1675. It was, however, revived by a descendant in the female line, through whom that race is still perpetuated.

Scarborough is principally an agricultural town, for which purpose it furnishes some rich soil, and has a large quantity of salt marsh.— Ship building, however, continues to be pursued here, although not to the extent it formerly was. Nousuck river passes through the whole length of the town. Its present name was given to it in 1658, when it submitted to the government of Massachusetts; previously the eastern side of the river and Marsh was called Black point, and the western, Blue point, names which are still in familiar use.

This town has the honor of being the birth place of the distinguished statesman Rufus King, and his half brother, William King, the first governor of Maine.

NEW ENGLAND GAZETTEER.

Schoodic Lakes, Me.

These are large collections of water, of very irregular form, united together, by boatable passages, lying principally in Washington county, but extending west into the county of Penobscot. Their outlet is by a large stream of the same name, into the river *Saint Croix*, on the west side, of about 9 miles in length. These lakes cover a large surface, they are navigable for large boats, and their borders, and indeed the whole country around them, are densely wooded. Vast quantities of timber and lumber descend from these waters to the St. Andrews, Eastport and Lubec markets, on the Passamaquoddy.

Scituate, Mass.

Plymouth co. This town, the Indian *Satuit*, lies at the mouth of North river, in Massachusetts bay, and has a convenient harbor, defended from the violence of the sea by several islands.

The *North River* rises near the sources of the Taunton. It passes Pembroke, Hanover and Marshfield, and meets the tide water here. This river is very deep, narrow and crooked, and is noted for the fine ships built on its banks. The manufactures of Scituate consist of leather, boots, shoes, tacks, vessels, &c. The value of vessels annually built is about $40,000. These vessels are of superior mechanism, and are built of native white oak, remarkable for its durability. There are a number of vessels belonging to this town employed in the merchant service and coasting trade. During the year ending April 1, 1837, Scituate had 22 vessels engaged in the fishery: they took 6,500 barrels of mackerel, valued at $46,000.

The town extends back from the bay a considerable distance; it contains large tracts of salt meadow and some valuable upland.

Scituate is 17 miles S. E. by S. from Boston and 20 N. W. by N. from Plymouth. First settled, 1633, Incorporated, 1637. Population, 1830, 3,470; 1837, 3,754.

The first settled minister in this town was the Rev. CHARLES CHAUNCY. He remained here twelve years previous to his becoming the second president of Harvard College.

Rev. THOMAS CLAPP, president of Yale College, was born in this town, in 1703. He graduated at Harvard College in 1722, and died in 1767.

Scituate, R. I.

Providence co. This town was a part of Providence until 1731, when it was incorporated. It lies 12 miles W. by S. from Providence, and, in 1830, had 3,394 inhabitants. The surface of the town is diversified by hills and valleys: in the north part of the town the soil is a gravelly loam, better adapted to grazing than tillage. Pawtuxet river with several of its branches give Scituate a good water power, and large manufactories, particularly of cotton and wool are found on their banks. There is a valuable quarry of free-stone in the western part of the town.

Seabrook, N. H.,

Rockingham co., is situated at the S. E. corner of the state, 17 miles S. S. W. from Portsmouth, and 7 N. from Newburyport, bounded N. by Hampton Falls, E. by the Atlantic, S. by Massachusetts, W. by South Hampton and Kensington. It was formerly a part of Hampton Falls, and was granted, 1768, to Jonathan Weare and others. Settlements commenced here in 1638. The rivers are Black, Brown's and Walton's rivers. Many of the rivulets abound with bog ore of iron. This town derives its name from the number of rivers and rivulets meandering through it. Whale-boat building is the most important manufacture, and is carried on to a greater extent than in any other town in New England. The larger part of the male inhabitants are mechanics and seamen. Perhaps no town in the state is better situated for carrying on the Bay and Labrador fisheries than this. Population, in 1830, 1,096.

Seaconnet Rocks, R. I.,

Or *Point*. See *Little Compton*.

Searsburgh, Vt.

Bennington co. Searsburgh is too elevated on the Green Mountains either for cultivation, population, or wool growing. It has 40 inhabitants, and 41 sheep. It is 11 miles E. from Bennington.

Searsmont, Me.

Waldo co. Searsmont has a good soil, and some beautiful ponds. It is a pleasant and flourishing town, 30 miles E. from Augusta, and 12 S. W. from Belfast. Population, 1837, 1,392. Wheat crop, same year, 2,792 bushels.

Seaville, Me.

Hancock co. This town was incorporated in 1838, and comprises a part of the island and town of Mount Desert, and Bartlett's, Robinson's, Hardwood and other smaller islands on the coast.

Sebago Lake, Me.

Cumberland co. This is a beauful sheet of water, about 12 miles in length, and of various breadths. The widest part is across from Baldwin to Raymond, about 7 miles. It receives the waters of Long and several other ponds, and of Crooked river, at and from the north. It discharges into Casco bay, at Falmouth, by the Presumpscot. The Cumberland and Oxford canal, completed in 1829, passes from this lake to Portland, and is the channel of considerable inland trade.

Sebago, Me.

Cumberland co. This town lies between Sebago lake and Hancock pond, and was taken from Baldwin in 1826. It lies 87 miles S. W. by W. from Augusta, and 30 N. W. from Portland. It has a good soil and is watered by small streams. Population, 1837, 646.

Sebasticook River, Me.

This valuable mill stream rises in Sangerville, Dover and Dexter, on the border of Penobscot and Piscataquis counties; it passes S. E. and S. through Ripley, Harmony, Hartland and Palmyra to Chandlerville; it then runs S. W. through Burnham and falls into the Kennebec between Clinton and Winslow, opposite to Waterville. This stream receives several tributaries; it is about 50 miles in length; it has numerous falls and passes through a delightful country.

Sebec, Me.

Piscataquis co. Sebec is a township of good soil, and is well watered by Sebec Pond and its outlet, Sebec river, which empties into the Piscataquis, on the north side, in the town of Milo. This town lies 87 miles N. N. E. from Augusta, and 9 N. N. E. from Dover. Incorporated, 1812. Population, 1837, 987. Wheat crop, same year, 7,650 bushels.

Sebec Pond lies in the towns of Sebec, Foxcroft and Bowerbank: it is about 10 miles long, and about a mile average breadth. Its outlet is a good mill stream of about 10 miles in length. The country around these waters is fertile and heavily timbered, and the scenery picturesque and beautiful.

Seboois Lakes and River, Me.

Seboois Lakes are connected sheets of water, of irregular form, of about 15 miles in length, varying in width from half a mile to a mile and a half. They lay near the Aroostook and constitute the head waters of the eastern branch of Penobscot river. *Seboois River* is their outlet. See *Penobscot River.*

Sedgwick, Me.

Hancock co. Sedgwick lies on the west side of Blue Hill bay, 87 miles E. from Augusta, and about 25 S. by W. from Ellsworth. Incorporated, 1789. Population, 1837, 1,784. This town has good harbors and enjoys great privileges for navigation. A number of vessels are owned here employed in the coasting trade and fishery, and ship building is an important branch of business. The soil of the town is not so productive as that more distant from the sea, still it is abundantly able to supply its own people with bread stuffs and all the varieties of fruits and vegetables common to a New England climate.

This town was named in honor of THEODORE SEDGWICK, an eminent statesman and jurist, a senator to Congress, and for many years a judge of the supreme court of Massachusetts. He died at Boston in 1813, aged 66, highly valued by his friends and country.

Seekonk, Mass.

Bristol co. This town is watered by Seekonk, or Pawtucket river, also by Ten mile river, a good mill stream. It lies 41 miles S. from Boston, 4 E. by N. from Providence, R. I., and 14 S. W. from Taunton. It was taken from Rehoboth in 1812. Population, 1837, 2,016. There are three cotton mills in the town, which constitute the principal manufactures; the annual value of which is about $80,000.

Seven Mile Brook, Me.

This stream rises by several branches in the counties of Somerset and Franklin; it runs in a south-eastern direction, about 35 miles, affording mill privileges to the towns of Kingfield and New Portland, and mingles with the Kennebec at Anson, 40 miles N. E. from Augusta.

Seymour Lake, Vt.

See *Charleston.*

Shaftsbury, Vt.

Bennington co. This town lies between the Battenkill and Walloomsac, and gives to those rivers some tributaries. West mountain lies in this town and Arlington. Shaftsbury lies 97 miles S. S. W. from Montpelier, and 8 N. from Bennington. First settled, 1763. Population, 1830, 2,143. Among the first settlers was the Hon. JONAS GALUSHA, late governor of the state. He was a captain in the militia in 1777, and commanded a company of the "Green mountain boys," at the battle of Bennington. Although the surface of Shaftsbury is elevated, the soil is generally of an excellent quality; it feeds 12,000 sheep, and its products of beef cattle and of the dairy are considerable. There are valuable beds of iron ore in the town, pine timber and quarries of beautiful marble. It has a number of manufacturing concerns on its small streams, a pleasant village and a school fund of $10,000.

Shapleigh, Me.

York co. Between Shapleigh and Acton are some pleasant ponds, the source of Mousum river which empties into the sea at Kennebunk. A bed of rich bog iron ore has recently been discovered in the town, which promises great usefulness. The surface of the town is generally level, and the soil favorable for the growth of wool, grass, wheat and other grain. Here are iron works and other manufactures. Shapleigh was incorporated, 1785.

Population, 1837, 1,547. It is 103 miles S. W. from Augusta, and 6 N. W. from Alfred.

Sharon, N. H.,

Hillsborough co., is bounded N. by Peterborough, E. by Temple, S. by New Ipswich and Rindge, and W. by Jaffrey. It is 18 miles W. by S. from Amherst, and 48 S. S.W. from Concord. The streams in Sharon are small branches of Contoocook river, and rise near the S. E. corner of the town. Boundary mountain lies on the line between this town and Temple, and has an elevation of 200 feet above the surrounding country. Sharon was incorporated, 1791. Population, in 1830, 271.

Sharon, Vt.

Windsor co. White river passes through Sharon and affords it an abundant water power. Here are mills for the manufacture of woolen goods, paper and other articles. It contains a handsome and flourishing village. The surface of the town is broken, but the soil is warm and productive. It keeps about 5,000 sheep. Sharon was first settled in 1763. Population, 1830, 1,459. It lies 22 miles N. from Windsor, and 34 S. by E. from Montpelier.

Sharon, Mass.

Norfolk co. Mashapoag pond in this town is one of the sources of Neponset river. Sharon has a good water power; one woolen and two cotton mills. There are also manufactures of axes, bed-steads, straw bonnets, leather, boots, shoes, wool cards, machinery, joiners' gages, &c.: annual value, about $75,000. Sharon is a very pleasant town; the scenery around Mashapoag, the Indian name of the place, is highly pleasing. There is good fishing in this pond. This town was incorporated, in 1765. It is 18 miles S. S. W. from Boston, 8 S. from Dedham, and 24 N. by E. from Providence, R. I. Population, 1837, 1,093.

Sharon, Ct.

Litchfield co. Sharon lies on the west side of Housatonick river, opposite to Cornwall. The eastern part of the town is elevated, mountainous, and stony, but is suited for grazing: the western part, which borders on the state of New York, is a fertile tract of undulating land, and very productive of all sorts of grain. Agriculture is the chief business of the inhabitants: they provide for about 10,000 sheep. Population 1830, 2,615.

Sharon was first settled in 1729. The village is situated principally on one street, on the eastern side of a beautiful valley, 16 miles W. N. W. from Litchfield, and 47 W. by N. from Hartford. There is a beautiful village called "Hitchcock's Corner," partly in Sharon and partly in the state of New York: this also is situated in a beautiful valley, and rich in agricultural resources.

"Considerable numbers of the Indians resided in the western and northwestern parts of the town, which are watered by two large ponds, and by the *Ten Mile river*, which touches the western borders of the town. Their principal village was on the east side of the *Indian pond*, so called, which is a body of water lying partly in the state of New York, and partly in Connecticut. On a romantic and beautiful plain, lying between this pond on the west, and the *Indian Mountain*, on the east, was a numerous village, where the natives continued to reside for many years after the whites came into the town. This tribe was visited by the Moravian missionaries, and one of them died and was buried there. He died in 1749, and a plain stone was placed over his grave, with the following inscription:

"David Bruce of Edinburgh in

Scotland, Minister of The Brethren's Church among the Indians. Depart'd 1749."

This town took an active part in favor of the liberties of the country.

" The approach of a large British army from Canada, under General Burgoyne, and the expedition up the North River, under General Vaughan, in 1777, filled the whole country with terror and despondency, and created strong fears and doubts as to the issue of the controversy : the firmness and confidence of Parson Smith, however, remained unbroken, and his efforts to revive the drooping spirits of his people were unremitted. In the month of October, he preached a sermon from these words : " Watchman, what of the night? The Watchman saith, the morning cometh." In this discourse he dwelt much upon the indications, which the dealings of Providence afforded, that a bright and glorious morning was about to dawn upon a long night of defeat and disaster. He told the congregation, that he believed they would soon hear of a signal victory crowning the arms of America ; and he exhorted them to trust with an unshaken and fearless confidence in that God, who, he believed, would yet crown with success the efforts of the friends of liberty in this country. Before the congregation was dismissed, a messenger arrived, with the intelligence of the surrender of Burgoyne's army. Parson Smith read the letter, conveying the intelligence, from the pulpit, and a flood of joy and gratitude burst from the congregation."

Shawsheen River, Mass.

This river rises in Lexington and Bedford. It passes Billerica, Wilmington and Tukesbury, and falls into the Merrimack, at Andover, 20 miles N. by W. from Boston.

Sheepscot River and Bay, Me.

The head waters of this river are derived from ponds in Palermo. Its course is south through the towns of Whitefield and Alna. It meets the tide water between Wiscasset and New Castle, and proceeds to a bay of the same name. The length of the river from its source to the bay is about 35 miles. This river is valuable on account of its hydraulic power and navigable facilities.

Sheepscot Bay sets up from the sea between Boothbay and Georgetown, and receives the waters of the river. It is about 3 miles wide at its mouth, and extends about 10 miles north. The whole of these waters are often called " Sheepscot River." The mouth of this bay or river bears about N. E., 6 miles, from Seguin Light, at the mouth of Kennebec river.

Sheffield, Vt.

Caledonia co. This town is 35 miles N. E. from Montpelier, and 16 N. from Danville. First settled, 1792. Population, 1830, 720.

This town lies on the height of land between Connecticut river and Memphremagog lake. Branches of Passumpsic and Barton rivers both rise here. It is watered by several ponds. The lands are generally broken and not very productive.

Sheffield, Mass.

Berkshire co. This is a very pleasant town, on both sides of the Housatonick. The river meanders circuitously and slowly through the town, and forms large tracts of rich alluvial meadow. In large freshets the river overflows its banks to a great extent, and forms the appearance of a large lake. The village is neat; situated in a beautiful valley, surrounded by hills, one of which is 3,000 feet in height, and presents a great variety of delightful scenery. There are manufactures in the town of leather, hats, ploughs, and spirits, but the principal business of the people is agricultural. In 1837, there were 6,892 sheep sheared in the town: the value of the wool amounted to $11,372. Marble and iron ore are abundant.

Sheffield is the oldest town in the county: it was incorporated in 1733. It lies 140 miles S. W. from Boston, 20 S. from Lenox, and 28 E. from Hudson, N. Y. Population, 1837, 2,308.

Shelburne, N. H.

Coos co. Androscoggin river passes through the centre of this town, into which fall the waters of Rattle river and some smaller streams. The soil on each bank of the river is very good, producing in abundance grain and grass: but as we rise from the river, the tracts are mountainous and unfit for cultivation.

Mount Moriah, an elevated peak of the White Mountains, lies in the S. part of Shelburne. Moses' Rock, so called from the first man known to have ascended it, (Moses Ingalls) is on the south side of the river, near the centre of the town. It is about 60 feet high and 90 long, very smooth, and rising in an angle of nearly 50°. In 1778, David and Benjamin Ingalls commenced a settlement at Shelburne, and not long afterwards, several families were added. In August, 1781, a party of Indians visited this town, killed one man, made another prisoner, plundered the houses, and returned to Canada in savage triumph. This town was incorporated in 1820. Population, 1830, 312.

Shelburn, Vt.

Chittenden co. On the east side of Lake Champlain, 33 miles W. by N. from Montpelier, and 7 S. from Burlington. Population, 1830, 1,123. Logan's and Potter's points were settled previous to the revolutionary war by men of those names. During the war these settlements were abandoned, but re-established at its close. Shelburn is finely watered by Platt river, a pond covering 600 acres, and by the waters of the lake.

Shelburn Bay sets into the township about 4 miles from the N. W., and affords the town a good harbor, and a depot of the interior trade on the beautiful Champlain. The soil of the town is strong, fertile, and generally well improved. About 10,000 sheep are within its limits.

Shelburne, Mass.

Franklin co. This town lies on the N. side of Deerfield river opposite to Conway. It is 100 miles W. by N. from Boston, and 5 W. from Greenfield. Population, 1837, 1,018. Incorporated, 1768. Deerfield river falls in this town a distance of 20 feet, and produces a valuable water power.

The manufactures of the town consist of woolen goods, leather, boots, shoes, scythes, palm-leaf hats, &c.: annual value about $40,000. The soil of the town is generally of a good quality; considerable wool is grown, and some cattle and products of the dairy are sent to market. More than common attention is paid to mental culture. This is a pleasant and flourishing town: the scenery about the falls is very handsome.

Sheldon, Vt.

Franklin co. The first settlements commenced here in 1790, by Elisha and Samuel B. Sheldon, from Salisbury, Connecticut. This is a good township of land, productive of wool, grain, and other northern commodities. The river Missisque passes through the town, and Black creek, a branch of that river, gives Sheldon an ample water power. The village is a thriving place, both in its manufactures and trade. It lies 46 miles N. W. from Montpelier, 32 N. by E. from Burlington, and 10 N. N. E. from St. Albans. Population, 1830, 1,427.

Shepaug River, Ct.

This river rises in Goshen, in the county of Litchfield; it receives several branches, and passes south, through the towns of Washington and Roxbury, and falls into the Housatonick at Southbury. This is a good mill stream, in some parts rapid, in others gentle and fertilizing.

Sherburne, Vt.

Rutland co. Killington Peak, 3,924 feet in height, several ponds, and Thundering brook, with a handsome fall, lie in this town. Queechy river rises in this town, and along its banks is some good land; but the lands are generally too elevated even for pasturage. Sherburne was first settled in 1785. It lies 22 miles N. W. from Windsor, and 10 E. from Rutland. Population, 1830, 452.

Sherburne, Mass.

Middlesex co. This town is watered by Charles and Sudbury rivers. It is 18 miles S. W. by W. from Boston, and 15 S. from Concord. Population, 1837, 1,037. Incorporated, 1674. The soil of Sherburne is very good and productive. The village is on elevated land; it is pleasant, and commands good prospects. The manufactures of the town consist of straw bonnets, boots, shoes, leather, axes, forks, ploughs, muskets and whips: annual value, about $60,000.

Sherman, Ct.

Fairfield co. Sherman was formerly the north part of New Fairfield, and incorporated in 1802. Population, 1830, 947. It is 60 miles S. W. from Hartford, 13 N. from Danbury, and bounded W. by the state of New York. There is a variety of soils in the town, but they are generally strong, warm, and productive of grass and grain. A branch of the Housatonick waters the town. Iron ore is found here.

Shetucket River, Ct.

This fine mill stream receives its head waters by several branches in the counties of Windham and Tolland. It passes between Lisbon and Franklin and uniting with the Quinnebaug at Norwich, flows into the Thames. Its principal branches are the Natchaug and Willimantic.

Shirley, Me.

Piscataquis co. This town was incorporated in 1834. It was formerly No. 3 in the 4th range of the Bingham Purchase. It is watered by the higher branches of Piscataquis river, and lies about 76 miles N. by E. from Augusta. Population, 1837, 213.

Shirley, Mass.

Middlesex co. This is a very pleasant agricultural and manufacturing town, 32 miles N. W. from Boston, 16 N. W. from Concord, and 18 S. W. from Lowell. There are some elevations in the town, but of warm and fertile soil. There are large tracts of intervale land along the streams, which are very fertile and valuable.

Shirley is separated from Groton by Nashua river, and from Pepperell by the Squanicook, a branch of the Nashua. These streams afford Shirley a fine water power, which renders it an excellent location for manufacturing establishments. There are 1 woolen and 3 cotton mills in the town, and manufactures of boots, shoes, paper, leather, palm-leaf hats, &c. Annual value, about $125,000. Population, 1837, 967.

Shoreham, Vt.

Addison co. This town lies on the east side of Lake Champlain, and is watered by Lemonfair river, a good mill stream. It is 12 miles

S. W. from Middlebury, and 26 N. from Whitehall, N. Y. The lake here is about a mile wide. Population, 1830, 2,137. The surface of the town is level and the soil remarkably good. This is one of the best farming towns in the state. In 1837, there was 26,584 sheep in Shoreham. There are some manufactures in the town, and a pleasant and flourishing village on the banks of the lake. Most of the waters here are impregnated with Epsom salts. See *Bridport*.

Shoreham was first settled in 1766, by a number of persons who adopted the plan of holding all things in common. This mode of holding property was, however, relinquished about the time of the revolutionary war.

Shrewsbury, Vt.

Rutland co. This town lies 22 miles W. from Windsor and 9 S. E. from Rutland. Population, in 1830, 1,289. This is a mountainous township, having Shrewsbury Peak within its limits, a summit 4,034 feet above the sea. Mill and Cold rivers and Peal's and Ashley's Ponds water the town, and fall into Otter Creek. There is some good land in this mountain town, and between three and four thousand sheep graze on its surface.

Shrewsbury, Mass.

Worcester co. This is an agricultural town of a pleasing variety of surface, and good soil, 36 miles W. by S. from Boston and 6 E. from Worcester. Quinsigamond or Long Pond lies principally in this town. It is nearly four miles in length and from 40 to 250 rods in width. It empties into the Blackstone river and canal, and produces a considerable hydraulic power. A floating bridge crosses this pond for the accommodation of the Worcester turnpike, 525 feet in length, built in 1818, and cost $6,000.

The manufactures of Shrewsbury consist of clothing, guns, hats, chairs, straw bonnets, leather, boots, shoes, &c: the value of which, during the year ending April 1, 1837, was $211,287. The town was incorporated, 1727. Population, 1830, 1,386; 1837, 1,507.

Levi Pease, the father of mail stages in this country, was a native of this town. He died here in 1824, aged 86. Mr. Pease was a man of great enterprise; he projected the first turnpike road in New England, and to his zeal and sacrifices the public is more indebted than to any other man for its excellent mail establishment. At the time Mr. Pease started his first line of mail stages between Boston and New York, in 1784, the mail between those places passed only once a fortnight, on horseback, in a pair of saddlebags.

Shutesbury, Mass.

This town is on high land, 10 miles E. from Connecticut river, 9 N. by E. from Amherst, 16 S. S.E. from Greenfield, and 78 W. by N. from Boston. Incorporated, 1761. Population, 1837, 816. Copper ore, and soapstone, are found here. On Swift river are three shingle mills and a wheel factory. There is a mineral spring of some note in this town, containing, in solution, iron, sulphur, &c. There is also a pond, covering about 700 acres, with an abundance of fine fish.

Ephraim Pratt lived in this town many years, and died here in 1804, aged 116 years. He married at the age of 21, and could count 1,500 descendants. He was a very temperate man, so much so that for 40 years he took no animal food. He was a farmer, and his health was so uniformly good that he was able to mow a good swath 101 years in succession. He was born at Sudbury, 1687.

Sidney, Me.

Kennebec co. Sidney is very

pleasantly situated on the west side of Kennebec river, and watered by a large and beautiful pond lying in this town and Belgrade. It is bounded N. by Waterville, and is 12 miles N. from Augusta. Incorporated, 1792. Population, 1837, 2,346. Wheat crop, same year, 6,569 bushels.

Simsbury, Ct.

Hartford co. The territory of this town was formerly a part of Windsor: its Indian name was *Massacoe*, and was incorporated in 1670. The surface of the town is greatly diversified by hills and valleys: a range of mountains pass through the town, and there is some level and good land within its limits on Farmington river. Population, 1830, 2,221.

Tariffville, a flourishing village, is situated at the northeastern extremity of this town, on the west bank of the Farmington river, which at this place passes south, at the base of a range of mountains, which divides this part of the State from the great valley of Connecticut river. This place is a carpet manufacturing village, owned principally by a company called the "New England Carpet Company;" they employ 175 hands, and manufacture yearly about 132,000 yards of carpeting. This flourishing village is between three and four miles south of Simsbury mines, in Granby, near the New Haven and Northampton canal, and 12 miles N. W. from Hartford.

Skitticook River, Me.

This is the most northern and eastern branch of the Matawamkeag.

Skootum Lake, Me.

A sheet of water of considerable size, the outlet of which passes through Kilmarnock.

Skowhegan, Me.

Somerset co. This town was formerly called Milburn: it took the Indian name of the place in 1836. It is situated on the N. side of Kennebec river, at Skowhegan Falls. The river runs here in an eastern direction. The local situation of Skowhegan, its admirable water power, and the fertility of the adjacent country, united with the enterprise of its inhabitants, has rendered the place, but recently a wilderness, one of the best cultivated townships in the state, the site of a great number of mills, and a mart of an extensive trade. There is much delightful scenery about Skowhegan; the village is neatly built, and its beauty is much enhanced by the whiteness of the houses contrasted with the blue and green of the river and its banks. Between Skowhegan and Bloomfield is a small island in the river. Across this island are noble bridges uniting the towns. This place lies 5 miles below Norridgewock and 33 N. from Augusta. Population, 1830, 1,006; 1837, 1,433.

Slaterville, R. I.

We regret to state that no account of the manufactures of this interesting manufacturing village has been received. See *Smithfield*.

Small, Cape, Me.

The eastern boundary of *Casco Bay*.

Smithfield, R. I.

Providence co. This is a large town, containing an area of about 10 by 6 miles, and a great variety of surface and soil.

Smithfield has generally an undulating surface, presenting an agreeable diversity of moderate eminences and gentle declivities; but in some sections it is considerably rough and broken.

The manufacture of lime is an important and extensive business, and affords employment to a great number of persons. There is also a quarry of white stone at what is called Woonsocket hill, that sustains heat remarkably well, which renders it very valuable for furnace hearths. About two miles distant from this, there is a quarry, containing excellent whetstones, for edge tools.

The soil is a gravelly and sandy loam, with some sections of a calcareous loam. It is generally rich and fertile, although in some places it has been reduced by an exhausting system of cultivation. There are, however, some low and marshy tracts, which are generally appropriated to mowing, and afford good crops of grass. The agricultural productions consist of the various articles common to the climate; Indian corn, rye, wheat, barley, oats, potatoes, flax, beef, pork, butter, cheese, apples, cider and hay.

The waters of the town consist of the Blackstone, which washes its northeastern border, and a branch of this river, nearly of equal size, which intersects the town, discharging its waters into the former, in the northern section of the town. After the union of these streams, the Blackstone is from one to two hundred feet in width. At some seasons of the year, it overflows its banks, and has been known to rise from 15 to 20 feet above its usual height. Besides these, there are numerous small streams, some of which afford valuable sites for mills and manufacturing establishments, which are mostly occupied. In the south part of the town, within about 4 miles from Providence, there is a considerable body of water, called Scots Pond. It is nearly a mile in length, about half a mile in width, and of great depth. What is remarkable in this pond, is the steep descent of its shores. Cases have occurred, of persons being drowned in attempting to water their horses at this pond.

There is a remarkable fall of water upon the Blackstone river, called Woonsocket falls, which is considered as quite a curiosity. The fall is about 20 feet, not perpendicular, but over a precipice of rocks, for some distance. The fall of the water upon these rocks through a succession of ages, has occasioned numerous excavations, all of which are smooth and circular, and some of them very large, being sufficient to contain several hogsheads.

The beautiful village of *Woonsocket* is situated at these falls, on the line of Cumberland; the river dividing the towns, and the village into nearly equal parts. In this village are 15 cotton and 2 satinet factories, a large furnace, machine shops, sash factory, &c. The Blackstone canal passes through this village, and it is in contemplation to construct a rail road to meet the Boston and Providence rail road, either at Providence or at Dedham, Mass. This village is indeed a beautiful place, and exceedingly flourishing. It is 14 miles N. N. W. from Providence.

Slaterville is another beautiful village in this town, on Branch river, about 2 miles W. from Woonsocket.

Smithfield is a large manufacturing town, containing many other pleasant villages, almost exclusively devoted to manufacturing objects. The centre of the town lies 9 miles N. W. from Providence. Incorporated, 1730. Population, in 1830, 6,857.

Smith's River, N. H.

Grafton co. This river rises from several ponds in Grafton and Orange, and after pursuing a winding, but generally an east course, of from 12 to 18 miles, through Danbury and Alexandria, falls into the Pemigewasset, between Bristol and Hill.

Solon, Me.

Somerset co. Solon is a flourishing farming town, on the east side of Kennebec river, opposite to Embden. It lies 44 miles N. by W. from Augusta, and 18 N. from Norridgewock. Population, 1830, 768; 1837, 1,129. Wheat crop, 1837, 6,567 bushels. The town is well watered by a pond and several streams: it has a pleasant village, and some manufactures.

Somers, Ct.

Tolland co. This town lies 22 miles N. E. from Hartford, 10 N. by W. from Tolland, and 12 S. E. from Springfield, Mass. First settled, 1713. It was incorporated by Massachusetts in 1734, and named in honor of Lord Somers, at the request of Governor Belcher.

Part of the town is level, and productive of grass and grain, and part is quite elevated, producing good pasturage for sheep, and presenting delightful views of the valley of Connecticut river. It is watered by Scantic river.

Somers has a very neat village, in which is a large establishment for the manufacture of straw bonnets. Population, 1830, 1,429.

Somerset County, Me.

Norridgewock, chief town.—Previous to the formation of Piscataquis and Franklin counties, in 1838, for which purpose a considerable portion of Somerset was taken, this county contained an area of about 8,785 square miles. Incorporated, 1809. About one third of this territory may be said to be settled, incorporated or granted, the residue, a wilderness. Its population, in 1820, was 21,787; 1830, 33,588; 1837, 40,963. Population to a square mile, 4 1-2. Gain in population, in seven years, 22 per cent.

The present county of Somerset is bounded N. by Lower Canada, E. by Piscataquis and a part of Penobscot counties, S. by the counties of Kennebec and Franklin, and W. by Franklin county and Lower Canada.

This county is watered by many ponds, some of the large tributaries of the Kennebec, and by the upper waters of many other important rivers in Maine; but its chief river is the noble Kennebec, which enters the county at its rise from Moose Head lake, and passing from that lake, which skirts the eastern boundary of the county, it traverses nearly in its centre about 75 miles. This river serves, at present, as a great thoroughfare to the ocean for an immense amount of timber, lumber and wood, the first fruits of the industry of pioneers to a heavily timbered country; and, in after times, will serve for the transportation of the productions of a fertile soil to distant markets, and of the wants of the inhabitants from abroad.

The surface of this county is diversified by considerable elevations and extensive valleys, which give it a varied and pleasing aspect. With the exception of the mountain range, which skirts the bounds of Canada, and the Bald Mountain ridge, nearly in the centre of the county, Mount Bigelow and Mount Abraham, on the border of Franklin county, are the most lofty.

So far as the march of improvement has been made in this interior and almost wilderness county, the soil of the lands, generally, is found to be fertile, as easy of cultivation, and as productive of all the varieties of grasses, grains, vegetables and fruits, as any portion of New England, with very few exceptions. The more interior portions of the county, those watered by the upper branches of the Penobscot and Walloomstook, now a wilderness, are said to be the most fertile. In 1837, there were in the old county of Somerset, 77,921 sheep; and, during that year, it produced 239,332 bushels of wheat, being the largest quantity of that valuable grain produced by any county in Maine, and probably by any county in New England.

Somerset, Vt.

Windham co. Mount Pisgah and other elevations give to the surface of this township so rough and drear an aspect, that but few are bold enough to attempt the cultivation of its soil. It is watered by the upper branches of Deerfield river. Population, 1830, 245.

Somerset *stands* 15 miles N. E. from Bennington, and 14 W. from Newfane. It would put the neighboring towns into a pretty pickle if it should *turn a Somerset*.

Somerset, Mass.

Bristol co. This town is pleasantly situated on the northern side of Taunton river, opposite to Fall River, and is the proposed depot of a rail road from Fall River to Providence, R. I. It is 16 miles S. E. from Providence, 13 S. from Taunton, and 45 S. from Boston. Population, 1837, 1,063. Incorporated, 1790.

There are some manufactures of stone and earthern wares, but ship building is the principal branch of mechanics in the town.

Somersworth, N. H.

Strafford co. This town was formerly a part of Dover. It was incorporated in 1754. It is bounded N. W. by Rochester, N. E. by Salmon fall river, which divides it from Berwick, Me., and S. W. by Dover. It is 11 miles N. by W. from Portsmouth and 45 E. from Concord. The White Mountains may be seen from the summit of Otis' hill; also the steeples of the meeting houses in Portsmouth, and the masts of the shipping in the harbor.

The soil of this town is well adapted to Indian corn, and almost all kinds of grain and grass. The tide flows on the east side of this town, four miles to Quamphegan falls. The river is of sufficient depth, till within a mile of said falls, for vessels of 250 tons. The S. part of this town is bounded on Cocheco river, from its confluence with the Piscataqua to the mouth of Fresh creek, near a mile; and from thence by said creek to its head, nearly a mile and a half.

There are but two ponds of note in this town: Humphrey's pond on the line of Dover, 200 rods long and 120 rods wide; and Cole's pond, 150 rods long and 75 wide.

Red and yellow ochre, also iron ore, have been found in this town. The ochre has been used in painting houses, and has been found to make a durable paint.

At Great Falls, are extensive manufactories, and a large and beautiful village.

This town was settled between 1650 and 1700, by William Wentworth and others. Many of the first settlers were killed or taken captive and carried to Canada. Ebenezer Downs, who was a quaker, was taken by the Indians at Indigo hill, in 1724, and carried to Canada. He was grossly insulted and abused by them, because he refused to dance as the other prisoners did for the diversion of their savage captors.

NICHOLAS PIKE, author of a popular system of arithmetic, was born in this town, October 6, 1743.

JOHN WENTWORTH, son of the Hon. John Wentworth, was born in this town, July 14, 1745; and was graduated at Harvard college, 1768. He entered on the study of the law, and settled at Dover. When application was made to him to put an action in suit, it was his practice to see the parties or to write to them, stating the consequences of a legal process, and advising them to settle their differences between themselves. By this mode of procedure he was instrumental in preventing many vexatious lawsuits; and was entitled to the appellation of *peacemaker*. He was a member of the continental congress in the revolution, and died January 10, 1787.

Hon. THOMAS WALLINGFORD, was born at Bradford, Mass., in 1697. He came to this town in the early part of his life; and by a diligent application to business, from a small beginning became one of the richest men in the province.

ICHABOD ROLLINS, was born in Somersworth in 1721. He was a judge of probate for the county of Strafford, and died January 31, 1800. Population, in 1830, 3,090.

Soucook River, N. H.,

Has its source in three ponds in the south part of Gilmanton, lying near each other, called Loon, Rocky and Shellcamp ponds. It passes through Loudon, receiving several branches, and forms the boundary between Concord and Pembroke, falling into the Merrimack below Garvin's falls.

Souhegan River, N. H.

Originally *Souhegenack*, the name of a river in Hillsborough county, and the former name of Amherst and Merrimack. The principal branch of this river originates from a pond in Ashburnham, Mass. It passes N. through Ashby, at the N. W. angle of the county of Middlesex, into New Ipswich, and through Mason, Milford, Amherst, into Merrimack, where it unites with Merrimack river. In its course it receives several streams from Temple, Lyndeborough and Mount Vernon, and just before it falls into the Merrimack, receives Babboosuck brook, a considerable stream issuing from Babboosuck pond. See *Amherst*.

South Hampton, N. H.,

Rockingham co., is bounded N. by East Kingston and Kensington, E. by Seabrook, S. by Amesbury, Mass., W. by Newtown; and is 50 miles S. E. from Concord, and 18 S. S. W. from Portsmouth.

The surface is generally even, and the soil of a good quality. Powow river passes through this town, affording valuable mill seats. South Hampton was incorporated in 1742.

Hon. PHILLIPS WHITE, who was a member of the old congress, a counsellor in 1792 and 1793, and for many years judge of probate, died June 24, 1811, aged 82. Population, 1830, 487.

Southampton, Mass.

Hampshire co. Manhan river waters the town and affords it mill privileges. The Farmington canal passes through the eastern part. Lead in various forms and qualities is found here, and here is a subterraneous passage leading to the lead mine in Westhampton. There are some manufactures in the town, but the people are generally employed in agricultural pursuits, and the soil is well adapted to that purpose.

Southampton is pleasantly situated, 9 miles S. W. from Northampton, and 97 W. by S. from Boston. Incorporated, 1753. Population, 1837, 1,216.

South Berwick, Me.

York co. This town is situated on the N. E. side of Salmon Fall river, 97 miles S. W. from Augusta, and 10 W. N. W. from York. The limits of the town have recently been increased by the addition of a portion of the territory of York. It was incorporated in 1814. Population, 1830, 1,577; 1837, 2,342. The Great Falls on the river at this place afford an hydraulic power of great magnitude and value. Manufacturing operations commenced here many years ago, and have been gradually increasing; but in 1837, the "Great Works Manufacturing Company" was incorporated. This company have a large capital, and are making arrangements for manufacturing on an extensive scale. When it is considered that this place is located on navigable waters, and only about a dozen miles from the beautiful harbor of Portsmouth, by water, these operations promise a favorable result, both to individual enterprise and the public.

The village of South Berwick is pleasantly situated; it is a place of considerable trade, and in the vicinity of delightful scenery.

Southborough, Mass.

Worcester co. This town was taken from Marlborough in 1727. It has a good soil, and is well cultivated by industrious and skillful farmers. It is watered by a branch of Sudbury river, and has manufactures of woolen cloth, boots, shoes, and straw bonnets: annual value, about $50,000. The Boston and Worcester rail road passes through this pleasant town. It lies 26 miles W. from Boston, and 15 E. from Worcester. Population, 1837, 1,113.

Southbridge, Mass.

Worcester co. Southbridge was taken from Sturbridge in 1814.—Population, 1830, 1,444; 1837, 1740. It is 54 miles S. W. from Boston, and 19 S. S. W. from Worcester. This town is watered by the Quinneboag, a branch of the Thames, and a good mill stream. There are one woolen and three cotton mills in Southbridge, and manufactures of boots, shoes and cutlery: the value of which, for the year ending April 1, 1837, was $262,212. This town has an excellent soil and a pleasant and flourishing village.

Southbury, Ct.

New Haven co. The principal village in this town is pleasantly situated on the Pamperaug, a fine mill stream, which passes through the town. This village is 20 miles N. W. from New Haven, and 40 S. W. from Hartford.

The village of South Britain is about 4 miles S. W. from the principal or central village: it is a flourishing place, containing a number of neat buildings, a carpet and several hat factories. This village is surrounded by high hills and precipices, and has a romantic and picturesque appearance. The surface of the town is generally uneven: there is some good meadow land on Housatonick, Pamperaug, and Shepaug rivers, and the uplands are warm and productive. Some traces of coal have been discovered.

The northern part of the town is called "White Oak," from an oak tree under which the first persons who explored the town encamped. Pieces of this tree are considered by some as precious relics. Southbury was formerly attached to Litchfield county. It was a part of Woodbury, and was first settled about the year 1672. It was incorporated as a distinct town in 1786. Population, 1830, 1,557.

South Hadley, Mass.

Hampshire co. Nature and art seem to have united to render this an interesting place. The falls on the Connecticut are 50 feet; not perpendicular, but in so short a distance as to render the river very rapid. These falls, Mount Holyoke at the north part of the town, and Mount Tom on the west side of the river, with the luxuriant meadows along this beautiful stream, would form a picture of no ordinary character. These falls are rendered passable for freight and steam boats by a canal of about two miles in length. In this canal is a cut through solid rock, 40 feet in depth and 300 feet in length. The hydraulic power, at this place, is very great, having the whole volume of Connecticut river and some smaller streams at command for manufacturing purposes. Much of the water power is yet unimproved, but its local situation is such as to insure its usefulness as the manufacturing interests of New England increase. There are in South Hadley 3 paper and 2 woolen mills, and manufactures of leather, boots, shoes, pearl buttons, iron, &c.: total value, the year ending April 1, 1837, $237,650.

South Hadley lies on the east side of Connecticut river, 90 miles, W. from Boston, and 5 S. by E. from Northampton. Incorporated in 1753. Population, 1837, 1,400.

South Hero, Vt.

Grand Isle co. Lake Champlain bounds this town on all sides.—The passage in the lake however, is very narrow between the towns of N. and S. Hero. It lies 12 miles N. W. from Burlington, and 16 S. S. W. from St. Albans. The lake is fordable a considerable part of the year on the Vermont side. This town was formerly a part of North Hero, and was separated from it in 1788. First settled, 1784. Population, 1830, 717. South Hero contains an area of about 9,065 acres of level land of an excellent soil. Its basis is limestone. It is supposed that all the lands of this island county were once covered by the waters of the lake, as clam shells are found incorporated with the rocks in the highest places. The scenery around these islands is beautiful. This vicinity was a favorite resort for the Indians, as appears from a large number of their implements found on the islands. It seems they manufactured hatchets, spear heads, chisels, arrows, and a variety of other implements at this place, from a flint stone not found in this region, but brought from a distance. This town furnishes a great abundance of food for the inhabitants, and some for exportation. It feeds about 6,200 sheep. This is a pleasant stopping place for the angler, the painter or the geologist.

Southington, Ct.

Hartford co. Southington was taken from Farmington in 1779. There are some elevations in the town, particularly in the eastern part; but the soil is generally very good for all kinds of grain and the pasturage of cattle. It is watered by the Quinnepiack, and the Farmington canal passes through it. It contains a neat village, 18 miles S. W. from Hartford and 21 N. from New Haven. Population, 1830, 1,844.

The inhabitants are generally engaged in agriculture; yet several kinds of manufactures receive considerable attention. Peck's patent for machines for making tin ware, a most valuable invention, is exclusively owned in this town, and the business of making them is extensively carried on, by Peck & Co., whose manufactory supplies almost the whole of the United States and the British provinces. The manufacture of water cement is very extensively carried on in this town, and furnishes a supply for the wants of the vicinity, and some for distant markets. There is an establishment for the manufacture of lasts, which are turned out by a machine: this is effected by having a model of the shape wanted, inserted into the apparatus connected with the machinery. Besides the above, there is a brass foundry; and several other establishments, for manufacturing various articles, such as saws of different kinds, tin ware, combs, spoons, clocks, brushes, &c., are in operation, more or less extensively, at different times, according to the demands of the market. Copper has been discovered, in several places, in the range of mountains on the eastern border of the town.

South Kingston, R. I.

Washington co. Chief town. This town was formerly a part of North Kingston, and was first settled in 1670. It is the largest town in the State, comprising 98 square miles, and within its limits is the noted *Point Judith*. It has an uneven surface, a soil of a gravelly loam, based on a granite foundation. Large quantities of grain of various kinds and of the productions of the dairy are annually sent to market from this town; also the fleeces of about 7,500 sheep. This town possesses great navigable advantages; its eastern and southern borders being washed by the Atlantic ocean and Narraganset bay. It contains a great number of fresh water ponds, and a large salt pond: one of the fresh water ponds, covers an area of between three and four thousand acres.

The fisheries on the shores and in the ponds of South Kingston are of considerable extent and value. The fish taken are principally bass, alewives, perch and smelts. Some portion of the inhabitants follow a maritime life for a livelihood.

The principal village in South Kingston is improperly called "Little Rest Hill," for it is quite a snug and comfortable place. It lies 30 miles S. from Providence, and 9 S. from North Kingston. Population, 1830, 3,663.

South Reading, Mass.

Middlesex co. This town was taken from Reading in 1812. It lies 10 miles N. from Boston, 18 E. by N. from Concord, and 10 W. from Salem. Population, 1830, 1,310; 1837, 1,488. The manufactures of the town consist of shoes, cabinet ware, chairs, shoe tools, razor straps, block tin and tin ware: annual value, about $60,000.

This town contains a large and beautiful pond, the source of Saugus river. The village is compact, neat and flourishing.

Southwick, Mass.

Hampden co. This town is bounded S. by the state of Connecticut, and is 100 miles W. by S. from Boston, and 10 W. S. W. from Springfield. Incorporated, 1779. Population, 1837, 1,291. It is watered by a considerable stream, and several ponds in the town supply water for the Farmington canal, which passes through Southwick. The manufactures consist of gunpowder, leather, and distilled spirits: annual value, about $70,000. The surface of the town is elevated, but the soil is generally good, particularly for grazing. The value of wool sheared in 1837, was $2,125.

Sowadabscook River, Me.

Penobscot co. This stream falls into the Penobscot at Hampden, 5 miles below Bangor. Within 3 miles of its mouth it falls 120 feet, furnishing many valuable mill privileges. The main branch, which rises in Stetson, unites with the Harvey stream from Levant, and the Kinsley stream from Etna, both affording excellent mill sites, near the village in Carmel. Below these, the Sowadabscook is deep and sluggish, from 15 to 25 yards in width, flowing through extensive meadows, and the Great and Little ponds in Hermon, with very little descent, to the head of the falls in Hampden. Near the east line of Carmel, this stream comes within about 20 rods of the Little Kenduskeag, a stream which flows through the N. E. part of Carmel, from Levant to Bangor; and the two streams are united by a branch from 20 to

30 feet wide and 3 feet deep, called the *Cross.* The Kenduskeag is so rapid that it rises and falls much quicker than the Sowadabscook. When the streams are rising, the current in the Cross sets towards the Sowadabscook, and when falling, towards the Kenduskeag. The country watered by the Sowadabscook is generally rather level and free from hills, though there are many swells of very fine farming land. In the towns of Hermon and Hampden is a large tract, very little elevated above the level of the stream, and liable to be overflowed by freshets. It is too low for settlement, and is chiefly covered with wood. The improvement of this land requires too great an outlay of capital for a new country, but it will probably at some time be among the most valuable in this country for mowing.

There are on this stream, in Hampden, five superior saw mills, a grist and paper mill, and the privileges are excelled by few in New England. Upon the Kenduskeag are 9 mills below the Cross, many of them superior double mills. The pine timber has been cut off upon the waters of this stream to such an extent, as to give a high value to that which remains, and to the hemlock timber, of which there are great quantities of fine quality.

Since our first pages went to press, we have received, from an obliging friend, the following information in regard to *Carmel.*

The township of Carmel, bordering on the Sowadabscook, is a very level tract of land; most of it of a very light and fertile soil, free of stone. The valleys have a fine growth of pine timber, which has been carefully preserved by the owners, and may be run, by means of the Cross, at a small expense, either to Bangor or Hampden.—There is probably no town in this section of the county, in which there was originally so valuable a growth of pine, or in which there is so large a quantity remaining. The swells are large, and are covered with the rock maple, beech, birch, &c., and are of a very superior quality for tillage. Near the streams are large tracts of intervale of great fertility, and making very fine meadows. There is little waste land in the town. The swamps are few and of small extent, but furnish cedars in sufficient quantities for fencing, for which use they are the finest and most durable material.

The settlement of this town is rapidly progressing, and many of the farms recently cleared are very superior, and the buildings, fences, and improvements, show an active, industrious and enterprising people.

The village near the centre of the town, is a very thriving and active place of business, on the stage road from Bangor to Skowhegan, 13 miles W. from Bangor, and 11 W. N. W. from Hampden. Here are four stores, two taverns, an apothecary shop, potash, blacksmiths, coopers, shoemakers, joiners, and other shops; an extensive tannery, mills, &c., and a meeting house is about being built. In the town are five good school houses, five saw mills, a clapboard and shingle mill, grist mill, and clothing mill.

There are found in this town some fine specimens of petrified shells, at an elevation of 125 to 130 feet above the Penobscot, and near the banks of the stream, showing that this valley was once covered by the ocean.

The roads in the towns watered by this stream are exceedingly well made, and creditable to the inhabitants, though it is remarkable, that several of them, which were made in the early settlement, pass over decidedly the most inferior lands in those towns. This is particularly true of the road from Hampden through Carmel and Etna to Newport: and the settlement of this section was formerly retarded, without doubt, by the unfavorable impression created by this circumstance. The projected rail road from Bangor to Augusta is surveyed to pass through this town, near the bank of the stream; and the level character of the country is exceedingly well adapted for that purpose.

Spafford's Lake, N. H.

See *Chesterfield.*

Speckled Mountain, Me.

Oxford co. This mountain lies on the line of New Hampshire, partly in the town of Riley, and is said to be 4,000 feet above sea level.

Spencer, Mass.

Worcester co. Seven Mile river, a branch of the Chickopee, waters this town. There are two woolen mills in the town, and manufactures of scythe snaiths, straw bonnets, boots, shoes, leather, cabinet ware, chairs, palm-leaf hats, harnesses, and barrels: annual value, about $80,000.

This township is quite elevated for the section of country in which it lies. It is stated to be the summit level between the waters of Boston harbor and Connecticut river, 950 feet above the former, and 880 feet above the latter. The surface of the town is agreeably varied by hills and valleys: the soil is fertile, and cultivated by men of industry and independence.

Spencer is 52 miles W. from Boston, and 12 W. from Worcester. Population, in 1830, 1,618; 1837, 2,085. It was taken from Leicester in 1753.

Spiggot River, N. H.,

Rises in Hampstead, and passes through Salem, and into the Merrimack between Methuen and Dracut, Mass., nearly opposite Shawsheen river, which comes from the S., through Andover.

Split, Cape, Me.

See *Addison.*

Springfield, Me.

Penobscot co. The Matakeunk, a branch of the Matawamkeag, rises here, and, with several ponds, gives the town a considerable water power. The soil of the town is fertile, and in 1837, with a population of 398, produced 9,429 bushels of wheat. Springfield was No. 5, 2d range N. of the Bingham Purchase, and was incorporated in 1834. It lies about 60 miles N. E. by E. from Bangor.

Springfield, N. H.

Sullivan co. This town is bounded N. by Grafton, E. by Wilmot, S. E. by New London, S. by Wendell and Croydon, W. by Croydon and Grantham. It lies 35 miles N. W. from Concord and 13 N. E. from Newport. A branch of Sugar river has its source in this town; and also a branch of the Blackwater river. The former empties into the Connecticut, the latter into the Merrimack. There are several ponds, viz. Station pond, about 250 rods long, 140 wide; Cilley pond, 240 rods long, and about 80 wide; Star, Stony, and Morgan's ponds. The land is rough and stony. This town was granted in 1769, by the name of *Protectworth.* Its first settlement commenced in 1772. It was incorporated by the name of Springfield, 1794. Population, 1830, 1,202.

Springfield, Vt.

Windsor co. Springfield is situated at the S. E. corner of the county, on the W. side of Connecticut river, and is 70 miles S. from Montpelier, 24 S. from Woodstock, and 110 N. W. from Boston. Population, 1830, 1,498.

The land in Springfield is generally rich, with a deep soil suitable for grass or tillage; on the rivers are extensive intervales, forming some of the most beautiful farms in the state. The principal agricultural products, are corn, rye, oats, beef, pork, butter, cheese; and wool, of which 17,872 fleeces were shorn in 1837. Many horses are raised in this town and sent to market.

The principal village is situated on Black River falls, near the centre of the town. These falls are about four miles from the confluence of Black river with the Connecticut; their descent is rapid over a rocky bed, about 60 rods, when the waters are contracted, and precipitated 50 or 60 feet down an abrupt ledge into a narrow channel. This ravine extends about 12 rods; it is 60 or 70 feet deep, and is walled by perpendicular ledges of mica slate. Over this ravine has been erected a bridge, from which may be had a full view of the falls. A mist constantly arises, in which may be seen, in a fair day, all the colors of the rainbow.

There are in Springfield 1 cotton and 2 woolen mills, a sand paper factory, on an extensive scale, which produces an excellent article, and manufactures of machine cards, machinery, iron ware, lead pipe, hats, chairs, tin and copper wares, scythes, leather, cabinet furniture, and various other articles. This is a very flourishing town, and the scenery around its neat and handsome village is delightful.

Springfield, Mass.

Chief town, Hampden co. This is one of the most beautiful and important inland towns in New England. It is situated on the east bank of Connecticut river, and is supplied with a good hydraulic power by Chickopee and Mill rivers. It is 87 miles W. by S. from Boston, 17 S. by E. from Northampton, and 27 N. from Hartford, Ct. Its Indian name was *Agawam.* First settled, 1635. Incorporated, 1645. Population, 1820, 3,914; 1830, 6,784; 1837, 9,234. Along the banks of the Connecticut are large tracts of fine alluvial meadow, which are very productive. Back from the river the land rises by a gentle acclivity to an extended pine plain.

The village and business part of the town, is on a street between 2 and 3 miles in length, running parallel with the river. This village is very pleasant, well built, and contains many beautiful buildings. A handsome bridge, 1,234 feet in length, connects this town with West Springfield. Boats for the transportation of passengers, and for towing freight boats, are continually plying between this place and Hartford, during the season of navigation. The rail road from Boston to Albany will pass through Springfield, which, with the great natural advantages it possesses, must render it one of the most important commercial depots on Connecticut river.

About 4 miles north of the principal village, near the confluence of Chickopee river with the Connecticut, stands the neat and enterprising village of *Chickopee*, one of the most beautifully located manufacturing villages in New England.

The *United States Arsenal* is delightfully situated on an elevated plain about half a mile east of the principal village. The buildings are arranged with great taste and judgment, around a level square of 20 acres, and make a fine appearance. The buildings are all of brick; on one of which is a cupola, from which an extensive and delightful view of Connecticut river and the surrounding country is presented. The water works are situated on Mill river, about a mile south of the arsenal. This establishment was founded in 1795, and is considered the most important arsenal of construction in the United States. There are 260 men constantly employed in the various branches of this manufacture. In 1837, the lands and buildings attached to this establishment were valued at $210,000; Machinery, $50,000; 170,000 muskets on hand, $2,040,000; muskets manufactured during the year ending April 1, 1837, 14,000, valued at $154,000: amount of ordnance and stock on hand, $80,000.

An establishment for the manufacture of brass cannon, employing 25 hands, lately commenced by a private company, will manufacture cannon to the amount of $50,000 per annum.

There are in Springfield 7 cotton and 4 paper mills, 3 tanneries, and manufactures of iron castings, cutlery, ploughs, chairs, cabinet and tin wares, boots, shoes, cards, hard ware, steam boats, joiners tools, paper machinery, shuttles, bobbins, rifles, stoves, machinery, swords, &c. The total value of the manufactures of Springfield, for the year ending April 1, 1837, exclusive of those by the U. S., amounted to $1,709,700. See *Register*.

Squam Lake, &c.

Squam Lake, N. H., lies on the borders of Holderness, Sandwich, Moultonborough and Centre Harbor. This is "a splendid sheet of water, indented by points, arched with coves, and studded with a succession of romantic islands." It is about 6 miles long, and in its widest part, 3 miles in width. It covers a surface of between 6,000 and 7,000 acres, and is well stored with trout and other fish.

Squam River is the outlet of the above mentioned lake: it passes through Squam pond in Holderness, and forms a junction with the Pemigewasset, at the S. W. corner of that town.

Squam Bay and Village, Mass.

The bay sets up between Gloucester and the mouth of Ipswich harbor. The village is on Cape Ann, about 4 miles N. from the principal village of Gloucester, and is the resort and residence of a large number of enterprising fishermen.

Squamanagonick, N. H.

The name of a village at the falls on Cocheco river, in Rochester, so called from the Indian name of the falls.

Squamscot River, N. H.,

Or *Swamscot*, called also Great or Exeter river. See *Exeter*.

Stafford, Ct.

Tolland co. This town lies 24 miles N. E. from Hartford, 6 N. E. from Tolland, 27 N. W. from Brooklyn, 36 N. from Norwich, 14 N. E. from Springfield, Mass., and 73 W. S. W. from Boston. Population, 1830, 2,515.

The surface of the town is rough; in some parts mountainous, abounding with rocks of primitive formation. Its soil is a coarse, hard and dry gravelly loam; generally not very productive. There are several minerals in the town, but iron ore is the principal. As early as 1779, a blast furnace was erected here, and cannon shot, hollow ware, &c., were cast.

The town is watered by Furnace river, and the Willimantic, which unite in Stafford, and afford a good water power. There are in the town several blast and cupola furnaces, a cotton mill, manufactures of pistols, axes, adzes, carpenters' chisels, tailors' shears, drawing knives, and several other articles of cutlery. There are also manufactures of cotton and woolen machinery, cabinet ware, brush handles, iron card cylinders, and two forges for making wrought iron.

Stafford Mineral Springs have acquired considerable notice, and are celebrated for their virtues in curing cutaneous diseases.

"The Indians first made the settlers acquainted with the virtues of these springs, when, in the year 1719, this part of the country began to be settled. 'It has been their practice, time immemorial, to resort to them in the warm season, and plant their wigwams round them. They recommended the water as an eye water; but gave, as their own particular reason for drinking it, that it enlivened their spirits.' It is said, that in 1766, these springs were carefully examined by Dr. Warren, who then had thoughts of purchasing the land on which they rise, with a view of establishing himself upon it. Subsequent events transformed the physician into a soldier, and Dr. Warren fell in the first great struggle of the Revolution. Dr. Willard afterwards put Dr. Warren's plan into operation, by building a large hotel for the reception of patients and others. The establishment is at present owned by Mr. Jasper Hyde, and its former reputation is fully sustained, and it is a place of much resort for the purposes of health or pleasure during the summer season. There are two distinct springs, the medical qualities of which are considered as essentially different. One of them contains a solution of iron, sustained by carbonic acid gas, a portion of marine salt, some earthly substances, and what has been called natron, or a native alkali. This spring has been known and used for a length of time, and has been pronounced by chemists to be one of the most efficacious chalybeate springs in the United States. The other spring, the medical virtues of which were not known till about the year 1810, contains, according to the opinion of Professor Silliman, (who examined it in that year) a large portion of hydrogen gas, of sulphur, and a small proportion of iron. These springs did not acquire much celebrity until about the year 1765, when a case occurred calculated to establish and extend their reputation. It was an effectual cure of a most obstinate cutaneous complaint, which had completely baffled all medicinal skill, and resisted all other applications. The publicity which was given to this case soon raised the reputation of these springs; and in consequence of which they immediately became a place of resort of persons afflicted with various diseases."

Stamford, Vt.

Bennington co. A mountain township on the line of Massachusetts. It is 9 miles S. W. from Bennington, and 21 W. by S. from Brattleborough. Population, 1830, 563. Branches of the Hoosack and Walloomsack rise here. There are several fine fish ponds among the mountains; and some good land; but the lands in Stamford are generally too elevated for culture.

Stamford, Ct.

Fairfield co. This beautiful town is bounded on the S. by Long Island Sound, and on the N. W. by the state of New York. Its Indian name was *Rippowams*, and was purchased of the natives for "twelve coats, twelve hoes, twelve hatchets, twelve knives, two kettles and four fathom of white wampum." The soil of Stamford is a rich gravelly loam, well cultivated and very productive. The surface is undulating, presenting a great variety of delightful prospects. The town is well supplied with mill sites by Mill and Miannas rivers, and, within its bay, between Shippan and Greenwich points, are good harbors for vessels of 8 1-2 feet draught of water. There are a number of vessels owned here, and Stamford is a place of an active trade with the surrounding country and New York. There are within the limits of the town an iron foundry, a rolling mill, a wire factory, and two large boot and shoe manufactories.

Stamford Borough is a neat village, beautifully situated near the Sound, and surrounded by a country full of interesting scenery. This was the residence of the Hon. ABRAHAM DAVENPORT, for many years one of the Counsellors of the colony, and afterwards of the state. He was the son of the Rev. John Davenport, the second minister of Stamford, and grandson of the Rev. John Davenport, the father of New Haven colony. Mr. Davenport was distinguished for his vigorous mind, Christian integrity, and for his uncommon firmness of character. An instance of his firmness is here quoted.

"The 19th of May, 1780, was a remarkable dark day. Candles were lighted in many houses; the birds were silent and disappeared, and the fowls retired to roost. The legislature of Connecticut was then in session at Hartford. A very general opinion prevailed, that the day of judgment was at hand. The House of Representatives, being unable to transact their business, adjourned. A proposal to adjourn the Council was under consideration. When the opinion of Mr. Davenport was asked, he answered, 'I am against an adjournment. The day of judgment is either approaching, or it is not. If it is not, there is no cause for adjournment: if it is, I choose to be found doing my duty. I wish therefore that candles may be brought.'"

Standish, Me.

Cumberland co. This township is bounded on the N. and N. E. by Sebago Lake, and S. W. by Saco river. It lies 68 miles N. from Augusta, and 16 N. W. from Portland. This is a good farming town with two pleasant villages. Incorporated, 1785. Population, 1837, 2,270.

Starks, Me.

Somerset co. Starks is very pleasantly situated on the W. side of Kennebec river, and is also watered by the Sandy, which unites with the Kennebec at this place. This town possesses great resources in the fertility of the soil, its location for trade, and its mill privileges. It lies 37 miles N. N. E. from Augusta, and 6 W. by N. from Norridgewock. Incorporated, 1795. Population, 1837, 1,424. Wheat crop same year, 7,614 bushels.

Stark, N. H.

Coos co. This town was named *Piercy*, until a few years since. It was then altered to compliment the memory of Gen. Stark. It contains about 20,000 acres, most of which is broken and extremely uneven. It was settled in 1788, but the progress of the settlement has been very slow. Population, 236. It lies 10 miles N. E. from Lancaster.

Starksborough, Vt.

Addison co. This town is watered by Lewis creek and Huntington river, which are good mill streams. There are three springs in the town, not more than 20 rods apart, which unite and form a stream of sufficient power for a number of mills, and is thus improved. The town is rough and mountainous. Hog's Back mountain skirts its western border, and East mountain passes through its centre, and divides the waters of the rivers. There is some good land in the town, but a large portion of the territory is too elevated for cultivation. Here are 2 villages, and the manufactures of iron are considerable.

Starksborough was first settled in 1788. It is 22 miles W. by S. from Montpelier, and 18 N. by E. from Middlebury. Population, in 1830, 1,342.

Sterling, Vt.

Lamoille co. *Sterling Peak*, in the South part of this town, ranks among the most elevated summits of the Green Mountain range. Some streams issue from this mountain town. It was first settled in 1799, and contains 23,040 acres of land. The quality of the soil may be known by the number of its inhabitants, 183; and by the number of its sheep, 350. It lies 24 miles N. by W. from Montpelier.

Sterling, Mass.

Worcester co. This town was first settled about the year 1721. It was taken from Lancaster, in 1781. It lies 40 miles W. from Boston, and 12 N. from Worcester. It is watered by Still river. Its surface is uneven, and its soil light. Population, 1837, 1,650. The manufactures of the town consist of boots, shoes, leather, straw bonnets, palm-leaf hats, scythe snaiths, chairs and cabinet ware: total amount, for the year ending April 1, 1837, $76,528, of which $53,228, was for chairs and cabinet ware.

Sterling, Ct.

Windham co. This town lies 10 miles S. E. from Brooklyn, and 44 E. by S. from Hartford. It was taken from Voluntown in 1794. Population, 1830, 1,240. The soil is a light gravelly and sandy loam, and produces good grain. Sterling is watered by two branches of Moosup river, a good mill stream, on which are four cotton mills.

"Near the centre of this town, there is a cavern, called the "Devil's Den," possessing very singular and curious features. It is situated within a ledge of rocks, and has a circular area of about 100 feet in diameter. The rock is cleft in two places, forming at each a chasm or fissure about 50 feet in depth, through one of which there runs a small stream of water; the other communicates with a room about 12 feet square, at the interior part of which there is a fire place, and a chimney extending through the rock above, forming an aperture of about 3 feet square. In another part of the rock there is a natural stair case, winding around it from the bottom to the top. In the cold season of the year, a large mass of ice is formed in the room above described, by the dashing of the water down the chimney, which continues there through nearly the whole of the warm months, the sun being almost excluded from this subterranean recess."

Stetson, Me.

Penobscot co. This town is bounded N. by Exeter, and S. by Etna and Carmel. It is 63 miles N. E. from Augusta, and 18 W. N. W. from Bangor. It is watered by branches of the Sebasticook and Sowadabscook, which rise here. It was incorporated in 1831. Population, 1830, 114; 1837, 437. The surface of the town is undulating, and the soil excellent. Wheat crop, 1837, 3,704 bushels.

Steuben, Me.

Washington co. This is a maritime township, and comprises *Dyer's Bay*, which sets up from the sea about 9 miles, and contains a number of good harbors. This bay lies between *Little Menan Point* and Goldsborough harbor. It is about a mile wide at its mouth.

Steuben is a place of considerable ship building, and a number of vessels are owned here, employed in the coasting trade and fishery. Narraguagus river passes its northeastern border.

Steuben lies 107 miles E. from Augusta, and about 35 W. by S. from Machias. Incorporated, 1795. Population, 1837, 802.

Stevens' River, Vt.

Caledonia co. This excellent mill stream rises in Peacham and Ryegate. It received its name in compliment to Captain Phineas Stevens, the brave defender of Charlestown, N. H. The waters of this river are remarkably clear, and its banks luxuriant and romantic. It meanders about 15 miles, and in its course through Barnet it receives Harvey's lake, a pellucid sheet of water, covering an area of 300 acres. This beautiful river mingles its crystal waters with those of the Connecticut, at Barnet, by a leap of 100 feet in the distance of ten rods, as it were in joy to meet a sister stream on its passage to the bosom of the ocean.

Stewartstown, N. H.,

Coos co., lies on the E. side of the Connecticut, which washes its W. boundary, a distance of 7 miles. It lies 150 miles N. W. from Portland, 150 N. from Concord, and is bounded N. by Canada.

The Connecticut river is about 15 rods in width at this place.— Bishop's brook, a considerable stream, rises in this town, and falls into the Connecticut at the N. W. corner. Dead water and Mohawk rivers have their sources here. Hall's stream, also, unites with the Connecticut in Stewartstown. There are two ponds in the E. part of this town, called Little and Great Diamond ponds, both well stocked with salmon trout. There are no large mountains in Stewartstown, although there are many elevations. The soil of the intervale is rich, and the uplands productive.

Stewartstown was incorporated in 1799. During the late war a block house or fort was erected in this town for defence by a company of militia, and occupied until August, 1814, when it was destroyed. Population, 1830, 529.

Stillwater, Me.

Penobscot co. A very flourishing village, on the lower falls of Penobscot river, in the town of Orono. An immense amount of lumber is sawed at this place, and rafted down to the Bangor market. See *Orono.*

Stockbridge, Vt.

Windsor co. This town lies 36 miles S. by W. from Montpelier, and 26 N. W. from Windsor. First settled, 1783. Population, 1830, 1,333.

White river passes through the town, and at a place called the "Great Narrows," it is compressed into a channel of but a few feet in width, and, affords the only good mill seat in town. The soil of the town is better for pasturage than tillage. It feeds about five thousand five hundred sheep.

Stockbridge, Mass.

Berkshire co. This is a fine farming town on both sides of the Housatonick river, 130 miles W. from Boston, and 6 S. from Lenox. Incorporated, 1739. Population, 1830, 1,580; 1837, 2,036.

The soil of this town is adapted to all kinds of culture; much of it is rich alluvial meadow, and the uplands produce excellent feed for cattle.

Here is an excellent hydraulic power, and a pleasant village on an extended plain, surrounded by delightful scenery.

There are one cotton and two woolen mills in the town, two tanneries, and manufactures of pig iron, iron castings, chairs, boots, shoes, and machinery for boring iron and wood: total amount of the manufactures, for the year ending April 1, 1837, $380,765. Marble is abundant.

A tribe of Indians had a reservation of 6 miles square in this town, from the year 1735 to their removal to New Stockbridge, Oneida county, New York. In 1735 there were 90 adult Indians in the tribe, of whom 52 were baptized by the Rev. John Sargent, a faithful missionary, and their first spiritual guide.

Stoddard, N. H.

Cheshire co. This town is bounded N. by Washington, E. by Windsor and Antrim, S. by Nelson and Sullivan, and W. by Gilsum and Marlow. It is 14 miles N. N. E. from Keene, and 42 W. S. W. from Concord.

This town is situated on the height of land between Merrimack and Connecticut rivers. It is mountainous and very rocky. The soil is better adapted to grazing than tillage. The south branch of Ashuelot river has its source near the centre of the town. The streams in the east section, fall into the Merrimack; those on the west, into the Connecticut. There are fourteen ponds, some of which are of considerable magnitude.

This town was formerly called *Limerick*. It was incorporated in 1774, when it received the name of Stoddard, from Col. Samsòn Stoddard, of Chelmsford, to whom with several others it was granted. The settlement commenced in June, 1769. The first family was that of John Taggard, whose privations and hardships were very great. Their grain was procured at Peterborough, at the distance of 20 miles, which was conveyed by him on his back through the pathless wilderness. At one time, they had nothing, for six days, on which to subsist, but the flesh of the moose. Population, 1837, 1,159.

Stoneham, Me.

Oxford co. Stoneham was incorporated in 1834. It lays westerly of Albany, and comprises the grant to Fryeburgh Academy. Population, 1837, 290.

Stoneham, Mass.

Middlesex co. This is a small town, rocky and uneven. It has some good soil and much wood. Incorporated, 1725. Population, 1837, 932.

During the year ending April 1, 1837, there were made in this town 380,100 pairs of shoes; valued at $184,717, employing more than half its inhabitants.

Spot Pond, a beautiful sheet of soft and pure water, lies in this town, 8 miles N. from Boston. It covers an area of 283 acres, and is 143 feet above high water mark, at Boston.

Stonington, Ct.

New London co. This town is situated at the eastern extremity of Long Island Sound; at the S. E. corner of the state, and on the line of Rhode Island. It contains an area of about six square miles. The land is rocky and uneven, but fertile and productive. A considerable amount of agricultural products is annually sent from this town to Nantucket and other places. It is watered by the Mystic and Paucatuck, considerable streams, on which are cotton, woolen and other factories. Stonington was first settled in 1649, and incorporated in 1658. Population, 1830, 3,401.

This place was bombarded by British ships during the revolutionary war, and again on the 10th of August, 1814, and gallantly defended.

The harbor of Stonington sets up from the Sound, opposite Fisher's island, and is well protected by an expensive Breakwater.

This place is noted for the commercial enterprise of its people. Large capitals are employed in the whale, seal, and cod fisheries. Five whale ships recently arrived, bringing each, on an average, 3,100 barrels of oil, and 25,000 pounds of bone. The sealing business in the Pacific Ocean, has been conducted here, very extensively, for many years, with great success. Many ships are built, and a large number of coasting vessels, and some in the West India trade, belong to this port. This place is accommodated with a marine rail way, and a light house at the entrance of the harbor.

Stonington Borough is located on a narrow point of land, extending into the Sound about half a mile. It was incorporated in 1801. It is handsomely laid out, is well built, and contains about 1,200 inhabitants. Many strangers visit this place in summer months to enjoy the marine air and delightful scenery. It lies 54 miles S. E. from Hartford, 12 E. from New London, and 62 E. from New Haven.

Stonington is an important point on the New York, Providence, and Boston Rail Road. The distance from New York to Brooklyn, on Long Island, across the ferry, is half a mile; from Brooklyn to Greenport, at the easterly part of Long Island, is 98 miles; from thence, across the Sound, to Stonington, 25; from Stonington to Providence, 47; and from Providence to Boston 41 miles. Total distance from New York to Boston, by this route, 211 1-2 miles.

Until the completion of the rail road on Long Island, passengers are conveyed to and from New York, daily, by safe and splendid steam boats.

Stop River, Mass.

This stream rises from ponds in Wrentham, and joins Charles river at Medfield.

Stoughton, Mass.

Norfolk co. Some of the head waters of Neponset river rise in this town. When the Indians sold their lands in Dorchester, a residence was established for them at this place, and called *Punkapog.* There were 12 families of Christain Indians here in 1674. Mr. Elliot, the apostle of the Indians, had the chief agency in their removal.

There are two cotton and a woolen mill in the town, and manufactures of boots, shoes, shoe tools, and boot forms: total value of manufactures, the year ending April 1, 1837, exclusive of cotton goods, $525,940; of which $487,390 was for boots and shoes. Hands employed in the various manufactures, 928.

Stoughton was incorporated in 1736. It lies 20 miles S. from Boston, and 10 S. from Dedham. Population, 1830, 1,591; 1837, 1,993.

Stow, Me.

See "Down East."

Stow, Vt.

Lamoille co. Waterbury river and its branches give this town a good water power, and by which several mills are put into operation. Stow is situated between the Mansfield and Hog's Back mountains, and contains a large tract of level, fertile land, which appears to have been of alluvial formation. This valley contains some very beautiful and productive farms. Between five and six thousand sheep are kept, and the exports of agricultural products are valuable. Stow is a flourishing town, and contains a neat and pleasant mountain valley village.

This town was first settled in 1793. It lies 15 miles N. N. W. from Montpelier, 12 S. from Hyde Park, and 26 E. from Burlington. Population, 1820, 957; 1830, 1,570.

Stow, Mass.

Middlesex co. Stow is watered by the Assabet river, and possesses a good water power. The soil is light and sandy, and good for the growth of hops. It lies 24 miles W. by N. from Boston, and 8 W. by S. from Concord. Incorporated, 1683. Population, 1837, 1,134. There are two woolen mills in the town, and manufactures of leather, boots, shoes, straw bonnets, and palm-leaf hats: total value, the year ending April 1, 1837, $231,611.

Strafford County, N. H.

Dover, Gilmanton, Gilford and *Rochester*, are the shire towns. Strafford county is bounded N. by the county of Coos, E. by the state of Maine, S. and S. W. by Rockingham and Merrimack counties, W. by the Pemigewasset river, which separates it from parts of the counties of Grafton and Merrimack, and N. W. by Grafton county. It is 63 miles in length, from the mouth of Lamprey river to the N. line of Albany; 33 miles wide at the centre. Its shape, like that of all the other counties in the state, is irregular. It contains an area of 1,345 square miles. This county, which extends to the neighborhood of the White mountains, has several considerable mountains within its limits. Chocorua Peak, in Albany, Sandwich mountain in the same range, Ossipee and Effingham mountains, Gunstock mountain, in Gilford, Moose, in Brookfield and Middleton, Teneriffe, in Milton, and the ridge denominated Blue Hills, are the most elevated. Red Hill, in Moultonborough, has a commanding elevation, and has long attracted visitors. Below, the waters of the Winnepisiogee lie open to the eye, and its numerous islands and bays present a fine appearance. This lake is much the largest body of water in the state, being 22 miles long, and varying from one to eight miles in width. Sullivan or Squam lake, lies partly in this county, and is 6 miles in length, and nearly 5 in width. Ossipee lake is also in this county. Great bay, Long bay and Merrymeeting bay, are connected with the Winnepisiogee lake. Smith's pond, in Wolfeborough; Sixmile, in Eaton, Merrymeeting, in New Durham, and Lovewell, in Wakefield, are the principal ponds. The larger rivers, are the Piscataqua, Salmon Falls, Cocheco, Saco and Swift rivers. The soil of Strafford county, though presenting a great variety, is generally good. The lands are generally hard of cultivation, but the patient laborer finds an ample reward for his industry. This county possesses a large hydraulic power, and manufacturing establishments are constantly increasing on its streams. Population, 1830, 58,916. Population to a square mile, 44. In 1837, there were 53,602 sheep in Strafford county.

Strafford, N. H.

Strafford co. This town lies 15 miles N. W. from Dover, and 25 E. N. E. from Concord, and is about 7 miles in length, 6 1-2 wide. Bow pond is in the S. W. part of the town, and is about 650 rods long, 400 wide; its waters form one of the principal branches of the Isinglass river. The range of Blue hills crosses the N. W. part of the town. The soil here is generally of a good quality. Strafford was formerly a part of Barrington, and was incorporated in 1820. Population, 1830, 2,200.

Strafford, Vt.

Orange co. This town is watered by a branch of Ompomponoosuc river, and lies 30 miles S. S. E. from Montpelier, 30 N. from Windsor, and 11 S. S. E. from Chelsea. Population, 1830, 1,935.

The surface of the town is rough, but the soil is productive. It feeds a large number of sheep. The manufacturing interests of Strafford are quite extensive.

" In this township is an extensive

bed of the sulphuret of iron, from which immense quantities of copperas are manufactured. The ore is situated on the east side of an elevation, and the bed is about half a mile in length, and from two to three rods in width. Its depth has not been ascertained. A company was incorporated by the name of the "Vermont Mineral Factory Company," in October, 1809, which immediately commenced the manufacture of copperas, at this place. In 1822, 180 tons of copperas were manufactured here, and in 1823, 158 tons; since that time the manufacture has increased. The ore is covered to the depth of about three feet with a stratum of earth. Below this is a stratum of ferruginous petrifactions, which exhibits forms of buds, leaves, limbs of trees, &c. in admirable perfection. This stratum varies from two to three feet in depth. Below this lies the bed of sulphuret of iron. It is very compact. Its colors are brilliant, varying from that of steel to a bright yellow, and its appearance is occasionally diversified by small quantities of green copper ore. It is also traversed in many parts by small veins of quartz. The ore is detached from the bed in large masses, by blasting. It is then beaten to pieces with hammers and thrown into heaps several rods in length, about 12 feet in width, and seven or eight in height. Here it is suffered to lie exposed to the action of the air and moisture until a spontaneous combustion takes place, and the whole heap is converted from the sulphuret to the sulphate of iron, which usually takes several weeks. After the process of burning is completed, the residue is removed to the leaches, where water is passed through it which dissolves the copperas and leaves the earthy matter behind. The water is then conveyed to the boilers, which are made of lead, and weigh about 2,500 pounds each. Here it is boiled and evaporated to a certain extent, and suffered partially to cool. It is then transferred to the crystalizers, where the copperas continues to crystalize, while cooling, and when the crystalization ceases, the water is again returned to the boilers, mixed with water from the leaches, and again evaporated."

Stratford, N. H.

Coos co. This town lies on the E. bank of Connecticut river, 16 miles above Lancaster. The town is large, extending 10 miles on the river, with a fertile intervale of 1-4 to 1 mile wide. This meadow is skirted in many places by a narrow plain, succeeded by the mountainous regions, covering the whole E. and N. divisions of the town. The soil, except along the river, is rocky, gravelly and cold. The Peaks, two mountains of a conical form, situated in the S. E. part of the town, are seen at a great distance. They are discovered immediately on entering Dalton, 30 miles below, and stand as land marks in front or to the right, till, on nearer approach, they are lost behind the intervening hills. Bog brook and several smaller streams, here fall into the Connecticut; and Nash's stream crosses the S. E. part of the town into the Amonoosuck. There is a pond in the S. E. part of the town, the waters of which pass into the Amonoosuck. Stratford was incorporated in 1779. Population, in 1830, 443.

Thomas Burnside, of this town, was one of Rogers' Rangers in the French war. Some years afterwards, he was desirous of becoming a justice of the peace. He procured Colonel Barr to assist his views, and carrying with him, by his direction, as a present, a firkin of butter and a piece of linen, waited upon Gov. Wentworth, at Portsmouth. He stated to the governor that the inhabitants of his town could not live peaceably any longer without a magistrate. The governor enquired how many inhabitants belonged to the town, and who was the fittest man for the office. Thomas answered that *himself* and his *neighbor* were the only inhabitants, and himself the only man qualified for the appointment; for his neighbor was no more fit for a justice of the peace than the d——l was. The governor gave him his commission, and was highly amused with the singularity of the application.

Stratford, Ct.

Fairfield co. This town was first settled in 1639, by persons from Boston, Roxbury and Concord, Mass. and Wethersfield, Ct. Its Indian name was *Cupheag.*

Stratford is about 6 miles in length from north to south, and its breadth from east to west is between 2 and 3 miles. It is bounded north by Huntington, west by Trumbull and Bridgeport, east by the Housatonick, dividing it from Milford, and south by Long Island Sound. The central part of the town is 13 miles S. W. from New-Haven, and S.E. by N. from Fairfield. The township is mostly level and free from stone, and there is a very rich alluvial tract of meadows on the river and harbor. The principal street in the town, is one mile in length, running north and south, parallel to the Housatonick; it is level, pleasant, and ornamented with shade trees. On this street, and others, in the immediate vicinity, there are about 200 dwelling houses, and 4 houses for public worship.

This place lies at the mouth of Housatonick river, and has considerable inland and coasting trade. *Stratford Point*, jutting out into the Sound, is very pleasant, and a noted landing place for passengers.

Gen. DAVID WOOSTER, was a native of this town, and was born in 1711. He was a brave and good officer, an ardent patriot, and in his various public and private relations, sustained a character distinguished for integrity, benevolence and virtue. He was mortally wounded in a skirmish with the British troops, at the time of their incursion to Danbury, in 1777.

Stratham, N. H.

Rockingham co. This town lies 39 miles S. E. by E. from Concord, 3 E. N. E. from Exeter, and is situated on the E. side of the W. branch of the Piscataqua river. Stratham is distant about 8 miles from the sea. The land is even, and well calculated for agricultural purposes. Farming is so exclusively the employment of the people, that although a navigable river adjoins it, there is little attention given to any other pursuit. In the east part of the town, in a swamp, is perhaps the largest repository of peat in the state. This town was a part of the Squamscot patent, or Hilton's purchase. It was made a town by charter, March 20, 1716. Population, in 1830, 833.

Stratton, Vt.

Windham co. A mountainous township in the west part of the county, 18 miles N. E. from Bennington, and 22 N. W. from Brattleborough. Branches of Deerfield and Winhall rivers rise here from two ponds. The soil is cold and generally unprofitable. Population, 1830, 312.

Strong, Me.

Franklin co. This excellent township lies on both sides of Sandy river, 45 miles N. W. from Augusta, and bounded South by Farmington. Population, in 1837, 1,091. There is a large body of intervale land on the Sandy, very fertile and productive. Strong contains a pleasant and flourishing village, some mills on the stream, and several very beautiful ponds. In Porter's pond, about two miles long, a salmon trout was taken, which weighed *twenty seven and a half pounds.*

Strong was incorporated in 1801, and named in honor of CALEB STRONG, LL. D., formerly a Senator to Congress, from Massachusetts, and Governor of that state 9 years. He died at Northampton, Mass., his native town, Nov. 7, 1819, aged 74 years.

Sturbridge, Mass.

Worcester co. This is a very pleasant town, and is well watered by Quinebaug river. It lies 60 miles W. S. W. from Boston, and 18 S. W. from Worcester. Incorporated, 1738. Population, 1830, 1,688; 1837, 2,004. The surface of the town is uneven and hilly, and the soil hard to subdue; but it has become productive by good management. There are some good fish ponds in the town, which serve to swell the Quinebaug. There are 6 cotton mills in Sturbridge and manufactures of boots, shoes, leather, chairs, cabinet ware, clothing, palm-leaf hats, trunks harnesses, chairs, wagons, sleighs and *pocket rifles;* total value, the year ending April 1, 1837, $182,415.

Success, N. H.

Coos co. There are several considerable mountains in this tract, and two or three ponds. Narmarcungawack and Live rivers rise here, and pass westerly into the Androscoggin. Success was granted Feb. 12, 1773, to Benjamin Mackay and others; and is 143 miles N. by E. from Concord. Population, 1830, 14.

Sudbury, Vt.

Rutland co. A part of Hubbardston, and Hinkum's ponds lie in this town, neither of which, nor Otter Creek, which passes through the eastern part, produce any considerable water privileges. The soil is generally a warm loam and productive: the surface is elevated, and, in the centre of the town, mountainous. There are about 5,500 sheep in the town. Sudbury is 43 miles S. W. from Montpelier, 47 S. by E. from Burlington, and 17 N. W. from Rutland. Population, 1830, 812.

Sudbury River, Mass.

This river rises in Hopkinton and its neighborhood, and after passing Framingham, Natick, Sudbury, Wayland and Lincoln, it joins the Assabet at Concord.

Sudbury, Mass.

Middlesex co. This ancient town is situated on the west side of a river of the same name, 19 miles W. by N. from Boston, and 8 S. W. from Concord. Population, 1837, 1,388. It is watered by a small stream, a branch of Sudbury river. There is a paper mill in the town, a plough factory, and manufactures of boots and shoes annual value about $20,000.

Sudbury was first settled in 1635. In 1676, about 70 men, on their march for the relief of Marlborough, fell into an ambuscade with the Indians: twenty six of the English were left dead on the field; the residue were captured, and many of them afterwards tortured and slain. West of Sudbury causeway, is a monument erected to their memory, by president Wadsworth, of Harvard College, a son of the Captain of the Band.

Suffield, Ct.

Hartford co. Suffield lies on the west side of Connecticut river, and is bounded N. by Massachusetts, to which state it was attached until 1752. This territory, 8 by 5 miles, was purchased about the year 1670, of two Indian Chiefs, for one hundred dollars. The surface on the banks of the river, are elevated, and although the town is without much alluvial meadow, the soil being of a strong deep loam, is very fertile, and productive. Suffield contains some of the best farms in the state. It lies 16 miles N. from Hartford, and 10 S. from Springfield. Population 1830, 2,690.

The principal village is pleasantly located on rising ground; it contains many handsome buildings; it is the site of the "Connecticut Literary Institution," and commands delightful views of the river and circumjacent country.

GIDEON GRANGER, post master general of the United States from 1801 to 1814, was born in Suffield, in 1767. He died at Canandaigua, N. Y., in 1822.

OLIVER PHELPS, Esq., "a man of extraordinary enterprise and extensive business, was for many years a resident of this town. He was the 'maker of his own fortunes.' He was a native of Windsor, but was bred in this town, and received a mercantile education. He engaged in business in Granville, Mass., and soon became a very enterprising, sagacious and successful trader. During the revolutionary war, he was employed by the state of Massachusetts, in the commissary department. Whilst in this situation, his transactions were of a most extensive and responsible nature, and his own paper formed a kind of circulating medium. Afterwards he purchased a large estate, and returned to this town. In 1789, he, in connection with the Hon. Mr. Gorham, purchased of the commonwealth of Massachusetts, a tract of land in the western part of the state of New York, in what is commonly called the Genesee country, comprising 2,200,000 acres. This is probably the greatest land purchase, or speculation, ever made by two individuals in the United States. This is a very excellent tract of land, having a mild climate, and fertile soil, and an abundance of waters, and is now comprised in the extensive counties of Ontario and Steuben. In 1795, Mr. Phelps, together with William Hart and their associates, purchased of Connecticut, the tract of land in the state of Ohio, called the Western Reserve, comprising 3,300,000 acres."

Suffolk County, Mass.

See *Boston* and *Chelsea*.

Sugar River, N. H.

This river originates from Sunapee Lake; it passes through part of Wendell, the whole of Newport, and nearly through the centre of Claremont, where it meets the Connecticut. Red Water brook, in Claremont, is a tributary of Sugar river.

Sullivan, Me.

Hancock co. This maritime town is situated at the head of Frenchman's bay, 93 miles E. from Augusta, and 17 E. by S. from Ellsworth. Population 1837, 611. Sullivan has mill privileges, and is finely located for ship building, and other branches of business connected with navigation.

This town was incorporated in 1789, and received its name in honor of JOHN SULLIVAN, LL. D., a major general in the revolutionary war; afterwards member of congress, president of New Hampshire, and district Judge of the U. S. Court. He was born in Maine, and died in New Hampshire, 1795.

JAMES SULLIVAN, LL. D., a brother of Gen. Sullivan, was born at Berwick, in 1744. He early espoused the cause of his country, and sustained the offices of member of the provincial congress, attorney general and governor of Massachusetts, with great talents and faithfulness.

He died while governor, in 1808, at a period of great political excitement, honored and beloved by all parties.

Sullivan County, N. H.

Newport, chief town. This county is bounded N. by Grafton county, E. by Merrimack and a part of Hillsborough counties, S. by Cheshire county, and W. by Connecticut river, or the state of Vermont. It was taken from Cheshire county in 1827, and contains an area of about 533 square miles. Population, 1830, 19,687. Population to a square mile, 37. The surface of the county is elevated, but not mountainous: Croydon mountain is the highest.

Along the streams, particularly on Connecticut river, the soil is rich and exceedingly productive. The uplands produce good grain, and afford excellent pasturage for cattle, of which many are reared for market. Although this is the smallest county in the state; in 1837, it had 71,076 sheep, whose wool, being partly Saxony, would average as good as full blood Merino.

Besides the Connecticut, which waters its whole western frontier, the Ashuelot, Cold, Sugar, Little Sugar rivers, and other streams furnish the county with an abundant water power, and Sunapee Lake and numerous ponds give beauty to its otherwise varied and picturesque scenery.

Sullivan, N. H.

Cheshire co. The distance from Keene is 6 miles, from Concord, 42 W. S. W. The S. E. part of this town is watered by Ashuelot river. This town was incorporated in 1787, and received its name from President Sullivan, the chief magistrate of N. H. that year. Population in 1830, 555.

Sumner, Me.

Oxford co. This town is well watered by a branch of Androscoggin river; it has a fine soil, and produced in 1837, 7,144 bushels of wheat. It lies 44 miles W. from Augusta, and 8 N. from Paris. Population, 1837, 1,190.

This town derived its name from INCREASE SUMNER, who was governor of Massachusetts in 1798, when the town was incorporated. Gov. Sumner was a native of Roxbury, Mass. He died in 1799, aged 52 years.

Sunapee Lake, N. H.

This lake is situated in the W. part of Merrimack county, and the E. part of Sullivan, in the towns of Wendell, New London and Newbury. It is 9 miles long, and about 1 1-2 miles in width. Its outlet is on the W. side through Sugar river. The waters of this lake are more than 800 feet higher than the Connecticut or Merrimack, at the nearest points.

Suncook River, N. H.

This river rises in a pond between Gilmanton and Gilford, near the summit of one of the Suncook mountains, elevated 900 feet above its base. The water from this pond passes through two others at the foot of the mountains, and thence through a flourishing village in the S. E. part of Gilmanton, into Barnstead, where it receives several tributaries; thence through Pittsfield and Epsom, and between Allenstown and Pembroke, into the Merrimack.

Sunderland, Vt.

Bennington co. This town was first settled in 1765. It lies 87 miles S. S. W. from Montpelier, and 15 N. by E. from Bennington. Population, 1830, 463. The town is watered by several ponds, Battenkill river and Roaring brook. There is some fine land along the streams, in Sunderland, excellent mill sites, and lead ore in granular limestone.

Sunderland, Mass.

Franklin co. This town lies on the east side of Connecticut river, 90 miles W. from Boston, and 9 S. by E. from Greenfield. It was taken from Hadley in 1718. Population, 1837, 729. The settlement in this town is principally on a street running parallel with the river. Between the street and the river is a tract of fertile meadow: on the other side of the village is a more elevated plain, and back of that, Mount Toby rears its lofty front. This mountain is composed of pudding stone, and the small stones within it are round and smooth as though washed by the ocean; they are of various sizes, and of every color. On one side is a cavern 60 feet deep; and many other ruptures seem to indicate some great change in this mountain since its formation. This village is very pleasant, and the scenery around it is of a fascinating character. The people here are good farmers, and are noted for their good schools and philanthropic disposition.

Sunkhaze, Me.

Sunkhaze stream meets the Penobscot, from the east, about 15 miles above Old Town village, in Orono. The *plantation* of Sunkhaze lies on this stream, 82 miles N. E. from Augusta. The population of the plantation, in 1830, was 250.

Surry, Me.

Hancock co. Surry lies on the W. side of Union river, 6 miles S. from Ellsworth, and 87 E. by N. from Augusta.

This town is accommodated with navigable privileges, and water power of superior excellence.—There are some manufactures in the town, but the inhabitants are generally independent farmers.—Many of the farms are rendered very fertile by an inexhaustible bed of shell marl, of a very fine quality. Incorporated, 1803. Population, 1830, 561; 1837, 735.

Surry, N. H.

Cheshire co. This town lies 54 miles S. W. from Concord, and 6 N. W. from Keene. It is watered by Ashuelot river, on which there is a tract of valuable meadow land, extending almost the whole length of the town. On the east side of Ashuelot river is a steep and high mountain, on the summit of which is a pond of about 3 acres in extent, and about 25 feet depth of water.

Surry was originally a part of Gilsum and Westmoreland. It was incorporated in 1769, deriving its name from *Surry* in England. The first settlement was made in 1764, by Peter Hayward. Population, 1830, 539.

Sutton, N. H.

Merrimack co. This town lies 25 miles W. N. W. from Concord. The southerly and largest branch of Warner river enters this town on the south, runs a short distance, and passes off into Warner again. The northerly branch of this river runs nearly through the centre of the town from north to south, and affords several good mill seats. Stevens' brook, another considerable branch of Warner river, has its source on the W. side of Kearsarge, and runs about 4 miles in this town, in a S. E. direction. There is also a large branch of Blackwater river, which has its source about the western confines of Kearsarge, and flows through this town in a N. E. course about 3 miles. On the margin of this stream, there is some rich meadow and intervale land. There are several ponds, the most important of which are Kezar's pond, situated towards the N. part of the town, which is about 190 rods square; and Long pond, situated at the south part of the town. Kearsarge mountain extends more than half the length of Sutton on the E. side. King's Hill is situated on the W. part of Sutton. On the most elevated part of this hill, which rises within a few feet as high as Kearsarge, there is one of the most extensive landscape views in the country. On the W. is seen the Sunapee lake, the Ascutney, and highlands in Vermont to the Green mountains; on the S. the Sunapee and Monadnock; on the E. you almost overlook Kearsarge, and on the north the Cardigan and White hills.

Sutton was granted in 1749. It was called *Perrys-town*, from Obadiah Perry, one of its original and principal proprietors. The first settlement was made in 1767. Population, 1830, 1,424.

On the W. bank of Kezar's pond, were several acres of land, which appeared to have been cleared of their original forests. Here were found several Indian hearths, laid with stone, and with much skill and ingenuity. Here was found an Indian burial place. Gun barrels and arrows have been found in this sacred repository. Near the pond, have been found stone pestles, mortars and tomahawks.

Sutton, Vt.

Caledonia co. This town is watered by several ponds and by branches of Passumpsic river. It lies 18 miles N. E. from Montpelier, and 13 N. from Danville. First settled, 1791. Population, 1830, 1,005.

The surface of the town is level, and in some parts so low as to render the soil cold and unproductive.

Sutton, Mass.

Worcester co. This is a very pleasant and flourishing town, 44 miles W. by S. from Boston, and 9 S. by E. from Worcester. Incorporated, 1715. Population, 1830, 2,186; 1837, 2,457.

Sutton is watered by Blackstone river, and the Blackstone canal passes through the town. There are in the town four cotton and two woolen mills, two scythe factories, and manufactures of boots, shoes, shuttles and spindles: total value, the year ending April 1, 1837, $309,578.

The surface of the town is agreeably diversified, and the soil capable of producing good crops. Granite and soapstone are abundant.

"Purgatory Cavern," in this town, is a great curiosity. It is a fissure in gneiss, nearly half a mile long, in most parts partially filled by the masses of rock that have been detached from the walls. The sides are often perpendicular, and sometimes 70 feet high; being separated from each other about 50 feet.

Swanzey, N. H.

Cheshire co. This town lies 6 miles S. from Keene, and 60 S. W. from Concord. The principal streams are the Ashuelot and the South Branch rivers. The former passes through Swanzey in a S. W. direction, and empties into the Connecticut at Hinsdale. This is a stream of much importance, and is made navigable for boats as far up as Keene, excepting a carrying place about the rapids at Winchester. The South Branch unites with the Ashuelot about one mile north from the centre of the town. The surface here is somewhat diversified with hills, valleys, and swells of upland. There is one pond in the S. W. part of the town, the source of the South Branch. There is a mineral spring, the water of which is impregnated with sulphate of iron. Some iron ore has been discovered. Here are 2 cotton factories, 1 cotton and woolen factory, and other machinery.

Swanzey was first granted by Massachusetts, in 1733. After the divisional line was run, it was granted in 1753, by New Hampshire. Until that time it had been called *Lower Ashuelot*, from the Indian name of the river, which was originally *Ashaelock*.

From 1741 to 1747, this town suffered much from Indian depredations. Several of the inhabitants were killed and many were made prisoners. After Massachusetts withdrew her protection, the settlers collected together their household furniture, such as chests, tables, iron and brass ware, and concealed it in the ground, covering the place of concealment with leaves, trees, &c., and left their plantation to the disposition of the Indians, who were not tardy in setting fire to their forts, which, with every house except one, they reduced to ashes. Most of the people went to their former places of residence in Massachusetts. They returned about three years afterwards, and nothing about their former habitation was to be seen, but ruin and desolation. Population, 1830, 1,816.

Swanzey, Mass.

Bristol co. This town lies between Somerset, and Bristol, R. I. An arm of Mount Hope bay sets up some miles into the town, on which is some navigation and ship building.

There are two paper mills, a cotton and a woolen mill in the town, and manufactures of vessels, boots and shoes: annual value, about $50,000.

Swanzey is a very pleasant town, and is interesting as the scene of much savage aggression. Here it was that Philip commenced his war, in 1675, by plunder and murder. It lies 46 miles S. by W. from Boston, and 14 S. W. by S. from Taunton. Incorporated, 1667. Population, 1837, 1,627.

Swanton, Vt.

Franklin co. This township is situated on the east side of Lake Champlain, opposite to North Hero and Alburgh. It is 50 miles N. W. from Montpelier, 28 N. from Burlington, and is bounded by St. Albans on the south, and Highgate on the north. Population, 1830, 2,158. Swanton was first settled by the whites in 1787. At that time the St. Francois Indians had about fifty cabins here, and large plantations of corn.

Missisque river passes through Swanton, and fertilizes a considerable portion of its territory. This river is navigable for lake vessels to Swanton falls, six miles from its mouth. These falls descend twenty feet, and, with other smaller streams, give to Swanton a water power of great value.

Bog iron ore is found in this town, and an abundance of beautiful marble. This marble is of various colors, and large quantities of it is wrought into all desired patterns, polished, and transported.

The surface and soil of the town is favorable to agricultural pursuits, with the exception of a part bordering the lake, which is low, wet and cold; and which is the favorite abode, in summer, of wild geese, ducks and other water fowls.

The village of Swanton is pleasantly located, and is the site of a number of manufactories, and of an increasing trade from the interior country, and to New York and Canada.

Swanton may boast of the purity of its air and water, and of *a* Walter Scott, who died in 1815, aged 110 years.

Swanville, Me.

Waldo co. This town lies 8 miles N. from Belfast, and 46 E. by N. from Augusta. It was incorporated in 1818. It is watered by Paasaggassawakeag lake and river, and possesses a pleasant surface and fertile soil. Population, 1837, 794.

Wheat crop, same year, 2,556 bushels.

Sweden, Me.

Oxford co. The waters from Kezer pond in Lovell, pass through this town, and give it mill privileges. Sweden lies 9 miles N. E. from Fryeburg, 19 S.W. from Paris, and 62 W. S. W. from Augusta. Incorporated, 1813. Population, in 1837, 621. Wheat crop, same year, 1,485 bushels.

Swift Rivers.

Swift river, in *Maine*, is a branch of the Androscoggin, from the N. These rivers unite at Mexico.

Swift river, in *New Hampshire*, rises among the mountains in the ungranted lands N. W. of Albany, and passes through the town from west to east with great rapidity, and falls into the Saco in Conway. Its whole course is rapid, and in one place it falls 30 feet in the distance of 6 rods, through a channel in the solid rock of about 12 feet wide—the sides being from 10 to 30 feet perpendicular height. At the upper part of these falls, are found several circular holes worn perpendicularly into the rock, several feet in depth and from 6 inches to 2 feet in diameter. There is another small river in Tamworth of the same name.

Swift river, in *Massachusetts*, rises in a pond in New Salem: it passes through the towns of Prescott, Greenwich and Belchertown, and joins the Chickopee at Palmer.

Tamworth, N. H.

Strafford co. This town is situated on the post road from Concord to Portland, about 58 miles from each, and 30 N. from Gilford.

There is no mountain situated wholly in this town. On the N. are the mountains of Albany, and the S. the line crosses a part of Ossipee mountain. The mountains to the N. have a romantic and picturesque appearance. The town lies in ridges and valleys, generally rocky and fertile. The principal rivers are Bearcamp, which passes through the town in an easterly direction, and discharges its waters into Ossipee lake; Swift river, which rises near the N. W. corner of the town, and passing through its centre, mingles its waters with the Bearcamp; and Conway river, proceeding from Conway pond, near Albany; and crossing the S. line of Tamworth, near the S. E. corner of the town, near which it empties into Bearcamp river. By these rivers, and other small streams, the town is uncommonly well watered. On these streams is a great number of excellent mill privileges. Tamworth was granted in 1766, and was settled in 1771. Population, 1830, 1,554.

Tariffville, Ct.

See *Simsbury*.

Taughkannic Mountains.

This range of mountains skirt the western border of New England, and separate the waters of the Housatonick and Hudson.

Taunton River.

This river rises in the county of Plymouth, Mass., and falls into Mount Hope Bay. The Taunton and its branches, water the towns of Abington, Hanson, Halifax, and Plympton, all the Bridgewaters, Raynham, Taunton, Berkley, Dighton, Freetown, Fall river, Somerset and Swansey. It is navigable to Taunton, for small vessels, and with its contemplated improvements, steam boats will be enabled to run to Taunton, and thus become another channel of conveyance between Boston and New York. This river is celebrated for the great and widely distributed water power it produces, and for the multitude of alewives within its waters.

Taunton, Mass.

One of the chief towns in Bristol co. This very beautiful town is situated at the junction of Canoe, Rumford and Taunton rivers, and possesses an excellent water power. There is some excellent land in this town, and its proprietors display much taste in its cultivation. The business of the place is, however, rather in manufactures than agriculture. There are 8 cotton mills and a print works, in the town; also a paper mill, 3 nail factories, a forge, a furnace, and manufactures of boots, shoes, leather, hats, chairs, brick, vessels, straw bonnets, and britannia, stone and cabinet wares: total value of the manufactures, the year ending April 1, 1837, exclusive of cloth printing and iron castings, $1,425,552. The number of hands employed in these manufactures was 1,308. There is some navigation owned in this town, which is employed in the coastwise trade, and domestic fishery.

The manufacture of britannia ware at this place, is of recent origin in this country, and proves successful. The articles manufactured, are tea sets, castors, urns, and all the varieties of that description of ware. The quality of the metal, and beauty of the polish of this ware, is said to equal any imported from "Britannia."

The village contains a large number of handsome public and private buildings, tastefully located around a beautiful enclosure, called "Taunton Green." This public walk is ornamented with trees, which heightens the beauty of this delightful village.

Taunton is 32 miles S. from Boston, 20 E. by N. from Providence, and 32 N. E. from Newport. A rail road connects this town with Boston. Population, 1820, 4,520; 1830, 6,042; 1837, 7,647.

The settlement of this place commenced in 1637. Its principal founder was Miss Elizabeth Poole The following is on her grave stone:

"Here rest the remains of Elizabeth Poole, a native of Old England, of good family, friends, and prospects, all which she left in the prime of her life, to enjoy the religion of her conscience, in this distant wilderness; a great proprietor of the township of Taunton, a chief promoter of its settlement, and its incorporation in 1639 —40; about which time she settled near this spot, and having employed the opportunity of her virgin state in piety, liberality, and sanctity of manners, died May 21, 1664, aged 65."

Temiscouata Lake, Me.

See *Madawaska River*.

Temple, Me.

Franklin co. This was formerly a part of Kennebec county. It lies 40 miles N. N. W. from Augusta, and is bounded N. by Farmington. It was incorporated in 1803. Population, 1837, 871. Wheat crop, same year, 5,798 bushels.

Temple, N. H.

Hillsborough co. Temple is 12 miles W. by S. from Amherst, and 40 S. S. W. from Concord. The several streams which empty into Souhegan river at Wilton, rise among the mountainous tracts on the W., and generally from sources within the limits of Temple. This town is of considerable elevation. The prospect towards the E. and S. is very extensive, and presents a rich and diversified scenery. From the highest point of elevation, in a clear atmosphere, about 20 meeting houses may be seen by the naked eye. The surface is uneven and pleasant. The soil is tolerably good. Temple is the easterly part of what was called *Peterborough Slip*. It was incorporated in 1768. Population, in 1830, 641.

Templeton, Mass.

Worcester co. Several streams, affording good mill seats, water this town, and pass to the Connecticut, by Miller's and Chickopee rivers. The surface of the town is uneven, but not mountainous; the elevated parts afford good pasturage, and the valleys, excellent crops of grain and hay. The manufactures consist of woolen goods, boots, shoes, leather, iron castings, shovels, hoes, spades, forks, palm leaf hats, chairs, carriages, and cabinet, tin and wooden wares: value, the year ending April 1, 1837, $145,400. The village is very pleasantly located, and presents some beautiful landscapes. This town lies 60 miles W. N. W. from Boston, and 26 N. N. W. from Worcester. Incorporated in 1762. Population, 1837, 1,690.

Tewksbury, Mass.

Middlesex co. The Indians called this place *Wamesit*. It lies on the south side of Merrimack river, 19 miles N. W. by W. from Boston, and 6 E. S. E. from Lowell. Incorporated, 1734. Population, 1837, 907. The surface of the town is level, and the soil light and sandy.

Thames River, Ct.

This river is formed by the union of Quinebaug, Shetucket and Yantic rivers, near Norwich, and is navigable from that place to New London, 14 miles. The banks of this river are romantic and beautiful, and possess great interest, as the residence of the once powerful, noble hearted and brave Mohegans.

Thatcher's Island, Mass.

See *Gloucester*.

Thetford, Vt.

Orange co. This town is pleasantly situated on the west side of Connecticut river, opposite to Lyme, N. H. The Ompomponoosuc and its branches, give the town an excellent water power. There are several ponds in Thetford, one of which is worthy of notice. It covers about 9 acres, and is situated on an elevation, the base of which is only 4 rods from Connecticut river, and 100 feet in height. It is very deep; it has neither inlet or outlet, and contains large quantities of perch and other fish. The surface of the town is generally rocky and uneven; it has but little intervale, but the soil is strong and productive: It feeds between 7 and 8,000 sheep. There are some manufactures in the town, a rich vein of galena, and three neat villages. Thetford was first settled in 1764. It lies 34 miles S. S. E. from Montpelier, and 18 S. E. from Chelsea. Population, in 1830, 2,113.

Thomaston, Me.

Lincoln co. This is a very flourishing maritime town, situated between the western entrance of Penobscot Bay and St. Georges' river, and comprises the celebrated peninsula of *Owl's Head*. It lies 36 miles S. E. from Augusta, 37 E. from Wiscasset, and is bounded N. W. by Warren. Incorporated, 1777. Population, in 1820, 2,651; 1830, 4,221; 1837, 5,272.

Thomaston is the site of the State prison, which is located on the bank of the St. George. The buildings occupy a plat of 10 acres, including a marble quarry; they are all of stone, and are surrounded by a high stone wall. The convicts are principally employed in cutting granite into various forms for building, and which, when prepared, is transported by water. The granite is of an excellent quality, and is found in large quantities on the river.

Thomaston is a place of considerable maritime commerce and ship building; but the most important business of its people, is the quarrying and burning of lime, from inexhaustible ledges of limestone within its limits. There are annually made at this place, no less than 350,000 casks of lime, the same in quality and reputation as that prepared at Camden, 10 miles distant. This manufacture, united with those of granite and marble, give constant employment to a large number of men and vessels. Thomaston is a beautiful Atlantic town, and commands a great variety of marine scenery.

Thompson, Ct.

Windham co. This town lies 47 miles E. N. E. from Hartford, 14 N. from Brooklyn, 27 W. N. W. from Providence, R. I., and 53 S. W. from Boston. It is bounded N. by Massachusetts, and E. by Rhode Island. It was formerly a part of Killingly, and was first settled about the year 1715. The surface of the town is hilly, but not mountainous: it presents a pleasing variety of elevations and valleys. The soil is a gravelly loam, strong, and productive of good crops of corn and hay, and affords excellent pasturage. French river meets the Quinnebaug near the centre of the town, and Five Mile river, issuing from several ponds, waters the eastern part. These streams give to the town a valuable water power, and on their banks are the pleasant and thriving villages of Masonsville, Fishersville and New Boston. These are manufacturing villages, and contain 10 cotton and woolen mills, and a number of other manufactures. This town is large, and very pleasant; it contains a class of enterprising and intelligent agriculturalists and mechanics. The population of Thompson, in 1837, was about 4,100. The Indian name of the place was *Quinnetessett.* The plantations of the natives are still apparent.

Thorndike, Me.

Waldo co. This is an agricultural town of pleasant surface and fertile soil, 59 miles N. E. from Augusta, and 17 N. W. from Belfast. It is watered by a branch of Sebasticook river. Thorndike was incorporated in 1819. Population, 1837, 763. Wheat crop, same year, 6,975 bushels.

Thornton, N. H.,

Grafton co., is bounded N. by Peeling and Lincoln, E. by ungranted land, S. by Campton, and W. by Ellsworth and Peeling. It is 12 miles N. from Plymouth, and 58 N. by W. from Concord. It is watered by Pemigewasset river, passing through the town from N. to S., by Mad river at the S. E. extremity, and by several small brooks. On Mill brook, there is a cascade, at which the water falls 7 feet in 2 rods, and then falls over a rock 42 feet perpendicular. The intervales on the Pemigewasset are productive. There are many elevations, but none distinguished for a remarkable height. Thornton was granted in 1763. It was first settled in 1770. Thornton was incorporated in 1781. Population, 1830, 1,049.

Tinmouth, Vt.

Rutland co. This town is separated from Wallingford by Otter Creek. Furnace brook rises from a pond in the south part of the town, and passing through Tinmouth and Clarendon, falls into Otter Creek, at Rutland. This stream has been noted for great quantities of fish of a remarkable large size.

The surface of the town is hilly, in some parts mountainous. There is some good land on the streams, and a large portion of the high land is good for the pasturage of sheep, of which between 3,000 and 4,000 are kept. There are several quarries of beautiful marble in the town, iron ore in abundance, and several iron works. Tinmouth was first settled in 1770. It lies 8 miles S. from Rutland. Population, 1830, 1,049.

Tisbury, Mass.

Dukes co. Tisbury lies on the north side of Martha's Vineyard, and contains the noted harbor of "Holmes' Hole." This harbor is large and safe, and of a sufficient depth of water for the largest merchantmen. It is much frequented by vessels passing through Vineyard Sound; particularly when the winds are contrary. From this harbor, across the Sound, to Falmouth, on Cape Cod, is 6 miles.

A number of small vessels belong to this place, and one of 388 tons is employed in the whale fishery.

There are some manufactures of salt, boots, shoes, leather, and hats; and, in 1837, there were 2,655 sheep in the town.

Tisbury is 77 miles S. S. E. from Boston, 8 W. from Edgarton, and 23 S. E. from New Bedford. Incorporated, 1671. Population, 1837, 1,461.

Tiverton, R. I.

Newport co. Tiverton is bounded N. and E. by Massachusetts, S. by Little Compton, and W. by the eastern passage into Mount Hope and Narraganset bays. It is connected with Portsmouth, on the island of Rhode Island, by a stone bridge at a place called "Howland's Ferry."

The surface of the town is varied by hills and valleys. Its structure is granite, and the land, in some parts, is stony. The soil is principally a gravelly loam, and capable of producing good crops. There are valuable forests of timber in the town, and a considerable number of sheep.

The navigable privileges of Tiverton are of a superior kind; and are improved, to some extent, in the fishery, and foreign and domestic trade. There are large ponds in the town, well supplied with fish. These ponds produce a water power which is applied to the manufacture of cotton and other materials.

This town was attached to Massachusetts until 1746. It is 24 miles S. E. from Providence, and 13 N. E. from Newport. Population, 1830, 2,905.

The captor of the British General Prescott, was a native of Tiverton. His name was Tak, a slave, the property of Thomas Sisson, a wealthy farmer. "During the Revolution, Tak was sent by his master into the army, to serve as a substitute for another man who was drafted. When Col. Barton took Gen. Prescott on Long Island, Tak was one of Col. Barton's chosen men; and the one on whom he most depended. Having entered the house where Gen. Prescott was quartered, Col. Barton, followed by Tak and two or three others, proceeded silently to the door of the chamber where General Prescott was sleeping. The colonel finding the door fastened, turned and whispering to Tak, 'I wish that door opened, General Prescott taken, and carried by the guard to the boat, without the least noise or disturbance.'

"Tak stepped back two or three paces, then plunging violently against the door, burst it open, and rushed into the middle of the room. At the same instant General Prescott sprang from his bed and seized his gold watch, hanging upon the wall. Tak sprang upon him like a tiger, and clasping the general in his brawny arms, said in a low, stern voice, 'One word, and you are a dead man!' Then hastily snatching the general's cloak and wrapping it round his body, and at the same time telling his companions to take the rest of his clothes, he took the general in his arms, as if a child, and ran with him by the guard towards the boat, followed by Colonel Barton and the rest of his little company.

Tak was more than six feet in height, well proportioned, and remarkable for his shrewdness, agility and strength. He attained great age, and was never known to taste of any kind of meat.

Tolland, Mass.

Hampden co. Tolland is situated on the border of Litchfield county, Connecticut, and is watered by the upper branch of Farmington river. The surface is elevated, but the lands are finely adapted for grazing.

There are manufactures in the town of shovels, spades, forks, hoes, and wooden ware; and here is a large tannery, but the inhabitants are chiefly farmers.

Tolland was incorporated in 1810. Population, 1830, 570. It lies 110 miles W. S. W. from Boston, and 20 W. from Springfield.

Tolland County, Ct.

Tolland is the chief town. This county was taken from Hartford and Windham counties in 1786. It is bounded N. by Massachusetts, E. by Windham, S. by New London, and W. by Hartford counties. Its greatest length from N. to S. is 30 miles. It covers an area of 337 square miles. Population, 1820, 14,330; 1830, 18,700. Inhabitants to a square mile, 56.

The western part of the county lays within the great valley of the Connecticut: it is generally free from stone, undulating, fertile and productive: the eastern section is within the granitic range which extends through the state: much of this portion of the county is covered with forests; that part which is cleared affords good grazing. In 1837, there were in the county 23,096 sheep. The Scantic, Willimantic, Salmon, Hockanum and Hop rivers, with their tributaries, afford the county a good water power, and manufactures flourish within its limits.

Tolland, Ct.

Shire town of Tolland county. This town has a population of 1,700 inhabitants, and is situated on the nearest mail route from Hartford to Boston. Its products are English grain, grass, potatoes, &c. It contains two small woolen manufactories, with water power sufficient to operate a greater number with corresponding machinery. It lies 18 miles E. N. E. from Hartford, 17 N. from Windham, 27 W. N. W. from Brooklyn, and 30 N. from Norwich. The land is rather sterile, mountainous and uneven. The inhabitants are industrious and intelligent.

Topsfield, Me.

Washington co. This township was number eight in the second range north of the Bingham Penobscot Purchase. It was incorporated in the year 1838. We *guess* that this town lies about 25 miles N. N. E. from the mouth of *Matawamkeag River*. We should like to *know* "how the land lies." See "Down East."

Topsfield, Mass.

Essex co. This is a very pleasant town, watered by Ipswich river and its branches. The surface is agreeably diversified by hills and valleys. There are some fine tracts of intervale in the town, and the uplands possess a strong soil, rendered productive by industrious and skilful farmers. The principal manufacture is that of boots and shoes, in which between 500 and 600 hands are employed, making annually about $100,000 in value. This town lies 21 miles N. by E. from Boston, and 9 N. by W. from Salem. Population, 1837, 1,049.

Topsfield was first settled about the year 1642. It was incorporated in 1650. Among the names of the first settlers were Peabody, Perkins, Clark, Cummings, Bradstreet, Gould, Town, Easty, Smith, and Wildes; many of whose descendants now cultivate the soil of their progenitors.

Topsham, Me.

One of the shire towns of Lincoln co. Topsham is pleasantly situated on the N. side of Androscoggin river, opposite to Brunswick. This is a good farming town, and, in common with Brunswick, enjoys a great hydraulic power, and accommodations for ship building and navigation. It is a place of considerable trade, and much lumber is annually shipped. Topsham was incorporated in 1764. Population, 1837, 1,778.

Topsham, Vt.

Orange co. This town is on elevated ground; with a rocky, strong soil, adapted to grazing. It contains much granite, and is watered by the upper branches of Wait's river, which propel a number of mills. The town was first settled in 1781. Population 1830, 1,384. It is 19 miles S. E. from Montpelier, 47 N. from Windsor, and 15 N. E. from Chelsea.

Torrington, Ct.

Litchfield co. This town was first settled in 1757. Its surface is diversified by hills and valleys, and the soil is better adapted to grazing than the culture of grain. There are many sheep in the town, and the products of the dairy are considerable. Population, 1830, 1,654.

Two branches of Naugatuck river meet at *Wolcottville*, a beautiful village, in the south part of the town; 26 miles W. N. W. from Hartford, 40 N. by W. from New Haven, and 7 N. by E. from Litchfield. This village is situated in a valley, and contains an extensive woolen factory, a church, an academy, and a number of handsome dwelling houses. Near this village, a good bed of copper ore has recently been discovered; and Mr. Israel Coe, the proprietor, has commenced the manufacture of brass kettles, the first establishment of the kind, it is believed, in the United States.

Wolcottville owes its rise, principally, to OLIVER WOLCOTT, secretary of the United States Treasury, during the administrations of Washington and John Adams; and governor of Connecticut 10 successive years. He was born at Litchfield, and died in New York, 1833, aged 74.

Townsend, Mass.

Middlesex co. The surface of this town is rather level; some parts are pine plains. The soil is generally light, but in some sections it is productive, particularly of fruit trees. It is watered by a branch of the Nashua, a beautiful mill stream, on which are divers mechanical operations. "Townsend Harbor," on the road from Groton to New Ipswich, N. H., is an active, pleasant village. The manufactures of this town consist of leather, palm-leaf hats, boots, shoes, ploughs, straw bonnets, fish barrels, nail kegs, and dry casks; annual value, about $75,000. This town was incorporated in 1732. Population, in 1830, 1,506; 1837, 1,749. It lies 38 miles N. from Boston, and 22 N. W. from Concord.

Townshend, Vt.

Windham co. This town was first settled in 1761. Among the first settlers, was Gen. Samuel Fletcher, who was a sergeant at the battle of Bunker Hill, in 1775, and a captain at Ticonderoga, in 1777. He afterwards rose to the rank of major general of the militia; was high sheriff of the county 18 years, and finally became judge of the court. He was formerly a blacksmith; but having welded himself to a buxom lass, he came to this, then wilderness spot, and, with his axe cut his way to fortune, usefulness and renown.

West river passes through the town with considerable rapidity: along its banks are some tracts of good intervale; but the surface of the town is generally hilly, and the soil more calculated for grazing than tillage. There are some manufactures in the town, a high school of good reputation, and two pleasant villages. Townshend lies 12 miles N. N. W. from Brattleborough, 28 N. E. from Bennington, 95 S. from Montpelier, and is bounded S. by Newfane. Population, 1830, 1,386.

Trenton, Me.

Hancock co. Trenton is situated on a navigable passage between Frenchman's bay on the E., Union river on the W., and N. of the island town of Eden. It possesses great advantages for navigation, and a large portion of its people is engaged in ship building, the coasting trade and fishery. Incorporated in 1789. Population, in 1837, 924. Trenton is 7 miles S. by E. from Ellsworth.

Trescott, Me.

Washington co. This is an Atlantic town, and bounded N. E. by Lubec. It comprises Moose cove, Bailey's mistake and Haycock harbors, and is flourishing in its trade and navigation. It was incorporated in 1827. Population, in 1830, 480; 1837, 713.

Trout River, Vt.

Franklin co. This river is formed in Montgomery, by several branches; it runs in a N. W. direction and falls into the Missisque on the border of Enosburgh and Berkshire. This is a good mill stream, and with its tributaries, fertilizes considerable tracts of country.

Troy, Me.

Waldo co. This territory was called Joy from 1812 to 1826: it was then called Montgomery, and changed again in 1827, to its present name. If these Trojans are fickle about the name of their town, they are good farmers, and produced in 1837, 9,194 bushels of wheat. The surface of the town is undulating and fertile; a large part of it is covered with heavy timber. It is watered by a branch of the Sebasticook, from which river it lies about 6 miles S. E. It is 39 miles N. E. from Augusta, and 25 N. W. from Belfast. Population, in 1830, 803; 1837, 1,140.

Troy, N. H.

Cheshire co. This town is bounded N. by Marlborough, E. by Jaffrey, S. by Fitzwilliam, and W. by Richmond and Swanzey. It is about 60 miles S. W. from Concord, and 12 S. E. from Keene. The inhabitants are principally agriculturalists. This town was taken from Marlborough and Fitzwilliam, and incorporated in 1815. Population, in 1830, 676.

Troy, Vt.

Orleans co. Troy lies 47 miles N. from Montpelier, 51 N. E. from Burlington, 11 N. N. W. from Irasburgh, and is bounded N. by Canada. First settled in 1800. Population, 1830, 608. During the war for "sailors' rights," most of the inhabitants left the town, which greatly retarded its growth. It is finely watered by Missisque river, and its tributaries: the surface is generally level, and the soil productive, particularly on the sides of the streams.

The Falls on the Missisque, produce a great water power, and propel some machinery. These falls pass down a ledge of rocks about 70 feet. A rock projects over them, 120 feet in perpendicular height. From this rock, the falls, the deep still water in the gulph below, with the romantic scenery around the place, present a spectacle of great

Trumbull, Ct.

Fairfield co. This territory was formerly called North Stratford, and was taken from Stratford and incorporated as a town, in 1798. This is a small town of about 5 by 4 1-2 miles. It lies 5 miles N. from the city of Bridgeport. It is watered by the Pequannock which empties into Bridgeport harbor. The surface is varied by hills and valleys: the soil is a gravelly loam, productive of good crops of grain and hay. Population, 1830, 1,242. *Tamtashua hill*, in the north part of the town, is the first land seen, in this direction, from the ocean.

Truro, Mass.

Barnstable co. Truro lies on Cape Cod bay, between Welfleet and Provincetown; it is nearly surrounded by water;—by Pamet river, which sets in from Cape Cod bay on the south, and by Cape Cod harbor in Provincetown. Truro was the *Pamet* of the Indians, and after its settlement, in 1700, was called *Dangerfield* for some years. Pamet river affords a good harbor for fishermen; it lies about 5 miles S. E. from Provincetown harbor. There is in this town, near the light house, a vast body of clay, called the "Clay Pounds," which seems providentially placed, in the midst of sand hills, for the preservation of this part of the cape. Although there is but little vegetation at Truro, and the people are dependent almost entirely for their fuel, and most of their food on other places; yet there are but few towns in the state where the people are more flourishing, and independent in their circumstances. To such towns as this old Massachusetts looks with pride for one of her chief resources of wealth—the fishery; and for men of noble daring in all her enterprises on the ocean. In 1837, there were 63 vessels owned at Truro, employed in the cod and mackerel fishery, measuring 3,437 tons; the product of which, in one year, was 16,950 quintals of cod fish, and 15,750 barrels of mackerel, valued at $145,350. The number of hands employed was 512. The value of salt manufactured, annually, is about $20,000. There are also, manufactures of palm-leaf hats, boots, shoes, &c.

No one would suppose that this was much of a wool growing place; and it is not so in regard to the quantity grown, but much so as it regards its means. In 1837, the people of Truro sheared 400 sheep of their own rearing. If the single county of Penobscot, in Maine, would produce as much wool, in proportion to its territory and the quality of its soil, as the town of Truro, there would be no cause of strife about the tariff on wool or woolen cloths; for the quantity would be sufficient to clothe all the inhabitants on the globe.

Truro was incorporated in 1709. It lies 41 miles below Barnstable, and 106 from Boston, by land. Population,1830, 1,549; 1837,1,806.

Tuftonborough, N. H.,

Strafford co., is about 50 miles E. by N. from Concord, situated on the N. E. shore of Winnepisiogee lake; bounded N. E. by Ossipee, S. E. by Wolfeborough, S. W. and W. by the lake, and N. W. by Moultonborough.

There are several ponds in this town, together with many small streams running into the lake.— There are several arms of the lake stretching far into the town, and presenting to the spectator, from the elevated parts of the town, a succession of beautiful views.

Tuftonborough was originally granted to J. Tufton Mason, and took its name from him. It was settled about 1780, and incorporated in 1795. Population, 1830, 1,375.

Tunbridge, Vt.

Orange co. A branch of White river passes through this town, on which are mills of various kinds. The soil is generally a rich loam: on the stream the intervale land is extensive and valuable. In some parts of the town the surface is elevated.

Tunbridge contains a medicinal spring of some notoriety in cutaneous diseases. Considerable quantities of the products of the farms are sent to market. Many sheep are reared; in 1837, the number in the town was 8,260.

Tunbridge was first settled in 1776. It is 26 miles S. by E. from Montpelier, 7 S. from Chelsea, and 30 N. by W. from Windsor. Population, 1830, 1,920.

Turner, Me.

Oxford co. A tributary of the Androscoggin meets that river in this town, and finely waters it. The soil of Turner is good, and its surface pleasant. There are a number of thriving villages in the town: there is considerable trade, and some manufactures; but the business of the people is generally agricultural.

Turner was incorporated in 1786. It is 38 miles W. S. W. from Augusta, and 14 E. from Paris. Population, 1830, 2,218; 1837, 2,435. Wheat crop, in 1837, 7,081 bushels.

Turtle River, Me.,

Or the *Meriumpticook*, a branch of St. John's river, which empties about 7 miles S. W. from the mouth of the Madawaska.

Tyngsborough, Mass.

Middlesex co. This is a pleasant town on both sides of Merrimack river, 8 miles N. W. by W.

from Lowell, and 29 N. W. from Boston. Incorporated, 1789. Population, 1837, 870.

The river here is wide, placid, and majestic, and adds much to the beauty of the place. There is not much water power in the town, and the soil is light and sandy. Large quantities of granite are quarried here, hammered and fitted for various uses, and taken down the river. Here are also manufactures of brushes, barrels, boots and shoes.

Tyringham, Mass.

Berkshire co. There are several ponds in this town, from which issues a branch of Housatonick river.

Tyringham lies 125 miles W. from Boston, 14 S. E. from Lenox, and 35 E. from Hudson, N. Y. Incorporated, 1762. Population, in 1837, 1,288.

The manufactures of the town consist of paper, iron castings, boots, shoes, leather, forks, rakes, palm-leaf hats, chair stuff, and wooden ware: annual value, about $35,000.

The surface of the town is uneven, and in some parts mountainous. "Hop Brook Valley," is a beautiful and romantic spot. There is a society of "Shakers" in Tyringham. See *Canterbury, N. H.*

Umbagog Lake,

Is a large body of water, situated mostly in the state of Maine, and extending about 300 rods in width along the east of the townships of Errol and Cambridge, in New Hampshire. This lake is very imperfectly known; is said to be about 18 miles long, and in some parts 10 wide; being but little inferior to the Winnepisiogee, in extent and beauty. Its outlet is on the west side, in Errol, its waters flowing into the Androscoggin.

Uncanoonook Mountain, N. H.

See *Goffstown*.

Underhill, Vt.

Chittenden co. The head branches of Brown's river water this town. The surface is hilly and broken, and the soil hard; but tolerable for sheep, of which a considerable number are reared.

Underhill was first settled in 1786. It lies 15 miles N. E. from Burlington, and 26 N. W. from Montpelier. Population, in 1830, 1,052.

Union River, Me.

Hancock co. The head waters of this river proceed within a few miles from the Passadumkeag. It flows south through the towns of Hampton, Amherst, and Mariaville: it meets the tide water at Ellsworth, and passes to the ocean by Blue Hill bay. This stream has numerous tributaries, the recipients of a great number of ponds, which are scattered over the interior parts of the county. This beautiful river is in some parts gentle and fertilizing, in other parts rapid, producing a valuable water power for mills. Its length, from Ellsworth, is between forty and fifty miles.

Union, Me.

Lincoln co. This pleasant and flourishing town is watered by Muscongus and St. George rivers, and by several beautiful ponds. The soil is fertile, and the surface generally swelling.

Union was incorporated in 1786. It is 28 miles S. E. from Augusta, and 7 N. by W. from Warren. Population, 1837, 1,750. Wheat crop, same year, 4,249 bushels.

Union, Ct.

Tolland co. The surface of Union is hilly, with a hard and unproductive soil. Mashapaug and Breakneck ponds, lying in this town, are the principal sources of Quinnebaug river. A branch of the Natchaug also rises here.

The town was incorporated in 1734. First settled, 1727. It is bounded W. by Stafford, and is 33 miles N. E. from Hartford, and 14 N. E. from Tolland. Population, 1830, 711.

Unity, Me.

Waldo co. This is a flourishing farming town, 33 miles N. E. from Augusta, 22 W. S. W. from Belfast, and bounded S. W. by Albion. It is well watered by a branch of Sebasticook river, which passes N. W., about 9 miles distant.

Unity was incorporated in 1804. Population, 1837, 1,520. Wheat crop, same year, 11,099 bushels.

Unity, N. H.

Sullivan co. This town is bounded N. by Claremont and Newport, E. by Goshen, S. by Lempster and Acworth, and W. by Charlestown. It is 43 miles W. by N. from Concord, and 9 S. from Newport.

Little Sugar river has its source in Whortleberry pond and Beaver meadow, in the N. part of the town, passes through its centre, and empties itself into the Connecticut at Charlestown. Cold pond, the head of Cold river, is partly in this town. From Gilman's pond, in the E. part of Unity, proceeds a branch of Sugar river, flowing through Newport. Perry's mountain is in the S. W. part, and partly in Charlestown.

Unity is an uneven township, but the soil is highly favorable for grazing. It is excellent for flax, few towns in the state producing a greater quantity.

Unity was granted in 1764. It was called Unity, from the happy termination of a dispute which had long subsisted between certain of the inhabitants of Kingston and Hampstead, claiming the same tract of land under two different grants.

The first settlement was made in 1769. Population, 1830, 1,258.

Upton, Mass.

Worcester co. Upton was taken from Mendon, Sutton and Hopkinton, in 1735. The surface of the town is plain land, and partly rough and hilly, with a strong soil capable of yielding good crops of grain and hay. Much attention has been paid to fruit trees in this town, and many fine orchards of various kinds of fruit have been the result. West river, a branch of the Blackstone, rises from a pond in Upton, and furnishes a power for a number of mills. The manufactures consist of woolen goods, boots, shoes, leather, straw bonnets, sashes and blinds: annual value, about $175,000.

This pleasant town lies 35 miles W. S. W. from Boston, and 15 S. E. from Worcester. Population, in 1830, 1,155; 1837, 1,451.

Uxbridge, Mass.

Worcester co. This very handsome and flourishing town lies 40 miles S. W. from Boston, 17 S. by E. from Worcester, and 24 N. N. W. from Providence, R. I. It receives an excellent water power from Mumford and West rivers, and the Blackstone canal passes through it.

The manufacturing villages are delightfully situated, in valleys surrounded by picturesque elevations. There are 5 woolen and 3 cotton mills in the town, and manufactures of yarn, straw bonnets, boots, shoes, leather, chairs, cabinet and tin wares: total value, the year ending April 1, 1837, $402,450.

Uxbridge was formerly a part of Mendon. It was incorporated in 1727. Population, 1830, 2,086; 1837, 2,246. Iron ore is found here, and an abundance of beautiful granite.

Vassalborough, Me.

Kennebec co. This is a large and flourishing town on the east side of Kennebec river, 12 miles N. by E. from Augusta. There are several large and beautiful ponds in the town, from which issue two excellent mill streams: one a branch of the Sebasticook, the other of the Kennebec.

This is a place of considerable interior trade, and business on the river. Vessels of considerable burthen pass to the ocean from Vassalborough, by means of the Kennebec Dam.

The valleys are very pleasant; and the surface and soil of the town varied and fertile. Vassalborough was incorporated in 1771. Population, 1837, 2,929. Wheat crop, same year, 10,272 bushels.

Vergennes, Vt.

Addison co. Vergennes was first settled in 1766. The territory, which comprises an area of 480 by 400 rods, was invested with city privileges in 1788. It lies 12 miles N. W. from Middlebury and 21 S. by E. from Burlington. Population, 1830, 999. Vergennes is beautifully located on Otter creek, at the falls on that stream, and is 7 miles from Lake Champlain. Otter creek, at this place, is about 500 feet wide, and, at the falls, is separated by two islands, which form 3 distinct falls, of 37 feet. These falls produce a great hydraulic power, rendered more valuable by being situated in the heart of a fertile country, and on the navigable waters of the lake.

The creek or river, between the city and the lake, is crooked, but navigable for the largest lake vessels. During the late war, this was an important depot on the lake. Here was fitted out the squadron commanded by the gallant McDonough, who met the British fleet off Plattsburgh, N. Y. on the 11th of September, 1814, and made it his.

This is a very favorable position for ship building: it now possesses important manufactories and considerable trade. Although the territory of this city is quite small, its peculiarly favorable location, and the enterprise of its people, warrant it a great degree of prosperity.

VERMONT.

The people of the territory now called the state of Vermont, having been connected with New York, and having experienced great dissatisfaction with their connexion with that state, assembled in convention and on the 15th of January, 1777, declared themselves independent, and organized a government for themselves.

The hardy mountaineers, who had become impatient under their connexion with and dependence on the great state of New York, in pursuance of their own peculiar views of the rights and duties of a free and independent people, adopted many singular and peculiar provisions in their constitution. Some of them are herein stated.

Their government consists of three parts; the legislative, the executive, and the judicial.

The Supreme Legislature consists of a Senate and House of Representatives, chosen annually by the freemen of the state, on the first Tuesday of September. The Senate consists of 30 members; each county being entitled to at least one, and the remainder to be apportioned according to population. The House of Representatives is composed of one member from each town. The Senators are to be thirty years of age; and the Lieutenant Governor is *ex-officio* President of the Senate. The body so chosen is called THE GENERAL ASSEMBLY OF THE STATE OF VERMONT. *The General Assembly* meets annually on the second Tuesday of October. They have power to choose their own officers, to meet on their own adjournments, to terminate their sessions at pleasure; to enact laws, grant charters, to impeach state criminals, &c. And, in conjunction with the council, they annually elect the Justices of the Supreme, County and Probate Courts; also the Sheriffs, High Bailiffs, Justices of the Peace, &c.; and, when occasion requires, they elect Majors and Brigadiers General. The General Assembly have full and ample legislative powers, but they cannot change the constitution.

The supreme executive power is vested in a Governor, Lieutenant Governor, and twelve Counsellors, chosen annually by the people on the first Tuesday of September. They meet at the same time with the General Assembly, prepare and lay before them the business apparently necessary; examine the laws in the progress of legislation, and approve or disapprove of them, and propose amendments. They cannot negative any act of the General Assembly, but can suspend the operation of any act till the next annual meeting of the Assembly. They commission all officers; sit as judges in all cases of impeachment; have power to grant pardons and remit fines in all cases, excepting in cases of murder and treason, in which cases they can grant reprieves till the next legislative session, and excepting also cases of impeachment. They may lay embargoes for thirty days, when the assembly is not in session.

The General Assembly, in joint meeting with the Governor and Council, annually elect the Judges, Justices of the Peace, Sheriffs, High Bailiffs, &c.

The Governor is Captain-General, but he cannot command in person, unless by advice of his council. The Lieutenant Governor is Lieutenant General of the forces.

The judicial power is vested in a Supreme Court and Court of Chancery, a County Court in each county, consisting of one of the Justices of the Supreme Court, and two Assistant Justices; a Probate Court in each District; and Justices of the Peace, who have a limited criminal and civil jurisdiction.

The Judges of Probate appoint their own Registers, and the Sheriffs and High Bailiffs appoint their own deputies.

The several Town Clerks are Registers of deeds of conveyance of lands in their respective towns; and if there be no town clerk, the deeds shall be recorded in the County Clerk's office.

A council of 13 Censors is chosen by the people once in 7 years, on the

NEW ENGLAND GAZETTEER.

last Wednesday of March, and meet on the first Wednesday of June following. Their duties are, to inquire if the constitution has been violated; if the legislature, &c. have performed their duty; if the taxes have been justly levied and collected; and if the laws have been obeyed. They may pass public censures; order impeachments; recommend the repeal of laws; propose amendments in the constitution, and call conventions to act on them. Their power expires in one year after their election.

Succession of Governors.

Thomas Chittenden, 1791—1796. Isaac Tichenor, 1797—1806. Israel Smith, 1807. Isaac Tichenor, 1808. Jonas Galusha, 1809—1812. M. Chittenden, 1813, 1814. Jonas Galusha, 1815—1819. Richard Skinner, 1820—1822. C. P. Van Ness, 1823—1825. Ezra Butler, 1826, 1827. Samuel C. Crafts, 1828—1830, William A. Palmer, 1831—1835. Silas H. Jenison, 1836—

Succession of Chief Justices.

Samuel Knight, 1791—1793. Isaac Tichenor 1794, 1795. Nathaniel Chipman, 1796. Israel Smith, 1797. Enoch Woodbridge, 1798—1800. Jonathan Robinson, 1801—1806. Royal Tyler, 1807—1812. Nathaniel Chipman, 1813, 1814. Asa Aldis, 1815. Richard Skinner, 1816. Dudley Chase, 1817—1820. C. P. Van Ness, 1821, 1822. Richard Skinner, 1823—1828. Samuel Prentiss, 1829. Titus Hutchinson, 1830—1833, Charles K. Williams, 1834—

The state is bounded N. by Lower Canada, E. by Connecticut river, S. by Massachusetts, and W. by New York. Situated between 42° 44′ and 45°N. Latitude, and 73° 16′ and 71° 20′ W. Longitude.

Vermont is divided into 14 counties, to wit: Bennington, Windham, Rutland, Windsor, Addison, Orange, Chittenden, Washington, Caledonia, Franklin, Orleans, Lamoille, Essex and Grand Isle. The population of the state in 1790, was 85,539; 1800, 154,465; 1810, 217,895; 1820, 235,764; 1830, 280,657. This state contains an area of about 10,212 square miles. Population to a square mile, in 1830, was $27\frac{4}{10}$. The number of sheep in the state, in 1837, was 1,099,011.

The important enterprise of a rail road from Boston to the outlet of the great lakes, on St. Lawrence river, will doubtless be accomplished. An enterprise of this kind, well worthy the consideration of the intelligent citizens and capitalists of Massachusetts, New Hampshire and Vermont, will greatly benefit those states, and make the capital of New England a powerful competitor with New York, for a large portion of the immense northern and western trade.

NEW ENGLAND GAZETTEER.

Although this fourteenth state was not admitted into the union until after the revolutionary contest was over, yet she vigorously resisted British oppression. A range of mountains covered with spruce, hemlock and other evergreens divides this state nearly in its centre; hence its name; and hence the epithet "Green Mountain Boys," celebrated for their bravery in the war of independence.

From these mountains many rivers take their rise; the most important are, Otter Creek, Onion, Lamoille and Missisque, which empty into Lake Champlain, on the west; and West, White and Passumpsic, which pass to the Connecticut on the east. This state is very fertile and produces all sorts of grain in great abundance. Cattle of various kinds are raised here with great facility. Wool is an important staple. Manufactures flourish on many of the delightful streams of Vermont, and its hills produce marble, granite and iron ore of superior excellence. The scenery of this state is very romantic and beautiful; the air is pure and healthful; the people industrious, intelligent, hospitable.

The trade of this state, on the west, passes to New York by lake Champlain, the northern canal and Hudson river; that on the east, to Connecticut river. Some of the trade of this state reaches Boston, and some goes to Montreal. See *Register*.

Vernon, Vt.

Windham co. Vernon lies on the west side of Connecticut river, opposite to Winchester, N. H. That river bends abruptly at this place, but in consequence of its elevated and rocky shore, affords this town but litle intervale land. The surface is generally mountainous, rocky and unproductive. There are in the town, fine forests of oak and chesnut timber, and quarries of slate. Vernon was settled at an early period, and for many years was subject to Indian depredations. The remains of an old fort built in 1740, are now seen: many persons were killed and carried into captivity; among the latter was the celebrated Mrs. Howe. From its settlement until 1802, Vernon was called Hinsdale.

Vernon is 18 miles S. E. from Newfane, and is bounded S. by Brattleborough. Population, 1830, 681.

Vernon, Ct.

Tolland co. This town lies 12 miles E. N. E. from Hartford, and 7 S. W. from Tolland. Rock village, and Tankerooson are pleasant and flourishing manufacturing villages, containing 18 cotton and woolen mills. The former is 14, the latter 10 miles from Hartford. The Hockanum, and a branch of that river, the Tankerooson, are the principal streams.

Vernon was first settled in 1716. It was a part of East Windsor and

Bolton until 1808. The surface of the town is varied by hills and valleys; the soil is a gravelly loam and sandy, but good for grain and grass. Population, 1830, 1,164.

Vershire, Vt.

Orange co. The surface of this town is uneven and stony, but furnishes pasturage for a large number of sheep, horses and neat cattle. Branches of Ompomponoosuc river rise here, but give the town no valuable water power. Vershire was first settled in 1780. It lies 25 miles S. E. from Montpelier, 35 N. from Windsor, and 6 E. by S. from Chelsea. Population, 1830, 1,260.

Victory, Vt.

Essex co. This township was chartered in 1781. Moose river, a branch of the Passumpsic, passes through it. It lies 10 miles W. from Guildhall, and, in 1830, had 53 inhabitants.

Vienna, Me.

Franklin co. A branch of Sandy river and several ponds water this fertile and pleasant town. It lies 25 miles N. W. from Augusta, and 10 S. E. from Farmington. Incorporated, 1802. Population, 1837, 793. Wheat crop, same year, 4,068 bushels.

Vinalhaven, Me.

Waldo co. Previous to 1838, this town was attached to the county of Hancock. It is situated 12 miles S. E. from Camden, 6 E. from Owl's Head, and is formed of the *Fox Islands*, at the mouth of Penobscot bay, about fifty miles below Bangor. There are three islands of considerable size, belonging to this group, besides several smaller islands on their coast. This island town possesses in an eminent degree all those advantages to be derived from a bold shore and good harbors, in the centre of an extensive maritime commerce, and of the domestic fishery. These privileges are well improved by the inhabitants of Fox Islands: they also make their soil tributary to their wants. In 1837, their crop of wheat was 1,611 bushels. So long as the *sea* island towns of Mount Desert, Eden and Vinalhaven, afford wheat, and Truro, wool, in such abundance; there seems, at present, no great cause for the Yankees going west to escape either nakedness or starvation. These islands are finely located for summer excursions, either for health or pleasure. The passages between the principal islands, are delightful; and the scenery around them beautiful. Population, 1837, 1,768.

Vineyard, Vt.

Grand Isle co. This town, comprising an island in Champlain Lake, covering an area of 4,620 acres, was chartered in 1799, by the name of *Isle La Motte*. Its name was changed to Vineyard in 1802. It lies about 4 miles W. from North Hero, and was first settled in 1785. It is a very pleasant island, fertile, and abounding in excellent cedar and limestone. Pop. 1830, 459.

Vineyard Sound, Mass.

This is a great thoroughfare for vessels bound along the coast between Cape Cod and the mouth of Buzzard's bay. It lies between the island of Martha's Vineyard and the islands of Nashawn and Nashawenna. The tides in this Sound are rapid, and the passage dangerous, without a good pilot.

Voluntown, Ct.

Windham co. This town was incorporated in 1719. It derived its name from the circumstance that most of its territory was granted, in 1696, to *Volunteers* in the Narraganset war. The surface is, in some parts, hilly; but the prevailing character of the surface and soil is a sandy and gravelly loam.

Voluntown is 14 miles E. from Norwich, and is bounded by Rhode Island on the east, and North Stonington on the south. Population, in 1830, 1,304. The town is watered by Wood river, a branch of the Pawcatuck, on which are one woolen and two cotton mills.

Wachusett Mountain, Mass.

Worcester co. See *Princeton*.

Wait's River, Vt.

Orange co. Branches of this river rise in Orange, Topsham, and Washington; they meet at Bradford, and fall into the Connecticut. This river, and the streams that compose it, are rather rapid in their course, and furnish many valuable mill privileges. Below the falls, in Bradford, this river is more gentle, and in its course it fertilizes a tract of intervale. Its longest branch is about 20 miles. Its mouth, on the Connecticut, is about 100 feet in width.

Waitsfield, Vt.

Washington co. Mad river, a small, rapid stream, passes circuitously through this town, fertilizing the soil, and affording it good mill seats. The uplands are a deep loam, fertile, and productive of all the varieties of a northern climate. Here are fine pastures, and between 5,000 and 6,000 sheep.

There are some manufactures in the town, but the people are generally farmers, and make a good business of it. Good clay for making earthern ware, iron ore, and rock crystal are found here. This town lies 11 miles S. W. from Montpelier, and 30 S. E. from Burlington. Population, 1830, 985.

The settlement of Waitsfield was commenced in 1789, by General BENJAMIN WAIT, from Sudbury, Massachusetts. General Wait entered the service of his country at the age of 18, and performed much difficult service with great bravery and success. At the age of 25 he had been engaged in forty battles and skirmishes: his clothes were several times perforated with musket balls, but he never received a wound. In 1776, he entered the revolutionary army as captain, and acquired the rank of colonel. After the war, he was made a brigadier general of militia, and was high sheriff of the county of Windsor seven years. General Wait, having lived to see the town he had planted in its wilderness state, covered with fruitful fields, and peopled by independent yeomen, died in 1822, aged 86 years.

Wakefield, N. H.

Strafford co. This town lies 50 miles N. E. from Concord, and 30 N. by W. from Dover; bounded N. W. by Ossipee and Effingham, E. by Maine, S. E. by Milton, W. by Middleton and Brookfield.

Lovewell's pond, in the S. part of the town, is about 700 rods long, 275 wide. Province pond lies between Wakefield and Effingham, and is 450 rods long, 400 wide. Pine river pond is the source of the river of that name flowing N. W. into Ossipee lake. The principal branch of the Piscataqua has its rise in East pond, between Wakefield and Newfield, Maine. The soil of this town is generally good.

The town was formerly called *East-town*, and was incorporated in 1774, by its present name.

There are several cotton mills in this town, and various other manufactures.

Lovewell's pond, in this town, derived its name from Captain John Lovewell, of Dunstable, who, on the 20th February, 1725, surprised and destroyed a party of Indians encamped on the side of the pond. Robert Macklin, distinguished for longevity, died here in 1787, at the age of 115. He was born in Scotland. Population, 1830, 1,470.

Walden, Vt.

Caledonia co. This is an elevated township between the head waters of Onion and Lamoille rivers. Cole's pond, a large sheet of water, lying in the town, produces a small mill stream, called "Joe's Brook." The surface is generally rough, but the soil in some parts of the town produces good crops. Walden was first settled in 1789. It lies 22 miles N. N. E. from Montpelier, and is bounded S. E. by Danville. Population, 1830, 827.

Waldo County, Me.

Belfast is the shire town. This maritime and agricultural county is bounded N. by Penobscot and Piscataquis counties; E. by Penobscot bay and river; S. by Lincoln county, and W. by the county of Kennebec. It contains an area of about 812 square miles. Its population in 1830, was 29,290; and in 1837, 36,817.

On the eastern side of the county, the noble Penobscot spreads its broad bay and river, embosoming Belfast and other beautiful bays, and indented with numerous capacious harbors, affording this county every desirable facility for navigation and the fisheries. The relative position of this county with the great basin of the Penobscot, is such as to give to it a large share of the commerce of that fertile and rapidly increasing section of New England.

Waldo county possesses within itself great resources of agricultural wealth. The surface is generally undulating: no portion of the county is too elevated or too low for cultivation. It is heavily timbered and abounds in limestone, of which large quantities are annually manufactured and transported. The soil is fertile, and congenial to the growth of every northern staple commodity. This county is interspersed with excellent mill streams, and its numerous ponds give it a varied and picturesque appearance.

Waldo county was, as it were but yesterday, a desert; at present not more than two-thirds of its territory may be said to be settled. In 1837, it produced 109,140 bushels of wheat, and contained 55,000 sheep, with a population of 45 to a square mile.

Waldo, Me.

Waldo co. This is a *Plantation*, but it is high time it was incorporated with town privileges, for its surface is pleasant, and its soil fertile: it abounds with mill sites, and its increase of population, for the last seven years, was 35 per cent. Waldo is 44 miles E. N. E. from Augusta, and 7 W. N. W. from Belfast. Population, 1837, 718. Wheat crop, same year, 1,903 bushels.

Waldoborough, Me.

Lincoln co. This is a large, pleasant, and flourishing commercial town; a port of entry, situated on both sides of Muscongus river, and at the head of navigation on Muscongus bay.

This town, surrounded by a fertile country, enjoying navigable accommodations, a great water power, and peopled by an enterprising and industrious class of agriculturalists, mechanics and sailors, cannot fail of advancing in wealth and population. The tonnage of this district, in 1837, was 39,960 tons.

The surface of the town is agreeably diversified; the soil of a quality just hard enough to promote a proper circulation of the blood of its cultivators, with air and water as pleasant, as pure, and as favorable to health and longevity, as those of any prairie, of which we have any account, west of the Alleghany mountains. It is true that these people have to encounter the dangers of the seas, in the navigation of their numerous vessels engaged in foreign and domestic commerce; to accidents attendant on launching their trig ships, brigs, and schooners, and in preparing various kinds of lumber for their cargoes; and that they sometimes get drowned in crossing their rapid streams, and break their limbs by riding too fast on their wintry snows; yet they are perfectly satisfied with their location and condition, and have no hankering for the balmy breezes of the south, nor thirst for the sweet waters of the west.

Waldoborough is an ancient town for this section of country: it was incorporated in 1773. It lies 37 miles S. E. from Augusta, and 22 E. N. E. from Wiscasset. Population, 1820, 2,449; 1830, 3,113; 1837, 3,420.

Wales, Me.

Lincoln Co. There is a beautiful pond lying partly in Wales and partly in Lisbon; its outlet meets the Androscoggin a few miles above Topsham. Wales is an agricultural town of good soil and even surface, 20 miles S. W. from Augusta, and 26 N. W. from Wiscasset. Incorporated, 1816. Population, 1837, 667. Wheat crop, same year, 2,232 bushels.

Wales, Mass.

Hampden co. This town is watered by a branch of Quinnebaug river, and has a considerable water power. The surface of the town is uneven, but the soil affords good pasturage. Here is a woolen mill, and manufactures of leather, boots, shoes, axes, hatchets, palm-leaf hats, &c.: annual value, about $70,000. Wales is 67 miles W. S. W. from Boston, and 17 E. by S. from Springfield. Population, 1837, 738.

Wallingford, Vt.

Rutland co. This town is watered by Otter creek, Mill river, and by three ponds, one of which, Hiram's pond, covering an area of 350 acres, lies on very elevated ground, and is one of the principal sources of Otter creek. The other ponds are of less size, and less elevated. These mountain ponds are very handsome, and contain fish. The soil of the town is generally good: that on the banks of Otter creek, is very fertile and productive. Wallingford produces all the varieties of grain, grass, &c., and feeds a large number of sheep.

" A range of primitive limestone passes through the western part of the township, in which have been opened several quarries of excellent marble. Green hill, situated near the centre, is composed almost entirely of quartz. A part of White rocks, belonging to the Green Mountain range, appears to be granite, the rest quartz. At the foot of White rocks, are large cavities formed by the fallen rocks, called the *icebeds*, in which ice is found in abundance through the summer season." There are some valuable manufacturing establishments in the town, and a flourishing trade. The village is pleasantly located on the banks of Otter creek, near one of the ponds. It contains some handsome buildings, and presents a variety of picturesque scenery. Wallingford was first settled in 1773. It lies 10 miles S. by E. from Rutland and 42 N. N. E. from Bennington. Population, 1830, 1740.

Wallingford, Ct.

New Haven co. " Wallingford is bounded N. by Meriden, W. by Cheshire, E. by Durham and Middletown, and S. by North Bradford and North Haven. Its length from east to west is nearly 7 miles, and its breadth about 6. The central part of Wallingford is 13 miles N. from New Haven, 23 S. from Hartford, and between 11 and 12 miles S. W. from Middletown. The prevailing surface is pleasantly diversified with moderate hills and dales; the eastern extremity of the township is mountainous. The soil is generally excellent, excepting a tract called Wallingford plain, consisting of coarse sand, situated on the eastern bank of the Quinnipiac. It is nearly 4 miles in length, and about ¾ of a mile in breadth. It is the most extensive tract of level land in the state, and one of the most sterile and barren. The town is watered by the Quinnipiac, a valuable mill stream, which passes through the extent of the town, upon which are several mills and manufactories. Yaleville is a little manufacturing village in the northern section of the town, where britannia and tin ware is manufactured to some extent. There is an establishment westward of the main street, on the Quinnipiac, for the manufacture of wood screws, of which there are about 1,000 groce manufactured daily. The principal village of Wallingford is beautifully situated on a fine elevation upwards of a mile east of the river, on two parallel streets extending along the ridge of the hill. The western street, on which the principal part of the village is situated, is upwards of a mile in length."

Wallingford originally belonged to New Haven, and was called New Haven Village. It was first settled about the year 1669. Population, 1830, 2,418.

Walloostook River, Me.

This is the western or main branch of St. John's river. Its head waters are in the counties of Somerset and Franklin, and on the border of Canada. It receives the waters of many lakes, ponds and rivers, and drains a large section of wilderness country. This river is called the Walloostook until it meets the waters of the St. Francois. The lands on the borders of this river are said to be fertile and heavily timbered. See St. John's river under *Fundy, Bay.*

Waloomsack River, Vt.

This good mill stream is formed in Bennington, by several branches: it passes N. W. and joins the Hoosack. Between the Waloomsack and Hoosack the famous "Bennington Battle" was fought.

Walpole, N. H.

Cheshire co. This place lies 60 miles S. W. by W. from Concord, 13 N. W. from Keene, and 90 N. W. from Boston. Population in 1830, 1,979. The face of this town is beautifully diversified by hills and vales. The soil is similar to that of other towns on Connecticut river. The intervales afford excellent tillage; the uplands are inferior to none in the state. Cold river passes through the north part, and forms a junction with the Connecticut. There is a lofty hill, called Fall Mountain, a part of the range of Mount Toby; the highest parts of which are about 750 feet above the level of the river. The village of Walpole is situated at the foot of this hill, on a plain; the margin of the intervales. The principal street runs N. and S. and is bordered on both sides with dwelling houses, stores and shops.

Drewsville, in this town, is a pleasant village, romantically situated near the falls: it is a place of some trade, and considerable manufactures.

Bellows Falls, on Connecticut river, separates this town from Rockingham, Vt. At the bridge, which crosses the river at this place, built in 1785, and 365 feet in length, the traveller is presented with a most interesting and sublime view. The river here is compressed into a narrow strait, between steep rocks, and for nearly a quarter of a mile is hurried on with great rapidity and loud roaring. In no place is the fall perpendicular, to any considerable extent; but in the distance of half a mile the waters descend 42 feet. A canal, with 9 locks, passes round these falls on the west side.

Col. Benjamin Bellows was one of the first settlers of this town, in 1749. He was a man of great enterprise and bravery. His descendants are numerous and highly respectable.

Bellows' Falls village, is in Rockingham, Vt., opposite to Drewsville.

Walpole, Mass.

Norfolk co. This town is finely watered by three branches of the Neponset which meet at this place. The face of the town is rough, but capable of producing good crops.

There are three cotton, two woolen and two paper mills in the town, and manufactures of iron castings, hoes, hats, leather, straw bonnets, and twine: total value, the year ending April 1, 1837, $240,364. This pleasant and flourishing town was taken from Dedham in 1724. Population, 1837, 1,592. It is 20 miles S. W. from Boston, 10 S. W. from Dedham, and 21 N. by W. from Providence, R. I.

Waltham, Me.

Hancock co. Population, 1837, 207. Wheat crop, same year, 356 bushels. See "Down East."

Waltham, Vt.

Addison co. Buck mountain lies near the centre of this town, and as it is the highest land in the county, west of the Green mountains, its summit exhibits a good view of a delightful section of country.

Waltham lies on the east side of Otter Creek, which separates it from Panton. Otter Creek, at this place, is sluggish in its course, and affords no mill privileges. The soil is generally good; that along the stream is excellent. The number of sheep in Waltham, in 1837, was 3,890. Population, 1830, 330. It is 9 miles N. W. from Middlebury, and 24 S. from Burlington.

Waltham, Mass.

Middlesex co. This is one of the many beautiful towns which environ the capitol of New England. It is 10 miles W. by N. from Boston, and 9 S E. from Concord. It was incorporated in 1737. Population, 1830, 1,859; 1837, 2,287.

The surface is moderately level, with some elevations. "Prospect Hill," 470 feet above the level of the sea, presents a delightful view of Boston, its harbor, and the adjacent towns and country. The soil is generally not very fertile, but is rendered productive by industry. "Waltham Plain" is a beautiful tract of land, under a high state of cultivation. It is about two and a half miles in length, and a mile in width. On the road over this plain is a continuous village, containing many handsome dwellings and beautiful gardens; among the number, that of the Hon. Theodore Lyman is pre-eminently beautiful. Mr. Lyman's garden, of many acres in extent, decorated with almost every variety of fruit tree, shrub and flower, both native and exotic, is probably unsurpassed, in costliness and splendor, by any private establishment of the kind in the United States.

In this town the first cotton mill, on an extensive scale, was erected, in 1814. The capital of the company was $600,000. By extraordinary skill and good management, through all the various commercial changes, this establishment proved lucrative to the proprietors and highly beneficial to the public. The waters of Charles river, which glide through the town, being fully improved, the proprietors extended their manufacturing operations at Lowell.

There are in Waltham three cotton mills, a bleachery, a machine shop, a paper mill, and manufactures of boots, shoes, hats, carriages, wagons, chairs, cabinet and tin wares: total value, the year ending April 1, 1837, $348,067. The roads in this and the neighboring towns, are uncommonly excellent. Perhaps in no section of country in the world, are the roads better than within 10 miles of Boston.

Wardsborough, Vt.

Windham co. This town is 15 miles N. W. from Brattleborough, 20 N. E. from Bennington, and 10 N. W. from Newfane. It was first settled in 1780. Population, 1830, 1,148.

The surface of the town is hilly, and in some parts rocky: the soil is hard, but rendered productive by the industry of its people. Wardsborough is watered by West river, and contains a number of minerals, of which tremolite and zoisite are the most important, and of which fine specimens are found. There are some mills in the town, but the water power is not extensive.

Ware River, Mass.

Branches of this large and powerful mill stream rise in Hubbardston, Barre and Oakham. It passes through Hardwick, New Braintree and Ware, and joins the Chickopee at Palmer.

Ware, Mass.

Hampshire co. Ware possesses an admirable water power by Ware and Swift rivers. The surface of the town is rough and hilly, and the soil more fit for grazing than tillage. In 1837, there were 1,380 sheep in the town: value of wool, $1,667. Ware is 66 miles W. by S. from Boston, 22 E. by S. from Northampton, and 23 N. E. from Springfield. Incorporated, 1761. Population, 1830, 2,045; 1837, 2,403.

Ware contains a beautiful village which commands an active and flourishing trade. There are two cotton and two woolen mills in the town, and manufactures of boots, shoes, leather, hats, tin ware, straw bonnets, palm-leaf hats, augers, sheet iron, starch, carriages, harnesses, and boxes: total value, the year ending April 1, 1837, $645,121.

Wareham, Mass.

Plymouth co. The surface of this town is generally level, with a light, sandy soil, not very productive. It is favorably situated for manufacturing purposes, being watered by two fine mill streams, and for ship building, the fishery, and foreign and domestic commerce, having a number of good harbors at the head of Buzzard's bay.

Wareham lies 50 miles S. S. E. from Boston, 16 S. from Plymouth, and 15 E. N. E. from New Bedford. It was incorporated in 1739. Population, 1830, 1,885; 1837, 2,166.

There are in this town six nail factories, six air and cupola furnaces, two rolling mills, 2 cotton mills, a paper mill, and manufactures of vessels, salt, nail casks, chairs, cabinet ware, leather, boots, shoes, &c.: the total value of these manufactures, the year ending April 1, 1837, was $1,260,637. The number of hands employed in these manufactures, was 682. One whale ship, of 374 tons, belongs to this place: the cargo of oil, in 1837, amounted to $78,286.

In 1836, there arrived and cleared at Wareham, 2 ships, 7 brigs, 86 schooners, and 193 sloops: aggregate tonnage, 20,140 tons. During that year there were exported from this place 7,107 tons of nails, 421 tons of iron hoops, 1,969 tons of hollow ware, 144 tons of iron castings, 98 tons of nail rods, 386 dozen of shovels, and 4,180 bushels of salt. The number of tons of manufactured iron, exported that year, was 9,765.

Warner, N. H.

Merrimack co. This town is bound N. by Sutton and Salisbury, E. by Boscawen, S. by Hopkinton and Henniker, and W. by Bradford. The distance of Warner from Hopkinton is 8 miles, and from Concord, 15. It is watered by Warner river, a handsome stream, which rises in the Sunapee mountain in Newbury. It passes through Bradford, enters Warner at the N. W. corner, and running in an E. and S. E. direction, divides the town into nearly two equal parts, and falls into Contoocook river in Hopkinton. The lands, though broken, have, in general a good soil. Mink hills lie in the W. part, and furnish fine orchards and good pasturage. There are four ponds, viz: Tom, Bear, Bagley and Pleasant ponds. Pleasant pond, the waters of which are clear and cold, deep, and of a greenish cast, has no visible outlet or inlet, and overflows its banks in the driest seasons.

This town was granted in 1735, by the general court of Massachusetts, to Dea. Thomas Stevens and others. It was incorporated in 1774, by the name of Warner. The first settlement was made in 1762, by David Annis and his son-in-law, Reuben Kimball, whose son Daniel was the first child born in town. Population, 1830, 2,221.

The following account of a terrible tornado, in this section of country, is by the Rev. John Woods, published in Professor Silliman's Journal, Vol. XXXV.—No. 2.—January, 1839.

Mr. Woods says, "The event occurred about half past 5 o'clock, Sunday evening, September 9th, 1821. The wind, I suppose, was a proper whirlwind, precisely such as occasion water-spouts at sea. A very intelligent woman in Warner, who, at a distance of two or three miles, observed its progress, compared its appearance to a tin trumpet, the small end downward, also to a great elephant's trunk let down out of heaven, and moving majestically along. She remarked, that its appearance and motion gave her a strong impression of life. When it had reached the easterly part of the town, she said the lower end appeared to be taken up from the earth, and to bend around in a serpentine form, until it passed behind a black cloud and disappeared. Its course was southeasterly. It was attended with but little rain in some parts of its course, more in others. The rain, or what appeared like it, was in my opinion taken from bodies of water which it passed over. It was said, that it lowered the water in a small pond in Warner, about three feet. To people near Sunapee lake, in New London, I was told, it appeared as if the lake was rushing up towards heaven. The appearance of the cloud to beholders at a little distance, was awfully terrific. It commenced its desolating progress east of Grantham mountain, in Croydon. In Wendell, beside other buildings, it demolished a dwelling house, and carried a child who was asleep upon a bed, into Sunapee lake. In New London and Sutton it did considerable damage, but met with few dwelling houses and destroyed no lives. From Sutton it passed over the southwest branch or spur of Kearsarge mountain, with a gore of land belonging to Warner, called Kearsarge gore. At the foot of this mountain, it entirely demolished five barns, unroofed another, and utterly destroyed two dwelling houses and so rent another as to render it irreparable.

"The houses wholly destroyed belonged to two brothers, Robert and Daniel Savary. They contained fourteen persons. In the house of the latter were their aged parents, seventy years old, I should think, or upwards. The old gentlemen, as he saw the cloud coming, went into a chamber to close a window, and was there when the wind struck the house. He was carried four or five rods, dashed upon the rock, and instantly killed.

A part of his brain was left upon the rock where he fell. His wife was very badly wounded, and it was thought would not recover. A child of Daniel Savary, in the same house, was also killed. In the house of Robert Savary, several were much wounded and bruised, but no lives lost. The houses and barns and other buildings at this place were not only levelled with the foundation, but the materials and contents were dashed in ten thousand pieces, and scattered in every direction. Carts, wagons, sleighs, ploughs, and sleds which were new and strong, (one ox-sled, I recollect, was entirely new,) were carried to a considerable distance—from twenty to sixty rods—and so broken and shattered as to be fit only for fuel. Stone walls were levelled, and rocks, weighing two, three, or four hundred pounds, were turned out of their beds, apparently by the bare force of the wind. Large logs, also, two feet or more in diameter, which were bedded into the ground, and were fifty or sixty feet long, were not sufficiently weighty to retain their location. In one instance I recollect to have seen one large log lying upon another in such a condition, that it was thought by good judges, that ten yoke of oxen could not have moved the lower one from its bed; but both were removed by the wind several feet. An elm tree near where old Mr. Savary fell, which was one foot at least in diameter, and too strongly rooted to yield, was twisted like a withe to the ground, and lay prostrate across the path like a wilted weed. Not an apple or forest tree was left standing. One barn was seen to be taken up whole, with its contents of hay, grain, &c. After being carried several rods, it came to pieces, and flew like feathers in every direction.

From the neighborhood of the Savarys, it passed over another spur of the mountain, and fell with great violence on the buildings of Peter Flanders and Joseph True. Their houses, which were but a few rods distant, one in Warner, the other in Salisbury, were utterly demolished. In Mr. F.'s house were nine persons, two of whom were instantly killed. Mr. F. and wife were very badly wounded, but at length recovered. In Mr. T.'s house were 7, all of whom were most wonderfully preserved, except that 2 children, 10 or 12 years old, were badly burnt by hot bricks, the oven having been heated and the bread then in it; one of whom lingered several weeks in extreme suffering and then died. The father and mother of Mrs. T., who lived about half a mile distant, were visiting there. They had just left the tea table. Mr. T. and his father-in-law went out at the door and saw the cloud, but thought at first they were so under the hill it would pass harmless over them. But they were soon convinced that its track was marked with desolation. Mr. T. just gave an alarm to his family, then ran under the end of his shop, which happened to stand beyond the violence of the wind so as not to be demolished. His father-in-law, (Jones,) stood his ground until the wind struck the barn, a few rods to the northwest of him, and he saw the fragments of it flying thick in the air over his head. He then threw himself flat upon the ground by a heavy pile of wood. Instantly a rafter fell endwise close by him, entering the ground a foot or two in depth, and immediately a beam grazed down upon the rafter and lay at his feet. He and Mr. T. were entirely unharmed. In a moment they saw, instead of a new and strong and very comfortable dwelling house, a perfect desolation. Not even a sill remained upon its foundation. Even the cellar stairs, and the hearths, which were of tile or brick eight inches square, were taken up and removed. The bricks of the chimney lay scattered along, partly covering Mrs. T., and covering to a considerable depth two of the children. Mrs. T. was soon taken up with but little injury. The shrieks and cries of the two children, under a weight of hot bricks, next pierced the heart of their father. In removing them, he burnt his hands to the bone. They were at length taken out alive, but in a state of great suffering, one of whom, as I have mentioned, after a few weeks, died. All were now found but the babe, about one year old. Supposing it to be under the bricks, Mr. T. renewed his labor; but soon it was heard to cry in the direction of the wind. Such as could run, ran in search of it, and soon found it lying safe upon the ground beneath a sleigh bottom, 10 or 15 rods from where the house had stood. When the wind came, the sleigh was in the barn, six or eight rods north or northwesterly from the house. The two last mentioned houses were one story, well built, and well furnished dwellings. Their materials were not merely separated, but broken, splintered, reduced to kindling wood, and scattered like the chaff of the summer thrashing floors. It was the same with furniture, beds, bedding, bureaus, chairs, tables, and the like. A loom was, to appearance, carried whole about forty rods, and then dashed in pieces. The width of the desolation here was about twenty or twenty-five rods. On the higher grounds over which it passed it was forty, fifty, or sixty rods. The deeper the valley, the narrower and *more violent* was the current. From the last mentioned neighborhood it passed on to the east part of Warner, but met with no other dwelling houses, and did but little damage, except to fences and forests. The appearance of the ground where it passed, was as if a mighty torrent had swept over it, up hill as well as down. Near the boundary, between Warner and Boscawen, the desolation ceased. It was taken up from the earth, but spruce floor boards, which were taken from New London, were borne upon its bosom and dropped in the Shaker village in Canterbury, a distance of about thirty miles. In following its track in Kearsarge gore, I came to a considerable stream of water, across which had been a bridge, covered with large oak logs, split in the middle, instead of planks. These half logs were scattered in every direction, some carried, I should think, ten rods in the direction from which the wind came, others sixty rods in the direction it went, and others were dropped near the margin at the right and left.

One remarkable fact is, that the same day, and about the same time in the day, two other similar whirlwinds were experienced, which moved in nearly parallel lines, one passing through Warwick, Mass., and the other about the same distance to the northeast."

Warren, Me.

One of the county towns of Lincoln county. This town is situated on both sides of St. Georges' river, at the head of the tide waters, and is bounded N. by Union, S. by Campden and Thomaston, S. by Cushing, and W. by Waldoborough. Incorporated, 1776. Population, 1830, 2,030; 1837, 2,143. It is 34 miles S. E. from Augusta.

The location of this town is very favorable for manufactures and navigation. The lumber business is not so large as formerly, yet considerable quantities are now sawed and shipped. Ship building is an important branch of business, and the manufacture of lime, from a superior quality of limestone, with which this section of country abounds, is carried on extensively, and is annually increasing. The village is well located and pleasant: it contains a well conducted academy or high school, for youth of both sexes; in which all the languages and other branches of education may be obtained, and such as are necessary to prepare them for future usefulness in society.

Warren, N. H.

Grafton co. This town is 10 miles S. E. from Haverhill corner, and 63 N. by W. from Concord. It is watered by the N. branch of Baker's river, which has its source on the E. side of Moosehillock mountain. It passes in a N. direction to Wentworth, and, near the S. line of Warren, furnishes several valuable mill seats. The S. E. part presents a mountainous aspect, having a large portion of Carr's mountain on its southeastern border. Warren was granted by charter, in 1763. Population, in 1830, 702.

Warren, Vt.

Washington co. This town was first settled about the year 1797, by Samuel Lard and Seth Leavitt. It lies 16 miles S. W. from Montpelier, and 31 S. E. from Burlington. Population, 1830, 766. This town is watered by Mad river, and although between the two Green mountain ranges, the surface is not much broken; it has some good mill sites, and some mechanical operations by water. Many cattle are reared in the town, and about 4,000 sheep are kept.

Warren, Mass.

Worcester co. This town was called Western from 1741 to 1834. It lies 60 miles W. by S. from Boston, and 23 W. S. W from Worcester. Population, 1837, 1,196. It is watered by Chickopee river, and contains one cotton and two woolen mills, a scythe factory and manufactures of palm-leaf hats. The value of goods annually made in the town, is about $75,000. A large portion of the lands in Warren are uneven and hilly, but the soil is warm, and favorable to the growth of grain, and the support of sheep, of which 1,110 were kept in 1837. The village is quite pleasant.

Warren, R. I.

Bristol co. This small town, comprising an area of only about 2,600 acres, is situated on the E. side of Narraganset bay, and is bounded N. and W. by Palmer or Warren river, E. by Massachusetts, and S. by Bristol. It is 11 miles S. E. from Providence, and 19 N. by E. from Newport. Incorporated, 1746. Population, 1830, 1,800.

The surface of Warren is undulating, with a soil of rich mould, very fertile and productive. Great attention is paid in this place to agriculture, and particularly to horticulture; and all the varieties of fruits and culinary vegetables are produced in abundance and perfection. Warren has a safe and commodious harbor for vessels of 300 tons burthen: a number of vessels are owned here, engaged in foreign commerce, the coasting trade and fishery. Ship building has been pursued here to a great extent, and some vessels are now built, but not so many as formerly. This place has produced a great number of excellent sailors and ship masters, as well as ship builders.

The village is delightfully situated on a rise of ground fronting the harbor: it is neatly built, and is surrounded by a variety of interesting scenery. This town is noted for the healthiness of its climate, and the longevity of its inhabitants. In 1834, there were only 19 deaths in the town, and the average age of 7 of those was 85 years. Warren is a fine resort in summer, and is much frequented.

Warren, Ct.

Litchfield co. Warren was taken

from Kent, in 1786. It is bounded on the E. by Litchfield, and is 38 miles W. from Hartford. The town is watered by Shepaug river, a branch of the Housatonick, and by a large and handsome pond, called Raumaug. Warren is hilly and rocky, and in some parts mountainous. It however produces butter, cheese, beef, pork, some grain, and considerable wool. Population, in 1830, 986.

Warwick, Mass.

Franklin co. This town is elevated, and contains Mount Grace, from which a delightful prospect is presented. The soil is strong, warm, and produces excellent pasturage. There are no considerable streams in the town, and its manufactures consist only of leather, scythes and palm-leaf hats. Moose pond, a pleasant sheet of water, furnishes an abundance of fine trout, pickerel and perch.

Warwick was incorporated in 1763. Population, 1837, 1,111. It is 78 miles W. N W. from Boston, and 14 E. by N. from Greenfield.

Warwick, R. I.

Kent co. This important town, the Indian *Shawomet*, is situated on the W. side of Narraganset bay, 5 miles S. from Providence. Population, 1820, 3,443; 1830, 5,529. It contains an area of 54 square miles. The surface of the town, along the bay, is generally level, but the westerly part is hilly, so much so that from some of the elevations, a large part of the state may be seen in a clear day. The prevailing soil is a gravelly loam, strong, and productive of grain, grass, fruits and vegetables. The town is well supplied with a great variety of fish, and forests of walnut, oak and chesnut.

Pawtuxet river washes the northern part of the town, and meets the waters of the Narraganset at this place, separating Warwick from Cranston. An arm of the bay extends westward, giving to Warwick and East Greenwich a number of excellent harbors. Vessels of 50 tons burthen pass to the flourishing village of Apponaug, between 4 and 5 miles from the bay. This village is pleasantly located, 10 miles S. from Providence, and is the site of considerable enterprize in ship building, the fishery, and the coasting trade.

Pawtuxet village is at the mouth of Pawtuxet river, a port of entry, and lays partly in Warwick, and partly in Cranston. This beautiful village, 5 miles S. from Providence, is celebrated for its great hydraulic power on navigable waters. Warwick is eminently distinguished as a manufacturing town; but all we can at present state is, that but very few villages in our country can boast of a more valuable manufacturing interest, particularly in cotton goods. As early as 1822, there were 15 cotton and 2 woolen mills in Warwick.

Warwick is the birth place of two distinguished patriots and warriors.

Col. CHRISTOPHER GREEN was born in 1737. He was in the ill-fated attack upon Quebec, in which the brave Montgomery fell. He was afterwards selected by Washington to take charge of Fort Mercer, or Red Bank, N. J. For his gallant defence of that Fort against a superior force, in 1777, he acquired the reputation of a brave, judicious and faithful officer. He was assassinated in the most brutal manner, in 1781, by a party of American royalists, while stationed on the border of Croton river, New York.

Major General NATHANIEL GREEN was born in 1741. He died in Georgia, in 1786. General Green early received the particular favor of Washington. This favor was continued throughout the war, and was strengthened by his ardent patriotism, undaunted courage, prudence, and superior military knowledge. "Within a mile from the village of Apponaug may be seen a huge rock, so completely balanced upon another, and its equilibrium so exact, that a boy 14 years of age may set it in such motion that the contact or collision caused thereby, produces a sound somewhat like that of a drum, but more sonorous, which in a still evening may be heard a distance of 6 or 8 miles. Hence, from time immemorial, it has gone by the name of the *Drum Rock*. From the ponderous weight of that part which is thus nicely balanced, it is generally believed that no other than the hand of nature ever could have done it. Yet some are inclined to believe, that it was thus placed by the herculean labor of some tribe of the natives. There remains no doubt, but that this was a place of their resort or encampment; and that the *Drum Rock* served them either to give an alarm in case of danger, or to call the tribe together from their daily avocations. This rock is considered as a great curiosity, excites much attention, and consequently is at the present day a place of much resort, particularly in the pleasant season of the year.'

Washington County, Me.

Machias is the shire town. This county is of a singular form. It extends from the Atlantic ocean to the border of Lower Canada, a distance of more than 3 1-2 degrees of latitude. Its interior part, for more than 175 miles, is but 14 miles in breadth: that part near the sea is about 50 miles in width. This territory is bounded N. by Lower Canada, E. by New Brunswick, S. by the ocean, and W. by the counties of Hancock and Penobscot. It contains an area of about 4,150 square miles. About a third part of this county may be said to be settled; the residue is a densely wooded wilderness. The character of the surface and soil of this county, is much the same as that of the adjacent counties of Hancock and Penobscot. In common with all the Atlantic counties in Maine, Washington county possesses its numerous bays, inlets, capacious harbors, and pleasant islands, so admirably adapted to foreign and domestic commerce, the fisheries and ship building.

The St. Croix is its most important river. The banks of this noble stream are rapidly settling, by Yankees on one side and Englishmen on the other; and long may it be a channel, not only of individual and national wealth, but of " good nature and good humor, between people, who, though under different governments, have the same language, a similar religion, a kindred blood."

The tonnage of the two districts in this county, Machias and Passamaquoddy, in 1837, was 19,072 tons. In 1837, the number of sheep in the county was 19,008: the same year it produced 27,014 bushels of wheat. The population of the county in 1820, was 12,744; in 1830, 21,294; and in 1837, 28,495: increase in 7 years,34 pr. ct., and in 17 years, 123 pr. ct. Pop. to sq. m., 7.

Washington, Me.

Lincoln co. This town contains several ponds, and some branches of the Damariscotta and Muscongus rise here. It lies 35 miles E. from Augusta, and 25 N. N. E. from Wiscasset. Population 1837, 1,378. Wheat crop, same year, 2,269 bushels. Incorporated, 1811. It was formerly called Putnam.

Washington, N. H.,

Sullivan co., lies, 22 miles N. N. E. from Keene, 20 E. by S. from Charlestown, and 35 W. from Concord. This town is hilly, but not mountainous. Lovewell's mountain, so called from Capt. Lovewell's killing 7 Indians near it, is of a conical shape, about 3-4 of a mile in diameter, and may be seen at a considerable distance. Washington abounds with springs, rivulets, and natural ponds, of the last of which, there are no less than 16, and some of them of considerable magnitude. Island pond, so called from its being full of islands, is 2 miles long, and 1 1-2 wide. Half moon pond is 1 1-2 miles in length. Ashuelot pond is 1 1-2 miles long, and 1 mile wide, and is the source of one of the principal branches of Ashuelot river. Brockway's pond, a beautiful sheet of water, lying on a white sand, is 1 mile long and 1-2 a mile wide. Long pond, lying in this town and Stoddard, is 5 miles in length. These ponds abound with a variety of fish. A branch of Contoocook river has its source from several small ponds in the E. part of the town. The soil is generally deep and moist, better for grass than tillage. Washington was settled in 1768. It was first called *Monadnock, No.* 8. From its settlement, it was called *Camden,* till December 13, 1776, when it was incorporated by its present name. The first settlers had 150 acres of land each for settling. Population, in 1830, 1,135.

Washington County, Vt.

MONTPELIER is the chief town. This county is nearly in the centre of the state, and the principal part of it lies between the two ranges of the Green Mountains. It is bounded N. by Lamoille and parts of Chittenden and Caledonia counties, E. by Caledonia county, S. by Orange and Addison, and W. by Addison, and Chittenden, counties. It was incorporated in 1810, by the name of Jefferson, and took its present name in 1814. The county is finely watered by its chief river, the Winooski, or Onion, and many of its important branches. These streams afford the county an abundant water power, and manufacturing establishments increase and flourish in this mountainous region.

The surface of the county is uneven, hilly, and in some parts mountainous, but there is much valuable land along the streams, which in many parts are sluggish, and form large tracts of excellent intervale. The agricultural productions consist of neat cattle, horses, hogs, wool, and of the productions of the dairy. In 1837, there were 60,025 sheep in Washington county. There are large bodies of beautiful granite, in the county, and slate of various kinds. Population, 1820, 14,113; 1830, 21,378.

Since 1830, there have been some small changes in Washington county, in regard to territory. We will thank any of our Green Mountain friends to give us all the necessary information respecting it, for future editions. The rail road from Boston to Ogdensburgh will probably pass through this county, but we beg them not to wait for that event.

Washington, Vt.

Orange co. Branches of Onion, Wait's and White rivers rise in this town, but afford no considerable water power. The two former are called *Jail Branches,* from the circumstance that the proprietors were required by their charter, of 1781, to erect a jail within the limits of the town, at an early period. There is some excellent land along the streams, and the uplands are generally arable, and afford good pasturage. There is a neat village in the town, some trade and manufactures, and between 3,000 and 4,000 sheep are annually sheared. Washington is 15 miles S. by E. from Montpelier, and is bounded S. by Chelsea. Population, 1830, 1,374.

Washington, Mass.

Berkshire co. This mountainous town is watered by branches of Westfield and Housatonick rivers

The soil is well adapted for grazing. In 1837, 5,209 sheep were sheared in the town, producing 15,627 pounds of wool, principally merino. There is found in this town a porous quartz, which is used as buhr stones, for mill stones; and is remarkable for resisting heat. Washington was incorporated in 1777. It is 122 miles W. from Boston, and 8 E. from Lenox. Population, 1837, 758.

Washington County, R. I.

South Kingston is the shire town. This is a maritime county situated in the southwestern section of the state; bounded on the north by Kent county, on the east by Narraganset bay, on the south by the Atlantic ocean, and on the west by the state of Connecticut. The average length of the county, from east to west, is about 20 miles, and it has a mean breadth of more than 18 miles, comprising about 367 square miles. The geological character of this county is primitive; the rocks consist of granite and other original formations. The surface is generally diversified with moderate hills and narrow dales; there are, however, some considerable eminences in the northwest section of the county, and some flats of considerable extent in the south section, bordering upon the Atlantic. The prevailing soil is a primitive gravelly loam, strong and fertile; there are some considerable tracts of sandy loam, and some of alluvial. A considerable section of this county was formerly called the Narraganset country, and was celebrated for an excellent breed of pacing horses; the other section was called the Shannock country, and was equally distinguished for a valuable breed of neat cattle. This county still maintains a high reputation as a grazing district, and affords many extensive and valuable dairies. But the agricultural interests are not confined exclusively to the objects of the grazing business; in some sections of the county considerable attention is paid to the cultivation of grain, particularly Indian corn and barley; some rye also is raised. The inhabitants are distinguished for their habits of industry and frugality, and in general enjoy their necessary results, health and competence.

The waters of the county are extensive and important, possessing a maritime border upon the Atlantic ocean and the Narraganset bay, of more than 50 miles extent. There are, however, but 2 or 3 harbors; the principal of which is Wickford, in the northeastern section of the county; the next most important is the Pawcatuck. The principal interior waters of the county are embodied in the Pawcatuck river, which forms part of the western boundary of the state. The principal branches of the Pawcatuck are the Wood and Charles rivers; which, with their tributary streams, water a large portion of the western section of the county, and afford numerous sites for mills, and other hydraulic works.

There are, in the county, several salt and fresh water ponds, which are well supplied with fish.

The fisheries of the county are extensive and valuable, affording employment to considerable industry, which is usually well rewarded. The fish taken, not only supply the home consumption, but constitute an article of exportation.

Although the commercial business carried on within the county is not very considerable, yet its maritime situation has had its natural influence upon the habits of the people; a considerable portion of whom are employed in seafaring business.

The manufacturing interests of the county are considerable, and consist principally of the woolen and cotton manufactures, and the business of ship building. Besides these, there is considerable mechanical industry in the other departments of mechanical business.

In 1837, there were 81,619 sheep in the county. Population, in 1800, 16,135; 1810, 14,963; in 1820, 15,687; 1830, 15,411. Population to a square mile, 42. From this statement of the population, it appears that this county must have suffered greatly by emigration.

Washington, Ct.

Litchfield co. Judea, the first society in this town, was a part of Woodbury until 1741. It was first settled in 1734. It was incorporated as a town in 1779.

This town is 40 miles S. W. from Hartford, and 10 S. W. from Litchfield. Population, 1830, 986.

"A large part of this town is elevated and mountainous. Limestone abounds in many of the valleys. Several quarries of marble have been worked, from which considerable quantities have been raised. Iron ore has been found in various places. Ochre, fuller's earth, and white clay, have also been found. The town is watered by the Shepaug river, a branch of the Housatonick, which passes through the whole length of the town, dividing it into two nearly equal parts. The town is divided into two societies, Judea and New Preston. There is in Judea, or Washington as it is called, about two miles S. W. of the centre of the town, a place called "Steep Rock." From the top of this eminence, which is easy of access, the beholder has one of the most interesting and beautiful prospects in the state. The scene presents an area in the form of an amphitheatre, the sides of which are covered with a dense forest. The Shepaug river is seen flowing in a beautiful circle at the base of the bluff. Within the circle of the river, there are several cultivated fields, affording a beautiful landscape to the beholder.

"This town has been the theatre of one of the most atrocious murders ever committed in New England. The murderer was a man or rather fiend, by the name of Barnett Davenport. From his own confession, it appears that his parentage and early education were exactly fitted to produce his wicked life and his tragical end. Untutored and unrestrained by parental government, he was left to grow up at random. In the morning of life, no morality was inculcated upon him, and no sense of religion, either by precept or example. On the contrary, he was, from early years, unprincipled, profane, and impious. Before he was 9 years old, he was expert in cursing and swearing, and an adept in mischief. At 11 years he began to pilfer. At 13 he stole money. At 15 he entertained thoughts of murder, and rapidly waxed harder and bolder in wickedness. At 19, he actually murdered a family in cold blood. As a friendless wandering stranger, he was taken into the house of Mr. Caleb Mallory, and treated with the utmost kindness, in December, 1779. Scarcely two months had elapsed, before the murder was determined on. The night of February 3d, 1780, was fixed on to execute the horrid purpose. With a heart hard as adamant, he lighted a candle, went into the lodging room of his benefactors, and beat them to death with a club. A little grand child being with its grand parents shared the same fate, and two others were left in a sound sleep to perish in the flames. Having kindled a fire in three of the rooms, he fled, after robbing the house of its most valuable articles. But from an accusing conscience, and from the hand of justice, which followed hard upon his steps, he was unable to flee. He was taken, and executed at Litchfield in the May ensuing."

Waterborough, Me.

York co. This town is watered by a large and pleasant pond, which empties into Little Ossipee river, a branch of the Saco, and by the head branches of the Mousum, a stream which meets the ocean at Kennebunk. This is a flourishing town, with a pleasant surface and good soil. It lies 81 miles S. W. from Augusta, 24 W. from Portland, and is bounded S. by Alfred. Incorporated, 1787. Population, 1830, 1,816; 1837, 1,953.

Waterbury, Vt.

Washington co. The surface of Waterbury is generally level, with some pleasant swells. The soil is warm and fertile: the meadow lands on the rivers, of which there are large tracts, are not excelled, in richness, by any in the state. This town is separated from Duxbury by Onion river, which, with Waterbury river and other streams, afford the town a good water power. It was first settled in 1784. Population, 1830, 1,650. It lies 12 miles N. W. from Montpelier, and 24 E. S. E. from Burlington.

In the southwest corner of the township, the passage of Onion river through a considerable hill, is considered a curiosity. The stream has here worn a channel through the rocks, which in times past, undoubtedly, formed a cataract below of no ordinary height, and a considerable lake above. The chasm is at present about one hundred feet wide, and nearly as deep. On one side the rocks are nearly perpendicular, some of which have fallen across the bed of the stream, in such a manner as to form a bridge, passable, however, only at low water. On the same side the rocks which appear to have been loosened and moved by the undermining of the water, have again rested, and become fixed in such a posture as to form several caverns or caves, some of which have the appearance of rooms fitted for the convenience of man. Several musket balls and flints were found in the extreme part of this cavern, a few years since, with the appearance of having lain there many years, which makes it evident that it was known to the early hunters.

Waterbury River, rises in Morristown, and runs south through the western part of Stow and Waterbury into Onion river. In Stow, it receives one considerable tributary from the east which rises in Worcester, and two from the west which rise in Mansfield. It also receives several tributaries from the west, in Waterbury, which originate in Bolton. The whole length of the stream is about 16 miles, and it affords a number of good mill privileges.

Waterbury, Ct.

New Haven co. The Indian Mattatuck, a territory comprising this and some of the neighboring towns, being 18 miles in length and 10 miles in width, was sold by the red men to the whites,, in the year 1684, "for divers good causes and thirty-nine pounds." This piece of ground was supposed by the white men, to afford sufficient room and accommodations for *thirty families.* The territory now contains 8,000 people; and if its population was as dense as that of England, in 1831, it would contain no less than 20,610, or of Belgium, 35,370 souls.

There are some good lands on the borders of the streams, within the present limits of Waterbury; but the surface of the town is generally rough, and the soil difficult of cultivation.

This town lies 28 miles S. W. from Hartford, and 20 N. by W. from New Haven. Population, 1830, 3,070.

"The site upon which the borough of Waterbury stands, is situated in a valley which is washed by Mad river on the east, and the Naugatuck on the west; and in its central part is about a mile in breadth. The main street runs east and west; but since the increase of the manufacturing establishments within the last twelve years, a large share of the new buildings have been erected in their vicinity, which is in the southeast part of the village. On either side of the village, hills gradually rise to a considerable elevation, presenting to the eye the galleries of an amphitheatre, the village forming the area. The number of houses is about one hundred and fifty, and the population fifteen hundred; which it is calculated has doubled itself during the last twelve years; most of the factories having been established within that time. Some of the private dwellings may be called splendid, and a majority of them neat, convenient, with handsome court yards in front.

"Of the articles manufactured in the village, those of gilt buttons and the rolling of brass and copper metals for a great variety of uses, constitute the greatest business. There are three factories of this kind upon an extensive scale, two in the village, and one about two miles north, connected with which is a gold refinery. There are likewise two factories of gilt buttons upon a considerable scale, unconnected with rolling mills. One extensive rolling mill connected with the brass wire and tubing manufacture, two satinet factories, one woolen factory, besides a great number of minor establishments, in which buttons of various kinds and other articles are manufactured to a considerable extent. The number of persons in the village, of both sexes, who are employed in the manufacturing establishments, is between six and seven hundred. It is not precisely known what amount is manufactured yearly, but it has been estimated by good judges to exceed a million of dollars, and is upon the increase. The route has been surveyed by a practical engineer, for constructing a canal to bring the Naugatuck on to the bank at the west end of the town, which will, when completed, afford a supply of water power, capable of employing as much or more capital than has been already invested."

SAMUEL HOPKINS, D. D., the founder of a religious sect, denominated *Hopkinsians*, was born in this town, in 1721. He died at Newport, R. I., in 1803. See *Religious Creeds, and Statistics.*

Dr. LEMUEL HOPKINS, a poet, and an eminent physician, was born in Waterbury, in 1750. He died at Hartford, in 1801.

Waterford, Me.

Oxford co. This town is watered by a number of beautiful ponds, and Crooked river passes through its northeast border. The surface is generally level and the soil good. It produced in 1837, 5,545 bushels of wheat.

Waterford was incorporated in 1797. It lies 57 miles W. by S. from Augusta, and 10 W. by S. from Paris. Population, in 1837, 1,297.

Waterford, Vt.

Caledonia co. This town was chartered in 1780, by the name of Littleton, which name it retained until 1797. It was first settled in 1787. It lies on the west side of Connecticut river, 32 miles E. N. E. from Montpelier, and 12 E. S. E. from Danville. Population, 1830, 1,358. The west part of the town is watered by the Passumpsic, and the north border by Moose river. Here is a water power, and some manufactures. A part of the town borders on Fifteen Mile Falls, in Connecticut river. The banks of that river are steep at this place, and form but little intervale. The uplands are rough and stony, but good for sheep, of which 3,500 are kept.

Waterford, Ct.

New London co. This town was taken from New London in 1801. It is washed on the east side by the river Thames; and on the south by Long Island Sound, from which a bay or inlet extends, between Millstone and Black Points, quite into the centre of the town, affording a harbor for small vessels. This is a resort for fishermen on the Sound, and many species of the finny tribe are taken captive.

There are a number of ponds in the town, three considerable mill streams, and two woolen factories. The surface of the town is rocky and uneven, with a gravelly loam, productive of corn, vegetables, fruits, and feed for cattle. In 1837, it contained 2,582 sheep.

Waterford lies 37 miles S. E. from Hartford, and 4 W. from New London. Population, 1830, 2,463.

Waterqueechy River, Vt.

See *Queechy River*.

Watertown, Mass.

Middlesex co. Charles river gives this town a valuable water power, which is well improved. The river is navigable to the centre of the town for vessels of 6 or 7 feet draught of water.

The surface of the town is diversified by hills and valleys, which is rendered very beautiful by a high state of cultivation, and by the numerous villas, neat farm houses, cottages, and delightful gardens which meet the eye in every direction. A part of the beautiful sheet of water, called "Fresh Pond," and a part of the celebrated Mount Auburn Cemetery lie in this town.

On the north bank of the river, a short distance below the principal village, the United States Arsenal, containing a large amount of munitions of war, occupies a site of 40 acres of ground. At the commencement of the revolutionary war, this place was the chosen seat of the continental congress. That body of patriots was in session at Watertown on the day of the battle of "Bunker Hill."

There are two paper mills in the town, a cotton mill, print works, an establishment for finishing woolen goods, and manufactures of soap, candles, boots, shoes, boxes, &c. Large quantities of beef, pork, bacon, &c., are annually packed at this place for the Boston market, and for transportation. In 1837, three soap and candle manufactories used 300 tons of tallow, 350 tons of barilla, 50 tons of palm-oil, 1,750 barrels of rosin, 2,000 casks of lime, and 1,000 bushels of salt.

Watertown was first settled in 1630, by the sons of Sir Richard Saltonstall and others. It was incorporated the same year. Population, 1830, 1,641; 1837, 1,739. It is 7 miles W. from Boston. Its Indian name was *Pigsgusset*.

Watertown, Ct.

Litchfield co. This town lies 30 miles S. S. W. from Hartford, 26 N. by W. from New Haven, and 10 S. E. from Litchfield. Population, 1830, 1,500.

Watertown was formerly a parish in Waterbury, by the name of Westbury. It was incorporated as a town in 1780. It is bounded N. by Litchfield, E. by the Naugatuck river, separating it from Plymouth, W. by Bethlem and Woodbury, and S. by Middlebury and Waterbury. It is about 6 1-2 miles in length, and 4 in breadth. The township is generally uneven, or rather hilly; but some sections are level. The prevailing soil is a dry gravelly loam, and best adapted to grazing, but the different grains common to this part of the country are cultivated

Steel's brook, a sprightly stream, passes through the central part of the town, and for a mile below and some distance above the centre of the town, a chain of rich meadows, though small in extent, border the sides of this stream.

This is the birth place of JOHN TRUMBULL, the celebrated author of "McFingal." He graduated at Yale College, and studied law with John Adams, in Boston. The first part of his McFingal appeared in 1775. It was completed in 1782. He was a judge of the Superior Court of Connecticut from 1801 to 1819. In 1825, he removed to Detroit, where he died, in 1831, aged 81 years.

The people of this town make some boast of the size of their forest trees. It is said, as an extraordinary fact, "that one of the first settlers, having no shelter for the night, peeled off the bark of one of the trees he had felled, and lay down upon the inside. In the morning when he awoke, he found the bark rolled up so closely that it was with some difficulty he could extricate himself."

This story will do to tell as far west as Connecticut, but the 'Down Easters' would laugh at it. It would take Dame Nature more than a night to screw up the bark of one of their common pines even to the circumference of the New Hampshire Giant. The Maine folks willingly grant to Connecticut the *tallest poets*, but claim to their state the *biggest trees*.

Waterville, Me.

Kennebec co. This town is situated on the west bank of the Kennebec river, 18 miles N. from Augusta. It was incorporated as a part of Winslow in 1771, and as a separate town in 1802. Population in 1820, 1,719; in 1830, 2,216; in 1837, 2,905. It contains 30 square miles, mostly of the best quality of farming land of the Kennebec region. Seven twelfths of the population is estimated to be agricultural. The principal village, of about 180 houses, is on the Kennebec, at Ticonic Falls. These falls are 18 feet in height, extending quite across the river. In the town, there are 17 saws, four grist mills, carding machines, three plaster mills, two extensive tanneries and a machine shop. One iron foundry, a branch of the celebrated Fairbanks establishment in Vermont, supplies a great portion of the interior of the state with ploughs. The public structures are 4 meeting houses, an Academy, and the Liberal Institute, a Seminary founded by Universalists. This latter edifice, though small, is one of the most beautiful specimens of architecture in the state. Ticonic bridge, crossing the Kennebec, 550 feet in length, is a fine specimen of Col. Long's plan of construction.

Waterville College is pleasantly situated near the village, on the bank of the river. There are 2 edifices for rooms, a chapel, and a commons hall. This Institution was founded in 1813, as a Theological school; in 1821 it was converted into a College, and has 143 graduates. It was founded by Baptists, but is open to all denominations, and affords facilities for manual labor. Its Faculty is a President, three Professors, and two Tutors.

From Augusta, the head of slop navigation, goods are transported to Waterville in large flat-boats, some of which carry 40 tons. This renders the place an important depot of merchandise for an extensive country above, and of produce and manufactures brought down to be shipped for a market: great quantities of oats, shingles and other lumber, leather, potash and potatoes, are thus transported from this place. The erection of a dam at Augusta, is thought to have improved the navigation, and affords facilities for making Waterville the centre of trade for the country above. A steam boat now runs between this place and the lower towns. The village of West Waterville is on Emerson stream, a tributary of the Kennebec. Here is a remarkble cascade, the highest known in the state, and is much resorted to for its picturesque scenery. At this village are manufactories for cutting out last blocks, which are exported in great quantities to Massachusetts, and a scythe factory of high reputation, which made 300 dozen scythes in the year 1838. The water power at Waterville and in the vicinity, is singularly great. A circle described from the Ticonic falls, before named, as a centre, with a radius of five miles, includes two falls across the whole Kennebec, at Kendall's mills, two miles above Waterville; two falls, 5 miles distant, on the Sebasticook, a large tributary stream; and an indefinite series of falls upon the Emerson stream, from the cascade to its confluence, besides numerous rapids, which could easily be dammed, on all these streams. It is believed that no similar circle of 10 miles diameter in New England, comprehends so large and convenient water power. But a very small part of this power is yet occupied, and situated as Waterville is, in the centre of these manufacturing facilities, enjoying convenient boat navigation to the sea ports, with an extensive region of the best agricultural advantages in the rear, it promises to become a thrifty and populous town.

Waterville, N. H.

Grafton co. This town comprises the territory called *Gillis and Foss' Grant*, until its incorporation, in 1829. It is bounded N. by ungranted land, E. by Albany, S. by Sandwich, and W. by Thornton. It was granted June 29, 1819, to Josiah Gillis, Moses Foss, jr. and others. It is watered by Mad river, which rises among the mountainous tracts on the N.; runs S. W. about 20 miles, and falls into Pemigewasset river in Campton. Swift river has its source in this town, pursues an E. course through Albany, into Conway, where it unites with Saco river. There are 2 ponds, and several considerable elevations. Moses Foss, jr. commenced the settlement some years since. It has 96 inhabitants.

Waterville, Vt.

Lamoille co. This town is environed by mountains, and is itself mountainous. It is watered by a branch of Lamoille river, and is bounded E. by Belvidere, W. by Fletcher. It lies about 25 miles S. E. from St. Albans. Population, 1830, 488.

Wayland, Mass.

Middlesex co. The name of this town was East Sudbury, from 1780 to 1835. It lies on the east side of Sudbury river, and is bounded east by Weston. The surface of the town is pleasant; the soil is generally good, and contains some well cultivated farms. There are 4 forges in this town, and manufactures of chairs and cabinet ware; but the principal manufacture is that of boots and shoes; the annual value of which is about $25,000. Wayland is 16 miles W. from Boston, and 7 S. from Concord. Population, 1837, 931.

Wayne, Me.

Kennebec co. Wayne lies N. of Leeds, and is situated a little below the centre of a chain of beautiful lakes or ponds, whose outlet, which passes through the town, falls into the Androscoggin. The centre of the town is about 4 miles east of the Androscoggin, and 16 W. from Augusta. The surface of the town is undulating, and the soil fertile. It was incorporated in 1798.

NEW ENGLAND GAZETTEER.

Weare, N. H.

Population, in 1837, 1,170. Wheat crop, same year, 3,268 bushels.

Hillsborough co. The only river in Weare, is the N. W. branch of Piscataquog, which enters the west boundary from Deering, and meanders through the N. and E. sections of the town, and passes the S. line about half a mile from the S. E. corner. This river affords the best mill seats in the town. There are three small ponds in this town. Rattlesnake hill, nearly in the centre of the N. line of the town, abounds with shelving rocks, abrupt precipices, forming dens and caves. During the summer season, the reptile from which the hill takes its name, is frequently found. The town, though rather broken, is not mountainous. It has small swamps, and some good meadows. It is now settled and cultivated to its extreme limits by industrious and wealthy husbandmen. It was incorporated in 1764, and received its name in honor of Meshech Weare, chief justice of the province of N. H.

Weare is 15 miles S. W. from Concord, and 17 N. N. W. from Amherst. Population, 1830, 2,430.

Weathersfield, Vt.

Windsor co. [Those who wish to find the course and distance to the onion fields in Connecticut, or to their fair cultivators, will please see *Weth*ersfield, Ct.]

Weathersfield was first settled about the year 1778. It is bounded S. by Springfield, N. by Windsor, and is 61 miles S. by E. from Montpelier. Population, in 1830, 2,213. This town lies on the west side of Connecticut river, at the " Bow," so called from a bend in the river. It contains large tracts of rich meadow land, and the uplands are of a good quality.

William Jarvis, Esq., for many years a resident here, owns a large and superior farm, and has greatly benefited this section of country by the introduction of new modes of agriculture, and more valuable breeds of stock. The agricultural products of Weathersfield are very valuable: about 15,000 fleeces of fine wool are annually sheared. This town is large, and contains a number of pleasant villages. It is watered by several ponds, and by Black river, which gives it a water power, and which is applied to manufacturing operations to some extent. In common with all the towns on Connecticut river, Weathersfield has its share of delightful scenery; and there is no better place to find it, in all its richness, than on the *Ascutney,* at the north part of the town.

Webster, Mass.

Worcester co. This town was incorporated in 1832, and named in compliment to Hon. DANIEL WEBSTER, including a part of Dudley and Oxford, and a tract of land previously unincorporated. It is bounded N. by Oxford, E. by Douglas, S. by Thompson, in Connecticut, and W. by Dudley. It is 46 miles W. S. W. from Boston, 16 S. from Worcester, 45 E. by S. from Springfield, and 28 N. W. from Providence, R. I. Population, 1837, 1,210.

There are in operation in this town two woolen and four large cotton mills, a cotton thread mill, 1 machine shop, 1 bleachery, a tannery, and a manufactory of tin ware: total value of manufactures, the year ending April 1, 1837, $312,277.

French river and a pond give this place a large and unfailing water power. The original name of this pond, as appears from ancient deeds, was *Chabanakongkomom,* the same name by which Dudley was known, though the latter probably borrowed it from the former. Some records and maps of New England have given the name of *Chargog-gagoggmanchoggagogg.* The fall at the outlet of this pond is 24 feet, which is increased after it empties into French river to about 90 feet before it passes into Connecticut. This afforded ample water power for the late Samuel Slater to concentrate here a large portion of his manufacturing capital; and it is to the enterprise of this 'Father of American manufactures,' that this place is indebted for most of the prosperity which it at present enjoys. It was his favorite residence, and where his remains now rest.

A remnant of the Dudley, or more properly of the Nipmuck Indians, reside here. They are about 40 in number, though but few of them are of pure blood. These Indians formerly owned a considerable tract of reserved land in the centre of Chabanakongkamon or Dudley. This was sold by order of the legislature, and the proceeds appropriated to their support, and to the purchase of about 30 acres, on which they now reside. This money is now expended, and they are dependent on the bounty of the state for support.

Weld, Me.

Franklin co. This town contains a large and beautiful pond, the outlet of which forms a considerable river, which passing south falls into the Androscoggin at Mexico.

The surface of the town is remarkably pleasant, and the soil fertile. Wheat crop, 1837, 6,039 bushels. Weld lies 53 miles W. N. W. from Augusta, and 14 W. from Farmington. Population, in 1830, 766; 1837, 953.

Wellfleet, Mass.

Barnstable co. This township lies on both sides of Cape Cod: it is bounded N. by Truro, S. by Eastham, and is 33 miles below Barnstable.

The town is on the west side of the Cape: it is neatly built, and although it is surrounded by sand hills, and almost entirely destitute of vegetation, it makes a handsome appearance. Wellfleet bay sets into the town from the south, and is separated from Cape Cod bay by several islands, which form a good harbor, at a place called "Deep Hole."

In 1837, there were 120 vessels, measuring about 6,000 tons, belonging to this place, employed in the cod and mackerel fisheries, and a number engaged in the coasting trade. The fishermen took 3,100 quintals of cod fish, and 17,500 barrels of mackerel: the value of which was $128,500. The quantity of salt used was 29,350 bushels: the number of hands employed was 496. During that year there were 39 establishments for the manufacture of salt in this place; the quantity made was 10,000 bushels.

There are several ponds and streams in the town, which afford water power sufficient for a large cotton mill. There are some manufactures of leather, boots and shoes; but the people are principally employed in the fishery, coasting trade and manufacture of salt.

Wellfleet was incorporated in 1723. Population, 1830, 2,044; 1837, 2,303.

Dr. Morse stated in 1797, that "since the memory of people now living, there have been in this small town thirty pair of twins, besides two births that produced three each."

This is one of the most thriving towns in the state. One of its former residents, Col. Elisha Doane, is said to have acquired a fortune of 120,000 pounds sterling on this sandy spot. The Indian name of the town was *Rinonakannit.*

Wellington, Me.

Piscataquis co. Wellington is bounded E. by Parkman, S. by Harmony, and W. by Brighton. It is watered by one of the head branches of Sebasticook river, and lies about 22 miles N. by E. from Skowhegan. A part of the town is elevated, but its surface, generally, is undulating, with a productive soil. Population, 1837, 721. Wheat crop, same year, 4,290 bushels.

Wells, Me.

York co. Wells lies on the sea coast between York and Kennebunk, and is 85 miles S. W. by S. from Augusta, and 30 S. W. by S. from Portland. The first settlers came from Exeter, N. H., about the year 1640. A noted Indian chief, Wawwaw, lived here about one hundred years ago, pretending to claim this and some adjoining towns. There is no evidence of any purchase of Indian title to the soil. The town charter from Thomas Gorges is dated Sept. 27, 1643.

There are a number of small streams or brooks running through the town in various directions, on which are 1 fulling, 16 saw and 10 grist mills. The principal river is near the middle of the town, and was called by the Indians *Webhannet*, but is now generally called the "Town river." A sand bar at the entrance renders the navigation somewhat difficult. Ogunquit river, in the southerly part of the town, forms a harbor for small coasting and fishing vessels.

The town contains about 35,000 acres, of which one fifth may be considered waste land, or unfit for cultivation. It contains large tracts of salt meadow. Wood for fuel is exported to Boston and other places, in considerable quantities. Some trade is carried on with the West Indies, and vessels of various size are built from timber in the town. Incorporated, 1653. Population, 1837, 3,042. This town furnished a large number of revolutionary officers.

Wells River, Vt.

This river has its source in Kettle pond, which lies at the northwest corner of Groton and a part of it in Marshfield. It runs nearly southeast about two miles, and falls into Long pond in Groton, which is about two miles long and 100 rods wide. From this pond it continues its southeasterly course half a mile, and falls into another pond, which is about half a mile long and a quarter of a mile wide. It then runs a mile and a half, and meets the south branch, which rises near the southwest corner of the town, and runs nearly east to its junction with the main stream; it then runs east southeast about a mile, and receives the north branch, which has its source near the southeast corner of the town. Continuing the same course, it passes through the northwest part of Ryegate into Newbury, and running near the line between Newbury and Ryegate about 4 miles, falls into Connecticut river about half a mile south of the northeast corner of Newbury. This is generally a rapid stream, furnishing many excellent mill privileges.

Wells, Vt.

Rutland co. A part of this township is level, and a part mountainous. The soil is generally good, and productive of grain, and of pasturage for sheep, of which between three and four thousand are kept. The principal stream in the town issues from Wells or St. Augustine lake or pond, a beautiful sheet of water, partly in Poultney, 5 miles in length, and covering 2,000 acres. At the outlet of this pond is a snug village, with some water power machinery.

Wells was first settled in 1768. It lies 65 miles S. S. W. from Montpelier, and 13 S. W. from Rutland. Population, 1830, 880.

Wendell, N. H.,

Sullivan co., is bounded N. by Springfield, E. by Sunapee lake, separating it from New London and Newbury, S. by Goshen, W. by Newport and Croydon. It is 35 miles N. W. from Concord, and 7 E. from Newport. A considerable part of lake Sunapee, a noble sheet of water, lies in this town. The surface of this lake is said to contain 4,095 acres, of which 2,720 acres are in Wendell. Here is the principal source of Sugar river, which flows from the lake near its centre from north to south; passes through the centre of the town into Newport, from thence into Claremont, where it unites with the Connecticut. There are three small ponds, containing an area of about 300 acres. This town was granted by the name of *Saville* in 1768. It was settled in 1772, and was incorporated in 1781, when it received its name from John Wendell, one of the principal proprietors. Population, 1830, 637.

Wendell, Mass.

Franklin co. The surface of Wendell is uneven, and in some parts hilly; but the soil is strong and productive. Miller's river passes through the north part of the town, giving mill privileges, fertility and beauty in its course. There is a curious kind of stone found here, embedded with mica slate; and Chalk pond furnishes a substance from which chalk is made by burning it.

The manufactures of this pleasant town consist of palm-leaf hats, boots, shoes, leather, cabinet ware, chairs, &c.

Wendell was incorporated in 1781, and named in honor of Oliver Wendell, Esq., a very worthy man, for many years president of Union Bank, in Boston, the second institution of the kind in Massachusetts. Mr. Wendell was a great patron of this town, and frequently visited it.

Wendell is bounded north by Erving, east by Phillipston, south by Salem, and west by Montague.

The mill privileges on Millers river in this town are very valuable; many of which remain unimproved.

Wendell lies 80 miles W. by N. from Boston, and 14 E. from Greenfield. Population, 1837, 847.

Wenham, Mass.

Essex co. This town is 20 miles N. by E. from Boston, 6 N. from Salem, and 16 S. from Newburyport. First settled, 1639. Incorporated, 1643. Population, 1837, 698.

Wenham or *Enon* pond is a beautiful sheet of water, about a mile square, and affords an abundance of excellent fish. It is much visited. The first sermon preached in this place was on the border of this pond, by the celebrated Hugh Peters, minister of Salem, about the year 1636. His text was, "At Enon near Salem, because there was much water there."

Mr. Peters went to England, as agent for the colony, 1641; engaged in the civil wars on the side of the parliament, and was executed after the restoration of Charles II.

The surface of the town is pleasant: the soil is generally of a good quality, and well cultivated by industrious and independent farmers.

John Duntan, an Englishman who travelled in this country in 1686, and on his return to England published a journal of his travels, gives the following account of Wenham, and of its minister, Joseph Gerrish, who was ordained Feb. 13, 1675, and died Jan. 6, 1719.

"Wenham is a delicious paradise, it abounds with rural pleasures, and I would choose it above all other towns in America to dwell in; the lofty trees on each side of it are a sufficient shelter from the winds, and the warm sun so kindly ripens both the fruits and flowers, as if the spring, the summer, and the autumn had agreed together to thrust the winter out of doors. It were endless to enter on a detail of each faculty of learning Mr. Gerrish is master of, and I therefore take his character in short hand. The *philosopher* is acute, ingenious and subtle. The *divine*, curious, orthodox and profound. The *man* of a majestic air, without austerity or sourness; his aspect is masterly and great, yet not imperious or haughty. The *christian* is devout without moroseness, or starts of holy frenzy, and enthusiasm. The *preacher* is primitive without the occasional colors of whining, or cant, and methodical, without intricacy or affectation; and which crowns his character, he is a man of public spirit, zealous for the conversion of the Indians, and of great hospitality to strangers. He gave us a noble dinner, and entertained us with such pleasant fruits, as I must own, Old England is a stranger to."

Wenlock, Vt.

Essex co. This mountain town gives rise to a principal branch of Nulhegan river. The lands here are too elevated for cultivation. Wenlock lies 53 miles N. E. from Montpelier. Population, in 1830, 24.

Wentworth, N. H.

Grafton co. This town is bounded N. by Warren, E. by Rumney, S. by Dorchester, and W. by Orford. It is 15 miles N. W. from Plymouth, and 52 N. N. W. from Concord. This town is watered by Baker's river, on which is a fall of 18 or 20 feet, affording an excellent privilege for all kinds of water machinery. The South branch of Baker's river passes through the southerly part of this town and joins the main branch near Rumney line. There are but few ponds. Baker's, situated on Orford line, is the most considerable; the outlet of which is called Pond brook, and affords water sufficient for several valuable mill seats. In the east part of the town, lies part of Carr's mountain, covered in its natural state with a heavy growth of forest trees. A part of the elevation called Mount Cuba lies in the W. part of Wentworth. This mountain contains inexhaustible quantities of the best limestone, of which a constant supply of good lime is made, and sold at a low price. Iron ore is found in various parts. The soil is generally good; the lands in the vicinity of the rivers are of the first quality. Wentworth was granted in 1766. It received its name from governor Benning Wentworth.— The first settlement commenced a few years before the revolutionary war. Articles of subsistence, potatoes and seeds for the propagation of vegetables, were transported thither from the lower part of the state on pack horses, hand-sleighs and in knapsacks. Population, in 1830, 624.

Wesley, Me.

Washington co. We should like to know the particular circumstances of Wesley, which doubtless was named in honor of one of the best of men that ever lived—JOHN WESLEY. It must be a thriving town, for its population, for the last 7 years, has increased from 80 to 232. But very little information can be obtained respecting a town, from merely its act of incorporation.

Westborough, Mass.

Worcester co. This town lies on the route of the Boston and Worcester rail road, 32 miles W. from Boston, 10 E. from Worcester, and 8 1-2 N. W. from Hopkinton Springs. It was taken from Marlborough in 1717. Population, 1830, 1,438; in 1837, 1,612.

As several persons were engaged in a field spreading flax, in 1704, the Indians rushed upon them from the woods, and seized 4 boys, and killed one, named Nahor Rice, about 5 years of age, who was the first white person buried in the town. The men made their escape to the house. One of the boys was redeemed, the others remained and mixed their posterity with the French and Indians. Timothy Rice, the youngest, 7 years of age, when taken, became a chief of the Cognawaga Indians. He visited Westborough in 1740, and remembered the house where he had lived, and the field where he was captured, and some aged people. He had lost the English language, and was accompanied by an interpreter. He was sent for and visited Gov. Belcher, at Boston, but chose to return to his Indian habits.

The waters of this town consist of some of the sources of Concord and Blackstone rivers, which furnish a good water power. There are several handsome ponds in the town, well stocked with fish.

The manufactures consist of boots, shoes, leather, axes, chairs, cabinet and tin wares, ploughs, straw bonnets, sleighs, and harnesses; total value, the year ending April 1, 1837, $169,476, of which amount $148,774 was for boots and shoes.

This is a very pleasant town: the surface is diversified by hills and valleys: the soil is good, and appears to be cultivated by men who understand their business. A brief statement of the products of Mr. Samuel Chamberlain's farm of about 100 acres, in 1833, is here given.

Butter, 3,486, lbs. $767.
Cheese, 3,836, 221.
Beef, - - 603.
Pork, - - 652.
Veal, - - 152.

Total, $2,395.

This is the native place of ELI WHITNEY. Soon after he graduated at Yale College, he went to Georgia, where he resided many years. He died, and was buried in the city of New Haven. The following is inscribed on his monument.

Eli Whitney,
the inventor of the
Cotton Gin.
Of useful Science and Arts,
the efficient patron
and improver.
Born December 8th, 1765. Died
Jan. 8th,1825.
In the social relations of life,
a model of excellence.
While private
affection weeps at his tomb, his
country honors his
memory.

See *New Haven, Ct.*

West Boylston, Mass.

Worcester co. This territory was a part of Boylston until 1808, and was first settled about the year 1720. It is 42 miles W. from Boston, and 8 N. from Worcester. Population, in 1830, 1,053; 1837, 1,330. The surface of the town is very pleasant; the soil good, and well cultivated. The Quinepoxet and Stillwater rivers meet the Nashua in this town. These streams fertilize a large portion of the town, and afford a water power to propel a number of mills.

There are in the town 7 cotton mills, and manufactures of boots, shoes, leather, palm-leaf hats, cotton machinery, baskets, boxes, straw braid, hatchets and school apparatus; annual value about $200,000.

The venerable Robert B. Thomas, author of the Farmer's Almanac, is a resident of this town. There are some mineral treasures in West Boylston, and a spring, the waters of which are strongly impregnated with iron.

West Bridgewater, Mass.

Plymouth co. This is the second daughter of the venerable Bridgewater, who found it difficult to find names for her progeny. This daughter was born in 1822, and although not so stout as her sisters, is healthy, comely and industrious. The manufactures of West Bridgewater consist of iron castings, shovels, forks, hoes, ploughs, boots and shoes: annual value, about $100,000. West Bridgewater is supplied with mill privileges by a branch of Taunton river; and is 25 miles S. from Boston, 19 N. W. from Plymouth and 9 N. N. E. from Taunton. The number of her children in 1837, was 1,145; increase in 7 years, 103.

In 1820, ancient Bridgewater contained 5,662 children: the whole family, in 1837, consisted of 7,865 members.

Westbrook, Me.

Cumberland co. This flourishing town was taken from Falmouth in 1814. It is 52 miles S. S. W. from Augusta, and is bounded E. by Portland. The Presumpscot river passing through the town from west to east, furnishes it with rich intervales, and numerous valuable mill privileges. The Cumberland and Oxford canal also passes through the town. This town is noted for its working cattle which are said to equal any in the country.

The principal place of business in Westbrook, is at the pleasant village of Saccarappa, where are large operations in the manufacture of lumber, and where has recently been erected, by citizens of Portland, a large brick cotton mill, containing 2,900 spindles, and 104 looms, and which is in successful operation.

Stroudwater, another village, has some navigation employed in the fishery and coasting trade, and has been celebrated for the fine ships built there. In Westbrook are extensive manufactures of tin ware and combs, which are sent to all parts of the United States.

The scenery along the canal, and about the falls on the Presumpscut, is very pleasant. Population, 1830, 3,238; 1837, 3,755

West Cambridge, Mass.

Middlesex co. This was a parish of Cambridge, called "Menotomy," until its incorporation, in 1807. A part of the lands are low and swampy, but the general features of the town are pleasant. Spy, Little, and a part of Fresh ponds lie in this town; they abound with fish, and add much to the beauty of the place. These ponds cover an area of about 200 acres, and furnish large quantities of ice for transportation. In this town are some very pleasant villages, numerous country seats, and well cultivated farms. Large quantities of milk are daily taken to the Boston market, and this place is a considerable mart for cattle from the interior country.

Sucker brook, though a small stream, furnishes a good water power. The descent of this stream is so great, that dams are erected in the town for appropriating its water nine different times. The mechanical operations of West Cambridge consist of dying and printing calico, pulverizing drugs, medicines and dye-stuffs, a turning and sawing mill, and the manufacture of saws, cards, boots, shoes, cabinet ware and chairs; total value, the year ending April 1, 1837, $312,500. West Cambridge is 6 miles N. W. from Boston, and 12 E. by S. from Concord. Population, 1830, 1,308.

Westerly, R. I.

Washington co. Westerly is washed by the Atlantic ocean on the south, and Pawcatuck river, which separates this state from Connecticut, on the west. This maritime town has its principal harbor at the mouth of the Pawcatuck, in which vessels are built, and in which some navigation is employed in the fishery and domestic trade.

The Pawcatuck affords a great variety of scale and shell fish.

The surface of the town is generally uneven; in some parts it presents rugged features. Its soil varies from good to bad, but its average quality is well adapted to the culture of all the varieties of grains, grasses, fruits and vegetables common to the climate. The business of the dairy is extensive and lucrative.

The *village of Pawcatuck* is very handsome; it is finely located 6 miles from the sea, at the head of navigation on the Pawcatuck, and at the falls on that stream. This village is the site of valuable manufactures, and of a large interior trade. It is crossed by the Providence and Stonington rail road, and lies 40 miles S. S. W. from Providence, 5 N. N. E. from Stonington, and 35 W. by S. from Newport.

There are a number of pleasant ponds in the town, well stored with fish. Westerly was incorporated in 1669. Population, 1830, 1,904. Its Indian name was *Misquamicut*.

West Fairlee, Vt.

Orange co. This town is watered by Ompomponoosuc river, and by a part of Fairlee pond. The surface is rough and mountainous, but capable of sustaining a considerable number of cattle.

West Fairlee was chartered in connexion with Fairlee, in 1761; and incorporated as a distinct town in 1797. It lies 28 miles S. E. from Montpelier, and 12 E. by S. from Chelsea. Population, 1830, 841.

Westfield, Vt.

Orleans co. A number of the branches of Missisque river meet in this town, and afford a good water power. A part of the surface of Westfield is mountainous; through which is the pass in the Green mountains, called Hazen's Notch. Westfield was first settled about the year 1800. It lies 42 miles N. from Montpelier, and 44 N. E. from Burlington. Population, 1830, 353.

Westfield River, Mass.

This river, often called the Agawam, rises in the north part of Berkshire county. It has many tributaries, and is exceedingly wild and romantic in many places. Its main branch traverses the towns of Plainfield, Cummington, Goshen, Worthington, 'Chesterfield, Norwich, Montgomery, Russell, and Westfield, and meets the Connecticut at West Springfield, 30 miles N. from Hartford, Ct.

Westfield, Mass.

Hampden co. This is a place of singular beauty, on Westfield river. It lies in a valley or basin of about 4 miles in diameter, surrounded by high hills, and is supposed to have been the bed of a lake whose waters burst the Mount Tom range of mountains and discharged itself into Connecticut river.

The Hampshire and Hampden canal passes through this town, and promises great advantages to its trade and hydraulic power.

About a third part of the population of the village is engaged in making whips. The annual amount of that article manufactured here is about $160,000. There are also three powder mills in the town, and manufactures of tin ware, ploughs, boots, shoes, leather, cigars, palm-leaf hats, chairs, cabinet and wooden wares: total annual value, about $250,000.

The Westfield academy is in high standing: it has considerable funds, and its annual number of scholars is about 400.

Westfield was first settled in 1659. Incorporated in 1669. It lies 99 miles W. S. W. from Boston, 9 W. by N. from Springfield, and 16 S.

by W. from Northampton. Population, 1837, 3,039.

Westford, Vt.

Chittenden co. This township was settled soon after the revolutionary war, by Hezekiah Parmelee and others. It lies 13 miles N. N. E. from Burlington, and 32 N. W. from Montpelier.

Westford is well watered by Brown's river, a branch of the Lamoille. The surface is rough, and the soil good for grazing. Between 3,500 and 4,000 sheep are kept. Population, 1830, 1,290.

Westford, Mass.

Middlesex co. This is a good farming town, on elevated ground, 26 miles N. W. from Boston, and 10 N.W. from Concord. Incorporated, 1729. Population, 1837, 1,451. The surface and soil of the town are well adapted to the growth of grain, grass and fruit, and large quantities of hay and vegetables are annually sent to Boston and Lowell. Quantities of fine granite, commonly called "Chelmsford granite," are found here, quarried and transported. Westford is watered by several beautiful ponds, and by Stoney brook which rises in the town and gives it mill privileges.

The manufactures of Westford, consist of bar iron, shoes and leather: annual value, about $25,000.

The village is handsomely situated on a swell of fine land, commanding a beautiful prospect, of great extent, and contains an Academy of ancient date and respectable standing.

West Greenwich, R. I.

Kent co. This town was taken from East Greenwich in 1741, by which it is bounded on the east. It lies 18 miles S. W. from Providence. Population, 1830, 1,818. This town possesses a primitive geological character, and its surface presents a diversity of hills and valleys. Hopkin's Hill, affords an agreeable view of the surrounding country. The waters of the town consist of the south branch of the Pawtuxet, which rises here; and of the upper branches of Wood river, which pass through it. There are some manufactures in the town, but the people are generally engaged in agricultural pursuits.

Westhampton, Mass.

Hampshire co. This township is rough, but the soil is generally good, particularly for grazing. There is a valuable lead mine in the town; about 1,000 merino sheep are kept, and some hats and leather are manufactured. It lies 8 miles W. by S. from Northampton. Incorporated, 1772. Population, 1837, 818.

West Haven, Vt.

Rutland co. This town was set off from Fair Haven in 1792. It lies 19 miles W. from Rutland, and is bounded W. by lake Champlain, and S. by Whitehall, N. Y.

This town is well watered by Hubbardston and Poultney rivers, and Cogman's creek; on the former of which are handsome falls and mill sites. The soil is productive of grain and grass: there is much limestone and clay in the town, and a large number of sheep are annually sheared.

The site of the village is pleasant; it is a place of some trade, navigation and manufactures. Population, 1837, 724.

Westminster, Vt.

Windham co. This town is bounded N. by Rockingham, E. by Connecticut river, and S. by Putney. It lies 82 miles S. from Montpelier, and 13 N. E. from Newfane. Population, 1830, 1,737.

This town was one of the first settled townships in the state, and being situated near a fort for the protection of the country, it prospered rapidly. For some years the courts of law were held here; here the legislature of the state held several sessions, and here the massacre of the 13th of March, 1775, was perpetrated.

The surface and soil of this town are favorable for agriculture; and various articles of produce are annually sent to market. In 1837, 13,766 sheep were sheared in Westminster

The principal and oldest village is delightfully situated in the east parish, on the bank of Connecticut river. The main street, which is perfectly level, crosses a table of land about one mile in diameter, considerably elevated above the river, and also above the large and fertile meadows by which it is approached on the north and south; and the whole is enclosed by a semicircle of hills which touch the river about two miles above and below the town. It is this barrier which, while it contributes to the natural beauty of the place, has, by turning the water course in another direction, deprived it of all those facilities of access, and of water power, which have so much contributed to the rapid growth of some of the neighboring villages.

Westminster, Mass.

Worcester co. This town lies on the range of high lands which separate the waters of the Connecticut and Merrimack. From the village a prospect is presented of lake and mountain with all the varied scenery which renders a New England town peculiarly delightful.

Several streams, rising from large ponds in this town and its neighborhood, produce a considerable water power, which is improved for manufactures of various kinds. These waters are so elevated and constant that, with a small expense, they might be rendered exceedingly valuable. They deserve particular attention of those in search of mill sites in this part of the state.

This town lies 50 miles W. N. W. from Boston, 20 N. by W. from Worcester, and 7 S. W. from Fitchburgh. Incorporated, 1759. Population, 1830, 1,640.

The manufactures of Westminster consist of chairs, cabinet and wooden wares, hats, boots, shoes, straw bonnets, palm-leaf hats, card boards, saddlery, and leather: annual value, about $60,000.

Westmore, Vt.

Orleans co. This town contains Willoughby's lake, a handsome sheet of water, surrounded by mounts Hor, Pico, and other elevations. This lake is about 6 miles in length, and one and an half in width. Branches of Barton, Clyde and Passumpsic rivers rise in this and other ponds in the town.

Westmore appears to be too high for the habitation of many people or sheep: in 1830, it contained 32 inhabitants, and in 1837, 10 sheep.

Westmoreland, N. H.

Cheshire co. Westmoreland is bounded N. by Walpole, E. by Surry and Keene, S. by Chesterfield, and W. by Dummerston and Putney, Vt. Its distance from Concord is 65 miles S. W. Population, 1830, 1,647.

This town is watered by several small streams which empty into the Connecticut. The one issuing from Spafford's lake in Chesterfield is the largest, and affords some of the best water privileges in town.

The present charter of the town was granted by New Hampshire, in 1752. The first settlement was made in 1741. The early settlers were several times attacked by the Indians. In one of their excursions, they killed William Phips, the first husband of Jemima How; and in another, carried Nehemiah How, the father of her second husband, a captive to Canada, where he died. The surface of Westmoreland is less varied by mountains, vales, rivers and ponds, than the neighboring towns.

West Newbury, Mass.

Essex co. This is a part of the ancient town of Newbury, and was taken from it in 1819.

This pleasant town lies on the S. side of Merrimack river; 33 miles N. from Boston, 20 E. from Lowell, and 4 W. from Newburyport. Population, 1837, 1,448.

This is a fine township of land, and many excellent farms and country seats are found within its limits. Asbestos and marble are found here.

Although most of the inhabitants of the town are *professional* farmers, still there are manufactures of bar iron, combs, chaises, leather, and shoes: annual value, about $75,000.

Weston, Me.

Washington co. This town was incorporated in 1835. It is the half township granted to Hampden academy. It lies a few miles west from Grand Lake: it is watered by Baskahegan river, and is about 90 miles N. E. from Bangor. Population, 1837, 213. Wheat crop, same year, 4,706 bushels.

Weston, Vt.

Windsor co. West river passes through this town, and on its banks are some good land, some manufactures and two pleasant villages. It was set off from Andover in 1790, and organized as a town in 1800.

Weston lies 66 miles S. by W. from Montpelier, and 22 S. W. from Windsor. Population, 1830, 972.

Weston, Mass.

Middlesex co. This is a township of good land with a neat and flourishing village. It lies 14 miles W. from Boston, 9 S. by E. from Concord, and is watered by Stony brook. Population, 1837, 1,105.

The manufactures of the town consist of boots, shoes, leather, machinery, ploughs, chairs, harnesses, pottery ware, &c.: annual value, about $60,000. Incorporated, 1712.

Weston, Ct.

Fairfield co. Weston was taken from Fairfield in 1787. It was settled in 1738. The town is watered by Saugatuck and Mill rivers, and a pleasant brook, which furnish a good water power. There are some valuable mills for manafactures in the town, but the chief business of the inhabitants is agricultural. The soil is a gravelly loam, with an uneven surface.

Weston is 60 miles S. W. from Hartford, and is bounded N. W. by Fairfield. Population, 1830, 2,997.

"On Monday, the 14th of December, 1807, at about the break of day, or a little after, the weather being moderate, calm, and the atmosphere somewhat cloudy and foggy, a *meteor* or *fire ball*, passing from a northern point, disploded over the western part of this state, with a tremendous report. At the same time several pieces of stony substance fell on the earth in Fairfield county. One mass was driven against a rock and dashed in small pieces, a peck of which remained on the spot. About three miles distant, in the town of Weston, another large piece fell upon the earth, of which a mass of about thirty pounds weight remains entire, and was exhibited the same day at town meeting. A small mass has been sent to Yale College, and examined by a number of gentlemen. It was immediately perceived by Professor Silliman to contain a metal, and on presenting it to a magnet a powerful attraction proved it to be iron. This is, we believe, the first instance in the United States, in which the substance of this species of meteor has been found on the earth, though it has often been found in Europe."

Westport, Me.

Lincoln co. This town is surrounded by the waters of Sheepscot river and bay, and is bounded N. by Wiscasset, E. by Edgecomb and Boothbay, and S. and W. by Sheepscot's bay and Georgetown. It is 29 miles S. by E. from Augusta. Population, 1837, 580. Incorporated in 1828.

Westport, Mass.

Bristol co. This town is pleasantly situated on Acoakset river, near the mouth of Buzzard's bay, on the line of Rhode Island; 18 miles N. N. E. from Newport, 25 S. from Taunton, 10 S. by E. from Fall River, 10 S. W. from New Bedford, and 60 S. from Boston. Five vessels belong to this place, engaged in the whaling business, and a number of small vessels are employed in coasting and fishing.

The value of whale oil imported into Westport, the year ending April 1, 1837, was $53,670. The value of the manufactures of this town, the same year, was $69,375; they consisted of cotton yarn, salt and hoes. The number of sheep sheared that year, was 2,392; value of the wool, $2,551. This town was incorporated in 1787. Population, in 1837, 2,618.

Westport, Ct.

Fairfield co. This pleasant town was called Saugatuck, the name of a river that passes through it, until 1835. It was taken from the towns of Fairfield, Norwalk and Weston. It is about 5 miles in length from north to south, and is bounded E. by Fairfield, S. by Long Island Sound, and W. by Norwalk. Population, 1835, 1,800.

There are in the town, 2 or 3 cotton mills, 2 carriage factories, and manufactures of shoes, hats and various other articles. The village is quite a business place, and commands considerable trade.

The Saugatuck is navigable for vessels of 7 feet draught of water to the village, which is 6 1-2 miles W. from Fairfield, 3 1-2 N. E. from Norwalk, and 27 S. W. from New Haven.

About 2 1-2 miles south of the village of Westport, is a smooth and beautiful elevation, called *Compo.* It was at this place that the British troops landed in April, 1777, when on their expedition to Danbury. They also returned to this place when they embarked on board of their shipping. Seven or eight men were killed in the vicinity of the Congregational church in Westport. *Ball Mountain,* a conical eminence, covered with large trees from its base to its summit, is situated a little south of the village, and is a striking feature in the landscape.

West Quoddy Head, Me.

See *Quoddy Head.*

West River, Vt.

This river rises in Weston, in the county of Windsor, and passing S. through the towns of Londonderry, Jamaica, Wardsborough, and Newfane, in the county of Windham, it falls into the Connecticut at the north part of Brattleborough. This river receives many branches in its course, which are good mill streams: the main river is rather sluggish, and fertilizes large tracts of meadow. West river traverses a distance of about 50 miles, and waters a basin of 440 square miles.

West River Mountain, N. H.

See *Chesterfield* and *Hinsdale.*

West Springfield, Mass.

Hampden co. This town is beautifully situated on both sides of Westfield river, at its confluence with the Connecticut, opposite to

Springfield, to which it is connected by a beautiful bridge. Some parts of the town are rough and uneven, and in some parts are stony plains; but the general character of the town in regard to soil is alluvial meadow of an excellent quality. On the summits of the hills and along the rivers, a great variety of wild and delightful scenery is exhibited.

There are 1 cotton and 2 woolen mills in the town, and manufactures of leather, boots and shoes; annual value, about $100,000. In 1837, there were 3,374 fleeces of wool sheared in the town, which weighed 8,512 lbs., and sold for $5,107. Good iron ore is found in West Springfield, and a species of limestone, used for making water proof cement. Incorporated, 1774. Population, 1837, 3,227.

West Stockbridge, Mass.

Berkshire co. Williams river which rises in Richmond, runs through the whole length of this town, and gives it a great hydraulic power.

This town is bounded W. by the state of New York, and lies on the route of the great western rail road from Boston to Albany. A part of the town is hilly; but the soil is generally good. Along the river is a valley of fine land which gives beauty to the village, and value to the town. Mines of iron ore are found in this town, and an inexhaustible quantity of beautifully variegated marble.

The manufactures of the town consist of bar iron, axes, brads, machinery, marble, leather, wooden ware, &c; annual value, about $50,000.

West Stockbridge lies 135 miles W. from Boston, 9 S. S. W. from Lenox, 26 E. by N. from Hudson, N. Y., and 37 1-2 S. E. by S. from Albany, by the proposed rail road. Incorporated, 1774. Population, in 1837, 1,244.

Wethersfield, Ct.

Hartford co. This town, the Indian *Pyquag*, was one of the first settled towns in the state. It is supposed that most of the Wethersfield settlers came round from Boston by water, and arrived in July, *before* the Windsor and Hartford settlers, who came through the wilderness, and did not reach the Connecticut until about the 9th of November.

Wethersfield is bounded N. by Hartford, E. by Connecticut river, S. by Middletown, and W. by Berlin. It lies 4 miles S. from Hartford. Population, in 1820, 3,825; in 1830, 3,853.

Piper's river and other small streams water the town, but afford no important mill sites.

The area of the town is about 6 miles square, containing 23,000 acres. This is an excellent township of land, having an undulating surface, and exhibiting a beautiful diversity of hill and dale. The soil is generally a rich gravelly and sandy loam, but in the western part of the town, argillaceous loam prevails; and some small sections in the centre, may be considered as a garden mould. It is well adapted to grass and grain, and particularly to esculent roots. The tract of alluvial upon Connecticut river is extensive and beautiful, and very productive.

Among other agricultural interests in this town, the cultivation of onions has long held a conspicuous rank. This is an important agricultural pursuit, although it occupies but a small portion of land, and the service is principally performed by females. Wethersfield onions have long been justly celebrated, and large quantities are exported to the southern states and the West Indies for a market.

The changing of the bed of the river in this town has been the occasion of much litigation respecting the title to the soil. Mr. Butler, who owned a tract upon which the river was encroaching, found after a while, some of his land appearing on the opposite side of the river, and accordingly laid claim to it. His claim was disputed, as he never owned land on *that side* of the river. It was a long time before this case was decided. There appeared some difficulty in making the jury who sat on the case, to understand the merits of the question. Mr. Ingersoll, a relative of the Ingersoll family in New Haven, was the counsel employed by Mr. Butler. He illustrated the case by supposing that Mr. B. had built a castle on the land in question. Although the ground on which it stood might be overflowed, yet still it was his castle, and also the ground on which it stood, and he had a right to his property wherever he could find it. The case was finally decided in accordance with these views.

The *State Prison* of Connecticut was erected in this town in 1826, and the prisoners from Newgate prison, in Granby, were removed here the next year. This building is situated on the south margin of the cove, which sets back from Connecticut river, at the north end of Wethersfield village. The buildings of the prison form very nearly a quadrangle, on the south side of which, stands the building which is more properly *the Prison*. The apartments of the warden are situated in the east end of this building; the centre surrounds the block of cells 4 stories high, in which the male prisoners are locked up. This hall or centre is 154 feet long, 43 feet wide, and 30 feet high; the number of cells or night rooms is 200. The west end, is used as the female department, containing cells, rooms for labor, kitchen, and apartments for the matron. The east, north, and west sides of this quadrangle, are formed by a wall 20 feet high. Within this yard are situated two ranges of shops; one on the east side, and one upon the west, in which the convicts perform their daily labor. The passage into the prison, is through the warden's apartment, into the guard room, thence into the hall surrounding the cells, thence into the yard. This is the only passage, except through a large gate on the north side of the yard.

Rocky Hill, the south parish of Wethersfield, lies on a collection of hills which are a continuation of the Middletown range: one of these eminences, Rocky hill, has given name to the parish. It has a pleasant little village on an elevated situation, 7 miles from Hartford, with a landing at some distance, where considerable commerce and ship building were formerly carried on.

Newington, the 2d society in Wethersfield, was formerly called *Cow plain*. The village is pleasantly situated in a fertile valley, west of Cedar mountain: the central part is 6 miles from Hartford, and 4 from Wethersfield village. The inhabitants are chiefly engaged in agriculture, and are distinguished for their general intelligence, and attachment to the institutions of morality and religion.

Many years since, a gentleman of Newington, who was a very religious and conscientious man, married for a wife, one of the most ill natured and troublesome women which could be found in the vicinity. This occasioned universal surprise wherever he was known, and one of his neighbors ventured to ask him the reasons which governed his choice. The gentleman replied, that having had but little or no trouble in the world, he was fearful of becoming too much attached to things of time and sense. And he thought by experiencing some afflictions, he should become more weaned from the world, and that he married such a woman as he thought would accomplish the object. The best part of the story is, that the wife hearing of the reasons why he married her, was much offended, and *out of revenge,* became one of the most pleasant and dutiful wives in the town, declaring that she was not a going to be made a *pack horse,* to carry her husband to heaven.

Wethersfield was the scene of one of the most horrible butcheries ever committed; that of the *Beadle family,* in 1782.

Beadle was an Englishman, and came to this country in 1762. He settled in Fairfield, where he married, and remained until about 10 years before this tragedy. The following are extracts from an account of this event, written by a neighbor, and attached to the funeral sermon of Mrs. Beadle and her children.

"When the war commenced, he had on hand a very handsome assortment of goods for a country store, which he sold for the currency of the country, without any advance in the price; the money he laid by, waiting and expecting the the time would soon arrive when he might therewith replace his goods, resolving not to part with it until it should be in as good demand as when received by him. His expectations from this quarter daily lessening, finally lost all hope, and was thrown into a state little better than despair, as appears from his writing: he adopted a plan of the most rigid family economy, but still kept up the outward appearance of his former affluence, and ever to the last entertained his friends with his usual decent hospitality, although nothing appeared in his outward deportment, which evinced the uncommon pride of his heart. His writings show clearly that he was determined not to bear the mortification of being thought by his friends poor and dependent.

On this subject he expresses himself in the following extraordinary manner: 'If a man, who has once lived well, meant well, and done well, falls by unavoidable accident into poverty, and then submits to be laughed at, despised and trampled on, by a set of mean wretches as far below him as the moon is below the sun; I say if such a man submits, he must become meaner than meanness itself, and I sincerely wish he might have 10 years added to his natural life to punish him for his folly.'

"He fixed upon the night succeeding the 18th of November for the execution of his nefarious purpose, and procured a supper of oysters, of which the family eat very plentifully: that evening he writes as follows: 'I have prepared a noble supper of oysters, that my flock and I may eat and drink together, thank God and die.' After supper he sent the maid with a studied errand to a friend's house at some distance, directing her to stay until she obtained an answer to an insignificant letter he wrote his friend, intending she should not return that evening—she did however return; perhaps her return disconcerted him and prevented him for that time. The next day he carried his pistols to a smith for repair: it may be, the ill condition of his pistols might be an additional reason of the delay.

"On the evening of the 10th of December some persons were with him at his house to whom he appeared as cheerful and serene as usual; he attended to the little affairs of his family as if nothing uncommon was in contemplation. The company left him about nine o'clock in the evening, when he was urgent as usual for their stay: whether he slept that night is uncertain, but it is believed he went to bed. The children and maid slept in one chamber: in the grey of the morning of the 11th of December he went to their bed chamber, awaked the maid and ordered her to rise gently, without disturbing the children, when she came down stairs; he gave her a line to the family physician, who lived at the distance of a quarter of a mile; ordered her to carry it immediately, at the same time declaring that Mrs. Beadle had been ill all night, and directing her to stay until the physician should come with her: this he repeated sundry times with a degree of ardor. There is much reason to believe he had murdered Mrs. Beadle before he awaked the maid. Upon the maid's leaving the house he immediately proceeded to execute his purpose on the children and himself. It appears he had for some time before, carried to his bedside every night an axe and a carving knife; he smote his wife and each of the children with the axe on the side of the head as they lay sleeping in their beds; the woman had two wounds in the head, the skull of each of them was fractured; he then with the carving knife cut their throats from ear to ear; the woman and little boy were drawn partly over the side of their beds, as if to prevent the bedding from being besmeared with blood: the three daughters were taken from the bed and laid upon the floor side by side, like three lambs, before their throats were cut; they were covered with a blanket, and the woman's face with a handkerchief. He then proceeded to the lower floor of the house, leaving marks of his footsteps in blood on the stairs, carrying with him the axe and knife, the latter he laid on the table in the room where he was found, reeking with the blood of his family. Perhaps he had thoughts he might use it against himself if his pistols should fail. It appears he then seated himself in a Windsor chair, with his arms supported by the arms of the chair; he fixed the muzzles of the pistols into his two ears, and fired them at the same instant: the balls went through the head in transverse directions. Although the neighbors were very near and some of them awake, none heard the report of the pistols.

"The line to the physician obscurely announced the intentions of the man; the house was soon opened, but alas, too late! The bodies were pale and motionless, swimming in their blood, their faces white as mountain snow, yet life seemed to tremble on their lips: description can do no more than faintly ape and trifle with the real figure.

"Such a tragical scene filled every mind with the deepest distress: nature recoiled, and was on the rack with distorting passions: the most poignant sorrow and tender pity for the lady and her innocent babes, who were the hapless victims of the brutal, studied cruelty of an husband and father, in whose embraces they expected to find security, melted every heart. Shocking effects of pride and false notions about religion!

"To paint the first transports this affecting scene produced, when the house was opened, is beyond my reach. Multitudes of all ages and sexes were drawn together by the sad tale. The very inmost souls of the beholders were wounded at the sight, and torn by contending passions. Silent grief, with marks of astonishment, were succeeded by furious indignation against the author of the affecting spectacle, which vented itself in incoherent exclamations. Nature itself seemed ruffled, and refused the kindly aid of balmy sleep for a time.

"Near the close of the day on the 12th of December, the bodies being still unburied, the people who had collected in great numbers, grew almost frantic with rage, and in a manner demanded the body of the murderer: the law being silent on the subject, it was difficult to determine where decency required the body should be placed: many proposed it should be in an ignominious manner where four roads met, without any coffin or insignia of respect, and perforated by a stake. Upon which a question arose, where that place could be found which might be unexceptionable to the neighborhood, but no one would consent it should be near his house or land. After some consultation it was thought best to place it on the bank of the river between high and low water mark: the body was handed out of the window and bound with cords on a sled, with the clothes on as it was found, and the bloody knife tied on his breast, without coffin or box, and the horse he usually rode was made fast to the sled: the horse, unaccustomed to the draught, proceeded with great unsteadiness, sometimes running full speed, then stopping, followed by a multitude, until arriving at the water's edge, the body was tumbled into a hole dug for the purpose, like the carcase of a beast.

"On the 13th of December, the bodies of the murdered were interred in a manner much unlike that of the unnatural murderer. The remains of the children were borne by a suitable number of equal age, attended by a sad procession of youths of the town, all bathed in tears; side by side the hapless woman's corpse was carried in solemn procession to the parish church yard, followed by a great concourse, who with affectionate concern and every token of respect were anxious to express their heartfelt sorrow in performing the last mournful duties.

"The person of Mr. Beadle was small, his features striking and full of expression, with the aspect of fierceness and determination; his mind was contemplative; when once he had formed an opinion, he was remarkably tenacious: as a merchant or trader, he was esteemed a man of strict honor and integrity, and would not descend to any low or mean artifice to advance his fortune. He was turned of 52 years of age when he died.

"Mrs. Beadle was born at Plymouth in Massachusetts, of reputable parents, a comely person, of good address, well bred, and unusually serene, sincere, unaffected and sensible. She died in the middle of life, aged 32 years.

"The children, (the eldest of which was a son, aged 12 years, the other three, daughters, the youngest aged 6 years) were such as cheered the hearts of their parents, who were uncommonly fond of displaying their little virtues and excellencies, and seemed to anticipate a continuance of growing parental satisfaction: alas, like early, tender buds nipped by untimely frosts, they did but begin to live!

"It is more than probable, that this man had for months past desired that some or all of his children might be taken out of the world by accident: he removed all means of security from a well near his house, which he was careful heretofore to keep covered. His little boy he often sent to swim in the river, and has been heard to chide the child for not venturing further into deep water than his fears would suffer him. He has at times declared it would give him no pain or uneasiness to follow his children to the grave: his acquaintance knew these expressions could not arise from want of affection or tenderness for his children, but rather imagined him speaking rashly in jest. He ever spoke lightly of death as a bugbear the world causelessly feared. It appears from his writings, he at first had doubts whether it was just and reasonable for him to deprive his wife of life, and offers against it only this reason, that he had no hand in bringing her into existence, and consequently had no power over her life. She set out on the 7th of November on a journey to Fairfield, which he thought was by direction of Heaven to clear him of his doubts and remove her out of the way, at the time the business was to be done; and his intention was to have executed his design on himself and children in her absence. She proceeded no further than New Haven, and by reason of some disappointment, returned ten days earlier than expected: he appeared chagrined at her early return, and soon began to invent some justifying reasons for depriving her of life also. He finally concludes it would be unmerciful to leave her behind to languish out a life of misery and wretchedness, which must be the consequence of the surprising death of the rest of the family, and that since they had shared the frowns and smiles of fortune together, it would be cruelty to her, to be divided from them in death."

Weybridge, Vt.

Addison co. Weybridge is watered by Otter Creek, which affords it good mill sites. Lemonfair river, a sluggish stream, also waters the town. Some parts of the town are mountainous, but the soil is generally good: the basis being limestone, it yields good crops, and pastures about 6,000 sheep. It lies 30 miles S. by E. from Burlington, and is bounded on the S. E. by Middlebury. Population, 1830, 850.

Weymouth, Mass.

Norfolk co. This was the second settlement made by white men in New England. Mr. Thomas Weston, a respectable merchant of London, who had been active in promoting the interests of the Plymouth colonists, sent two ships and 50 or 60 men to plant a colony at this place, in the year 1622. The fate of the colony was as unfortunate as the designs of Mr. Weston were philanthropic. By the unjust and wanton conduct of his agents towards the natives, the colony would have been totally destroyed, were it not for the timely assistance afforded it by a band of men from the Plymouth Colony, commanded by the gallant Standish. The colony was broken up, and Mr. Weston lost his life on the coast in attempting to reach it. This place, the Indian *Wessagusset*, named Weymouth from a town in England, was however permanently settled by the Rev. William Morrill, Capt. Robert Georges and others, in the year 1624.

The surface of the town is pleasantly diversified by hills and valleys. Some of the elevations are commanding, and present delightful views of Boston harbor, Massachusetts bay and the adjacent country. The soil is a strong gravelly loam, with a granitic superstructure.

This town was formerly noted for its excellent dairies, particularly for its cheese of a superior richness and flavor; but little of which is now made in consequence of the increased value of the lands.

Weymouth is finely watered by large and beautiful ponds, and by two important arms of Boston harbor, called Fore and Back rivers. These rivers are navigable for large vessels, and at their head are valuable mill privileges. Between these rivers, and between the towns of Braintree and Hingham is a large tract of gently swelling land of good soil, extending to Quincy, and is united to " Quincy Point " by a bridge across Fore river. Over this ground the turnpike road between Quincy and Hingham passes.

There are several pleasant villages in Weymouth, but the principal place of business in the town is at " Weymouth Landing," so called, or Washington Square, at the head of Fore river, on the line of Braintree. This place, being at the head of navigation for a large and flourishing section of country, has long enjoyed, and must ever possess superior privileges as a place of trade. About 1,000 tons of shipping is owned here, employed in the fishery and domestic trade. At this place are a number of wharves, ware houses, a steam saw mill, and manufactures of various kinds. Ship building is carried on to some extent, and large quantities of lumber, flour, grain, lime, coal, wood, &c., are annually sold.

This village lies on the Plymouth and New Bedford roads, 11 miles S. by E. from Boston, 24 N. N. W. from Plymouth, 14 S. E. from Dedham, 5 W. from Hingham, and 9 S. S. W. from Boston Light.

The village at the south part of the town is pleasantly situated on elevated ground, about 3 miles S. from Washington Square. The people here are extensively engaged in the manufacture of boots and shoes.

Stages pass between these villages and Boston, daily; and packets, for the transportation of merchandize, navigate the rivers about nine months in the year.

The roads in this section of the country are remarkably fine, and many citizens of Boston make Weymouth their summer residence.

The manufactures of the town are various, but those of leather, boots and shoes, are the most considerable. The annual amount of these manufactures varies from $500,000 to $800,000.

Weymouth was incorporated in 1635. Population, 1820, 2,404; 1830, 2,839; 1837, 3,387.

This ancient town has been the birth place and residence of many men of great usefulness in society. Among the number, the name of COTTON TUFTS, M. D., M. M. S. S. A. A. S., will long be remembered as a revolutionary patriarch and skillful physician.

Whately, Mass.

Franklin co. This town lies on the west side of Connecticut river, 9 miles N. from Northampton, 11 S. from Greenfield, and 92 W. by N. from Boston. Incorporated in 1771. Population, in 1837, 1,140. There are some pine plains, and a part of Sugar Loaf mountain extends into the town from Deerfield; still there are some tracts of good intervale land on the Connecticut, and smaller streams, by which it is watered. The number of sheep in Whately, in 1837, was 1,650; weight of wool, 4,953 lbs.: value, $2,862. There are 3 woollen mills in the town, 3 tanneries, 3 distilleries, and manufactures of gimblets, augers, hammers, brooms, brushes, palm-leaf hats, boots, shoes, pocket-books, &c. Annual value, about $90,000.

Wheelock, Vt.

Caledonia co. There is some good land in this town, but a great part of it is mountainous or hilly, and fit only for the pasturage of sheep, of which about 3,000 are kept. The streams flow N. W. into the Lamoille; and S. E. into the Passumpsic.

This town was granted in 1785, to the charity school at Dartmouth College, and named in honor of John Wheelock, who was, at that time, president of that institution. Wheelock lies 30 miles N. N. E. from Montpelier, and 9 N. from Danville. Population, 1830, 834.

Wheelwright's Pond, N. H.

See *Lee.*

White River, Vt.

This is the largest stream in the state on the east side of the Green Mountains. It waters a basin of about 700 square miles, and traverses in its course from Kingston, in

Addison county, about 60 miles. It passes through Hancock, Rochester, and Pittsfield, in Rutland county, and Stockbridge, Bethel, Royalton, and Sharon, in Windsor county, to its fall into the Connecticut at Hartford, about 5 miles above the mouth of Queechy river. White river receives many large tributaries; the most considerable of which are the three branches, so called, from the north; and Broad brook and Locust creek from the south. This stream and its branches, afford a great hydraulic power; and large tracts of country are fertilized by its waters. It passes through a country of lofty mountains, deep ravines and fertile valleys; the scenery of which is much enhanced by the devious course of this beautiful river.

White Cap Mountain, Me.

See *Andover*.

Whitefield, Me.

Lincoln co. Sheepscot river passes through this town, giving it fertility, beauty, and a good water power. It lies 16 miles S. E. from Augusta, and 14 N. from Wiscasset. Incorporated, 1809. Population, in 1837, 2,136. Wheat crop, same year, 3,637 bushels.

Whitefield, N. H.

Coos co. This is an irregular township, lying S. from Lancaster, W. from Jefferson, N. from Carroll and Bethlehem, and E. from Dalton. It is 120 miles N. from Concord. Its soil is generally thin and light, of easy cultivation and tolerably good; though in the N. part low spruce swamps abound. In this town lie part of Blake's, Long, Round and Little river ponds, beside two other small ponds. The second of these is a beautiful pond of considerable size, abounding with fish. John's river passes through this town. Whitefield was granted July 4, 1774, to Josiah Moody and others, and soon after settled by Maj. Burns and others. Population, 1830, 685.

Whitehead, Me.

Lincoln co. An Island off the town of St. George, with a light and tower 30 feet in height. The light bears about S. W. by S. 9 miles from Owl's Head.

White Mountains, N. H.

These mountains are situated in the county of Coos, in the north part of the state. They extend about 20 miles from S. W. to N. E., and are the more elevated parts of a range extending many miles in that direction. Their base is about 10 miles broad and their central latitude is 44° 15′ N., and 71° 20′ W. longitude.

The Indian name of these mountains, according to Dr. Belknap, was *Agiocochook*. An ancient tradition prevailed among the savages, that a deluge once overspread the land, and destroyed every human being, except a single powow and his wife, who sheltered themselves in these elevated regions, and thus preserved the race from extermination. The fancy of the natives peopled this mountain with beings of a superior rank, who were invisible to the human eye, but sometimes indicated their presence by tempests, which they were believed to control with absolute authority. The savages therefore, never attempted to ascend the summit, deeming the attempt perilous, and success impossible. But they frequented the defiles and environs of the mountain, and of course propagated many extravagant descriptions of its appearance; declaring, among other things equally credible, that they had seen carbuncles at immense heights, which, in the darkness of night, shone with the most brilliant and dazzling splendor.

President Alden states, that the

White mountains were called by one of the eastern tribes *Waumbekketmethna:* Waumbekket signifies *white*, and methna, *mountains.*

Before we attempt a description of these mountains, we shall endeavor to direct the traveller, in his course, from the east, the south and the west, to this magnificent exhibition of Almighty power.

Routes from Boston, through Concord, N. H. Travellers take the rail road to Lowell, pass to Nashua, by rail road, and then by stage through Amoskeag to Concord, or take the Mammoth road at Lowell, through Manchester and Londonderry, or pass through Andover and Haverhill, Mass. The distance from Boston to Concord, by the Mammoth road, is 65 miles: by Nashua, 72, and by the way of Haverhill, 70 miles. From Concord you pass to Meredith bridge, either by the Shaker village in Canterbury, 12 miles; or Sanbornton bridge, 16 miles from Concord. The distance from Concord to Meredith bridge is 26 miles. From Meredith bridge to Meredith village, is 9 miles; from thence to Centre Harbor, at the north western extremity of Winnepisiogee lake, is 4 miles. Here you have a fair view of the lake for 15 miles, and here you can be accommodated with a passage down the lake, to Alton, any day in the season of navigation. From Centre Harbor to Moultonborough is 5 miles, to Sandwich, 2, to Tamworth, 12; to Eaton, 6, to Conway, 8, to Bartlett, on the south east side of the mountains, 10; to the entrance of the Notch, 12 miles; and from thence to the "Crawford House," is 12 miles. The Crawford house is about 9 miles from the summit of Mount Washington. About two thirds of this distance is traveled by horses, procured at the accommodation house of Crawford; the residue is traveled on foot, by a pretty good path, cut for the purpose. The total distance from Boston to the base of Mount Washington, is 171 miles. These are very pleasant routes; you pass through the capital of New Hampshire, a beautiful town; you enjoy a great variety of delightful and romantic river and lake scenery, and are accommodated with good houses, gentlemanly landlords, skillful and obliging stagemen.

There is another route from Concord to these hills, by the way of Plymouth, through the Franconia Notch, that is very pleasant and frequently traveled. From Concord through Boscawen, Franklin, Andover, Hill, Bristol, and Bridgewater, to Plymouth, is 40 miles; from thence, through Campton, Thornton, Peeling, Lincoln, to Littleton, through the Franconia Notch, is 40 miles. From Littleton to Crawford's, is 18 miles. Total distance from Boston, by this route, 163 miles.

From Plymouth to Littleton the roads are remarkably good, and the landscape delightful; but the scenery is not so beautiful as by the Winnepisiogee, nor so magnificent as through the Notch of the White Mountains.

The *Portsmouth and Dover route*, from Boston, is very pleasant: you exchange the beautiful scenery along the Merrimack, for a visit to some of our most delightful Atlantic towns. On this route we pass through the principal towns of Salem, Beverly, Ipswich, Newburyport, Hampton, to Portsmonth, 56 miles from Boston. From thence we go to Dover, 12 miles, to Alton, at the southeastern extremity of Winnepisiogee lake, 28 miles; from thence up the lake, by steam boat, to Centre Harbor, 20 miles, and from thence, to Crawford's, at the base of Mount Washington, as by the Concord route. Total distance, by this route, 183 miles.

The *Portland route*, from Boston, by steam boat and stage, is another very pleasant way to reach this mountainous region. You leave Boston in the evening, on board one of our beautiful, seaworthy steamers, and take an early breakfast, the next morning, at our friend Haskell's, at the "Elm House," in Portland. The distance from Boston to Portland is about 120 miles; but distance, in this case, is generally lost in sleep. After breakfast you take the northern stage, and passing through Gorham and other towns, to Fryeburgh, you arrive at Conway, (the centre of all the eastern routes,) 57 miles from Portland, and, find excellent accommodations for the night. The next day you have ample time to go to the Crawford house, and to prepare for an aerial excursion the next morning. The distance from Boston, in this way, is 211 miles. This is the most expeditious route, and has the charms of both ocean and inland scenery.

The *Connecticut River route*, to the "Crystal Hills," is full of beauty in almost all its course. You leave Hartford and ascend one of the most delightful rivers in the world, to Littleton, N. H., a distance of 188 miles. Some of this distance may be travelled by water, but the most agreeable mode of travelling is by land, on either side of the river. As you pass the principal towns of Springfield, Northampton, Deerfield, Greenfield, Brattleboro', Walpole, Windsor, Hanover, Norwich, Haverhill and Newbury, you are charmed with all the varieties of scenery, which elevated mountains, placid and rapid waters, a wide, luxuriant and densely populated alluvial basin can yield. The distance from Littleton through Bethlehem to Crawford's House is 18 miles. Total distance from Hartford, by this route, 206 miles.

The Hudson River Route. Excursions to these mountains from New York by the Hudson river, Lake Champlain, and back by the way of Boston or Hartford, affords our southern and western friends a rich repast of New York and New England scenery.

The distances on the Hudson from New York to Troy are given under *Long Island Sound.*

From Troy to the far famed Mineral Springs, at *Ballston and Saratoga*, is a pleasant ride, by the rail road. The distance to the former is 25, and to the latter 32 miles. The distance from Albany to Saratoga Springs, by the way of Schenectady, is 36 miles.

The waters of these springs have long been justly celebrated for their medicinal and exhilarating qualities; and a vast number from all parts of the United States, and even from foreign countries, resort to them, either for health, or to join the gay and fashionable throng who hold an annual festival around these hygeian fountains.

The accommodations at these villages, for the entertainment of strangers, are of the first order: no expense seems to be spared to render them acceptable to their numerous visitants.

These springs are numerous, but generally contain the same substances, only in a greater or less quantity. The most celebrated of them is the *Congress*, at Saratoga, which has given, in analysis, 471,5 grains muriate of soda; 178,4 3-4 carbonate of lime; 16,5 carbonate of soda; 3,3 1-2 carbonate of magnesia, and 6,1 3-4 carbonate of iron, to one gallon of water: carbonic acid gas, 343 cubic inches. Temperature through the year, 50° of Farenheit.

A few miles east from Saratoga village is Fish Creek, memorable as the scene of the surrender of Burgoyne's army, of 5,791 men, to the Americans, under General Gates, October 17, 1777.

From Troy to Whitehall, N. Y., is 70 miles by stage, and 72 by the Champlain canal. In this distance we pass Bemis' Heights, and forts Miller, Edward, and Anne; important stations during the revolutionary war.

Whitehall is at the southern extremity of lake Champlain, and at the junction of the canal with the lake. This place is an important location for trade on Lake Champlain, and of an extensive tract of country. The lake is navigable here for all classes of lake vessels; and from this place steam boats ply along the shores of this beautiful lake to St. Johns in Lower Canada. This is a pleasant and flourishing town, and a great thoroughfare for travelers in the season of navigation. It is situated in the county of Washington, and contains a population of about 3,500.

About a dozen miles west from Whitehall lays *Lake George*, celebrated for the purity of its waters, its enchanting island and mountain scenery, its salmon trout, and above all, for its history, as connected with the memory of our fathers in their glorious struggle for liberty. This lake is about 35 miles in length, and averages about 2 miles in breadth. It discharges its waters into Lake Champlain, near the ruins of Ticonderoga, by an outlet of 3 miles in length; in which distance the fall is about 150 feet.

On some of the islands in this lake, crystals of quartz are found of uncommon transparency and perfection of form.

Rogers' Rock, is on the west side of the lake, near the outlet. It rises abruptly between 300 and 400 feet. It received its name from a Major Rogers, who, to elude his Indian pursuers, deceived them by asscending the rock, throwing his pack into the lake, and changing his snow shoes heels foremost;

thus inducing them to believe that he had leaped into the lake.

This is indeed one of the most beautiful and romantic sheets of water in the world.

From Whitehall to Burlington, Vermont, is 70 miles. On this route we pass the memorable fortresses of Ticonderoga and Crown Point; Mount Independence, and a great number of beautiful towns which skirt the lake on each side.

Opposite to Charlotte, Vermont, 11 miles S. from Burlington, in the town of Essex, N. Y., is *Split Rock*, a great natural curiosity. This rock projects into the lake 150 feet. The point is separated from the main rock about 20 feet: it contains about half an acre, and is covered with trees. The height of the rock, on each side of the opening, is about 20 feet; and appears to have been rent asunder by some great convulsion.

From the beautiful town of Burlington we cross the mountains to Montpelier, situated in a delightful valley amid the hills. The distance is 38 miles. On this route we travel along the romantic banks of the Winooski; we listen to the rushing of its waters down its mountain course; view its foaming cataracts, and stop to admire the wonderful fissures and fantastic mechanism, which, in the course of ages, that stream has wrought, by its ceaseless current, amid these adamantine hills.

From Montpelier we pass to Connecticut river, and Littleton, N. H., a distance of 40 miles, and from Littleton to the base of Mount Washington, a distance of 18 miles.

By this route from the city of New York, the distance is 386 miles: from that city by the way of Stonington, Providence, and the nearest route from Boston, the distance is 383 miles. This route may be varied so as to enjoy the beauties of Winnepisiogee lake, by leaving Troy, 150 miles, for

Bennington, 30 miles, 180; Brattleborough, 40—220; Keene, 20—240; Concord, 55—295; to the base of the mountains, 106; total distance, 401 miles.

These mountains are the highest in New England; and, if we except the Rocky mountains, whose height has not been ascertained, they are the most lofty of any in the United States. Their great elevation has always rendered them exceedingly interesting both to the aboriginal inhabitants and to our ancestors. They were visited by Neal, Jocelyn, and Field as early as 1632: they gave romantic accounts of their adventures, and of the extent and sublimity of the mountains. They called them the CRYSTAL HILLS.

Since that time this mountainous region has been repeatedly explored by hunters and men of science. Their height has been a subject of much speculation; but from the best surveys, Mount Washington is 6,234 feet above the level of the sea. The following is the height of the principal mountains above Connecticut river at Lancaster, to wit:

Mount Washington, - 5,850 feet.
" Adams, - - 5,383
" Jefferson, - 5,281
" Madison, - - 5,039
" Monroe, - - 4,932
" Franklin, - 4,470
" La Fayette, - 4,339

Although these mountains are 65 miles distant from the ocean, their snow white summits are distinctly visible, in good weather, more than 50 miles from shore. Their appearance at that distance is that of a silvery cloud skirting the horizon.

The names here given are those generally appropriated to the different summits. *Mount Washington* is known by its superior elevation, and by its being the southern of the three highest peaks. *Mount Adams* is known by its sharp terminating peak, and being the second north of Washington. *Jefferson* is situated between these two. *Madison* is the eastern peak of the range. *Monroe* is the first to the south of Washington. *Franklin* is the second south and is known by its level surface. *LaFayette* is known by its conical shape, and being the third south of Washington. The ascent to the summits of these mountains, though fatiguing, is not dangerous; and the visitant is richly rewarded for his labor and curiosity. In passing from the Notch to the highest summit, the traveller crosses the summits of Mounts La Fayette, Franklin and Monroe. In accomplishing this, he must pass through a forest, and cross several ravines. These are neither wide nor deep, nor are they discovered at a great distance; for the trees fill them up exactly even with the mountain on each side, and their branches interlock with each other in such a manner, that it is very difficult to pass through them, and they are so stiff and thick as almost to support a man's weight. Mount La Fayette is easily ascended. Its top, to the extent of 5 or 6 acres, is smooth, and gradually slopes away in every direction from its centre. It even has a verdant appearance, as it is every where covered with short grass, which grows in little tufts to the height of four or five inches. Among these tufts, mountain flowers are thinly scattered, which add life and beauty to the scene. The prospect from this summit is beautiful: to the N. the eye is dazzled with the splendor of Mount Washington; N. W. are seen the settlements in Jefferson; W. the courses of the Amonoosuck, as though delineated on a map: S. W. the Moosehillock and Haystack are discovered; S. Chocorua peak; S. E. the settlements and mountains in Bartlett; E. only dark mountains and forests. On descending this mountain, a small patch of water is found at its base; from which the ascent is gradual to the summit of Mount Franklin. After crossing this mountain, you pass over the east pinnacle of Mount Monroe, and soon find yourself on a plain of some extent, at the foot of Mount Washington. Here is a fine resting-place, on the margin of a beautiful sheet of water, of an oval form, covering about 3-4 of an acre. The waters are pleasant to the taste, and deep. Not a living creature is to be seen in the waters, at this height on the hills; nor do vegetables of any kind grow in or around them, to obscure the clear rocky or gravelly bottom on which they rest. A small spring discharges itself into this pond at its southeast angle. Another pond, of about 2-3 its size, lies N. W. of this. Directly before you, the pinnacle of Mount Washington rises with majestic grandeur, like an immense pyramid, or some vast Kremlin in this magnificent city of mountains. The pinnacle is elevated about 1,500 feet above the plain, and is composed principally of huge rocks of granite and gneiss piled together, presenting a variety of colors and forms.

In ascending, you must pass enormous masses of loose stones; but a walk of half an hour will generally carry you to the summit. The view from this point is wonderfully grand and picturesque. Innumerable mountains, lakes, ponds, rivers, towns and villages meet the delighted eye, and the dim Atlantic stretches its waters along the eastern horizon. To the N. is seen the lofty summits of Adams and Jefferson; and to the east a little detached from the range stands Mount Madison. Mount Washington is supported on the N. by a high ridge, which extends to Mount Jefferson; on the N. E. by a large grassy plain, terminating in a vast spur extending far away in that direction; E. by a promontory, which breaks off abruptly at St. Anthony's Nose; S.

and S. E. by a grassy plain, in summer, of more than 40 acres. At the southeastern extremity of this plain, a ridge commences, which slopes gracefully away towards the vale of the Saco; upon which at short distances from each other, arise rocks, resembling, in some places, towers; in others, representing the various orders of architecture.

It would be vain in us to attempt a description of the varied wonders which here astonish and delight the beholder. To those who have visited these mountains, our descriptions would be tame and uninteresting; and he who has never ascended their hoary summits, cannot realize the extent and magnificence of the scene. These mountains are decidedly of primitive formation. Nothing of volcanic origin has ever yet been discovered on the most diligent research. They have for ages, probably, exhibited the same unvarying aspect. No minerals are here found of much rarity or value. The rock which most abounds, is schistus, intermixed with greenstone, mica, granite and gneiss. The three highest peaks are composed entirely of fragments of rocks heaped together in confusion, but pretty firmly fixed in their situations. These rocks are an intermediate substance between gneiss and micaceous schistus; they are excessively rough and coarse, and grey, almost black, with lichens. The mica in them is abundant, of different colors, red, black, and limpid, and though sometimes several inches in diameter, yet most often irregularly stratified. The granite contains emerald, tourmaline, of which are found some beautiful specimens, and garnets, besides its proper constituents. Crystals of quartz, pyrites, actinote, jasper, porphyry, fluate of lime, and magnetic iron ore, are sometimes obtained.

During 9 or 10 months of the

year, the summits of the mountains are covered with snow and ice, giving them a bright and dazzling appearance. On every side are long and winding gulleys, deepening in their descent to the plains below. Here some of the finest rivers of New England originate. The Saco flows from the east side of the mountains; the branches of the Androscoggin from the north; the Amonoosuck and other tributaries of the Connecticut from the west; and the Pemigewasset from the south, its fountain being near that of the Saco. The sides of the hills are in many parts covered with soil; but this is very superficial in all cases, and every spot, that can be reached by running water, is left destitute of every thing but rocks and pebbles, of which likewise the river bottoms are exclusively composed. In these cold and elevated regions, the period for the growth of vegetables is extremely brief; the mountains must be forever sterile. Moss and lichens may be found near the summits, but of meagre and scanty growth—looking as if they had wandered from their proper zone below, into these realms of barren desolation.

A visit of Mr. Vines to the White Mountains, described by Winthrop, is worthy of notice. It was performed in the month of August, 1642, by him in company with Thomas Gorges the deputy-governor. Darby Field, who was living at Exeter, 1639, has the credit of being the first traveller to these mountains. His journey also is described by Winthrop, who says it was performed in the year 1632. He appears to have returned by the way of Saco. "The report he brought," says Winthrop, "of shining stones, &c. caused divers others to travel thither, but they found nothing worth their pains. Mr. Gorges and Mr. Vines, two of the magistrates of Sir F. Gorges' province, went thither about the end of this month," (August.) They set out, probably, a few days after the return of Field, dazzled by visions of diamonds and other precious minerals, with which the fancy of this man had garnished his story. "They went up Saco river in birch canoes, and that way they found it 90 miles to Pegwagget, an Indian town, but by land it is but 60. Upon Saco river they found many thousand acres of rich meadow, but there are 10 falls which hinder boats, &c. From the Indian town they went up hill (for the most part) about 30 miles in woody lands, then they went about 7 or 8 miles upon shattered rocks, without tree or grass, very steep all the way. At the top is a plain about 3 or 4 miles over, all shattered stones, and upon that is another rock or spire about a mile in height, and about an acre of ground at the top. At the top of the plain arise 4 great rivers, each of them so much water at the first issue as would drive a mill: Connecticut river from two heads at the N. W. and S. W., which join in one about 60 miles off; Saco river on the S. E.; Amascoggin, which runs into Casco bay, at the N. E.; and the Kennebeck at the N. by E. The mountain runs east and west 30 or 40 miles, but the peak is above all the rest. They went and returned in 15 days." This description of the mountains was probably communicated by Mr. Vines to Gov. Winthrop. It conveys a very accurate idea of them, as they now strike the traveller.

The Notch of the White Mountains, is a phrase appropriated to a very narrow defile, extending two miles in length between two huge cliffs apparently rent asunder by some vast convulsion of nature: probably that of the deluge. The entrance of the chasm on the east side, is formed by two rocks standing perpendicular at the distance of 22 feet from each other: one about 20 feet in height, the other about 12. The road from Lancaster to Portland passes through this notch, following the course of the head stream of the Saco. The scenery at this place is exceedingly beautiful and grand. The mountain, otherwise a continued range, is here cloven quite down to its base, opening a passage for the waters of the Saco. The gap is so narrow, that space has with difficulty been found for the road. About half a mile from the entrance of the chasm is seen a most beautiful cascade, issuing from a mountain on the right, about 800 feet above the subjacent valley, and about 2 miles distant. The stream passes over a series of rocks almost perpendicular, with a course so little broken as to preserve the appearance of a uniform current, and yet so far disturbed as to be perfectly white. This beautiful stream, which passes down a stupendous precipice, is called by Dwight, the *Silver Cascade*. It is probably one of the most beautiful in the world.

At the distance of 3-4 of a mile from the entrance of the chasm is a brook, called the *Flume*, which falls from a height of 240 or 250 feet over three precipices—down the two first in a single current, and over the last in three, which unite again at the bottom in a small basin formed by the hand of nature in the rocks. The water is pure and transparent, and it would be impossible for a brook of its size to be modelled into more diversified or delightful forms.

It is by no means strange that the unlettered Indian fancied these regions to be the abodes of celestial beings; while the scholar, without a stretch of fancy, in calling to mind the mythology of Greece, might find here a fit place for the assemblies and sports of the Dryads, Naiads and Oreades.

Avalanches or *slides* from the mountains. On the 28th of August, 1826, there occurred one of the most remarkable floods ever known in this mountainous region; and which was attended by the awful calamity of the destruction of a whole family, by an Avalanche or slide from the mountains.

These Avalanches, as they are termed in Switzerland, are produced by heavy rains: they commence generally near the highest limits of vegetation on the mountains, which, on some of them, is near their summits; the slides widening and deepening in their downward course, carrying along all the trees, shrubbery, loose rocks and earth from their granite foundation. At this time there were probably thousands of acres reft from the sides of the mountains and carried to the valley in the Notch below.

The house inhabited by Capt. Samuel Willey and his family, stood on the westerly side of the road, in the Notch, and a few rods distant from the high bluff which rises with fearful rapidity to the height of 2,000 feet. Adjoining was a barn and woodhouse; in front, was a beautiful little meadow covered with crops, and the Saco passed along at the foot of the easterly precipice.

Nearly in range of the house, a slide from the extreme point of the westerly hill came down in a deep and horrible mass to within about five rods of the dwelling, where its course appears to have been checked by a large block of granite, which, falling on a flat surface, backed the rolling mass for a moment, until it separated into two streams, one of which rushed down by the north end of the house, crushing the barn, and spreading itself over the meadow; the other passing down on the south side, and swallowing up the unfortunate beings, who probably attempted to fly to a shelter, which, it is said, had been erected a few rods distant. This shelter, whatever it might have been, was completely overwhelmed: rocks weighing 10 to 50 tons being scattered about the place, and indeed in every direction, rendering escape utterly impossible. The house remained untouched, though large stones and trunks of trees made fearful approaches to its walls, and the moving mass, which separated behind the building, *again united in its front!* The house alone could have been their refuge from the horrible uproar around, the only spot untouched by the crumbling and consuming power of the storm.

The family consisted of 9 persons; Capt. Willey, his wife, 5 children, and two men by the names of Nickerson and Allen.

Travelers visiting this section of country, in autumn, will be gratified with the rich and varied beauties of *Autumnal foliage*, common in this country, but more particularly so at the north; and which is thus described by Dr. Dwight.

"The bosom of both ranges of mountains was overspread, in all the inferior regions, by a mixture of evergreens, with trees, whose leaves are deciduous. The annual foliage had been already changed by the frosts. Of the effects of this change it is, perhaps, impossible for an inhabitant of Great Britain, as I have been assured by several foreigners, to form an adequate conception, without visiting an American forest. When I was a youth, I remarked, that Thompson had entirely omitted, in his seasons, this fine part of autumnal imagery. Upon enquiring of an English gentleman, the probable cause of the omission, he informed me, that no such scenery existed in Great Britain. In this country it is often among the most splendid beauties of nature. All the leaves of trees, which are not evergreens, are by the first severe frost changed from their verdure towards the perfection of that color, which they are capable of ultimately assuming, through yellow, orange, and red, to a pretty deep brown. As the frosts affects different trees, and the different leaves of the same tree, in very different degrees; a vast multitude of tinctures are commonly found on those of a single tree, and always on those of a grove or forest. These colors, also, in all their varieties are generally full; and in many instances are among the most exquisite, which are found in the regions of nature. Different sorts of trees are susceptible of different degrees of this beauty. Among them the maple is preeminently distinguished by the prodigious varieties, the finish, beauty, and the intense lustre, of its hues; varying through all the dyes, between a rich green and the most perfect crimson; or more definitely, the red of the prismatic image."

Whiting, Me.

Washington co. This town lies at the head of Machias bay, and is watered by several ponds and a good mill stream. It lies 152 miles E. N. E. from Augusta, and 6 N. E. from Machias. Incorporated, 1825. Population, 1837, 462.

Whiting, Vt.

Addison co. Whiting lies 40 miles S. W. from Montpelier, and 10 S. from Middlebury. It is washed on the eastern border by Otter Creek, but is without any valuable mill stream.

This is a fine farming town: the soil is composed partly of marl, and affords excellent crops of grain and hay: about 7,000 sheep are kept here. Some years since fish were introduced from the lake, to Otter Creek, at this place, and have been found to multiply exceedingly.

Whiting was first settled in 1772. It was named in honor of John

Whiting of Wrentham, Mass. Population, 1830, 653.

Whitingham, Vt.

Windham co. Deerfield river passes through this town and forms considerable tracts of valuable intervale. The surface of the uplands is diversified; with a good soil for sheep, of which many are kept.

Sawdawga pond, in Whitingham, is rather a curiosity. It is a handsome sheet of water, covering about 500 acres. For many years past earth has been forming over its surface, and from 75 to 100 acres of land now rise and fall with the waters of the pond.

Among the first settlers of Vermont, many remarkable instances of longevity and fecundity are found. A Mr. Pike had 28 children; 19 of whom were living a few years since; the youngest aged 25 years. Mr. Benjamin Cook died in this town, a few years since, aged 106 years. He had followed the business of shoemaking through life. He celebrated his hundredth birth day by making a pair of shoes, without the use of spectacles.

Whitingham was first settled in 1773. It lies 17 miles W. by S. from Brattleborough, and 18 E. S. E. from Bennington. Population, 1830, 1,477.

Wickford Village, R. I.

See *North Kingston*.

Wilbraham, Mass.

Hampden co. The people of this pleasant town are principally employed in agricultural pursuits, and are remarkable for equality of property. This town is watered by the Chickopee and several of its small tributaries. The surface is agreeably diversified by hills and valleys, and the soil is well adapted to agricultural and horticultural pursuits. The products of Wilbraham are numerous; among others, the weight of 2,292 fleeces of wool, sheared in this town, in 1837, was 6,110 pounds, valued at $3,669. There are some manufactures in the town of boots, shoes, leather, straw bonnets, palm-leaf hats, wagons, &c.

The "Wesleyan Academy," in Wilbraham, is an institution of great value, and in high reputation. It has considerable funds, and about 240 scholars attend throughout the year. Scholars are received at this seminary from ten years of age and upwards. The annual cost to a scholar, for board and tuition, is from $80 to $90. This institution was incorporated in 1824, and is governed by a board of trustees.

Great excitement existed in this quiet town and vicinity by the murder of Marcus Lyon, on the 9th of November, 1805. The murder was committed by two foreigners, Halligan and Daley, who were hanged at Northampton on the 5th of June, 1806.

Wilbraham lies 80 miles W. S. W. from Boston, and 10 E. from Springfield. It was incorporated in 1653. Population, 1837, 1,802.

Williams' Rivers.

Williams' river, in *Vermont*, is formed in Chester by the union of three considerable branches, which originate in small streams in the townships of Ludlow, Andover, Windham, and Grafton. These three branches unite about a mile and a half to the southeast of the two villages in Chester, and their united waters, after running 15 miles in a southeasterly direction, fall into Connecticut river in Rockingham, three miles above Bellows' Falls. Along this stream is some fine intervale, and it affords several good mill privileges. Williams' river derives its name from the celebrated Rev. John Williams, who was taken by the Indians at Deerfield, Mass., in 1704. and who, at the mouth of this stream, preached a sermon to his fellow captives. Williams' river, in *Massachusetts*. See *West Stockbridge*.

Williamsburgh, Me.

Piscataquis co. This town was incorporated in 1820. In 1834 the easterly part of the town was set off and called *Barnard:* this fact was unknown to the editor when the first pages of this edition were printed.

The lands in Williamsburgh and Barnard are undulating, heavily wooded, with a fertile soil. The population of Williamsburgh, in 1837, was 120.

Williamsburgh and Barnard are at present but thinly settled; but in consequence of a vast body of slate for roofing houses and other purposes being found within their limits, the lands within these towns must enhance in value and increase in population. These quarries are common to both towns; they lie at an elevation of from 150 to 200 feet above Pleasant river, a branch of the Penobscot, which passes their northern and eastern borders, about two miles distant.

These quarries are inexhaustible in quantity, and are stated to be fully equal to the celebrated Welsh slate. They are situated 40 miles N. from Bangor; and, by the Bangor and Piscataquis rail road, now in operation to Orono; and in progress from Orono to these quarries, the Bangor of the new world seems likely to become as celebrated for its fine slate as the Bangor of the old. See *Barnard*.

Williamsburgh, Mass.

Hampshire co. The surface of this town is elevated and uneven; but it is pleasant, and has a warm and fertile soil. It is watered by a good stream which meets the Connecticut at Northampton. It lies 8 miles N. W. from Northampton, and 100 W. from Boston. Incorporated in 1771. Population, 1837, 1,345.

The manufactures of the town consist of woolen cloth, (3 mills,) boots, shoes, leather, hats, iron castings, axes, gimlets, screw drivers, augers, punches, bitts and bitt stocks, flexible and japan buttons, stocking yarn, and lather boxes; annual value, about $200,000.— The value of *buttons*, manufactured the year ending April 1, 1837, was $102,500.

In 1837, there were 2,815 sheep sheared in this town, whose fleeces weighed 8,362 pounds, and sold for 5,017.

Williamstown, Vt.

Orange co. This town lies on the height of land between Onion and White rivers; 10 miles S. E. from Montpelier, and about the same distance N. W. from Chelsea. First settled, 1784. Population, 1830, 1,487. This mountain town produces good crops of grain and hay. It pastures about 7,500 sheep.

The "Gulf Road," so called, between Royalton and Montpelier, passes through this town. This mountain pass is some miles in length, wild and picturesque. The mountains on each side of the gulf are very high, and the sides are so steep as to leave only a narrow passage for the turnpike, and a gurgling branch of White river on the south side, and of a branch of Onion river on the north.

Williamstown, Mass.

Berkshire co. This town is situated in a large and fertile valley, surrounded by romantic elevations, and watered by Hoosack and Green rivers. These beautiful streams unite their hydraulic powers and fertilizing qualities, to render this remote valley a scene of competence and peace, and a delightful retreat for the muses.

Williamstown lies at the N. W. corner of the state, on the lines of Vermont and New York; 135 miles W. by N. from Boston, 27 N. from

Lenox, and 36 E. by N. from Albany, N. Y. It was incorporated in 1765. Population, 1837, 1,981.

There are 1 cotton and 2 woolen mills in the town, and manufactures of potatoe starch, cabinet ware, chairs, palm-leaf hats, shovels, hats, leather, &c.: annual value about $75,000.

The number of sheep in this flourishing agricultural town, in the year 1837, was 8,000—viz: 2,000 Saxony, 5,800 Merino, and 200 common. The fleeces of these sheep weighed 23,200 lbs., and sold for $13,965.

The village in this town is delightfully situated on a gentle rise from the river. The buildings are generally tastefully constructed and command a great variety of superb scenery. This town contains a tepid spring, of some repute in cutaneous diseases.

Williams College, in this town, is handsomely located. It derived its name from COL. EPHRAIM WILLIAMS, a native of Newton, and a distinguished benefactor of Williamstown. Col. Williams was a man of talents, brave, witty, polite and popular. He commanded the line of forts on the west side of Connecticut river, in the French and Indian wars from 1740 to 1748. In 1755, he received the command of a regiment, and joined general Johnson. He fell at the head of 1,200 men, near lake George, on the 8th of September of that year. Col. Williams, being a bachelor, gave the most of his estate for the establishment of a free grammar school at this place. The school went into operation in 1791, and in 1793 the legislature vested it with college privileges. See *Register*.

Willimantic River, Ct.

Also *Village*, see *Windham*.

Willington, Ct.

Tolland co. This town was sold by the Connecticut colony, to Roger Wolcott, Esq. and others, for £510, in the year 1720. It is about 7 miles in length, and 4½ in width. There is an abundance of granite in the town, and good iron ore. The surface is uneven and the soil hard. The Willimantic and other streams give Willington some excellent mill privileges, some of which are profitably improved.—There are about 2,500 sheep in the town. Population, in 1830, 1,305. It is 24 miles N. E. from Hartford, and bounded W. by Tolland.

Williston, Vt.

Chittenden co. This is an excellent farming town of a rich soil, with an uneven surface, but not mountainous. It is very productive of all the varieties common to a northern climate: its product of wool, in 1837, was 9,225 fleeces. Williston is watered by Onion river, and some smaller streams; but its water power is small. It is 27 miles W. N. W. from Montpelier, and is bounded on the W., by Burlington. Population, 1830, 1,608.

THOMAS CHITTENDEN was the father of this town. He came here in 1774. He was a member of the convention, which, in 1777, declared Vermont an independent state, and was active in procuring its admission into the Union. When the Vermont Constitution was established, in 1778, Mr. Chittenden was selected as a candidate for governor; to which office he was annually elected, with the exception of one year, till his death in 1797. He was 67 years of age.

Wilmington, Vt.

Windham co. The east and west branches of Deerfield river unite in this town, which, with the waters of Beaver and Cold brooks, and of Ray's pond, a large and beautiful sheet of water; a valuable mill power is produced. There are some fine tracts of land in the town, and a considerable portion that is rough and hard to till. There are a number of mills of various kinds in the town, and a pleasant and thriving village.

Wilmington was settled before the revolutionary war, but increased but slowly until the peace. It lies 46 miles S. S. W. from Windsor, 14 S. W. from Newfane, and 17 E. from Bennington. Population, 1830, 1,367.

Wilmington, Mass.

Middlesex co. The surface of this town is generally level, with a light and sandy soil. The wood is chiefly pine, and much charcoal is made. This kind of soil, although unfit for the generality of crops, is well adapted for the growth of hops, of which large quantities, of a fine quality, are produced in Wilmington, and which frequently afford the cultivator a large profit.

During the period of 32 years, 1806—1837, inclusive, there were inspected at Charlestown, Mass. 76,860 bags of hops, weighing 16,467,182 lbs. The price varied from 3 4 to 5 cents a pound. The highest price was in 1817, the lowest, in 1819; average price, 13 1-5 cents. Total value, $2,169,430.

The town is watered by a branch of Ipswich river: the Middlesex canal passes through it, and adds much to the beauty of its scenery. Wilmington was incorporated in 1730. It is 14 miles N. N. W. from Boston, and 10 S. E. by E. from Lowell. Population, 1837, 795.

Wilmot, N. H.

Merrimack co. Wilmot is 30 miles N. W. from Concord, and 87 from Boston. The streams forming Blackwater river have their origin in the vicinity of Wilmot.— They afford a number of good mill seats. The 4th N. H. turnpike from Concord to Hanover passes through this town. It was made in 1803, through an entire forest, without any inhabitants for 14 miles above, and about 6 miles below Wilmot. The land near the turnpike appears rude and barren; but the acclivities on either side are susceptible of cultivation. The town is composed of hills and valleys, presenting a rough surface. There are no large collections of water, nor any mountains, excepting Kearsarge, whose summit forms the southern boundary. It was incorporated June 18, 1807. It received its name in honor of Dr. Wilmot, an Englishman, who, at one time, was supposed to be the author of the celebrated letters of Junius. Population, 1830, 835.

Wilson, Me.

This town was incorporated in 1836, as "township number 9 in the 9th range, north of the Waldo Patent in the county of Somerset." We repeat, that but very little information respecting a town is gained from its act of incorporation. We beg our friends "Down East" to write to us.

Wilton, Me.

Franklin co. This is one of the most flourishing agricultural townships in the state. It has a fertile soil, a beautiful surface, and two pleasant villages. It lies a little distance from Sandy river, 5 or 6 miles S. W. from Farmington, and 38 W. N. W. from Augusta.

Wilton has an adequate water power for common purposes, produced by streams issuing from beautiful ponds in the town. The people are principally agriculturalists, and tested their skill in that delightful pursuit, in 1837, by producing 11,071 bushels of good clean wheat.

Wilton was incorporated in 1803. Population, in 1830, 1,140; 1837, 2,102.

Wilton, N. H.

Hillsborough co. This town is bounded S. by Mason, and W. by

Temple. It is 9 miles W. by S. from Amherst and 37 S. by W. from Concord. Souhegan is the principal river. Its main branch enters this town near the S. W. corner and proceeds in a N. E. course till it forms a junction with several branches running from Lyndeborough and Temple. These flow through the N. part, and are sufficiently large for mill streams. On these streams are some valuable manufactures, and a pleasant village has sprung up within a few years. This town has neither mountains, ponds or swamps. It is in general of strong and excellent soil. Good clay is found in plenty near the streams. There are several quarries of excellent stone for splitting and hewing. The first settlement was made in 1738, by 3 families from Danvers, Mass., 2 by the name of Putnam, and 1 by the name of Dale. Hannah, the daughter of Ephraim Putnam, was the first child born in town. The town was incorporated June 25, 1762, and derived its name from Wilton, an ancient borough in Wiltshire, England. A distressing accident occurred in raising the second meeting house, September 7, 1773. The frame fell, and three men were instantly killed; two died of their wounds soon afterward, and a number of others were badly injured. On July 20, 1804, the same meeting house was struck by lightning and considerably shattered. Population, 1830, 1,039.

Wilton, Ct.

Fairfield co. Wilton was taken from the north part of Norwalk, in 1802. The surface of the town is broken by two ridges of hills, but the soil is a gravelly loam and productive of grain and a great variety of fruit. Agriculture is the principal business of the inhabitants. The town is watered by Norwalk river, and has a satinet factory and other mechanical operations by water. A classical school, of high reputation, was established here in 1818, by Hawley Olmstead, Esq. This school is worth a million of the silver mines that were discovered and worked in this town during the revolutionary war. Wilton lies 34 miles W. S. W. from New Haven, and 6 N. from Norwalk. Population, 1830, 2,095.

Winchendon, Mass.

Worcester co. This town was incorporated in 1764. It is 60 miles N. W. by W. from Boston, and 34 N. N. W. from Worcester. Population, 1830, 1,463; 1837, 1,802. The surface of the town is uneven and rocky, with a strong soil, which, when subdued, is quite productive of grain, grass and fruit trees. There are fine quarries of granite in the town; and a spring tinctured with iron and sulphur, but which is less visited than formerly. Miller's river rises in this town and Ashburnham, and affords convenient mill seats. There are 2 pleasant villages in the town, a cotton mill, a woolen mill, and manufactures of cotton and wool bobbins, leather, palm-leaf hats, chairs, cabinet and wooden wares: annual value, exclusive of cotton goods, about $100,000.

Under *Warner*, N. H., we gave an account of a frightful tornado in that and the neighboring towns in 1821. It appears that this part of the country was visited by a similar desolation, *at the same time*, more than 40 miles distant. A Worcester paper thus describes it:

"About 6 o'clock, Sunday evening, September 9th, a black and terrific cloud appeared a little south of the centre of Northfield, Franklin county, nearly in the form of a pyramid reversed, moving very rapidly and with a terrible noise. In its progress it swept away or prostrated all the trees, fences, stone walls, and buildings which came within its vortex, which in some places was not more than 20 rods and in others 40 or 50. It passed from Northfield through Warwick and Orange, to the southwesterly part of Royalston, where its force was broken by Tully Mountain. Its path was strewed for the distance of 25 miles, through the towns of Royalston, Winchendon, Ashburnham and Fitchburg, with fragments of buildings, sheaves of grain, bundles of corn stalks, clothing, &c.

"Several persons were killed and wounded, numerous houses, barns, &c. demolished, and many domestic animals, in the track of the tornado, were destroyed. Large trees were taken 200 feet into the air, and logs which would require 4 oxen to remove them were swept out of the bed of Tully river where they had lain for more than half a century. The ground was torn up from the river to the mountain, about 40 rods, from 1 foot to 6 feet deep. The surface of the earth was broken throughout the whole course of the whirlwind, as with the ploughshare of destruction. Stones of many hundred pounds weight, were rolled from their beds. Lots of wood were whirled into promiscuous heaps, with roots and tops, and tops and roots. The appearance presented by the track of the whirlwind, indicated, as near as the writer can judge from actual inspection, that the form of the cloud, and the body of air in motion, was that of an inverted pyramid, drawing whatever came within its influence towards the centre of motion."

Winchester, N. H.

Cheshire co. This pleasant town is bounded N. by Swanzey and Chesterfield, E. by Richmond, W. by Hinsdale, and S. by Massachusetts line. It lies 13 miles S. W. from Keene, 65 S. W. from Concord, 80 W. from Boston, 80 N. from Hartford, Ct., and 12 E. from Brattlebo', Vt. Population, 1837, 2,500. The face of this town is diversified with hills and valleys. The soil is of an excellent quality, furnishing in abundance, all the agricultural products natural to this section of the country. Ashuelot river passes through the centre of this town, affording a number of mill privileges, and is bordered on each bank by extensive intervales, of a fertility rarely excelled.

There are other small streams running in various directions through the town, affording facilities for water power.

The centre village is on the S. E. bank of the Ashuelot, and the principal street, running parallel with its border, has a number of dwelling houses, with stores and shops, 3 meeting houses, an elegant district school house, saw and grist mills, shops for turning wood and iron, an extensive establishment for the manufacture of musical instruments of all kinds, and 2 organ manufactories; and, at the lower end, the street is adorned with a beautiful row of native ever-green trees, which extends nearly half a mile.

Two miles west is another considerable village, containing 1 large woolen factory, 1 cotton factory, 1 satinet factory, saw, grist and oil mills, two furnaces, together with shops, stores, meeting houses, &c.

In the S. E. part of the town there are saw mills, grist mills, clothier's works, and 1 satinet factory.

This town was sacked by the Indians, and the inhabitants taken prisoners or driven off in 1745 or '6, and did not return under about 5 years to resume the settlement of the place. The former name of the town was Arlington, and it was incorporated by its present name in 1753.

Winchester, Ct.

Litchfield co. Winchester was

incorporated in 1771. Population, 1830, 1,766. The geological character of the town is primitive; the rocks consisting of granite, mica slate, &c. The soil is gravelly, hard and coarse: it affords good grazing, and its products of butter, cheese and wool are considerable.

The Borough of Clifton was incorporated in 1832. It is a flourishing village, consisting of about sixty or seventy dwelling houses, and 4 mercantile stores. The village is principally built in a narrow valley, on the banks of a mill stream, called Mad river, which is a tributary of Farmington river. The valley at this place is but barely of sufficient width to admit of a street, with buildings on each side, the ground rising immediately in every direction. Westward of the main street in the village, a road passes up a steep hill for nearly a quarter of a mile, where, upon an elevated plain, is an interesting lake or pond, which is one of the largest bodies of water in the state, being 3 1-2 miles in length and 3-4 of a mile in breadth. The outlet of this lake presents a novel scene; it consists of a small stream, compressed within a narrow channel, and literally tossed from rock to rock till it unites with Mad river. Most of the manufacturing establishments in the village are situated on this outlet, upon which there are some of the best natural sites for hydraulic works in the state. In this village are four large scythe factories, one machine shop, and five forges. The ore to supply these forges is brought from Canaan, Kent and Salisbury.

Winsted, or the East village, is very pleasant, and contains a large woolen mill, an extensive clock factory, an iron foundry, and an axe factory. This village is 26 miles N. W. from Hartford, 49 N. by W. from New Haven, and 17 N. by E. from Litchfield.

Winchester lies within the "evergreen district," so named from the forests of hemlock and other evergreen trees with which it abounds. These "Green Woods" present one of the most impressive scenes which can be found in an American forest. The branches of the trees are thickly covered with a deep green foliage, closely interwoven overhead, nearly excluding the light of the sun. The scene forcibly reminds the contemplative traveler of the words of Thomson, in his celebrated hymn:

"Oh, talk of Him in solitary glooms!
Where, o'er the rock the scarcely waving pine
Fills the brown shade with a religious awe."

Windham, Me.

Cumberland co. Windham lies on the N. E. side of Presumpscut river, which separates it from Gorham. It is 76 miles S. W. from Augusta, and 14 N. N. W. from Portland. This is a valuable farming town, and the inhabitants are principally employed in agriculture. Branches of the Presumpscut give the town good mill privileges. There are 2 pleasant villages in the town, some manufactures, and several beautiful fish ponds. Population, 1837, 2,207.

Windham, N. H.

Rockingham co. This town is 34 miles S. by E. from Concord, and 45 W. S. W. from Portsmouth. Policy pond lies in this town and Salem, about one half in each. Cabot's pond lies E. of the centre of the town. Golden pond is in the south, and Mitchel's is in the northeast part of the town. Beaver river or brook forms the W. boundary, upon which are some meadow lands. The town is also well supplied with small streams.

Windham was originally a part of Londonderry; and was detached and incorporated in 1739. The inhabitants, principally derived from the first settlers of Londonderry, have firmly adhered to the religious principles of their fathers, to the doctrines and forms of the presbyterian church as originally established in Scotland, and administered in this country. Population, 1830, 998.

Windham County, Vt.

Newfane is the shire town.—This county is bounded N. by Windsor county; E. by Connecticut river; S. by the state of Massachusetts, and W. by the county of Bennington. It contains an area of about 780 square miles. Population, 1810, 26,760; 1820, 28,457; 1830, 28,748. Incorporated, 1789. For some years it bore the name of Cumberland. Population to a square mile, 37.

The surface of the county is much broken by hills and valleys: the western part is very elevated, and contains a part of the Green Mountain range. The geological character of the county is primitive. Immense quantities of granite are found in all parts of the county, both in quarries and boulders, most of which is of fine grain and very handsome. It also contains gneiss, hornblende, serpentine, primitive limestone, and mica, talcose, chlorite, and argellite slates.

The soil of the county is various; from the rich and alluvial meadows on the Connecticut, to the cold and rugged lands on the sides of the mountains. The general character of the soil may be considered as tolerable for grain and excellent for grazing. In 1837, there were 76,582 sheep in the county. Some of the wool is of a fine quality, but generally it is about half blood.

Windham county is finely watered by Williams', Saxton's, and West rivers, with their branches, and by numerous other streams. These waters give the county a great hydraulic power, which is rapidly coming into use for manufacturing purposes.

Windham, Vt.

Windham co. Branches of West, Williams' and Saxton's rivers give this town a good water power. The surface of the town is elevated; the soil, though strong, is better adapted for grazing than tillage. About 4,000 sheep are kept here. Windham was formerly a part of Londonderry. It is 30 miles N. E. from Bennington, and 25 S. W. from Windsor. Population, 1830, 847.

The actynolite embedded in talc, is found in this town, in slender four sided prisms of a leak green color. The crystals vary in size; some are six inches in length and an inch in breadth. These crystals are abundant. Chlorite, garnets, serpentine, and steatite are also found.

Windham County, Ct.

Brooklyn is the county town. This county is uniformly hilly, yet no part of it is mountainous or very elevated. The prevailing soil is a primitive gravelly loam. The greatest portion of the county is stony and considerably rough, and the lands generally best adapted for grazing, and many sections afford some of the richest dairy farms in the state. The Quinnebaug and Shetucket, with their branches, intersect this county, and afford many valuable water privileges for mills and manufacturing purposes. The valley of the Quinnebaug river comprises the best land in the county. The inhabitants of this county are more extensively engaged in the manufacturing business than in any other county in the state. Cotton and woolen goods are the principal articles manufactured.

Windham county originally belonged to the counties of Hartford and New London. It was incorporated as a county in May, 1726.

This county is bounded N. by

Massachusetts; E. by Rhode Island; S. by the county of New London, and W. by Tolland county. It contains an area of about 620 square miles. Population, 1810, 28,611; 1820, 31,684; 1830, 27,077. Population to a square mile, 44. In 1837, there were 26,017 sheep in Windham county.

Windham, Ct.

Windham co. The territory of this town, Mansfield and Canterbury, was given by Joshua, a son of Uncas, the celebrated Mohegan sachem, to John Mason, James Fitch and others, in the year 1675.

"Lieut. *John Cates*, a pious puritan, who served in the wars in England, holding his commission under Cromwell, when Charles II. came to the throne, fled to this country for safety. He landed first in Virginia, where he procured a negro servant to attend him. But when advertisements and pursuers were spread through this country, to apprehend the adherents of the Protector, he left Virginia, came to New York, and from thence to Norwich. Still feeling that he should be securer in a more retired place, he came to this new plantation, dug the first cellar, and with his servant, raised in Windham the first English habitation, in the spring of 1689. The settlers, rapidly increasing, petitioned the general court, and obtained a grant of town privileges in May, 1692. It was made a county town in May, 1726."

Windham is bounded N. by the towns of Hampton, Chaplin and Mansfield; E. by Franklin and Lisbon, and W. by Lebanon and Columbia. It contains an area of about 8 by 6 miles. It has an uneven surface, with a tolerable soil.

The following is a copy of the inscription on Lieutenant Cates' monument, in the village burying ground.

In
memory of
Mr. John Cates.
He was a gentleman born
in England,
and the first setteller in the
Town of Windham.
By his last
Will and Testament,
he gave a
generous Legacy
to ye first
Church of Christ in
Windham,
in plate, and a generous
Legacy in Land
for ye support of ye Poor,
and another
Legacy for ye support
of ye School
in said town for ever.
He died
in Windham,
July ye 16th, A. D.
1697.

Since the removal of the county courts from this place to Brooklyn, and the establishment of the village of Willimantic, the ancient village of Windham has somewhat declined in its trade and population. It is pleasantly located, compactly and neatly built, and contains the charm of antiquity, in as great perfection as can probably be found in New England. This village is 30 miles E. from Hartford, 14 N. by W. from Norwich, 44 W. S. W. from Providence, R. I., and 12 S. W. from Brooklyn. Population of the town, 1820, 2,489; 1830, 2,812.

The *Borough of Willimantic* is 3 miles W. from Windham village. It is well situated on Willimantic river: it is built principally on one street, and contains some very handsome buildings. In this village are six cotton mills, containing 13,000 spindles; a paper mill and a satinet factory. This flourishing village has grown up in the course of a few years. The population of this borough, in 1837, was 2,000.

Willimantic River rises in the county of Tolland, and with the

Natchaug, forms the Shetucket in Windham.

"Much pleasantry," says Mr. Barber, "has been indulged at the expense of the inhabitants of Windham, on account of a singular occurrence which happened in the year 1758, by which the inhabitants were very much frightened. There is probably some exaggeration in the account, though the foundation of the story is believed to be a matter of fact." We copy it as an amusing relic.

"On a dark, cloudy, dismal night in the month of July, A. D. 1758, the inhabitants of Windham, a small town in the eastern part of Connecticut, had retired to rest, and for several hours, all were wrapped in profound repose—when suddenly, soon after midnight, the slumbers of the peaceful inhabitants were disturbed by a most terrific noise in the sky right over their heads, which to many, seemed the yells and screeches of infuriated Indians, and others had no other way of accounting for the awful sounds, which still kept increasing, but by supposing the day of judgment had certainly come; and to their terrified imaginations, the awful uproar in the air seemed the immediate precursor of the clangor of the last trumpet. At intervals, many supposed they could distinguish the calling out of paticular names, as of Colonels DYER and ELDERKIN, two eminent lawyers, and this increased the general terror. But soon there was a rush from every house, the tumult in the air still increasing—old and young, male and female, poured forth into the streets, "*in puris naturalibus*," entirely forgetful, in their hurry and consternation, of their nether habiliments, and with eyes upturned tried to pierce the almost palpable darkness. Some daring "*spirits*," concluding there was nothing supernatural in the hubbub and uproar over head, but rather, that they heard the yells of Indians commencing a midnight attack, loaded their guns and sallied forth to meet the invading foes. These valiant heroes, on ascending the hill that bounds the village on the east, perceived that the sounds came from that quarter, and not from the skies, as first believed, but their courage would not permit them to proceed to the daring extremity of advancing eastward, until they had discovered the real cause of alarm and distress, which pervaded the whole village. Towards morning the sounds in the air seemed to die away. In the morning, the whole cause of alarm, which produced such distressing apprehensions among the good people of the town, was apparent to all who took the trouble to go to a certain mill pond, situated about three fourths of a mile eastward of the village. This pond, hereafter, in the *annals of Fame*, forever to be called the *Frog Pond*, in consequence of a severe drought, which had prevailed many weeks, had become nearly dry, and the Bull Frogs (by which it was densely *populated*) at the mill fought a pitched battle on the sides of the ditch which ran through it, for the possession and enjoyment of the fluid which remained. Long and obstinately was the contest maintained; and many thousands of the combatants were found defunct, on both sides of the ditch, the next morning. It had been uncommonly still, for several hours before the battle commenced, but suddenly, as if by a preconcerted agreement, every frog on one side of the ditch, raised the war cry, *Col. Dyer, Col. Dyer*, and at the same instant, from the opposite side, resounded the adverse shout of *Elderkin too, Elderkin too*. Owing to some peculiar state of the atmosphere, the awful noises and cries appeared to be directly over their heads."

Windsor, Me.

Kennebec co. Windsor was incorporated by the name of Malta, in 1809. In 1821 it took the name of Gerry, and in 1822 it received its present name. It lies 12 miles from Augusta, by which it is bounded on the west. Population, 1837, 1,660. Wheat crop, same year, 5,947 bushels.

This town is watered by the upper branches of Sheepscot river, and by several handsome ponds. The surface of the town is diversified: the soil is generally good, and its agricultural condition improving. There are some manufactures in the town.

Windsor, N. H.

Hillsborough co. This town contains only 5,335 acres. It is diversified with hills: its soil is strong, good for grazing, and for bread stuffs, of which quantities sufficient for use at home, and some for the markets are raised. Black pond, near the centre, is said to be 160 rods long and 80 broad; and one near the S. E. corner of the town, is about 80 rods long and 40 wide.

Windsor was formerly called *Campbell's Gore.* It was incorporated with town privileges in 1798. Population, 1830, 226.

Windsor County, Vt.

Woodstock is the county town. This county is bounded N. by the county of Orange, E. by Connecticut river, S. by Windham county, and W. by Rutland and a part of Addison counties. It contains an area of about 900 square miles. Population, 1810, 34,877; 1820, 38,233; 1830, 40,625: population to a square mile, 48. Incorporated in 1781.

Windsor county is watered by White, Queechy, Black, West and Williams' rivers, and by other excellent mill streams. The surface of the county is uneven, and in some parts mountainous, but generally, it is not too elevated to admit of cultivation. The soil produces fine crops of grain, hay, vegetables and fruits: the lands are peculiarly adapted for grazing, and about 200,000 sheep graze on its varied surface of hills and valleys.

The beautiful Connecticut, which washes its whole eastern boundary, gives to this county large tracts of alluvial meadow land, and affords it a navigable channel to the sea board, for its surplus productions, and for its wants from abroad.

The hydraulic power of Windsor county is very large, and its local position is such as to induce men of enterprize and capital to embark in manufacturing operations, which are annually increasing with fair prospects of success.

Windsor, Vt.

Windsor co. Windsor was first settled in 1764. Its surface is uneven, but there are but few parts of it unfit for cultivation. It contains large tracts of alluvial meadow, and the uplands are generally fertile. Mill brook waters the south part of the town, and furnishes it with excellent mill sites. The manufactures of the town are numerous and valuable. The agricultural interests are also valuable: 10,000 sheep are annually sheared in the town, and many neat cattle, horses and productions of the dairy are annually transported to its various markets.

This town has become the centre of an important commerce, both from the river and a fertile interior country. The favorable position of Windsor, as a place of trade, was early discovered, and it has been fortunate in possessing a succession of men, who, by their enterprise and wealth, have rendered it one of the most flourishing towns on Connecticut river.

Windsor is situated on the west side of that delightful river, 55 miles S. by E. from Montpelier, 105 N. W. from Boston, 55 N. E. from Bennington, 95 S. S. W. from Burlington, and 127 miles above Hartford, Ct. Population, in 1820, 2,956; 1830, 3,134.

The village of Windsor is on elevated ground, on the bank of the river: it is compactly, and somewhat irregularly built, but very beautiful. There are but few villages in our country which make a more delightful appearance. It contains a great number of handsome dwelling houses and stores. Some of the private houses, churches and other public buildings are in a style of superior elegance. This is the site of the Vermont State prison. The streets are wide and beautifully shaded. The scenery around Windsor is highly picturesque; from the high lands across the river, in Cornish, which is united to Windsor by a bridge, or on the Ascutney at the south part of the town, some of the best landscapes in our country are presented to view.

Windsor, Mass.

Berkshire co. This town is situated on the ridge of high lands which divides the waters of the Housatonick and Connecticut. Branches of the Housatonick and Westfield rivers rise here. There are some good fish ponds in the town, but no important streams. The surface of the town is much broken, but the soil is warm and finely adapted for grazing. There are some excellent farmers in Windsor, and the productions of the dairy and of cattle are considerable. In 1837, there were 7,157 sheep in the town, principally of the Saxony and Merino breeds. Their wool weighed 21,337 lbs., and sold for $10,521. This town is remarkable for the longevity of its inhabitants; which is doubtless owing to the purity of its air and water.

Windsor contains beds of serpentine and soapstone. It is 117 miles W. by N. from Boston, 18 N. N. E. from Lenox, and 12 E. N. E. from Pittsfield. Incorporated in 1771. Population, 1837, 887.

Windsor, Ct.

Hartford co. This most ancient town in Connecticut is situated on the west side of Connecticut river, 6 miles N. from Hartford. Population, 1830, 3,220. The surface of the town is generally level, having some extensive plains. The soil is various, and free from stone: some of it is light, but a large proportion of it is fertile, containing extensive tracts of rich meadow.

Farmington river passes through the town, and meeting the Connecticut, gives the town a good hydraulic power.

There are in Windsor 4 paper mills, 2 manufactories of cotton batting, and factories of satinet, Kentucky jean, wire, &c. The business in these manufacturing establishments is very considerable. At a place called Pine Meadow, at the commencement of the locks on the Enfield canal, a variety of ship and other timber is prepared for market. Pine Meadow is opposite to Warehouse Point, in East Windsor.

The centre village in Windsor is pleasantly extended on the banks of the Connecticut: it is well built, well shaded, and commands delightful prospects.

Poquonnuck village is a few miles N. from the centre. It is a manufacturing village, delightfully situated at the head of navigation on Farmington river.

"In 1631, Wahquimacut, an Indian sachem, living near Connecticut river, made a journey to Plymouth and Boston, and earnestly entreated the governors of each of the colonies to send men to make settlements on the river. He represented the fruitfulness of the country, and promised the English, that if they would make a settlement, he would annually supply them with corn, and give them eighty beaver skins.

"The governor of Massachusetts, although he treated the sachem and his company with generosity, paid no attention to his proposals. Mr. Winslow, the governor of Plymouth, judged it worthy of attention. It seems that soon after that, he went into Connecticut, and discovered the river and the adjacent parts. It appeared that the earnestness with which the sachem solicited the English to make settlements on the river, originated from the distressed state of the river Indians. Pekoath, the great sachem of the Pequots, was at war with them and driving them from the country, and they imagined that if the English made settlements on the river, they would assist them in defending themselves against their too powerful enemies.

"Governor Winslow of Plymouth, being pleased with the appearance of the country, having visited it, the Plymouth people made preparations for erecting a trading house, and establishing a small company upon the river. In 1633, William Holmes, with his associates, having prepared the frame of a house, with boards and materials for covering it immediately, put them on board of a vessel and sailed for Connecticut. Holmes landed and erected his house a little below the mouth of Farmington river, in Windsor. The house was covered with the utmost dispatch, and fortified with palisadoes. The Plymouth people purchased of the Indians the land on which they erected their house. This, governor Wolcott says, was the first house erected in Connecticut.

"In June, 1634, the Dutch sent Jacob Van Curter to purchase lands on the Connecticut. He made a purchase of about twenty acres at Hartford, of Nepuquash, a Pequot captain, on the 25th of October. Curter protested against Holmes, the builder of the Plymouth house. Some time afterwards, the Dutch governor, Van Twiller, of Fort Amsterdam, sent a reinforcement to Connecticut, in order to drive Holmes from the river. A party of seventy men under arms, with banners displayed, assaulted the Plymouth house, but they found it so well fortified, and the men who kept it so vigilant and determined, that it could not be taken without bloodshed. They therefore came to a parley, and finally returned in peace.

"A number of Mr. Wareham's people came, in the summer of 1635, to Connecticut, and made preparations to bring their families and make a permanent settlement. After having made such preparations as they judged necessary, they began to remove their families and property. On the 15th of October, about sixty men, women and children, with their horses, cattle and swine, commenced their journey from Massachusetts, through the wilderness, to Connecticut river. After a tedious and difficult journey, through swamps and rivers, over mountains and rough grounds, which were passed with great difficulty and fatigue, they arrived safely at the places of their respective destination. They were so long on their journey, and so much time and pains were spent in passing the river, and in getting over their cattle, that after all their exertions, winter came upon them before they were prepared.

"About the beginning of December, provisions generally failed in the settlements on the river, and famine and death looked the inhabitants in the face. In their distress, some of them in this severe season attempted to go through the wilderness to the nearest settlement in Massachusetts. A company of thirteen, who made the attempt, lost one of their number, who, in passing a river, fell through the ice and was drowned. The other twelve were ten days on their journey, and had they not received assistance from the Indians, would all have perished. Such was the general distress by the 3d and 4th of December, that a considerable part of the settlers were obliged to leave their habitations. Seventy persons, men, women and children, were obliged, in the severity of winter, to go down to the mouth of the river to meet their provisions, as the only expedient to preserve their lives. Not meeting the vessels which they expected, they all went on board of the Rebecca, a vessel of about 60 tons. This vessel, two days before, was frozen in, twenty miles up the river; but by the falling of a small rain, and the influence of the tide, the ice became so broken, that she made a shift to get out. She however ran upon the bar, and the people were forced to unlade her to get her off. She was reladed, and in five days reached Boston. Had it not been for these providential circumstances, the people must have perished from famine.

"The people who remained and kept their stations on the river, suffered in an extreme degree. After all the help they were able to obtain, by hunting and from the Indians, they were obliged to subsist on acorns, malt and grains. The cattle, which could not be got over the river before winter, lived by browsing in the woods and meadows. They wintered as well, or better, than those that were brought over, and for which all the provision was made, and care taken, of which the settlers were capable. A great number of the cattle, however, perished. The Dorchester or Windsor people lost, in this species of property, about two hundred pounds sterling. Upon the breaking up of winter, and during the summer following, the settlers came in large companies, and the settlements at Windsor, Hartford and Wethersfield were firmly established."

The first of the four following epitaphs is supposed to be the most ancient monumental inscription in the state.

Heere
lyeth Ephraim Hvit,
sometimes
Teacher to ye chvrch of
Windsor, who
died September 4th,
1644.

Who when hee lived wee drew ovr vitall breath,
Who when hee died his dying was ovr death,
Who was ye stay of s'ate, ye chvrches staff,
Alas, the times forbid an epitaph.

Here
vnder lyeth the body of
Henry Wolcot,
sometimes
a Maiestrate of this Ivrisdiction,
who died ye 30th day
of May,
Anno Salvtis 1655,
Ætatis 77.

Here lyeth
the body of the
Hon. Roger Wolcott, Esq.
of Windsor, who
for several
years was Governor of the
Colony of
Connecticut, died
May 17th,
Anno Salutis 1767,
Ætatis 89.

Earth's highest station ends jo "Here he lies;"
And "dust to dust" concludes her noblest song.

To the memory of *Oliver Ellsworth*, LL. D., an assistant in the Council, and a judge of the Superior Court of the State of Connecticut. A member of the Convention which formed, and of the State Convention of Connecticut, which adopted the Constitution of the U. States.—Senator and Chief Justice of the U. States; one of the Envoys extraordinary and Minister Plenipotentiary, who made the convention of 1800 between the U. States and the French Republic. Amiable and exemplary in all the relations of the domestic, social and christian character.

Pre-eminently useful in all the offices he sustained, whose great talents under the guidance of inflexible integrity, consummate wisdom, and enlightened zeal, placed him among the first of the illustrious statesmen who achieved and established the independence of the American Republic. Born at Windsor April 29th, 1745, and died Nov. 26, 1807.

The ancient boundaries of Windsor extended 46 miles in circumference, lying on both sides of the river. Within these limits there were ten distinct Indian tribes or sovereignties. In the year 1670 there was a large Indian fortress at Windsor, and nineteen natives to one Englishman: but another race has arisen:—

"The chiefs of other days are departed.
They have gone without their fame.
The people are like the waves of the ocean:
Like the leaves of woody Morven,
They pass away in the rustling blast,
And other leaves lift their green heads on high."

Winhall, Vt.

Bennington co. Winhall is bounded on the W. by Manchester, and is 33 miles S. W. from Windsor. This town was chartered in 1761, and its settlement commenced during the revolutionary war. Population, 1830, 571. The surface is rough, and the soil not very productive.

Winhall River rises in this town and affords it a good water power. It passes through a part of Jamaica, and joins West river in Londonderry.

Winnepisiogee Lake, N. H.

This lake possesses singular charms. However romantic and beautiful Lake George, the charmer of all travelers, appears in its elevation, the purity of its waters, its depth, its rapid outlet, its 365 islands which bespangle its bosom, its mountain scenery, its fish, its mineralogy; still in all, but its historic fame, it has a rival at the east, in the Winnepisiogee of New Hampshire.

There are more than forty different ways of spelling the name of this lake. It was formerly written as though it had six syllables; but the pronunciation which has generally obtained with those best acquainted with the region of the lake, and the Indian pronunciation of the name, was *Win·ne-pe-sock-e.* The following authorities show this:

Winnapusseakit: Sherman and Ince's Report, 1652.
Winnipesocket: Bartlett's Narrative, 1708.
Winnipissocay: Penhallow's Wars, 1726.
Winaposawgue: Canterbury charter, 1727.
Winnepissocay: Petition, 1733.
Winnipeshoky: Petition, 1744.
Winnepesocket: Stevens' Journal, 1746.
Winepesocky: Surveyor Clement, 1746.
Winipiseoce: Theodore Atkinson, 1746.
Winnepesacket: Governor Shirley, 1747.
Winipesockee: Bryant's Journal, 1747.
Winnapessocket: Map of New Hampshire, 1750.
Winipisoky: Hon. George Boyd, 1785.
Winnepisiogee: The present mode of spelling, pronounced *Winipisoky,* or *Win-ne-pe-sock-e.*

This lake is situated in the county of Strafford. Its form is very irregular. At the west end it is divided into three large bays; on the north is a fourth; and at the east end there are three others. Its general course is from N. W. to S. E.; its length is about 22 miles, and it varies in width from one to ten miles. This lake is environed by the pleasant towns of Moultonborough, Tuftonborough,

Wolfeborough, Centre Harbor, Meredith, Gilford, and Alton, and overlooked by other deligtful towns.

The waters of the Winnepisiogee are remarkably pure, and its depth in some places is said to be unfathomable. Its sources are principally from springs within its bosom. Its outlet is the rapid river of its own name. Its height above the level of the sea is 472 feet. It is stored with a great variety of excellent fish: in the summer season, steam boats, sloops and smaller vessels ply on its waters, and in the winter season it presents an icy expansion of great usefulness and beauty.

Like Casco bay and Lake George, this lake is said to contain 365 islands. Without supposing the days of the year to have been consulted on the subject, the number is very great; several of which comprise farms of from 200 to 500 acres.

The beauties of this lake were thus described, by the celebrated Dr. Dwight, many years ago.

"The prospect of this lake, and its environs, is enchanting; and its beauties are seen with great advantage from a delightful elevation a little distance from the road towards Plymouth. The day was remarkably fine. Not a breath disturbed the leaves, or ruffled the surface of the waters. The sky was serene and beautiful. The sun shone with a soft and elegant lustre; such as seems peculiar to that delightful weather, which from the 20th of September to the 20th of October, so often elicits from the mouths of mankind the epithet of charming. Mildness tempered the heat; and serenity hushed the world into universal quiet. The Winnepisiogee was an immense field of glass; silvered by the lustre which floated on its surface. Its borders, now in full view, now dimly retiring from the eye, were formed by those flowing lines, those masterly sweeps of nature, from which art has derived all its apprehensions of ease and grace; alternated at the same time by the intrusion of points, by turns rough and bold, or marked with the highest elegance of figure. In the centre a noble channel spread twenty-two miles before the eye, uninterrupted even by a bush or a rock. On both sides of this avenue a train of islands arranged themselves, as if to adorn it with the finish, which could be given only by their glowing verdure, and graceful forms.

"Nor is this lake less distinguished by its suite of hills, and mountains. On the northwest ascends a remarkably beautiful eminence, called the Red Mountain; limited every where by circular lines, and in the proper sense elegant in its figure beyond any other mountain, among the multitude, which I have examined. On the south ascends Mount Major; a ridge, of a bolder aspect, and loftier height. At a still greater distance in the southeast rises another mountain, more obscure and misty; presenting its loftiest summit, of an exactly semicircular form, directly at the foot of the channel above mentioned, and terminating the watery vista between the islands, by which it is bordered, in a magnificent manner. On the northeast the great Ossipee raises its long chain of summits with a bold sublimity, and proudly looks down on all the surrounding region.

"As we did not cross the Winnepisiogee, I am unable to determine in what manner an excursion on its waters might be compared with that which I made on Lake George. That the internal and successive beauties of the Winnepisiogee strongly resemble, and nearly approach those of Lake George, I cannot entertain a doubt. That they exceed them seems scarcely credible. But the prospect from the hill at the head of Centre Harbor is much superior to that from Fort George; a fact of which hardly any thing could have convinced me, except the testimony of my own eyes. The Winnepisiogee presents a field of at least twice the extent. The islands in view are more numerous; of finer forms, and more happily arranged. The shores are not inferior. The expansion is far more magnificent; and the grandeur of the mountains, particularly of the Great Ossipee, can scarcely be rivalled. It cannot be remarked without some surprise, that Lake George is annually visited by people from the coast of New England; and that the Winnepisiogee, notwithstanding all its accumulation of splendor and elegance, is almost as much unknown to the inhabitants of this country, as if it lay on the eastern side of the Caspian." See *Centre Harbor.*

Winnepisiogee River, N. H.,

Is the great outlet to the lake of that name; and issues from the southwest arm of the lake. It thence passes through two bays between Meredith and Gilford, entering the Great Bay in the northeast part of Sanbornton. From thence it passes through two other bays, forming the boundary between Sanbornton on the northwest, and Gilmanton and Northfield on the southeast; and unites with the Pemigewasset a short distance below Webster's falls. The stream is rapid in its course, and has a fall of 232 feet from the lake to its junction with the other branch of the Merrimack: this name being given to the confluent stream.— There are numerous bridges over the Winnepisiogee; which also furnishes many excellent privileges for factories or other machinery. See *Merrimack River.*

Winnicut River, N. H.,

Or the *Winniconett,* a tributary of the Piscataqua, rises in a swamp between Hampton and N. Hampton, and passes north into the Great Bay at Greenland.

Winooski City, Vt.

See *Burlington.*

Winslow, Me.

Kennebec co. This is a beautiful town, opposite to Waterville: it is watered by Kennebec and Sebasticook rivers, by several ponds, and by a fine stream, a branch of the Sebasticook. Its water power is constant and abundant. The soil of the town is fertile; the surface is diversified, and rendered productive by industrious and independent farmers. Winslow is 18 miles N. by E. from Augusta. It was incorporated in 1771. Population, in 1837, 1,557. Wheat crop, same year, 6,910 bushels.

Winthrop, Me.

Kennebec co. This town is finely situated, having a fertile soil, an undulating surface, and comprising six beautiful sheets of water; the *Cobbessecontee* and some of its tributaries. The largest of these lakes or ponds is ten miles in length, and from one to three miles in width. These waters give to Winthrop a valuable water power, and which is partly improved by a large cotton mill, a flour mill, carding and cloth dressing establishments, saw mills, &c. There are also in the town extensive manufactures of leather, boots and shoes.

The principal village is delightfully located, in the form of a crescent, at the union of the North lake, extending into Readfield, about six miles, with the South lake extending into Monmouth, about the same distance. This village is 10 miles W. from Augusta. The East village likewise is pleasantly situated at the northern extremity of the large lake, and is about 6 miles from Augusta.

These villages are neatly built, and are flourishing places of business. The lakes add much to the beauty of the town. The descent of their banks is gently sloping, with a dispersion of acclivities, which serve to heighten the beauty of the scenery: their waters are deep, clear, and are stocked with an abundance of trout, pickerel, perch, and other fish.

There is in this town an elevated tract of land containing an inexhaustible quantity of iron ore, or the material from which copperas is manufactured. Large quantities of copperas were made here during the late war, and it is thought that this ore might be advantageously used in times of peace.

Winthrop is an excellent farming town, and the moral character of its inhabitants is said to be uncommonly good. It was incorporated in 1771. Population, 1837, 2,003. Wheat crop, same year, 5,194 bushels.

Wiscasset, Me.

Lincoln co. Shire town. Wiscasset is a port of entry, situated on the west side of Sheepscot river, 20 miles from the sea; 24 miles S. S. E. from Augusta, 42 N. E. from Portland, and 10 N. E. from Bath. It was incorporated in 1760. Population, 1837, 2,246.

Wiscasset contains a noble harbor for vessels of the largest class: it is easy of access and seldom obstructed by ice. For many years previous to the commencement of the commercial restrictions, in 1807, Wiscasset was one of the most active and flourishing sea ports in Maine. During the disastrous period which followed, Wiscasset suffered severely, in common with all towns largely engaged in navigation.

Since the termination of the war the town has been slowly but safely progressing in wealth and prosperity. In addition to its commerce in lumber and ship building, this place is largely and profitably engaged in the fishery, for which pursuit it is admirably located. The tonnage of this district in 1837, was 11,662 tons.

The village of Wiscasset is delightfully situated on rising ground, in view of the harbor. The court house, churches, stores, and dwelling houses are built with taste, and many of them with elegance. A more beautiful village is rarely seen.

Woburn, Mass.

Middlesex co. This town is situated 10 miles N. W. by N. from Boston, 12 E. by N. from Concord, and 14 W. from Salem. It was incorporated in 1642, and first settled in 1640. Population, 1830, 1,977; 1837, 2,643.

There are some elevations in Woburn which give the surface a variegated and pleasing aspect. There is considerable wood land in the town, and some pine plain land; but the soil is generally strong, fertile and well improved. It contains some beautiful farms.

The manufactures of the town consist of leather, boots, shoes, india rubber, chairs, door sashes, blinds, tin, cabinet and wooden wares: total value, the year ending April, 1, 1837, $421,042.

Horn Pond in this town is a delightful sheet of water, surrounded by evergreens, and is so remarkable for its rural beauties as to attract many visitors from a distance. This pond serves as a passage for the Middlesex canal; it also furnishes the town with a water power of some value. The waters of this and several smaller ponds in Woburn fall into Mystic river, through Mystic pond in Medford.

Wolcott, Vt.

Lamoille co. Wolcott is well watered by Lamoille river, and by Green and Wild Branch, its branches. "Fish Pond," in Wolcott, is a pretty piece of water, and bears an appropriate name. There is some good grain land in the town, but most of the lands are fit only for pasturage. There are some mills in the town, and about 1,500 sheep. Wolcott was chartered in 1781. It is 22 miles N. from Montpelier, and 7 S. E. from Hyde Park. Population, 1830, 492.

Wolcott, Ct.

New Haven co. This is a small town, watered by a branch of Naugatuck river; 22 miles N. from New Haven. Population, 1830, 843. The town was incorporated in 1796. The territory was formerly a parish in the towns of Farmington and Waterbury; and from that circumstance was called "Farmingbury." The lands in Wolcott are elevated, rough, stony, and hard to cultivate. One of the highest hills in this part of the state lies in this town: it commands a very extended prospect of Long Island Sound, and the adjacent country.

Wolcottville, Ct.

See *Torrington.*

Wolfeborough, N. H.

Strafford co. This town is 45 miles N. N. W. from Portsmouth, and 45 N. E. from Concord. It is bounded S. E. by Brookfield and New Durham, S. W. by Winnepisiogee lake and Alton, N. E. by Ossipee, and N. W. by Tuftonborough.

The soil is rocky, but productive, and the face of the country level. The wood is principally oak and other hard timber. The only river is Smith's, so called from a hunter of that name: it issues from a large pond of the same name in the S. E. part of the town, and discharges its waters into the lake. There are four other ponds of considerable magnitude, called Crooked, Rust's, Barton's, and Sargent's ponds. There is a bridge over Smith's river about 60 feet long, near its entrance into the lake. Near this bridge is a pleasant village.

The charter of Wolfeborough was granted in 1770, to Gov. John Wentworth, Mark H. Wentworth and others. Gov. Wentworth, distinguished for his enterprise and taste, and a fondness for agricultural improvements, erected a splendid mansion about 5 miles east of the bridge, and made it his summer residence.

At the foot of a hill, near one of the ponds in this town, is a mineral spring, the waters of which are of a quality similar to those of Saratoga, but not so strongly impregnated. Population, 1830, 1,928.

Wonasquatucket River, R. I.

Providence co. This river rises in Smithfield, and after passing nearly through that town, it runs between North Providence and Johnston, and forms the head of Providence river. This stream is celebrated for its hydraulic power and the numerous manufacturing establishments erected on its banks.

Woodbridge, Ct.

New Haven co. The territory of this town belonged to the towns of New Haven and Milford, and was called the parish of "Amity," from 1739, until its incorporation in 1784. West river runs on the west side of West Rock, a range of mountains on the eastern border of the town. The surface of the town is hilly, but the soil is excellent for grazing, and much butter and cheese is annually taken to the New Haven market, from which it lies 6 miles S. W. Population, in 1830, 844.

The regicides, Goffe and Whalley, had a number of places of concealment in the limits of Woodbridge, the most noted of which is *Hatchet Harbor* or the *Lodge*, near a beautiful spring, in a valley, about 7 miles from New Haven.

Woodbury, Vt.

Washington co. Woodbury is watered by branches of Onion and Lamoille rivers, and contains a greater number of ponds than any other town in the state. These ponds afford a great variety of fish. Woodbury lies 15 miles N. by E. from Montpelier. Population, 1800, 23; 1820, 432; 1830, 824.

Woodbury, Ct.

Litchfield co. The settlement of this town commenced in the year 1672: in 1674, it was incorporated.

This is a good grazing township; the soil is generally warm and fertile. Between four and five thousand sheep are annually sheared in Woodbury.

The village is situated in a pleasant valley, and watered by a number of small streams, which form the Pomperaug. It is surrounded by high hills on every side, forming a kind of amphitheatre, which renders it strikingly romantic. The village contains some handsome buildings, three satinet, one tin and two nail factories. This place lies 25 miles N. W. from New Haven, 36 W. S. W. from Hartford, and 15 S. from Litchfield. Population, in 1830, 2,049.

Bethel Rock, near the village of Woodbury, is about forty feet in height, and projects over 3 or 4 feet, forming a kind of shelter from the wind and rain. There is a fine grove near it. This spot is frequently visited: it excites solemn and pleasing impressions.

Woodford, Vt.

Bennington co. This mountain town is 7 miles E. from Bennington, on the road to Brattleborough. Population, 1830, 395.

Woodford contains several large ponds, from which issue branches of Woloomsack and Deerfield rivers. There is a good deal of wild scenery on the road in crossing the mountains from Bennington through Woodford and Searsburgh: the gurgling of the streams down the mountain sides, allay, in a great degree, the fatigue of the journey. The greater part of this township is too elevated and broken for cultivation. It is a good location for the sportsman; for fish and fowl are abundant, and the deer, the bear, and other wild animals, roam with almost undisputed sway

Wood's Hole, Mass.

See *Falmouth.*

Wood River, R. I.

See *Hopkinton.*

Woodstock, Me.

Oxford co. A part of this township is mountainous; but it contains large tracts of undulating, fertile land. It is bespangled with beautiful ponds, forming mill streams, which pass to Little Androscoggin river.

Woodstock was incorporated in 1815. It lies 42 miles W. from Augusta, and 10 N. W. from Paris. Population, in 1837, 699. Wheat crop, same year, 2,669 bushels.

Woodstock, Vt.

Shire town, Windsor county. This town was first settled about the year 1768. It is well watered by Queechy river and its branches, which propel a woolen mill, a scythe and axe factory, an establishment for the manufacture of woolen machinery, and several smaller manufacturing works.

The soil of the town is generally very fertile, with a pleasant surface of hills and vales. The agricultural productions are large and valuable: they consist of beef, pork, butter, cheese, apples, cider and wool, of which 9,000 fleeces were shorn in 1837.

"Woodstock Green," so called, is a beautiful village. It is the seat of a flourishing country trade, and contains many very handsome buildings. The court house, planned, and built under the supervision of Ammi B. Young, Esq., a native architect of great promise, is one of the most chaste and classical structures in New England. The south village is neat and pleasant: it is about 5 miles from the "Green."

Woodstock lies 46 miles S. from Montpelier, and 11 N. W. from Windsor. Population, 1830, 3,044.

Woodstock, Ct.

Windham co. Woodstock is bounded N. by the Massachusetts line, E. by Thompson, W. by Union and Ashford, and S. by Pomfret and Ashford. It is 8 miles long, and upwards of 7 in breadth. The surface of the town is characteristically hilly, but not mountainous or broken, and comprises very little waste land, most or all of the eminences being capable of cultivation. The prevailing soil is a deep gravelly loam, which is strong and fertile. It is best adapted to grazing, but generally admits of tillage; and considerable quantities of grain are annually raised, consisting principally of rye and corn; and it may be considered one of the richest agricultural towns in this part of the state. There are 4 woolen and 4 cotton factories in the limits of the town. There are also about 900 persons engaged in the shoe making business, principally in the western part of the town. The town is divided into three parts, viz. the old society of Woodstock, West Woodstock or New Roxbury, and Muddy Brook society or North Woodstock.

The villages of Thompson, North Killingly, and Dudley in Massachusetts, on corresponding elevations, are in fair view, from the village in Old Woodstock, which is 41 miles E. N. E. from Hartford, 32 N. from Norwich, 32 W. N. W. from Providence, and 12 N. by W. from Brooklyn. First settled, in 1686. Population, 1830, 2,915. The village of Muddy Brook, or North Woodstock, is about three miles distant, situated in a beautiful valley, through which Muddy Brook, a fine mill stream, passes. The village is in two parts, in each of which is a Congregational church, upwards of one mile distant from each other. The houses in this village are more clustered than in any other part of the town, and viewed from the surrounding hills present an uncommonly beautiful appearance. The west part is called "Village corner."

General WILLIAM EATON, a consul to Tunis, from 1797 to 1803, and the hero of Derne, in 1804, was born in this town in 1764. He died at Brimfield, Mass., in 1811.

"Gen. Eaton was a very extraordinary character; he possessed much original genius, was bold in his conceptions, ardent in his passions, determined in his resolutions, and indefatigably persevering in his conduct. He possessed considerable literary acquirements, and the style of his writings was characteristic of his mind; bold, energetic and decisive. His courage was equalled only by his resolution, and the boldness of his enterprises, by his ability and perseverance to execute them."

Woolwich, Me.

Lincoln co. Woolwich lies a little above Bath, on the east side of Kennebec river, 32 miles S. from Augusta, and 7 W. from Wiscasset. It was incorporated in 1759. Population, 1837, 1,433. Woolwich has several ponds and small streams, and its navigable privileges are valuable.

Woonsocket Falls, R. I.
See *Smithfield*.

Worcester, Vt.

Washington co. This town is situated 10 miles N. from Montpelier and 30 E. by S from Burlington. First settled, 1797. Population, 1820, 44, and in 1830, 432. A branch of Onion river gives the town a good water power, and which is used for various purposes. Much of this township is mountainous; but there is some good land along the stream, and the highlands afford pasturage for cattle.

Worcester County, Mass.

Worcester is the county town. This county was incorporated in 1731. Population, in 1820, 73,635; 1830, 84,365; 1837, 96,551. It contains an area of 1,500 square miles.

This county crosses the state from New Hampshire on the north, to Connecticut and Rhode Island on the south. It is bounded W. by the counties of Franklin, Hampshire, and Hampden, and E. by Norfolk and Middlesex counties. This is the largest county in the state. Its territory is larger than the state of Rhode Island, and its population is greater than that of the state of Delaware. Its surface is rather undulating than hilly. The soil is generally strong, and produces all kinds of grain, grasses, fruits, &c. common to its climate. Its water power is abundant in almost every town, and perhaps in no section of New England are the interests of agriculture, commerce and manufactures more completely blended; nor can there be found better resources for their united support. Its principal rivers are the Blackstone, Quinabaug, Nashua, Ware, Millers, and Mill. There are in this county 54 towns, and 64 inhabitants to a square mile.

In 1837, the value of the manufactures in the county of Worcester was $11,407,790: the number of sheep in the county was 24,901; value of the wool, $37,267.

Worcester, Mass.

County town, Worcester co. This town was incorporated in 1684, but in consequence of Indian hostilities, the first town meeting was not held until 1722. This part of the country was called by the Indians, *Quinsigamond*, and *Tatmuck* and *Bogachoak* hills were Indian residences.

The central situation of the town, both in regard to the county and state, the fertility of its soil and that of the surrounding country, the salubrity of its climate, and the industry, intelligence and wealth of its people, have long since entitled it to the honor of being called the chief town in "the Heart of the Commonwealth." The town is situated in a valley, and surrounded by hills of gentle acclivity. It is well built and beautifully shaded, and travellers from every direction, are delighted with its neatness and beauty.

A number of the streams which form the head waters of the Blackstone meet in this town, and furnish a considerable water power.

Worcester is 40 miles W. from Boston, 51 E. from Northampton, 38 S. W. from Lowell, and 41 N. N. W. from Providence, R. I. Population, 1820, 2,962; 1830, 4,172; 1835, 6,624; 1837, 7,117.

There are in Worcester 8 woolen, 3 cotton and 2 paper mills; an air and cupola furnace, 9 woolen machinery factories, 3 tin factories, and manufactures of coaches, chaises, boots, shoes, hats, cutlery, chairs, cabinet ware, ploughs, straw bonnets, palm-leaf hats, wire, lead pipe, paper machinery, &c.: total value, the year ending April 1, 1837, $1,042,369.

Worcester is the centre of a large inland trade. The Blackstone canal, from Providence, R. I., 45 miles in length, terminates here; and here is a permanent depot on the great western rail road from Boston to the Hudson river. This is the seat of many religious, literary, and philanthropic societies.

The *State Lunatic Asylum*, established in this town in 1832, is an institution honorable to the nature of man. It is a beautiful building, delightfully located, and admirably conducted. Its plan and arrangements are so excellent as to render it a model for similar institutions in other states.

This institution is a receptacle for all persons arraigned as criminals, but found to have committed the offences in a state of insanity; of paupers, and of those who are so furiously mad as to render their continuance at large dangerous to the community. Although the worst cases of insanity are found here, yet experience has proved that there are very few cases of derangement which may not be ameliorated by the kindly influence of humane treatment. The average recoveries, to the present time, is about 56 pr. ct.

The *American Antiquarian Society*, was founded in 1812. By the liberality of the late ISAIAH THOMAS, LL. D., one of its first benefactors, a spacious hall was erected in 1820, for the reception of its large and valuable cabinet of antiquities, and its library of about 12,000 volumes of American publications, particularly of all works pertaining to American history, and literature generally.

Mr. Thomas was the father of New England printers. He published the first newspaper in this town, in 1775, and, a few years after, the first bible in America. He was a gentleman of great patriotism and liberality. He was born in Boston, January 19th, 1749, and died in this town, April 4, 1831.

Worthington, Mass.

Hampshire co. This town has a good soil: it is pleasantly situated on elevated ground: it has some mineral treasures, and is washed by a branch of Westfield river. It is 103 miles W. from Boston, 55 E. from Albany, N. Y., and 17 W. N. W. from Northampton. Incorporated, 1763. Population, 1837, 1,142.

The manufactures of Worthington consist of leather, boots, shoes, curtains, children's wagons, and hats: annual value, about $50,000.

In 1837, there were sheared in this town 9,050 merino sheep: the wool weighed 27,000 pounds, and sold for $16,875.

Wrentham, Mass.

Norfolk co. There is a large pond near the centre of this town, from which issue several streams which flow to the Charles, Neponset and Taunton. In this town are one woolen and four cotton mills, an axe manufactory; boat building to a considerable extent; and manufactures of boots, shoes, hats, hoops and straw bonnets. The total value of the manufactures of this town, for the year ending April 1, 1837, was $204,806; of which $77,815 was for straw bonnets.

Wrentham is a pleasant town, with a tolerable soil and diversified surface. It was taken from Dedham in 1673. Population, 1837, 2,817.

A family of Indians once resided in a cavern in this town, called "Wampum's Rock," which place is rather a curiosity. The Indian name of the town was *Wallomapogge*.

Wrentham is 27 miles S. by W. from Boston, and 15 S. by W. from Dedham. This town is bounded S. E. by Mansfield, and within the region of a vast bed of anthracite coal.

Yantic River, Ct.

New London co. This stream

rises by several branches in the northwest part of the county, and passing in a southeast course meets the united waters of the Quinnebaug and Shetucket at Norwich, where the waters of the three rivers fall with great rapidity, forming the Thames, and producing a valuable hydraulic power. See *Norwich.*

It is said that a party of Mohegan Indians plunged themselves down the Yantic falls, when pursued by their foes, the Narragansets.

Yarmouth, Mass.

Barnstable co. Yarmouth extends across Cape Cod, and has a good harbor on each side. There are several ponds in the town, from which issue a small stream, called Bass river, and from which a small water power is derived. The soil of the cape here becomes thin, sandy and unproductive. The people of this town are principally devoted to the fishing business, coasting trade, and the manufacture of salt. There are, however, some manufactures of vessels, cordage, leather, cabinet and tin wares, chairs, boots and shoes. Some sheep are kept, but the agricultural productions are small. A large number of vessels are engaged in the coasting trade, and in 1837, 13 vessels, of about 50 tons each, were employed in the cod and mackerel fishery: the product, that year, was $26,622.

During that year there were in operation in this town, 52 establishments for the manufacture of common salt, and 4 for the manufacture of Epsom salts. The quantity of common salt made was 365,200 bushels. The value of common salt was $109,560; of Epsom salts, $1,350. Hands employed, 55.

In 1837, there were in the state of Massachusetts 743 establishments for the manufacture of salt: 758,392 bushels were made, valued at $246,059, employing 708 hands. Yarmouth is bounded W. by Barnstable, and lies 72 miles S. E. from Boston. Incorporated, 1639. Population, in 1830, 2,251; 1837, 2,454.

York County, Me.'

Alfred is the county town. This county is bounded N. by Oxford county, N. E. by the county of Cumberland, E. by the ocean, S. by Portsmouth harbor, and W. by Strafford county, N. H. It comprises an area of about 818 square miles. Its population in 1810, was 41,877; 1820, 46,283; 1830, 51,722; and in 1837, 53,781. Population to a square mile, 66. The surface of the county is rough and uneven, but not mountainous; its highest elevation is Mount Agamenticus. Its soil is hard and rocky, particularly on the sea coast, which extends about 35 miles. There is, however, much good land within the limits of York county: it produces large quantities of English and salt hay, potatoes and other vegetables, corn, and some wheat; but the latter grain is not so abundant in this as in the more eastern counties. The quantity of wheat grown in this county in 1837, was but 17,795 bushels. There is much good grazing land in the county, and in 1837, there were 60,392 sheep within its limits.

The sea coast is lined with fine harbors for the fishery, and many vessels are built of native timber. The county contains many capes, points and necks of land, on which are well conducted light houses. The tonnage of the three districts within the county, Saco, Kenne bunk and York, in 1837, was 11,505 tons. York county contains many excellent mill streams; and the value of its hydraulic power is beginning to be seen and felt.

This ancient county was the lodgement of some of the first settlers of New England. See *Saco.*

York, Me.

York co. This is an ancient maritime town, on the coast, between Kittery and Wells. It is bounded W. b·· South Berwick. This was for many years the shire town, and the place of holding the courts and keeping the records for the whole province, until the counties of Cumberland and Lincoln were set off in 1760. The town was incorporated in 1653.

York has a court house and gaol, but all the county courts have been, within a few years past, removed to Alfred. The principal harbor is York river, about 6 miles from Portsmouth, N. H., with water sufficient for vessels from 200 to 300 tons burthen. The entrance, however, is difficult, being narrow and crooked. The other harbor is cape Neddock, about 4 miles N. E. of the former, navigable about a mile from the sea at full tides only; it having a sand bar at its mouth, sufficient to prevent vessels of any considerable burthen from passing at low water.

Cape Neddock and Bald Head are the head lands. The former is a little to the south of cape Neddock river. At the end of this cape is a small hillock called the Nubble, on which Congress has recently authorised the erection of a Light house. Boon Island lies about 9 miles southeast of this point. Bald Head makes the S. W. part of Wells bay.

The settlement of this place began about the year 1630: it was then called Agamenticus, from a mountain of that name in the north part of the town. This is of considerable elevation, and a noted land mark. From its summit, there is an extensive prospect bounded by the great ranges of the N. H. mountains on the N. and N. W., and the Atlantic on the coast from Cape Ann to Cape Elizabeth.

This town was nearly destroyed by the Indians and French in 1692, who, coming on snow shoes, surprised the unwary inhabitants at early morning. This calamity was so desolating, that the few remaining inhabitants had thoughts of abandoning the place altogether; but a number remained, though suffering under severe privations from the destruction of almost every thing that could give them shelter or sustenance.

The population of the town in 1830, was 3,485; but has been reduced since that time, by the annexation of a portion of its northern angle to South Berwick. Its population in 1837, was 3,001.

York is situated 99 miles S. W. from Augusta, 45 S. W. by S. from Portland, 22 S. S. E. from Alfred and 9 N. by E. from Portsmouth, N. H.

www.ingramcontent.com/pod-product-compliance
Lightning Source LLC
Chambersburg PA
CBHW071231300426
44116CB00008B/996